GEORGE CUKOR, MASTER OF ELEGANCE

Other Books by the Author

The Habima—Israel's National Theater: A Study of Cultural Nationalism (1980). Winner of the 1980 National Jewish Book Award

The History of the Habima and the Hebrew Theater (1982)

And the Winner Is: The History and Politics of the Oscar Awards (1987)

John Wayne: Prophet of the American Way of Life (1988)

Small-Town America in Film: The Fall and Decline of Community (1991)

GEORGE CUKOR, MASTER OF ELEGANCE

Hollywood's Legendary Director and His Stars

Emanuel Levy

William Morrow and Company, Inc.
New York

Copyright © 1994 by Emanuel Levy

Title page photograph courtesy of the Academy of Motion Pictures Arts and Sciences.

It is the policy of William Morrow and Company, Inc., and its imprints and affiliates, recognizing the importance of preserving what has been written, to print the books we publish on acid-free paper, and we exert our best efforts to that end.

Library of Congress Cataloging-in-Publication Data

Levy, Emanuel, 1947–
   George Cukor : master of elegance : Hollywood's legendary director and his stars / Emanuel Levy.
     p. cm.
   Filmography: p.
   Includes bibliographical references and index.
   ISBN 0-688-11246-3
   1. Cukor, George Dewey, 1899– . 2. Motion picture producers and directors—United States—Biography. I. Title.
PN1998.3.C8L48 1994
791.43'0233'092—dc20
[B]   93-31894
                                         CIP

Printed in the United States of America

First Edition

1 2 3 4 5 6 7 8 9 10

BOOK DESIGN BY LISA STOKES

To Rob Remley

Contents

Foreword

There are several books about George Cukor, but I believe that none has addressed the chief concern of my book—namely, what made Cukor so special as a filmmaker. When I set out to write this biography, I was intrigued by such seemingly simple yet challenging questions as how Cukor actually worked with his actors. What was it like to be on a Cukor movie set? How did Cukor feel about being labeled a woman's director? What were the effects of his being an outsider—an unattractive, Jewish, homosexual director—in a business that worshiped good looks and perceived its role as nothing less than defining and transmitting the American dream to millions of viewers in the United States and abroad.

I also wished to question, and dispel, some of the prevalent myths and long-held notions about Cukor as an artist and a man. Prominent among these was the widespread belief that he was dismissed from *Gone with the Wind* because of his preferential treatment of Vivien Leigh and because of Clark Gable's contempt for him. My book suggests that Cukor was fired because of a "classic" authority conflict between him, a strong visionary director, and Selznick, an even stronger and more obsessive producer, who consciously set out to produce the greatest movie ever made.

I never believed that Cukor was such a "gentleman" as to forgive Selznick for dismissing and humiliating him. Though Cukor continued to socialize with Selznick and his family, he was always ambivalent about the producer and made every possible effort not to work with him again.•

The charges that Cukor's film oeuvre wasn't interesting cinematically, that his pictures were filmed plays, that his cameras didn't move enough, that the quality of his films was static also required reexamination. *George Cukor, Master of Elegance* attempts to deal with all these issues, providing, I hope, a fresher perspective on Cukor's subtle mise-en-scène and distinctive visual style.

Several discussions have attributed too much importance to Cukor's stage career in Rochester and then Broadway. My belief is that even though he began his career in the theater, Cukor really came into his own in 1929, when he moved to the West Coast and became a Hollywood director. Contrary to popular notion, even though Cukor used this "theatrical baggage" to an advantage once he became a filmmaker, he never had been a prestigious or even major Broadway director.

There is also the issue of his gay life-style and its impact on his standing in the Hollywood community and on the kinds of films he made. Despite accepted beliefs, Cukor didn't live a double life; he was just discreet about it. Everybody, from Louis B. Mayer to gossipers Hedda Hopper and Louella Parsons, knew that he was gay, but because people respected his work and liked him, they went out of their way not to damage him. This is not to say that Cukor's personal life didn't suffer from his total commitment to his work. For Cukor, career always came first; personal life and leisure were a distant second.

Moreover, as a homosexual director Cukor neither favored actresses nor worked in a different way with his female stars. Instead his homosexuality was expressed in his unique sensibility as an artist, in the kinds of stories he directed, the types of female protagonists and dilemmas that attracted him. It is significant that most of Cukor's films were about women who tended to be strong and eccentric, outsiders who wished to assimilate but without giving up their idiosyncratic habits and traits—just like him.

When I began researching the biography, I failed to realize the amount of work involved. Ambitious that I was, I wanted to be comprehensive and examine each of Cukor's films, television productions, and projects that were in extensive preproduction but never materialized. Cukor died at the age of eighty-three as one of Hollywood's most accomplished and most prolific directors. In a career that spanned more than half a century and saw the making of more than fifty films, Cukor never lost his gusto for the movies—or life, for that matter.

The scope of *George Cukor* further expanded when I decided to draw some comparisons between him and other major directors of his generation, specifically Alfred Hitchcock, who made as many films as Cukor, most of them—again, like Cukor's—commercially successful. At the same time, unlike Hitchcock's or even Howard Hawks's career, Cukor's suffered from a lack of assertive ego and showy style. Unlike the Master of

Suspense, Cukor was never a director "above the title." Indeed, to this day Cukor still is a director whose films' titles are better known than is his own name.

Whenever I mentioned to my friends that I was writing a biography of George Cukor, the typical reaction was: George who? What movies did he make? Yet invariably it was only a matter of seconds after I mentioned such Cukor smash hits as *What Price Hollywood?*, *Dinner at Eight*, *Little Women*, *David Copperfield*, *Holiday*, *The Women*, *The Philadelphia Story*, *Gaslight*, *Adam's Rib*, *Born Yesterday*, *A Star is Born*, and his Oscar-winning *My Fair Lady* before they realized that all these pictures had been made by the same director. On one level, their reactions may be the ultimate compliment to a director who never thought of himself as extraordinarily talented and never believed his range was as diverse as his movies displayed.

George Cukor, Master of Elegance is my sixth and most ambitious book to date. When I undertook to write this biography, I had no idea that it would take so long—by the standards of my previous productivity. The research process was so extensive that I ended up using only 50 percent of the data I collected.

Two sources of materials distinguish this book from others about Cukor. First is the George Cukor Special Collection, a treasure trove of letters, screenplays, production notes, and photographs. Cukor was kind enough to donate this collection to the library of the Academy of Motion Picture Arts and Sciences, with which he had a long-standing relationship. Second, no previous author has interviewed as many actors and actresses as I have. This research strategy was crucial for substantiating the book's main concern: Cukor as an actor's director. Though Cukor's movies were often marked by strong screenplays and witty dialogue, in the final account he expressed himself through—and identified with—his performers.

I began collecting materials for the book in the summer of 1988. A grant from the National Endowment for the Arts facilitated my travels to Los Angeles—practically every January and then from June to August, while I was teaching at Wellesley College and Columbia University.

Two grants from Wellesley College's Stone Center for Research on Women helped expand the scope of my research and focus on the issue of male versus female sensibility in the arts. Out of this grant came a seminar on women directors, focusing on Dorothy Arzner, a friend and contemporary of Cukor's, and the only woman to have a sustained directorial career in the studio system of the 1930s and 1940s.

George Cukor is the first completed project with my dear and loyal agent, Maria Carvainis. Over the past five years—with all the changes of editors that this book saw—Maria has provided a staunch support and a tough, matter-of-fact approach with my editors. She was always there in moments of unsound anger and frustration to lend her rational advice and soothing voice of reason. If I proved difficult at times, I extend my apologies to her. Maria's two assistants, Jan Barcena and Beazie Chase, also lent their help in executing some necessary administrative tasks.

Many friends and colleagues have read and commented on earlier drafts of the manuscript. I would like to thank especially Rob Remley, John Ryan, Bill Shepard, and Jeff Farr for their extremely useful and detailed comments on the book.

Three dedicated assistants worked first on the research and then on the manuscript. While I was at Wellesley College, Erin collected information about the critical and commercial reception to each and every Cukor movie. At Arizona State University I had the benefit of working with Jeff Farr, who transcribed most of the taped interviews, and Daniel Stamps, who worked on the Filmography and Bibliography.

This book owes an intellectual debt to the writings of Andrew Sarris on auteurism. Sarris's brief discussion of Cukor in his magnum opus, *The American Cinema,* is nothing short of brilliant. I have attempted to apply some notions of auteurism—both thematic and stylistic—to Cukor's accomplished film oeuvre.

I have learned a good deal about George Cukor from Gavin Lambert's excellent interview book *On Cukor,* a unique volume in structure and contents. Mr. Lambert was later kind enough to grant me an interview that supplemented his book with excellent insights into the artist and the man.

The numerous performers, writers, and colleagues of Cukor's I have interviewed are listed elsewhere. Here I just want to say that it was a pleasure to talk to each one of them and hear their praise of and comments about Cukor. Even those who didn't get along with Cukor— Stewart Granger, for one—had to concede his uniqueness and greatness as a director.

Though she was at first reluctant to talk to me, I ended up spending a lovely day at Katharine Hepburn's house in Manhattan. At one point during our early communication I had found myself saying, "But, Ms. Hepburn, you made ten movies with Mr. Cukor. I can't write the book without your collaboration." The scarce knowledge I had of her at that time made me believe she would not change her mind about seeing me. But she did, and the following week I received a telephone call at Wellesley College. "Professor Levy," said a familiar voice that made me tremble, "we can meet on Monday at ten o'clock in my house." My only regret now is that out of shyness and my desire to get as much information from Ms. Hepburn as possible, I declined to take a lunch break and thus missed my opportunity to taste a Hepburn homemade soup!

My students at Columbia University, Wellesley College, and Arizona State University have contributed to this book by challenging my ideas about classic Hollywood cinema and Cukor's narrative paradigms and by providing illuminating insights into his movies. Over the last five years I have introduced many of my students to Cukor's films, the best and famous ones, like *Holiday, The Women, The Philadelphia Story,* as well as the less popular and less known, such as the still-underrated Garbo swan song *Two-Faced Woman,* the overlooked Crawford melodrama *A Woman's Face,* the campy Sophia Loren vehicle *Heller in Pink Tights.*

In 1989–90 I spent an enjoyable sabbatical at the New School for Social Research before moving out West. Peter Haratonik and Jennifer Sharp of the Film Department were kind and generous enough to let me teach a course dealing with Cukor's work. The course coincided with an evening series in which ten of Cukor's movies were shown to students and the public.

The collection of data took place in many libraries on the East and West coasts. I would like to thank the personnel of the Margaret Herrick Library of the Academy of Motion Picture Arts and Sciences (AMPAS), arguably the best film library in the United States. I enjoyed the generosity of Linda Mayer, director of the library, and her staff. I am particularly grateful to Sam Gill, curator and archivist for special collections, and his assistant, Howard; Sandra Archer, head of reference services; Patrick Stockstill, academy historian and awards coordinator; and the late Douglas Edwards, special projects coordinator.

The staff of the Lincoln Center Library for the Performing Arts helped me locate invaluable materials on Cukor's stage career in Rochester and Broadway. Additional work was conducted at the libraries of the American Film Institute, the Museum of Modern Art, the University of California at Los Angeles, and the University of Southern California.

My editor Robert Shuman and his staff at William Morrow, who worked on the final version of the manuscript, helped shorten it and make it tighter.

Finally, I would like to stress that *George Cukor* could not have been written without the practical assistance and moral support of my two best friends, Rob Remley and Nathan Waterman. Until his untimely death in 1989 Nathan was the kind of friend one dreams about having—loyal and generous to a fault. I owe to him a good deal of my literary career, which began during our friendship with my book about the

Habima theater, which went on to win the 1980 National Jewish Book Award.

George Cukor is dedicated to Rob Remley, without whom the book could not have been completed. No writer could ever hope for more supportive encouragement than that which Rob provided. I can't think of another individual who has influenced my writing and helped me become the film critic and scholar that I am. Those who know me as a person and a critic will understand exactly what I mean.

—EMANUEL LEVY

Los Angeles

CHAPTER ONE:

A Life in the Theater, 1899–1928

GEORGE CUKOR ARRIVED IN LOS ANGELES IN FEBRUARY 1929. HE had been born and bred in New York, but his relocation to the West Coast was the single most important event of his life. The move involved a pivotal career change and a major transformation of life-style. It began what could be described as Cukor's love affair with the movies, an infatuation with movie personalities and movie culture that consumed the director until his death half a century later, in January 1983.

"Still another Broadway stage director has come to Hollywood to conquer new worlds in the realm of talking pictures," announced the *Los Angeles Times* as Cukor joined a host of other directors who abandoned the New York stage for the exciting movie industry. The young, ambitious Cukor, however, soon proved to be more than just "another Broadway stage director" seeking fame and fortune in Hollywood. Within three years his achievements in *A Bill of Divorcement* and *What Price Hollywood?* began to define the art of screen acting. And by his fifth year in Hollywood, after the critical and commercial successes of *Dinner at Eight, Little Women,* and *David Copperfield,* Cukor became one of the industry's top filmmakers and Metro-Goldwyn-Mayer's highest-paid director.

The transition from the theater to the film world, and from the urban intensity of New York City to the sunny sprawl of Los Angeles, was actually easier than he could have anticipated. Cukor loved the energy and sophistication of New York. "It never occurred to me that I could live in California," he said in later years. "I was really a New Yorker."

But once he set foot in Hollywood, he took an immediate liking to the city and the new life-style it afforded him. Both the movie industry and Los Angeles felt like home. "I can't image living anywhere else," he said. "I'm not a sun worshipper, but here I live close to my work, and in country surroundings." Unlike other "émigrés" from the East, Cukor never looked back. His transition to Southern California was swift and smooth.

Cukor, in fact, became an ardent defender of California. "It bothers me when people disparage Los Angeles and say they miss the culture of New York, that New York is so stimulating." His response to this snobbery was true to his buoyant nature: "Well, if you're not dull yourself, you'll find it just as stimulating here."

Cukor's fondness for L.A. was inseparably tied to his immersion in movies. In his first RKO publicity bio, he was described as a person who directs as a "vocation, avocation, and hobby." For Cukor, making movies was the most fascinating work in the world. "It has never bored me," he once noted. "It's an enormous challenge, because with each picture I must prove myself all over again."

As his career developed, Cukor came to know almost everyone in Hollywood. His closest friends were movie personalities, mostly actors and writers. Cukor's work, in many ways, eclipsed his personal life. Socially and culturally resplendent, Cukor's life was emotionally barren. To some extent it was a matter of choice: Early on Cukor determined that his homosexuality would not be an obstacle to his career. Working in a highly conservative setting, Hollywood of the studio era, Cukor was extremely careful ("discreet" was the word he liked) about his gayness. But he didn't live a double life; everybody in Hollywood knew he was gay, and he was never ashamed of it. "I never had any problems accepting myself," he confided in a friend. "I never had any guilt about it."

As a single gay man, without a long-term partner, Cukor was, as friend and collaborator Garson Kanin said after his death, lovingly married to the movies. It was a marriage in every sense, involving love, passion, and commitment—as well as disappointment, pain, and betrayal.

Hollywood was a much-desired new beginning for Cukor. Reared in a middle-class Jewish family of immigrant Hungarian stock, he was always sensitive about his social status. Once in Hollywood, Cukor avoided talking about his family or his past. Privately, though, he was interested in tracing his family's genealogy. Over the years Cukor spent a good deal of time, energy, and money trying to reconstruct his family tree.

As much as Cukor would have liked to turn up a respectable or elevated lineage, his was not a family of wealth or rank. And as much as he would have liked to boast a privileged upbringing, he could not. It became one of Cukor's lifelong aspirations to be accepted and assimilated, to become a member of Hollywood's elite. He wanted wealth, social position, and the life-style that went along with them. Cukor's ambition was to be rich and famous—ironically, the title of his last film.

To a large degree he succeeded. He attained professional and economic success in Hollywood and cultivated an international social network that included literary and cultural luminaries, nobility, and upper crust society as well as movie celebrities. Cukor was particularly drawn to English culture and English actors, who seemed to represent a more refined culture.

Cukor consciously created his home as a social salon, receiving people renowned all over the world. Cukor must have been heartened when, during preparations for *Gone with the Wind,* writer Sidney Howard asked him to receive some friends from abroad. "Let them see in your mode of life," Howard said, "that Hollywood is the peer of, if not superior to, the capitals of Europe."

When the subject of family was broached, Cukor talked more about his ancestors in Hungary than about his immediate family. They seemed to be a more prestigious and cultured lot than his parents were. Joseph Cukor, his paternal grandfather, had prepared a long manuscript that described the family's origins. Cukor knew that the document was not entirely accurate, but he preferred to hold it as fact.

The Cukors, according to Joseph, were descendants of a tribe that had migrated to India. His grandfather believed that Chukor, the original family name, derived from a word for the Himalayan hill partridge. In both Sanskrit and Hindi, *chukor* does mean "partridge," a symbol that graced the family crest. For centuries the name remained unchanged, but in 1790, after the clan had made its way to Europe, the name was "Magyarized" to Czukor.

In 1859 Joseph dropped the Z to make the name easier to pronounce and to avoid what he considered the Slavic connotation of two successive consonants. In later years, during Cukor's brief tenure at Paramount, there was always some confusion between him and the studio's president, Adolph Zukor, also of Hungarian-Jewish descent, owing to the similarity of their names. Cukor often joked that he might have fared better at Paramount, had Joseph dropped the C instead of the Z.

His great-grandfather owned an estate in Hungary, an unusual situation for Hungarian Jews at the time. Cukor never learned the reason why his handsome grandfather left the landed gentry of Central Europe and emigrated to the United States. Whatever the reason, Cukor liked to emphasize that Joseph's arrival in New York City preceded the great Hungarian immigration of the 1900s; this somehow set his family apart from the masses.

Joseph and his wife, Victoria, arrived in New York in 1884 with their four children—two boys and two girls. Victor, Cukor's father, was the eldest, and Morris the youngest. Between them there were two girls, Bertha and Irene. "We landed at this God blessed coast of free America," Joseph wrote; "now you are in the land of possibilities." Both sons, no doubt with their father's blessing, went to law school and ultimately practiced law. The daughters married and, like their brothers, settled close to their parents in New York.

Unlike her dashing husband, Victoria Cukor was not known for her beauty, but her vibrant, witty personality dominated the family. Cukor was extremely fond of his paternal grandmother. She was hard-of-hearing, and the young Cukor was endlessly amused by the ear trumpet she carried as she shopped, cooked, and managed the household. Though she lived in the United States for decades, she never really learned to speak English. She was, however, fluent in Hungarian and German.

At family gatherings all these languages were spoken, sometimes all at once. From an early age Cukor developed a sensitivity to the spoken word. He had a knack for picking up funny expressions in other languages; he liked to accent his conversation with bits of foreign tongues. "George had a good ear for languages, but he didn't really speak any language fluently," said his friend and physician Hans Kohler. "Sometimes he used a few words of 'kitchen Hungarian,' but just for joking. He had some knowledge of French and German, but he did not really speak either."

Cukor's mother, Helen ("Ilona") Gross, was the daughter of a Hungarian prison administrator. Five years younger than Victor Cukor, Helen was an attractive woman, with beautiful brunette hair and fine, delicate, features. Her family had also emigrated to the United States in the late 1880s. The Grosses, however, were better educated than the Cukors. One of Helen's brothers was a photographer, who later started a business in Ohio, where most of her family settled.

Helen and Victor were married in 1894. Their eldest child, Elsie, was born in 1895. Her younger brother, George Dewey Cukor, was born four years later, on July 7, 1899. He was named after the hero of the Spanish-American War, Admiral George Dewey. The name was a source of patriotic pride, and Cukor flaunted it to his friends.

Cukor and his sister were not close. He never liked Elsie, never had a good rapport with her. She was a "shadowy figure," Cukor said in later years, singling out her long nails and her difficult, bullying manner. Elsie was jealous of her brother, who was brighter, better at getting his way with the family, more charming.

Like most immigrant families, the Cukors had endured some hardship when they arrived in America. But Cukor later emphasized that despite hardships, his family was middle-class. The early struggle made the family intimate and proud; "dignity" was a word Cukor used frequently to describe his family.

The family lived closed to one another. Cukor's aunts and uncles and their children assembled for dinner almost every night at his grandparents' brownstone on East Sixty-eighth Street. Meals were a central part of family life for the Cukors. George Cukor was brought up socializing around the table, a tradition he continued for the rest of his life. The adult Cukor hated eating alone; his friends believed he seldom ate dinner by himself.

Cukor learned a lot from watching his grandmother conduct the family dinners. That was when he picked up his lifelong habit of urging people to eat. "When people come to dinner, I urge them to have second helpings, just like my grandmother," Cukor commented. His love of food and his propensity to overeat also stemmed from his grandmother. Cukor admired rich cooking, sweets, iced cakes. Never athletic, he was inclined to chubbiness; for most of his adult life he was on a strict diet.

Sundays were special and ceremonial for the Cukors. Before dinner they would shake hands and wish one another *gesegnete Mahlzeit*, German for "blessed mealtime." But this tradition was not as formal as in other Hungarian households, where children kissed their mothers' hands to thank them for their meals. What Cukor remembered most fondly was that at the end of every long Sunday he would fall asleep and then miraculously wake up the next morning in his own bed.

Although the Cukors were good Hungarians—always weeping when listening to Hungarian songs—they did make an effort to assimilate, to become Americans. No matter where they were, the American flag was always hanging outside, a custom Cukor kept at his own home.

Cukor remembered vividly the decor of his grandparents' house. Displayed prominently on the walls were reproductions of the Stuart portrait of George Washington, a color picture of Betsy Ross sewing the American flag, a picture of the Lincoln family, and a steel engraving of Lajos Kossuth, the Hungarian leader, as well as a facsimile of the Declaration of Independence.

The Victor Cukors lived in an apartment just down the street from the grandparents' brownstone. The noise of the elevated train on Third Avenue was a constant disturbance. This childhood memory was one reason why Cukor later built high walls around his secluded house in California.

Cukor loved the distinct aroma of that neighborhood: the smell of a local brewery, or chicken roasting, or rich Hungarian cooking. The smell of musk melons reminded Cukor of the summers the family spent at Bath Beach in Brooklyn. The smell of camphor recalled their strange housekeeper and other females of the family.

In 1904, when Cukor was five, his aunt Irene died while only in her forties. Her death left a void in the family, especially for Cukor's grandparents; Irene and her husband lived with them. Cukor remembered painfully how his grandmother cried for months.

In their determination to be middle-class, the Cukors lived beyond their means. They did what wealthier people did: went away for the summer, patronized the theater. As a child Cukor was brought up in a manner out of all proportion to that which his father could afford. "When I tore my pants," he recalled, "it wasn't the tragedy that it was for the other boys I played with." Uncle Morris simply supplied the extra money needed.

The young Cukor admired Uncle Morris, who was more outgoing, charming, and, most important, successful than his father. Though both brothers completed law school, Morris graduated with honors and went on to become a known civic leader and a distinguished (a common Cukor adjective) lawyer. Cukor's father had the more humble status of assistant district attorney. The brothers were close, but there was rivalry. Cukor couldn't help noticing that Victor was overshadowed by the more eminent Morris.

Although Morris didn't support the family, he made their life more comfortable with his generosity of spirit—and money. Morris, who married late in life, had no children of his own. He fell in love with his secretary, Cora Woodruff, who was not Jewish. Cukor's grandfather didn't approve of the marriage, and although Cora learned to speak German in order to communicate with her mother-in-law, Cukor's grandmother accepted her only after Joseph Cukor died.

Cukor looked up to Morris as his role model. His uncle lived in a nice brownstone and was a pillar of the Hungarian-American community. He was a member of the Hungarian cultural society and adviser to the Austro-Hungarian consulate. What Cukor called "hyphenated" organizations were always being entertained at Morris's house. In time Cukor came to believe that his uncle would have had a more lucrative career had he worked harder to assimilate. Early in life Cukor vowed to become a fully fledged, not hyphenated, American in his own life. The adult Cukor was offended when and if he was introduced as a Jewish or Hungarian-American filmmaker.

Cukor's relationship with his father was always distant. He rarely spoke about him, even to close friends. In truth Cukor was embarrassed by his father. Despite Victor's education and decades of living in this country, his knowledge of English was limited; Cukor communicated with him mostly in Hungarian. In fact, Cukor had little in common with his father. As the years passed, Victor showed little parental pride or involvement in his son's success.

Once Cukor had established himself in Hollywood, he bought a house for his parents in Beverly Hills. But even in California Cukor's parents showed little interest in his career; unlike his friends, they rarely visited the studio. After his mother died in 1936, his father took to sitting on the front porch of his house all day long. For a man of Cukor's energy, his father's passivity and despair were intolerable. Once, when a friend of Cukor's pointed out to his father that his son was a famous director, Victor didn't seem to understand what he was talking about.

With the exception of Uncle Morris, Cukor could not rely on his family for moral, or any, support. And he seldom derived any pleasure from their company. "He was a pretty good son to his mother and father," Katharine Hepburn said, "but I don't think he was close to them the way I was close to mine. George's parents presented him to the world, but then he walked alone. George made his own life."

Cukor was closer to his mother than to his father. She was the only family member he liked to talk about—albeit in moderation. Protective and indulgent, his mother spoiled him. He was not expected to do any work around the apartment; his bed was made, and food was always served to him.

Helen had a sweet, gentle personality and a restrained, docile temperament. Cukor believed that she was overwhelmed by the more spirited and talkative members of the family. She occasionally wrote poetry, for which she was relentlessly teased by the Cukors; her son said he felt her "unrealized yearnings."

Cukor's closeness to his mother and the fact that he was surrounded with women in his childhood later contributed to his sensitive understanding of the female characters in his movies. From the beginning Cukor felt more comfortable with his actresses than with his actors. Throughout his life he found the greatest pleasure and solace in the company of women.

Cukor's childhood was essentially happy; there was lots of laughter, exchange of gifts, picnics, family summers at Bath Beach. He was an independent boy—"full of infatuations." When he went shopping with his mother, he knew exactly what he wanted. "I want this, not that," he would say. "I was never disciplined," he recalled. "If my parents were tough, my grandfather would have turned on them, so I learned to work them against each other."

Cukor's renowned personal and professional generosity was an outgrowth of his childhood. As an adult he refused to economize, throwing glorious parties and dinners that cost him a fortune. Cukor enjoyed gift giving; birthdays and special occasions always involved presents. And Christmas was a grand production every year. Cukor went to great expense to decorate his house and took pains to ensure that all his friends were included in his gift list. It was an inside joke in Hollywood that Cukor—a Jew—hosted the best Christmas fetes in town.

Actress Signe Hasso, who became a close friend on the set of *A Double Life,* remembered Cukor as a "great humanitarian." She related a telling example of his generosity. A group of forty blind people from Sweden, all educated as professional divers, were in L.A. to work with blind Americans. Hasso wanted to entertain them, but her house could not accommodate such a large group. "Why don't we give them a big lunch here?" Cukor said, and invited the whole group to his home. "We spent a whole day around the pool," Hasso recalled. "George had Swedish food cooked and presents for each one of them. They still talk about this luncheon in Sweden."

Cukor was constantly doing favors for friends and colleagues. People in need often came to him for loans. "He did an awful lot for people he knew and an awful lot of good that people never knew he did," said Hasso. Cukor befriended most of the actresses he worked with and kept track of them. He also quietly supported a number of aging actresses whose careers were over. Said Hasso: "I don't know how he found time to keep in touch with all his friends, but he always did."

His generosity and disregard for money later worked against Cukor. His business skills were not acute; he didn't think of filmmaking in terms of budgets or shooting schedules. And unlike some of his colleagues, Cukor never became a producer of his movies. As Cukor aged and his directorial opportunities began to dry up, his financial resources withered as well. In the last decade of his life Cukor lived well beyond his means just as his father had.

Cukor did not grow up in a particularly Jewish neighborhood, nor were the Cukors particularly religious. As a boy he was taught Hebrew, but he had no clue to the meaning of the words he learned phonetically. Jewish holidays were not regularly celebrated, and pork was one of the family's favorite foods. The young Cukor liked Jewish holidays for only one reason: They provided a legitimate excuse to miss school.

Although the Cukors did not speak Yiddish, the common tongue of Eastern European Jews, later in his life he learned some phrases from his friends actors Paul Lukas and Fanny Brice. The vulgar and suggestive phrases in Yiddish intrigued him. But on Sixty-eighth Street Yiddish was regarded as the language of the poor downtown Jews. The Cukors were uptown Jews.

From his childhood Cukor was ambivalent about his Jewishness. He treated traditional Jews with a slight contempt. Being Hungarian was acceptable, but Jewish beliefs and ceremonies made him uncomfortable. This early ambivalence carried over into adulthood. In Hollywood Cukor, like many others of his background in the industry, was a self-effacing Jew, fervently desiring assimilation and integration. His manners and style had nothing to do with his Jewishness. Cukor even went to lengths not to sound Jewish. The native New Yorker cultivated a mid-Atlantic accent. A close friend commented, "If he had been a woman, we would have called it a finishing school accent."

Cukor was much more comfortable identifying himself as a Hungarian. His conversational and social gifts as well as his sharp-edged humor were attributed to his Hungarian heritage. In one of this first European trips, in 1937, he could not wait to visit Hungary, a country he went back to several times. He was always eager to meet Hungarians in Hollywood: actors Paul Lukas, Tony Curtis, even Zsa Zsa Gabor, agent Robert Lanz, playwright Ferenc Molnár.

As a film director Cukor was anxious to blend in. "George was the self-reliant type of man; he respected Christianity and the Protestant Ethic," said director Paul Morrissey. "In his time self-reliance was like an American religion. George didn't like people who traded on their Jewishness; he simply paid no attention to them. There were two things in George's life he was determined never to make an issue of: his Jewishness and his homosexuality." Cukor never dated Jewish men; "Me no like my kind," he told his friends.

But as much as Cukor wanted to blend in, he appeared stereotypically Jewish, particularly as he grew older. Cukor's vulnerability about his looks began during his adolescence (he had been an attractive child). "It's hard to believe," Cukor used to say, "but I was a good-looking child, though it soon wore off." As he matured, his so-called Semitic features seemed more pronounced to him.

When he was a young man, Cukor's looks were defined by curly black hair, a sharp nose, and a pronounced chin. At five foot eight and a half, he was of average height, but he tended to be fat—"sensuously plump," he said. As a director he showed sympathy for performers who had talent but weren't attractive. He felt especially close to Spencer Tracy, Marie Dressler, Ruth Gordon—plain, "ugly duckling" performers who became high achievers despite their looks.

When, at age ten, it was discovered that Cukor was nearsighted and would have to wear glasses, his grandfather thought it a tragedy. The glasses gave the boy a bookish look and "just didn't fit in" with Joseph's concept of a Cukor. But Cukor *was* somewhat bookish; uninterested in sports, he loved to read. He was particularly fond of books on history; the Civil War was a favorite topic.

What Cukor lacked in good looks, he made up in demeanor and personality (a key word in his language when he described people). He was courteous and thoughtful, always bearing a gift or making a compliment. Even as a child he went out of his way to exhibit confidence and self-assurance—despite his looks.

Cukor maintained a buoyant energy throughout his life. Claire Bloom, who worked with him in *The Chapman Report*, always thinks of him in terms of "his excitement, his gesturing with his hands, and a very strange tongue which kind of darted in and out. His body, his hands, everything about him were always in motion, very electric. He was full of intellectual energy." In an early interview a journalist noted that Cukor spoke with "every terminal part of his body." Even detractors, such as Stewart Granger, who did not get along with Cukor on the set of *Bhowani Junction,* conceded, "The greatest thing about George was his excitement; he was enormously enthusiastic about everything."

Claudette Colbert grew up in New York at about the same time as Cukor. When they worked together on *Zaza* in 1939, they joked about their first meeting. Colbert said: "I had a mother who insisted that every day after school I go to Central Park with my brother. During the winter there was a hill by Seventy-second Street, called Pilgrim Hill, where we used to go sledding. I must have been about seven or eight, but I remembered seeing a well-dressed boy, standing on the hill and watching us. And I said to George once, 'I think it was you; you were watching us.' It was only a joke, but after that George always sent me postcards of Pilgrim Hill."

Whom Colbert actually saw at Pilgrim Hill remains a mystery, but the image of a well-dressed boy standing apart, watching the raucous activity of other children, is entirely consistent with the picture of the young Cukor.

Going to the theater was a lifelong habit Cukor acquired from his family. The Cukors often went to the Irving Place Theater, which was managed by Rudolf Christians, to see classic German plays. Cukor later kept in touch with Christians's daughter, Mady, who became an actress. Hungarians constituted most of the audience at the Irving Place. Hungarians were bilingual or trilingual and better educated than the German immigrants of the time.

The stage, the lights, the costumes, and, above all, the actors enthralled Cukor. His exposure to the theater was not limited to highbrow fare. Uncle Morris took him to see musicals at the Hippodrome on Sixth Avenue. They sat close to the stage, where Cukor could watch the incredible machinations of the elaborate productions. He was also fascinated by the performers' costumes and makeup.

Every detail was absorbed by the young Cukor. Bewitched by the nuts and bolts of the theater, he developed acute powers of observation. He could isolate and remember details that stood out on the stage: an article of clothing, a hairdo, a piece of furniture that didn't fit, an actor who missed a line.

Working as a director, Cukor borrowed elements from the plays and revues he loved as a child. Though the adult Cukor was well known for his use of foul language, when it came to theater and culture, he disliked anything vulgar or banal. His tastes were always conservative.

Cukor admired beauty—in people, in objects, in architecture. Ugliness of any kind appalled him. As a director he talked endlessly about the beauty and elegance of his female stars: Ina Claire, Greta Garbo, Vivien Leigh, Ava Gardner, Marilyn Monroe, Sophia Loren, Audrey Hepburn, Liz Taylor. "You put Ava Gardner in a fur coat or in a tent and she is attractive," he said, "and you get a girl who isn't attractive and you stuff her breasts and put everything in tight around the bottom and it just doesn't work."

Cukor's childhood experience in the theater was not limited to the audience side of the footlights. As an adolescent he directed his neighborhood chums in plays. He remembered one in which the prince, the leading man, was so short he played a love scene with the princess's elbow on his shoulder.

Cukor also took dancing lessons at Neuberger's, at Fifty-eighth Street and Lexington Avenue. Once a year Neuberger's put on a school show, in which all the boys wore coats and dancing pumps. When Cukor was seven, he got to play Neptune and sing a song. Decades later, when Cukor looked at a program of this performance—throughout his life Cukor saved everything—he was surprised to see that David O. Selznick, his friend and mentor, was also there! By that time Selznick was dead, and Cukor never got the opportunity to reminisce with him.

Cukor's grandparents died within a year of each other when he was about to start high school. With these central figures gone, Cukor's social world changed. He began spending more time with his new friend Mortimer Offner, who was a year younger, and Mortie's cousin Stella Bloch. To Cukor the Offners were an ideal family. They were more cultural than the Cukors: They read books, went to museums, talked about art (Mortie's brother Richard later became an expert on Florentine art). The Offners lived just down the street, and Stella often stayed for the night. Cukor sometimes saw his friends two or three times a day. The threesome spent endless time talking about art, literature, theater, and film.

They of course went to the theater together. Cukor's parents complained that he was squandering too much time and money on the theater, but he never listened. Mortie and Stella exposed Cukor to the likes of Isadora Duncan and famed French singer Yvette Guilbert. He in turn introduced them to vaudeville shows at the Palace. The friends would cut classes, lunch in Central Park, then mount the great marble staircase of the theater to see the leading entertainers of the day, including the legendary Fanny Brice. Cukor remembered rushing home afterward to intercept any mail from the school asking about his absence. He looked back upon those halcyon days as "delicious, nothing to do, with slight feelings of guilt."

Silent movies were also on Cukor and his friends' agenda. Film was in its infancy and had not yet garnered cultural cachet, but directors like

D. W. Griffith and Cecil B. De Mille were making epic movies, which Cukor saw. "I saw the movies, too, when I was a kid," Cukor later recalled, "but I was rather hoity-toity about them. I was only interested in the theater."

Mortie and Cukor both attended DeWitt Clinton, one of the better public high schools in New York, across town at Fifty-ninth Street and Tenth Avenue. Since high schools were not coed in those days, this was one activity the boys could not share with Stella. As well as offer a solid academic curriculum, DeWitt Clinton was dedicated to the development of its students' literary and cultural skills. There was an array of activities to engage the students' imaginations: language clubs, drama clubs.

Though bright, Cukor was never a good student; school simply didn't interest him. He would much rather play hooky with his friends or buy half-priced tickets at Gray's Drugstore and go to a Broadway show, as he did at least once a week. "I don't know how the hell I finished high school," he recalled, "I was so busy seeing every show from the second balcony."

Indeed, in 1917 and 1918, the New York theater was booming, affording Cukor a thorough theatrical education. He tried to see everything—good and bad. "If you read Alexander Woollcott [the noted theater critic]," Cukor once said, "you would become hooked on the theater within two weeks." He himself didn't need that; his passion for the stage was already keenly developed.

In those years Broadway was resplendent with great leading ladies, who drew Cukor to the theater. He had many favorites: Ethel Barrymore, Laurette Taylor, Emily Stevens, Pauline Lord, Mrs. Patrick Campbell, Elsie Ferguson. Cukor vividly remembered his first encounter with these luminaries and how he fell in love with each one of them. There were at least twenty distinguished actresses on the stage at the time, each endowed with "enormous personality" (a favorite Cukor expression), each leaving a profound impact on him.

In later years, when Cukor encountered these stars, most were flattered that he could quote famous lines from their heyday. But it was also a nasty reminder of how much older than he they were. Fanny Brice was reportedly offended when Cukor told her he had seen her at the Palace as a young boy.

Brice became a close friend, as did many of Cukor's childhood idols, like Ina Claire and Ethel Barrymore. His admiration for Claire never waned; he later directed her in the movie *The Royal Family of Broadway*, in a role based on Ethel Barrymore. Though he never had the pleasure of directing Barrymore herself, they became fast friends when he was a stage manager on a 1926 production of Somerset Maugham's *The Constant Wife* that she starred in.

In his senior year of high school Cukor worked at the Metropolitan

Opera as a "super." The job afforded him a few moments onstage and a wage of fifty cents a show, one dollar for blackface. What excited Cukor was the opportunity to see, close up, the stars of the Metropolitan. He was permitted to stand in the wings and watch artists like Geraldine Farrar sing her great roles: *Carmen, Tosca, Madama Butterfly.* The lyric soprano soon became another idol. He always remembered her backstage, talking to Caruso, bowing to her audience, "wafting by with her mother in a cloud of perfume."

In the late spring of 1917, near eighteen, Cukor graduated from De-Witt Clinton. With World War I in full swing, he enrolled in the Student Army Training Corps at the City College of New York, which he entered. But the war ended in November 1918, terminating Cukor's "military" stint.

Cukor's parents expected him to follow in the family tradition and study law, but he was not interested in pursuing further education. His ambitions were already focused. When he informed his parents that he wanted to direct plays, they were appalled: "They acted as if I had said I was going to be a bookie."

A stage director was neither respectable nor secure enough a profession for a Cukor. Only as the public image of the theater improved, and it became clear that there was money to be made, did the Cukors' attitude begin to change. However, his parents were never really supportive of his stage career.

Uncle Morris shared their disappointment, but true to his generous nature, he was willing to help. Through law school connections, Morris arranged a meeting with Arthur Hopkins, the distinguished Broadway producer-director.

Hopkins was innovative: Reacting against the mechanical stage direction of his day, he emphasized the play, the text. He was also a purist; under his direction actors' tricks and mannerisms seemed to fall away. Cukor came to admire him. Throughout his own directorial career Cukor also championed the importance of the writing, holding that "the script is the core, the heart, the lifeblood, the 'everything' of a picture."

But Cukor's meeting with Hopkins didn't turn out to be his entrée into the theater, though Hopkins did advise him to get his feet wet—get work, do anything he could.

At eighteen Cukor let everybody know he was looking for a job in show business. *The Better 'Ole,* a World War I musical import from London, was then on the road in the United States. Cukor answered an ad placed by producers Klaw and Erlanger, who needed a backstage man for the Chicago company. Hired as an assistant stage manager, Cukor handled technical and organizational details of the production, keeping the props in order, helping with the cues, posting cast call sheets.

Cukor also played a bit part in the show, but he did not like performing. He had never wanted to be an actor, and he now realized he was not made for the stage. "I don't have the physical thing," he said; "there are all sorts of funny-looking actors, but I'm not. I suppose I never had the temperament to be an actor."

Still, Cukor was fascinated by life in the theater. He liked its communal aspects—the camaraderie, the intensity of sharing adventures, onstage and off. He was an outsider—gay, Jewish, and unattractive—and the theater was a sanctuary for outcasts and "deviants" like him.

From the beginning Cukor found show business personalities intriguing—strange but also eccentric. He soon developed an ambivalent attitude toward actors. It was not exactly a love-hate relationship, but a mixture of admiration and contempt: admiration for the really gifted and devoted actors; contempt for the untalented, unintelligent, and lazy ones.

Cukor displayed heartfelt sympathy for show people in every capacity. Some of his most powerful films were about actors and the magic of the theater. Show business, in fact, became the most prevalent theme of his work; about one third of his fifty-one movies were about theater and movies. The grand actresses he adored were the protagonists of such films as *Zaza* and *The Royal Family of Broadway,* the ambitious ingenues in *The Actress,* the has-beens in *Dinner at Eight* and *A Star Is Born,* the traveling provincial performers in *Heller in Pink Tights.* Often the same movie included both types, the rising and falling, as in *What Price Hollywood?*

Theatrical personalities were also in the many Cukor projects that never materialized, including movies about Isadora Duncan, D. W. Griffith (with Gregory Peck), Laurette Taylor (with Judy Garland), and Fanny Brice (with Gwen Verdon).

Cukor could be critical of actors. He had little patience for what he perceived as the petty concerns of actors—their bickering, complaining, and gossiping. At one point in his stage career, fed up with the intrigues, quarreling, and temperament of his actors, he characterized them as having the "geniality of prostitutes" and behaving as a "typical bunch of gypsies."

Cukor displayed a nasty, sharp tongue when it came to actors he didn't like; he once described Louise Brooks as "a beautiful nothing." He was often too frank in his remarks. Samuel Goldwyn, Jr., remembered going with Cukor and his mother, Frances, to see Luigi Pirandello's *Enrico IV,* starring Rex Harrison and Rachel Roberts. Cukor hated the production and Harrison's pompous performance. At the end of the show they all went backstage, and Cukor told the actor straightforwardly what he thought of the play and his work. The Goldwyns were stunned at Cukor's "ultracandid reaction."

The Better 'Ole, which opened in Chicago in 1919 and then toured other cities in the Midwest, marked another first for Cukor, who had never been outside New York. Chicago became his first taste of travel. He fondly recalled that trip half a century later, when he went back to the Windy City to be honored at the Chicago Film Festival.

After *The Better 'Ole,* Cukor moved to another company in Chicago as the assistant stage manager of Mark Swan's *A Regular Feller.* Then Klaw and Erlanger sent him to Baltimore to supervise a musical, *Dere Mable.* Cukor was moving up the ranks; for this show he was promoted to stage manager.

On the road, Cukor met Howard Rumsey, a theatrical manager with the Belasco organization. Rumsey operated a stock company, the Knickerbocker Players, that presented plays in Syracuse and Rochester during the summer. His wife, the troupe's leading lady, was actress Florence Eldridge, who later married Fredric March (the star of Cukor's *Royal Family* and *Susan and God*).

Rumsey offered Cukor a job for the 1920 Knickerbocker season. His responsibilities were to organize the schedule of rehearsals and performances in both cities. Occasionally he had a walk-on part.

Cukor made the most of these jobs; they were his apprenticeship. He threw himself into theatrical work with all his energy and gusto. "There weren't schools in my day," he later said, "but there was an awful lot around to be observed." He soon discovered he was good at managing chaos, solving all kinds of problems—artistic, technical, administrative.

As the summer of 1921 approached, Cukor was again signed as stage manager of the Knickerbocker Players. The season turned out to be important for him, beginning one of the most enduring relationships of his life. Rehearsals were slated to begin in Syracuse in May, but earlier that spring the troupe was assembled at Tuxedo Hall on Madison Avenue in New York. When the season's strikingly beautiful ingenue, Frances Howard McLaughlin, arrived, Cukor was instantly smitten; she was the "prettiest girl" he had ever seen.

The actress and the stage manager fast became friends. They lived down the hall from each other first in Syracuse and later in Rochester and spent most of their free time together. Cukor talked incessantly about Frances's natural elegance and gorgeous skin. Frances became his protégé: He coached her, advised her what to wear, helped fine-tune her makeup and hair. He even convinced her to shorten her name to Frances Howard.

When the troupe moved to Rochester, Frances's hometown, for a week at the end of the summer (billed as the Manhattan Players at the Lyceum Theater), she introduced Cukor to relatives who had connections in the city. When Cukor became general manager of the Lyceum a year later, Frances moved with him. They were inseparable. Frances fell in love with Cukor, though she knew he was gay. Cukor's feelings for her also ran deep.

When, in 1925, movie mogul Samuel Goldwyn asked Frances to marry him, she consulted with Cukor. "I need you to tell me honestly," she said, "whether I have a future as an actress, or should I give it up for this man?"

Cukor, with the acerbic humor she admired, gave her his blessing. "Run, do not walk, to Samuel Goldwyn," he told her. "You have no future as an actress, but I suspect you have a considerable future as Mrs. Goldwyn." Frances and Cukor both wound up in Hollywood, where their close friendship endured until her death, in 1976.

"They were very close," recalls Frances's son, Samuel Goldwyn, Jr. "It was a romantic, though nonsexual, relationship; they were like brother and sister. They spoke every day on the telephone. My mother had a wonderfully wicked, offbeat sense of humor. She and George kidded and cracked jokes all the time."

During the summer of 1921 the proprietor of the Lyceum, Martin Wollf, died. Cukor befriended Mrs. Wollf and soon became the general manager of a newly formed company, the Lyceum Players. With his sharp tongue and congenial personality, he had a penchant for charming women, particularly older women.

In the 1920s Rochester was, according to Cukor, "a very American, very Yankee city, and so much fun." It had a bustling downtown, full of theaters, movie houses, restaurants, hotels. "Rochester was a good theater town then," Cukor remembered, even if the architecture, which was "Moorish and very twenties," offended his refined aesthetics. The Lyceum, however, with its huge, well-appointed stage was ideal. The first two years, 1922 and 1923, were modest in their offerings. Cukor was not yet directing, but he was important backstage, overseeing the productions' technical aspects.

Looking back on his early career, Cukor said: "I consider myself blessed, because when I was very young, I had a sense of what I wanted to do." Indeed, Cukor's tenure in Rochester reads like a success story from one of his productions. Within four years he was promoted from assistant stage manager to stage manager to director and finally coproducer of the Lyceum, considered the city's prime playhouse.

Cukor later recalled how "exciting and thrilling" the Rochester experience was. With a new production opening each week he was extraordinarily busy. But Cukor lived for his work. His approach to stock was brash, even experimental. He claimed credit for beginning the practice of bringing visiting stars to stock and trying out new plays that were destined for Broadway. "We did certain things that were not done before, and we did not know at the time that we were doing them," Cukor explained. "I didn't know that we were doing a new thing when we ushered in stock stars, like Billie Burke and Elsie Ferguson, to work with the regular players. Stock companies at that time never hired first-class stars. We could try them out for plays on Broadway."

Cukor understood that the survival of his troupe depended on its integration in the community. Most of the stock players settled in Rochester, becoming part of the town. Cukor, too, made an effort to socialize with the locals. According to Henry W. Clune, a local journalist, local theater buffs gathered around Cukor's company, members of the audience entertained them, stagestruck men dated the young women in the company. Cukor participated in these activities, even encouraged them. He loved the lavish parties and hobnobbing, the rewards of the profession he cherished; they were also considered vital to his job.

Louis Calhern, the talented and immensely popular star of the company, was something of a local hero, a hard-drinking, boisterous, and romantic leading man onstage and off. Cukor's friendship with the influential actor was of great value a year or two later, when Cukor set out to establish his own company in Rochester.

There were rival troupes, like the Temple Theater across the street, which at one time boasted Alice Brady as its star, and the Baker Theater, with its repertoire of melodramas. Cukor looked down on them; their productions lacked the sophistication and polish of his company.

Another rival center was the George Eastman House, which produced raw film stock and equipment. In 1923 Rouben Mamoulian, a Soviet immigrant, arrived in Rochester to direct the Eastman School of Music. Mamoulian mounted lavish spectacles that preceded the showing of films at Eastman. On Sunday nights Mamoulian staged grand operas at the School of Music: *Carmen, Faust, Tannhäuser.*

Cukor and Mamoulina maintained a distinct coolness toward each other. Though roughly the same age (Mamoulian was two years older), they came from different backgrounds. Mamoulian had trained for the stage at the Moscow Art Theater under Yevgeni Vakhtangov, a disciple of Konstantin Stanislavsky's. After Rochester Mamoulian began teaching and producing plays at the Theatre Guild; in 1927 he directed a successful Broadway production of *Porgy.* Because of his growing reputation as an inventive stage director, Mamoulian was approached by Paramount to make a movie, *Applause,* at its Astoria studio, in New York. Later he was one of the first stage directors to work in Hollywood.

When Cukor arrived in Hollywood, he didn't socialize with Mamoulian. In the 1930s the two were in competition, and Mamoulian directed Garbo in *Queen Christina,* three years before she worked with Cukor in *Camille*. However, in the long run Cukor's film career proved the more durable and more successful. By 1957, with only sixteen movies to his credit, Mamoulian's career was practically over; Cukor's continued for twenty-four years.

As summers ended, Cukor returned to New York for the regular theater season. He became the stage manager of the Empire Theater, the showcase of the Charles Frohman organization. From the start Cukor excelled in his methodic drilling of understudies and meticulous supervision of rehearsals.

Because Broadway-bound plays often began on the road, they required a good deal of traveling. Cukor liked going to Rochester for summer stock, but he didn't relish being on the road for long periods. This never changed. As a film director Cukor always preferred to work at home—close to his friends and his dogs. At the time, though, there were advantages to traveling. Cukor met interesting show business personalities, and there were also opportunities for one-night stands with the local gay men.

In 1923 Cukor met the respected British author Somerset Maugham while touring with *The Camel's Back,* a farce of three one-act plays. The older Maugham took an immediate liking to the young stage manager. The two men had a lot in common: Both were cultured, and neither was particularly attractive or fulfilled as a gay man.

Thus began a long-enduring friendship that ended only with Maugham's death in 1965. Maugham served as a role model for Cukor. Telling of his own unhappy marriage, he advised Cukor not to marry for the sake of facade; it wasn't worth it. Cukor appreciated the writer's Victorian sense of propriety, and over the years he learned the importance of self-discipline from Maugham, who was known for his rigid daily schedule. Above all, Cukor emulated the writer's need for control or, as Maugham's biographer noted, his attempt "to impose a pattern on his life—not merely his professional career but also his emotional and spiritual being." There was a price to be paid, however, for this discipline and control: Cukor was never to find personal happiness.

In Rochester Cukor was in the closet, never developing an overt homosexual attachment. His discretion as an homosexual prevailed in Hollywood. There was a contradiction in Cukor's personality: He never liked to talk about his own sex life, but he was extremely inquisitive about other people's private lives, wanting to know who was gay, how gay couples lived, what their sexual practices were. Immensely curious, Cukor bombarded Maugham and his companion, Alan Searle, with questions about their life-style.

On the tryout circuit Cukor was upset by changes made in the script as the producers tried to tighten the show. Maugham was nonplussed. "When you write easily," he said, "you don't mind cuts." Cukor learned an important lesson: For Maugham the writer, the ultimate test was whether the reader was tempted to turn the next page. Cukor applied Maugham's credo to his movies, becoming an audience-oriented director: "The primary purpose of movies is to capture audiences, entertain them—not to try to be arty or pretentious."

In Hollywood Cukor was to become a director of sophisticated films that were also commercially successful, some of them smash box-office hits. *Little Women, Dinner at Eight, Camille, The Philadelphia Story, Born Yesterday, A Star is Born, My Fair Lady* all were top-grossing films. In his best work Cukor combined literary and entertainment values in equal measure, creating popular pictures.

The summer of 1924 brought the devastating news that Mrs. Wollf was withdrawing her backing for the Rochester company. Cukor learned from Calhern that her decision, at least in part, was prompted by reports that Cukor was focusing too much attention and money on social concerns—parties and fun—and neglecting his work in the theater.

Cukor was hurt and angry particularly since he was devoting virtually all his time to the Lyceum. He believed his success in the community, which he had carefully forged and to which the fledgling company owed much of its existence, was being turned against him. He appealed to Mrs. Wollf, but to no avail; for the 1924 season the Lyceum was leased to another company.

With characteristic resilience, Cukor returned to New York and began making plans to start his own Rochester troupe. He consulted with Calhern, on whose friendship and loyalty he depended. At first he thought of naming it the Rochester Theater Guild, but Calhern warned him that the Theatre Guild had a highbrow ring, associated with such weighty works as G. B. Shaw's *Joan of Arc.* Since theater in Rochester was summer entertainment, why not simply call it the Cukor Company? "Don't be afraid to tack the Cukor name on it," Calhern advised; "you might as well start now to get it attached to programs. Keep on your toes—you can cut it, young feller."

Calhern was also willing to lend his name and considerable box-office clout to the endeavor. The difficulty, of course, was getting financial backing. Cukor approached George Eastman but was turned down. He then appealed to Walter Folmer, son of a wealthy Rochester manufacturer with interest in the theater, offering him a partnership. Folmer's father agreed to invest money in the next season. In the summer of 1925 Cukor returned to Rochester and the Lyceum at the helm of his new company, the C. F. and Z. Production Corporation—C for Cukor, F for Folmer, and Z for John Zwicki, the treasurer.

Ann Andrews and Ilka Chase joined Calhern as the company's leading actors. Later Calhern married Ilka Chase, the second leading lady, in what Cukor described as a "whirlwind" courtship. Most of the plays the following season were staged by Cukor or under his supervision. Calhern directed some plays, and there were also newcomers, like Irving Rapper, another Broadway stage manager who later went to Hollywood. About half the fourteen plays produced at the Lyceum in 1925 were new, which was unusual for summer stock.

Excited at the prospect of making his directorial debut on the Great White Way, Cukor returned to New York after the 1925 summer season. One of Broadway's foremost producers, and the manager of the Frohman organization, Gilbert Miller respected Cukor's skills as stage manager and knew of his work in Rochester. He decided to give the eager young director a shot at Broadway.

Arthur Richman's adaptation of Melchior Lengyel's Hungarian play *Antonia* premiered at the Empire Theater on October 20, 1925. Lengyel, who had directed *Antonia* in Hungary, was credited as Cukor's codirector. The story follows the adventures of a lusty country wife seeking romance and excitement in Budapest. The play is noteworthy for featuring the kind of heroine, strong and feisty, who appeared again and again in Cukor's movies.

Though billed as a musical comedy, *Antonia* had little music, and critics found it only moderately amusing. The production was designed to spotlight Marjorie Rambeau, a beautiful actress, then married to the heavy-drinking actor-writer Willard Mack. Rambeau was praised for her vigorous and varied performance, but the play closed after fifty-five performances.

Cukor went on to direct a number of plays on Broadway, but his stage career lacked distinction. None of his productions enjoyed a lengthy run, and only a few received good notices.

Cukor's inauspicious debut was followed a few months later by one of his more successful productions, *The Great Gatsby,* based on the F. Scott Fitzgerald novel, which premiered on February 2, 1926, at the Ambassador Theater. The play starred James Rennie, until then known primarily as Dorothy Gish's husband, and Florence Eldridge. It ran for 113 performances, Cukor's longest run on Broadway.

The Great Gatsby was Cukor's breakthrough as a stage director. Shrewdly adapted, carefully cast, and skillfully staged, it drew critical praise. "Mr. Cukor has done considerably more than drag the play behind the footlights," wrote the *New York Post*'s John Anderson . "In spite of its artificial nature, he has thrown a sheltering cloak of plausibility." This critic noted that on a wintry night Cukor so completely simulated heat and humidity that he drove this "parched larynx to the nearest soda fountain." The romantic scenes were also depicted as being credible and passionate.

Cukor gave much of the credit to Owen Davis's clever and sophisticated play. "Fitzgerald is very hard to translate to the stage," he said, "you really have to know the milieu of the whole thing and you've got not to overblow it. We had a wonderful adaptation, you could play it." Davis attended all the rehearsals, giving welcomed suggestions to the director and the actors.

At times Davis's script tended toward verbosity, but Cukor overcame this fault by speeding up the pace. Pacing was to become one of Cukor's signatures as a film director, best illustrated by the breakneck speed of *The Women.* The first thing Candice Bergen, costar of Cukor's last film, *Rich and Famous,* recalled was the eighty-one-year-old director yelling over and over again, "Pick it up, girls, pick it up, faster, faster."

The summer of 1926 found Cukor back in Rochester. The Lyceum Players moved to the Temple Theater for the season under the banner of the Cukor-Kondolf Stock Company, a newly formed partnership with Rochester native George Kondolf. The summer programs were heavily weighted toward comedy and melodrama. But the company enjoyed moderate prestige and publicity, too. Critics from New York ventured to Rochester to review the plays. Cukor encouraged them by importing an impressive array of talent from Broadway as guest artists, some on a regular basis. Among these performers were Helen Menken, Dorothy Gish and James Rennie, Billie Burke, Louis Wolheim, Wallace Ford, Elsie Ferguson, Ruth Gordon, and Helen Hayes. Some of these actors reprised their Broadway hit roles.

Big-name talents enjoyed working with Cukor; he understood their mentality and psychology. He felt comfortable around celebrities; he knew how to court them, how to treat them. He never forgot to send flowers or telegrams on opening night to his performers, years after he had become a big shot.

Two tendencies of Cukor's career—his interest in working with established stars and his ability to discover new talent—were already evident in the 1920s. "He could detect talent a mile off," observed Glynis Johns, who appeared in *The Chapman Report.* "He knew whether somebody had the talent and the magic right away." Many Hollywood figures owed their careers to Cukor: Katharine Hepburn, Angela Lansbury, Aldo Ray, Jack Lemmon, Anthony Perkins, Capucine, to name only a few.

From 1926 to 1928 the summer schedules in Rochester were extremely busy. In June and July a new play was presented every week, with performances six nights a week plus matinees. On Monday Cukor started rehearsals early in the morning and worked his actors straight through the week. The company rehearsed during the day and performed at night.

"I study my new parts until three in the morning, snatch some sleep, and rehearse a good part of the next day on the roof of the hotel," reported guest artist Helen Menken. "Then it's time to go back to work, and when that's over, I begin to study more on my new role again. Working in stock is very hard."

Cukor transformed his stock company into a substitute family for himself and his performers. As a stage and film director Cukor was a strange combination of a matriarchal and patriarchal figure, at once nurturing and stern. Aldo Ray, whom Cukor discovered, observed that while filming *Pat and Mike,* even though Cukor was relaxed with Tracy and Hepburn, he still acted "like a mother hen, nurturing them, holding them together."

In Rochester Cukor began what became a lifelong practice and his signature as an actors' director: lengthy talks with his actors. Cukor knew exactly what he wanted from his performers. Always firm, he was not beyond yelling and screaming if he didn't get a desired effect, but with a few exceptions of public outbursts on his sets, Cukor's direction was discreet. He developed a habit of whispering his remarks quietly in the actors' ears.

Cukor possessed a unique talent for pulling individuality out of an actor. Describing himself as full of "hot tips," he said: "I like to surprise the actors and surprise myself, it's awfully important that they be stimulated. You find out what the key is, make them feel right, bring out things in them that they don't know and you don't know." He perceived his role as a director as making his actors "lively all the time." That's why filmmaking continued to be a great adventure for him; there were always new performers to drill, new actors to stimulate and nurture.

Many future screen performers passed through the ranks of the Cukor-Kondolf Stock Company. Cukor never forgot them. In later years he proved a loyal friend, casting old colleagues in his movies. Louis Calhern, best known for his powerful MGM films, was cast in *A Life of Her Own.* Douglass Montgomery costarred in *Little Women* and was used in the screen tests for *Gone with the Wind.* Phyllis Povah was cast in *The Women* and *The Marrying Kind,* Ilka Chase in a bit role in *It Should Happen to You,* Reginald Owen in *A Woman's Face,* Elizabeth Patterson in *Tarnished Lady* and *David Copperfield,* Genevieve Tobin in *One Hour with You* and *Zaza.*

Bette Davis also passed through the company during the 1926 season. She was not, however, destined to join Cukor's Hollywood stable. Davis arrived in Rochester with a letter of introduction from Frank Conroy, an actor Cukor knew from the New York stage whom he later cast in *The Royal Family of Broadway.* Cukor first cast the ambitious actress as a tough chorus girl in the musical *Broadway.* When the show's star sprained her ankle, Davis stepped into the part. Her big scene, shooting the villain, was the climax of the play.

Cukor was immediately impressed with Davis's fiery talent. "Bette seemed to know this was her big chance and she took hold from the first moment," he said. "I was worried she might be overdoing it. The other girl had played it toughly, coldly, but Bette had a mind of maniacal fierceness—even seemed to be willing the actor to die. The audience was stunned." Cukor realized she had the same "white heat" that Jeanne Eagels had. Davis went on to appear in a number of plays that summer: *Excess Baggage, Cradle Snatchers, The Man Who Came Back, Laff That Off,* and *The Squall.* Cukor promised to rehire her as a resident ingenue but never did.

"Her talent was apparent," Cukor later said, "but she did buck at direction. She had her own ideas, and though she only did bits and ingenue roles, she didn't hesitate to express them. Her mother, as I recall, pushed her like crazy, and was always lurking about." Davis tended to argue whenever Cukor criticized her; she could never admit she might have been wrong. Other company members—Miriam Hopkins and Louis Calhern—also spoke against her, resenting her stubbornness and ambition. Finally, when Davis complained during a rehearsal of the melodrama *Yellow* that she looked more like Calhern's daughter than his mistress, Cukor replaced her.

Calhern later suggested that Cukor gave in to pressure from the other actors to get rid of her. The already headstrong Davis abruptly left the company, but Cukor continued to claim she was not asked to leave. "I did not fire Bette," he said. "She insists I did, and says I had a low opinion of her then. Somehow she got it into her head that I sacked her on the spot."

Davis's dismissal became Hollywood legend. Over the years Cukor grew sick and tired of hearing the story. Once, meeting Davis in a party, he said to her: "For Chrissakes, Bette, don't talk about how I always fired you. We've all been fired, and we all will be again before we're through." Cukor was always puzzled that such a minor incident would become such big trauma for her; "she thinks I have done her a great injustice." Cukor did, however, believe that Davis was not good in comedies.

With another Rochester season behind him, Cukor found himself on the road with Frohman, as stage manager in Maugham's noted play *The Constant Wife.* Though not directing, Cukor was thrilled to be working with the leading lady, Ethel Barrymore, Broadway's reigning queen and one of his childhood idols. George Miller received sole credit for directing the play, but Cukor worked extensively on the staging.

The play, about a modern, freethinking wife's indifference to her husband's philandering, was risqué at the time—"delightfully scandalous," one critic said. Alexander Woollcott noted that twenty years earlier police would have closed down the production. *The Constant Wife* toured extensively across the country and was successful everywhere. By the time the play reached Broadway in December 1926, it was already a bona fide hit. Its run in Washington, D.C., topped box-office grosses of the best plays on Broadway.

The first performance in Cleveland, however, was ragged because the cast members, including Barrymore, had not yet mastered their lines. They had to depend on the audible assistance of a prompter, concealed, as a disgruntled critic noted, "like Santa Claus in a stage fireplace." After the performance, approaching a distracted Maugham, Barrymore put her arms around him and kissed him. "Willie, Willie," she said, "I've spoiled your beautiful play. But it will be all right." It was more than all right.

As the run progressed, Cukor and Barrymore became close. Every night after the performance they talked in her room for hours. On weekends Cukor went to her country house. Barrymore became a surrogate mother—and an elder sister and a distinguished member of his burgeoning extended family.

"Friendships are of enormous importance to me," Cukor once said, "but every friendship must be handled according to its own logic." He explained: "You must maintain the relative position of the first meeting. When I first met Ethel Barrymore, I fell on my face. We became good friends and she was very dear to me. But when she stayed here, it was always the same. She'd contradict me and say, 'Go here, go there.' " Older by twenty years, Barrymore was the only actress who exerted such influence.

Friendships provided continuity in Cukor's life. He was extremely adept at making and maintaining long-term relationships with women—and men. In the early 1920s he befriended Alex Tiers and Whitney Warren, two young men who became close friends. Both were handsome and independently wealthy men who unsuccessfully attempted stage careers. Both had "social connections," the kind that Cukor desired and eventually achieved in Hollywood.

Whitney Warren was the son and namesake of the architect who had designed Grand Central Station. Well educated and well traveled, the younger Warren knew show business personalities of the caliber of Ina Claire and Tallulah Bankhead. As for Alex Tiers, he had inherited a fortune from his family's sulfur mine operations. Both men later moved to California—Tiers to Santa Barbara, Warren to San Francisco—and kept in close touch with Cukor until his death. They spoke on the telephone, wrote letters, visited each other. San Francisco was the only city Cukor frequented with some regularity; he could be freer and wilder there in his sexual escapades.

Humor, reflected in good company, was the basis of Cukor's relationships. Paul Morrissey recalled: "The element of fun was the most wonderful part of his friendships, not the mechanical fun, but a kind of humorous fun, a sense of absurdity." Cukor was a boisterous raconteur, but stories, not jokes, were his specialty. "George would characterize certain people and then tell anecdotes about them. And you would hear the same stories more than once, because he didn't remember he'd told them, but he would be the first to admit his memory was weak.

"George's favorite people were the Barrymores," Morrissey elaborated. "For him, they had a lot of class. They were great aristocrats, but they constantly made fun of themselves and didn't mind looking foolish." Cukor also had a special liking for the Irish of the likes of Spencer Tracy and Judy Garland. "The Irish drank a lot," he said, "but they just made you laugh."

Much of the professional bond between Cukor and his actors was based on laughter. Aldo Ray recalled that humor and laughter were a staple on Cukor's sets. "For some reason," he said, "Europeans seem to be able to laugh at almost anything. My mother is an eighty-three-year-old Italian, and she still laughs like hell." Cukor's unique laugh is the first thing actors mention about him. Capucine, whom Cukor directed in *Song Without End,* described his laughter as "epidemic and contagious."

Back at the Lyceum Theater in Rochester, the Lyceum Players' summer 1927 lineup was fairly typical: twelve plays in thirteen weeks. *Rain,* based on Maugham's short story "Miss Thompson," opened the season on May 16. Moving from stark tragedy to staccato comedy, the play concerns a missionary's ill-fated attempt to reform a girl of the streets. The production brought Helen Menken, the celebrated star of *Seventh Heaven,* to Rochester as a guest performer. She earned laurels under Cukor's direction, giving one of the season's finest performances.

On Broadway *Rain* broke records with 947 performances, then set records across the country, including Rochester. So many theatergoers had to be turned away from the Lyceum each performance that the management decided, for the first time in its history, to extend a run for a second week. Cukor and Kondolf sent a jubilant communiqué to Gilbert Miller reporting their success. Though the best seats were modestly priced at $1.65, *Rain* set new box-office records for stock, grossing $11,000 in the first week and $8,000 in the second.

As a result of Menken's tremendous success in *Rain,* she agreed to star in the Lyceum's next production, *The Dove.* Written by Willard Mack, the play had been first presented on Broadway in 1925. It began its run on May 30, with Menken and Minor Watson, another guest artist, in the leading roles. Set in a Mexican town near the border, *The Dove* was a colorful old-style melodrama of gamblers, firing squads, and dance hall maidens. The huge cast and many settings made heavy demands on the resources of a stock company. Cukor was praised for mounting an expensive and ambitious undertaking with his usual effectiveness—"admirably done," said the Rochester *Times Union*.

Applesauce, a comedy by Barry Conners, which premiered on June 6, brought a new lady to Rochester. At the last moment Miriam Hopkins was asked to replace Helen Menken, convalescing from a throat operation. Cukor assured Menken that she would rejoin the troupe as soon as she recovered. But Hopkins soon became a staple among the company's guest artists.

A slight comedy of love, marriage, and money, *Applesauce* was not well received on Broadway. In Rochester, however, it was a hit. Cukor played to his audience. Every line was exaggerated; the whole production was consciously caricaturistic. The laughter was so uproarious that the actors had trouble making their lines audible.

The Players' next offering, Arnold Ridley's *The Ghost Train*, on June 13, was a change of pace, a mystery melodrama set in a train station at night. Cukor, assisted by Arthur Wood, subjected his characters and the audience to a host of eerie atmospheric and mechanical effects. The play had little dramatic value, but Cukor and Wood's re-creation of a passing train was impressive.

The Ghost Train was followed on June 20 by Harry Delf's *The Family Upstairs*, an unpretentious play about a middle-class girl who can't reconcile her love of family with her aspirations for the finer things in life. Although the play was criticized for heavy-handedness, the lead actress, Roberta Beatty, was praised. However, Miriam Hopkins, as the mischievous younger sister, stole the show.

Helen Menken rejoined the company the following week as the star of *The Green Hat*, adapted by Michael Arlen from his novel. A story about class differences and frustrated love ending in the heroine's tragic suicide, *The Green Hat* was routine melodramatic fare. Cukor was drawn to this kind of material—melodramas with strong, independent female characters—because of their audience appeal.

Reaction to *The Green Hat* was mixed. While one critic dismissed the play as worthless and unpleasant, another praised it as the most sophisticated of the season. Most agreed, however, that the performances were above what might be expected from the minimal rehearsal time available to the company.

The Fourth of July marked the opening of *Drifting*, by John Colton and D. H. Andrews, a sprawling political drama set in China that was part adventure, part love story. In the leading role, Menken re-created her Broadway success of a few years earlier. *Drifting*, with its six changes of scenery and unusually large cast, was another difficult project for a stock company. Cukor again won kudos for his deft production. "That they are so successful with the show casts a lot of credit on George Cukor," wrote one critic.

A writer from the *New York Sunday Telegraph* was on hand for the opening of *Grounds for Divorce,* by Ernest Vajda, on July 13—again starring Helen Menken. "The smooth Parisian comedy I saw swelled into hearty burlesque under the directorial baton of George Cukor," she reported. "This change of direction was vital to the Rochester—shall we say—temperament." Though smirking at the gloved debutantes and dowagers entering the Lyceum Theater, she had kind words for the company. "The Lyceum Players constitute the only $1.65 top stock company in the country. Their productions not only merit comparison with Broadway offerings, they are even superior."

Mulberry Bush, a Broadway tryout by Edward Knoblock starring Fay Bainter and Hugh Wakefield, and *The Butter and Egg Man,* a George S. Kaufman farce about theatrical sharpshooters, rounded out the regular season, which was scheduled to close at the end of July. But response to the company from the Rochester community was so good that two more plays were added, extending the season to August 13.

No, No Nanette, which was not directed by Cukor, opened on August 1, and a new play, *Diversion,* by John Van Druten, followed. Estelle Winwood was brought in from New York to star in *Diversion*—another Broadway tryout. Winwood played a well-worn London actress in Italy whose love affair with a young British law student ends in tragedy. Strong acting could not salvage a play burdened with a long, talky first act. Critics recognized the shortcomings but attributed it to the difficulties of staging a brand-new play in a single week.

Cukor's work on Broadway in 1927 was less than stellar. The year began badly with the February opening of Martin Brown's *The Dark,* a production that had originated in Rochester in the 1925 season. The play is a psychological melodrama about a woman saddled with a blind, disfigured husband whom she cannot bear. For the New York production Louis Calhern and Ann Andrews re-created their original roles. After a long incubating period, however, the curtain rose on the Broadway production only thirteen times.

In the spring of 1927 Cukor directed another of his childhood idols, Laurette Taylor, in Valerie Wyngate's *Her Cardboard Lover.* Taylor starred as a liberated Parisian who engages a penniless young man—played by Leslie Howard—to masquerade as her lover, in this Americanization of a popular French play. It was one of the few comedies Cukor directed on Broadway—odd, considering that in Hollywood he became a specialist of the genre.

Neurotic and alcoholic, Taylor was not easy to work with. To make matters worse, bedroom farce was not her forte. When he realized that his revered star was uncomfortable in her role, Cukor tried to help her through the awkward moments. He set up special lighting, for instance, in scenes where she had to disrobe, to mollify her sense of exposure.

Although Cukor found Taylor's performance light and funny, the critics thought she was miscast and panned her. Following a preview in Atlantic City, Taylor was reportedly dismissed. After months of rumors and counterrumors and a lot of shuffleboard casting, *Her Cardboard Lover* opened at the Empire Theater on March 21, 1927, with another legendary actress, Jeanne Eagels. Leslie Howard and playwright Wyngate, who had a small role as a maid, retained their roles. Howard garnered universal raves from the New York critics, but Eagels, a brilliant dramatic actress, was not well received in this frothy comedy. As Brooks Atkinson of the *Times* put it, "In a play so dependent upon acting, the clumsiness of the leading part was fatal."

In the fall, after the 1927 Rochester summer stock season closed, Cukor was slated to direct Helen Hayes, another old friend, in a Broadway production of a new play entitled *Coquette*. Cukor had met Hayes in the fall of 1924, while stage-managing the Frohman production of *Dancing Mothers*. That cast also included David Manners, who later worked with Cukor on his first film with Katharine Hepburn, *A Bill of Divorcement*.

During the months he worked on *Dancing Mothers,* Cukor and Hayes became friends. It was because of their friendship that Cukor was engaged to direct *Coquette*. Hayes played a perfect Cukor heroine, a southern tart, a coquette, who finds herself in trouble when succumbing to a passionate love affair. But saddled with a poorly written play, Cukor could not make the material work. *Coquette* had originally been written as a comedy by first-time playwright Ann Preston Bridgers, then reworked as a drama. Both Cukor and Hayes were frustrated by the end result.

George Abbott, a producer-director who had helped Preston with the script, was brought in to rewrite the play. But he also insisted on directing, and Cukor left the production. Whether he was fired, asked to resign, or simply quit depends on which version of the story one hears. Hayes later noted that she was "too cowardly" to stand up and demand that Cukor stay. At any rate, Abbott took over and transformed the play into a successful production. It was a slap on Cukor's face when the drama critics hailed *Coquette* as one of the highlights of the season.

Cukor quickly began another play, the first of five he was to direct on Broadway over the next fifteen months. *Trigger,* by Lula Vollmer, was a saga of southern hillbillies brimming with religion and histrionics. Premiering on December 6, 1927, the play enjoyed a moderate run of fifty shows. Cukor typically dealt with the play's ups and downs of sentimentality and confusion by keeping the pace brisk. "Cukor has scraped through earnest layers of hard-caked local color and uncovered its patches of middling to good melodrama," one critic noted.

A murder mystery followed: Willard Mack's *A Free Soul,* based on a novel by Adela Rogers St. Johns. In the play an independent-minded daughter of a once-prominent jurist repudiates her social standing to marry a notorious gambler (played by the young Melvyn Douglas). The play ran more than three months—a respectable achievement.

In March 1928 Cukor again had an opportunity to direct Laurette Taylor in Zoe Akins's *The Furies,* a play centering on a woman accused of murdering her millionaire husband. Her brooding son, studying Shakespeare, is obsessively suspicious of his mother and her lover. Intended to boost Taylor's sagging career, the production was lavish. But despite its allusions to *Hamlet,* the play was jumbled and excessively maudlin. There was unanimous praise for Taylor's beguiling performance, but the play closed after forty-one performances.

One of Cukor's Broadway tryouts for the 1928 Rochester season opened in New York on October 29. *Young Love,* a sex comedy about a pair of lovers testing their relationship before marriage, starred silent film siren Dorothy Gish, in her Broadway debut, and her husband, James Rennie. Samson Raphaelson, who later became an accomplished screenwriter (*The Jazz Singer*), wrote the play. Adroit direction and excellent cast kept *Young Love* running for almost three months.

Cukor next tackled Maxwell Anderson's *Gypsy,* which opened regionally on New Year's Day, 1929, with Claiborne Foster and Louis Calhern. In the move to Broadway two weeks later, Calhern was replaced by Donn Cook. Another melodrama with a strong female lead, the play presented a portrait of a modern marriage between a forthright man and his false, insubstantial wife. "Few plays are lucky enough to be as well-acted as *Gypsy,* and so well-staged as George Cukor has staged it," noted one critic. Other notices, though were bad—bad enough for the show to close on its twelfth night.

By January 1929 Cukor was ready to walk away from the stage. In five years he had established one of the nation's most exciting summer stock companies and earned a modest reputation as a Broadway director. But he never attained greatness; really good plays never came his way, and the conditions under which he directed—especially the short rehearsal time—were far from ideal.

Cukor found summer stock and the traveling involved in Broadway tryouts wearying and arduous; the rewards, particularly the monetary ones, were not good either. Between 1918 and 1926 Cukor was earning $75 to $100 a month. Even as a director for Frohman and Miller his salary reached only $350 a month.

When an official of the Paramount Famous Lasky corporation approached Cukor with an offer to direct dialogue and assist actors in Hollywood, he couldn't resist the financial allure: $600 a week and the security of long-term contracts! Always a practical man, Cukor decided to move west. But money was not the only reason for embracing the new medium; Cukor somehow knew instinctively that movies were the future of mass entertainment.

Cukor's most outstanding traits as a director—and a person—were enthusiasm, boundless energy, and determination to succeed. Actors marveled at his endless exhilaration, which was contagious. Cukor knew how to channel his creative energies into the movies he made; he knew how to stimulate his performers. But perhaps most important of all were Cukor's tenacity and resilience—the basic instinct to survive professional failures, even to learn from them.

Cukor's credo, long before he moved to Hollywood, was "On to the next thing." The title of a later autobiography, which never materialized, was going to be *Getting On*. It was this quality that made him the oldest-working filmmaker when at the age of eighty-one he directed his last film, *Rich and Famous*. Cukor didn't die a rich man, but he did achieve fame and distinction (the latter one of his favorite words), in one of the toughest and most competitive businesses, the movies.

CHAPTER TWO:

The Making of a Movie Director, 1929–32

In THE EARLIER DAYS OF SOUND, BECAUSE THE TECHNOLOGY WAS new, a dialogue director—who worked with the actors, coaching them scene by scene—was sometimes present on the set. Stage directors were a logical choice for such a job. With the advent of sound in Hollywood, there was a sizable influx of theater directors who were interested in working in talking pictures.

Cukor was brought to Hollywood from Broadway, in early 1929, as a future film director. He followed the paths of Rouben Mamoulian, John Cromwell, and others from New York. Salisbury had approached Cukor with the offer "to direct the dialogue and to assist directors." He was not entitled to receive screen credit during the first six months, which were considered an apprenticeship, enabling Cukor to observe the manner in which pictures were made.

Cukor's first agreement at Paramount was signed on December 19, 1928. Walter Wanger, then general manager of Paramount, started Cukor on a six-month contract at $600 a week. In July 1929 it was extended for another six months, at $750.

Cukor's first assignment was to serve as dialogue coach for director Richard Wallace on Paramount's *River of Romance*. Based on Booth Tarkington's play *Magnolia,* the movie deals with the codes of honor in the South. The star of the film was Charles "Buddy" Rogers, who had appeared in the 1927 Oscar-winning film *Wings* and was then nicknamed America's Boy Friend. Rogers played a southerner who returns home after getting an education in Philadelphia. The big city has presumably changed him, for he commits the "unpardonable" sin of refusing to fight a duel. His father casts him off, and he ventures down the Mississippi (thus the title *River of Romance*).

Despite the potential awkwardness of what amounted to two directors, Cukor and Wallace worked well together. The actors felt no loyalty toward one or the other, according to the film's star Mary Brian, who was also to appear in Cukor's *The Royal Family of Broadway*. "George was subtle," Brian said. "He knew what he had to contribute—not just dialogue; analysis, too. George was more articulate than Wallace; he was really good in communicating his ideas." Bringing along his cumulative experience as stage director, Cukor worked with the actors on their big, important scenes. Brian remembered the film as one of the "great learning experiences" of her career.

Easy to work with, Cukor elicited great commitment from the actors. He knew exactly what he was after and the specific ways to get it. When an actor was headed in the wrong direction, Brian said, Cukor read the scene himself and illustrated his point. She remembered his readings as "always on the mark."

His early pictures were also an education for Cukor, whose aspirations went well beyond being a dialogue coach. On the set of *River of Romance,* he often observed the technicalities of moviemaking, absorbing all he could about the new exciting medium. He was using his time to learn and formulate his own techniques. "Some directors are the outdoor type," Brian said, "others are good with dialogue, but Cukor had complete control, with a well-rounded input to his pictures."

Cukor was serious, but not really formal, in his work. This attitude was reflected in the way he dressed. Unlike other directors, Cukor did not wear a suit, just a jacket and a tie. Brian recalled that he was round, "a bit fat," because he loved to eat. Unselfconscious about his appetite, however, Cukor laughed at his excessive eating. "One day," Brian recalled, "there was a strange sound on the set; it turned out to be Cukor's stomach growling from his lunch."

While working on this film, Cukor met editor Cyril Gardner, who soon became a director himself. In those days editors were on the set, and Cukor listened carefully to Wallace and Gardner's discussions about camera setups, angles, and cutting. He began to acquire not only technical skills but the jargon that went along with it.

Over at Universal, *All Quiet on the Western Front,* a big-budget prestige film, was in preparation. Carl Laemmle, Jr., the studio's young head of production, was building his reputation on making quality films on a grand scale. Laemmle committed $1.25 million to put Erich Maria Remarque's famous pacifist novel of World War I on the screen. It was a staggering budget for the late 1920s and a major risk for the studio.

Lewis Milestone was signed to direct through his agent, Myron

Selznick, the brother of David O. Selznick, who at the time was executive assistant to B. P. Schulberg, Paramount's general manager. Milestone, originally a film editor, was an expert with the camera but had limited experience with sound. Myron Selznick, who also represented Cukor, convinced Milestone to bring the young dialogue coach onto the picture to work with the actors. Though Cukor knew little about filmmaking, he understood acting and dialogue. David Selznick was glad to inform Cukor in the fall of 1929 that he had been lent to Universal at Milestone's request.

A bleak portrayal of trench warfare, *All Quiet* follows a group of German soldiers who are initially excited by the glories of war but then find disillusionment and death on the battlefield. In keeping with its pacifist theme, the movie, a stinging indictment of the inanity of war, officially went into production on Armistice Day, November 11, 1929.

It took seventeen weeks to shoot the picture. Interior scenes were filmed on the lot at Universal, but the extensive exteriors were shot at various locations around Southern California: the RKO-Pathé Studios in Culver City, Malibu Lakes, and Sherwood Forest in the San Fernando Valley. The crucial battlefield sequences were shot on the Irvine Ranch (now the University of California at Irvine), which in those days was mostly barren rolling hills, a perfect setting for a war film.

Though Cukor was consulted, Milestone handled the principal casting. William Bakewell, Louis Wolheim, Russell Gleason, and Owen Davis, Jr., were among the young men cast in lead roles. But it was Lew Ayres who gained "overnight" stardom for his portrayal of Paul, the sensitive soldier. At first Cukor was opposed to casting Ayres, for the actor had been in films for only one year and was inexperienced for a leading role. "George was doubtful about my capacity," Ayres said, "but we didn't have any trouble because of it."

On the first day Milestone introduced Cukor to the cast: "Now, there's a man out here from New York who's going to be the dialogue director. This is his first time out here." The actors knew that Cukor had been successful in the theater and had a renowned company in Rochester, but beyond that they didn't know what to expect.

Cukor possessed a disarming charm that tended to win people over right away. But on first impression he was markedly unattractive. "He was quite plump in those days," Bill Bakewell recalled, "with a gargoyle-like face, black curly hair and horn-rimmed glasses." Working in an industry that admired good looks, Cukor had reason to be sensitive about his homely appearance.

Writer Gavin Lambert, who befriended the director in the 1960s, said, "I suppose anybody would be [sensitive], wouldn't they? You are sensitive to the fact that you are not as good-looking as you would like to be."

Never one to be self-pitying, however, Cukor didn't talk about his looks, though he did talk about his weight. "Cukor's real fat period was in the 1930s and 1940s, but he took steps: He had a trainer who made him exercise and carefully watched his diet."

Bakewell remembered that Cukor was also sensitive about his Jewishness. "He would say with his biting and caustic wit, 'You boys are ashamed of me because I'm a Jew.' " Bakewell hastened to add that Cukor was only kidding, but most of Cukor's friends confirm that he shied away from the subject.

"Unlike a lot of American Jews," said Lambert, "who talk about it and sort of make fun of it, 'Well, you know that's a classic Jewish syndrome,' George never had that at all." In fact, Cukor preferred not to discuss his origins. "I don't know whether he was uncomfortable about it," said Lambert, "but he did not have an innate solidarity with the American Jewish movement. Perhaps he was embarrassed." Lambert elaborated: "Maybe he would like not to have been a Jew, but he was not going to make a big thing about it. He was going to play it down." This attitude, according to Lambert, stemmed from living in Hollywood in the 1930s, when Cukor's values took shape.

"There were so many things in George that were covered [up]," said Lambert, "things that were never discussed but, of course, [that] he must have felt about. Obviously George was in many ways an enormous outsider in his time. He was an outsider as a gay person, as a not-attractive gay person, and as a Jewish person." In Lambert's view, Cukor contended with these things with incredible resourcefulness: "George was basically optimistic about life. Optimism is an innate quality one either has or doesn't have."

Although Cukor had been in Hollywood only a year, his sexual preference was not a secret in the film community. Bakewell recalled, "People said, 'You guys be careful, watch out for this man, he is queer.' " One evening Cukor asked Ayres to his Hollywood apartment for some extra work. Ayres was nervous about it. "If anything happens," he told Bakewell, "you can forget it." Of course, nothing happened. "George never, ever tried or did anything like that," Bakewell said. "He was too intelligent, too nice, too professional. He couldn't have been straighter. He was not effeminate or swishy."

Shortly after his arrival in Hollywood Cukor befriended MGM's actor William Haines and his gay entourage. Cukor and Haines had some notoriously wild nights on the town and were even arrested. Friends of Cukor are vague about the incident, which he never talked about, but they held that his arrest was a turning point.

Said director Joseph Mankiewicz, who befriended Cukor through his sister-in-law, Sara Mankiewicz, Cukor's friend: "George got very frightened when he and Haines were arrested in public. Once he became an MGM director, he calmed and settled down." Mankiewicz recalled talks about "MGM fixing some public happening that involved George and Billy." After that incident Cukor became very discreet about his homosexuality. "George would never go to a gay bar," said a friend. "He would ask us to bring interesting men to his house."

Still, Cukor never hid his homosexuality, never pretended he was straight, and never lived a double life; he was just "discreet" about something he assumed everybody in Hollywood knew. Indeed, when Louis B. Mayer, who was "to the right of Attila the Hun" in politics, heard that his "distinguished director of memorable earth-moving loving scenes with the most glamorous actress, might himself not like women," he summoned Cukor to his office. Nearly whispering, he said, "George, this is a very important matter. A very serious matter. You must answer me truthfully because I must know." Hardly able to get the words out, the mogul then said, "Tell me, are you a . . . homosexual?" Cukor replied unhesitantly: "Dedicated."

That was the end of the conversation and the meeting. Louis B. simply turned away and began reading his mail. And while the conservative Republican never liked Cukor, the event didn't signal the end of his MGM career. As producer David Brown observed, "even Louis B.'s homophobia gave way to the higher needs of business, money, and stockholders." Cukor's career never suffered because he was gifted and his movies were box-office hits.

Mankiewicz claimed that there wasn't much gossip about Cukor. "He was not the first gay artist in Hollywood; it was not big news because there was always a new homosexual in town." Though discreet, Cukor wasn't shy: He was determined to help other new gay artists in the film colony. Said Mankiewicz: "Homosexuals would call George as soon as they arrived in Hollywood, and if he liked them, he would introduce them to other members of his elite."

Cukor's friends credited him for performing a vital function in the annals of Hollywood's gay life. Los Angeles *Times* critic Kevin Thomas held that "George created a civilized gay society in Hollywood. You could always meet intelligent gay men at his house." According to Thomas, this role was important in a city like Los Angeles, which is not like New York, and in a conservative industry. Said Thomas: "George left a tremendous gap in gay social life after his death."

Once *All Quiet* was cast, Cukor took the actors in hand and rehearsed them for two weeks before shooting began. He had his work cut out for him: They were young and green and were going to play German characters. Said Bakewell: "Cukor wanted to eliminate any localism in our speech; he was particularly concerned about the dialogue sounding too midwestern. He worked long and hard with actors to purify and soften their speech." He added: "George was an absolute genius as far as dialogue was concerned. I don't think there was ever a director more qualified. He was a perfectionist, we rehearsed over and over again." Ayres's repeated complaint to Bakewell was: "I don't think I can ever please him."

Present on the set every day throughout the picture, Cukor soon became much more than a dialogue director; he became an invaluable assistant to Milestone. Milestone was the kind of director who would say, "All right, now you're coming into this scene, you're cold and hungry, or you're angry or you're happy. Go and do the scene." But not Cukor. "George discussed the lines thoroughly," Ayres said. "He went on way beyond what you could hope to remember. He analyzed motivation and meaning in every line, every word. He had incredible capacity for analysis, more than we really wanted to hear."

Because Ayres played the leading role in the picture and was less experienced than the rest, he often bore the brunt of Cukor's tireless perfectionism. In retrospect, Ayres acknowledged the value of Cukor's coaching, but at the time he was unhappy about getting so much attention. Ayres never encountered another director who could analyze a script to the degree that Cukor did. Ayres postulated that perhaps "this is why actresses were so drawn to him: Women may enjoy lots of direction, but men don't want so much."

Cukor often stopped a scene to work on the reading of a specific line, and he persisted until he was satisfied with the tone of each word. Bakewell recalled that even while shooting the battle scenes, Cukor, with a white handkerchief over his head underneath a German steel helmet—to protect his hair from flying dirt—sat behind the camera, mouthing each and every line with the actors and making "sort of gargoyle faces." Cukor was so funny that the actors had to fight breaking out in laughter whenever they looked at him.

Ayres worked with Cukor again eight years later, on *Holiday,* this time with Cukor directing. "Generally speaking," Ayres said, "George worked in the same way, though in *Holiday* he was not as meticulous as he had been on *All Quiet.* That was his first job, and he wanted to make a statement about his capacity. When you're a director, you're concerned with many other things, you don't have the time to be so specific with the dialogue."

Principal photography on *All Quiet* was completed in the last week of March, and the film was released later that year. Proving to be a box-office hit, Universal's biggest success to date, it went on to win the 1930 Oscars for Best Picture and Best Director. *All Quiet* was Cukor's first major work in Hollywood, but because his name didn't appear in the credits, few people were aware of his role.

At the time Cukor didn't say a word about it, but he was offended. Years later, while dining at Ayres's house, with Bakewell in attendance, Cukor reminisced about how the studio had given him a handful of "dreadful boys" to whip into shape. The fact that he had not been given screen credit still bothered him. "That's the only ignoble thing I ever recall Millie [Milestone] doing," Cukor said..

Every film Cukor worked on resulted in new, long-lasting friendships. This became the norm, beginning with the relationships he formed with Mary Brian, Bakewell, and Ayres. Cukor remained good friends with Ayres and Bakewell through the years; both were asked to speak at a memorial for him.

Cukor went back to New York after *All Quiet*, but once he had tasted life on the West Coast, New York was not the same. All of a sudden the busy and congested streets, the noise and filth of the big city began to bother him. It was just a matter of time before he settled in California.

In 1930 Cukor was assigned to codirect *Grumpy* with Cyril Gardner, whom he had met during *River of Romance*. This was the first of three films Cukor codirected. Though Paramount elevated him to the position of codirector, Cukor's work was not fundamentally different from that of dialogue coach. He handled the acting and dialogue, leaving the shooting of action sequences to Gardner, who had learned his craft in silent films.

For the remake of *Grumpy* as a talkie, Paramount called on the actor Cyril Maude, who had brought the play to New York in 1913 with an English company. But even Maude's expertness as the senile and testy yet lovable old Grumpy could not save it. By 1930 the piece's moral standards and dramatics were hopelessly outdated. For the sophisticated post-Prohibition audience, the film's battles for honor were hardly worth talking about. Still, *Variety*'s critic wrote that the movie was "without allure," but the direction was "legitimate and intelligent."

Cukor's next assignment, *The Virtuous Sin*, codirected with Louis Gasnier, was appropriately described by *Variety* as an "average program flicker." Kay Francis starred as a dutiful wife, willing to make sacrifices to save her husband, a Russian soldier condemned to death by his general. Weak on theme, the film stands on the eloquent portrayal of Francis, who excelled in the climactic scene, when she meets the general with whom she has fallen in love.

The film's weaknesses were blamed on Cukor and Gasnier. "The directing duo," *Variety* complained, "have lingered over scenes which were not constructed to stand the amount of footage allowed." There was no excuse for the picture to run for eighty minutes, when seventy would have been plenty.

*   *   *

In July 1930 Paramount awarded Cukor with an amended contract, increasing his salary to a thousand dollars a week. Cukor directed no fewer than fifteen films in the 1930s, which became the most productive and, arguably, the most creative decade of his career.

Of the three films made in 1930, *The Royal Family of Broadway,* which Cukor was assigned to codirect, again with Cyril Gardner, was by far the most important. The division of labor between the two was clearly delineated: Cukor set up the scenes, and Gardner photographed them. This was an extension of how Cukor had worked with Milestone on *All Quiet,* except that now he was responsible for the staging of all the scenes—and he got credit for his work.

Herman Mankiewicz and Gertrude Purcell, who cowrote the script, actually improved on George S. Kaufman and Edna Ferber's play. The gossipy, thinly disguised satire of the Barrymore-Drew acting dynasty was a Broadway hit in 1927. Paramount bought the screen rights for Fredric March, who re-created his stage role as the flamboyant matinee idol—clearly a caricature of John Barrymore. Though his role is small (he is offscreen most of the time), March completely dominates the picture.

The zany plot outlines the wild fortunes of the Cavendishes—i.e., the Barrymores, Broadway's First Family. The hectic homelife of the incurably theatrical family provides riotous fun. March plays Tony, who returns to the Cavendish house with reporters at his heels after breaking with the family faith and going Hollywood. Now "America's Greatest Lover," he is fending off a director he hit in anger, while ducking legions of marriage-hungry females. Tony dazzles his family with his colorful dramatics and outlandish conduct.

March, who had met John Barrymore, carefully studied his model. His clever impersonation imitated every lifted eyebrow, gesture, and mannerism of the noted star. For an actor who generally lacked humor, March's inventive lampoon of Barrymore was remarkable. His bravura performance, which critics described with such adjectives as glamorous, lunatic, vital, spirited, boisterous, garnered March his first Oscar nomination.

Ethel Barrymore, a good friend of Cukor's, was initially livid about the gossipy material, regarding anything written about the Barrymores as "treason" or at the very least an "invasion of privacy." Between the play's many clues and March's exact impersonation, there was no doubt who the characters were. Ethel's anger, however, lasted only until she saw Cukor's movie, which she had to admit was great fun.

Though the film hosted a topflight cast, for Cukor the major reward was working with his friend Ina Claire, whose elegance he admired. Claire was cast in the Ethel Barrymore role, as Julie Cavendish, a woman who has long spurned marriage to her millionaire beau. "Her whole career was dedicated to perfecting herself," Cukor once said of Claire. "She learned that most difficult of arts, high comedy." Although a sophisticated stage comedienne, Claire never blossomed onscreen.

The Royal Family was shot at Paramount's Astoria studio in Queens. Edward Dmytryk, who was assigned to cut the film, remembered making a poor impression on the young Cukor. Cutters were known for being supercritical, examining every facet of a scene with microscopic eyes. They often overlooked clever staging or effective acting to nitpick at some bit of mismatched action.

"Cutters had a tendency to act tough," Dmytryk recalled, "and I was intent on playing the cutter." Dmytryk would first look at the dailies, then go down to the set. Cukor would anxiously inquire about the rushes, but Dmytryk's terse answers often left him standing in stony silence. Gardner, who had been a cutter, understood Dmytryk. "Gardner knew he had only to wait a little, and I'd soon be telling him everything he wanted to know," said Dmytryk. It was years before Dmytryk realized that regardless of stature, no director was secure enough not to welcome a reassuring word.

According to Dmytryk, film directors were insecure with the dialogue, and stage directors were insecure with the camera. At first Cukor felt uncomfortable in a medium where a look or a gesture could mean more than a spoken phrase, where upstage and downstage were replaced by camera right and camera left. Using codirectors was meant to solve this problem: The film person placed the camera and staged the scene physically; the stage man was in charge of playing the scene and the dialogue.

Static and stage-bound, The Royal Family shows all the signs of an early talkie. In one important scene when March invites the whole family upstairs while he takes a bath, however, Cukor's evolving cinematic eye is evident. Cukor suggested that the camera track March and his entourage as they made their way upstairs, cutting as he reached the bathroom. Huge, manually operated cranes were needed to execute this shot, but the mobility and fluidity of the camera in this scene were the beginning of a breakthrough for Cukor as a film director, stressing from then on the unique aspects of cinematic language.

Coming from the theater, Cukor got a special kick from one funny moment that reflected a fashionable attitude toward movies at that time. Ina Claire and her mother are returning home from the theater in a taxicab. Passing through Times Square, the old matriarch glances out the window at a movie marquee and comments: "All singing, all dancing, all terrible!"

A Christmas release, The Royal Family opened to excellent reviews. The New York Mirror singled out the "witty dialogue, brisk action, and eloquent direction which give the comedy a brilliant polish," much of which were shaped by Cukor.

In the 1960s, when Cukor saw the picture again, he was struck by its conventional ideas. Showing the charming, childish side of the actors, the film represented what people wanted to believe about the theater. "The smell of the greasepaint isn't real," Cukor told Gavin Lambert, "it's plastic." Even in 1930 the film was dated and clichéd, but it was a succès d'estime and enjoyed a good run.

The picture perpetuated the myth of the Barrymores as a crazy family, to whom nothing outside the theater matters. At the end the aging matriarch (Henrietta Crosman) decides to embark on a tour to keep the family name alive, but the thrill of applause brings on a fatal attack. In the spirit of the show must go on, Julie decides to continue the tour in her mother's place.

For Cukor, *The Royal Family* was the first of many movies in which he celebrated the magic quality of the theater and its performers. Thematically this notion became the most prevalent in his work, as evidenced in *What Price Hollywood?*, *Sylvia Scarlett*, *A Star Is Born*, *Heller in Pink Tights*, *Let's Make Love*, and others.

After the success of *The Royal Family,* Cukor's status at Paramount changed. His apprenticeship formally ended with his next assignment, which marked his debut as a solo director. The film was *Tarnished Lady,* a breezy comedy written by Donald Ogden Stewart from his short story "New York Lady."

Paramount had high aspirations for *Tarnished Lady,* which was conceived as a vehicle for Tallulah Bankhead; it was to be her first sound film. The studio hoped to cash in on the acclaim and notoriety Bankhead had earned as a stage actress. After a successful debut on the American stage the young Bankhead had gone to London and quickly became the toast of the town. The English were fascinated by her. Mrs. Patrick Campbell, the witty English actress whom Cukor admired, once said, "Watching Tallulah Bankhead on the stage is like watching somebody skating over very thin ice—and the English want to be there when she falls through."

She returned to the United States to make films, but Bankhead, the stage idol, like Ina Claire before her, never achieved film stardom. Cukor found her an exhilarating stage actress, but he realized that the qualities that made her exciting onstage did not translate onscreen. Excessively theatrical, with an inclination for overacting, Bankhead was not at ease in front of the camera.

Bankhead wanted to look like Garbo—high cheekbones—but she did not have Garbo's kind of face. Her presence was striking, but her face lacked the kind of animation the camera loves. For Cukor, being photo-genic was a question of movement, how the face projects under the piercing scrutiny of the camera. Despite her enormous talent, when Bank-head spoke, her mouth didn't appear graceful, and her eyes never lit up. "Movies were never easy for her," Cukor later said. "She wasn't born for them."

To make matters worse, Bankhead was miscast in *Tarnished Lady*. The narrative center on a popular heroine of the time, a socialite who marries for money when her family loses its fortune but is tormented when she falls in love with a poor writer. This classic setup, however, suffers from a weak climax. When she happens upon her lover talking—only talk-ing—with another woman, her trust is completely crushed. Bankhead handled the story's moments of high comedy brilliantly, but she was not credible in scenes that demanded vulnerability and helplessness.

Bankhead was slightly more established than Cukor at the time, though, as she recalled, "Here was I, a stage actress, with a stage director and stage writers on my first film. We were all swimming without wa-terwings, and we had never been in the water before."

Bankhead found Cukor gallant and kind. "If you're tired or not up to snuff," she told an interviewer, "he understands and makes things easy for you, instead of acting as if you'd contrived the complete feminine anatomy as a personal affront to him." When Cukor had a correction to make, instead of bawling it out over the whole set to assert his authority or relieve his nerves, as other directors often did, he took the time to walk a few steps and say whatever he had to say into her ear. "It's not a minor thing," she explained. "Try being bellowed at for eight or ten hours a day, six weeks on end, and then tell me how you feel about it." All the performers who worked with Cukor singled out this sensitivity as one of his most consistent qualities.

Bankhead's flamboyant temper flared only once, when she refused to put on a shabby dress she thought inappropriate for her character. But Cukor had the final word, commanding her to wear it. Bankhead said that Cukor was the only director ever to have talked to her as he did that day. In later years both joked about this incident, which contributed to Cukor's reputation as a director who could handle Hollywood's most eccentric and strong-willed stars.

Tarnished Lady launched one of Cukor's most enduring friendships. In 1981, celebrating his golden anniversary as a filmmaker, Cukor recalled his directorial debut with typically self-deprecating humor: "I could have fallen flat on my face—but with Tallulah's help it was quite a success." Bankhead and Cukor never worked together again, but they remained close friends until her death, in 1968.

Cukor again found himself in Astoria, Queens, for the filming of *Tar-*

nished Lady. About half the scenes were shot on location, giving the film an innovative ring of authenticity. Bankhead's proposal scene, for example, was shot on the actual terrace of a New York apartment. Cukor also attempted to keep the interior scenes from becoming too stagy by using a more realistic lighting.

The film was criticized for its inferior cinematography and production values. Though more cinematic than *The Royal Family, Tarnished Lady* failed to draw audiences. Credited as sole director, Cukor was blamed.

Despite the failure of *Tarnished Lady,* Cukor's career remained on track. On February 16, 1931, Paramount negotiated a new contract, five months before the existing one was to expire. Cukor's salary jumped from $1,000 to $1,500 a week, with a weekly expense account of $125. At the expiration of the fourth option, in July 1931, Cukor's salary was increased to $2,000. In fewer than two years, his income had quadrupled. His earnings from Paramount for 1931 amounted to $73,500, a huge income for a former stage director.

While Cukor never chose filmmaking for its glamour and financial rewards, once he got used to high fees and luxurious living, his commitment to Hollywood and his new life-style became stronger. Security-oriented, Cukor seldom took big risks with his money. With a soaring income and a sizable amount of cash on hand, he began to invest money in stocks; in the future he often turned to Selznick, who was more knowledgeable in these affairs, for business advice.

Cukor had not yet invested in a home, which later claimed much of his income. At the time he was renting a house above Hollywood Boulevard. His business affairs were handled by Elsa Schroeder, a secretary-manager who had worked for him in New York and eventually moved to Los Angeles.

The premiere of *Girls About Town,* in the fall of 1931, marked Cukor's last picture at Paramount for almost a decade. An inconsequential romp, in the gold digger comedy tradition, it is a tale of two smart girls acting as "professional" entertainers for out-of-town millionaires. One girl falls in love and reforms, while the other sends her lover back to his wife and keeps her life-style.

Tarts in the big city were not new ground for writer Zoe Akins. But fearing censorship, she bathed the film's heroines in a charming innocence. The women had lovely wardrobes, money, and a succession of rich men, but at the end of the evening they just smiled and said good night—as if this were the extent of their activities. "What if the audience wonders where do these girls get all those fancy clothes?" Cukor sarcastically teased Akins.

Cukor directed the film with a light touch, sharply pacing its comedy sequences. In one of the funnier scenes the girls attempt to raise money by auctioning off their ill-gotten clothes and jewels. A rowdy scene results that in tone and catty sophistication looks ahead to later and better Cukor comedies, such as *The Women* in 1939.

Despite the material's underlying dishonesty, Cukor finessed highly polished acting from his cast that ultimately saved the picture. Lilyan Tashman's excellent performance, reminiscent of Jean Harlow, was particularly surprising. Tashman, who usually played heavies, had never before been given the opportunity to tap into her comic persona. Cukor recognized her lively, outrageous personality immediately; his eye for casting was already well hewed from his days in the theater. Through his direction he was able to relax Tashman, allowing her to be as amusing onscreen as in life, something he had been unable to do with Bankhead in *Tarnished Lady*.

The rest of the cast was also more than adequate. Kay Francis's natural elegance (she wore clothes well) complemented Tashman's inherent vigor. The young and attractive Joel McCrea played the lover who won't fall for the careless girls unless they reform, and character actor Eugene Pallette, in the role of the old Michigan millionaire, was also amusing.

Aside from good acting, *Girls About Town* marked the emergence of what became Cukor's distinct cinematic style: elaborately staged scenes that seemed fresh and unobtrusive. Cukor was to perfect a mise-en-scène based on a precise definition of space and tempo: where the actors stood in relation to each other, how fast (or slowly) they moved and talked, etc.

In a scene where Francis and McCrea go to the zoo, Cukor's camera tracks their stroll past the cages with a long dolly shot, interrupting the dialogue from time to time with a casual look at the animals. This smooth and fluid camera work conveyed a natural quality to Cukor's technique, one that didn't call attention to itself and yet reflected the director's distinct approach.

Though *Royal Family* enjoyed more prestige when released, *Girls About Town* and *Tarnished Lady*, which at the time were considered routine, hold up much better today. Based on original screenplays, they were unencumbered by contrived stage conventions.

Following *Girls About Town*, Cukor was assigned his most important—and problematic—film to date: *One Hour with You*, with two of Paramount's major stars, Maurice Chevalier and Jeanette MacDonald. A remake of Ernst Lubitsch's silent movie *The Marriage Circle*, the film was to be directed again by Lubitsch, but when other obligations made it impossible, Cukor took over with the understanding that the film would be shot under Lubitsch's supervision.

Working closely with a director of the caliber of Lubitsch, then at the peak of his career, was very attractive. At the same time it was going to be *his* movie; Cukor made the screen tests and was consulted about the story, sets, and costumes. The production began in early 1931 with good humor and excitement, shared by both directors. In the first week Cukor directed without much input from Lubitsch.

However, in the second week Paramount's B. P. Schulberg informed Cukor that Lubitsch wanted closer contact with the production since the material was so close to his style. This, of course, meant Lubitsch's spending more time on the set. The studio general manager tried to smooth over the awkward situation by praising Cukor's generous cooperation and good sportsmanship.

Cukor considered it natural for Lubitsch to take a more active part: He was a distinguished director, and the project was right up his alley. Left with little choice, he consented to confer with Lubitsch about each scene. The two men would discuss a scene, then rehearse the actors together, or Lubitsch would watch Cukor rehearse them, after which Lubitsch would express his ideas about what needed to be changed. After reaching a consensus, the scene would be shot.

As shooting progressed, Lubitsch divided his time between editing the movie *The Man I Killed* and supervising *One Hour with You*. The arrangement was not perfect, but somehow the film proceeded without major problems—until the evening of January 26, 1932, when studio executives were invited to the first screening.

It was customary for the director to be present at a screening, but Cukor was not even notified. Two days later he received a letter from Schulberg, expressing regret at the oversight. Schulberg claimed he had simply taken it for granted that Lubitsch would tell Cukor about the event. Asking his forgiveness for the unintended affront, Schulberg assured Cukor the studio heads were delighted with the picture. Lubitsch also apologized to Cukor for the oversight.

Two weeks later, on February 9, a public preview was held at the Uptown Theater for an audience of twenty-one hundred people, including studio officials. The main title, "An Ernst Lubitsch Production," was in letters four times as large as those used for Cukor's credit. Moreover, it was followed by another card in large type: "Personally Supervised by Ernst Lubitsch." The predominance of Lubitsch's name in the credits was disconcerting, but the film was well received, and Cukor was given a complimentary write-up in the *Hollywood Reporter*.

Then, on February 11, Schulberg asked Cukor for permission to take his name off the picture. Lubitsch had told Schulberg that if Cukor's name was not removed, he would request removal of his own name. Shocked by the request and incapable of making a quick decision, Cukor told Schulberg he needed a day or two to think it over.

Cukor didn't sleep all night, debating what to do. Apart from the fact that withdrawing his name would be an embarrassment, he thought it would damage his reputation. The next morning he informed Schulberg that he would not remove his name from the picture. Not expecting one of Paramount's newest directors to have such a strong voice, Schulberg was shocked by Cukor's feisty attitude. The executive warned Cukor that if he did not consent, he would become a laughingstock. He even threatened to cancel Cukor's contract, suggesting that a man who showed so little rational judgment about screen credit could not be entrusted with the direction of a major production.

Schulberg then read a note from Lubitsch that further infuriated Cukor. Apparently, after reading the *Hollywood Reporter* article and hearing reports around the lot, Lubitsch feared that *One Hour with You* would be considered Chevalier's best picture, surpassing his own directorial efforts with the star, and that everything would be attributed to Cukor's better direction.

Lubitsch was overly sensitive to the issue because at the completion of *One Hour with You* his contract with Paramount expired. On February 13, 1932, Cukor received a letter from Lubitsch. "I cannot tell you," he wrote, "how uncomfortable I feel in this situation, but there was really no other choice for me. I would honestly prefer to have my name taken off the picture entirely than to allow my reputation as a director to suffer."

Initially Cukor was determined to go to court. In a prepared statement he expressed the importance of getting formal recognition. "Screen credit is as vital a part of the compensation which I am entitled to receive under my contract as is the salary," he wrote. "My professional reputation and prestige probably will be enormously enhanced, and I will be able to demand and receive a much higher salary than I am receiving at present."

At the heart of the matter was Cukor's belief that *One Hour with You* was more his than Lubitsch's movie. He was satisfied to remove Lubitsch's name and, as he wrote, willing to bear the full responsibility of the results. Cukor, however, lost the battle. The film was released with Lubitsch credited for the direction and Cukor's work remained unacknowledged in most of the prints.

As *One Hour with You* neared completion, Cukor was notified that his next project would be a film with Carole Lombard. Cukor asked to be relieved because he would not have time to prepare adequately. But as a contract director Cukor was not idle long. A week after finishing *One Hour with You,* he was assigned another film, this time starring his former leading lady from Rochester Miriam Hopkins. Much to Cukor's disappointment, this film never materialized.

Though the Lubitsch matter was finally settled out of court, it soured Cukor's relationship with Paramount. Not pleased with the material assigned to him, he became impatient, restless. Cukor felt that he was not properly treated and that the caliber of his talent was not appreciated by the studio.

At Paramount Cukor had befriended David O. Selznick, an ambitious young man who was to have tremendous influence on his career. When Selznick left Paramount in the fall of 1931 to become RKO's head of production, he asked Cukor to join him. Because Cukor was unpopular and undervalued at Paramount, Selznick had little difficulty in getting him out of his contract. Paramount's executives were in fact relieved to see Cukor leave.

The first major studio to be formed during the sound revolution, RKO was a fledgling company. The immediate problem Selznick faced was the lack of high-quality properties and the lack of good directors. At the same time his one-year contract made him, as his wife, Irene, noted, "a young man in a hurry."

At RKO Cukor was given better material to work with, though not in his first year. The three films he made there in 1932 had short shooting schedules and small budgets and, with the exception of *A Bill of Divorcement,* were not prestigious productions; RKO simply lacked the resources.

Cukor's first film at RKO was *What Price Hollywood?,* the tale of a gifted director (Lowell Sherman) who helps an ambitious waitress (Constance Bennett) become a movie star, while his career disintegrates into alcoholic ruin. Selznick and Cukor decided to produce a more honest and accurate portrayal of Hollywood, one that would combine comedy, pathos, and drama. Two working titles, "The Truth About Hollywood" and "The World, the Flesh, and the Movies," were dropped because they were pompous and failed to convey Selznick's more romantic view of Hollywood.

The inspiration for Adela Rogers St. Johns's story derived from the relationship between silent star Colleen Moore and her producer-husband, John McCormick. But Sherman's character also echoes the lives of Marshall "Mickey" Neilan, a silent movie director with a drinking problem, and John Barrymore (who would play a similar role in Cukor's 1933 *Dinner at Eight*).

Selznick originally envisioned Clara Bow as the female lead—the story needed an exciting actress to lift up its melodramatic aspects—but Bow's career was fading, and Selznick could not dissuade her from retiring. Instead Constance Bennett was offered the role, and the script was rewritten to fit her particular talents: sophistication, glamour, and wit.

Sherman, a fine actor from silent films who never achieved stardom and a director himself, was cast as the filmmaker. Though playing a drunken and disagreeable character, he succeeded in making the director's bitterness sympathetic and his suicide touching. Sherman gave a prophetic performance; he died two years later.

Cukor's handling of the climactic suicide scene was original for its time. It is preceded by a quick succession of shots, with the director reliving his life, from the early triumphant days to the more desperate ones. The sequence is accompanied by an extraordinary sound—an eerie whirring sound, which Slavko Vorkapich, who was working on the film, achieved by attaching a string inside a cigar box and spinning it around. The impact of this scene was so compelling that Cukor urged Selznick to give Vorkapich separate credit for "special effects."

The movie's incidental details are perceptively observed by Cukor. His ability to draw the audience to the characters is particularly telling in an early sequence that illustrates Bennett's dogged determination to succeed. Bennett has a small part—a throwaway line—in the film within a film, but her performance is terrible, and the director fires her. She then goes home and stays up all night rehearsing, trying to perfect her reading. Cukor lets the audience see her improvement as she slowly builds her confidence. When the producer sees the new dailies, he puts her under contract. In her finished performance, seen in rushes, a star is born right before the audience's eyes.

But the quality of *What Price Hollywood?* is uneven. Pushed into production too quickly, Cukor never approved of its script. The narrative is incoherent, shifting to a silly romance between Bennett and her polo-playing husband that ultimately weakens the film. Cukor fought to keep the story focused on the relationship between the star and the director, but Selznick overruled him. Wishing he had spent more time on developing the script, Selznick later admitted Cukor was right.

The writing credits on *What Price Hollywood?* turned out to be problematic, for a number of writers, including Jane Murfin, Ben Markson, and Gene Fowler, worked on the script. After being burned by Lubitsch, and remembering his experience with Milestone on *All Quiet,* Cukor was particularly sensitive to the credits issue. A committee from the Motion Picture Academy of Arts and Science writers branch took up the question of the script, which was nominated for an Oscar. After reading all versions, it stipulated that credit for the original story should go to Adela Rogers St. Johns and that Robert Presnell should also receive credit for his share of the adaptation, but the latter never did.

Cukor always showed concern for the quality of writing perhaps because he was a frustrated writer. In the production process he held the greatest respect for writers—to the point of not allowing performers to change one word once the script was finished. "Although every artist has his ego," Lambert commented, "George was not as egotistic as other directors I've known. For one thing, he was extremely generous to writers. George was modest, and that is one thing that delayed his just recognition for a long time. He never publicized himself a great deal."

Though Cukor held the highest regard for authors, he was dependent on actors for establishing his directorial style. He understood early that his forte was working with actors, helping them showcase their individual personas. And because he was assigned mediocre screenplays, over which he had little control, he placed extra emphasis on casting the best available performers. Cukor's stature as an actor's director rose after people in Hollywood saw the performance he coaxed out of Constance Bennett in *What Price Hollywood?*

"He is a rare thing," said Bennett in 1933, "an unselfish director. He doesn't make a show of what he's giving the actor. He doesn't specialize in so called 'directorial touches' to emphasize his own activity. He keeps himself in the background. To him, the story—and consequently the people through whom the story's being told—are the important thing." Actors trusted Cukor implicitly, as Bennett said, because they knew that "first and foremost, it's you and your part he's thinking of. Naturally you'll work like a slave, because you realize you're safer in his hands than in your own."

Given a lavish publicity campaign, the film opened in New York at the Mayfair Theater and soon became one of the year's top-grossing films. *What Price Hollywood?* is one of Cukor's most interesting films despite its contrived ending and shifting tone. It maintains a fresh, timeless quality in its commentary on movie stardom, making it one of the most enduring pictures about Hollywood. In 1937 Selznick used the same story for *A Star Is Born,* which Cukor was offered to direct but which he turned down. Cukor himself used the same theme in his 1954 musical of *A Star Is Born,* with Judy Garland. Though both succeeding films are better constructed, *What Price Hollywood?* stands on its merits.

During this time Cukor and David Selznick became closer. In fact, because of their physical resemblance, they were always mistaken for each other. It was mostly a facial resemblance, for Selznick was six inches taller than Cukor. But every time the subject of their similar appearance came up, Selznick's mother protested violently—in Cukor's presence—that they did not look alike. "It's all right, Mrs. Selznick," Cukor said one night. "My mother doesn't like it either." Stunned, Mrs. Selznick never talked about it again.

As usual, Cukor's friendship with Irene Selznick, who was Louis B. Mayer's daughter and Selznick's wife, was more intimate than with Selznick himself. Selznick encouraged their friendship; the producer knew that Irene needed friends of her own. Cukor was also friendly with Irene's sister Edith, who was married to William Goetz, a top Paramount executive. Soon Cukor became Irene's personal confidant, which, considering Selznick's womanizing, put him in an awkward position.

Stories from the set of *What Price Hollywood?* wafted across town. Rumors circulated that Cukor was vituperative in a way that not only was amusing but also got results; even his profanity was salutary. Irene Selznick described the young Cukor as a man who had "invigorating viewpoint and original personality" and was "full of beans, taste, and humor."

Cukor's accomplishment in *What Price Hollywood?* and his sharp eye for style made him a natural choice to direct *A Bill of Divorcement,* his second RKO feature. A family melodrama, the film raised genetic questions about mental illness and moral questions about the granting of divorce on the ground of insanity. The title refers to a bill for liberalizing divorce that was placed before the British Parliament. The story revolves around Hillary, a mentally unstable man who escapes from an asylum and returns home on the day his wife is to remarry.

Clemence Dane's play was a great success in 1921 in London and in 1928 in New York, where Katharine Cornell was an overnight sensation. However, by 1932, when the play was optioned for the screen, the material was already dated. Considering its subject matter, the play was also considered an unlikely property for Hollywood. Wishing to avoid the static feeling of most stage adaptations, Selznick realized that nuance and delicacy would be vital in successfully transferring the material to the screen.

John Barrymore was signed for Hillary, the husband-father. Billie Burke played the wife-mother, though Selznick was at first hesitant to pay her requested twenty-five hundred dollars a week. But knowing the actress and her work from the stage, Cukor demanded she be cast.

A small budget, under three hundred thousand dollars, precluded the casting of a big star for the pivotal role of Sydney, the daughter. Even RKO's two female stars, Constance Bennett and Irene Dunne, were too expensive. Dunne's contract, which stipulated fifty thousand dollars per film, put her out of the running. Selznick and Cukor had little choice but to find an unknown actress.

Cukor knew that Sydney was an extraordinary role for any actress, let alone a newcomer. The search first began at RKO among the contract players. Anita Louise and Jill Esmond, Laurence Olivier's first wife, were seriously considered, and Esmond was chosen. Olivier had been at RKO when Selznick took over the studio, but with little success in Hollywood at this point, he persuaded Esmond to pass on the role and return with him to England.

Again the search was on. It just happened that Merian Cooper, a director and friend of Selznick's brought to RKO as a producer, was given a photograph of a promising new actress, Katharine Hepburn, who was then playing on Broadway in *The Warrior's Husband.* The critics were unanimous only in praise of Hepburn's legs, but Kay Brown, Selznick's influential story editor, explored the matter. She reported: "She has done only three plays, but her salary demand, 1,000 dollars a week, is too excessive." Selznick thought that it was inadvisable to spend money on a test, but Cooper insisted that the New York office shoot one and send it to Hollywood.

When Cukor saw Hepburn's test, a scene from Philip Barry's *Holiday,* he was instantly taken. Hepburn was unlike anybody he had seen; she was odd-looking and had a peculiar voice. Though she had never made a movie, he could see that she had good instincts about the camera. His eye lingered over a lyrical moment in the test, when she reached down to pick up a drink. Though she had been shot from the back, Cukor sensed enormous feeling in the way she executed this simple gesture.

With Cukor convinced that Hepburn was the leading lady, Selznick agreed to take a chance, even though she negotiated a rather shrewd contract, demanding not only a high salary for a newcomer but also the option of going back to the theater from time to time.

Hepburn set out by train for Hollywood and arrived in early July 1932. Her initial encounter with Cukor was anything but auspicious. Along the way something lodged in Hepburn's eye, causing a terrible inflammation. "I arrived in California with a steel filing in my eye," Hepburn recalled, "and nobody paid attention, least of all George, that I was really quite ill. I had two red eyes!"

Wearing an expensive outfit purchased for the occasion, Hepburn entered the room where Cukor was waiting. He greeted her with an odd but cordial look, immediately sensing her self-assurance. "I thought her rather la-de-da," Cukor later commented. "She was wearing a rather arty dress."

Hepburn was actually shaky and a bit scared. "Mr. Cukor," she said, "I have something in my eye. Do you have a doctor?"

Ignoring her question, Cukor, who may have been as nervous as she was, said, "I want you to see the sketches," and proceeded to show her the costume design. "What do you think of them?" asked the director.

Hepburn looked at them and said, "They are horrible. I really don't think a well-bred English girl would wear anything like that."

"What do you think of what you have on?" Cukor retorted.

Taken aback, Hepburn said, "Well! I've paid three hundred and fifty dollars, and I think it's very smart."

"Well, I think it stinks," Cukor said. "You're the damnedest-looking girl I've ever seen, and that's an awful outfit you have on. What makes you think you know so much about clothes?"

Hepburn paused and with great forced amiability said, "Oh, do you think so?"

"Now we can proceed to business," Cukor said, taking Hepburn up to the hairdressing department, which styled her hair.

"Those were my lines," Cukor later noted, "and for once, Kate did not step on them."

Cukor then went home for dinner, leaving Hepburn alone, her eyes still irritated with no doctor in sight. Fortunately John Barrymore came in and helped solve the problem. Barrymore's behavior was much more sensitive than Cukor's. "Miss Hepburn," he said, "I've seen the test. You're going to be a great star." When Cukor heard rumors that the much older Barrymore tried to seduce Hepburn, he was not surprised; he kind of expected it.

By July Cukor had a reasonably good treatment of *A Bill of Divorcement*. Screenwriters Howard Estabrook and Harry Wagstaff Gribble worked hard on the dialogue after Cukor's complaints that it was too long-winded and overwritten. The quality of writing was one area in which Selznick blindly trusted Cukor. But when shooting began, despite Cukor's efforts, the script was still barely passable.

Hepburn remembered her very first scene with Barrymore. He came in, wearing a hat and a raincoat, and began fiddling around with some pipes on the mantelpiece. Barrymore turned around and looked at her; she was standing off camera. Watching him with the cold eye of youth, she thought he was overdoing it and was actually not very good. With all these unkind notions passing through her mind, Hepburn was acting away, full of sincerity, tears streaming down her face. She then realized she herself was doing a little too much. Barrymore could see that Hepburn was a kid to whom the movie meant a great deal. When the take was over, he took her chin in his hands and said, "I'd like to do it again." And he did, and differently.

Barrymore gave a restrained but touching performance in a subservient role. Cukor had never worked with the actor before, but found him open and accessible. Cukor was a bit cautious, considering Barrymore's stature in the industry, but they worked well together, even became friends.

While shooting Barrymore's crucial scene—when Hillary returns home, beaten and seedy, and pleads for love—Cukor felt the actor was working with the wrong kind of tension; it was too desperate. "Jack," he said, "the man is happy to be home, he doesn't know they don't want him." Barrymore understood Cukor's insight and adjusted his acting, playing it a little more softly.

There is a sequence lasting only a minute, with no dialogue, that contains essential elements of the Cukor style. Barrymore has escaped from the asylum and returns home. His daughter is alone in the house when he arrives. She hides halfway up the stairs and watches him wander around the room. All she knows about her father is that he was shell-shocked during the war. The audience, of course, knows that his wife is in love with another man and wants to divorce him. Cukor established the appropriate tone, the precise mood ("climate," in Cukor's jargon) of poignancy and tension for this particular scene, showing his masterful mise-en-scène.

Hepburn's performance was strikingly original. One senses how well she and Cukor worked together. Some of it was the part she was playing; Hepburn identified with a girl who rebels against her middle-class family. And some was her own personality; Cukor noticed immediately Hepburn's impatience and directness, which he found electrifying. He always singled out Hepburn's quality of "cutting through correctness," onscreen and off.

In a touching scene Hepburn asks her aunt if insanity runs in the family. Cukor forced her to do it many times, but after the seventeenth take, instead of getting peevish or bored, he came over to her. "Listen, kid," he said quietly, "are you holding out on me? Because if you are, you're doing the lowest thing one human could do to another." Hepburn wasn't holding out; she just didn't understand what he wanted. But taken by his honesty, she made a heroic effort and got it right on the eighteenth take.

On the set Cukor watched every move, gesture, and expression that crossed his actors' faces, striving to inject into the material his as well as their sensibilities. There was one scene in which Hepburn excelled, proving her potential as a screen personality. She takes a pillow and lies down on the hearthstone, displaying her lovely figure and graceful movement. Then she suddenly reveals a warm, forthright smile.

Hepburn was not really good in the movie, but her appearance was so angular, and her mouth a sign of such suffering, that she was riveting to watch. Though she was inexperienced, her honesty shines through. Hepburn didn't try to woo the audience; she took risks that a known actress with an established screen persona might not.

Cukor held that Hepburn was marked by a paradox: She was at once hard and tender, cocksure yet humble about her work, "straight as a knife and slippery as a snake." Her problem, he said, was that she had "more brains than she knows what to do with." At first she was "bumptious" and argued about everything, demanding to understand exactly what he wanted and why. "She cannot do anything mechanically, just because she was told to," Cukor said. "But when she understood, she'd do it like a saint." She once told Cukor, "Just because you don't know what you're doing, don't take it out on us!" The remark hurt him very much.

Cukor was not above overt displays of anger. On the set he hit Laura Harding, Hepburn's closest friend who was standing with her hand on a newel post, waiting for someone to ask her to dance. When she moved to the dance floor, the ball on top of the post came off in her hand. Not knowing what to do, she handed the ball to the man dancing with her, startling the actor so much he yelled out loud. Cukor came over and hit her in a fury; she had destroyed a wonderful take of a complicated shot.

Cukor's shrewd use of music in *A Bill of Divorcement* was reflected in a touching moment, when Hepburn sits down at the piano with Barrymore. In the film Barrymore's musical gifts are beginning to come back—he is going to write a great sonata—and they play together as the music rises to a crescendo of bittersweet laughter at the end. This scene was invented for the film, but the trick was so good that Cukor used it again in *Camille*.

After a preview of *A Bill of Divorcement* Merian Cooper congratulated Cukor. Reportedly every woman he talked to had cried during the screening. There was some inappropriate laughter in the wrong places, which concerned Cooper, but two friends who sat in the second row said it came from children. Cooper did suggest reshooting one of Hepburn's close-ups. She was going to be a major star, he reasoned, and it would be a mistake to have her appear as badly as she did in this shot.

Hepburn was convinced she was "rotten" and declined Cukor's invitation to go to the preview. She escaped to Santa Monica for the night and missed the glowing reviews the next day. "Hepburn's portrayal is exceptionally fine," wrote *The New York Times;* "her characterization is one of the finest seen on the screen." *Photoplay* magazine noted: "This picture makes history. Not since Greta Garbo first lashed before screen audiences has anything happened like this Katharine Hepburn."

Hepburn would have become a star even if she hadn't appeared in *A Bill of Divorcement,* but the fact that it happened in a Cukor film made a difference. Cukor was always proud that even though he didn't discover Hepburn, he was the one to have launched her screen career. The two made eight features and two TV movies together. Hepburn eventually became Cukor's best friend, though it took another film, *Little Women,* for their friendship to blossom.

Cukor directed Constance Bennett in two quickies in 1933: *Rockaby* and *Our Betters.* In *Rockaby* Bennett starred in a romantic tale of a Broadway actress who is denied the adoption of a child because of her underworld connections. She redeems herself in a love affair with a presumably honest playwright (Joel McCrea), only to realize he is married. A contrived story of a woman sacrificing her happiness, the movie was targeted to female viewers, containing some unusually passionate scenes between the two stars.

From the start Cukor could not tolerate actors behaving unprofessionally. He angrily complained to Selznick that Joel McCrea and Paul Lukas had a "God damn nerve" to be half an hour late to the set. Cukor told them he was "thoroughly annoyed," but he also asked Selznick to scold them in no uncertain terms.

When McCrea complained to Cukor that his part was too small, the director sent him to Selznick, who reminded McCrea that he was under contract, receiving a weekly salary, and that all decisions about his parts were made "by us, and not by you." Selznick stressed that McCrea had "the advantage of Cukor's direction," which he hoped the actor valued.

For his part, Selznick sent Cukor teasing cautionary notes with a message: "If you go into the moving picture business, be careful." The Russian art director Leonidov had been sentenced to life imprisonment, and two others had been executed for supposedly spending money "recklessly." Russia would be a dangerous place for some American movie experts who tended to spend too much money, Selznick noted.

Economy and efficiency were Selznick's hallmarks. In January Cukor received a memo about the status of *Our Betters*. After fourteen days of work, he was four days behind schedule; he had shot 44.6 minutes instead of the optimal 46.4 minutes. Selznick asked Cukor to stick to the original plan and shoot about the average daily footage of 3.2 minutes.

Our Betters, a farce about a free-spirited American social climber, was the only Somerset Maugham play Cukor directed for the screen. The British atmosphere in *Our Betters* was nicely handled, though the movie is stagy. English high comedy was a form seldom successful in Hollywood because American actors were not trained in vocal nuances. The material should have been—but was not—performed in the Noël Coward style, in which frivolous dialogue is taken seriously.

Maugham's play is darker than Coward's high comedies, a bitter exposé of expatriate American women who marry British nobility for their titles. Cukor thought the material was too brittle; Maugham's women are ambitious, catty, and adulterous. In his direction Cukor softened Maugham's harsh attitude toward women, achieving a tone that he used again in *The Women*. Some of the dialogue was witty and sparkling, and it moved fast, considering that the movie was all talk.

In retrospect, *Our Betters* stands as a crucial, personal work in Cukor's oeuvre. Its gallery of screen types appeared time and again in Cukor's later movies. As Lady Pearl Grayston, the American beauty who turns to gold-digging, Bennett embodied a role that Cukor understood well: a sophisticated, sharp-tongued woman, disillusioned with bourgeois marriage and bored with conventional behavior. The Duchess, another disenchanted woman desperately clinging to her cheating gigolo, undergoes one public humiliation after another. As a gay man Cukor could relate to Bennett's flirtatious woman running her house as a salon as well as to Violet Kemble-Cooper's Duchess, an aging woman who has to pay for sex.

As for the men, Grant Mitchell played an expatriate who hopes nobody can detect from his speech that he was born in America. There is also a genuinely virile American, played by Minor Watson as a "straight," proud of his nationality and practicality. Finally, the film contains the only overtly gay character in a Cukor film: a dancing teacher, played by Tyrell Davis with rouge on his cheeks and painted lips. One shocked critic noted that he was "the most broadly painted character of the kind yet attempted on the screen."

Dealing with the lascivious affairs of the upper class, Cukor excelled in bringing out the typically English drawing-room banter, the wickedly nasty humor of people who show no sign of repenting or changing their ways. Cukor's direction was described as "smart," particularly in his handling a sequence in a teahouse (to which Bennett goes with the gigolo), "which suggests everything and shows nothing."

Cukor had vivid memories of the stage production, which featured Ina Claire in the lead and Constance Collier as the Duchess. But unfortunately he was unable to assemble a company equal to the demands of the form. Only Kemble-Cooper came close to the desirable technique and manner.

Cukor instructed Bennett to talk as rapidly as Claire did onstage, but he realized that she lacked Claire's brilliant technique. One critic complained that perhaps out of desperation Cukor gave Bennett a mile-long cigarette holder, around which her entire performance was molded.

Cukor's model for comedy acting was Ina Claire's speedy, stylized delivery. On occasion he admittedly "stole" Claire's trick, recommending the technique to his friends. Indeed, during a visit to London Cukor saw Gladys Cooper in a Peter Ustinov play. He sensed something was wrong but could not put his finger on the problem. The next night he went back and realized that Cooper's delivery was too slow. He told her to speed up, and the actress was instantly rewarded; the audience applauded for the first time.

Ever concerned with speed, Cukor was ruthless with his performers on the issue of pace. From his first film to the very last, he had his actors talk much faster than they normally did.

Aiming to get peer recognition, Cukor invited King Vidor to a preview of *Our Betters*. Having made *The Crowd* and *Hallelujah*, Vidor was one of the most respected directors at the time. He complimented Cukor but conceded he would never tackle a subject with so "little locomotion." Vidor thought the picture was static, but that Cukor had somehow kept it interesting in spite of this obstacle.

Vidor's comment reinforced Cukor's commitment to high-quality texts and forte in staging lengthy dialogue scenes. There is very little action or conventional plot in Cukor's films, which are noted for their sharp characterization and keen dialogue. The typical Cukor film revolves around a strong character, almost always a woman, faced by a personal moral dilemma. This dilemma precipitates an inevitable chain of events that necessitate her self-examination and reevaluation of her values.

Cukor's unique mise-en-scène entailed the stylized orchestration of complex set pieces, usually involving half a dozen characters whose "action" consists of sharp verbal exchanges. Compared with American movies past and present, the amount of talk in Cukor's films is amazingly large. At their best Cukor's films are *talking* pictures about personal relationships, evoking the climate of comedy, without ever resorting to melodrama or pathos.

CHAPTER THREE:

The First Peak, 1933–37

SELZNICK MOVED TO METRO-GOLDWYN-MAYER IN FEBRUARY 1933 TO head one of its production units. Ruled with a firm hand by Louis B. Mayer, MGM was then the most prestigious studio in Hollywood. It wasn't very hard for Selznick to persuade Cukor once again to follow him. However, because Cukor was already assigned to a remake of Louisa May Alcott's *Little Women,* for which preproduction had begun, he promised to return to RKO as soon as the MGM picture was complete.

The all-star adaptation of *Dinner at Eight,* based on George S. Kaufman and Edna Ferber's popular Broadway play, was Cukor's first MGM film. For Cukor, Kaufman was not a profound writer, but he could write funny dialogue. Like *A Bill of Divorcement, Dinner at Eight* was a straightforward, unobtrusive adaptation of a stage work with little attempt to go beyond a proscenium perspective; neither film contained exterior shots.

Unlike *A Bill of Divorcement,* however, *Dinner at Eight* maintains its contemporary edge. For audiences in 1933, the ambience was timely because of the comedy's underlying sense of the Depression, a sense of anxiety below the surface. The characters are bitter or insecure. Husbands cheat on wives; the rich are scared about going broke; actors lose their looks—and jobs.

The story revolves around a dinner given by Millicent Jordan (Billie Burke), a foolish snob obsessed with status. As her guests arrive for a party in honor of VIPs (who never show up), the carefully planned evening falls apart. Her husband, Oliver Jordan (Lionel Barrymore), seriously ill and in danger of losing his business, has invited crass industrialist Dan Packard (Wallace Beery) and his vulgar wife, Kitty (Jean Harlow), in an attempt to salvage the fortunes of the Jordans. Their daughter, Paula (Madge Evans), falls in love with Larry Renault (John Barrymore), a pathetically fading matinee idol, and abandons her fiancé.

The script was written in four weeks by Herman Mankiewicz and Frances Marion, but Donald Ogden Stewart was brought in for additional script work. Stewart wrote the classic exchange between Harlow and Marie Dressler. Harlow says: "I was reading a book the other day, machinery is going to take the place of every profession." With a pointed glance at her sexy rear, Dressler retorts, "Oh, something *you* need never worry about, my dear." Dressler's quip became one of the most memorable lines in movie lore.

Preserving the play's caustic humor, the script softened some of its elements. Goaded by Kitty, for example, Packard decides against taking over Jordan's shipping company. And when Paula learns of Renault's death, she returns to her fiancé, who knows nothing of the affair. These concessions were made to accommodate the audience's taste at the time.

But some people were troubled by the film's ruthless cynicism, which was precisely what attracted Cukor to the material. People's deceits and self-deceptions, their double and triple natures are the film's thematic core. "You're two people really. One's magnificent and the other's very shady," says a long-suffering wife to her philandering husband. Motifs of deception and self-delusion were to be prevalent in Cukor's work.

Budgeted at $420,000, *Dinner at Eight* was made in the Thalberg tradition of literary quality, a modern drama with meaningful text. Because MGM had just released *Grand Hotel*, which won the 1932 Oscar, comparisons between the two movies were inevitable. The two films were multicharacter contemporary dramas, and both cashed in on MGM's gallery of stars.

But unlike the troubled and bumpy production of *Grand Hotel, Dinner at Eight* got off to a smooth start on March 16, 1933, and Cukor was able to complete it in four weeks. The film contains no sustained scenes, which helped Cukor to make it quickly. He credited his cast. "That was a wonderful record," Cukor said. "I owed it all to these marvelous performers; with them behind me, everything seemed possible."

Louis B. didn't want to cast Jean Harlow as the flashy smart-mouthed blonde. Unconvinced of her talent, he feared she might suffer in comparison with Dressler, who played Carlotta, the aging grande dame, but Cukor fought for Harlow. Admittedly Harlow had given weak, self-conscious performances, but Cukor had noted her natural talent for comedy in *Red Dust*.

Harlow was a wisecracker who conveyed at the same time toughness and vulnerability, qualities that made her attractive to male and female viewers. She also had an uncanny knack for delivering her lines as if she had no idea of what she was saying. During the film Cukor got to know Harlow well. He found her subtler and shrewder than she was given credit for. "She was a real actress," he later said, "with beautiful manners, a rather lady-like creature."

Cukor brought out the best in Harlow in his acute direction of her big scene where she tells off Wallace Beery. Beery finds her lying in bed wearing a new black hat in an all-white bedroom. She sits up, pushes back her hat (as if she were sitting on the toilet, Cukor said), and yells "You big windbag!" When Beery's big shot has to go to Washington, clearly bored but still impressed, she looks at him and says, "Yeah, you better go and *fix* things." Years later Cukor orchestrated a similarly effective scene with Judy Holliday and Broderick Crawford in *Born Yesterday*.

Barrymore's superb portrayal of the tragic Renault was done as black comedy. Playing a second-rate actor—which, of course, he was not—Barrymore used subtlety and wit to turn Renault into an ignorant ham. Barrymore's ability to immerse himself in a character and let that character transcend his personality was remarkable. In his first shot Barrymore is on the telephone trying to impress a society woman; his speech is well observed and accurate. But when he turns to ask for a drink from the bellhop, his fake grandeur instantly disappears.

Cukor was particularly fond of a scene in which Renault learns he has lost his job because he is not British. "I can be English," he says. "I can be as English as ahnnybohdy."

"Oh, that is wonderful, Jack!" Cukor enthusiastically said.

"Well, it ought to be," Barrymore reportedly said. "This is a combination of Maurice Costello [his father-in-law], Lowell Sherman [his brother-in-law], and me."

Under Cukor's direction, Barrymore was also effective in his death scene, one of the screen's most vivid and pathetic suicides. Cukor suggested that Renault, always the actor, would die in a picturesque way but would botch his suicide, like everything else in his life. As the scene was shot, Barrymore, again drawing heavily on Lowell Sherman and Maurice Costello, walks very grandly across the room, then trips over a stool, gets up, pulls himself together, sits down in a chair, and turns his profile to the light—in a suitable death pose. This marvelous scene taught Cukor that "If first-rate actors respect you, they'll try anything you suggest."

As a whole the casting could not have been better. Marie Dressler was outstanding as the gaudy, comical dowager. Dressler's specialty was low comedy, but she also knew how to play an actress with great aplomb. Homely, she herself found it incredible she was playing an ex-beauty with a host of suitors. To make Carlotta more theatrical, Cukor proposed a campy approach.

Cukor's only regret was his "great disservice" to Billie Burke, whom he cast as a featherbrained "flibbertigibbet." Burke was so convincing that she was typecast for the rest of her career. But Cukor knew that Burke "forgave" him; it was not in her character to hold grudges.

The cast did not escape the biting humor of screenwriter Herman Mankiewicz. "It must be awful tough for you to show Marie Dressler how to perform an old actress who's very ill," he quipped, "and I can see the difficulty in making Lionel Barrymore understand the emotions of a man who has an extravagant wife, or Jack Barrymore comprehending the feelings of a fading matinee idol." Mankiewicz also "sympathized" with Cukor for trying to make a sexy tart out of Jean Harlow and an uncouth creature out of Wallace Beery. Indeed, details of Barrymore's biography—Renault talks about his profile and drinking—were used to enhance his part. This interplay between the actors' offstage and onstage personalities enriched the plot.

In *Dinner at Eight,* arguably the best film from a Kaufman play, Cukor achieved a fine balance of comic and serious tonalities, a blend of high comedy and melodramatic pathos that became one of his specialties. He also managed to fuse a broad range of acting styles (Harlow's natural charm, Beery's mugging, Dressler's grand delivery) into a coherent ensemble piece. Yet he also let each star enjoy special vignettes that linger in memory.

Having directed half a dozen films, Cukor believed he had begun to know his way around the camera. *Dinner at Eight* marked a change, showing his deeper understanding of the kinds of performances that worked in film, the difference between stage and screen acting.

Maureen O'Sullivan, who a year later played Dora in *David Copperfield,* singled out Cukor's line reading and work with actors. She remembered talking to Ayres and Bakewell, who had worked with Cukor in *All Quiet.* "They were eternally grateful to George because they didn't know how to act for the camera." O'Sullivan herself learned "the intimacy of the camera, what it shows, what it picks up." As opposed to some directors who would just say, "Do it," Cukor showed her how to do "a second level of thinking for the camera."

Throughout his career Cukor trained many stage performers in acting for the camera. For instance, he helped Ruth Hussey acquire a movie technique, guiding her to an Oscar-nominated performance in *The Philadelphia Story.* "He showed me that screen technique was quieter and subtler," Hussey said. "He gave me one piece of advice that I always use: 'Keep your emotions near the surface so that you can call on them when you need to.'" Working with Cukor on two films (the other was *Susan and God*), Hussey was taught that "Actors onstage act with the voice, but onscreen they act with their eyes.

"The understatement of great screen acting," said Charles Brackett, who wrote and produced Cukor's 1951 film *The Model and the Marriage Broker,* was mostly Cukor's invention. "He was the one of the first to understand the difference between acting for the theater and acting for the camera." Cukor held that "acting for films has to be done freshly and spontaneously, you have to act as if it were being said for the first time." Cukor understood that a brilliant stage performance, particularly in comedy, would seem artificial onscreen.

Dinner at Eight was Cukor's biggest success to date and a smash hit. The night of the premiere, in the pouring rain, police had to keep back the crowds who gathered in front of the theater to watch the stars' arrivals. A live radio broadcast from the theater filled the airwaves with excitement. The rain went on for days but it did not keep audiences away from the theater.

The film was loved by the critics and public. The New York *Daily Mirror* critic called it "wholly splendid" and a "much improved version of play." Among the barrage of congratulatory notes, Cukor received an emotional note from Irene Selznick: "What are words? Nothing! But you must know how very great my feelings toward you are. My appreciation is no end."

Overcoming the dubious merits of his last RKO films, *Dinner at Eight* began the most creative phase of Cukor's career. It was followed by two great movies that demonstrated his distinctive style, *Little Women* and *David Copperfield*. All three films proved durable and solidified Cukor's reputation as one of Hollywood's best directors. But *Little Women* was a personal favorite in a way that *Dinner at Eight* or *David Copperfield* was not.

After seeing a preview of *A Bill of Divorcement,* Selznick thought *Little Women* would be a perfect vehicle for the young and vibrant Hepburn. When he approached Cukor about the project, the director confessed that he had not read the book. "It was always considered a little girl's story," Cukor recalled; "it seemed awfully syrupy." But once he read the novel, he found it strong-minded, full of solid virtues, and ripe for a new screen adaptation, especially with Hepburn in the lead. Hepburn was delighted at the prospect of working with Cukor again, though she teased him about never having finished the novel. Despite his vehement denials, this became a running joke between them.

Selznick met with staunch resistance from RKO's executives, who were concerned about the lack of commercial appeal of a period piece like *Little Women*. Indeed, finding an approach that would capture the work's essence was foremost in Cukor's mind. Asking himself why the novel had survived all these years, he found the answer in its heartfelt, multilayered portrait of family life—"an admirable New England sternness about sacrifice and austerity."

Set during the Civil War in Concord, Massachusetts, the film is dominated by women. Mr. March, off fighting the war, leaves his wife, Marmee (Spring Byington), to take care of their four daughters: Jo (Hepburn), an ardent tomboy; Beth (Jean Parker), gentle and sweet; Meg (Frances Dee), tender and romantic; and Amy (Joan Bennett), dainty and sly. With the exception of Jo, the sisters try to live up to their father's expectations to be responsible "little women," to fit into the traditional mold of femininity.

The Oscar-winning script for *Little Women,* by husband-and-wife team Victor Heerman and Sarah Y. Mason, was quite original. Rather than tighten the loosely constructed novel, it followed its episodic quality. Things happen, but they're not tied together, reflecting Cukor's belief in the book's vitality. When people commented on how well he handled the big scene, he would ask, "What big scene?" Cukor didn't think of the movie in terms of linear plot or one big climax; these concepts betrayed the spirit of the novel.

Cukor showed respect for his source material. Successful screen adaptation, he believed, meant accepting a book's weaknesses and strengths. For instance, Beth gets desperately sick, and it looks as if she's going to die. Then she recovers. Then she gets sick again. Then she becomes an invalid. Finally she dies. Cukor shot this sequence as it was written. When friends complained, "Why, the bitch seems to be dying all the time," he countered that this awkwardness was also in the book.

Similarly, Cukor refused to tamper with Jo's love interest, which develops awkwardly and late in the story. He also insisted that a version of the script, in which Jo's novel becomes a smash success, be modified to present a less idealized view. Cukor wanted to depict a family that accepts hardship and sacrifice as a matter of course—without nobility.

Jo, the most eccentric of the sisters, is the center of the movie, and Hepburn's superlative performance, singled out at the 1934 Cannes Festival, makes her all the more prominent. Hepburn was born to play the part; her Jo is fiercely proud but also funny and foolish. There were similarities between Hepburn's life and her character that gave greater depth to her portrayal. Like Jo, Hepburn was a New Englander, enormously devoted to her parents, particularly her mother, a feminist active in women's rights.

By this film, with an Oscar (for *Morning Glory*) to her credit, Hepburn had become an accomplished actress. She gave such an inspired performance that the viewers now went with whatever she did. Exuding charm and vitality, Hepburn brought out the elements that made the film alive and contemporary: family love; unselfishness; above all, truthfulness to one's self.

Cukor had an emotional affinity with Jo, who, like him, was not only an outsider but an artist. His direction conveys effectively how Jo's restlessness and frustration are channeled into her creativity. Jo's determination to make her own way as a writer leads her to decline marriage. "Look at me, world, I'm Jo March, and I'm so happy!" says Jo in a moment of exhilaration. When Hepburn said that love is "sickly and sentimental," audiences believed her.

Like Jo, Cukor was more interested in pursuing his career than in having a rich love life. He also related most personally to Jo's tutorship by an elderly gentleman. Jo meets a shy professor, Fritz Bhaer (played by Paul Lukas), who introduces her to the theater and opera and lends her his volume of Shakespeare. This was a role Cukor played in real life for numerous young men in his own house, which became one of Hollywood's chief cultural salons.

Working together for the second time, Cukor and Hepburn developed an intense relationship imbued with forthright honesty and humor. There was a sound strike the day they were filming Beth's dying scene, with Hepburn weeping at her bedside. Cukor did at least twenty takes of the scene, with Hepburn weeping day after day, but the amateur replacement sound man didn't get it right. Cukor was growing increasingly impatient; he could see Hepburn's hard work but didn't like the results. One day, after much crying, Hepburn was so tired and frustrated she threw up. Unsympathetic, Cukor said, "Well, that's what I think of the scene, too."

At one point in the shoot Cukor became so enraged he actually struck Hepburn across the face. Hepburn was to run upstairs with a plate of food. Beforehand Cukor warned her, "Be careful, don't laugh, because I'll kill you if you do." She didn't laugh, but in making her way up the stairs, she slipped and spilled ice cream on her one and only dress. Furious, Cukor hit her while screaming, "You amateur." Hepburn was taken aback but did not show it. "I probably didn't hit her hard enough," Cukor later mused.

Cukor's directorial touch was usually more lighthearted than that. In the scene where Jo goes to New York and sees opera for the first time, she is transfixed, suddenly wanting to be an opera singer. Cukor noticed that Hepburn was twirling around with great exuberance in an exquisite dress that had been copied from one of her grandmother's. He thought she was too high-minded, fancying herself a bit too much. After a long take, as Hepburn sank to the ground in a curtsy, Cukor had a large ham tied to a rope and lowered into view! He made his point.

Cukor was sensitive to his performers, always aware of their problems. At one point a schoolteacher who was visiting the set was asked to leave because she had an unsettling effect on the actors. He explained: "People are insensitive, they have no hesitation of coming here and standing in front of the actors and watching them, and the actors, instead of looking into their own imagination, are confronted with cold eyes."

If Hepburn was a natural choice for the tomboyish Jo, it did not immediately occur to Cukor that Joan Bennett might be right for Amy, the mischievous sister. Cukor perceived Bennett as a somewhat hard-bitten actress, certainly not a character out of Alcott's book. Amy, as he saw it, called for a soft, comedic touch. But one night he ran into Bennett at a party and observed her tipsy and amusing conduct. It was there and then that he got the idea to cast her. However, unbeknownst to Cukor, Bennett was pregnant, and as the film went on, her condition threatened the credibility of Amy's slim girlishness.

Douglass Montgomery, the actor from the Rochester days, was cast as Jo's love interest, the romantic Laurie. Montgomery looked strange in the picture, wearing too much makeup and lipstick, but he gave a sensitive performance. Fond of Montgomery, Cukor later considered him for the lead of *David Copperfield* and as Ashley in *Gone with the Wind*.

The only disappointing performance in an otherwise uniformly good cast, was Spring Byington's Marmee. *Little Women* was her film debut; Cukor gave her a break. Byington was too sugary and sentimental to capture the "tall stately lady" Alcott intended. The other false note that Cukor disliked was Max Steiner's insistently sentimental score.

Working on this film, Cukor discovered how stimulating the research process could be. The film's authentic look is a tribute to his meticulous attention to detail. He sent set designer Hobe Erwin to Concord, to get a feel for the place and ensure that the sets reproduce the locale with accuracy. *Little Women* was shot entirely on the RKO lot, including the winter scenes, which required the use of artificial snow; having grown up in New York, Cukor was sentimental about snow.

A humorous incident that occurred during *Little Women* taught Cukor the need to be discriminating in his choice of consultants. Hepburn insisted: "In New England, there is always a poinsettia on the breakfast table, it's an absolute law."

Cukor dutifully obliged and had a plant brought in. But when he shot the scene, a crew member said, "What is that doing on the table?"

"Well," Cukor said, "you should know, you're from New England."

"I never saw one before," the man said.

Cukor learned a lesson: "Be careful of what advice you take and from whom."

Walter Plunkett approached the costumes with the same desire for accuracy as Cukor. His designs reflected the notion that the girls were poor but high-minded. Plunkett arranged that the costumes be interchanged among the actresses in different scenes to suggest their frugal life. This struck a chord among the viewers because *Little Women* was released at the height of the Depression. In that context the treatment of social class was relevant: The March family, once rich, has lost its fortune. Hunger, poverty, and infant mortality all are in the background.

Tallulah Bankhead was vacationing in California when she saw a rough cut at Cukor's house; no one else had seen it yet. There was a frightful scream at the end of the showing. Typically flamboyant, Bankhead threw herself into Hepburn's arms and hugged her, then burst into tears. On her knees, holding three wet handkerchiefs, she was terribly shattered by the film and Hepburn's performance. Cukor looked at her with a cruel eye and said, "Tallulah, you're weeping for your lost innocence."

Under Cukor's delicate direction *Little Women* is a powerful depiction of lost innocence: the making of a sensitive writer, the maturation of a girl who transcends her milieu while retaining its heritage. *Little Women* was nominated for three Oscars, including Best Picture. It also brought Cukor's first nod as Best Director, which he lost to Frank Lloyd (*Cavalcade*). *Little Women* was dismissed for many years as a maudlin period piece, but reassessed in the 1970s, in the new context of feminism (of which Hepburn was an early exemplar), the picture held up well.

Selznick produced *Little Women* again in 1948 at MGM, but early on he realized something basic was missing. He called Cukor and asked for his honest opinion. "It's perfectly all right," Cukor said after looking at the rushes, "but it hasn't got magic." Cukor thought that the newer version made the mistake of slicking the novel up, and the acting did not measure up to his version. June Allyson, who played Jo in the MGM movie, was no Hepburn. Cukor knew it was Hepburn's great performance that cast magic over his film.

Dinner at Eight was so successful that Selznick wanted to make another film with Cukor and the Barrymores. He appreciated Cukor's ability to handle the temperamental siblings without the slightest difficulty—the only director who could do it. Cukor joined in Selznick's enthusiastic desire to film John Galsworthy's *The Forsyte Saga* with the Barrymores, but the project never materialized.

Selznick had a habit of keeping lists of literary classics he might want to film. Novels that had withstood the test of time, he believed, were a welcome change from Hollywood's conventional formulas. Selznick decided to push for an adaptation of Charles Dickens's *David Copperfield*. Although no one at MGM was silly enough to suggest modernizing the masterpiece, he encountered the same kind of opposition he had experienced at RKO over *Little Women*.

MGM's top brass was adamantly opposed to highbrow literary adaptations, which were expensive and risky in terms of box-office appeal. In a February 1934 memo to executives at Loew's (MGM's parent company), Selznick noted that the public was tired of the hackneyed and standardized movies that Hollywood was grinding out with workman-like efficiency. He went on to say that there were few producers with sufficient understanding and few directors with sufficient taste and talent to transcribe the classics with an accuracy of spirit and mood. He finally persuaded the studio heads that he had the understanding, and Cukor the taste and talent, to tackle *David Copperfield*.

Bringing Dickens to the screen ultimately changed MGM's attitude toward literary classics. The studio's last release in 1935, *David Copperfield* was both an artistic success and a financial bonanza—despite its huge price tag. With its sixty-nine-day shooting schedule, the movie cost more than $1 million. Cukor made a lot of money on it; his directorial fee amounted to $113,585.

Adapting such a monumental novel, with so many characters, was not an easy task. Howard Estabrook worked on the scenario's structure, but Cukor thought that Hugh Walpole, the English novelist, would do a better job with the dialogue. Walpole didn't know anything about screenwriting, but he understood Dickens and the tone that was needed. His contribution was not in dramatic terms but in giving the characters their authentic voices.

Selznick at one point suggested making two pictures out of *David Copperfield*, which would cost only a hundred thousand dollars more. The films, while related, would be complete in themselves. He also toyed with the idea of exhibiting the two films on successive weeks, a notion that was dropped for practical reasons.

David Copperfield enjoyed a barrage of advertising. AMERICA MAKES A BRITISH EPIC, read the headline of one newspaper. Originally the movie was going to be made with an entirely British cast. Selznick and Cukor were to prepare the script in Hollywood, then cast and shoot it entirely in England. Louis B. supported the idea, hoping it would boost the film's grosses in Britain and revitalize MGM's British company.

Once it was decided to shoot in England, Cukor became impatient, demanding to know "when the hell" they were leaving. Here was his great opportunity to go to London, the world theater capital, which he had been wanting to see but lacked either the time or money to do so.

On May 8, 1934, Selznick, Cukor, and Estabrook arrived in London to look for authentic types and scout locations. Cukor got to meet London's literary elite—Hugh Walpole, J. B. Priestley—at a special lunch. Selznick told reporters that an American Micawber or Peggotty "simply won't do."

In London Cukor got in touch with the head of the Charles Dickens

Society, who told him about every place associated with the novel. He carefully went all over the ground the fictional David had traveled, but in the end, only one second-unit shot, a charming view of him walking to Canterbury, was used.

David Copperfield was not destined to be shot in London. The alternative was to make the film in Hollywood but still use British actors. Cukor was lucky there were so many good British actors in Hollywood at the time. Thus Elsa Lanchester was cast as Clickett, Roland Young as Uriah Heep, and Basil Rathbone as Mr. Murdstone.

Early on Cukor decided that Charles Laughton would be a perfect Micawber. Having just won an Oscar for *The Private Life of Henry VIII*, Laughton would be the most prestigious name in the large cast. Selznick, too, thought Laughton was a good choice and was willing to do whatever necessary to sign him. But the capricious actor was not very interested and had to be persuaded to take the role.

Laughton finally agreed to play Micawber, but then a new set of problems arose for the always insecure actor. "If Charles had his way," wrote his wife, Elsa Lanchester, "he never would have acted at all, because in every part he played, after the first two or three days' work, he tried to get out of the picture." On the set of *David Copperfield*, the situation was worse than ever. Laughton lost his confidence. He considered Micawber a ham actor who was always "on", but Dickens's portrayal was so complete that Laughton believed he had nothing to add.

At first Laughton and Cukor got on very well, despite the director's fears of encountering the actor's alleged prejudice against Jews. Laughton's physical embodiment of Micawber was correct, right down to the meticulous makeup he devised. But his insecurity was too close to the surface, and he began exhibiting strange habits on the set. Laughton needed offstage noises to get himself into the mood, and he was the first actor Cukor encountered who prepared himself for a laughing entrance by walking around making "ha-ha" sounds for hours. Deep down Laughton felt he wasn't right, and soon Cukor himself sensed he lacked the geniality the part called for. After one week Laughton withdrew, and Cukor sighed with relief.

Selznick then went to Paramount and made hasty arrangements to borrow W. C. Fields, who, as anticipated, jumped at the chance of playing Micawber. Physically he wasn't right, but his spirit was ideal. "This is the first time in my life I ever played a real 'character' part," Fields told the press. "I've always gone over my dialogue and made it fit my style."

Some cast members were worried that Fields would "steal" the film, but Cukor reassured them there was nothing to worry about. "For the first time in his career," Cukor later said, "he followed the script because of his admiration for Dickens." It was that rare combination of personality and role meshing perfectly. "I've been playing Micawber all my life," the actor said, "under a lot of different names, and never knew it."

Finding an actor to play the young David Copperfield was the biggest problem. Louis B. wanted to cast Jackie Cooper, whom he liked after his performance as Wallace Beery's son in *The Champ*. Cooper was an appealing child star, but Cukor shuddered at the thought of the snub-nosed American youngster. Selznick and Cukor dug in their heels, telling Louis B. they wouldn't cast an American to play such a famous English character.

An extensive search spread out on both sides of the Atlantic. Maureen O'Sullivan recalled that her husband-to-be, director John Farrow, was sent to scout for a young actor to play Copperfield. She and Farrow went to Canada and London but didn't turn up anybody.

On their trip to England Cukor and Selznick had come upon an attractive kid, Freddie Bartholomew. Bartholomew's qualities—his stage experience, charm, and distinctly English manner of speech—made him a strong possibility. But there were problems with his parents: Bartholomew's father in interviews with the press implied that the boy had already been hired, falsely putting the studio in the position of violating British law against exportation of children for labor.

Selznick was determined to employ the child but only with permission of the British government, even though the delay was costly because the rest of the cast had been engaged. Cukor promised that the child's schooling would not be affected, that his future would in fact benefit by his having money for his education. And he continued to argue that the British would resent an American child cast as Copperfield.

Climaxing an eight-month search, the eventual casting of Bartholomew was highly publicized. The boy was brought to Hollywood with his aunt, but problems with his drunken father continued. A vindictive man, Mr. Bartholomew resented the fact that the aunt was earning fifty dollars a week to look after his son. Claiming rights to his son's earnings, he threatened to come to the United States and take his boy home.

Cukor thought it would be a disaster for the child to go back to his revolting father. The situation seemed right out of Dickens; it made Copperfield's plight lighthearted by comparison. But the "ordeal" was worth it: Bartholomew was credible, except for an air of British noblesse oblige and difficulty in crying.

By that time Cukor had developed his own rule about literary adaptations: the essence of the original should determine the film's style. But as with *Little Women,* this involved accepting the weaknesses of the source material. Cukor knew that there was excessive melodrama in *David Copperfield* and that dramatically the resolution was unsatisfactory. When people chided him that the film's second half was not as good as the first, he would say, "Well, the second volume of the novel is not as good as the first." It was a pity, Cukor said, that Copperfield grew up to be a "bore" and "typical Victorian." But the second part did not damage the film. *David Copperfield* was overall accomplished; it had vitality, and its feeling was right.

Cukor realized that Dickens's core was in his characters, and the challenge was to bring them to life, make them slightly grotesque yet human, funny yet frightening. Cukor made sure that his eccentric performers acted as an ensemble. Working two dozen principals into a unified cast, Cukor saw to it that no one, let alone Fields, slipped into routine.

So many unfavorable stories circulated about Fields that Cukor prepared himself for displays of capricious behavior, but they never happened. Even Fields's alleged trademark—his hatred of children—was not in evidence. Fields treated the eleven-year-old Bartholomew with kindness and respect. Bartholomew became like Fields's own son.

Fields, in fact, was endearing—"dignified," Cukor said. His suggestions and ad libs were always sound and in character. In a scene in which he had to sit at a desk writing, he asked Cukor if he could have a cup of tea on the desk. To show Micawber's agitation, Fields dipped his pen into the teacup instead of the inkwell. In another scene, sitting on a high stool, he asked for a wastepaper basket, in which he could get his feet stuck.

To simulate the white cliffs of Dover, Cukor used locations around Malibu. When he eventually saw the real cliffs, he thought that his cliffs were "better, whiter and cliffier." It was as if he had first created something and then found it in reality.

The research proved stimulating. "When you really look at things, you reeducate your eyes and your sensibilities," said Cukor, who regarded filmmaking as self-instruction. "Every picture is an education to me," he said. "Most of the education I have is from preparing pictures. I become sort of a half-assed expert on certain things. In a very profound way, I do a great deal of research purely for myself, and some of it sticks."

If the acting in *David Copperfield* and its mood were right, the art direction was uneven and inconsistent, hovering between realism and stylization. Cukor believed that the more artificial the film, the better; he wanted everything to be stylized, like the shipwreck scene. But under pressure from MGM, the picture ended up less coherent and more compromised than *Little Women*.

David Copperfield launched another enduring friendship, this one with Maureen O'Sullivan. According to the actress, Cukor didn't think she was good in the ingenue role. "I didn't quite understand what he wanted, and I felt I wasn't doing it right," she confessed. O'Sullivan and Cukor did not see eye to eye at first. "I went for hairdressing tests, and I came back to the set to show George my hairdo, which was the same as the one

I'd worn in *The Barretts of Wimpole Street*. I'd rather fancied myself in that and had pictured Dora as being a more fiery character, which was opposed to George's notion. George was very disappointed. 'Oh,' he said, 'I thought you were going to come up with a new hairdo.'

"George told you explicitly what line reading he wanted," she said. "He was very adamant about exactly what he wished you to do, where to stand, how to move. He wasn't really open to suggestions, and I didn't make any because I was in awe of him. George was not dictatorial or fussy; he just knew what he wanted."

According to O'Sullivan, Cukor's major qualities were his deep understanding of the material and his humor, which he used to get what he wanted. In one scene, O'Sullivan had to dance with a dog. "I had just done a Tarzan film, and I couldn't get this dog to face the camera." Cukor came over and said, "Maureen, pretend you're in the Tarzan film. Just wind that damn dog up and get his face on the camera; just twist it around."

Cukor's methods were not always so benign. During her death scene he didn't like what was coming through. "Off camera," she recalled, "George twisted my feet turning them this way and that way. It was rather painful, and I was in agony, but he got the right expression on my face." Cukor used the same gimmick with Olivia de Havilland in her birth-giving scene in *Gone with the Wind*.

The final cut that Selznick delivered had a running time of two hours and thirteen minutes—long by standards of the day. Nicholas M. Schenck, the president of Loew's, had serious misgivings. He reproached Selznick for letting the film run so long and for not organizing it better. "How long can it be?" Schenck pleaded. "How long is it good?" Selznick replied. Schenck had to concede that it was good all the way through.

Cukor was ill during the first three previews but rose from a pallet of pain for the fourth. "They were hectic, confusing times," he later recalled, "everybody urging different things, cut some of the stories, release the picture in two parts." But he always gave Selznick credit for his adamant insistence on releasing the picture in its present form.

A huge hit, *David Copperfield* grossed nearly three million dollars in its eighty-six-week-run, doing exceptional business abroad. Selznick was right in his prediction about the British response; the Commonwealth countries contributed 25 percent of the grosses. The film was nominated for three Oscars, including Best Picture, but lost in all categories. Cukor was hurt; for some mysterious reason, he had failed to receive a directorial nomination.

For the British premiere, a Copperfield luncheon was organized, with celebrities like Hugh Walpole, J. B. Priestley, Frank Lawton (who played the mature Copperfield), and two of Dickens's granddaughters in attendance. The British press came ready to attack the film, but they all were charmed by what they saw.

Walpole, who played the parson in the film, praised *David Copperfield*, particularly its editing, which was also nominated for an Oscar. Walpole very much wanted to work with Cukor again and tried to find the right classic for them to tackle. Though another literary friendship began, they never managed another collaboration. Years later Walpole dedicated a collection of his stories to Cukor with a personal inscription.

Cukor's *David Copperfield* is arguably the purest Dickens film ever made. Cukor, in fact, could not bring himself to see another version, filmed in London, when it was released in 1970. The new film, Cukor said after seeing it years later, "unfortunately zeroed in on the depressing parts and they didn't get the virtues." He repeated: "To get the strength of a novel, you've got to do the weaknesses."

Thirty years later Henri Langlois, founder of the Cinémathèque Française, reviewed *David Copperfield* in a perceptive critique. "Your words were music to my ears and eyes," wrote Cukor, touched by the way a director's work was treated in France. And while he didn't mean to sound disloyal to Hollywood, he conceded that American directors were not given the "thoughtful consideration and regard" they received abroad.

Meanwhile, Cukor was busy remodeling the house he had purchased at 9611 Cordell Drive. Nestled in the Hollywood Hills, above the raffish squalor of the Sunset Strip, the house became the center of Cukor's universe. Cukor rebuilt what was a small house with the assistance of architect Michael Delina. The house had one of the most famous swimming pools in Hollywood and a large terraced garden graced with Italian statues that were lit by tinted rays from concealed spotlights. Imposing ivy-covered walls, which surrounded the estate, ensured privacy and conveyed the atmosphere of a medieval castle. Cukor lived behind the high walls of "a bachelor pleasure-dome," as one journalist put it.

William Haines, the former actor and a friend of Cukor's, designed the interior. It took almost two decades to bring the house to its desired look. The restructured house had several living rooms but only one bedroom. As one reporter put it, although the director was a celebrated host, he disliked entertaining anyone overnight.

The furnishings, like the sets of some of Cukor's movies, were a curious mixture of modern and antique. For each room, paintings were selected with meticulous taste and discrimination. Cukor owned several Picassos and Toulouse-Lautrecs, a superb Rodin bronze, and works by Braque, Rouault, Renoir, and Henry Moore. One staircase wall was closely hung with works by such prominent artists as Matisse, Goya, and Dali.

A gallery of familiar faces, ranging from Olivier to Garbo, looked down from the walls. The photographs in the house were mostly of female stars; there was none of Cukor alone. Cukor particularly liked a gracious Sargent drawing of Ethel Barrymore, bequeathed to him by the actress.

Cukor had a passion for chinoiserie and collected Han dancing figures. "George is galvanized by objects," said a friend. "They perpetually astonish him. He adores possessing them, and if he catches you looking covetously at something he owns, he'll grasp it almost vengefully. Then he may give it to you for Christmas."

In 1934 the house was coming along beautifully, though its size and luxuriousness terrified him. "I've had to go to the Jews to pay for it," Cukor confessed, "and I'm afraid I shall have to work the rest of my life to pay it off completely." Maureen O'Sullivan recalled how Cukor described to her all the things he was going to do with his house. "My Lord," said the actress, "that's going to cost you a lot of money."

"Yes," he said, "Irving Thalberg told me, 'Go ahead, George, spend a lot of money. I love to have directors in debt, it forces them to work harder.' "

In 1935 Cukor purchased Grant Wood's "Near Sundown" in a frame designed by the artist for a modest $750. His dining room was designed at great expense around the painting. Other artworks were not obtained so cheaply: He bought a much-sought-after Renoir from the Courvoisier Gallery, at a cost of $3,500.

Cukor's opulent house became a most famous "showcase mansion" in the film colony. "The house suits me perfectly," he boasted. "I know I belong here. The rooms are more or less the way Billy Haines decorated them, but that is not to take away from my personal taste and knowledge."

There was elegance in every room, each filled with mementos. In later years there was a silver cigarette box, with a message from Marilyn Monroe, and a beautiful Renoir on a table easel, a gift from Vivien Leigh. A bronze head of Tallulah Bankhead rested on an inlaid demilune table in the lower hall, and displayed against a nineteenth-century puppet theater proscenium were figures of Katharine Hepburn and Spencer Tracy, two of his frequent players and dearest friends.

Given his new lucrative contract at Metro, Cukor could afford to spend money. On October 21 the "Selznick contract" was terminated and replaced with a five-year contract at a good salary. Cukor now hoped to achieve financial independence. His great wish was to maintain control of loan-outs, in the event that Selznick went to another studio and then asked him to direct a picture.

Whether working or not, Cukor was fastidious in his correspondence with friends. No event, be it the birthday of a friend or the opening night of an old stage star, passed without acknowledgment. There was always a steady flow of requests from friends of one kind or another. In 1935 his friend Laurette Taylor sent him a play she was writing as a movie for John Barrymore. Taylor hoped Cukor would help her break into films as an actress or a screenwriter. Unfortunately it never happened. As she grew older, Taylor was losing her confidence and became easily offended. She complained to Cukor about a young director who, after reading her play, had the nerve to ask her if she also wanted to act in it.

Over the years many of Cukor's friends asked for assistance to get into the film business, and he helped whenever possible. He cast Lenore Ulric, a former David Belasco star, as Olympe in *Camille*. Ulric was not an accomplished actress—and was not good in the role—but he had shown his loyalty to one of his oldest friends from New York. In later years, as Ulric struggled for her livelihood, Cukor occasionally sent her money. This kind of loyal generosity was characteristic of Cukor, who also provided occasional support for Billie Burke and Ethel Barrymore.

After *David Copperfield*, Cukor returned to RKO to direct *Sylvia Scarlett* because he owed the studio one picture. Although a commercial and critical failure when released in January 1936, *Sylvia Scarlett* was one of Cukor's most personal and original films.

Cukor was intrigued by the story of petty crooks on the run who give up crime to become vagabond actors. With three strong characters— Henry Scarlett (Edmund Gwenn), a hard-luck embezzler forced to flee France; his daughter, Sylvia (Hepburn), disguised as a boy to help him; and Jimmy Monkley (Cary Grant), a raffish cockney who joins them— Cukor had the making of an offbeat film.

Looking at the film today, one can see the eccentricities that must have attracted him. Sylvia was a suitable part for Hepburn's boyish quality: She played a young chap whom both men and women fell in love with. First, a rural artist (Brian Aherne) is attracted to her, saying, "There's something very queer going on here," and then a maid finds her attractive and kisses her. In its day the sexual ambiguities and misunderstandings were daring, but audiences didn't see the humor in the film's crossdressing and mistaken identities.

Neither did producer Pandro S. Berman, who disliked the "freak picture" from the beginning. "I hated it as a book," he recalled, "but George and Kate were crazy about it, and they ganged up on me. I'd never seen them so enthusiastic about a project." Cukor and Berman also disagreed about casting. Berman wanted Errol Flynn, then an unknown dashing Australian, as the rural artist, but after meeting Flynn for only five minutes, Cukor dismissed him, and the role went to Brian Aherne.

At the special request of Cukor's old friend actress Elsa Maxwell,

Natasha Paley, a bona fide Russian princess, was cast as Aherne's lover, even though her English was bad. Paley had fallen on hard times, and Maxwell was concerned about her financial welfare. Maxwell also took the liberty of asking a favor for herself—should the director come across a high-comedy Marie Dressler part.

Perhaps the most significant piece of casting was Cary Grant, featured here in a pivotal role that changed the course of his career. Under contract at Paramount, Grant was typed as a conventional leading man and cast in unimportant parts. It was not until Cukor directed him in *Sylvia Scarlett,* his first important role, that Grant's flair for comedy emerged. "George taught Cary how to be funny," Hepburn said. "He brought out the Archie Leach in him. George saw that Cary was not really a trained actor, that he was wooden, but he helped him discover he was a comedian."

Grant, who had been a circus stilt walker in his childhood, was familiar with his character's raffish personality. Playing a cockney trickster, Grant stole the picture and went on to a triumphant career as a romantic wise guy. Cukor periodically reminded Grant that he had made his breakthrough in *his* movie.

Cukor persuaded John Collier, a writer whose short stories he liked, to come to Hollywood and write the screenplay. But the final script, credited to Collier, Gladys Unger, and Cukor's childhood friend, Mortimer Offner, was a curious work, burdened by a jumbled plot and labored dialogue.

Cukor's treatment was in part whimsical, in part allegorical. Some of the film, like the sequence when Hepburn and Grant join up with the traveling players, was really good. But other scenes proved difficult and lacked credibility. It always worried Cukor when a scene didn't play: "A good scene falls into place and carries itself and everything else with it."

Hepburn is lovely in the first part, which is funny. The way she handles her body as the awkward heroine and her haircut were appropriately boyish. The actress's painful vulnerability and romantic sexual longings are as apparent in this film as they are in *Little Women.* But Hepburn seems affected in the second section—as a result of the script.

When they finished shooting, Cukor thought they had "something really fine"—until the infamous preview at Huntington Park. Cukor and Hepburn had an early supper with Natasha Paley and went to the theater. They were convinced that *Sylvia Scarlett* would be a great success. "I can quit the business now," Cukor joked, "and rest on my laurels." He added, "Wouldn't it be funny if the picture would flop?" He was certain this was out of the question.

But during the screening Hepburn realized that something was wrong: No one was laughing, even though it was supposed to be a comedy. Half the audience walked out, and those who remained began to talk. "It was an absolute agony," Hepburn recalled. "The audience had no idea what the film was about. I thought they were going to lynch me."

The preview was a nightmare, with people walking up and down the aisles. At one point Hepburn went to the ladies' room, where to her dismay she found a woman lying on a sofa. "What's the matter?" asked Hepburn. "Was the picture so bad? Did it finish you off?" The woman just rolled her eyes, never answering. Later, as they were leaving, Hepburn banged her head while getting into her car. "Thank God," she said, "I've knocked myself out." Hepburn remembered the evening as "a total disaster."

After the preview they all went back to Cukor's house. "Pandro, scrape this one," said Hepburn, "and we'll do another picture for you for nothing!"

Berman looked at them coldly and said: "I never want to do a picture with either of you again."

Usually Cukor could count on kind words from his friends, even about his weakest films. But when Fanny Brice saw the film, she responded with characteristic bluntness. She gave Cukor and Hepburn a discouraging look and said, "What the hell were you two thinking about making that picture?"

Hepburn later admitted that during the scene when she was reciting a poem, she began to lose confidence in the material and wondered if Cukor had lost his. She thought the picture ended too abruptly and again accused Cukor of not finishing the book, as she herself had not. "We've worked on other books we've never finished," Cukor said, referring to *Little Women*.

Cukor went out on a limb with *Sylvia Scarlett* and got clobbered, but he refused to indulge in self-pity. He was fond of Fanny Brice's dictum: "If ya stay in the game long enough, the deal comes round to you." Failure was not a pleasant experience, but Cukor believed it was better to forge new paths than to sit back and cry. Both he and Hepburn, as he later put it, had "many kicks in the ass" after that. Cukor's attitude was typical: "Get on with something else." Still, the failure of *Sylvia Scarlett* made him more cautious. "It slowed me up," he told Lambert. "I wasn't going to be so goddamned daring after that."

At the time, though, Cukor didn't have any inkling of disaster. It wasn't pleasant to have a flop, but it really didn't injure him. His direction even got some good reviews. Cukor later realized that it wasn't the daring part of *Sylvia Scarlett* that failed; it was the part where they tried to play it safe! The opening scene, after Sylvia's mother has died and she cuts off her hair to sell it, was put in later. Originally the story started aboard the ship, when Hepburn is already disguised as a boy. The prologue was tacked on as a sympathy device: Poor girl, her mother died;

what else could she do? The ending was also weak and contrived; its sole purpose was to get Hepburn away from Grant and back to the artist. Worse yet, the subplot of Natasha Paley, as Aherne's older woman who almost drowns, has nothing to do with the rest of the film.

A commercial flop, *Sylvia Scarlett* disappeared for some years, but then it began to acquire an underground reputation and even became a minor cult film. It never stopped playing at the art theaters. But Cukor used *Sylvia Scarlett* as a litmus test, to see if his friends were in their right minds. If they liked it, they were "a little batty." Indeed, years later, when Judy Holliday noted she loved the picture, Cukor said: "Now, I know about *you,* your mind is not too good."

Once the initial shock was over, Cukor's attitude toward the movie softened. He often joked how it took "a mere thirty-five years" to appreciate the film. Privately he continued to feel affection for it. Nothing delighted him more than the critics' comment that *Sylvia Scarlett* was ahead of its time. It was a great compliment for a contract director.

Cukor's next film, *Romeo and Juliet,* also turned out to be an interesting flop. Though faithful to Shakespeare, it succeeded neither as a passionate romance nor as a costume drama.

In June 1935 Irving Thalberg announced his intention to do *Romeo and Juliet* with his wife, Norma Shearer, under Cukor's direction. Once again Louis B. opposed the idea, reminding Thalberg that neither he nor Cukor had experience with Shakespeare and, more to the point, the public did not want to see a Shakespearean film. But Thalberg argued convincingly that a good production of the classic would enhance the studio's prestige. The film was finally approved, but Thalberg was urged to keep the budget down.

The casting of Romeo proved difficult. When Cukor's first choice, Fredric March, declined the role, he suggested Douglas Fairbanks, Jr., who was young and could project the image of a passionate lover, but Thalberg was not excited. Both Laurence Olivier and Robert Donat were considered, but the chances of getting either English actor were slim. Cukor and Thalberg finally settled on Leslie Howard. Cukor was not particularly happy about his two leads, knowing that neither Howard nor Shearer could convincingly play the fiery young lovers; they were too old and too stodgy.

Realizing her limitations, Shearer was intimidated by the part, but fueled by Cukor's enthusiasm, she labored diligently on her diction. Cukor instructed her to work with the character actress Constance Collier and to read poetry out loud every day. He wanted her to grasp the cadence of Shakespeare, without speaking in an artificial classical manner; his goal was to make the language real and comprehensible to contemporary audiences. Cukor managed to get Shearer's readings clear, but because she was not much of a dramatic actress, her performance never rose above adequacy.

It was Thalberg's idea to cast John Barrymore in the role of Mercutio. But because Barrymore had been drinking heavily, Thalberg insisted that the actor live at a Culver City home for alcoholics; he even assigned studio police to guard him. Despite precautions, Barrymore showed up for the first day of shooting hours late—and drunk. He told Cukor, who had been waiting all morning for him, that he had lost his voice. Trying to make the best of the situation, Cukor shot the duel scene first, thinking it might be easier for Barrymore to handle. There were a few harrowing moments, however, when Barrymore almost hit Howard during the sword play.

As usual, Barrymore was hard to handle, playing around with his lines, making jokes about the text. When Cukor could not control the actor's shenanigans, Thalberg was brought onto the set to straighten things out. Miraculously, in the next take, Barrymore said his lines correctly. Not taking any chances, Cukor ordered, "Print!" Cukor thought Barrymore, with his ranting and grimacing, gave an atrocious performance, missing the opportunity of being a great Mercutio.

A grand-scale production, *Romeo and Juliet* was Cukor's biggest assignment to date, and he took great care in planing the medieval sets and costumes. But the prestige of the literary source—the first and only Shakespeare Cukor ever directed—made him nervous. Although playwright Thornton Wilder was going to do a treatment of *Romeo and Juliet*, with samples of dialogue in modern adaptation, in the end, Talbot Jennings prepared the script. A Cornell professor was also brought in as an adviser "to represent the interests of the author."

Those interests were not served well at Metro as far as the look of the picture was concerned. Indeed, there was a tug-of-war about the "right" style. On one side were costume designer Adrian and resident art director Cedric Gibbons, and on the other were Cukor and Oliver Messel, who did the sets. The result was an incoherent look, pleasing neither side. Original at moments, like the ball scene, which was choreographed by the young Agnes de Mille, *Romeo and Juliet* was conventional at many others. Messel's ideas were severely compromised by the studio's art department. Cukor later regretted not having been more forceful with MGM, though at the time he lacked the clout for that.

Except for the style issue, Cukor respected Thalberg's feelings completely. Once he moved to MGM, Cukor got closer and closer to Thalberg in a relationship that Selznick resented. Well read, Thalberg displayed better literary and cinematic taste than Selznick. Cukor's arguments with MGM's wunderkind, who was generous and gentlemanly, were intellectual and congenial, unlike the heated and pretentious debates he had had with Selznick.

When they shot the parting scene, for example, Cukor thought it was moving, but Thalberg claimed the actors were too glum. "But, Irving," Cukor said, "they're parting in the morning."

"No," said Thalberg, "it could be done with a smile."

Cukor saw his point: What Thalberg meant was tenderness, a more romantic way of saying good-bye.

Curiously, one of the best and most complex scenes, the potion scene, was done with the least amount of trouble. It was shot in one take on a Saturday morning, when Thalberg was in the desert working on another script. The understanding was that nothing would be filmed during his absence; Thalberg insisted on seeing every scene rehearsed before it was shot. But that Saturday morning the set scheduled for shooting was not fully dressed, and the only one ready was Juliet's bedroom. Cukor asked Shearer if she would like to try the potion scene. "What about Irving?" she said in concern.

"Let's just knock it off and see what we get," Cukor said.

The suicide scene was done as one long, uninterrupted shot, from the point Juliet's mother leaves the room through Juliet's long soliloquy to the taking of the potion. Though the sequence hadn't been fully rehearsed, Shearer knew her lines, and Cukor decided to work out the camera movements. Then, just for luck, they did one take. "Okay, print it!" Cukor said. "We'll let Irving see it on Monday." The crew was stunned by Cukor's gutsy determination. Thalberg was a bit angry that Cukor had shot the scene without his permission, but when he looked at the rushes, he agreed that the footage had a spontaneity and an intimacy that could not be improved upon.

On the set of *Romeo and Juliet,* Cukor met child actor Lon McCallister, who later became a close friend. "I had been trying unsuccessfully to break into film," McCallister recalled, "and when the moment finally happened, it was my great good fortune to begin at the top, with Shearer, Howard, Barrymore, and Cukor." Only eleven, McCallister was a choirboy extra, but he remembered Cukor's kindness and patience, qualities that never varied during their friendship. "George shot a close-up of me singing with the choir," he remembered. "Fortunately we had prerecorded music, because when he said, 'Action,' I lost my voice. 'Pretend!' said Cukor. That was the first piece of direction I ever received in movies." After they became friends, Cukor confessed that the close-up was not his idea; he shot it at Oliver Messel's request.

McCallister didn't really get to know Cukor during *Romeo and Juliet:* "He was on the highest ring, and I on the lowest." The child actor continued to address him as Mr. Cukor up until 1944, when they worked again on *Winged Victory*. "George was a presence, and I respected him," he explained. "My six years as an extra taught me to be very courteous to directors."

Shooting wrapped on May 7, 1936, and the picture was released on August 20. *Romeo and Juliet* was another movie running over two hours. The negative costs of the opulent production had skyrocketed to more than two million dollars, way above Thalberg's original eight-hundred-thousand-dollar estimate. With added costs of advertising and distribution, the film lost money at the box office. But the response of the more literate viewers was favorable, and Cukor and Thalberg felt the effort was justified; Louis B. just kept quiet.

Still, Cukor wished he had given the exteriors of *Romeo and Juliet* a more Italian flavor. Short on passion, the whole picture was inhibited by MGM's concept of "literary prestige." Visually attractive, the movie was too formal. It was one picture, he said, that if he would do again, he'd get the "garlic and the Mediterranean" into it.

Cukor always felt uncomfortable about *Romeo and Juliet*. It was an incomplete experience; there were too many things he would have liked to change. But back in 1936 he was caught up in what he described as "production gloss," which meant giving the film a stately look. As a result, the picture suffered; there was too much of the old Hollywood in it.

If Cukor regretted being unable to film *Romeo and Juliet* in Italy, he felt the same way about not filming *Camille* in Paris. Garbo was under contract for two more pictures, and Cukor was given a choice: *Anna Karenina* or *Camille*. He chose *Camille*, and guided Garbo to her greatest performance in the role of Dumas's doomed heroine. In *Camille* he brilliantly created a psychological portrait of a victim trapped in her social milieu. The movie represented another achievement: It was Cukor's first costume film that had the right look.

Selznick was apprehensive about his first venture with Garbo, in part because of her stature and, more to the point, because of commercial disappointment of her historical film *Queen Christina*. Initially he was inclined to film *Dark Victory*, provided he could purchase the Broadway play at a reasonable figure and get Philip Barry to write the script. Cukor agreed that *Dark Victory* was a better vehicle for Garbo than *Anna Karenina*. Assuring Garbo that Cukor would put his best efforts into making a fine film of *Dark Victory*, Selznick asked for her permission to switch from *Anna Karenina*. But in the end he decided against doing the picture.

Over the years Cukor had seen Garbo at MGM, but he had not formally met her. When he was finally "treated" (as he put it) to the divine

Garbo in 1935, his first impression was not great. He found her to be nice and sweet but devoid of humor and rather pretentious. She was also depressing, as if she were carrying all the sorrows of the world around with her. Real lesbians, he told Hugh Walpole with unusual candor, were a little heavy-handed and so goddamned noble. Cukor made nasty jokes about the suffering that Garbo projected onscreen, imitating her famous line, "I want to be alone!"

Walpole was anxious to know how Cukor was getting on with the Swedish star. Was she rude to him? Other directors who had worked with Garbo had recommended toughness with her. Teasing Cukor for being too gentlemanly, Walpole feared Garbo would bully him.

Considering the subject matter of *Camille,* censorship problems were expected. The Production Code Administration (PCA), also known as the Hays Office after its founder, Will H. Hays, decreed that "the heroine is definitely an immoral woman" and demanded that the story be cleaned up. Stipulating that there should be no "courtesans" in the film other than Marguerite, they recommended that Olympe be married instead of being a mistress. They also suggested that Marguerite indicate she would not resume her life as a courtesan after breaking with the baron. Cukor was at once bemused and outraged when the censors wished to inject a stronger note of repentance and regeneration.

"You have put too much emphasis," Joseph Breen, director of the PCA, wrote, "on the point that living as a mistress is a highly profitable enterprise," wishing Cukor would tone down the fact that Marguerite goes about the business of procuring a master in a cold-blooded way. Breen also thought it would be better if Marguerite did not go to Armand's apartment at midnight. Why not play this scene in the café? And was it necessary to show Armand living with Marguerite in the country?

Cukor knew that *Camille* was a hackneyed piece of theater that could be elevated only by an extraordinary portrayal of the central character. With Garbo, it was the happy meeting of a gifted actress and the perfect part. A reigning star in Hollywood for twelve years, Garbo had made twenty films, but *Camille* became her most publicized performance. For the first time, the Hollywood press shouted, a screen actress had successfully challenged the immortals of the theater, Tallulah Bankhead, Ethel Barrymore, and Eva Le Gallienne, who had played Camille onstage. Cukor also knew that comparisons would be inevitable with Norma Talmadge, Alla Nazimova, and Theda Bara, who had tried their luck with the part onscreen.

For Cukor, the story's falsest note was the scene in which Armand's father talks Marguerite out of seeing his son. It was a difficult scene for modern audiences to comprehend—not so much the dialogue as the situation itself. "Armand is the world's worst part," Cukor said. "The only way for it to work was to cast a young man in the role." Regrettably Armand was usually played by middle-aged actors, and one can't forgive an older man for being so foolish and weak.

Though it was not his idea, Cukor was satisfied with the casting of Robert Taylor as Armand. Handsome and six years younger than Garbo, Taylor made Armand more convincing. He also had the advantage of projecting a romantic image; for many viewers, he was the most credible Armand they'd ever seen. A leading man, Taylor possessed classical beauty and a great profile. "One practically forgets the meaning of real beauty," Cukor said, "or what true beauty should really represent."

Under Cukor's direction, Garbo played her most demanding role: *Camille* consisted of 156 scenes, of which she had 57. Cukor's challenge was to provide continuous stimulation for her. "With Garbo," he said, "you must make a climate in which she trusts you. You watch carefully what she's doing and you make suggestions, but you let the impulse come out of her."

Indeed, after seeing the rushes of the first few days, Thalberg said: "George, she's awfully good, she's never been so good."

"But, Irving," Cukor said, "she just sitting in a theater box."

"She is relaxed and she's open," the producer said.

That night, running some of Garbo's previous movies, Cukor realized what Thalberg meant: There was a new, unguarded quality about Garbo, never shown before.

Cukor found Garbo to be a most imaginative actress; her performance was built of many small, inventive gestures. For example, the way Garbo responds when Taylor says, "No one has ever loved you as I love you!" "That may be true," she says with a casual smile, "but what can I do about it?" In another scene, when Garbo bursts into tears, she is so convincing it isn't just an actress crying.

Garbo's previous tendency to flatness and lugubrious drone was absent from *Camille;* revitalized, she went beyond her vocal limitations. And her deathbed scene was truly heartbreaking. Cukor's mother was dying just before shooting began. While visiting her, he noticed certain facial expressions and gestures, which he used in *Camille.* "Part of me is always clocking something I can use," he said about his habit of always observing. It was Cukor's idea, in fact, that Garbo play her death scene in a whisper.

Not subscribing to the view that Garbo's main asset was her "physique," Cukor allowed Garbo to register deep feeling and thinking on-screen. Garbo was distant; she categorically refused to speak to Robert Taylor during the shoot. Not that she didn't like Taylor, but she wanted to save her love for the screen character he portrayed. In this fashion she retained the illusion that Taylor was really Armand, her uncompromising lover. Garbo knew that if they socialized, Taylor would become just another actor.

One of the film's most erotic scenes—when Garbo and Taylor convey passion for and impatience with each other—was filmed without any instructions from the director. Cukor let Garbo use her own ideas. Garbo just leaned over, making sure her body didn't touch his, and gave Taylor small kisses all over his face. In a scene where Garbo had to walk through a theater lobby, Cukor instructed her to walk slowly, so that the men would have time to examine her. Instead Garbo walked very fast. She knew instinctively that a beautiful woman does not have to walk slowly to get attention.

"Garbo has a magic that can't be defined," Cukor said at the time. "She is a rare creature who touches the imagination, and no one will replace her," he noted after her untimely retirement. "She submits herself to the camera, and retains her privacy before it." For Cukor, Garbo's greatest, undecipherable quality was her mystery onscreen: "Garbo had this rapport with an audience. She could let them know she was thinking things, and thinking them uncensored."

Cukor admired the gambling scene, in which Garbo drops her fan and the Baron de Varville makes her pick it up. Garbo doesn't kneel to pick it up—bending down would signify a loss of dignity—but instead leans sideways in a most natural, elegant way. In the scene in which she gives up Armand, Garbo surprised Cukor when she slowly sank to her knees and threw up her arms.

Garbo was a pragmatic actress. She would leave the studio at a certain hour but not because she was indifferent. After long hours on the set she would get nervous, and she wanted to look fresh the next day. And there were certain things Garbo demanded, conditions under which she worked well. Privacy was one of them. She didn't like people standing and staring at her. Cukor once asked Garbo, "Why do you mind people looking at you?"

"When people are watching," Garbo answered, "I'm just a woman making faces for the camera. It destroys the illusion."

Garbo didn't talk an awful lot about what she was planning because that would have lessened the magic when she actually performed. Cukor rehearsed her in the mechanics of the role, but often when the cameras were turning, she added something totally new. Cukor also learned that Garbo was very good in the first five or six takes, but then lost her freshness. Unlike most actors, Garbo never watched her rushes. Challenged by Cukor, she simply said: "I have some idea of what I am doing, and every time I see it it falls so short that it throws me."

In later years, accused of perpetuating Garbo's mystery, Cukor's response was "bullshit." Offscreen Garbo was actually a simple girl. Once

Ferenc Molnár asked Cukor to arrange for a meeting with her. Garbo went to see him at the Plaza Hotel, and they talked about doing one of his plays. Their meeting was so awkward that the disappointed Molnár complained to Cukor that Garbo was dull.

Cukor immersed himself in the period of *Camille*, researching the sets and costumes. The cancan dance, meant to evoke Toulouse-Lautrec, was an approximation of the dance Alexandre Dumas saw, which was later forbidden by the Paris police. Cukor had many discussions with William Daniels, Garbo's favorite cinematographer, about the lighting. They used a shallow depth of field and lush, romantic lighting. Karl Freund completed the cinematography when Daniels got sick, but the film maintains a coherent look.

The film's music had an exceptionally emotional impact. Cukor instructed Henry Daniell, as the nasty Baron de Varville, to play the piano louder and louder when Armand is ringing the doorbell and Garbo stands agonized beside him. He chose to end the scene that way. Cukor also introduced a scene in *Camille* where Daniell and Garbo were to laugh. Both were worried, because neither laughed easily onscreen, but Cukor was able to put them at ease.

Cukor thought the scene at the casino was lacking something even though he had planned and approved it. It was getting late, six o'clock, and they were due to shoot on the set the following day. To his surprise, at nine the next morning, there was a huge statue of the Goddess of Chance on the set; it was precisely what was needed. Resources like that made life much easier for directors under the studio system.

Thalberg died in September in the midst of the work on *Camille*. On the last day of shooting, October 27, 1936, Eddie Mannix, Louis B.'s right-hand man, asked Cukor: "This is Irving's last picture. Is there anything you can do to improve it?"

"There's always something one can do," he said, asking for three more shooting days to make some fine points.

The loss of Thalberg was so heavily mourned that the L.A. premiere of *Camille* became a veritable celebrity wake. Even Garbo showed up—not a minor achievement. Thrilled by the results, Norma Shearer told Cukor: "I think it is something to be really proud of. I am so grateful for all you contributed to Irving's life."

The word of mouth on *Camille* was so good that it alarmed Cukor, fearing its potential effect on reviewers. "Now you'll go to see it," he told a friend, "and just sit there and grit your teeth and wonder why anyone should have said so much about it." Cukor took the film to New York and showed it to a distinguished audience that included Tallulah Bankhead and Noël Coward. At the end of the screening, with some viewers still sobbing, Coward got up and announced that Garbo gave "the finest performance ever put on screen." He declared it in such way that his words had weight.

MGM announced "Garbo Talks" for *Anna Christie* and "Garbo Laughs" for *Ninotchka;* now it could publicize *Camille* as "Garbo Acts!" Garbo's performance was refreshingly ironic: Her Camille was too intelligent for the character's frivolous life, too generous for the historical circumstances. But it was consistent with a film that presented a romantic view of a courtesan life.

Garbo was so good that Cukor violated his habit of not seeing his movies more than once; he saw *Camille* four times. Arguably her greatest screen performance, Garbo won a well-deserved Oscar nomination and the New York Film Critics Award as best actress of the year. Garbo was obviously pleased, but she never said a word to Cukor, which upset him very much.

Most of the reviews talked at length about Garbo's splendid work. "Through the perfect artistry of her portrayal," wrote Frank S. Nugent in *The New York Times,* "a hackneyed theme is made new again, poignantly sad, hauntingly lovely. . . . Miss Garbo has interpreted Marguerite Gautier with the subtlety that has earned her the title, 'first lady of the screen.' " When *Camille* came out, Cukor was not given any particular kudos for either the film or Garbo's work. Some critics believe it's time for *Camille,* often called Garbo's finest picture, be recognized as Cukor's greatest picture.

CHAPTER FOUR:

The Greatest Disappointment of His Life, 1937–39

AFTER PRODUCING A STRING OF HIGHLY SUCCESSFUL FILMS (*ANNA Karenina, A Tale of Two Cities*) at MGM, David O. Selznick achieved his lifelong ambition and founded his own production company, Selznick International. The informal understanding was always that Cukor would direct movies for Selznick's company.

In the summer of 1936 Selznick received a wire from Kay Brown, his New York story editor, urging him to buy the film rights for a new novel by an unknown writer about to be published. The book was Margaret Mitchell's *Gone with the Wind*. Selznick was skeptical: Mitchell had no track record, and her first novel was too long. He also had misgivings about filming a story of such epic scope, but in the end he changed his mind. In July Selznick purchased *GWTW* for fifty thousand dollars, a bargain considering that once published, the book quickly topped best-seller lists.

Cukor was still at MGM finishing up *Camille,* but his contract was due to expire in October. After Thalberg's death Cukor was given the option of canceling the remainder of his contract. Indeed, on October 1 Mitchell was informed that Cukor had been assigned as director of *GWTW*.

With the novel's popularity sweeping the country, word quickly got out that a film was in the making. A modest woman, passionate about the South, but not interested in being in the public eye, Mitchell was suddenly in the limelight. She was deluged with letters demanding that Clark Gable be cast as Rhett Butler or that Tallulah Bankhead not be considered for Scarlett O'Hara. Strangers grabbed her on the street, insisting that Hepburn would never do.

The casting of this picture soon became a favorite drawing-room game, with newspapers around the nation badgering Mitchell to divulge her choices for the leading parts. Though it was increasingly difficult, Mitchell managed to keep her mouth shut, but in her correspondence with the filmmakers, she urged them to announce the cast and relieve her of "this burden!"

Mitchell wanted to help, but she confided to Brown that if the news got out that she was responsible for any deviations from the book, her life wouldn't be "worth living." The South took the book to heart; Mitchell's loyal readers felt they had "part ownership" in it. Mitchell found herself besieged by people who told her they would never speak to her again if she "let the movie people change one line." Brown pompously assured the novelist that they were just as concerned as the "rest of the world" about not making mistakes on the adaptation of *GWTW*.

Many southerners thought that the scenario needed to be written by someone who understood the region. Lamar Trotti, a writer from Atlanta who had studied the period, was touted as the logical choice. By October 1936, however, Selznick had decided to turn the script over to playwright Sidney Howard. Howard, who had done a superb job adapting *Dodsworth* for William Wyler that year, was a dramatist of the first rank.

Selznick asked Mitchell to talk to Cukor and help guide him from any pitfalls. Plans were made for Cukor and Howard to go south together to meet Mitchell and discuss the script. Howard promised to have a preliminary outline ready before the trip.

Mitchell, too, was anxious to meet Cukor, but she also recommended Wilbur Kurtz, a southern architect and an authority on the Civil War, to show him around. Cukor's meeting with Mitchell went well; in fact, he began a lively correspondence with her. Always the gentleman, Cukor sent her charming notes and gifts of perfume; she sent him yet another book about the South. "You charmed all the regions you visited," wrote Mitchell in April 1937; "everyone liked you so much and felt that *GWTW* was in perfect hands."

Selznick was deluged with letters recommending actors for the leads, but he believed that any well-known actress as Scarlett would be accused of playing herself. He told Cukor that if they had an unknown person, audiences would be more satisfied that she was their conception.

Early on Selznick demanded of Cukor: "[U]nder no circumstances should you send script scenes or discuss test scenes with anyone we have under consideration for *GWTW*, until the proper papers have been signed." And of course, Cukor should not spend much time on rehearsals for the screen tests. Not only was this considered a waste of valuable time and money, but it might have bad psychological effects on those under consideration, making them believe their chances were better than they were.

In August 1937 Selznick informed Cukor that a silent test in color cost $509.80, and in black and white $349.08. This included production staff, equipment, camera rentals, and raw stock developed and printed. Under these circumstances, Cukor was asked not to test his friend Ina Claire, whom he wanted to cast, because she had not made any film since 1932. Selznick preferred to save the money "until and unless" something came along that seemed right for Claire. As usual, Selznick advised Cukor to keep their memos "strictly confidential."

Cukor performed many chores for Selznick during preproduction for GWTW. The mogul involved him in projects he was not going to direct. Cukor jokingly described himself as "The Boy Test Director" because one of his responsibilities was to call the other Selznick directors and inquire if they needed tests to be made. Unlike other directors, Cukor enjoyed making tests with aspiring actresses and soon became famous for this. Through his testing Cukor played a crucial role in the development of acting talent in Hollywood, though he never received full credit for it.

Selznick asked him to rehearse and shoot the tests for Intermezzo, a film that introduced Ingrid Bergman to the American public. Cukor also took care of some of Selznick's unpleasant correspondence. In 1938, when Selznick had no time to meet Romola Nijinsky, he asked Cukor to get him out of this duty gracefully. Nijinsky's widow wished to write the script for a picture about her legendary dancer husband.

Casting GWTW, however, was the main topic on everybody's mind. In November 1937 Irene Selznick noted in Time magazine an interesting photograph of possibly a cousin of Tallulah Bankhead's; a young Tallulah was what they were looking for. Pressured by Irene's excitement, Cukor made inquiries and found out that Bankhead did have a cousin, Blossom, aged sixteen, and a younger sister, Louise, aged fourteen, but neither was tested.

Some newcomers who were tested, however, later became stars. Susan Hayward was reportedly discovered when Irene saw pictures of her in a Saturday Evening Post article about the Walter Thornton modeling agency. "All those stories are pure bull," Cukor later said. "I never saw the story." Cukor claimed he met Hayward in Selznick's New York office after a swing through the South. Impressed by her, he recommended that she test for Scarlett. In late 1937 Hayward and her sister Florence boarded the same California-bound train as Cukor and the Selznicks.

Cukor directed and shot Hayward's tests in December, but she was never seriously considered; she was too green to take on such a demanding role. Her test, the library scene at Twelve Oaks, which was not very good, confirmed Cukor's initial impression. But Cukor liked Hayward, who was attractive and "dignified," and he introduced her to agent Ben Medford and Gertrude Folger, Metro's acting coach.

When Hayward landed one of her first parts, in *The Sisters,* in 1938, she asked for Cukor's advice on how to control her grimacing; her acting apparently created the feeling she was cold and unfeeling. Cukor instructed her supervisors to "let her overact, let her be a ham—so long as it comes from the heart!"

"Life at present, is not as exciting for your self-appointed protégé as it might be," the grateful Hayward wrote. "How can I ever thank you for making possible my entry into this world? The only way I can think of is to some day soon win the Academy Award for the finest performance and in return present it to you, to whom I owe so much." Hayward did become a star and did win an Oscar, in 1958, for *I Want to Live!* but didn't stay in touch with Cukor. Offended by her failure to acknowledge publicly or privately her debt to him, Cukor held a grudge against her.

During the extended script preparations and casting of *GWTW,* which took more than two years, Cukor was assigned to direct Philip Barry's Broadway play *Holiday* at Columbia. Selznick hoped that by the time Cukor finished *Holiday,* they would have a wonderful script. Cukor found *Holiday* a pleasant distraction from the frantic activities of *GWTW;* it was fun to work on a picture that had a definite shooting schedule—with a beginning, a middle, and an end.

Cukor directed two of Barry's best plays, *Holiday* in 1938, starring Katharine Hepburn and Cary Grant, and *The Philadelphia Story,* in 1940, also with Hepburn and Grant. Both plays had been directed in the theater by Arthur Hopkins, whom Cukor admired; Hopkins was the first big director he had met.

When *Holiday* was produced on Broadway in 1928, Hope Williams played Linda Seton. Her understudy was Hepburn, then an unknown and inexperienced actress. For two years she marked time offstage, but her chance to perform never materialized. Ironically, Hepburn used a scene from this play in her screen test for *A Bill of Divorcement*

Upon learning that Columbia had acquired the rights to *Holiday,* Hepburn began a personal campaign to win the role, since her career at this point was in trouble. After *Bringing Up Baby,* an artistic success but a commercial failure, Harry Brandt, the president of the Independent Theater Owners Association of America, published a list of stars who were "box-office poison." Hepburn headed a roster that included other "Cukor girls," Garbo and Kay Francis. Brandt's slur, which was picked up by the press and received a lot of publicity, damaged the status of these stars at their studios.

But Columbia was a relatively small studio, and Hepburn had little difficulty in persuading its boss, Harry Cohn, to cast her. She also talked

Cohn into borrowing Cukor as director and casting Cary Grant as costar. In fact, in advertising the film, Columbia used the "box-office poison" label as a selling point. "Is it true what they say about Hepburn?" a public message provocatively asked, ensuring the audience that this time the studio had a high-quality, commercially viable film.

Once again Hepburn was cast in a role that seemed tailor-made. Linda Seton, a rebellious society girl from Park Avenue, falls in love with her sister's fiancé, Johnny Case (Cary Grant), a boy from the slums with a knack for making money. When Johnny decides to take a holiday to explore the world, Julia (Doris Nolan) is horrified, but he finds a kindred spirit in Linda. "I've got all the faith in the world in Johnny," Linda proudly declares. "Whatever he does is all right with me. If he wants to sit on his tail, he can sit on his tail. If he wants to come back and sell peanuts, how I'll believe in those peanuts!"

Hepburn delivered her lines with conviction, eloquence, and commanding authority. Linda, in fact, became an archetypal Hepburn heroine: a tomboy rebel endowed with intelligence and individuality. One of Hepburn's most accomplished characterizations, the role touched all aspects of her complex personality, her toughness as well as vulnerability.

To be effective, Barry's language required a particular kind of acting, lightly stylized but not affected. The witty dialogue seemed realistic, but it was not; the words had a distinctive rhythm. Hepburn understood Barry's lyric quality and accentuated the rhythm of his lines with a kind of "singsong" voice. It was a technique she would refine to perfection in *The Philadelphia Story*.

Donald Ogden Stewart and Sidney Buchman's brilliant script was faithful to the play, forwarding its story almost entirely with dialogue—most of it Barry's. To update the story, Stewart also introduced some satirical allusions, which enriched it.

Like all good comedies, Barry's could be played seriously as well. Cukor relished taking a serious subject and treating it with "impertinence and gaiety." His fluent adaptation actually improved on the play, creating a new genre: comedy-drama. Cukor held that true comedies spring from painful realities, that without the tragic underlayer the comedy becomes trivialized. "I believe in the detached approach for comedy," he told Lambert. "If you *really* look at anything, there's always a comic note, and a painful note too. One brings the other to life." Cukor understood that directing a screen comedy was different: "On stage, you can play for laughs and wait for them, but on the screen, you have to get the laughs without playing for them."

Both Barry and Cukor excelled in nuance. Barry was a subtle writer full of surprises. The characters in his plays are rarely what they seem to be; each reacts in unexpected ways, underlining the difference between appearance and reality. The surface closeness of the two sisters actually hides mutual dislike, which neither of them is aware of. And when Julia realizes that Johnny is going to walk out on her, she's not crushed but relieved. Cukor handled these transitions with tremendous ease and delicacy, giving the film a fresh, endearing quality.

When the play was written, the stock market was booming and prosperity was in abundance. Barry's view of the rich was that of an outsider; they were seen through Johnny's eyes. For Barry, there was nothing ostentatious about their way of life. The wealthy owned grand houses, but they didn't flaunt them; everything was understated.

It was interesting for Cukor to present a young man who wanted to enjoy life, instead of just conforming to it. Johnny is initially patronizing toward Linda but later realizes she's the one for him. In his second film with Cukor, Cary Grant gave a dazzling performance. In his knockout scene, which he did with restraint, Grant tells the rich where to go, dashing off with a disdain of conventionality. Grant's performance in this film made him one of Hollywood's most popular leading men.

Holiday completed shooting on April 20 and opened in New York, at Radio City Music Hall, on June 15. Despite favorable reviews, the film failed with Depression audiences, for whom selling peanuts was a reality, not a joke. Linda, the little rich girl who stays in her nursery and denounces the filthy rich, was more appropriate for audiences of earlier times. But it was personally gratifying for Cukor that Barry regarded the movie as "a brilliant and beautiful piece of work."

Throughout the making of *Holiday* preproduction work on *GWTW* continued. By February 1938, however, Selznick had depressing news to report. With more sequences still to come, the film's estimated length was 22,250 feet—far too long. Its running time had to be reduced, and that, of course, meant more work, more time, and more money.

With no clear idea when shooting would begin, Selznick and Cukor discussed an assignment to succeed *Holiday*. On February 3 Selznick agreed to lend Cukor's services to Paramount to direct *Zaza*. Under the loan-out terms, Cukor was to receive separate card credits on the main credit title, and his name would be in type at least 60 percent as large as the type used for the title.

Zaza was based on an old French play about the loves and sorrows of a tumultuous music hall siren. The play had an illustrious history: In 1889 the great French actress Réjane played the title role, and in 1920 the legendary diva Geraldine Farrar sang it at the Metropolitan Opera. Cukor perceived Paramount's remake as "terribly French," what with "that endless exploration of unfaithfulness and the suffering of love."

Claudette Colbert was cast as Zaza, a music hall performer who falls in love with a handsome chance acquaintance, Dufresne (Herbert Marshall), only to become heartbroken upon learning he is married and has a child. What intrigued Cukor was not the illicit affair but the examination of performers' public and private lives, the tension between life onstage and off. In his movie the audience got a real sense of a company's routine, in which privacy was impossible; the whole troupe knows and talks about Zaza's affair.

For Cukor the period feeling was as good as *Camille*. Hans Dreier, known for his atmospheric sets, came up with an interesting design for *Zaza*, creating an authentic outdoor cabaret complete with dirt on the floor. The picture was photographed by Charles Lang, known for his special skills in making women look ravishing; *Zaza*, for example, features stunning shots of Colbert in big feathered hats.

Shooting began with an Italian actress, Isa Miranda, but her accent was so heavy she could hardly be understood. After a week Cukor demanded a new actress. Claudette Colbert, then under contract to Paramount, remembered the incident's causing quite a stir on the lot; Cukor was after all *not* a Paramount director. "George came to my dressing room," she recalled, "and told me what a great play it was, how it had always been a vehicle for stars, and blah, blah. He really knew how to talk you into things."

Cukor and Colbert had never worked together, but they had met years before, when both were in the theater. According to Colbert, Cukor was a very personal director who, owing to his stage career, was particularly good with actors. "In my whole experience onscreen I never felt there was enough rehearsal to discuss things with the director. The camera was given much more time than the actors. But with George, you really felt you had worked your part out; he went into deeper explanations than other directors."

"Cukor was a whiz with dialogue," said Edward Dmytryk, *Zaza*'s editor, "but was never quite at home with the camera." Cukor would rehearse and stage a scene, then allow Dmytryk to work out the camera setups. When the cameras rolled, Cukor was again in charge.

Cukor knew what he wanted and continued shooting until he got it. "He took quite a few takes," Colbert conceded, "but he never took unnecessary takes. He knew when it was good and when it was bad." Cukor held that there comes a time when the scene is done. "You have to let it go, for that's going to be as good as it's going to be. You accept it as such and don't beat it to death."

Occasionally Cukor failed to get the results he wanted. Colbert recalled a scene in which Zaza, dressed in her finery, gathers up courage and goes to Dufresne's house. His daughter answers the door. "The child was very beautiful," Colbert said, "but not a good actress. George said to her,

'Here is this beautiful lady, and I've got to see what you think.' So I knocked on the door, and she opened it and just looked at me. And George said, 'No, no, no, you've got to show me that you have never seen a lady dressed like this.' We did it so many times, but the girl would open the door with this blank expression on her face." After a dozen takes, realizing he wasn't getting anywhere, Cukor sent his star home so that he could work with the child alone.

The next day Colbert went to see the rushes at lunchtime as was her practice. "I laughed so much," she said. "Here is the girl, and you could only hear George's voice as he said to the cameraman, 'Don't cut, we'll just keep doing it a few times while I talk to her.' But the same thing happened again and again. He said, 'Here is this beautiful lady,' and there was this very blank look. Finally Cukor said to her, 'Look, I'm a Christmas tree, I'm a Christmas tree, and I'm covered with silver balls you have never seen before!' The little girl gave him the same blank look." Cukor was forced to use a long shot of this scene.

Few children appear in Cukor's films. "The idea of working with a child absolutely appalls me, as working with an animal appalls me." Cukor understood that manipulation is the key to getting a good performance from children, and he hated that. He was devastated by reports that Vincente Minnelli told Margaret O'Brien that her dog was dead to get her to cry in *Meet Me in St. Louis*.

Colbert seemed more personal in *Zaza* than in previous films. Cukor thought that as a comedienne Colbert used only part of her talent and elegance; her range was wider than she displayed. *Zaza* was the only film in which Colbert used her pretty voice to sing. Cukor brought his friend Fanny Brice onto the set to coach Colbert. "It was wonderful," she said. "No other director would do such a thing. That's going a long way and indicative of the kind of director he was."

Brice taught Colbert how to contact an audience, how to command the stage. "You know, kid," she told Colbert in her heavy Brooklyn accent, "when you sing a ballad, if you touch your own flesh, it's a kind of comfort to ya." Brice placed her hands at the base of her neck and showed Colbert how to make each theatergoer feel she was looking directly at him with her penetrating eyes and radiant smile. "When they calm down," Brice said, "especially if it's a serious song, I fasten my eyes right below the balcony, and I sing."

Said Colbert: "When I did out-and-out comedy with Lubitsch, it was heaven, because I understood comedy, Lubitsch understood comedy, and he was very funny himself." But *Zaza* wasn't really a comedy, and there was a difference between Cukor and Lubitsch, though she was "crazy" about both. "Lubitsch was a personality in his own way," she said. "He always had a piano on the set, and he would play and make jokes between sets. George's humor was with you, personally, just talking; he did not spend the day entertaining his cast."

If Colbert was perfectly cast, Cukor didn't think Herbert Marshall was right as the married lover: He was too stuffy, too much of an English gentleman; his adulterous duplicity was not believable.

Cukor had a wonderful habit of using older actresses in need of a job. One of these, Mrs. Zimmerman, an elderly stage actress, was always on the set. She was quite a character, according to Colbert, wonderful but very foul-tempered. Bert Lahr, who played Cascart, Zaza's faithful manager, was very annoyed by her. "Bert was a great comedian," Colbert said, "but he was playing a dramatic part, and Zimmerman didn't like what he was doing. She would sit under that camera like a little Buddha and everything would show on her face. Bert was distracted by her."

Finally, Lahr said to Colbert, "She's driving me crazy. I'm going mad."

"Oh, just ignore her," said Colbert, "don't look at her, she's Russian, she's got her own ways."

Lahr then said, "I'd like to ask her if she can do a time step."

Colbert replied, "Bert, don't ask. From what I've seen she might be able to."

At this point, having overheard the conversation, Cukor burst out laughing.

Cascart became Lahr's breakthrough role. "Cukor edited me," Lahr later said. "He would take me aside and say, 'Act simple, Bert, simple. Cut it down to half. You've got a microphone above you. You don't have to kick it out and project to an audience of a thousand people. Let the camera do the work.' " Cukor was the first director to help Lahr learn the film medium.

As always, Cukor's direction was very precise. When Cascart is encouraging the depressed Zaza, Lahr has a line, "Oh, come now, you'll cry your eyes out over a dozen worse fellows yet." During rehearsals Lahr had difficulty making the scene work. "When you see she is unimpressed," Cukor suggested, "you try some other way to cheer her up. Use that funny laugh from your act." Lahr ran through his repertoire of laughs until Cukor singled out the one he liked. But later, when they shot the scene, his laugh was different. Cukor stopped the cameras and insisted on reshooting until Lahr gave him the "right" laugh.

Regrettably *Zaza* got an absolute turndown by the Production Code Administration, which demanded cuts. "It was stupid," Colbert said, "because *Zaza* had been a success at the turn of the century, and all of a sudden the Hays office thought it was risqué." But morals in 1939 were so rigid and the authority of the Hays office so strong that most of the film's pristine shock had to be expunged. "These long despairing scenes were all cut," Cukor later lamented.

Despite the problems with the PCA office, Paramount's top brass thought the film was one of studio's best in years. With confidence, the company traveled to a double preview, in Oakland and San Francisco. At the first night in Oakland the preview began well, and the film played beautifully for almost an hour, but then, according to Dmytryk, "all hell broke loose." In the story, after Zaza goes to Paris and meets Dufresne's daughter, she returns home and awaits his arrival. As Marshall entered, preceded by a huge bouquet of roses, the audience began to hiss. "Not Friday-night-students-at-the-flicks hissing, but the real hissing," Dmytryk recalled. Though a very good scene unrolled, no one heard it; the audience's angry reaction continued right through the bitter end.

Shocked by this turn of events, Cukor was forced to make a few emergency cuts the next morning. The studio now hoped that a more cosmopolitan San Francisco audience would find the film acceptable. The viewers were indeed somewhat younger and more sophisticated, but the reaction was the same. Audiences simply could not forgive the hero for deceiving Zaza, making a "loose woman" out of her. Interestingly there was evidence that watching the film alone, a person would accept its morality, but the same person, surrounded by others, joined in a "mob" reaction. *Zaza* demonstrated that, as Dmytryk observed, "censorship never led, it merely reflected the common attitudes of the public."

The return to Hollywood was a "nightmare of despair," said Dmytryk. The ending was reshot, and further cuts were made. But each time the film was tested with an audience, in or outside big cities, the reaction was similar. There was little more Paramount could do.

Colbert was shooting *Midnight* when her brother came onto the set with bad news. "I have just seen *Zaza*'s final version," he said. "They've cut it; they've ruined it." The actress said years later: "I was very upset. I couldn't see the film for a long time." Cukor, too, was furious; the film he had made would never be seen.

Zaza was quietly released on January 5, 1939, and just as quietly died. Negative reaction from the press, led by Louella Parsons, did not help either. Nor did the condemnation from local and state religious organizations. The film became one of the few big box-office failures in Cukor's career. The winter of 1939 was a particularly bad one for Cukor: One month after *Zaza*'s disastrous opening, he was fired from *GWTW*.

All along Selznick had had some doubts about Cukor's skills for an epic like *GWTW*. Periodically he conceded that his decision to use Cukor was held "through difficulties." One major concern was the huge amount of money the director was paid even though shooting had not yet begun. They were "in danger" of paying Cukor about three hundred thousand dollars for *GWTW*, Selznick complained to his associates in September 1938.

While preparations continued, Selznick tried to keep Cukor busy on other pictures, but the director turned down both *A Star Is Born* and *Intermezzo.* "I think the biggest black mark against our management to date is the Cukor situation," wrote Selznick, "and we can no longer be sentimental about it. We are a business concern and not patrons of the arts." There was talk about making a new deal with Cukor for *GWTW* or using the project to lure a new director, Victor Fleming or Frank Capra, for a long-range contract with Selznick International.

In February 1938 Selznick told Cukor of the arduous task he and Sidney Howard had undertaken in putting together the script. With each word carefully weighed, they double-checked the text against the book and substituted valuable lines for the script's more ordinary lines. Then they double-checked against the story notes, production notes, cutting suggestions, even the PCA office.

Concerned that their painstaking work was going to be in vain, Selznick asked for Cukor's pledge *not* to use the book anymore and not to add any lines, as he had been doing for the tests, because anything extra would be costly. The addition of five or six words per scene, Selznick noted, mounted up to a thousand feet or more that had to be taken out with "terrific agony and intense work." Selznick was not averse to Cukor's raising points before shooting began, but he wanted assurances that Cukor would shoot only what was written.

Selznick hoped to have every set of the film designed at least three weeks before shooting and decided to proceed even if the script was not final. Considering the picture's scale and expense, he wanted everyone to realize the vital importance of organizing the film as never before. Selznick "suggested" regular discussions with Cukor, so that he would have "no worries" once shooting began.

Casting remained the greatest concern. The overwhelming sentiment was that Rhett Butler was made to order for Gable. Cukor thought Gable would be good but by no means believed Gable was the only actor who could do it. Cooper or Gable, he told an interviewer. "To me it's six of one, half a dozen of the other. Perfect for either."

Getting Gable, MGM's most popular star, was complicated, however, and Selznick feared MGM would have the upper hand in the deal. Negotiations were conducted through Loew's vice-president Al Lichtman because Selznick didn't want to deal directly with Louis B., his father-in-law. A tough trader, Lichtman set these terms: Metro would lend Gable and half the production costs, estimated at $2.5 million, on the condition that it release the film. After production costs and a distribution fee of 15 percent of the grosses, MGM and Selznick would share equally in the profits. The deal meant that Selznick, still committed to a distribution deal with United Artists, would have to hold back *GWTW.*

The deal was signed in August 1938, and MGM promised to "deliver" Gable on January 5, 1939. Gable was asked to call Cukor to discuss his costumes, hair, and mustache. Cukor was concerned about Gable's accent, but Selznick assured him that Gable would be in touch soon: "He is as much concerned as we are, perhaps more."

Casting Scarlett, however, was more problematic. Numerous tests were taken of just about every actress between twenty and thirty-five, an illustrious list that included Hepburn, Paulette Goddard, Jean Arthur, and Lana Turner among others. To cover himself, Selznick even considered stars who were unlikely candidates, Joan Crawford and Barbara Stanwyck.

Selznick wanted to test any potentially castable actress, but at the same time he put continuous pressure on Cukor to economize on tests: "Any money we waste is going to be money that is unavailable, if and when we need it on the picture itself, as we have a definitely limited budget. Under no circumstances will we go beyond the budget, even if it involves cuts and sacrifices during shooting."

Uncharacteristically Selznick soon began to meddle in the tests themselves. Making recommendations for Cukor's choice of cameraman, he urged greater care in the selection of actors playing opposite the women. Selznick even advised Cukor on camera angles that would best feature those under consideration. Cukor, who prided himself on his ability to test actors, was offended by Selznick's "friendly advice."

Selznick's extensive involvement—interference, from Cukor's perspective—eventually became a major source of tension between producer and director. Cukor received so many memos from Selznick that he once sent him a note saying: "You see, I am getting the Selznick habit (or vice) of sending memos."

Early in the search Norma Shearer was considered for Scarlett. She owned a piece of Selznick International, and the success of *Marie Antoinette* proved that she could carry an expensive film. Shearer was eager to make a big picture, but she was concerned that the willful and ruthless Scarlett was too extreme a departure from her screen persona as a morally upright lady of refinement.

Selznick said that Scarlett was right for her, promising the part could be tailored to make her more sympathetic; they discussed how Scarlett's "bitchy" aspects could be softened. The fact that Cukor was assigned to direct was another incentive for Shearer. Cukor, however, was against softening the role; what intrigued him about Scarlett was that she was a bitch. In truth, Cukor thought Shearer was absolutely wrong. She lacked sex appeal, and it was impossible for him to imagine her killing in cold blood or bargaining with her body.

In the end Shearer's concern about the public's reaction won out. When rumors that she was thinking about the role leaked to the press, the studio was flooded with fan letters from across the country, urging her not to accept the "bad woman" role; columnist Ed Sullivan also advised her against playing Scarlett. This, combined with her own misgivings, forced her to remove her name from the contenders.

Cukor prepared Joan Bennett for her test in 1937, but at first she refused to take it. "I could not associate myself with a part," Bennett recalled, "that I felt Paulette Goddard was practically set for." Bennett agreed to go before the cameras only after Goddard had tested; she didn't want to feel guilty about wasting Cukor's time and the studio's money.

Goddard was one of the more serious contenders, though Selznick feared questions about the respectability of her marriage to Charlie Chaplin might turn the public against her. But Goddard's major asset for Selznick was that she was not "stale," and he asked Cukor to devote particular attention to the dramatic sections of her test.

Hepburn had unsuccessfully tried to talk RKO into purchasing GWTW after Mitchell had sent her a copy of the book. When Selznick acquired the property, Hepburn begged him: "I'd be perfect, the part was written for me." But she refused to test, telling Selznick, "If you don't know whether I can act by now, you never will."

Hepburn explained: "'By the time they came around to ask me to play it, I felt they must do what Selznick had advertised: find an unknown girl. If I had been signed up to do the picture," she observed, "Selznick would have found Vivien Leigh anyway. He would have paid me twenty-five thousand or whatever, dumped me, and made the picture with her." But Selznick thought Hepburn was not beautiful or feminine enough for Scarlett, and her screen image was too established. Cukor was also ambivalent about Hepburn and for a change kept his mouth shut.

When Tallulah Bankhead, a southerner with a theatrical personality, asked for a test, Cukor saw a potential strain on their friendship. He knew Bankhead was wrong but still gave her a chance. "Take it easy, Tallulah, relax," he told her on the phone when she informed him that her flight to L.A. had been delayed. It was a bad idea to test Bankhead when she was tired and tense.

Cukor shot Bankhead's first test in black and white, which she liked, but Cukor wanted a second, with softer lighting. They both agreed, however, that her third test, in color, was a disaster. In a characteristically diplomatic manner Cukor later said, "Tallulah just wasn't fresh enough"—a polite way of saying that she was too old and too harsh to be a convincing Scarlett.

When gossip columnist Louella Parsons learned that Tallulah was testing, she was outraged: "George Cukor, her friend, is going to direct, and Jack Whitney, another friend, is backing it. So I'm afraid she'll get the part. If she does, I personally will go home and weep, because she is not SCARLETT O'HARA in my language, and if David O. Selznick gives her the part, he will have to answer to every man, woman, and child in America."

Perceiving Scarlett as a woman with distinctive looks, great courage, and vitality, but essentially humorless, Cukor thought it would be a great chance for an unknown. But because he thought that the part of Melanie was difficult, much harder, he wanted a good experienced actress. "She shouldn't be too pretty," Cukor said, "but she must be able to act. It's a more subtle character, finer, perhaps equally humorless, but quite as strong in another way."

The young Joan Fontaine never tested for Scarlett, but she did for Melanie. "I made a big mistake," she recalled. "I had just come from a luncheon wearing something terribly elegant. 'Oh, my God,' George said, 'too chic, too chic. Melanie must be a plain girl.' It was then that I said, 'What about my sister [Olivia de Havilland]?,' not meaning she wasn't chic but that she probably would have been more sensible and not wear high-style clothes to an interview for a simple character."

Melanie was exactly the kind of part De Havilland had been looking for. As she related it, "One day the phone rang at my house, and on the line was George, a man I had never met. George asked me if I would be interested in playing Melanie, and of course, I replied yes. He then inquired if I would be willing to come secretly to his office and read for the part." De Havilland was instructed to arrive as inconspicuously a possible and slip in through a private entrance to his office.

Cukor reacted favorably to de Havilland's reading, immediately arranging for an appointment with Selznick. He asked her to commit to memory the scene they had been working on. The following Sunday afternoon De Havilland arrived at Selznick's southern-style mansion on Summit Drive and reenacted the scene, this time with Cukor giving a particularly impassioned reading of Scarlett. "He did it with such fervor and dynamism," de Havilland said that Selznick was beside himself with enthusiasm. To this day the actress thinks it was *Cukor's* performance that won her the role!

De Havilland was told right away she would play Melanie, but Cukor still watched clips of other actresses, among them Andrea Leeds, Anne Shirley, and Frances Dee. "I sat there spellbound," de Havilland recalled. "I could never understand why George and David wanted me when they could have any of these actresses." Before leaving, the startled actress was directed not to tell anyone about getting the role of Melanie: "It was the hardest secret I ever had to keep."

Time was passing, and *GWTW* had no leading lady. Testing of every major actress in Hollywood was obligatory for such a plum role, but from the onset Selznick had thought about casting an unknown. In fall 1938 he still hoped that "somehow, some way" they would be able to "dig up a new girl." With the search for Scarlett intensifying in the public eye, Cukor began getting telephone calls in the middle of the night from hysterical stage mothers, willing to do anything to get screen tests for their hopeful daughters.

By November Selznick was really worried. He insisted that if things were run right, Cukor could interview as many as twenty girls in an hour. Cukor could just exchange two sentences with each girl and decide whether she had a chance or not. Selznick wrote:

> *If we finally wind up with any of the stars, we must regard ourselves as absolute failures at digging up talent; as going against the most violently expressed wish for a new personality in an important role in the history of the American stage or screen; as wasting the opportunity to create a new star; as actually hurting the drawing power of the picture by having a star instead of a new girl; and as actually hurting the quality of the picture itself by having a girl who has an audience's dislike to beat down, as in the case of Hepburn, or identification with other roles to overcome, as in the case of Jean Arthur.*

Cukor thought this memo was pompous and silly.

Scarlett had become the most talked-about woman of the decade. Exploiting the public's obsession, Selznick fed the press by dropping rumors on his casting plans. In this respect *GWTW* is still the most publicized movie ever made. Selznick was ardently conducting the most celebrated talent hunt in Hollywood's history, a judicious combination of calculated strategy and genuine effort.

In December Selznick decided to start production without Scarlett. The back lots of his studio in Culver City had to be cleared to build the O'Hara plantation. Art designer William Cameron Menzies came up with a brilliant idea: torch the old sets and use the fire to shoot the burning of Atlanta, one of the film's highlights. Selznick immediately took to such a practical idea. Long shots of stunt actors could be used to depict Scarlett and Rhett escaping from the burning city in a wagon. Close-ups could be intercut later by Cukor, once they had found their actress.

The burning of Atlanta was scheduled for the night of December 10. The beginning of this eagerly awaited film became an "event," with many Hollywood celebrities and press in attendance. It was in this dramatic context that British actress Vivien Leigh, virtually unknown in America but destined to be the long-sought-after Scarlett, entered the scene.

Leigh was brought to the lot by Selznick's brother, Myron. They arrived on the set just as the flames of Atlanta were rising. Myron is reported to have tugged Selznick by the sleeve, Leigh at his side, saying, "I want you to meet Scarlett O'Hara." When Selznick looked at the beautiful actress, he immediately knew the long search for his leading lady was over.

This famous story smacks of a publicist's brainstorm. Leigh later said she had been eyeing the role for more than a year. Her trip to the United States, ostensibly to visit her then lover, Laurence Olivier, who was filming *Wuthering Heights,* was suspiciously well timed, since Myron had apparently made plans for her to be tested. There are also reports that Selznick had talked to Cukor about Leigh, having liked her work in *A Yank at Oxford* and *Fire over England.* Still, Leigh was just what Selznick and Cukor were looking for, an attractive, vibrant new face. On December 12 Cukor's scheduled interviews with other actresses were canceled so that he could rehearse exclusively with Leigh.

Within a few days Cukor was instructed to make full-color tests for the four finalists: Joan Bennett, Jean Arthur, Paulette Goddard, and Vivien Leigh. Cukor chose three sequences: Scarlett's corset scene with Mammy, to test sex appeal; her attempted seduction of Ashley, for romantic image; and her drunken proposal to Rhett, for dramatic and comic power.

For Cukor it was an instantaneous meeting of the actress and the part. In the tests he shot, Leigh didn't use a southern accent, but she demonstrated authority. In her test scene with Ashley, Leigh is even better than in the finished film. The scene highlights her neurotic, desperate power; Fleming's version is tame by comparison. Cukor performed an important service for Leigh, acting out her role in the tests and rehearsals.

Though Leigh was cast in December, the decision was not made public until January 13, 1939. The announcement brought protests from fans all over the nation. But Leigh immediately threw herself into perfecting a southern accent; she had never heard one before. Susan Myrick, a friend of Margaret Mitchell's and a consultant for the film, coached her.

Cukor was known for his "allergy" to accents: They were usually phony and interfered with the acting. "I'm appalled when people try to play certain parts with a kind of terror accent [*sic*]. It's intrusive, it's not true. I'm ruthless when I'm working with an actor who's trying to show off at the expense of the picture." Most southern accents Cukor heard onscreen were "absolutely preposterous," as if the actors had mouths full of mush. But Selznick held that if Leigh overcame the accent problem, all remaining dangers of her casting would be over.

Selznick informed Cukor that shooting would definitely start on Monday, January 23. "We simply cannot fool around another day in connection with the casting," he wrote, "and we must decide on the various roles remaining to be cast on Monday." The picture finally went before the cameras on January 26.

From the very first day of shooting, Cukor sensed that Selznick was on edge. On January 28 the producer notified Cukor that Menzies was to have the *final* word on the physical aspects and color values of the production. This increased the tension between Cukor and Menzies, whose greater authority the director now perceived as a threat. A few days later Selznick announced that he wanted to see the block rehearsal of each scene before it was shot. He also demanded that Cukor call him before making any changes in a scene or in the dialogue. This was done to avoid what the producer termed "projection-room surprises."

Cukor was shocked. "I was the director, after all," he later said, "and a director should shoot the scene before the producer sees it. That's when the producer's opinion is important, when he sees it on the screen for the first time. But David started coming down on the set, giving hot tips which weren't very helpful."

This was a marked change in the working relationship they had established over the years. "We worked very well together," Cukor said. "He was the producer I respected; I was a director he had some regard for." But they had not teamed for several years, during which time Cukor's stature and confidence had substantially grown. Cukor was now a director in full command of his skills.

Though Selznick had always been involved in casting, writing, and art design, now he seemed to want to muscle in on the direction as well. Selznick could not bear being away from the set, and this infuriated Cukor. He was constantly at Cukor's side, bothering him about one thing or another. Selznick became obsessive, completely absorbed in making *GWTW* the greatest film ever produced.

Few people knew that at the time Selznick was on drugs that were affecting his behavior and was not getting any sleep. "George never emphasized the drugs as a weapon against Selznick," said Paul Morrissey, "but he really resented his interference. 'You'll see it in the rushes!' Cukor would say. 'You're not going to be on the set when I'm directing!' What George did on the set," he said, "every director does: command. People know he is driving the ship. If somebody else is there, it deflates his authority."

Any director of Cukor's rank would have found Selznick's actions unacceptable. Cukor's resentment was magnified by the fact that they were friends and had made so many successful pictures together. "Knowing Cukor's temper," said Gerald Ayres, who later wrote *Rich and Famous*, "he could not tolerate Selznick saying, 'You directed this scene without my permission.' "

Selznick also resented the fact that shooting moved too slowly, that after two weeks the production was seven days behind schedule. In those two weeks Cukor directed only one scene with Gable, who was on the set every single day. Cukor liked having his cast around, even when he didn't need them—just in case. The picture was shot out of sequence, and because the initial scenes centered on Scarlett, Leigh received most of Cukor's attention.

Practically everything Cukor shot remained in the final cut. He directed two important scenes: the first, early in the war, when Scarlett nurses Melanie through her labor pains and has to deal with the hysterical servant Prissy (Butterfly McQueen), and the second, after the war, when a marauding Yankee soldier breaks into Tara and Scarlett kills him.

When De Havilland was preparing for the birth scene, Cukor suggested primary research since she knew nothing about childbearing. "Olivia," Cukor said, "we've got to time these spasms exactly right. We've got to get the technique for it." Arrangements were made for de Havilland, dressed as a nurse, to sit by the beds of women in various stages of labor at a local hospital. She observed their hands and the sounds they made during contractions.

As an unmistakable cry rang out when one of the women was about to deliver, de Havilland was whisked into the operating room to witness the birth. "It was one of the most moving and awe-inspiring experiences of my life," she recalled. "I made notes about the exclamations, the cries, the breathing rhythm, everything—just as George demanded."

When they shot the actual scene, Cukor sat at the foot of the bed, outside the camera range. "Every time I was supposed to have a spasm, George twisted my ankle." Years later, when de Havilland really gave birth, she sent him a wire: "You weren't there to twist my ankle, but I still had the baby. I did it without your help!"

On February 12 there was a dramatic turn of events when Cukor was suddenly dismissed and shooting suspended. In production less than two weeks, but with a number of its most important scenes done, the two-million-dollar property faced another extended delay.

De Havilland recalled that it was during the bazaar sequence that news of Cukor's dismissal hit the set. "I at once spoke to Vivien, commiserating with her in this calamity, and we went together to call on Selznick in his office. We remained there for three hours, pleading with him not to let George go." Ironically, both women were dressed in black, their widows' garb for that day's work. When reports of their efforts reached Cukor, he was deeply touched but also amused by their "appropriate" clothes for the occasion.

"The only solution," Selznick said, "is for a new director to be selected at as early a date as is practicable." In a February 13 memo, Selznick noted: "Cukor's withdrawal is the most regrettable incident of my rather long producing career." The memo was meant to give the impression that the dismissal was based on a mutual decision.

Selznick had a knack for firing directors; Cukor was not the first. On the set of *GWTW* Selznick behaved like a dictator; no one could be trusted. "I was put off," Cukor later said, "because David, in all honesty, felt that I wasn't doing things quite right. I really never knew the facts, but there came a point, after I'd been shooting for a few weeks, when he obviously didn't think I could do it."

Selznick did express dissatisfaction with the tempo of Cukor's direction. Strongly against stylization, he thought Cukor's pace was too slow and his emphasis too strong on the female characters. Irene Selznick claimed in her memoirs that "George's work was simply not up to David's expectations," implying that the project, an epic film, might have been too big for him.

Once the film was in production, there were constant ego struggles on the set. Gable's relationship with Cukor was never more than formally cordial. From the start Gable protested vigorously that Cukor's direction would not be to his advantage. Everybody knew Gable fretted about Cukor's already known reputation as a "woman's director." And he was unnerved by the speed with which Cukor established rapport with Vivien Leigh. Gable wanted a "man's director"—a Victor Fleming or even Jack Conway.

When Cukor asked his actors to begin their "southern" lessons, Gable took his first rebellious stand. "I am informed by MGM," Selznick wrote to Cukor on December 8, "that Gable refuses under any circumstances to have any kind of a Southern accent." From then on the informal agreement was whatever the King wanted, the King got.

"I'm not sure that Clark really thought I was much good," Cukor later said. "Perhaps he mistakenly thought that because I was supposed to be a 'woman's director,' I would "throw" the story to Vivien, but if that's so, it was very naive of him and not the reaction of a professional actor. It's not the director who 'throws' things and puts the emphasis the wrong way," he explained. "That would be like singing certain notes very loudly or heavily to divert attention from the others."

Cukor's friends suspected that Gable had other compelling reasons for wanting him off. Cukor knew of Gable's days as a hustler on the Hollywood gay circuit, when the actor first arrived in L.A. One of these sexual encounters was with William Haines, the actor who later became Cukor's friend and designer. Cukor's very presence might have reminded the macho actor of his dubious past.

Lambert, who wrote a book about *GWTW*, dismissed the notorious sex story about Gable. "The episode between Haines and Gable may have happened," he said, "but I don't think that Gable would ever have done that—he was too professional. He would have made it a condition at the start." Lambert said that Cukor was pretty honest about his dismissal.

The distrust between Gable and Cukor reached unpleasant proportions. Cukor further irritated the actor by calling him "dear" and "darling" on the set, as was his habit with all his stars, male and female. Gable took advantage of the fact that Selznick had to beg MGM to get him. He went on payroll on January 23, a day after his wife Ria announced their divorce, and Selznick feared that he would leave the production to marry his new love, Carole Lombard.

"Selznick did fire George," Katharine Hepburn said, "but I don't think he really understood it. I think Gable didn't like George because he would be very careful with Vivien Leigh. He would be much more interested in the woman's character." According to Hepburn, Cukor probably thought of Gable as "just one more character to present himself, whereas Leigh was a new personality. Gable might have thought, 'What the hell am I going to do? George is fascinated by Vivien Leigh and doesn't pay attention to me.' "

Cukor knew Gable didn't want to do the film but needed the money for his divorce. "Gable went into the movie very insecure," Lambert said, "and he did see at once that George and Vivien had a terrific rapport. That, combined with George's reputation as a woman's director, made Gable feel he was going to be on the less attentive end of the stick. His insecurity made him more demanding." According to Lambert, "Gable was not George's kind of actor, though George thought he was right for the part. They didn't have a deep rapport, not in the sense that George had with Cary Grant."

Lambert also refuted the claim that Selznick didn't think Cukor was good enough. "George's account basically was that Selznick kept rewriting the script and that he did hold things up. They were getting behind schedule." In *Bhowani Junction,* the 1955 film about India, Lambert said, "Cukor handled the crowd and action scenes brilliantly, so I don't see any reason to suppose he couldn't have done it. Especially in that kind of operation, where there was so much technical backup.

"It's hard to know where George begins and Selznick ends," Lambert noted about their relative contribution, though in the final account, he thought Selznick was the auteur of that movie. But Morrissey and other critics disagree. Morrissey claimed Cukor should get more credit for *GWTW*: "George did the casting, and he shaped the level of performances. George had this gift of knowing what was good acting. It's not just dialogue; it's performing. In *GWTW* all the performances belong in history. Hattie McDaniel, Butterfly McQueen, Laura Hope Crews are totally theatrical and artificial, but when you can be funny and artificial and get away with it, that's great acting. George never said, 'Now, be realistic, this is a serious movie.' There are a lot of dopey, awful directors who smother actors. He could see that Laura Hope

Crews [who played Aunt Pittypat] was over the top, but she was good."

"It is nonsense to say that I was giving too much attention to Vivien and Olivia," Cukor told a reporter. "It is the text that dictates where the emphasis should go. Gable didn't have a great deal of confidence in himself as an actor, although he was a great screen personality; maybe he thought that I didn't understand that."

Gable thought that a "he-man" director like Victor Fleming would put guts into the film. He did complain a lot about Cukor and worked on Selznick until he got Fleming. Selznick used Gable's complaints as an excuse to get rid of Cukor, whose direction he didn't like. Interestingly, when the foulmouthed Fleming saw the footage that had been shot, he is reported to have said, "David, your fucking script is no fucking good."

"George won from me total confidence," said de Havilland, "just as he did from Vivien. He had a wonderful sense of detail in shaping a characterization. The greatest difficulty after he left was the change of directors. There were three of them. For Vivien and I, the loss of Cukor was a terrible blow. He had so much to do with our having been chosen for our roles; he had helped us so much in setting our characterization. We thought that without him we would flounder and fail."

Though de Havilland liked Fleming's direction, there were times she missed Cukor's insights. One day she called Cukor to ask if he would give her counsel. He invited her to lunch at a Beverly Hills restaurant. "We read over the scene about which I felt uneasy, and he gave me marvelous advice."

On at least two other occasions de Havilland turned to Cukor, who always responded with "grace, kindness, and wisdom." "My consultations with George lasted about an hour," she said, "and aside from the first luncheon, they took place at his house." De Havilland felt guilty about moonlighting with Cukor, as if she were running her scenes behind Leigh's back, until she found out that Leigh was doing exactly the same thing.

Leigh liked Cukor the minute she saw him because he "smelled" of theater and was imaginative. She was extremely angry at Selznick's decision; Cukor was her only hope for enjoying the film. But even after being fired, Cukor continued to coach Leigh, who trusted him more than she trusted Fleming—or herself. Leigh's regular three-hour rehearsal with Cukor on Sundays was her favorite part of the week. It is ironic that Cukor ended up directing Leigh and de Havilland after all.

Unlike de Havilland, Leigh actually resented Fleming. She kept going back to her screen test and stuck as closely as she could to Cukor's direction. "I was an awful bitch on the set," she once told Cukor. They had been working on her big scene with Ashley, and she felt it wasn't right. "Let's see how George handled it," she said, forcing Fleming to screen her test. Nothing could irritate him more.

The picture went on and on, and Leigh missed Olivier, who was in London. Exhausted and impatient, she spent Sundays at Cukor's. One day she took a swim, lay down on a chair in the sun, and fell asleep for hours. Cukor just sat next to her, watching this beautiful creature with delight.

Cukor had spent two years on *GWTW*, preparing, researching, making tests. It was no consolation that other artists on that project also failed to last. After Sidney Howard was taken off, innumerable writers, including Scott Fitzgerald, worked on the script. Although *GWTW* finally came off effectively, Cukor held that it contained Selznick's "seeds of destruction": "Some producers want to direct, believing they can do it better, but they don't, so it frustrates them and spoils their relation with their director." Selznick's strength, his relation with people, began to fall apart as his stars, Ingrid Bergman, Joan Fontaine, and Vivien Leigh, left him.

Selznick and Cukor continued to be friends of sorts, but Cukor never really forgave him. The problem was that Cukor could not talk about his bitterness. "When something like this happens," he told Lambert, "it's the luck of the game." But it is hard to believe he really meant it. At the time Cukor pretended that "when you've finished a picture and it's ruined by other people's cutting, that's much worse, it stays with you."

Cukor had to be careful, because everything he said was interpreted as too critical of Selznick. A lot of water had gone under the bridge, Cukor would say about *GWTW*. Asked if he hated being taken off the picture, he answered, "I've long ago reconciled myself to what can best be termed the vicissitudes of war out here." But Frances Goldwyn observed: "When Selznick fired him, he didn't yell or scream, but he ate a great many cakes."

"What in the world happened about *GWTW*?" asked the disgusted Hepburn, who learned about it while performing in Boston. "I simply can't imagine the picture not directed by *you*. But then it has been a pain in the neck and I should think that you are probably relieved of an interesting but very problematical venture." Revolted by the whole thing, and to console him, Hepburn reported that Cukor's girls had finally redeemed themselves, referring to her success in *The Philadelphia Story* and Tallulah Bankhead's in *The Little Foxes*. "Darling, how much I wish you were here to see *Little Foxes*!" Bankhead wrote. "It's all been worth it. I'm not only in a good play, but really the *best* play, and we're the talk of the town."

After his suspension from *GWTW* in February 1939 Cukor did not remain idle for long. His new MGM contract began in late March; the studio wanted him on another project right away. Fortunately his next two pictures—*The Women* and *The Philadelphia Story*—were among the best and most satisfying of his career.

Louis B. had originally assigned Ernst Lubitsch to direct *The Women*, with producer Hunt Stromberg's blessing. When Cukor was suddenly left without a film, however, Lubitsch was moved to *Ninotchka*, Garbo's first comedy. Cukor was then put in charge of "that feminine kennel," as Hedda Hopper later dubbed *The Women*. Louis B. hoped that Cukor—a master of women's psychology—would be able to "handle" the large cast of female stars.

Still reeling from the *GWTW* debacle, Cukor put on a cheerful facade, telling reporters he was truly in his element, prepared to have the time of his life. *The Women* was a perfect choice—the kind of film Cukor really excelled in making. Clare Boothe's stinging play about the cattiness of upper-crust wives and mistresses was a smash hit on Broadway. Desperation underscores the comedy, though Boothe's work is less cynical than, if somewhat reminiscent of, *Dinner at Eight*. Unfortunately a great number of the funniest lines were blue-penciled by Hollywood's censors. "The most innocent jokes about sex were banned," recalled Anita Loos, who, along with Jane Murfin, was credited with the script.

Loos was instructed to sit beside Cukor and ad-lib "clean" jokes. This did not prove difficult. Quick and witty, Loos found plenty of humor in the ordinary bitchiness of women. Loos invented one lively scene, where all the women go to the ladies' room at the same time to gossip, in a matter of seconds.

Under Cukor's direction, the dialogue in this scene moves at a dizzying pace; the action was to be played as quickly as possible. Cukor instructed Rosalind Russell to pick up a towel mid-sentence and say, "Cheap Chinese embroidery," then toss it away, without losing a beat. These catty remarks ("Only ten cents a bar!") were almost subliminal, sandwiched between the women's rapid banter.

Cukor's contribution was in pacing the dialogue, which was fast, crisp, and beautifully timed. Aware that the story's central character (played by Norma Shearer) was weak, Cukor created a circus ambiance, emphasizing the funny episodes and eccentric characters around her. No men appear in the movie, even in minor roles—a novel idea for 1939. At the end of the story a male shadow is visible onscreen. Cukor reportedly tested three actors for their ability to cast the shadow!

When the film was made, kept women and marital breakups were big moral questions. In later years Cukor mused that considering changing times and conventions, if *The Women* had been remade, "everybody would be screwing everybody, and everybody would know about it." But even by today's standards, Cukor's film is remarkably fresh.

Cukor's genius for casting was again evident. The all-female ensemble was particularly appropriate to the facilities of MGM, which always boasted more impressive female than male stars. "The ensemble was a wonderful combination of personalities," Joan Fontaine recalled. "George cast each woman very skillfully." And Loos, who considered Cukor one of the few truly creative directors, observed: "George could detect hidden qualities in an actress that would make a star of her."

The first to be cast was Norma Shearer. Owning a large piece of MGM stocks, Shearer was still powerful in 1939, and with this privileged position, she had no trouble snagging the lead role. Though a straight and humorless character, Mary is the center of the story or, as Cukor said, the glue that holds everything together.

As soon as she heard about the film, Joan Crawford announced that she wanted to play Crystal Allen, the tough perfume girl who steals Mary's husband. Crawford, who had been labeled "box-office poison" after a string of lackluster films, knew that the prestige of *The Women,* with its all-star cast, could boost her career. She began an active campaign to win the role, but Louis B. was appalled at such a radical divergence from her established screen image; Crawford usually played strong career women. "It would offend your fans if you played such a cold-hearted bitch," he told her. Louis B. did not stand in her way, but he refused to go out of his way to help, telling his star she would have to convince producer Hunt Stromberg and Cukor.

Stromberg was also dubious about Crawford, fearing her inclusion would upset the film's balance. Besides, the part was too small for an actress of her stature. But knowing the part was a gem, she held to her guns. The part was small, but the hard-boiled Crystal had bite; Crawford knew she would stand out as the other women played sympathetic parts. Stromberg left it up to Cukor.

At the time Cukor had little respect for Crawford; she was too much of a mannered movie queen. They had met in 1935, on the set of *No More Ladies,* a vehicle that Cukor took over when director Edward H. Griffith fell ill. "Miss Crawford," he said, during that shoot, after a long speech he particularly disliked, "you remember your lines, which is fine, now try to put some meaning into them." Crawford was shocked. No director had spoken to her in this manner before. "George is a hard task-master," she later said; "he took me over the coals, giving me the roughest time I have ever had. And I am eternally grateful." Cukor did respond to Crawford's feisty personality; he respected her fierce determination to succeed.

But another factor motivated Crawford's campaign. She relished a direct confrontation with Shearer now that Thalberg was dead. Thalberg and

Shearer had always condescended to Crawford, perceiving her as a pushy working-class girl; a duel had been building up for a decade. Now, for the first time, MGM's two queens would be in a film together—cast as rivals.

Cukor anticipated a showdown, and it finally happened when Crawford and Shearer were preparing their big confrontation scene at the fashion show. The actresses were running through their dialogue together, a common courtesy. Crawford, sitting in a chair, was feeding lines to Shearer while knitting with large needles that clicked noisily. Shearer took it for a few run-throughs, then asked her to stop. Conspicuously rude, Crawford continued to knit. Irritated, Shearer finally turned to Cukor, asking that *he* give her her lines. Outraged at Crawford's behavior, Cukor reprimanded her and asked her to leave the set. Later that night she received one of his famous lectures.

But Cukor secretly enjoyed the temperamental feuds of his stars. The fan magazines also needed such stories. Both women were in their own ways experts at self-publicity, and the "feuds" were good copy. Rumors circulated that Shearer had actually encouraged Crawford's casting, knowing that their juicy scene, fighting over the same man, would attract audiences to the theaters. Still, the two actresses never spoke to each other again after this scene had been completed.

Rosalind Russell, another ambitious actress, was also trying to get away from her nice girl image when she begged for the part of Sylvia Fowler, the gossipy gadfly. "I must have taken several particularly deep drags of oxygen," she recalled in her book, *Life Is a Banquet,* "the day I went after a flashy part in *The Women.* MGM had tested everybody, but Lassie and Mrs. Roosevelt, for the film." Competition was fierce; even the maids' roles were fought over.

One day, looking very smart after a visit to the Elizabeth Arden salon, Russell drove out to Metro and marched straight into Stromberg's office. "I want to play Sylvia," she said. "Why haven't you tested me?"

"Well, Roz," he said, "you're too beautiful." This caught her by surprise. "We want somebody, who gets a laugh just by sticking her head around the door." Russell was considered a dramatic actress, not a comedienne. But in the spirit of fairness Stromberg arranged for a test.

Cukor was less than thrilled. "I don't want you in this part," he said. "I want Ilka Chase, she's a friend of mine, she played it in New York, and she's right for it." But they went onto a sound stage for the test, and Russell asked if the camera was fully loaded. She then proceeded to play the scene in three different ways: as drawing-room comedy; realistically; and in a flat-out exaggerated style. Impressed, Cukor told Russell she could start the fittings for Sylvia's wardrobe.

Russell was only a few lines into her first scene when Cukor stopped her. "No, no, no," he said, "do it like you did it in the test. The very exaggerated version is the one I want."

Russell was horrified. "Mr. Cukor, I can't do that, the critics will murder me."

"You have a big following at Loew's State in New York," said Cukor, "but in Waukegan, Illinois, they've never heard of you. Now you do it the way I tell you." Cukor explained that Sylvia was breaking up a family and there was a child involved. "If you're a heavy, audiences will hate you. Just be ridiculous." Though frightened to death, Russell did it exactly the way he said. "Everything that came to me from *The Women*," Russell later acknowledged, "my reputation as a comedienne, I owe to George."

Cukor was an endlessly inventive director, always coming up with bits to enhance a scene or characterization. When they were shooting the ladies' room scene, Cukor suggested to Russell, "After they leave, I want you to look at your teeth."

"Why?" she asked.

"When you girls make up in front of people," he explained, "you make up one way, and when you're alone, you make up another."

Russell bared her teeth to the mirror and eventually got credit for an inspired moment—courtesy of Cukor.

Under Cukor's direction, the nuances in all the women's speeches were witty. Uncharacteristically Cukor even made a few textual suggestions, like adding the famous line—*"l'amour, l'amour"*—of Mary Brian, who played the countess.

The day the fashion show sequence was shot Russell was running lines with Shearer while practicing her knitting, a skill she needed for the scene. Russell was chewing gum, her head bent over her needles, and her glasses had slipped down her nose. She was unaware that Cukor was watching. When Cukor announced he was ready to shoot, an assistant gave Russell a Kleenex for her gum, but Cukor stopped her: "I want her to chew gum in this scene." The observant Cukor was always alert to new possibilities.

Shearer was not thrilled by the idea. As it was, Russell, with her nonstop chatter, dominated their scenes together. "Is she going to knit and chew gum and let those glasses hang down on the end of her nose in a scene with *me*?" Shearer complained. "Who can compete with that?"

"Yes, she is," was Cukor's assured answer. "Now let's go."

Feigning sympathy, Russell said, "I don't blame you, kid, it's rough." Then she went ahead joyfully with her lines.

Shearer was much more genial with Russell, however, than with Crawford, displaying a healthy sense of humor. At a party during the shoot Cukor was dancing with Russell. Ernst Lubitsch danced by and winked at her. "Trying to get a close-up in the picture?" he quipped. "If you want to *stay* in the picture, you'd better dance with Miss Shearer." Word got back to Shearer of Lubitsch's wisecrack, and a few minutes later, to everyone's amazement, Shearer grabbed Russell's arm and danced her around the floor.

Cukor derived enormous pleasure from drawing out Russell's unique comic gifts. Her first comedic role, Sylvia is one of Russell's funniest and most original performances. Though broad, her delivery rang true. With Cukor's help, she grabbed hold of the role without worrying about being unsympathetic. She played the bitchy gossip so outrageously that audiences found her irresistible.

One of the film's comic climaxes was the fight at the divorce ranch in Reno between Russell and Paulette Goddard, who steals Russell's husband. The two women scratched, bit, and kicked their way through seven sets, requiring eight changes of costume before the sequence was completed. The fight took three days to shoot. Cukor shot it at the end, so that any black eyes or sprained ankles resulting from the fight would not affect the budget.

Her teeth clenched, Goddard starts the fight by giving Russell a kick in the ass. Russell loses her balance and pitches forward on her face. Shearer ineffectively tries to stop Goddard from hitting Russell, who bites Goddard's left leg. At the end Goddard rubs her bitten leg, while Russell sits up and squeals in tearful rage. Goddard took the bite only in the long shot of the scene. In the close-up, the leg belongs to actress Mary Beth Hughes, who was chosen because her underpinnings resembled those of Goddard.

To prepare his actresses for the scene, Cukor made them study famous female screen fights, which included the battle between Marie Dressler and Polly Moran in *The Callahans and the Murphys,* Ginger Rogers and Frances Mercer in *Vivacious Lady,* and Alice Faye and Constance Bennett in *Tailspin.*

Goddard, a woman with exceptional allure, usually played the coquette on the screen, but in this movie Cukor wanted something else. "Look, kid," he told her, "just forget those female tricks of yours, and try to give the best imitation you can of Spencer Tracy!"

The Women was also a breakthrough film for Joan Fontaine, whose career as a leading lady at RKO had not been successful. She was terribly insecure about her acting, and Cukor's direction gave her the confidence she lacked. "This film was a turning point," Fontaine said. "It was the first time I had a director who showed me that acting was not standing in front of a camera reading lines. Up to that point directors had not bothered."

"The magic words of acting," Cukor told Fontaine, "are 'think and feel'; the rest will take care of itself." Cukor's simple advice was the best any actor, male or female, could get. "We just rehearsed a scene and shot it," Fontaine said about his technique. "We didn't do any intellectualizing. George was against Method acting because it kills the spontaneity and emotion of the role."

Cukor's aversion to Stanislavsky (and later Lee Strasberg's Method) was known from his stage days. A famous story circulated of how Dorothy Gish asked Cukor during rehearsals for *Young Love* to explain her motivation for crossing the stage. "Just motivate your ass over there and sit in that chair," Cukor told her.

Fontaine recalled Cukor's habit of standing behind the camera, acting a scene as it was being shot: "He moved as if his whole soul was reaching out to you to call the performance from you." Cukor's distinctive talent was empathy; his actors believed he cared about their work. Kindness, humor, and wit were tools Cukor used to produce consistently strong, often surprising performances from his stars. "He wasn't a marshmallow by any means," Fontaine added. "He could be caustic, but he did all he could to help you do the best job.

"George could do no wrong with me," said the actress. "I wish we had more directors like him today. I have missed Mr. Cukor in every piece of work I have ever done. I just wish he were there to show me the way and help me. I don't know what he did for other people, but I felt he was my God. I felt total sympathy from him."

Fontaine had the most sentimental scene in *The Women* when she reconciles with her husband on the telephone. Though small, this role had a great deal to do with Fontaine's getting the lead in Hitchcock's *Rebecca*. "George recommended me for the part," Fontaine noted. "I'm sure Selznick called him up and said, 'What's this woman like?' and George probably was very favorable."

Indeed, while Cukor was preparing *The Philadelphia Story*, Selznick was testing actresses for *Rebecca*. Vivien Leigh and Laurence Olivier tested together, but as much as he liked the duo, Cukor's reaction to their test was not favorable. Still trusting Cukor's casting savvy, Selznick asked for his opinion on the finalists: Anne Baxter, Margaret Sullavan, and the feuding sisters, Olivia de Havilland and Joan Fontaine. Cukor indeed recommended Fontaine on the strength of her breakthrough in *The Women*. Hitchcock concurred, and Fontaine landed the role, for which she received her first Oscar nomination.

As the shooting on *The Women* progressed, Stromberg was ecstatic about the rushes, writing almost daily memos praising Cukor and the cast. "Today's rushes great," he noted on May 9. "Norma's positively magnificent, completely natural and convincing." On May 10 he wrote again, "I'm plumb crazy about today's rushes. Joan looks stunning, and scenes are knockout in every respect." He noted on May 13: "Thursday's rushes very good, and you can use this note for Wednesday's rushes too."

But Cukor's dealings with Stromberg were not uniformly positive. Cukor had to compromise his vision in terms of MGM's notions of how to please an audience. Cukor emphasized the satirical elements of the characters. With the exception of Mary, Shearer's straight, humorless lady, none of the women seems to mind how awful or bad she is; this is why the comedy has aged well. But MGM still stressed the happy ending, which was meant to reassure audiences that a nice woman can always keep her husband.

Cukor also lost the battle with Stromberg over the fashion show scene, which had nothing to do with the film but was inserted to make the picture more exciting. Imposed by the front office, this color sequence reflected Stromberg's silly wish to give the public something extra. This scene, however, wasn't very good, and it made the black-and-white footage that followed look strange.

For his research Cukor went to a real fashion show, but he realized that the nuances were difficult to duplicate onscreen. Color was such a novelty in 1939 that the fashion show sequence received considerable attention. But it was too long, about five minutes, and halted the narrative flow.

Shooting was completed on June 28, 1939, but a new problem emerged: the credits. Shearer demanded that her name appear above Crawford's in all the ads. But having lobbied hard for a role designed to elevate her status, Crawford managed to slip her name above the title, too. The billing was settled to read "Norma Shearer and Joan Crawford in *The Women*." Then Russell demanded her name over the title as well. Her strategy was a four-day sick leave from the set. Russell's "sickness" ended only when MGM moved her name above the title, albeit in type only half as large as that of Shearer and Crawford.

Faced with an all-female cast, studio publicists couldn't feed gossip columnists the usual spicy tales about romance, so they embellished stories about the feuding stars. Poor Cukor, they were saying, referring to his directing 135 women, a dozen of them stars. "I learned a few tricks from a lion tamer," Cukor said, though he always held that women were much more realistic and tougher than men. "I'd rather handle ten women than ten men," he said, "because they have less vanity." Defending his cast, Cukor dismissed rumors that they were demanding and temperamental.

The Women was actually one of the easiest films Cukor ever directed.

He explained it simply: "When one deals with stars, he is dealing with intelligent people. If they weren't intelligent, they wouldn't have arrived at the star pinnacle. Stars understand the business. They have learned that a show of temper gets them nothing, save perhaps a salary suspension or at least a headache."

There was going to be a premiere to end all premieres, Cukor told Russell, inviting her to enter the theater on his arm, with thousands of their fans cheering. Cukor quipped that it might be good publicity if they were married in the theater's forecourt after the show. For her part, Russell said she would settle for the proper vehicle with him, acknowledging that "if Sylvia contributed in anyway to *The Women,* it is because of you, your faith, your generous help."

Cukor was next assigned to *The Wizard of Oz,* starring Judy Garland. The picture had taken six months of preparation, with a number of directors coming and going. When Richard Thorpe was fired, producer Mervyn LeRoy brought in Cukor, though it was never clear whether he would just look at the rushes and provide advice or also direct the picture. LeRoy had doubts whether it was the right property for Cukor. He knew that Cukor didn't like fantasy films, and he didn't relish working with children.

After only three days on the set Cukor expressed his dissatisfaction and was removed. In the end the movie was directed by Victor Fleming. Ironically, Fleming replaced Cukor on the two pictures he is best known for: *GWTW* and *The Wizard of Oz.* Cukor, however, did make one major contribution: He got rid of Judy Garland's blond wig and cute doll-face makeup and restored her down-to-earth look.

Cukor didn't worry much about *The Wizard of Oz* because the reviews of *The Women* were really great. Cukor had won the major critical and commercial success he needed to boost his morale after *GWTW,* as well as a lucrative new contract. "Marvelous, every studio should make one nasty picture a year," wrote *The New York Times.* Cukor's direction was intentionally coarse and broad—it was one of his few low comedies—but *The Women* became one of his most popular successes and later acquired a cult status.

It was also a huge commercial triumph. In its sixty-fourth week in New York, it ran longer and stronger than other recent releases. In Syracuse, Baltimore, New Orleans, and Atlanta, it was more successful than *The Wizard of Oz.* However, none of the actresses received an Oscar nomination, nor did the picture, in a year considered the best in Hollywood's history. *GWTW* swept all the 1939 awards, including Best Picture, Director, and Actress.

With all the success of *The Women,* Christmas 1939 was one of the saddest in Cukor's life. Always the gentleman, he sent a telegram to

Selznick on the opening night of *GWTW:* "I don't know whether to be wistful, noble, or comic, but tonight I send you my love." And he treasured for life a letter from Margaret Mitchell: "The premiere was exciting and fine, but we did miss you. You were almost our first contact with the movies—and a most pleasant one—so we naturally had you and the film linked up together in our minds. It seemed strange not having you here with us at the 'birthday.' "

CHAPTER FIVE:

The End of an Era, 1940–43

THROUGHOUT HIS CAREER CUKOR WAS A PRODUCT OF TYPECASTING. He once admitted in an interview: "In 1929 I was a young blade who constantly made jokes, so they said I had no heart. Then I did a couple of sob pictures, and they said I was all heart. Then I did a few comedies, and they decided I was a funny fellow."

Cukor had no strict guidelines on material he wished to direct. "It is disconcerting to people," he noted, "when they are unable to peg you properly. I did some comedies, and it was assumed that I was better at comedy than anything else. Then I did a spate of costume pictures, and for years no producer would send me anything to read but a costume picture."

One issue, however, was consistent in Cukor's choices: a reluctance to use violence. He shunned violence, not on moral grounds but because he did not find it scary: "[v]iolence doesn't really frighten me." Cukor may well have been the only major Hollywood director whose celluloid record was completely free of crime fare. The only gangsters he chose to portray were funny ones, as in his 1952 sports film *Pat and Mike*.

The other omission from Cukor's repertoire was the socially conscious film. "There's nothing more awful than being preached at," he once said. It is doubtful that he would have chosen to do the antiwar film *All Quiet on the Western Front*. "I certainly don't want a message from a lot of half-baked people, I don't respect what they have to say. I'd like to be able to deduce my own message." "I would rather be dead," he said on another occasion, "than see *On the Beach*," Stanley Kramer's antinuclear message film. He also refused to see Richard Lester's *How the War Was Won*; as gifted as Lester was, Cukor didn't care what the Brit thought about war.

Nonetheless, there were some pictures that touched Cukor's conscience. John Ford's 1940 classic *The Grapes of Wrath* was a film that "did make a change." He saw it with the Oliviers, who called it *Grapes of Wrought* because they were so touched. But for Cukor, Ford's film was first and foremost a work of art and only secondarily a work that awoke the conscience.

Bored with pretentious films about the world's big issues, Cukor believed that movies were not meant to solve problems. "I haven't solved the big burning questions," he said, holding that a director can stimulate an audience, "maybe impart some wisdom along the line, but not much more than that."

At one time Cukor showed interest in religious films but was discouraged by Hollywood's tendency to make them "heavy going, sanctimonious and humorless." He was appalled by the "De Mille variety," preposterous stories that evoked laughter. Granted, De Mille was a master storyteller, but his stories were ludicrous and absurd: "De Mille wasn't bothered by good taste," Cukor quipped. Regrettably Hollywood's epics had neither the wit nor the courage to deal with religious subjects in a light and charming way.

After his dismissal from *GWTW*, and the allegation that he favored Leigh over Gable, and after directing an all-female cast in *The Women*, Cukor was typecast as a woman's director. This label stuck with him until his death. "It's rather a nice label," Cukor once said, "although I've never understood the reasons for it. Perhaps it's because in the 1940s the emphasis was on movie queens, and I did work with them all."

Indeed, from 1940–1942 Cukor directed all four reigning MGM queens: Garbo (*Two-Faced Woman*), Hepburn (*The Philadelphia Story*), Joan Crawford (*Susan and God, A Woman's Face*), and Norma Shearer (*Her Cardboard Lover*). The titles of these and later movies (*Les Girls, My Fair Lady*) reinforced his label. Along with his being "a woman's director" came his reputation of a "lion tamer," of his ability to handle temperamental female stars.

But Cukor's colleagues thought the label was justified. According to Joseph Mankiewicz, who produced *The Philadelphia Story*, "What was special about George was his serene relationship with actresses. They felt comfortable with him; they knew he would never get them into bed. George was not threatening to them as were the more masculine directors, William Wellman or Victor Fleming. Actresses felt at ease in his company. They knew he adored women, understood them; they also trusted his impeccable taste in makeup, costumes."

Mankiewicz elaborated: "George made sure to befriend his actresses' families, particularly mothers." Indeed, Cukor knew and kept in touch with Hepburn's family, and Judy Holliday was always invited to his house with her mother. He was kind to Shelley Winters, letting her have Monday or Friday off in order to spend more time with her daughter. Cukor's relationship with their families not only made his actresses closer to him but also fulfilled emotional needs for him, substituting for the lack of warmth within his own family.

Most of Cukor's films featured female protagonists, and the few focusing on men (*Edward, My Son*) contained costarring female roles. Cukor did place women at the center, honoring them with respectable treatment. But there was no glorification of the eternal feminine or exaltation of the feminine mystique. His heroines were flesh and blood—"realistic" he said—reflecting his female friends: Ethel Barrymore, Ina Claire, Tallulah Bankhead, Katharine Hepburn.

The most erroneous misconception about Cukor was that he worked better with women. While he undoubtedly enjoyed exceptional rapport with actresses, he also worked extremely well with men. Cukor was the first to discern and develop the comic talent in Spencer Tracy and Cary Grant, and he helped John Barrymore reaffirm his stature in *Dinner at Eight.* Teresa Wright, who appeared in *The Actress,* said, "I don't understand why he is called a woman's director. He has had some great male performers. Certainly you cannot get many actors better than Spencer Tracy."

Under Cukor's direction Tracy received an Oscar nomination for *The Actress* and gave distinguished performances in other films. Cukor was also the director to coach James Mason (*A Star Is Born*), Jimmy Stewart (*The Philadelphia Story*), Ronald Colman (*A Double Life*), and Charles Boyer (*Gaslight*), in Oscar-winning or nominated performances. Cukor was quick to point out that more men than women won Oscars in his pictures.

Though Mankiewicz defined him as "Hollywood's greatest woman's director," he conceded that Cukor didn't like the label. But he quickly added: "Victor Fleming also didn't like the label of men's director." Joan Fontaine said, "George didn't like it because it limited him, but he was indeed the finest woman's director I have ever worked with."

For Fontaine, "George was a better woman's director because he was more feminine by nature. We all knew he was homosexual. He made no bones about it." Fontaine held that Cukor's nature was also reflected in the sensitivity of his work. "He cared about detail, about clothes, about ambiance," she said. "These are feminine traits. He had a tremendous sense of costume appropriateness, a sense of chic and style." Fontaine elaborated: "Hitchcock worked from a masculine point of view, and George from a feminine. Hitchcock would allow the makeup and wardrobe departments to take care of their business. He would never fuss over the clothes, he wouldn't say, 'You're prettier if you wear this.' George did all that."

Claudette Colbert recalled that on the set of *Zaza* Cukor didn't go into as complete an analysis about Herbert Marshall's role as he did with hers. "He may have been better with women," Colbert allowed, "because of the usual thing—that he was not going to tell a man what to do—whereas he wouldn't hesitate with a woman. Don't forget that men have the upper hand."

Cukor's reputation became more restricting as his career progressed. "I'm staging a one-man rebellion!" he once said humorously. "I am tired of the tag. This rebellion in no way alters my belief, however, that women are the realists of the sexes and the better sports." Cukor knew he lost some prime projects on account of his label. "I don't think I behave any differently when I direct a woman," he said; "you talk the same to a man as you do to a woman."

After *The Women* Cukor was assigned to direct *Susan and God,* based on Rachel Crowther's play. Its heroine, Susan Trexel, is a flightly, self-deluded upper-crust woman who drives her family away when she experiences a religious conversion. Susan comes home from Europe obsessed with a new belief that she tries to impose on her friends. But gradually she realizes that her withdrawn daughter and alcoholic husband need her, that true charity begins at home.

Unlike most of Cukor's films, *Susan and God* lacked a sympathetic character at its center. What Susan needed, Cukor jokingly said, was a good spanking from a man. As much as he tried, he could not overcome the stuffy dialogue and tedious plot.

MGM had purchased the rights to *Susan and God* for Shearer, who turned it down because she didn't want to play a mother with a teenage daughter; it would have revealed her age. As in the past, the next star down the line was Joan Crawford.

Because *Susan and God* was high comedy, Cukor hoped to transform Crawford into a comedienne, as he had with Rosalind Russell in *The Women*. He thus demanded that Crawford submit completely to his unrelenting discipline. But the star lacked the necessary skills to pull off the role. Cukor was frustrated, for he was unable to stretch Crawford's range; she was simply not a comedienne.

Fredric March, who had worked with Cukor on *Royal Family,* was cast as the distressed husband. But March was not above nasty humor, suggesting that if Cukor were not up to the task, he could always call in Cyril Gardner, his former codirector. He sent Cukor a newspaper clipping that said: "After three weeks of production, Selznick decided that Cukor failed to grasp the magnitude of the picture, that his action sagged, that he favored the female characters over the male." The last statement was underlined with a message: "hope you've learned your lesson!"

"Now that we've got you in the bag, signed, sealed and almost delivered," Cukor teasingly responded, "I don't have to be so Goddamned polite to you anymore." Though sensitive about *GWTW*, Cukor could still show humor about it: Gardner was old stuff; for future ribbing, March should use Victor Fleming.

By Cukor's standards, none of the performances in *Susan and God* were good. As the husband who takes to drinking to escape from his frivolous wife, March was listless. There was a small society woman role in the film, and Cukor, against MGM's advice, cast a youngster by the name of Rita Hayworth. Sensing there was something special about Hayworth, Cukor gave the makeup people specific instructions on how to make her even more beautiful. This film served as another step on Hayworth's way to stardom.

Lon McCallister, the child star Cukor had met during *Romeo and Juliet,* was also briefly involved. Cukor walked down a line of would-be stars, selecting some young actors. As he passed McCallister, he recognized him. "You've grown!" he said with a smile. McCallister was given a bit part in a party sequence that was eventually cut, a scene that required wearing a tuxedo. "I didn't own one," McCallister noted, "but I lied, and the next day I bought one 'on time.' " Years later Cukor inquired, "Whatever happened to the tuxedo?" McCallister told him that he had worn it in other pictures, that it hadn't been a bad investment after all.

Cukor worked on eleven films in the 1940s. The decade started well (*The Philadelphia Story*) and ended well (*Adam's Rib*), but in between these successes he directed some of his weakest pictures (*Winged Victory, Desire Me*).

Philip Barry wrote the great romantic comedy *The Philadelphia Story* for Katharine Hepburn, shaping it to her strengths and eccentricities. Opening on Broadway on March 29, 1939, and running for 416 performances, the play was a critical and commercial success and a personal triumph for Hepburn.

All the major studios wanted to buy the play, but Hepburn shrewdly purchased the screen rights with the help of Howard Hughes. She cleverly had written into her contract a stipulation that the two leading men must be major stars, preferably Gable and Tracy. Instead the film was made with Jimmy Stewart and Cary Grant. Neither actor was top-notch at the time, but perfectly cast, both later became Hollywood icons.

From the beginning it was tacitly understood that Cukor would direct; Hepburn's and Cukor's previous collaboration on Barry's *Holiday* had been a critical success. They had talked about this film from the moment she secured the rights. Having seen the play numerous times in New York, Cukor knew it inside out.

Cukor sent producer Joseph Mankiewicz to New York to record the show in order to determine where the laughs came. Checking the film against the recording, he realized that the laughs came in different places. In the theater Barry's verbal wit carried the play, but in the movie the comedy was more visual, and the fun derived from the actors' gestures. Cukor believed in letting comedy happen on the screen, allowing the material to determine its tempo. He was pleased by complaints from his friends that the laughter drowned out many funny moments. "Well, go and see it again," he said.

Knowing Barry had a precise vision of the locale and characters, Cukor sought his input. He asked Barry to provide a description of the Lord house, particularly its style and furnishings. He wanted to know if the house was patterned after any particular structure. But all Barry asked Cukor was not to overdo it: The house should be impressive but not forbidding, handsome but warm. These comments influenced Cukor's understated sets.

Cukor saw the play as a fairy tale with a moral: Tracy Lord meets her prince but gums it up and has to rediscover her humanity. A smart, cold-blooded, hot-tempered girl needs to transform herself into a human being. The priggish Tracy, contemptuous of everyone who doesn't live up to her standards, has to learn humility and tolerance of other people's lapses.

What distinguishes *The Philadelphia Story* as a comedy is its suspense. Up to the end the viewers aren't sure whom Tracy is going to marry. As for its comedy, it derives from her dilemma: In love with three men, Tracy behaves as if it's the most important problem in the world, but only she sees the situation as tragic. Cukor knew the film's effectiveness depended on Hepburn's high-strung thoroughbred winning the audience's hearts. Orchestrating what is Hepburn's greatest screen performance, Cukor brought forth her radiance and intelligence.

Both *Holiday* and *The Philadelphia Story* contain a lot of dialogue, but Cukor made sure his films wouldn't be stage-bound. Transferring a play to the screen didn't mean tearing it apart. Cukor's challenge was to find a new rhythm for the screen, which meant treating the dialogue as action.

Doubtful whether Barry could adapt his play, Cukor turned to Donald Ogden Stewart, a friend of Barry's with whom Cukor had worked successfully on *Dinner at Eight* and other films. Stewart handled the play effectively, but with modesty; his subtle work was deservedly honored with an Oscar for Best Screen Adaptation.

Cukor shot a brilliant new prologue without his actors uttering one line. It sums up how the marriage between Hepburn and Grant ended as well as explains her fury when Grant reappears on the eve of her wedding. Grant walks out of the house carrying a bag of golf clubs. Hepburn appears at the doorway, carrying a club he's forgotten, but instead of giving it to him, she breaks it in two. Furious, Grant advances on her as if he were going to hit her, then simply gives her a contemptuous push that sends her into a pratfall.

Other than that sequence, simplicity was the norm. When Jimmy Stewart was struggling with his big romantic line to Hepburn "You've got hearth fires banked down in you," Cukor told him not to emote at all. Unfortunately, just before Stewart got his line right, Noël Coward stepped onto the set and the actor nearly collapsed. Aware of Stewart's shyness, Coward went up to him and told him how fantastic his acting was. "Roll them," said Cukor, taking advantage of this genuine flattery.

Cukor found Stewart most agreeable, but there was a problematic scene in which he had to swim. "If I appear in a bathing suit," he told Cukor, "I know it's the end of my career and also the end of the motion picture industry." Cukor decided to shoot the scene in a long take.

Ruth Hussey, nominated for a supporting Oscar for her wisecracking photojournalist, said she learned more from Cukor than from any other director. "He'd take you aside after a scene," she remembered, "and discuss with you the motivations, what went before, what's coming after, but all his comments were made in privacy.

"George didn't say, 'Well, let's try it again,' as other directors do when they don't know what they want. His corrections were more like 'A little more color' or 'A little more depth,' or 'Lighten it up a bit.' " According to Hussey, "George gave you a feeling he was really concerned. He wanted you to do well for your sake as well as his. George spent a lot of time with the actors, always demanding more detail for their characterization."

Cukor's mouthing of Hussey's part, as she was doing it herself, surprised her, as it did other actors. "His gestures were hilarious," she said. "If I was supposed to be smiling, he was smiling. If I was frowning, he was frowning. He just acted the whole thing. He was the only director I ever knew who did that." At first she found it disconcerting because "your mind is on him, instead of on what you're supposed to be doing," but then she got used to it.

Cukor showed great stylistic authority in *The Philadelphia Story*. His camera movement is elegant and smooth, confirming his belief that the audience shouldn't be aware of camera tricks. His rule of thumb was: "Unless you have to move the camera, unless it does something for you, be quiet. When you cut, you have to do it delicately, not adventurously. You mustn't show off with the camera."

His philosophy served the text as inconspicuously as possible. "If you're going to do a story about a murder in a Victorian house," he said about *Gaslight,* "you make it claustrophobic, clouded. You research the period," he told Lambert, "not just to reproduce things physically, but for the emotions to stir up. The text dictates the whole style, which may not be to the director's advantage, because it means his touch is not immediately recognizable."

The Philadelphia Story was completed on August 14, 1940, and the movie opened on Christmas Day at Radio City Music Hall. By January 21, 1941, the film had broken the all-time attendance record, held by Disney's *Snow White.* A commitment to exhibit *Rebecca* forced the end of its run after six weeks. But in those six weeks every show was sold out, with 850,000 people seeing the movie in New York alone.

Cukor was amused by reports of the inadvertent effects of *The Philadelphia Story* on liquor consumption. One critic charged that it was a story about smart folks trying to cure their emotional blindness with alcohol: "The W.C.T.U. doesn't know it, but it ought to stop this film, because it sells liquor better than any million-dollar advertising campaign."

This kind of unanticipated impact surprised Cukor. At the same time the prevalence of sympathetic alcoholics in his oeuvre is noteworthy. There are the heroes of *Dinner at Eight* and *What Price Hollywood?,* and drinking features prominently in *Holiday* and *The Philadelphia Story.* Later in the decade Tracy played an alcoholic tyrant in *Edward, My Son,* and James Mason a dipsomaniacal actor in *A Star Is Born.* Cukor himself refrained from excessive drinking; at his parties he would have one cocktail before dinner and a glass of wine with dinner. But all his life he was surrounded by people who drank; some, like Barrymore and Tracy, had severe drinking problems. This firsthand familiarity resulted in fresh, compassionate portraits of alcoholics, avoiding the familiar Hollywood clichés.

Cukor's most admired friends were prominent writers: Somerset Maugham, Noël Coward, Aldous Huxley, Edith Sitwell. It pleased him to orchestrate the sometime incongruous introduction of literary and cinematic celebrities at his house. At one party an English writer asked to meet Joan Crawford; after meeting her, he said she reminded him of an "unnamed Du Pont product."

"The best times of my life I remember having here—in my own house," Cukor said. "It's been an intimate part of my life." He reminisced: "We used to work six days a week, and usually on Sundays, I don't know how I managed it all, but we had lunch here. There were the regulars, like Katharine Hepburn, Irene Selznick, and Vivien Leigh when she was in town. Through the years, particularly during the War, everyone seemed to come. The regulars would sit at the end of the table, and the new people sat close to me."

"George gave wonderful Sunday luncheons," Fontaine confirmed. "He would combine interesting theater and movie people together. At times there were as many as twenty people, and tables were set out in the garden. His lunches were charmingly informal. George did everything terribly well."

Conversation, of course, was the center of the gatherings. Cukor liked to talk about everything; he was very well informed. "I don't think any of us talked much about movies," said Fontaine. "It was our day off; we tried not to talk about ourselves. Its being Sunday, with all of us over-worked and tired, we wanted to relax. George always related something that might be amusing to all of his guests."

Ilka Chase, who had been in his Rochester stock company, observed that the Hollywood pasha Cukor was not so very different from the Rochester pasha Cukor: "The only difference is that now he is rich and gives Sunday luncheons which are eaten by Ina Claire and Billie Burke and Aldous Huxley, and in the old days the luncheons were sometimes Dutch, but they were also eaten by Ina and Billie."

Tallulah Bankhead also recalled with great fondness her afternoons at Cukor's: "Katie [Hepburn] and I used to go nearly every Sunday to Cukor's for lunch, as nearly everybody did in Hollywood at one time or another. We were so different that it used to kill George, but we liked each other very much." Fontaine recalled how Bankhead once showed up for brunch with her makeup still on from the night before.

When Anita Loos, who became fast friends with Cukor, arrived for her first Sunday brunch, Bankhead was floating nude in the pool, while Constance Collier and Hugh Walpole were conversing under a huge Japanese parasol. Cukor had class—Loos thought "he bestowed MGM with whatever cultivation it could boast"—and liked to be surrounded with the rich, beautiful, and talented. But even beautiful guests were not invited again unless they contributed to the conversation.

Since Cukor never liked to have dinner alone, it was not unusual for him to have lunch and dinner parties on the same day—often on Sundays. Cukor was offended when one writer noted that he had those lovely Sunday lunch parties for his friends, but then in the evening "all those strange young men come to eat up the crumbs." A friend countered: "It was not true. The boys would have wonderful meals there as well."

Like his straight soirees, Cukor's gay parties followed a structured pattern. The guests arrived around six-thirty and had one drink in the library and were ushered into the dining room. The bar was in the hall, and often one of the guests served drinks.

Cukor couldn't tolerate his guests' being late. Artist Don Bachardy re-called that once he and his companion Christopher Isherwood happened to be late: "We both felt bad and had to apologize profusely." The French actress Simone Signoret observed that Cukor was the kind of man "who phones you at 7:26 and is furious to find you at home, when the dinner to which he has invited you is at 7:30." When Signoret told him that she and Yves Montand were only five minutes from his house, Cukor retorted, "You are still late." But in his endearing way he proceeded to explain he had called because he wanted her to consider "the hazards of the journey!"

Serving dinner late also irritated him. Cukor got bored with Hollywood dinners at which people drank for hours but didn't get any food. He would say: "I go to these dinners, but if there's no food by nine, I just leave."

Cukor's dinners usually consisted of six to ten friends. The maid served him first, and he was notorious for eating fast. "George just wolfed his food," Elliott Morgan, MGM librarian and Cukor's friend, recalled. "By the time the servant had gone around and served the last person, his plate was already empty. That made everybody else rush, which was a pity, because he served delicious food."

According to writer George Eells, who met Cukor when Eells was *Look*'s entertainment editor, "Despite the fact that George had two maids serving, he would often be so impatient that he might jump up and serve, to get things going." Eells once took to Cukor's a friend who was interested in a screen career. "He had some talent, and I thought George could give him some tips. But it turned out to be a disaster because he ate very slowly. George said afterwards, 'You know, your friend ate slowly just to annoy me.'

"He was a wonderful host except that he wasn't a drinker," noted Eells. "It was annoying to some people as he offered only one drink. George would have one drink, but it was merely to be polite." Cukor believed that people didn't behave well after a couple of drinks and that it "dulled down the conversation." He proudly boasted that there were few Jewish alcoholics.

If the food was usually good, the wine was terrible. Cukor's friends offered different explanations of this "anomaly" in an otherwise class act. Some maintained that because he didn't drink, he wasn't sensitive to the wine's quality, but others claimed it derived from his frugality. [The wine was always served in carafes, so that the guests would be unable to tell its price.] "Guests would be either amused or horrified," one friend noted. "It was the cheapest wine you could get. It was always a puzzle to me because the food was uniformly delicious."

Hans Kohler first met Cukor in 1940, when he came to L.A. with a letter of introduction from a mutual Austrian friend. He talked to Cukor's secretary and, a few days later, was invited to MGM, where Cukor was shooting *A Woman's Face*. "He let me watch the moviemaking process, which was fascinating to me. That was the beginning of a friendship which only ended when George died."

Kohler was trained as a lawyer, then took up medical studies. After the war he became Cukor's dermatologist, and Cukor occasionally consulted with him about other health matters. Cukor was proud of Kohler because he had been an Army officer as well as a lawyer and later a physician: "George liked ambitious people who achieved." Indeed, though the range of people entertained in his house was diverse, at heart Cukor was a snob. His visitors had to be distinguished in some respect. Three kinds of distinction were particularly appealing: wealth, noble origins and good upbringing, and professional achievement.

Few of Cukor's friends liked Lady Juliet Duff, the only child of the fourth earl of Lonsdale, but he went out of his way to see her whenever he was in London. A noted figure of Edwardian society Lady Duff could have been Cukor's mother, but he was awed by the luminaries, Winston Churchill, General de Gaulle, Jean Cocteau, Picasso, Stravinsky, Arthur Rubinstein, he could meet at her salon.

"As a host and guest," said writer James Leo Herlihy, "Cukor played to the ones he wanted and ignored those he didn't care about. He knew his power and how to play it." The only exception to this rule were young gay men, preferably blond, and it helped if they had good education and good manners.

But Cukor was "hundred percent reliable if you were his friend," said Kohler. "You could always come to him." Los Angeles *Times* critic Kevin Thomas recalled that when he met Katharine Hepburn on the set of *Guess Who's Coming to Dinner?* and Cukor's name came up, she said, "When Cukor is your friend, you *really* have a friend." Thomas said: "The words 'loyalty' and 'friendship' had meaning for him." Cukor's intimate friendships, said producer Allan Davis, were based on "trust and regard." He showed respect for people's careers and the sacrifices made to maintain them. "George understood better than anyone else work schedules and pressures," Thomas allowed.

Cukor's friends singled out the fact that he was discreet and didn't like to "divulge in nasty gossip." According to Davis, "He didn't like vicious gossip and hated actors' bitchery." Davis wanted to introduce Cukor to actress Coral Browne, known for her witty tongue, but the director dismissed her as a gossiper. However, director Arthur Lubin, who also attended his salon, claimed that "mostly what George and his guests did in those Sunday evenings was criticize others in the movie business."

At his dinners Cukor excelled as a witty raconteur, favoring "cross-examining" stories. Restless, he moved around a great deal in the course of the evening. Don Bachardy recalled that he often asked Cukor questions about his work and that he was always "full of insights." Cukor's comments about movies or actors struck his friends as "very precise and very sound."

Cukor couldn't tolerate any kind of complaining—from his actors or his friends. Thus, he was critical of MGM veteran actor Lewis Stone because he pouted a lot on the set. Herlihy held that Cukor "didn't want any browbeating, any sense of suffering, any display of pain in his house. He recalled a hot summer day when one of the guests complained about the humidity and traffic. Cukor listened patiently, then said, "So what are you going to do about it?"

"Well, I can't do anything about it," the embarrassed guest said.

"Precisely!" Cukor retorted. "Now, let's get on with the evening."

Signe Hasso remembered: "George never complained. If I'd complain about something, he'd say, 'Oh, that's hogwash,' or 'Don't be stupid, don't pay attention to what *they* say, just go ahead and do what *you* think you should do.' "

According to some friends, Cukor was superficial in his socializing. He never liked to get "too deep" or "too personal." However, on one occasion Cukor asked Herlihy about his work as a writer. "I was pretty candidly open about my writing problems," Herlihy said, "but George was taken aback, and said, 'I should think that you should be ashamed to admit this.' "

Kohler met with Cukor alone and with his entourage. "A great many of his friends were in the entertainment field, and they were talking about movie stars, of whom I didn't know much," Kohler noted. "Cukor talked about theater and film, but he was also very knowledgeable about Victorian literature. He liked his guests to discuss literature, art—not just movies." Cukor conceded he had no feeling for poetry—"I just don't get it." As a reader he was interested in biographies about people's lives; always suspicious, he favored facts over fiction.

"Cukor would decide whether or not he would be the center of conversation," recalled Herlihy. "It all depended on his whim and mood that night." According to Kohler, "When George was talking, he didn't like other people to make conversation. If he had something interesting to say or of he was explaining something, he disliked other people talking at the same time. He didn't like interference."

Cukor often surrounded himself with "good listeners." Friends suspected that Cukor liked his rich but boring neighbor Harris Woods because he knew that whatever he said, Woods would nod in agreement. Woods was an easy companion, who always answered the way he was expected to. Said Kohler: "I was a much better listener than talker. George liked that."

From his childhood Cukor excelled in carrying on a witty conversation—with anybody. It proved a useful talent in Hollywood, where socializing is integral to the business. But it was also useful to him as a host. "He had a special gift for conversation and for social situations," said

Herlihy. As Cukor aged, his memory began to wan, but he never lost his sharp tongue. Gary Essert, cofounder of the international film festival called Filmex, recalled that Cukor was incredibly bright and incredibly witty with language. "I could be carrying on a conversation with him, and there would be people talking on the other side of the room. And suddenly George would just turn his head away and make the most witty line to them because he had heard what they were talking about."

An "acquisitive" person, Cukor continued to enlarge his art collection. In 1942 he bought a Braque painting, "Still Life," for $3,700, and in 1944 Georges Rouault's "Le Maillot Rose" (The Pink Tights) painted in gouache in 1917, for $1,230. Cukor joked about the fascination art held for him and how he couldn't resist adding to his collection, relating how he purchased a 1929 ink drawing by Henri Matisse or a Rodin bronze head of a woman.

The theater and its interiors always had a great appeal for him. That is why he owned so many paintings and drawings on the theater. A particularly favorite was "At the Matinee" by Giovanni Boldini. Simone Signoret observed that there was no projection room at Cukor's house, but a collection of photographs made his little Victorian drawing rooms look like a still *cinémathèque*.

Asked to describe his house for *Flair* magazine, Cukor began with his sleeping quarters. His bedroom was small, no bigger than a sleeping porch, because he believed that most bedrooms were "uselessly large." Three sides of the room were made completely of glass and overlooked the garden. The curtains were green, of handwoven mohair. Everything in the room was functional. The furnishings included a rubber-tired cart with two shelves for books, scripts, a thermos bottle, fruit, a paper knife, and scissors. Cukor often worked and napped in his bedroom. All he had to do was shut the door, "not to feel the life of the house swirling around me."

The upholstered furniture was slipcovered for his comfort. The paintings and photographs on the walls were changed from time to time. Aldous Huxley once used a misquotation of Psalms 69:9 to describe the constant rebuilding of the house: "For the zeal of *mine* house hath eaten me up." The most beautiful view, overlooking Hollywood, was from the bathroom. His guests were known to take very long showers!

As much as Cukor enjoyed entertaining, he liked to be invited to Hollywood's literary salons, like the soirees at Salka Viertel's in Santa Monica. Throughout the war years Viertel and husband director Berthold held a salon for the creative people in L.A. It was there that Cukor could meet in the same evening Christopher Isherwood, Aldous Huxley, Anita Loos, Thomas Mann, Bertolt Brecht.

*   *   *

There was some talk about involving Cukor, left without a project, in *The Blue Bird*, with Shirley Temple. But Cukor feuded with Fox's Darryl Zanuck about the screenplay. "Cloud-cuckoo-land," he mourned; "of all forms of cinema waste, the most extreme is tossing away talent." Even calloused souls with antipathy for child players complained about those choosing Temple's projects. The film was finally made by Walter Lang, but ironically, in 1976, Cukor directed another version of *The Blue Bird*.

Looking for a movie, Cukor came across a Swedish film in which Ingrid Bergman portrayed a woman whose scarred face embitters her into a life of crime. Intrigued by the character, he mentioned it to Joan Crawford, who immediately became interested in playing the role. Louis B. was horrified: "Do you want the public to see you ugly?" But sensing her persistence, this time fully supported by Cukor, the powerful studio chief said: "Go ahead, if you want to destroy your career."

Crawford applied herself uncompromisingly to the role of Anna Holm in *A Woman's Face*. While Jack Dawn devised a horrific makeup for her face, Cukor infused her with the psychology of a disfigured woman. He suggested that Crawford rely on the scar as a prop, the way actors used artificial noses. Cukor rehearsed her mercilessly, impatiently waiting for her to assume the hopeless fatigue that such disfigurement would engender. Whenever he thought she was lapsing into her customary glamour routines, he imitated Lon Chaney's Hunchback of Notre Dame off camera. He was funny, but he also made his point.

The Swedish setting was inexplicably retained in the American version. The first part of the film is interesting: a character study of a stigmatized woman taking out her bitterness on the world. But in the second half the story changes gears, describing her spiritual transformation after a plastic surgeon (Melvyn Douglas) heals her face, turning her into a good person who wants to live down her past and become a governess.

Cukor was embarrassed by the second part because it turned the story into conventional melodrama. In the first, Anna Holm is a real character, but as soon as she regains her looks, she becomes Joan Crawford. Viewers could actually see touches of the movie queen gradually sneak in: artificial eyelashes, lifted breasts.

The first sequence was also the most risqué that Cukor ever got past the censors in showing a gay theme. The decadent ambiance of a restaurant, used as a front for a criminal gang, is established with a shot of two lesbians dancing together.

Cukor always stressed the manner in which women made their entrances in his movies; it was a theatrical convention carried over from his stage career. In *A Woman's Face* the camera cuts to a dark stairway with Crawford coming down. The camera holds back from her face as she walks, then suddenly reveals her scarred face.

Cukor was concerned about the courtroom scene in which Anna reveals her story. The text was so dramatic there was no need for Crawford to do any acting or show any self-pity. Wishing to steer clear of melodrama, Cukor instructed her to play it as if she were reading the telephone book. When this ploy didn't work, Cukor asked her just to speak the lines as if she were saying the multiplication table. Crawford tried, but again Cukor said: "No, no, no, it's still got emotion. I want no emotion at all, just say it." It took many takes, but she finally rendered the dreary monotone he was seeking.

Opening on May 16, 1941, *A Woman's Face* received mixed reviews and failed at the box office. For Cukor, however, the major reward was his having coaxed out of Crawford one of her best performances.

After successfully teaming on *Camille*, Cukor looked for other projects with Garbo. One day, trying to dig up a story for Garbo, Salka Viertel, who had written some of her scripts, said in her rich *alt Wien* accent: "These are the qualities necessary for a good Garbo movie: comedy, tragedy, box office, sex appeal, and nothing bourgeois!"

Cukor agreed with Garbo that no matter what the film did, they must have a finished script. There was some talk about *Madame Curie,* a biopicture of the French scientist. Aldous Huxley, perceived by Cukor as a distinguished author, was enthusiastic about the project. Huxley was a good choice, being well informed on the scientific and human aspects of the story.

However, Cukor's next film with Garbo, the comedy *Two-Faced Woman,* turned out to be a dismal experience. World War II broke out, and the closing of the European market, where Garbo was always popular, made another picture with her risky, especially at her high salary. Hoping to make Garbo more "accessible" with American audiences, Cukor talked her into playing a part not suitable to her talents. He reasoned that Garbo had played tragedy and comedy. Why not stretch and try a "typical" American girl?

Seeing the film as a "frothy and light entertainment," Cukor tried to make it "gay and funny." The story (previously known as *The Twins*), based on the old formula of mistaken identity, was silly. Publisher Larry Blake (Melvyn Douglas) goes to a ski resort, where he meets and then marries Karin (Garbo), a ski instructor. He promises to give up his sophisticated New York life, but his ex-flame, Griselda (Constance Bennett), plots to get him back. Realizing she can't compete with the glamorous Griselda, Karin decides to impersonate her own twin, a worldy-wise woman.

In the tradition of "Garbo Talks" and "Garbo Laughs," MGM's publicity machine announced that in her new movie "Garbo plays a dual role, swims, wears a new hairdo, dances Rumba, skis, and even wrestles."

In her first publicity stills since 1929, Garbo displayed her boyish physique in a bathing suit—but not before holding up production for a couple of days when Cukor insisted on filming her emerging from a pool. Scorning Adrian's fancy design, Garbo designed her own bathing suit. Cukor managed to relax Garbo enough so that to everyone's surprise, she allowed the crew to watch even her more intimate scenes.

The critics were in agreement that there was no excuse for the film's tedious repetition and distasteful heartlessness. "Open the windows, Messrs. Cukor, Behrman, et al.," wrote one critic. "This is 1942, and Theda Bara's golden age is gone." Cukor's *Two-Faced Woman* became Garbo's twenty-seventh and last film.

The film caused a run-in between MGM and Joseph Breen. In June 1941, when the first eighty-four pages of the incomplete script were submitted, the dialogue was found to be full of sexually suggestive inferences. A line like "If you got snowed in with Karin, you'd be married, too," was not approved. The office also wanted to omit the scene in which Blake takes a shower because of its sexual flavor. Their embrace on the bed was objectionable, too: Neither could be seen in a horizontal position.

But since the script was sent to Breen's office in segments, it became difficult to render an opinion about its overall acceptability. Cukor knew that the drinking had to be kept down to a minimum; he was reminded of the numerous protests about *The Philadelphia Story*. There were other objections: Karin's line "I have no past before last night" was questionable; it took place in the morning after their reunion, giving it a decidedly suggestive flavor.

The script was sent in sections because nobody—least of all Cukor—knew how the tale was going to end. When the picture was finally submitted for review, it was approved with the elimination of one line. But then Cukor did considerable retakes, and the Production Code Administration demanded to see them. On October 6, after reviewing the picture, Breen issued his approval.

Cukor still had to face the more conservative Legion of Decency, which condemned the "immoral" movie for its un-Christian attitude toward marriage, suggestive scenes, dialogues, and costumes. This time the PCA supported Cukor, claiming the story was about the preservation of marriage as a permanent institution: "the wife came to recognize the proper relationship between a husband and wife and went back to him."

A telegram from MGM to the legion's office, on December 5, made the case for leaving *Two-Faced Woman* intact. "Pictures have been so cleaned up," stated the memo, "that they are becoming uninteresting. There are groups who would remove all the spice of life and make this world a very drab place to live." On December 17 the legion reviewed Cukor's revised version and voted to lift the movie from the C (condemned) list. Controversial publicity of this kind was hoped to be a pull. It was not.

Perceived as "disastrous" at the time, *Two-Faced Woman* was reevaluated in later years. Like *Sylvia Scarlett*, the movie enjoys a higher regard today, holding up better than other Garbo vehicles. Contrary to popular opinion, it does not feature Garbo's worst performance. Still, Cukor regretted asking Garbo to do such a light comedy: "I'm still not sure, whether or not I was responsible for the complete lack of success of this film."

On the plus side, *Two-Faced Woman* saw the beginning of a new friendship with Ruth Gordon and Garson Kanin, who in the next decade became Cukor's closest friends and collaborators. He had first received a note of praise from the Kanins about the greatness of *The Philadelphia Story*. Then Gordon was cast in the Garbo film in a secondary role.

Fearful of flying, Gordon asked for Cukor's permission to take a train to Hollywood—making her late by a few days—and he consented. At the end of the shoot she praised Cukor for being "the finest magician." Not only had he pulled a rabbit out of an impossible old hat, but he had turned it into a knockout rabbit. Cukor was now admired for his "chaperonage" and for making her look elegant in Adrian's couture. Considering how bad she looked in the tests, his transformation of her was no minor achievement.

Whenever the Kanins were in town, Cukor was ready for a party. As was his habit, he felt more relaxed and spent more time with Gordon than with Kanin. "Honey" or "Dream Boy" was the way Gordon addressed Cukor, always sending him humorous notes about gifts he had given her. One, a bottle of perfume, made her want to go "the pace that kills." When she visited him alone, they had nights on the town with Tallulah Bankhead, going from one party to another and screaming in laughter to the point of losing their voices. Tallulah was fun, but she often misbehaved; on one occasion Cukor ordered a taxicab and sent the noisy and drunk Bankhead home.

Cukor's next film, *Her Cardboard Lover,* proved as ill starred as the Garbo film. It became Norma Shearer's swan song, just as *Two-Faced Woman* had been Garbo's. Although Cukor had directed *Her Cardboard Lover* as a stage vehicle for Jeanne Eagels and Laurette Taylor in the 1920s, the creaky French farce didn't engage his interest anymore.

The movie was the last of a six-picture deal that Shearer, now at a crucial phase of her career, had signed with Metro after Thalberg's death. Louis B. tried to persuade Shearer to do a more timely film, but the star was offended when he said, "This is 1942, not 1922." For his part, Cukor was delighted that Shearer asked for his services; he desperately needed an assignment.

Cukor knew that comedy was not Shearer's strong suit, but as in the past, they got on extremely well. He let her come up with her "inspirations," though he wouldn't tolerate her overacting. It was always easier for him to tone down an excessive performance than to ask for more. "Please, Mr. Cukor, let's call it a day," Shearer suggested one day after hours of shooting.

"One more scene," said the indefatigable director. "Remember, you're supposed to be exhausted in this shot!"

Ultimately Cukor's direction was a wasted effort, producing no great performances. The critics agreed that Shearer overacted and lacked comic finesse; she herself dismissed the picture as one of her lesser ones. But Shearer gave full credit to Cukor for being "helpful and clever with ideas." She said: "He was a gentleman, always talked things over with me first; never tried to push anything on me."

The film's failure signaled Shearer's retirement from the screen. Working with three grand movie queens, Crawford, Garbo, and Shearer, and producing three failures in a row was not easy to digest even for a director with a track record like Cukor.

In 1942 Donald Ogden Stewart sent Cukor his adaptation of an unpublished novel by I. A. R. Wylie, *Keeper of the Flame*. It dealt with a woman whose life is distorted by her continuing love-hate relationship with her dead husband. MGM was not thrilled with the choice as a follow-up to Hepburn's success in *Woman of the Year*, but she persuaded the studio to make the film with Spencer Tracy.

Hepburn had just met and fallen in love with Tracy on the set of *Woman of the Year*. Her ambition was to find good scripts for the two of them; it was also an effective way to keep an eye on the boozy Tracy. Hepburn soon became Tracy's secretary, companion, chauffeur, and nurse. She drove him to the studio and stayed on the set even when not needed. At the end of a working day she drove him home and cooked dinner. Tracy and Hepburn were not cast as lovers in the film; Tracy had a much bigger part, but she didn't mind. An added inducement to do the film was the fact that Cukor agreed to direct.

Cukor's last project before his military service, *Keeper of the Flame* was his first and only film with an explicit political message. "The screen is a powerful factor for the expression of those ideals in which we believe and today are fighting for," Cukor said in one of his rare political statements. It was a suspense mystery that also spoke "the truth of democracy and Americanism." Stewart, who had become politically active after the start of World War II, stuffed the script with strong anti-Fascist messages.

Tracy plays a journalist who sets out to write the biography of Robert Forrest, a leader he admired. Refusing to cooperate, Forrest's widow

(Hepburn) puts obstacles in his path. As it turns out, she's trying to conceal that her husband headed a vast secret organization that was going to turn the country over to fascism. Made during a period of undercover fascism in the United States, the film was filled with contemporary references to hero worship, the effects of leaders on youth, and strong speeches about patriotism.

Considering that the book was portentous, the unfolding of the mystery onscreen was well done. Cukor built a strong atmosphere for *Keeper of the Flame*, using an interesting Gothic style. He almost managed to conceal the fraudulent story, but then it disappointingly resorted to melodramatics—a fire, chase, noble death. The whole film had a "waxwork quality" because everything was shot on the sound stage.

Christine, the mysterious widow, was Hepburn's first mature screen woman. She looked beautiful, but she spoke in a mournful manner and "suffered" too much. "Kate had to float in, wearing a long white gown and carrying a bunch of lilies," Cukor said in her defense. "That's awfully tricky." But he also conceded that her performance was a bit phony, what with those long, piercing looks at the portrait of her husband.

Keeper of the Flame was the first—and weakest—movie Spencer Tracy, MGM's most respected actor, made with Cukor. Tracy went on to make five more movies with Cukor—the most he made with any director. Although Tracy gave a monotonous performance, Cukor praised him for playing a difficult part, specifically for "plugging all that integrity and honesty."

The impressive supporting cast included Frank Craven, Donald Meek, and Howard da Silva. Best of all was Margaret Wycherly, who, as Forrest's mother, played the madness scenes so hauntingly that the viewers almost forgot the melodrama she was in.

Whenever possible, Cukor liked to get new people into his movies. In this one Percy Kilbride, who later became Pa Kettle in the popular film series *Ma and Pa Kettle*, made his debut as a taxi driver. "I have always rejoiced coaching untried performers," Cukor said, "and do not prefer to work exclusively with established actors, as has sometimes been said." (In the next decades Cukor launched the screen careers of such actors as Angela Lansbury [*Gaslight*], Judy Holliday [*Winged Victory*], Tom Ewell, Jean Hagen, and David Wayne [all in *Adam's Rib*], Anthony Perkins [*The Actress*], Aldo Ray [*The Marrying Kind*], Jack Lemmon [*It Should Happen to You*], Capucine [*Song Without End*], and Meg Ryan [*Rich and Famous*].)

By 1943 most of Cukor's colleagues—John Ford, George Stevens, Frank Capra—were in the military, but it was not easy for him to go. Cukor was in the midst of shooting *Keeper of the Flame*, "an important picture in a propaganda way," when the other directors were enlisted.

In July 1942 Cukor spoke to Major W. J. Keighley, the Washington representative of the First Motion Picture Unit, who was in charge of the applications for commissions. At his physical examination at March Field, Cukor's eyes were found below standard for combat. Cukor complained to MGM's publicity head, Howard Strickling, that his papers hadn't arrived. Conflicting stories disquieted him: after an order to report for induction in September, he received a deferment for sixty days. Unable to enlist on his own, Cukor asked for the assistance of David Selznick and Spencer Tracy.

In September Selznick sent a strong letter on Cukor's behalf to Major Keighley. Having known Cukor for ten years as an employee and friend, Selznick unhesitatingly recommended him as a man of the most splendid character and of extraordinary intelligence, readily adaptable to any work, and gifted with qualities of personality and leadership. Selznick thought Cukor, one of the industry's most able directors, with unquestioned "integrity and patriotism," would make an excellent officer in any branch connected with the making of motion pictures.

Selznick's letter was followed with one from Tracy to Colonel Melvin E. Gillette at the Signal Corps Photographic Center in New York. Tracy stressed Cukor's knack for "handling" difficult people and so well that they didn't realize they were being handled, a quality that could be put to use in the Army. Cukor's boundless energy and quick mind could add to his potentialities as an officer. In short, as a man with great understanding of human nature, Cukor would be of inestimable value to the Army.

On October 21, 1942, Cukor finally started basic training at Camp Edison. He was then assigned to the Signal Corps Photographic Center in Astoria, Queens. He worked on a number of training films until he passed the Army's age ceiling and was discharged.

Ever since Cukor directed gossiper Hedda Hopper in *The Women,* he had gone out of his way to be cordial to her, fearing the power of her tongue. Cukor corresponded with Hopper during the war. He once teasingly warned her that if she published one of his more private stories, he would be ruined, but with his "dying gasp" he would tell the world why she, a girl named Elda Fury, had to leave Altoona, Pennsylvania.

For her part, Hopper confessed that she got "hell" for what she had written about Cukor's wild parties at the St. Regis Hotel. She declared her greatest admiration and regard for him, but also conceded that as a newspaperwoman with a regular column to fill, she was always after good stories. If he didn't come out of this war a major general, Hopper teased, she wouldn't speak to him; the rank of private simply didn't become Cukor.

Hopper reported to Cukor that Hollywood went on living in much the same way; all the shenanigans over the Oscars were just the same. She resented the kind of awful pitch director Mervyn LeRoy had put on to get the Oscar for *Random Harvest*. He had apparently called up in person dozens of people and asked them to vote for him. "Isn't that disgusting!" declared Hopper. "If I wanted an Oscar so badly, I think I'd go out and earn one, won't you?" Inadvertently Hopper managed to offend Cukor, who at this point had not yet won an Oscar.

Rumors that Cukor's difficulties in enlisting and his release after a short time were due to his homosexuality could not be confirmed. There are also different opinions about the general extent to which Cukor's career suffered as a result of his homosexuality. "There was always a double standard in Hollywood," Lambert said. "George was talented and very successful; most of his movies did well. People were very nice and polite to him. But that, of course, wouldn't stop them from gossiping about him when he left the room. After some conference with executives they might say, 'that old faggot.' "

But Lambert didn't think Cukor's homosexuality had any effect on his assignments. Lambert once asked Cukor if there were any films he wanted to do and couldn't do. "He mentioned a couple of things, but that didn't have anything to do with his gayness." Cukor wished to direct *Escape*, a movie assigned to Mervyn LeRoy, because he was interested in the figure of the actress, played by his friend Alla Nazimova. But he was turned down by the studio simply because he hadn't done a thriller before.

It was only in the late 1960s, according to Lambert, that Cukor became really open about his homosexuality: "He felt it was in the air." Lambert explained: "George had grown up and functioned in the era when you had to be very careful about what you said; he was conditioned by the time he came to fame, when you had to be absolutely discreet. That context almost pushed you to the hustler scene; it was hard to keep a gay relationship under that pressure."

Indeed, Cukor didn't make close friends of other gay directors. Lambert remembered that when they were talking about James Whale (*Frankenstein*), Cukor was "surprisingly cool." Lambert got the feeling that he had something against Whale. "You didn't like him?" asked Lambert. "Well, you know," Cukor said, "he was too indiscreet." Lambert said: "Of course, Whale lived openly with a producer for several years, and that's what George meant."

Lambert said that Cukor and Arthur Lubin (*Phantom of the Opera*) were not close friends either but were amicable. There was also coolness toward Irving Rapper (*Now Voyager*), whom Cukor had met back in Rochester. When Lambert mentioned Rapper once, "George simply froze."

Cukor always felt more comfortable around women, particularly rich socialites. "It was absolutely all right to be gay in Hollywood," Cukor once told Lambert, "as long as you were not living with a man. In fact, you were often very useful socially, as a desirable bachelor, the single man needed for the party." Cukor always escorted female companions to public events, premieres, benefits. Longtime friend Frances Goldwyn became a regular escort in the 1970s, especially after Goldwyn's death. But he also went to parties by himself. Said Lambert: "Whether they were large parties or small dinners, you would just invite George by himself."

CHAPTER SIX:

Up and Down and Up, 1944–49

CUKOR'S MILITARY SERVICE LASTED ONLY TWENTY-NINE WEEKS AND five days. On July 9, 1943, Metro informed him that his employment had been suspended for the duration of his service. Except for that, the old contract was not changed.

One of the projects Cukor lost because of the war was a musical. Producer Arthur Freed originally assigned Cukor to direct *Meet Me in St. Louis* with Judy Garland. The musical was handed instead to Vincente Minnelli, then a beginning director. In the future Cukor lost other valuable projects (*Gigi* in 1958) to Minnelli, who emerged as one of MGM's top directors.

Upon his release from the Army, Cukor's first assignment at Metro was *Gaslight,* based on the 1938 English hit play. On Broadway it was called *Angel Street* and enjoyed a run of two years. MGM bought the rights to the 1940 British film *Angel Street,* starring Anton Walbrook and Diana Wynyard, and withdrew it from circulation for fear of competition.

Gaslight became one of Cukor's best pictures. His version was thirty minutes longer, and marked by rich detail, had a more substantial narrative and greater psychological depth, than the British. The superbly crafted script was cowritten by John Van Druten, who was strong in dialogue, and Walter Reisch, who excelled in plot construction. Moving the narrative out of the confines of the stage, *Gaslight* became one of Cukor's most disguised adaptations of a play.

Set in 1885, the story chronicles Gregory Anton's wooing of and marriage to Paula, who has inherited the mansion of Anton's murder victim, singer Alice Alquest. Upon their return from idyllic honeymoon, Anton

(Charles Boyer) sets out to drive his rich wife (played by Ingrid Bergman) insane so that he can conveniently put her in an institution. The title derives from the gas jet in the bedroom, which ominously dims whenever Anton turns on the lamp in the attic, in search of the jewels.

In the best Hitchcockian tradition, Cukor early tips off the audience to Anton's duplicity and sordid scheme. Because this vital information is given away before the heroine finds out, the suspense in *Gaslight* is prolonged. The tension builds steadily to a climax in which Paula finds out that her husband has never had any genuine feelings for her. Cukor also hints at Anton's perverse fetishism for jewelry, a notion that was ahead of its time.

A noir thriller, *Gaslight* belongs to a cycle of films that could be labeled "Don't Trust Your Husband/Lover" and include *Rebecca* (1940) and *Suspicion* (1941). One of *Gaslight*'s unanticipated effects that amused Cukor was the expression "Don't you gaslight me," meaning "Don't try to drive me crazy."

Since *Gaslight* was an indoor film set mostly at night, Cukor used dark and claustrophobic sets. He successfully created a mood of paranoia, with the house becoming a trap of terror, menacing in all its clutter. Cukor requested that Paul Huldschinsky, a German refugee, design the sets. Along with Huldschinsky, Edwin Willis is credited as set designer; their creations are an example of the dazzling resources of the big studios. Cukor didn't have to go out and get any of the period pieces; they all were there. "You just had to take a firm stand and get the right personnel to work with you," Cukor told Lambert. "Once you made it clear what you wanted and how desperately you wanted it, the studio would go for it."

Selznick didn't interfere much in the making of the film, even though the two stars, Ingrid Bergman and Joseph Cotten, were under contract to him. Both actors complained to Cukor about Selznick's rigid hand, perceiving themselves, as Cotten noted, as "slaves bound in golden chains." Selznick actually praised Cukor's meticulous attention to atmosphere and made only one suggestion: a retake of the final sequence, to emphasize Paula's release from bondage.

Cukor had met Ingrid Bergman when he tested her for *Intermezzo*, her first American film. Upon her arrival in Hollywood, Bergman sent flowers to her compatriot Garbo, whom she long admired. But Garbo's thank-you note came only days before Bergman left town, making it impossible for them to meet. Knowing they were friends, she asked Cukor about Garbo's strange behavior. "But of course," Cukor told Bergman, "Greta wouldn't have sent the telegram unless she were certain you were leaving."

Cukor arranged for Bergman to visit a mental hospital in preparation for her role. To sustain tension on the set, he told her the point of each and every scene. It was his habit to talk with actors between takes, to "keep them at a pitch," stimulate them for the next scene. When he first approached Bergman with his talk, she froze him with a cold Swedish stare. "You know," she said, "I'm not stupid, you told me that before."

"I'm sorry," said Cukor, and walked away. Bergman had him so spooked that when he had something important to say, he was afraid to.

A few days later Margaret Booth, MGM's cutter, complained to Cukor that Bergman was underacting. Cukor saw her point and, before the next take, burst into Bergman's room and told her what he had been holding back for some time. Moments after storming out, he went back and told her *again*. "Piss on that!" he said to himself. "Damn it, she's got to get used to the way *I* work. Actors have to listen."

Bergman did listen and won her first Oscar under Cukor's guidance. Bergman could hardly express herself in any language, but she was grateful to Cukor for his "help and understanding of my poor Paula." *Gaslight* enhanced Bergman's reputation as Hollywood's most popular actress; Hitchcock was so taken with her that he cast her in *Spellbound* and *Notorious*.

But Cukor's casting coup was a young British girl, Angela Lansbury, in the important role of Nancy, the conniving maid who attempts to lure Anton away from his wife. Writer Van Druten told Cukor, looking for a girl to play the sluttish maid, of a British actress, Moyna MacGill, who was in town with her daughter, Angela, and her two sons. The entire family was working at Bullock's in the Christmas rush.

Cukor asked Lansbury for a test, which was excellent. She had the right poise, and her cockney accent was authentic. But she was too young and didn't seem sexy enough. Overweight and spotty, Lansbury looked like a salesclerk. "I don't think you're going to get the job," Cukor told her, "but I think you're a very talented girl." Lansbury went back to Bullock's with a mixed reaction of dejection and encouragement.

A week later Cukor looked at Lansbury's test again and called her in for a second audition, which turned out to be even better. In the end Cukor liked her so much that he had her role rewritten and expanded. When Lansbury told her manager at Bullock's that she had found a better job, he proposed to raise her pay to twenty-seven dollars a week. He was shocked when she said that Mr. Cukor at MGM had signed her for a seven-year-contract at five hundred dollars a week!

There were some unanticipated problems with Lansbury, however. At five feet eight she was as tall as Bergman. To add to her height and contribute to the suspense of the scene in which she threatens Paula, Cukor made her wear platform shoes. "They thought my towering over

Ingrid would make me more sinister," recalled Lansbury. Another unexpected problem was a scene in which she lights a cigarette in defiance of her mistress. This scene was postponed until Lansbury had her eighteenth birthday; the studio's teacher would not allow her to smoke until then. When this eagerly awaited day arrived, Cukor and Bergman threw a surprise party for her.

Cukor later said that Lansbury was the only other actress aside from Hepburn who took to film so quickly. Even though *Gaslight* was her first picture, he said, she had the "ability to transform herself into the character she was playing as soon as the cameras turned." Ordinary-looking, Lansbury became the character by just drooping her mouth. "Some people have experience, but still remain eternal amateurs," Cukor elaborated, "but Angela was a pro from the very first day." Lansbury's stunning debut certified her talent and honored her with the first of three Oscar nominations. "I was really very young," recalled Lansbury in a tribute to Cukor, "and I didn't know my ass from a hole in the ground. George introduced me to style."

A huge box-office hit, *Gaslight* was nominated for eight Oscars, including Best Picture, though Cukor failed again to receive a nomination. The movie won two awards: Best Actress for Bergman and Best Art Direction for Cedric Gibbons.

Cukor's next movie, *Winged Victory,* was just a chore that unsurprisingly became one of his least distinguished endeavors. Moss Hart, who wrote and directed the stage version, wanted to acquaint the public with the Army Air Force's indomitable spirit. To gather material, Hart put on a cadet's uniform and set out on a jaunt by bomber that covered every phase in a pilot's training.

Lon McCallister, cast as one of the cadets, recalled that the picture was a trying experience for him as well as for Cukor. "We were both replacements. William Wyler had originally been announced to direct, but George was released from the Army before Wyler returned to civilian life."

In May 1944 the Broadway cast arrived in Hollywood to make the movie. The entire crew, including technicians and set designers, was recruited from the ranks of the Army Air Force. But the studio needed box-office insurance, so they added Jeanne Crain and McCallister to the cast after the success of their film *Home in Indiana* that year. McCallister was the only man in the film who had not been in the original show.

The film had very few roles for women, and those mostly mothers and sweethearts. One was played by Judy Holliday, who in the next decade became Cukor's quintessential actress, appearing in five of his movies. The first time Cukor heard about her was when Darryl Zanuck mentioned "these clever kids," Adolph Green, Betty Comden, and Judy Holliday, from New York's Greenwich Village. But Zanuck couldn't convince anyone to use them.

First tested by Cukor for one of the housewife roles, Holiday was heavily made up and dressed in clothes she thought a movie star should wear. Cukor thought she was decidedly not the "motion-picture type but pretty in an odd way." Holliday had little acting experience, but her phrasing was poignant, moving, and intensely personal. "Can you do this again?" asked Cukor. Holliday did and landed the part.

The premiere, held at the Grauman Chinese Theater, on December 27, 1944, was attended by high-ranking military officers. One thousand grandstand seats, the most ever, were erected in the theater's forecourt for the festive gala, with antiaircraft searchlights used to augment the regular studio lights.

Cukor came into the project with little preparation. "It would have been a better picture if he had been given more time to work with Hart," said McCallister. "The brilliance of *A Star Is Born*, in 1954, proved the value of their complete collaboration."

While Cukor was shooting *Winged Victory,* Selznick asked for his help. He was not pleased with the work of director William Dieterle on *I'll Be Seeing You,* an overblown production in which Ginger Rogers plays a convict who, at home on parole, falls in love with a disturbed soldier (played by Joseph Cotten). Zanuck was especially dissatisfied with a sobbing scene between Rogers and Shirley Temple. Selznick wrote a replacement scene, and Cukor was brought in to direct. Dieterle had featured Rogers at the actress's insistence, but Cukor's direction favored Temple.

Kneeling at Rogers's bedside, Temple began to blurt her sad emotional confession of how she tattled to her boyfriend that Rogers was a convict. Suddenly Cukor shouted, "Where did you learn this business?" Without waiting for an answer, he added, "That's awful!" Removing his horn-rimmed glasses and letting both arms hang limp, he stared helplessly at the door.

It was the first time a director had "openly declared me a dunce," Temple observed, and that it came from someone of Cukor's stature was even more humiliating. "Look," Temple said, "all you want is a good cry. Give me five minutes and you'll get a good cry."

"Cry, nothing," Cukor retorted. "I want emotion, not tears." There was complete silence on the set.

The next try resulted in another Cukor explosion of dismay. "Unnerved by his violent reaction," Temple recalled, "whatever capacity I had for emotional versatility simply vanished." Angered by his bullying direction and frustrated by her failure to please, she said her lines with an increasingly hysterical inflection. By the twelfth take both Cukor and the actress were exhausted. To Temple's surprise, Cukor put his arm around her affectionately and told her he had finally got what he wanted. "Harange and insult the woman," she observed, "that was his way of getting results."

Never before had Temple been bullied into an emotional reaction, let alone delivered a better performance because of it. To this day Temple believes that with each successive verbal buffeting she produced a less convincing result and that Cukor picked her worst rendition. Critics, however, sided with the director. Applauding her final scene, Elsa Maxwell noted "a remarkable metamorphosis of a performer, who, frankly, used to bore me with her glibness."

In 1944 Somerset Maugham's agent gave Cukor a new manuscript called *The Razor's Edge*. "Willie's written this thing," he said, "and wants you to read it." Cukor read the story and immediately became interested in making a movie. The same night he happened to be at a party at Zanuck's where he saw Orson Welles. "I'm not really an educated man," Cukor overheard Welles saying, "and I wish I were. I'd love to read *The Odyssey* in the original Greek and the Bible in the original Hebrew."

"That's strange." Cukor thought, "Where have I heard that before?" He suddenly remembered it was from Larry's speech in *The Razor's Edge*.

The incident struck Cukor as odd. He was supposed to be the only person in Hollywood who had read the book; the galley's weren't even out. But he soon discovered that Maugham's agent had saturated the town with copies.

Soon afterward Maugham sold the book to Zanuck for $250,000. "If you can get Willie to do the script," Cukor told him, "I'd do the picture." But Zanuck said Maugham would be too expensive. Cukor called Maugham in New York and was shocked when the writer said he'd do it for nothing. This was against the prevalent view of Maugham as tight about money. Cukor invited him to work on the script at his house.

Cukor was fascinated with Maugham's working habits. The writer got up early, sat at a desk in the guest room, and wrote all morning in longhand. In the afternoon he read proofs or went out to the movies with Ethel Barrymore, whom he had met back in 1926, when she starred in *The Constant Wife*, which Cukor stage-managed.

Hepburn displayed her sense of occasion when Maugham was staying with Cukor. One evening she invited the two men to dinner at the house she was renting from King Vidor. Not knowing who would be there, they came in to observe Ethel Barrymore wearing an elegant black dress and Hepburn a white dress. With his precise camera eye, Cukor paused for a second to observe these "creatures of distinction and bearing" who were his favorite actresses.

When Maugham showed Cukor the script, all he said was: "It's anti-pragmatic writing." Cukor didn't know what he meant until sometime later, when the two were driving back to London from the country. They were playing a literary game, putting odds on which contemporary writers would survive. "I'm not a practicing writer anymore," Maugham suddenly said. "I no longer write for profit." He had made up his mind that at the age of seventy-five, after years of hard work and undertaking projects for profit, he would finally start to do things differently.

Cukor thought the script for *The Razor's Edge* was wonderful; the prologue contained useful instructions to the director, noting that it was a comedy and should be played lightly. "The actors should pick up one another's cues as smartly as possible, and there's no harm if they cut in on one another as people do in ordinary life." Maugham was "against pauses and silences" and in favor of "speed, speed, speed." It was a perfectly acceptable instruction for Cukor, who always believed in increasing the pace of the dialogue.

But Zanuck didn't like the script; it was too sophisticated. And there were other problems: Cukor was still under contract to Metro, and Tyrone Power, whom Zanuck wanted for the lead role, was still in the Army. By the time Power became available, Cukor would be starting a new picture at Metro.

In a typically Hollywood manner, Maugham's wonderful script was never used; Edmund Goulding's *Razor's Edge* in 1946 was based on Lamar Trotti's. It was a severe blow to both Maugham and Cukor, who tried to take the episode in stride. "Willie behaved very well about it," Cukor later said, "considering he couldn't bear that script. I'm sure he was deeply disappointed, more than he let on."

But *The Razor's Edge* episode did end nicely in another way. Zanuck wanted to give Maugham a present for his free-of-charge script; he didn't like the idea of gratis work. He summoned Cukor to his office for consultation about the gift. Cukor dismissed every idea Zanuck had: cuff links, a gold cigarette case, even a car. Maugham had all those items. Finally, in desperation, Zanuck said, "What the hell would he like?"

"I think he'd like a picture," Cukor said most calmly. Zanuck then authorized fifteen thousand dollars for Maugham, who bought his first Impressionistic painting, a work by Camille Pissarro.

Far more important was the intimate friendship that evolved during Maugham's three-month stay. He was treated better than a family member: Cukor's personal manager, Elsa Schroeder, bought him comfortable socks, and Cukor lent him his own slippers (which he later took back to England). The cook gave him some recipes for dishes he liked, though when he tried, they were "prose rather than poetry." There were also financial rewards: *Good Housekeeping* offered Maugham a lot of money for a story about his stay at Cukor's house. But to Maugham, the offer meant nothing because, as he noted, "the months I spent with you earned me such spiritual riches."

Like many writers, Somerset Maugham was ambivalent toward Cukor's work: He looked down on Hollywood, but at the same time he liked the potential amounts of money to be made there. Upon learning of Cukor's financial stature, he expressed jealousy at his enormous salary and huge pension. Maugham wondered why he did not become a movie director instead of a "struggling author."

In March 1945 Cukor's lawyers worked out a new Metro contract for seven years, with a compensation of four thousand dollars a week. Cukor's best contract to date, it reflected, as Metro's memo stated, his high standing in the industry.

Along with a new contract, came a new secretary, Irene Burns. Burns soon had a stabilizing effect on Cukor's professional life and remained his secretary for thirty-eight years—until his death. Appropriately Burns began working in 1945, on VE-Day. "It was a very historical day," she recalled. "Mr. Cukor was on loan-out at Fox preparing *The Razor's Edge*. There was so much commotion that day we just barely said hello."

They had met before, on the set of *The Women,* when Burns was working for MGM producer Hunt Stromberg. Cukor called Burns while she was working for Samuel Goldwyn and asked if she would be interested in becoming his secretary. She immediately said yes. "I didn't know him," she recalled, "but I knew of his reputation.

"I did work at the house," Burns said, "but when we were shooting, I was always at the studio with him." Burns did not travel; Cukor preferred that she oversee things at his house. "At the studio all films are made with a great staff, but at his house I was his only secretary."

A working day for Burns began at nine-thirty in the morning and ended around six. However, it was flexible. At times there was a lot of pressure and life was hectic. But sometimes, when things weren't so busy, she went home earlier. "My schedule wasn't anything formal. Mr. Cukor would come in the morning into the office, always cheerful and on a humorous note. He would either start dictating letters or there would be telephone calls to be made to his associates and friends. He was an avid letter writer, although he claimed he didn't do it well."

For a while Schroeder and Burns were served lunch in the office. "He wanted us to be there in case he needed us," said Burns. "But I didn't enjoy that much. It was too confining; I wanted to get out of the place for a while. At first he didn't like it, but it finally evolved I didn't lunch there anymore."

What impressed Burns about Cukor as a boss was his "innate sense of kindness and humanism. He'd go out of his way to express warmth to everyone at the studio or in his home." Cukor's charm and humor made everyone feel at ease. "He was certainly demanding," she said. "You had to watch your P's and Q's not to do anything to disturb or offend him."

Burns also singled out Cukor's love of his dogs. "When I first came," she recalled, "it was fashionable to own cocker spaniels. You know how dogs go, they change in different periods. At that time he had five cocker spaniels. Then his friend George Hoyningen-Huene had dachshunds, and Mr. Cukor fell in love with them and got into a dachshund period. At one time Ruth Gordon gave him a beautiful black poodle, Sasha. Then Whitney Warren, his friend from San Francisco, gave him a golden labrador retriever. He adored that dog, the last one he had."

Cukor kept photographs of each and every dog; he had the habit of counting them before he went to bed to make sure they all were indoors. Working or not, Cukor spent hours with his dogs and an equally long time talking or writing about them to his friends. In 1939 he had nine cocker spaniels, each boasting an amusing name. One pair was called Romeo and Juliet, another (black) was named Tallulah, a golden dog Scarlett, and one Connie, after his friend actress Constance Collier.

One of Cukor's favorite tales concerned Connie's disappearance. He was walking with Vivien Leigh and Connie up the hills around his house when all of a sudden the dog vanished. They searched for her, but to no avail. Finally Cukor called the police, and Connie was declared lost. Later that evening Ethel Barrymore called, but all Cukor could talk about was Connie. "Have you notified the police?" asked Ethel.

"Yes," said Cukor, "they have been very kind about it."

"I suppose the papers will be full of this tomorrow," said Ethel. She couldn't believe it when Cukor told her it was the dog, not the actress, who was missing.

Cukor's love of dogs extended to all animals. "George wouldn't allow anything to be killed, including moths and flies," recalled George Eells. "The only things you were allowed to kill in his house were mosquitoes."

Cukor's preferential treatment of his dogs upset his guests. "I don't like dogs," Allan Davis recalled. "I'm a bit allergic to them. I hated when I'd come into the room and there'd be some dog jumping on me. George's dogs would be on the most comfortable chair, and I'd shoo them out. 'Don't do that, Allan,' Cukor would say. 'I want them to sit there.' " It bothered him that Davis didn't like animals. "You're the only friend I have who doesn't like animals," he would say with slight anger in his voice.

Burns got quite close to Cukor, though, as she said, "there was a fine line between knowing him well and not knowing him well. I knew his temperament and character well, but I wouldn't say I was a personal friend. There was a feeling of closeness, and I think he felt that toward me. But I addressed him as Mr. Cukor, which never varied. He respected me for it and never corrected me." Burns heard some secretaries call him George. That offended him because he expected respect from them.

George Hoyningen-Huene came into Cukor's life at about the same time as Burns. Hoyningen-Huene was first mentioned to Cukor by their mutual friend John Darrow, an actor who became a successful agent. Hoyningen-Huene was an intelligent and imaginative photographer with great potential. As movies became more spectacularly designed, not only in their sets and costumes, but also in color, Cukor benefited from knowing him. Hoyningen-Huene became Cukor's closest collaborator and changed the look of his 1950s color films. He also became Cukor's most intimate friend, following a brief romantic interlude.

Hoyningen-Huene first approached Cukor in a letter, dated October 6, 1945. He was preparing a book on Mexico but, fed up with twenty years of fashion photography, he wanted to work in pictures. He therefore asked for permission to observe Cukor on the set of *The Razor's Edge*. In return he promised to make himself useful and prepare publicity stills for the studio.

Cukor immediately responded to the request. The most "practical" thing for the photographer was to observe how films were being made. Cukor was sure he would catch on to the whole system after two films. He also talked about Hoyningen-Huene to Arthur Freed, MGM's influential producer, who was always interested in new talent for his unit. Genuinely touched, Hoyningen-Huene couldn't believe Cukor's efficiency and generosity; he had been waiting for years for such opportunity.

Cukor was wild about a lovely canvas that Hoyningen-Huene painted for him. Hung over his desk against a green background, it was a constant reminder of his friend. Cukor invited him to stay with him until he found a place to live. He also encouraged him to do a "bang-up" photo book about Hollywood, that would gain him entry to every nook and cranny. Dismissing Hoyningen-Huene's hesitation that he would be in the way, Cukor said his presence would be like "a precious ornament."

Hoyningen-Huene was not to observe *The Razor's Edge* since the proper actor and script were still lacking. Finally, when *The Razor's Edge* was assigned to another director, Cukor invited Hoyningen-Huene to observe his next MGM film, *Desire Me*, which went into production in February 1946.

Produced by the estimable Arthur Hornblow, Jr., *Desire Me* was touted as Metro's most important production of the year. Cukor got to work with Louis B.'s favorite actress at the time, Greer Garson. Louis B. told

Cukor that Garson desperately needed a hit after *Adventure,* her disastrous film with Clark Gable. This put additional pressure on Cukor, who, from the start, didn't like the project or actress, whom he found unbearably stiff.

Cukor began to work with Casey Robinson's muddled script, first titled *Sacred and Profane* or *Karl and Anna.* Three women, Zoe Akins, Marguerite Roberts, and Sonya Levien, then tried to revamp the screenplay, changing its name to the vapid *Desire Me.* It was a dreary melodrama about a Normandy villager's wife (Garson) who, after hearing that her husband (Robert Mitchum) died in a concentration camp, marries his best friend (Richard Hart). But complications ensue when the news bearer turns out to be psychotic and the presumably dead husband comes home.

The Brittany sequences were filmed in California's picturesque Monterey. Along that eighteen miles of the rock-studded coast, a crew of 150 people worked for sixteen weeks. They erected a French village, including a city hall, a tobacco shop, and a wine inn. Permission was obtained for schoolchildren to appear in the crowd scenes—a school was set up on location for classes between takes—and men from a nearby military base were used as French soldiers.

It was a troubled production from the start. First, Richard Hart, a recruit from the New York theater, had replaced Robert Montgomery, who walked out soon after shooting began. Cukor thought Hart had no talent, but the actor was imposed on him by Hornblow. Worse yet, Hornblow pressured Cukor to use Robert Mitchum, then an emerging star, as Garson's husband.

Impatient at the numerous rewrites and constant reshooting, the cool Mitchum began to clown it up, incurring Cukor's wrath. Cukor thought the actor was lazy because he treated the film with irreverence. For his part, Mitchum complained that he was forced to act like a serious Shakespearean actor, which he detested.

Unable to conceal his contempt for the material, Cukor demanded to be replaced after shooting about half the film. *Desire Me* was finally taken away from him when Hornblow looked at the rushes. The film was reshot by two MGM directors, Mervyn LeRoy and Jack Conway, but no credit was given to any director. *Desire Me* may be the only Hollywood film released without a directorial card. To Cukor's embarrassment, his name did appear on some of the prints in England.

Whenever a picture didn't turn out, Cukor said, the studio assumed that it was the director's fault. He was put off because the front office blamed everything on him. After his dismissal Cukor showed up at MGM, but some people did not speak to him. "Now I know who will come to my funeral," he said to himself.

In December 1946 a preview of *Desire Me* proved to be disastrous. "Much to my disappointment," Mitchum later recalled, "the audience didn't seem to like it." After the first reel, with many viewers fleeing the theater, Mitchum put his collar up and sneaked out himself. The preview audience found the film poorly motivated and full of cutbacks. Some sequences were then reshot, and the film was finally released in September 1947, a year and a half after its production began.

Cukor had several failures in his five-decade career, though none as embarrassing as *Desire Me*. However, as often happens in Hollywood, in 1948 Cukor was asked to replace Mervyn LeRoy on Selznick's remake of *Little Women*. He refused. When LeRoy showed signs of desperation, Cukor told him: "I was put off *GWTW*, maybe the biggest movie ever made, and I'm still here to tell the tale; so don't despair."

It was not that Cukor was insensitive to LeRoy. In 1938, when he was brought in to tidy up *I Met My Love Again,* codirected by Joshua Logan and Arthur Ripley, Cukor told Logan: "I would make it as painless as possible for you and Arthur, because of what I had endured myself on *One Hour with You*."

Years later, when Ruth Gordon was dismissed from a film shortly after wining an Oscar, George Eells felt sorry for her. "It must be awful for Ruth," he told Cukor, who said, "Don't worry. It won't stop her. That's the difference between those who really have it and those who don't." Cukor's motto continued to be: "You must have faith in yourself and keep going." Cukor kept going on, and his next film, *A Double Life*, turned out to be a success.

A Double Life was Cukor's first collaboration with Ruth Gordon and Garson Kanin. Their story concerned a famous actor, whose personality and life are completely taken over by playing Othello onstage. Drawing on the professional hazard of actors who immerse themselves so passionately in their roles that they fail to distinguish between life onstage and off, the Kanins dealt with the issue seriously rather than satirically.

British actor Ronald Colman, whom Cukor had known for years, was cast as Tony, the distinguished performer who becomes paranoid and eventually commits murder. Cukor respected Colman's qualities as a screen actor—his photogenic, emotional face—but he had doubts whether the gentlemanly Colman possessed the madness to play Othello. Though gifted, Colman lacked the demonic and sinister quality needed for the part to be scary.

The leading lady in the film, Brita, was played by Signe Hasso, a Swedish actress. "George had directed Garbo and Ingrid Bergman, he loved Swedish women," Hasso recalled. "He thought they were extraordinary. 'Oh, you strange women,' he would say."

A Double Life is interesting for providing the only negative view of the theater in Cukor's work. In the past—and future—he celebrated the magical quality of performers. Cukor knew the theater world well, but it still held mystery for him. Indeed, even in this story's sordid milieu of jealousy and murder he managed to convey his love for show business.

Cukor wished to capture an accurate impression of being onstage. When performers step onto a stage, the light blinds them. To create the illusion, the crew had to experiment with the camera and lighting. "Don't worry about whatever curious effects happen," Cukor told cinematographer Milton Krasner; "let all kinds of things hit the lens as if they're hitting the audience." Since cameramen fear such things, Cukor said he would take responsibility if it failed.

But it worked, and the theatrical scenes heightened the story's atmosphere of terror and excitement. Cukor chose to shoot the theater scenes on location, in New York's famous Empire Theater. This helped the visual contrast between the interior theater world and the exterior squalor of the city.

Universal International had good reasons to fear the Production Code office, which didn't like the project, least of all its initial title, *The Art of Murder*. In June 1947 Breen submitted a list of items for revision. Cukor was urged to avoid a light attitude toward marriage and make sure that when Tony stabs himself, it is the action of an insane man. There should be no openmouthed, prolonged, or lusty kissing anywhere in the picture. And under no circumstances should the film suggest that Tony has beaten Brita; Cukor should show that she has bitten her lip.

Hasso remembered a small scene, that for some reason she could not do right. "What's the matter?" Cukor asked. "It's a very easy scene." Cukor decided to turn for help to her brother, who was visiting on the set. "Val, do you know what to say to irritate her?" Cukor asked. "Yes, I do," her brother said.

"Good," Cukor said. "Now *you* do the scene with her."

"My brother said the worst things to me in Swedish, with a big smile. He just cursed me out really good," said Hasso, who was so shocked she did the scene in one take.

"That was marvelous," said Cukor with a gleam in his eye. "What did you tell her?"

A British gentleman, Colman didn't want to hurt Hasso in the scene where he chokes her. "Come on, Ronnie," Hasso said, "just go ahead and do it." But Colman didn't dare. Cukor worked on that scene for a long time. "But the last time we did it," Hasso said, "Ronnie really dug deep into my throat. By the time George said, 'Cut,' he had almost choked me to death."

When the scene was over, Colman asked, "Did it hurt?"

"Not at all," Hasso said.

Cukor just stood aside and smiled.

Colman experienced some trouble with the Shakespearean scenes because it had been a long time since he had performed onstage. Cukor brought noted coach Walter Hampden from New York to rehearse the sequences. "This was indicative of George's work," said Hasso. "He was very thorough. If something wasn't absolutely perfect, he would take his time and do as many takes as needed. He was a director who followed his intuition, but he also let you follow your intuition. It was very easy to work with George. I learned a lot from him."

For the death scene Cukor gave the same advice to Colman as he had to Lowell Sherman in *What Price Hollywood?* He said, "When you die, all your life, everything that's happened, comes into your eyes for a brief moment." Colman did it, but Cukor didn't see it. The next day, however, it was in all the rushes; Colman was a subtle actor who knew how to register his thinking on camera.

Cukor perceived thinking as a photogenic quality; it had to register. "Cukor understood that words are a result of thoughts, and thoughts are a result of emotions," said Shelley Winters, cast in the small role of Pat, the waitress. "Don't close your eyes," Cukor instructed her. "The eyes are the mirror to your soul. You must think every moment." She remarked: "George knew how delicate the actor's psyche is and that with good actors you can see their thoughts."

Winters had also read for Scarlett in *GWTW*, but to this day she is not sure whether Cukor recognized her when she auditioned for *A Double Life*. Of her test, Winters said, "I was only fifteen, and I wore wobbly high heels, looking pretty funny. I am probably the only girl who played Scarlett with a terrible Brooklyn accent, which made George laugh." Trying not to offend her, Cukor sent for two bottles of Coca-Cola and chased everybody out of his office. "Are you serious about acting?" he asked. He then instructed Winters to go to college to work on her speech and visit public places to see how ordinary people walked.

At the audition for *A Double Life* Cukor told Winters, "The first thing you have to do is go to the bathroom and take off your false eyelashes and makeup. It's not a movie star part; you are playing a waitress." Winters recalled: "I looked around the office, and when I saw there was no casting couch, I determined to take a risk and follow all of his instructions."

Cukor then had an appointment, but he gave her the script to read. Winters bought a tuna sandwich and read the entire script in one reading at a public park. Her first reaction was "God meant for me to play this part," which she later repeated to the director, using the same words. Afterward Cukor questioned her in detail about each of the characters. "Don't you want to hear me read?" asked Winters. "No," said Cukor. He then asked Winters to rehearse with a coach before taking the test.

Cukor and Winters rehearsed for two or three times, but then, just when she thought they were going to shoot, Cukor said, "You already did it." Said Winters: "George knew that words like 'roll 'em' and 'action' made actors nervous, so he shot my last rehearsal."

Not having heard the verdict about *A Double Life,* Winters persistently called Cukor at home. One day Cukor informed her she got the part. "Mr. Cukor," she said in tears, "I can't do it. I just signed a contract for the musical *Oklahoma!*" She went on to say: "It was a marvelous scene. I was crying and George was hysterically laughing." He said: "You better get a lawyer and an agent soon."

To express her gratitude, Winters brought Cukor flowers and a bottle of champagne. "Shirley," he said, "you are not allowed to have champagne." It was only when she put a pink flower in her hair that she suspected Cukor might have recognized her from her *GWTW* audition. "Wait a minute," he said, "there is something familiar about you." They both broke out laughing.

Working on this film was not easy for Winters. "One day I became comatose," she recalled. "We had many takes of the same scene, and I inadvertently poured water on Colman's hand. I couldn't function. George must have thought he hired the village idiot. To put my mind at ease, he asked Colman to take me to lunch."

The insecure Winters could be exasperating, too. "Mr. Cukor," she said one day, "I don't like this line. I think I should say something else."

"You nincompoop!" Cukor raged. "How dare you! Ruth and Garson have written this wonderful part, and *you,* you nothing, want to rewrite the dialogue." Later on, however, Cukor came to an odd phrasing that did need changing. He read it to her and shouted, "And don't say it this way." He then reached out and slapped her across the face. After that Winters didn't dare open her mouth.

In this, her first important part, and the start of her career, Winters made the waitress's sexiness disgusting. Cukor thought she was both funny and sleazy. He was proud of the scene where she makes passes at Colman, which he ignores. She sits on the arm of his chair, and he runs his hand over her arm, signaling that he'll decide when to bed her. This erotic feeling was ahead of its time—the kind of tease Cukor admired.

In another scene Cukor turned off the light and told Winters to put perfume between her breasts and keep one foot on the floor. "George had excellent intuition about women," Winters said. "He really knew how women felt. I used to go in the corner and cry because I wanted to look glamorous and he wouldn't let me. I was finally in a Hollywood movie, and I looked awful.

"Many of the things I tell my students," Winters said, "Cukor told me." One of these was: "As soon as the director says 'action,' you have to come to life and have fun. When the camera turns, it must be absolutely real." There was also the issue of punctuation. Cukor didn't like to emphasize one line in a long speech. And of course, there was the notion that in film the audience is looking through a keyhole, so there was no need "to project."

At the end of the shoot Cukor gave Winters a bust of Colman. For her part, realizing that the film showed off her talent, Winters thanked Cukor for "opening the door" and gave him a box of pills for stomach pain and heartburn.

Released on February 20, 1948, *A Double Life* scored a huge success and enjoyed nice reviews. The film was nominated for four Oscars, this time including Best Director. Winning his first and only Oscar, Colman thanked Cukor for his "grand qualities" of patience and kindness. Without his valuable direction, he couldn't have done "half the job."

Cukor failed to win the Oscar; the winner that year was Elia Kazan for *Gentleman's Agreement.* But Cukor was pleasantly surprised to find himself on *Variety*'s list of Hollywood's top directors however, one that included John Huston, George Stevens, and David Lean.

Unfortunately after *A Double Life* not much happened professionally. Cukor was "at liberty" reading scripts, but nothing tantalizing showed up. He went a lot to the movies but hated most of them. Selznick had asked him to see a preview of King Vidor's western *Duel in the Sun,* which he produced for his wife, Jennifer Jones. Cukor dubbed the box-office bonanza "duel for my sins." The film had the "subtlety, sincerity and fine writing" of *Since You Went Away,* another Selznick picture he detested.

There were, however, always new and distinguished visitors, like Diana Vreeland of *Vogue* magazine, to revive his social scene. In November 1947 Mrs. Elizabeth Gray Vining, who had recently been awarded Nobel Prize for Peace, visited California. The tutor of the thirteen-year-old Japanese prince Akihito was honored at a tea reception given by Cukor and Olivia de Havilland at the Beverly Hills Hotel.

Through the initiative of Irene Selznick, Cukor also met Tennessee Williams, whose *The Glass Menagerie* he admired. Irene arranged for the playwright to spend a few days at Cukor's house. Cukor envied Williams for living an openly gay life, even using his homosexuality to an advantage in his creative work. The age difference between the two men was only a decade, but they represented totally divergent life-styles.

Although they never became intimate friends, Cukor was impressed by Williams's stories about his cultured grandfather and trips to London. Despite a simple and humble appearance, there was good background and tradition in Williams's family. For his part, the writer praised Cukor's wonderful gift in "dissolving walls" between people, a gift he lacked. "I have never been treated like that before, anywhere," wrote Williams, "and I will not soon forget it." As a gesture of friendship for his kind hospitality at his "heavenly place," Williams sent Cukor a scarf, which the director promised to model for him in person in New York.

Williams consulted Cukor about bringing his new plays to the West Coast. When the playwright mentioned that he had just written a new script, *The Pink Bedroom,* Cukor saw in it a good part for Garbo. "I want you to show it to Garbo," he said. "I'll arrange for her to see you." To Williams's utmost astonishment a few weeks later, Garbo received him alone in her New York apartment.

What really excited Cukor in 1947 and 1948 was the prospects of a Garbo comeback under his direction. After all these years he still felt guilty that her last film, *Two-Faced Woman,* was done under him. The talk about a comeback revolved around a film concerning the eccentric romance of writer George Sand and composer Frédéric Chopin.

Salka Viertel had told Cukor that while Garbo was anxious to perform, she was afraid of work. Cukor sympathized with the star: after six years of idleness, work was a habit that Garbo had lost. Conducted indirectly, Cukor dealt with George Schlee, who acted as Garbo's manager. In some respects communication was worse with Schlee, who was even more elusive than Garbo.

Garbo wanted to do the Sand project as a foreign film so that Hollywood would finally value her taste and artistic integrity. In May 1947 Garbo gave her approval to Peter Cusick, of the William Morris agency, for shooting the film in Paris, in English, under Cukor's direction. Cukor's first move was to secure Roger Furse, who did the costumes and sets for Olivier's prestigious *Henry V,* to design the new picture.

Garbo demanded that in terms of quality the movie must be a "Grade A photoplay." But she was soon upset, when the film was publicly announced before negotiations were completed. An international project, the movie was going to be based on an equal three-way partnership: The Americans would provide story, star, director, finance, and distribution; the French, studio space, costumes, sets, production facility, and finance; and the British, cast, designer, and finance.

Cukor knew that this film would have to be made in England or France—or never made at all—and it worried him. The production was set to start shooting on April 1, 1948, but he suggested not being bound by a firm date until there was a finished screenplay; the last Garbo picture had taught him a lesson. Cukor was also unsure if Olivier, slated to play Chopin, would be willing to commit to a specific date because he had scheduled an Australian tour.

Unfortunately a good shooting script never materialized. Cukor was disappointed, though he knew all along that the longer everyone waited for Garbo, the less the chances for a comeback. Garbo, in fact, withdrew. In the next few years Cukor made several attempts to bring Garbo back, but he invariably came up against "that unbending Swedish stubbornness."

Idle, Cukor devoted further attention to his house, which was decorated in phases. Though Billy Haines had basically a free hand, Cukor always had to stick in his two cents. Cukor told Haines to go ahead with the library, because it was used a lot, but to wait with the other rooms until he finished paying for his artworks.

The Braque painting added to the atmosphere of the oval room, and he enjoyed Toulouse-Lautrec's "Bicyclist," though occasionally he had a twinge of conscience about its price. Art dealer Eric Charrell was always reminded to look for "important" paintings, preferably in one of Paris's bargain counters.

With his next assignment, *Edward, My Son,* Cukor became the first American director to work at England's Metro studio since the war. He arrived a few weeks before shooting began and spent an amusing time with his friends in London and in the country. But as soon as the film began, he said good-bye to "the great social world." Cukor now hoped to finish the movie in August and go to Paris for a vacation.

Based on Robert Morley and Noel Langley's hit play, the movie concerns an egotistical father (played by Spencer Tracy) who ruthlessly drives his son to suicide and his wife to alcoholism. An underrated work, *Edward, My Son* stands out in Cukor's repertoire as featuring one of his few male protagonists. Most of his films revolve around strong females, the main reason why Cukor's label—Hollywood's best woman's director—persisted. Stylistically, too, *Edward, My Son* boasts some long, uninterrupted sequences that distinguished Cukor's later films.

The part of the alcoholic and bitter wife was assigned to the young British actress Deborah Kerr. Despite initial reservations, Cukor was soon taken with Kerr, who showed a knack for acting with a "disarming reality." He predicted that despite Kerr's youth, she would be extraordinarily good, healing the "scars" of her two previous MGM pictures.

There were some problems with casting Eileen, the secretary. While it was not a big enough part to tempt a major star, Cukor thought it needed to be played by a commanding actress. Because Katharine Hepburn was in London with Tracy, there was some talk of her playing the secretary. But intriguing as the idea was, Cukor saw obstacles. Tracy and Hepburn didn't want to act together too frequently. And by using an important a star as Hepburn, the balance of the film would be off, making it an

"unfair" situation for Kerr. The part was finally cast with Leueen Mac-
Grath.

Two Cukor gimmicks marked this movie: Tracy addresses the camera
directly, and the title character, Edward, never appears onscreen. "It was
a very clever piece of theater," Kerr recalled. "You get a remarkable
picture of the son without ever seeing him."

The film was stolen by the actors who played the smaller parts instead
of being illuminated by its central character; all along Cukor claimed that
the father's role was superficially conceived. Moreover, in its transfer to
the screen the story became safer and tamer. For censorship reasons, the
film contains a retribution scene that didn't exist in the play: Setting fire
to his shop to collect insurance, the father goes to prison.

Shooting began on time and progressed smoothly. On the eighth day
Cukor was one day ahead of schedule. Always partial to his own work,
this time Cukor thought the rushes had exceptional vitality and freshness.
By July 14 Cukor was four days ahead of schedule, no small accomplishment, for British crews worked at a more leisurely rhythm than Americans. "It has been said by my enemies that I am a very slow director,"
Cukor quipped, "but no more!"

Cukor worked extensively with Kerr on the development of her character from a young woman to an old, sad drunken lady. "George had a
wonderful way with actors," said Kerr. "He would talk and talk about a
particular scene, and then say, 'Now forget everything I've said, and go
and do it your own way.' This was very clever psychologically because
everything he said had already gone into your head." Kerr admired
Cukor's ability to convey what he wanted without actually saying, "I
want you to do this or that."

"George helped me with being aged," Kerr said. "He was always encouraging and open to ideas, but I was very young and in awe of him."
Cukor put the shy actress at ease with his disarming humor. "I was just
a schoolgirl starting out, but I enjoyed getting to know him. I only wish
I had more chances to work with him. He was an enchanting man," she
elaborated. "George was absolutely one of my favorite directors, and I
worked with some wonderful directors: John Huston, Fred Zinnemann.
I was extremely young to play that woman. It was tremendously exciting
to have gotten my first Academy nomination quickly after going to Hollywood." In one film Cukor succeeded in establishing Kerr as one of
Hollywood's most important leading ladies.

"We had the same understanding about particular scenes," Kerr said.
"We got on with each other because we agreed enormously on that." The
ambience on the set was friendly, with everybody working very hard. At
times Tracy wasn't happy, but one could feel, Kerr said, "that George and
Spencer had worked together and knew each other a great deal."

Before the movie Tracy told Cukor he was nervous about his ability to function in a foreign country. He put Cukor under pressure because he wanted to spend as little time in London as possible. But it turned out this was the first film in years during which Tracy wasn't sick from nerves and wasn't drinking much.

Tracy had to carry the whole picture; he appeared in almost every scene. But Tracy had become such an assured actor that he was able to do long scenes, five pages at a time, in one take without cutting. Cukor ended up doing fewer takes than the usual, adapting himself to Tracy's new assurance.

Cukor urged Tracy to help the less experienced actors. In one scene Kerr, as a gray plumped-up, sad-looking lady, had to pour a drink for herself. Tracy stood in the background as she sipped the drink. "George," he suddenly said, "do you mind if I tell her something?" "No, of course not," Cukor said. "You know, darling," Tracy then told Kerr, "when you're an alcoholic, you don't sip, you just throw the whole thing down." Kerr later remarked: "Being young and not alcoholic, I didn't know that."

Tracy became an enthusiastic cricket fan during his stay. With his interest in the game aroused by the front-page stories, he attended a match one weekend and soon became a regular. Every Sunday he drove his car to the country and picnicked on the grounds of Winston Churchill's large estate in Kent. At the end of the shoot Cukor presented Tracy with a cricket bat.

Cukor stayed at the Savoy Hotel, in an apartment facing the river. Metro had kindly provided him with a chauffeured car, and he felt he was living in the lap of luxury. The food at the Savoy was not all it should be, but that pleased him because he was determined to lose a little weight on his "big hips."

He "prudently" spent his weekends lying in bed at the Savoy, instead of being "brilliant and scintillating," telling his comical stories. He spent a good deal of his free time at the hotel, entertaining his friends there. On his birthday, in July, he invited Alfred Hitchcock and his wife, Alma, Ingrid Bergman, Lady Juliet Duff, and director John Farrow for dinner. Cukor derived great fun from listening to Hitchcock's complaints about David Selznick's obsessive interferences with his work.

The reports from Irene Burns that the dogs were waiting for him at the gate, always on the lookout, made him feel pretty important to be missed. Burns wished he could have seen the dogs the day she took them for a bath; crowded in her little Ford, they were overcome with excitement at the idea of going someplace. "Far away on alien shores," Cukor was not exactly depressed, but he had more than occasional "twinges of sickness" for his dogs. He never liked to travel for long periods.

What Cukor did ask Burns for was more supplies of instant coffee; the one thing he could never reconcile himself to was English coffee. Wanamaker soap, a dozen boxes of Kleenex (preferably Bullock's), Earl Grey tea, wild rice for Oliver Messel, and seeds of sweet corn for Maugham were also put on a list of items that were to be sent to Lady Duff's house.

Cukor also asked Burns to get autographed photos of Joan Crawford and Barbara Stanwyck for the cute telephone operator at the Savoy, who had been kind to him. When the photographs arrived, Cukor invited the handsome guy up to his room for a more intimate session. The boy got such a thrill that afterward Cukor could almost use the telephone for free.

In August Cukor threw a dinner party at the Savoy for writer Peter Quennell, set designer Oliver Messel, Noel Langley, the author of *Edward, My Son,* Emlyn Williams, and theater manager Hugh Beaumont. For another all-male party at the hotel, he invited Aldous Huxley, Maugham and Alan Searle, and director Peter Glenville. Irene Selznick happened to be in London and, with her usual efficiency, planned a busy week. They went every night to see plays, most of which Cukor found ordinary and not well done.

It was exciting for Cukor to be in London during the premiere of *A Double Life,* which went off with a "bang" (a typical Cukor expression) and got good notices. Whenever Cukor passed the Leicester Square Theatre, he was happy to see long lines. At the premiere gala Colman devoted half of his speech to Cukor, who was sitting in the balcony. Unfortunately the Universal people had completely fumbled the ticket arrangements, and many of his friends could not get in.

Edward, My Son was done in forty days. That was an unheard-of feat, and Cukor boasted, "We made time and that's because of *me*." He now planned to go to Nice to see Maugham, then join Eric Charrell at Antibes and drive to Paris in grand style.

On October 19, 1948, the first preview of *Edward, My Son* took place. It went well, except for a snag with the dubbing. Cukor sat around twiddling his thumbs for more than a month before he finally caught on to how to use the new sound equipment. He brought a rough cut of the picture back to California and showed it to his bosses. He believed that with some discreet cutting and minor retouches, it would be an entertaining picture.

When *Edward, My Son* premiered in London in March 1949, it received mostly good reviews in the British press. "They are billing it as a great British picture and they are right," wrote the *Star*. "In every way, it is a prestige picture." However, in the United States the film received mixed notices and barely recouped its cost.

Edward, My Son marked the last collaboration between Cukor and Donald Ogden Stewart, who, singly or jointly, wrote no fewer than eight of his movies. With the exception of his teaming with Ruth Gordon and Garson Kanin that produced seven films, Stewart was the only writer with whom Cukor had worked continuously for close to two decades. Unfortunately Stewart was blacklisted during the McCarthy era; *Keeper of the Flame* was among the "evidence" used against him by the House Un-American Activities Committee.

Back in California, after a long absence, Cukor got in touch with his closest friends. He had been worried for some time about Billie Burke, who had not made a movie since *The Bachelor's Daughters* in 1946 and had no money. For the last couple of years she had a hard time of it. Through his connections Cukor helped the actress sell her life story and arranged for the book to get published. Cukor was touched when Burke inscribed her book, *With a Feather on My Nose,* to him. She wrote: "I hope you will accept this simple dedication behind which lies such a world of loving devotion to all you have meant in my life."

At the same time he was concerned about the health and welfare of his niece Evelyn. Aside from the agony, bad health was regarded by Cukor as "infuriating and a waste." His sister, Elsie, had asked him to buy a house for Evelyn in Westwood. But Cukor said he couldn't afford it and also didn't think it would really be a solution. However, Cukor got the proper staff and set up a comfortable setting for Evelyn. With the exception of Uncle Morris, family for Cukor always signified problems—and money.

Though generous with family and friends, Cukor could be frugal, too— two traits that some of his friends found contradictory. Meticulous and detail-oriented to a fault, Cukor kept every receipt from a restaurant at which he ate or a store at which he shopped. When it came to paying for services or merchandise, he demanded the best. Back from London, Cukor returned slacks and two suits he had purchased there. Angry and determined not to take any nonsense from them, Cukor asked for an immediate cash refund. When the store failed to comply, he threw a tantrum on the phone.

There was plenty of time for socializing. Cukor's friendship with the Kanins had grown after *A Double Life,* and they started to correspond, at times exchanging two letters a week. Ruth Gordon reported that her autobiographical play *Years Ago* was a hit and might be a viable film for Cukor. For his part, Cukor made arrangements for the Kanins to stay at his house while he was gone. The ground rules were quite simple: They could use the house as their own for picnics and parties—"within reason"—and the limit was two weeks.

On March 7, 1949, Cukor gave the Kanins a farewell dinner that included Garson's brother Michael and his wife, Fay, Dore and Miriam Schary, Tracy and Hepburn, Ethel Barrymore and her son, Sammy Colt, Cole Porter and Fanny Brice.

Cukor always balanced the number of men and women at his dinner table. For each of his single female friends, Cukor arranged a companion, usually a gay man. For example, for a big dinner on April 19, 1949, Irene Burns was asked to invite Ina Claire with Hoyningen-Huene, Constance Collier with Orry-Kelly, Ethel Barrymore with Cole Porter; Cukor was Garbo's partner that night. The "regulars" at Cukor's parties included: Garbo, Gladys Cooper, Ethel Barrymore, Judy Holliday and her mother, Tracy and Hepburn, and three of Cukor's close homosexual friends, Hoyningen-Huene, Cole Porter, and Orry-Kelly. In addition to the regulars, there were always visitors, often show business people from New York, like Arthur Rubinstein or Irene Selznick.

It was Cukor's idea to have a big celebration for Ethel Barrymore's seventieth birthday on August 15, 1949. At his initiative, the Academy of Motion Picture Arts and Sciences became the sponsor of a radio broadcast in honor of Barrymore. Greetings from some of her friends were to be introduced by no less than President Truman. Cukor didn't expect such an immense response from the actress's colleagues and friends, all wishing to be included. Gladys Cooper, Clark Gable, John Huston, Barbara Stanwyck, Robert Taylor, and others reported to Cukor's MGM office to record messages for the actress.

Cukor himself drafted a cable from Ethel Barrymore to Winston Churchill. It stated: "Dear Winston. It would be wonderful if you would wish me a happy birthday on August 15, when I shall be all of 70 years, more than 50 of them made proud by having known you."

On August 15 Cukor was actually vacationing in Colorado, but with a personal campaign, he got half the townspeople to listen to the broadcast. It was one of the few big social gatherings he missed by being away from Hollywood.

During this time Cukor solidified his position not only as a director but as Hollywood's chief information center. Old and new directors often consulted with him about writers, designers and especially casting problems.

Few people know that Gloria Swanson's great screen performance in the classic film *Sunset Boulevard* was a direct result of Cukor's intervention. Billy Wilder's idea was to use a star whose career was similar to Norma Desmond's, so that the audience would be shaken by the double masquerade. He first asked Pola Negri, but she was offended by the notion of portraying a has-been. Wilder then considered Mae West, who also turned him down, while aging star Mary Pickford agreed to do it on the condition that the role be enlarged.

One afternoon Wilder was sitting in Cukor's garden, sipping tea and pouring out his heart. After listening attentively to his younger colleague, Cukor suddenly said, "Billy, I have the ideal Norma Desmond for you, Gloria Swanson." Wilder admitted that he had somehow forgotten the declining star. But when Wilder called Swanson, she absolutely refused to test. "I got a phone call from darling George," Swanson recalled in her memoirs. "He is so persuasive, charm the birds out of the trees."

Cukor told Swanson that it would be "the greatest part," one for which she would always be remembered, and that Wilder was becoming the number one director in Hollywood. Reassuring her that Wilder would "do justice" to her, he talked the star into testing. The rest is film history: Norma Desmond became Swanson's best-known role, for which she won a well-deserved Oscar nomination.

In 1949 the Garson Kanins came up with a fine screen comedy for Tracy and Hepburn, under Cukor's direction. After their great experience with *A Double Life*, the new movie, *Adam's Rib*, was meant to be another happy partnership for all concerned.

Cukor thus began an extensive collaboration with the Kanins, one that involved six more movies between 1949 and 1954. This became the most important collaboration in Cukor's career and one of the most productive in Hollywood's history. Cukor gave credit to the screenwriters not only for their comic inventiveness but for their contribution to some of his directorial touches. In fact, he showed too much respect for their scripts, at times slavishly chained by them. Eventually Cukor was to regret this selfless devotion when the witty husband and wife failed to acknowledge his contribution.

Originally called *Man and Wife*, the script for *Adam's Rib* was completed on February 27, 1949, and Cukor began the principal photography on May 31. At one level the film is a sitcom about married lawyers who find themselves on opposite sides of a court battle. On a deeper level the film provides a serious meditation on a modern marriage. Cukor's funny but poignant portrait of the Bonner alliance distinguishes *Adam's Rib* from other comedies. A commercial "feminist" film with arguments about law and order, *Adam's Rib* was ahead of its time. But in 1949 it provoked more comment about its marital than legal issues.

Of course, the PCA office was concerned with the portrait of marriage as well as the legal process. It demanded that there be no suggestion that the trial was a travesty of justice or any unfavorable reflection on the legal process. Cukor was urged to stay away from any situation that might make comedy out of the "unholy" alliance of the philandering husband and his mistress: "adultery is not a proper subject for comedy."

For Cukor, great comedies were first and foremost human. "You've got to be funny," he once said, "but to elevate the comedy, you've got to be human. That's why anything that works as a comedy should also work as a tragedy and vice versa." A chief source of the comedy in *Adam's Rib* is the lack of rapport between Hepburn's militant lawyer, who uses feminist principles, and Judy Holliday's submissive housewife, all too willing to accept her guilt.

Cukor imbued the film's settings—the apartment, the courtroom, the tax consultant's offices, the farm, the New York streets—with authenticity. He would go to people's apartments and pick up all kinds of "illogical" details that later would be used in his sets. Because the sets were reproductions of what he had seen, his films with the Kanins have a semidocumentary feel.

Cukor gave the script the verisimilitude of actual observation. The opening sequence—Judy Holliday tracking down her husband—was done in the cinema verité style, showing realistically the rush and crush of a New York business district at 5:00 P.M.

The courtroom scenes were especially fresh. Just before shooting began, there was a murder trial for Betty Ferreri, who stabbed a man in L.A. Attending the Ferreri trial for a solid week, Cukor took pictures of the woman, from the first time she was brought into the court to the very end, to show how the evolution of the trial was reflected in her looks. At first Ferreri looked tough and was heavily made up, but gradually she appeared more discreet and more modest. Cukor used this idea for the transformation of Judy Holliday's character.

Cukor took Hepburn with him to the courtroom to observe how judges and attorneys behaved. He noticed that they worked differently from the way they were portrayed in movies. "The judge shouldn't have a gavel; judges pound gavels only in the movies." He also disliked the "frozen" and "formal" ways that courtroom scenes were treated in Hollywood movies.

Cukor's two favorite stars, Tracy and Hepburn, were given freedom to experiment with their roles, which were basically an extension of their natural offscreen interaction. Tracy played Adam, the stern prosecuting attorney, and Hepburn his lawyer wife, who defends Holliday's accused woman and strikes a blow for equal treatment of her gender. There was added realism to the way Tracy and Hepburn, who were intimate in real life, played together. Their onscreen rapport had an extra dimension of authenticity. The dialogue seemed improvised because of the actors' offscreen relationship.

Cukor loathed the word "improvisation." "It's just bullshit," he said. He favored "creativity, spontaneity, and freshness," but "improvisation" was "the wrong word." "When I go on the set, I have a general idea of what I'm going to do. I don't like to say, 'here's a close-up,' because it ties you in. But the discovery is how you have the inspiration of creating it."

"Cukor never gave Spence any suggestions," Hepburn recalled, "but he gave them all to me." He would say, "You know, Spencer, I think of a lot of things to say to you, and I don't say them. But then I see the rushes, and it's all there, but I never see you do it." A director's job is "to know when to shut up and to know, when you see it happening, not to give a lot of hot tips." Tracy was so original about everything, Cukor said, "that you would only intrude yourself." Besides, he knew Tracy would not listen to him anyway.

"Spencer liked to work with George very much," Hepburn said. "George understood him. Spencer was not interested in a lot of intellectualizing about why a character did this or that." Cukor took it as a compliment when Tracy said he liked working with him. "I must have some virtue," Cukor quipped, which he summed up in one sentence. "It's in making a *climate*." "Climate" was another of Cukor's magic words and his greatest talent: "A director should make a climate where people can make fools of themselves with freedom."

Tracy was always careful and economical with himself. He knew the strength of his face and personality and used both sparingly, with discretion. Neither Tracy nor Hepburn paid much attention to the camera; they trusted Cukor implicitly. Once, when Tracy and Hepburn were doing a scene together, Cukor screamed, "It's a great scene, but I don't see either of you."

In *Adam's Rib* Hepburn's character reflected the way she felt about sexism in real life. Ambitious and intelligent, Amanda challenges male authority and male supremacy. She is determined to show evidence of women's accomplishments to prove their equality with men. But she stoops to unscrupulous methods; her antics with the absurd characters she introduces turn the court into a circus. A lady wrestler (a great turn by Hope Emerson) lifts Tracy onto her shoulders, making him a laughingstock.

Throughout, Adam remains a solid citizen who maintains his honor and decorum. He argues that though one may be against the law, one still has to respect it. At the end Adam loses his case, but he is restored to dominance when he is asked by the Republicans to run for judge. Still, a note of ambiguity is inserted at the very last shot, when Amanda poses the question "Have the Democrats chosen a candidate yet?"

In *Adam's Rib*, Cukor introduced four promising stage actors: Judy Holliday from *Born Yesterday*, Tom Ewell from *John Loves Mary*, Jean Hagen from *The Traitor*, and David Wayne from *Mister Roberts*. Given their first chance, all four established themselves in the next couple of years.

Cukor cast Tom Ewell and David Wayne as two different sides of masculinity. Ewell played Doris's creepy and loutish husband, and Wayne, Amanda's gay sidekick, Kip. As a composer neighbor, a Cole Porter type, Kip is Amanda's ally, a character who possibly stands for Cukor himself. Kip sympathizes with Hepburn and, in marital feuds, takes her side against Tracy's virile "straight" man. At the end Adam resorts to he-man tactics, beating up Kip.

The latent homosexual character, one of the few in Cukor's oeuvre, is a comic plot element that neither the Kanins nor Cukor bothered to develop. It could be that they were restricted by the Production Code: "There should not be even the slightest indication that Kip is a pansy." It is also possible that Cukor's realization that Kip was based on himself or Cole Porter made him uncomfortable even talking about the character with the Kanins. It was the only element in the script he remained silent about.

The film reconciles the tension between certain "male" qualities—stability and stoicism—and certain "female" qualities—volatility and intuition. But under the right circumstances, each gender can exchange these qualities; Adam demonstrates that he can fake tears. That each can do almost everything the other can is established pointedly during the courtroom session, when the faces of Doris (Holliday) and Warren (Ewell) are transposed, each becoming the other.

But *Adam's Rib* also shows that the success of Adam and Amanda's marriage derives from their individuality, its stability based on a fluctuating balance of power. Adam can be humiliated and still rebound without loss of male ego. Amanda can defer to Adam and still not lose her identity. Based on their willingness to listen to each other, their marriage celebrates accommodation and compromise.

As a comedy *Adam's Rib* was weak cinematically, but the witty sex battle was well written, overcoming the technical shortcomings and uninventive visuals. Hepburn's intense, high-strung performance nicely balanced Tracy's usual solid acting.

But it was Judy Holliday who lifted the picture to a more spontaneous level of wit. In the first scene the desperate Doris waits outside her husband's office with a candy bar and a gun in her purse. But on the first day of shooting Holliday was inept and couldn't hit the mark; Cukor had to do the scene over and over again. She later offered the crew tickets to see her in *Born Yesterday* onstage, so that they wouldn't think she was a complete idiot.

The public was somehow "prepared" for Holliday's dazzling emergence as a star. During the shoot stories in the press stated that she was stealing the picture from the two old pros. Curious to know who was planting the notices, Cukor found out that Hepburn had gone to MGM's head of publicity, Howard Strickling, and suggested the strategy. It was

Hepburn's personal campaign to get Holliday the Billie Dawn role in the upcoming production of *Born Yesterday.*

Cukor, the Kanins, and Hepburn all "plotted" to enhance Holliday's part to help persuade Harry Cohn to cast her in *Born Yesterday,* which she had played with great success on the stage. "The woman is a frump," Holliday told Cukor. "When Harry Cohn sees it, he won't let me do Billie Dawn." But Cukor reassured her that her look would change as the picture progresses. He was right. Holliday scored a huge triumph. When *Adam's Rib* opened, Holliday got all the press. Not realizing her willing accomplices had orchestrated the feat, critics claimed she stole the film.

The scene in which Hepburn visits Holliday in the detention center was long, but Cukor shot it in one take. Amanda's interview of Doris, the most famous sequence in *Adam's Rib,* runs more than five minutes, but Cukor presents it without any cut or camera movement. In a medium shot, Amanda is at the left, and Doris at the right, describing her unhappy marriage and absurd crime. This sequence works largely because of Holliday's stunning portrait of a wacky woman who is smart enough to know she is abused. By maintaining the spatial unity, Cukor gave Holliday the opportunity to create something special—and uninterrupted; Cukor used no action-reaction shots, the way most dialogue scenes were filmed in Hollywood.

There was no reason to cut, and besides, the camera couldn't be moved; the whole scene took place in a cell. It was Holliday's first talking scene in the picture. In those days there was a lot of chatter about scene stealing, which Cukor usually dismissed. "You can't steal a scene in a movie," he maintained, "because it's all controlled by the camera and editing." The most an actor could do was use little tricks, which as a director he didn't approve of.

Cukor said that it wasn't Hepburn's generosity or Holliday's stealing the scene; it was *her* scene, and the full shot had to be on her. Cukor believed that there was one perfect place to shoot from, where the scene falls into place. It was the text, not the director, that determined how a scene should be shot. Cukor thought there was no need to cut to Hepburn because the audience knew her face. In fact, Hepburn played the scene in profile, facing away from the camera.

Blending comic and melodramatic elements, the overall quality of *Adam's Rib* is uneven. Though lively and ingenious, the script contained easy laughs, and it had a neat, but weak, resolution. The coy "happy" ending testifies, as Molly Haskell notes, that the film strikes deeper into the question of sexual roles than its comic surface would indicate and that Cukor raises more questions than he could possibly answer. Cukor's direction was commercially clever, down to title cards that announced the changes in scenes ("Later that night"). Despite some brilliant sequences, however, *Adam's Rib* is not totally satisfying because of its blend of different styles.

The only part that was badly performed was Amanda's secretary, played by Hepburn's friend Eve March. They sometimes stubbed their toes casting chums, the resentful Cukor told Garson Kanin; in a perfectly cast film March stood out like a "sore toenail."

The other sour note was Cole Porter's dismal song "Farewell Amanda," which *Time* magazine suspected he wrote "while waiting for a bus." Actually, Porter had written the song on a cruise and originally called it "Bye, Bye, Samoa." Cukor was disappointed: It was the first Porter song to be used in his films; neither man ever mentioned the song again.

Cukor had met Porter during World War II, and they developed mutual respect and friendship; they also wanted to work together. In 1937 Porter had suffered a riding accident that resulted in multiple operations and finally the amputation of his leg. Cukor admired the composer's stamina; despite years of agonizing pain, Porter continued to travel, entertain, and write popular songs for Broadway and Hollywood that were known for their witty and risqué lyrics.

There was some rivalry between Cukor and Porter. Cukor envied his creative brilliance and social skills; like him, Porter had formed a salon for Hollywood's interesting gay men. Cukor's senior by five years, Porter was more handsome, though just as much a snob. There was always a note of ambiguity when Cukor talked about Porter. "Beneath that social exterior and that fancy-schmantzy way of talking, he was a tough businessman," Cukor once said.

Cukor was a handsome child
(here at age three), but he
was the first to admit that his
good looks didn't last long.

As a young man, Cukor bore a strong physical resemblance to David O. Selznick.
Needless to say, neither man liked the
comparison.

Cukor on the set of *Tarnished Lady*, his first film as a solo director; Tallulah Bankhead is on his right.

COURTESY OF THE ACADEMY OF MOTION PICTURE ARTS AND SCIENCES

Cukor *(bottom center)* orchestrates the kind of complex mise-en-scene for which he later became famous in *What Price Hollywood?* Leading lady Constance Bennett is at center in a white dress.

COURTESY OF THE ACADEMY OF MOTION PICTURE ARTS AND SCIENCES

Rehearsing John Barrymore and Billie Burke in the family melodrama *A Bill of Divorcement*, the film that introduced Katharine Hepburn to the American public.

COURTESY OF THE ACADEMY OF MOTION PICTURE ARTS AND SCIENCES

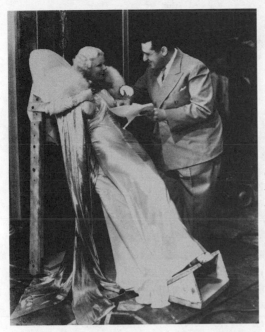

Jean Harlow gets one of Cukor's famous "personal talks" while resting between takes of *Dinner at Eight*. Her tight, elegant dress became intimately associated with her image and set a fashion trend in the 1930s.

On the set of *Little Women*, Cukor gives one too many instructions to an angry Katharine Hepburn. On the left is Douglass Montgomery.

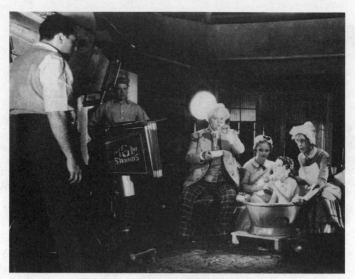

Testing the lighting for an early scene in *David Copperfield*.
W. C. Fields is on the left, Freddie Bartholomew in the tub,
and Edna May Oliver on the right.

Sylvia Scarlett was one of Cukor's
most risky and innovative films. For
most of it, Katharine Hepburn
appeared as a boy, flirting with
Cary Grant, at right.

Camille featured Garbo's finest
performance, but it was also one of
MGM's best-produced films, due to
the contributions of Cukor
(center) and the famous designer
Adrian *(right)*.

Holiday, the first Philip Barry play Cukor adapted to the
screen, was a superlative example of Cukor's favorite
genre, comedy with serious overtones. Cary Grant and
Katharine Hepburn gave top-notch performances.

COURTESY OF THE ACADEMY OF MOTION PICTURE ARTS AND SCIENCES

Cukor hated making films with children. *Zaza,* the
exception, proved to be extremely trying, because of a
little girl and despite the charming presence of Claudette
Colbert *(right).*

COURTESY OF THE ACADEMY OF MOTION PICTURE ARTS AND SCIENCES

Celebrating his birthday on the set with the crew and all-female cast of *The Women,* Cukor stands between MGM's two rival queens, Norma Shearer *(right)* and Joan Crawford *(left).*

Katharine Hepburn shone in *The Philadelphia Story* in a performance that should have won the Oscar, but didn't. Cukor observes as her character interrogates the two journalists, Jimmy Stewart *(left)* and Ruth Hussey *(right),* who have come to do a story about her wedding

Cukor directed the eighteen-year-old Angela Lansbury in her film debut, *Gaslight,* which won her the first of three Oscar nominations.

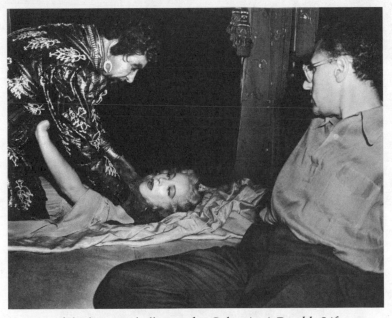

One of the biggest challenges for Cukor in *A Double Life* was instructing Ronald Colman (as an actor playing Othello) how to strangle Signe Hasso (as Desdemona).

Cukor gives William Holden
and Judy Holliday a lesson
in American history in
Washington, D.C., during the
filming of *Born Yesterday*.
Holliday plays Billie Dawn,
her best-known, Oscar-
winning role.

In *The Marrying Kind,* one
of his few movies about the
working class, Cukor
shows novice Aldo Ray,
whom he discovered, how
to interact with Judy
Holliday.

There was a lot of laughter between Cukor
(*second from right*) and Judy Holliday on the
set of *The Marrying Kind*. Holliday's large
behind later became an ongoing joke between
Cukor and screenwriters Garson Kanin and
Ruth Gordon, who called her Fatso.

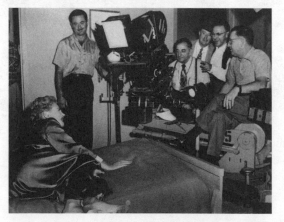

CHAPTER SEVEN:

Collaborating with the Kanins, 1950–53

AFTER THE SUCCESS OF *ADAM'S RIB*, CUKOR'S FIRST ASSIGNMENT IN 1950 was a minor picture starring Lana Turner and Ray Milland, called *A Life of Her Own*. Though the acting was better than in other Hollywood melodramas about adultery, for Cukor this forgettable picture became the nadir of the entire decade. This movie soon became a negative point of reference, the kind of film he *should not* be doing.

Nobody, least of all Turner, liked the picture, designed as a star vehicle. The bad script was never finished, and both Cukor and Turner disliked the actor cast as the married man, Wendell Corey. The actor, Cukor protested, projected anything but the image of a rich and suave married man. But as if to demonstrate *his* power, Dore Schary cast him. Cukor was furious, and in a show of anger over the situation, Turner decided to stay home for a few days, halting the entire production. Finally, the tension between Turner and Corey, compounded by Cukor's continuous protests, led to the quick recasting of another actor he didn't respect, Ray Milland.

Cukor was also unhappy about working with costume designer Helen Rose, a friend of Schary's and a "conniving bitch." Untalented and devoid of taste, Rose designed clothes for Turner that almost destroyed the actress's image as a glamour girl. For the first scene her dress was an ugly red chiffon whose seams were unsewn. To speed things up, Rose pinned the dress so that Turner could do the master shot. Rose's work nearly succeeded in undermining Cukor's rapport with his leading lady.

However, Turner gave a surprisingly subtle performance, better than Cukor expected of her. He found Turner to be practical, as far as acting was concerned, though he detested her barbarous taste, particularly in men. To his surprise, Turner could be campy, too, even poke fun at herself. Before shooting began, she came to him and said, "Mr. Cukor, I want you to know one thing: I can do it if I can understand it." Cukor thought that was very funny; it was the kind of story he relished telling at his dinner parties.

Shortly after Cukor's return from Europe, in April 1950, Harry Cohn assigned him to direct *Born Yesterday*. The new assignment meant he would not be available to work on Selznick's production of *Tender Is the Night,* planned as a star vehicle for Jennifer Jones. Cukor derived no small pleasure from turning down Selznick's offers. The wheels had turned: With Selznick's career in decline, it was now he who needed Cukor.

Getting *Born Yesterday* was an achievement because Cukor was not the first choice. All the studios had been after Garson Kanin's play. In one of its biggest deals Columbia purchased the Broadway hit for one million dollars in 1948, but the project was put on the shelf for months because of casting problems. Harry Cohn assigned it to his star, Rita Hayworth, but she was too busy as Aly Khan's new wife to make up her mind to do it.

In January 1950 the studio announced that as Cukor wanted, Judy Holliday would play Billie Dawn. Kanin had written the play for Jean Arthur, but the insecure actress had withdrawn during rehearsals, and Holliday was asked to learn the role in three days. Holliday scored a huge success in the theater, playing Billie Dawn for four years and 1,643 performances.

Before Cukor came aboard, Cohn's maladroit handling of the situation alienated Kanin and the actors involved with the New York production. Cohn riled up Paul Douglas, who played Brock, the junk dealer, so much that the actor would have nothing to do with the movie. Instead Broderick Crawford, who had recently won an Oscar for *All the King's Men,* was cast in the role.

Crawford was a better actor than Douglas, but he lacked the latter's sex appeal. When Douglas punched Holliday, it was at once painful and erotic. Crawford, in contrast, punched her like a policeman, and the two didn't generate any sexual tension. Onstage Holliday and Douglas worked so well together that the audience didn't really want her to go back to the journalist, who was a stuffed shirt. But because of casting, in the film William Holden's journalist was perceived as the sympathetic romantic hero.

Cohn was polite with Cukor, and the director did his best to keep him that way. Sorry that Kanin was determined to remove himself from the final script, Cukor how hoped that "les frères Epstein," the bright Julius and Philip, who had written *Casablanca,* would produce a respectable script. He was absolutely wrong.

The Epsteins' draft significantly altered the original. To spend a million dollars, Cukor told Cohn, and arbitrarily throw out some awfully good things in the play was incomprehensible to him. A tough businessman, Cohn had paid a lot of money for the script and wouldn't spend anymore. He agreed, however, for Kanin to do a rewrite, if no more money was involved, and he didn't get screen credit (which ultimately went to Albert Mannheimer).

To Cukor's dismay, Columbia treated the project as if it were a dreary play that had just happened to "limp along" for four years on Broadway. But he didn't feel bad about burdening Kanin with the rewrites because his assistance might make the difference between success and disaster.

Kanin, like Cukor, thought it was an error to stress the plot, which was never the play's strongest point. Cukor and Kanin suspected a certain kind of censorship was at work. The omissions—the script didn't detail Brock's greedy scheme to sweep all the scrap iron from the world—were absolutely disastrous. To have rewritten the script into a snide piece of mushmouthery, was "a terrible whiff from the stench of cowardice." Kanin wondered why certain sentences were changed to such vague formulations as "It used to be called fascism, now it's called by other names," which made no sense. It was idiotic to make an intelligent man like Paul utter such words; it would be better to cut the whole thing. Kanin begged Cukor to protect the play's integrity at all costs.

The third draft, a combination of the play and the first script, proved better. Cukor perceived it a "personal triumph over dark forces" that Kanin's lines stayed. Boldly overriding Cohn's resistance, he reverted to the original play, with all of Kanin's suggestions incorporated into the final draft.

Once the script was done, Columbia encountered nearly insurmountable difficulties in passing the censors' scrutiny. Cukor was urged to take the greatest care in photographing Holliday's dresses: It was mandatory for the intimate parts of the body—specifically breasts—to be fully covered. The censors also requested avoiding any suggestion that Billie was trying to get Paul into bed. It initially didn't like Billie's line "Are you one of these talkers, or would you be innarested in a little action?" Miraculously, at Cukor's insistence, the line remained intact.

Cukor knew audiences would accept the idea that innocence could be born afresh in a "fallen woman." He directed Billie's reaction when kissed by the young journalist as virginal, as if she'd never been kissed before. For him, this was one of the film's charming points: Billie was born yesterday, but she was also born again.

Cukor's preparatory work was innovative: The actors rehearsed for two weeks, then performed before an audience of studio employees. This procedure gave the actors a chance to develop "dimensional characters" and also to clock laugh values. It was a pre-preview of the film, long before the cameras began rolling. Cukor held that if a scene was funny, there was no need to play with it. When people complained, "That laugh overrode the line. I did not hear the next line," his standard answer remained: "Go and see it again." But he did make changes, adding some visual detail, when the laughter was long and loud.

To increase authenticity, Cukor decided to go to Washington, D.C., for locations. The city actually became a dramatic personage in the story. Observing tourists at the Lincoln Memorial, he noticed that sightseers chewed gum and gave the place only a cursory glance, if any at all. In Hollywood movies, however, sightseers invariably stood in rapt attention. Avoiding these clichés, Cukor considered the outdoor scenes among his best efforts.

Harry Horner was chosen as production designer. Horner, who was Viennese, had worked with Cukor on several films. "As designer," Horner recalled, "I did more than the sets, I worked with George on the whole visual concept." Cukor instructed Horner not to be influenced by the play, which was confined to one set. He based his design on a real hotel, which he built on the lot. The sets were set up in a way that allowed for the shifting locales of the story. "To work with George was a pleasure," said Horner. "Other directors I worked for, like William Wyler, were very serious, but George was always amusing in his comments. I had a lot of freedom in suggesting ideas, which he always accepted; he had complete trust in me."

Onstage Judy Holliday wore five costumes; for the film Jean Louis designed thirteen elaborate creations. Holliday made a great entrance with a corsage hanging behind her right ear; it looked like a displaced bunch of grapes. Cukor asked Louis to "characterize" the clothes, with obviously expensive and ornate clothes at the beginning, when Billie is dumb and acquisitive, but as she acquires culture, with a simpler, more elegant wardrobe.

Billie Dawn became Holliday's most famous role, even though her later role in Cukor's *The Marrying Kind* was richer and more textured. With *Born Yesterday*, Holliday became an accomplished actress, for which Cukor took credit. "It was all me," he joked. "My job was to see that she made all the points, but not too obviously."

Cashing in on Holliday's unique voice, Cukor refused to let the sound department tamper with it, insisting on a true recording. But the first time he heard her voice in the rushes, it seemed strange. "We just cut out some of the crud in her lower register," a sound technician said. "You've also cut out the comedy and the heart," Cukor dryly noted.

"Let's go back to the original recording."

Like *Adam's Rib*, *Born Yesterday* is an uneven film, with a hilarious opening, talky middle, and preachy finale. Pauline Kael pointed out its chief problem: As Billie gains in virtue, she diminishes in interest. But as far as Cukor's work was concerned, he continued his exploration of the long, uninterrupted takes. The silent gin game is technically the film's most brilliant sequence.

During the shoot Cukor entertained very little. When he was working, his habit was to crawl into bed early in the evening. Friends invited for dinner were warned in advance that by nine they would be "out into the night."

As soon as shooting was over, on August 12, Cukor again engaged in a busy social schedule. His closest friends in the 1950s included Tracy and Hepburn, the Colmans, Ethel Barrymore, Judy Holliday, Constance Collier, Lucile Watson, Clifton Webb, and Joan Crawford. As usual, in addition to the "regulars," special guests, often writers or artists, were invited. At a big dinner party he gave in September, with Ethel Barrymore, Ava Gardner, Joan Crawford, Sam Goldwyn, Jr., and Hoyningen-Huene, the outsider was piano virtuoso Vladimir Horowitz.

Cukor made an effort to see Katharine Hepburn and Irene Selznick whenever he was in the East. After her divorce from Selznick, Irene became a major theater producer, orchestrating such plays as *A Streetcar Named Desire*. From time to time she consulted with Cukor, as when she took an option on *Anastasia*. Cukor thought it was an interesting but poorly written play, but she went ahead, and it was a smash hit before eventually becoming a popular picture.

In April 1951 Cukor was in New York for a few days to see his friends. He hosted a big dinner party at the "21" Club for Irene Selznick, to which he invited Garbo and George Schlee, Lucile Watson, Constance Collier, Judy Holliday, and the George Kaufmans. Garbo's presence was unusual. His friendship with her was ambiguous and mostly on a one-to-one basis. Once in a while Garbo teased Cukor about returning to the screen, hoping he was still waiting for her comeback!

While Cukor was in New York, there was a press screening of *Born Yesterday* in Hollywood that created a big hoopla: nothing but enthusiasm for the film and endless praise for Holliday, with predictions of an Oscar for her. Cukor was not as sure as Cohn that she would win an Oscar, but he knew Holliday would give contenders Gloria Swanson (*Sunset Boulevard*) and Bette Davis (*All About Eve*) a run for their money.

When the movie opened, Kanin was wonderfully generous in his praise, claiming the film was better than the play. It ought to be, Cukor held, not too modestly. At Oscar time *Born Yesterday* was nominated for the top awards (Best Picture, Actress, Director). Cukor was relieved to be out of town during the race, planning to return after the "Academy dirt" was safely over. He felt unable to give again the big "clown laugh" with tears in his eyes if he didn't get the award for the fourth time; he was just too old for that.

Cukor listened to the ceremonies on the radio in a New York club, with two of the nominees, Holliday and Gloria Swanson. Upon winning, Holliday wanted to call her mother, but the press monopolized all the telephones. Cukor tried to get her a booth, but a reporter elbowed his way ahead of them. With rain pouring outside, he put his coat on Holliday's shoulders and took her to a Chinese restaurant to make the call.

Knowing that Cukor would be embarrassed if she told him how wonderful he was, Holliday instead sent him a letter: "I love every minute of working with you." For his part Cukor sent her a cable from the Oliviers in London, praising the movie and Holliday. Despite all the adulation, however, when Cukor returned to California, he was disappointed to find himself idle, with nothing interesting to do.

Cukor's closest male friend in the 1950s was George Hoyningen-Huene, who became his favorite traveling companion. After their stimulating trip to Greece, Cukor hoped to go on "the road to romance" with Hoyningen-Huene to other countries. When the photographer was not available for a trip to Spain Cukor was planning, he took another old companion, Bob Wheaton. They saw all the sights, but it was not the same as traveling with the exciting and knowledgeable Hoyningen-Huene.

Priding himself as a bountiful gift giver, Cukor did some shopping in Spain, buying rugs, lanterns, handbags. His friends were delighted with their Spanish presents; Ethel Barrymore and Billie Burke got beautiful leather handbags.

Cukor was asked to do an article for *House & Garden* about Spain, but, afraid to display his ignorance, he asked Luis A. Bolín, director of the Spanish Tourist Department, for a well-written book from which he could plagiarize, wishing to "cut a fine figure" (a common Cukor expression) not only as a traveled director but as a literary light as well. Cukor agonized for days over the piece but, frustrated with his writing, was too embarrassed to submit it. He was now interested in shooting a film in Spain just to get a free trip.

Every year, as soon as September arrived, Cukor was already thinking of Christmas. He enjoyed giving presents but hated the work involved. He much preferred to have other people do the shopping—the likes of Hoyningen-Huene, or a decorator friend, Jerry Wunderluck, or on occasion his neighbor director, Arthur Lubin. Lubin recalled: "Around Christmastime, we would go shopping to places I knew where they sold wholesale. George would then have people come in and wrap the presents for him."

Lubin had introduced Wunderluck to Cukor in 1947. At that time he had a flower shop downtown and helped Lubin with his parties. Wunder-luck recalled: "George liked me because I was useful. I would get things done quickly and cheaply." Wunderluck would do the flowers, reuphol-ster a chair, buy a cashmere sweater for Frances Goldwyn. Cukor called him Mr. Wonderful.

Gift giving was a big effort, but because he wasn't always endowed with good memory and didn't pay attention, he often recycled gifts, passing them from one friend to another. Hans Kohler remembered that Cukor once gave a friend the present he had received from him the year before. Cukor's friends joked about his "impractical gifts," usually items that were given to him: ashtrays, trays, blankets.

Hoyningen-Huene was the chief engineer of Cukor's Christmas oper-ation—particularly the cards. For Cukor's 1950 cards, the photographer came up with an original idea of showing him leaning out of a cloud. But it made Cukor self-conscious: Wasn't it too angelic for him to lean out of heaven? Having gained fifteen pounds that year, he sure didn't feel or look like an angel.

Cukor usually purchased about a hundred objects, the gifts equally divided between men and women. Hoyningen-Huené knew the sort of "classy" friends Cukor had—"pretty elegantsia who had everything"—in his words. One year the photographer was asked to buy nice but inex-pensive presents—silver boxes or trays from Mexico. "The cheaper the better," Cukor instructed him. Close friends, like Spencer Tracy, got bigger presents, like a red rug from Spain; the others got pins, trays, or other knicknacks.

Every January was the same. The month was devoted to the exchange of thank-you notes for Christmas presents. No matter what else was going on in Cukor's life, Christmas celebrations were never neglected. There was the routine exchange of presents with David Selznick, who had moved into a new apartment, overlooking New York's East River. Selznick extended a standing invitation, which Cukor never used. When-ever Cukor gave Selznick a painting, the latter asked for the artist's name, intimating that perhaps the work was not by a famous enough artist.

A recurrent problem during the holiday season was that most parties Cukor attended played havoc with his ongoing diet. Gifts of food from his friends (a delicious cake from Billie Burke), who knew how much he loved to eat, compounded the problem. After the holidays Cukor sent humorous notes to Doré Schary, who was also always dieting. Cukor reproached Schary for living in a dreamworld, reminding him that oil and butter were "Instant Death," that "anything anybody eats too much is fattening."

In 1951 Cukor began extensive correspondence with the writer Edith Sitwell about a possible film adaptation of her novel *Fanfare for Eliza-*

beth, an original look at King Henry VIII and Anne Boleyn. It was the first of a handful of promising projects Cukor couldn't get off the ground in the 1950s.

Cukor met Sitwell with Maugham and Ethel Barrymore when they all attended an event at which Sitwell read the sleepwalking scene from *Macbeth.* "She knocked me right on my ass," he later said of her illuminating performance, one that only a real artist could convey. He believed that with his guidance she would write a first-rate screenplay.

Because *Fanfare* provided great roles for the Oliviers, Cukor wished to make a deal as soon as possible. In 1951 he had the Garson Kanins deliver Sitwell's script to the Oliviers in person. But after reading it, Olivier told Cukor he couldn't visualize the material as a film—the incidents were diffused, there were too many characters, and the king didn't emerge as a recognizable figure—but the Oliviers were thrilled at the prospect of working with him.

Cukor maintained that the material had dramatic excitement, casting a fresh light on a familiar story. Written insightfully, the royal characters had the breath of life, missing the waxwork characters of more conventional historical novels. But as usual, the first job was to get a clean story line, with a beginning, a middle, and an end.

Sitwell was sad that the Oliviers weren't enthusiastic and proposed another British actor with a marvelous voice, John Gielgud. *Fanfare* dragged on at MGM, then moved to Columbia, but it was never made. The time was bad for such literary projects; the film industry was changing, and it was difficult to get any projects into production. Metro axed eleven films that were ready to go, and Fox six. Cukor saw the lack of interest in Sitwell a reflection of the death of the Old Hollywood. For the first time, he could see himself as a victim of the new technologies: CinemaScope, 3-D, Todd-AO.

It was at this juncture of his career that Cukor grew more dependent on the Kanins' screenplays. Their working relationship was mutually rewarding, and it also deepened their friendship. The Kanins knew that under Cukor's direction their stories would remain intact and be tastefully done; Cukor displayed a sacred attitude toward writers and the printed word. Two pictures were ready to go, *The Actress* and *Pat and Mike,* but Cukor left the prioritizing up to the Kanins; he was "that versatile."

In the meantime, Cukor's estate at Cordell Drive was coming along. Spencer Tracy moved into one of the houses, which became his permanent residency. When a prospective tenant who was to move into the other house proved difficult, Cukor approached the Kanins, who had once suggested he build a house for them. How about using his house as a third place, along with New York and St.-Tropez? Cukor even promised to decorate it with wonderful objets d'art.

Cukor enjoyed chiding the Kanins for their "luxurious" life-style in southern France, contrasting it with his modest existence in California. While the couple were having fun abroad, he had to work hard, making a living as a director of their "indifferent scripts." Truth to tell, Cukor was taken aback when the Kanins declined his offer to rent one of his houses—shocked that $450 a month seemed a wild extravagance to them.

Charles Brackett, a Fox writer-producer, wrote a mildly amusing comedy-drama in 1951 about a woman who runs a lonely hearts racket, called *The Model and the Marriage Broker*. The script detailed the efforts of Thelma Ritter, who played cupid for a model (Jeanne Crain) and an X-ray technician (Scott Brady). Ritter got third billing, but it was really her film, for which she received an Oscar nomination.

Cukor had reservations about Brackett's cynical, heartless approach to human frailty. But there was enough in it to engage his imagination; he was attracted to the collision of fact and fantasy among lonely hearts, a motif that recurred in his work. The reviews, however, were bad, and *The Model* was one of Cukor's big flops.

The Model was made as part of Cukor's contract for Fox. At first it was not easy for Fox's top brass to sell Jeanne Crain for the lead. Zanuck was willing to wait for the results of the test with Joanne Dru, Cukor's first choice. Dru was young and attractive and possessed sex appeal, but under pressure Cukor relented and agreed to use Crain, whom he perceived as "a flat tire." Shooting began in June and was scheduled to be completed in thirty days. But things proceeded so smoothly Cukor was done in twenty-nine days. "Count 'em," he told Zanuck.

The mogul wished to have at least one big name in the film, to prevent it from being labeled a "character actors' film." Substantial changes were made in the script, which Zanuck thought was too "talky." But the film was in danger of receiving a secondary status, a little item, as it finally did. The New York front office wanted a more youthful title, fearing that because of Ritter's prominent role, audiences might think it was a "middle-aged" film.

After working with Cukor, Brackett said he never believed the director until he said something four times. "He would look at a page of dialogue," he recalled, "and tell us it was phony, phony, phony, phony. When Cukor got to the fourth one, we knew he meant business."

At the end Cukor thanked Zanuck for his encouragement, "the shot in the arm" that every director needs. Never beneath flattery, Cukor pretended to have appreciated his comments. With all his criticism of the moguls—Louis B., Harry Cohn, Zanuck—Cukor seldom had the guts to confront them, the way Katharine Hepburn did. He moaned and groaned, wrote protest letters—without mailing them—but avoided direct confrontations at all cost.

During the shoot Cukor's father died, at age eighty-six, in his Beverly Hills home. The last year had been agonizing for Victor Cukor; he had been semicomatose, in pain and discomfort. Cukor arranged for modest services at Malinow and Simon Mortuary.

In the same season Cukor was shocked by Fanny Brice's death, though it happened in a wonderfully merciful way. Suddenly stricken, Brice never suffered the slightest pain and never regained consciousness. It was a "model death" that Cukor wished for himself.

Though her last years were not very good, Brice didn't go like Laurette Taylor, who died in misery in 1946. Cukor had donated his correspondence to her daughter, Marguerite Courtney, for a book she was writing. It broke Cukor's heart when Courtney told him he was the only person Laurette really trusted, the only man, she believed, who could help her comeback.

In August 1951, with his work on *The Model* complete, Cukor left for a one-month vacation in New York, luxuriously ensconced, courtesy of Columbia, at the Waldorf. He used some of his free time to interview actors and scout locations for his next film, *The Marrying Kind*.

In New York, Cukor was pleasantly surprised when producer Gilbert Miller asked him to direct a stage version of Colette's *Gigi*. Cukor had not seen the French play, but he praised Anita Loos's excellent adaptation. It was going to be an adventure; the last time Cukor had worked in the "theatah" was in 1928. "I must take care," he told a friend, "lest I direct the actors in a way that has gone out with Edwin Booth." The enthusiastic director hoped that getting Metro's approval would not be an insurmountable problem.

From time to time Cukor was asked to do a play, but he wasn't tempted until *Gigi* came along. *Gigi*, a play with great roles for women, was his kind of material, described by him as a story about three generations of tarts trying to marry off a heroine who was half child and half woman. Anxious to direct, Cukor quipped: "I'm sure large audiences of mine have been waiting for my comeback for many years."

He was not encouraged, however, by Bert Allenberg, his William Morris agent. There were complications in getting a release, and in the end Cukor was unable to fit the play into his schedule. Anita Loos was terribly disappointed. For her, no one but Cukor was cut for the job, and she trembled to think of the play's success if it was not handled properly. Shortly thereafter Cukor's friend actress Constance Collier withdrew from the pivotal role of Gigi's grandmother. A French director, Raymond

Rouleau, who spoke little English, was chosen, and Collier didn't think she could render an effective performance. "I've never had such a good press in my life," the touched Cukor told Collier. "It certainly makes me sound mighty important when I read that you chuck a part because I'm not doing the play."

Based on a script by the Kanins, Cukor's next film, *The Marrying Kind*, dealt with the breakup of a blue-collar marriage between Florence (Judy Holliday) and Chet Keefer (Aldo Ray). It starts off as a light romantic comedy, but then the tone changes to melodrama. Though warm and likeable, inadvertently, the comedy seems condescending to the "little" people."

What set the movie apart was its unspectacular milieu. In the 1950s there weren't many films about the working class. In its style, too, *Marrying Kind* was innovative, using a kind of American neorealism. Extensive location shooting in New York gave the film authenticity in conveying the blue-collar milieu.

Several scenes were actually shot at a post office. If he ever had to show hell or purgatory, Cukor said, a New York post office would be the perfect setting. It was a place devoid of any emotion—ambition, anger, jealousy. Workers just blankly sort letters. Cukor enhanced this monotonous feeling with the lighting. Years earlier, on a flight from Europe to New York, his plane had stopped at Gander. He noticed that the light inside and outside the plane was exactly the same; it was neither day nor night. Cukor remembered this image and used it for the post office scene.

A more realistic approach was also attempted with the studio sets. The Keefers' apartment was deliberately small and cluttered, to convey a stifling sense of confinement that reflected the couple's marital tension. A stickler for research, Cukor attended some divorce sessions in a Brooklyn court. The Kanins had placed the divorce proceedings around a conference table, rather than a regular courtroom table, but Cukor found out this was a procedure only in juvenile court.

The hearings Cukor attended were presided over by a woman, which gave him the novel idea of casting a female star in the role of Judge Kroll. He first thought of Ina Claire, who expressed her wish to do a down-to-earth part. She once told Cukor that her stylish, sophisticated acting was something she had to impose on herself. But Claire turned the role down, suggesting instead Ethel Barrymore. "Oh," said Cukor, "Ethel would never consider so small a part for such little money. We could never aspire that high." Offended, Claire did not react with her customary laughter.

The role was played by Madge Kennedy, another old friend: She needed money, and work was good for her spirits. A Broadway ingenue in her youth, Kennedy had made some silent films. *The Marry Kind* was her first film since 1926; Cukor used Kennedy again in *Let's Make Love,* in 1960.

Cukor knew that casting was the most important element for *The Marrying Kind.* As a team he and the Kanins had developed a casting method called "The Blackball System." If one tried long enough, one could always find an actor who was acceptable to every member of the team. But if one member felt strongly opposed to an actor, it was enough to rule that actor out.

The role of Florence was specifically written for Judy Holliday, then at the peak of her career. Holliday came back from her vacation looking slender; she had lost twenty pounds, and the loss was very becoming. Because Holliday was a compulsive eater, Cukor used a double standard with her. If Holliday came to dinner while she was working with him, he watched her carefully to see that she didn't overeat. But when Holliday was in another film, Cukor reverted to his childhood and urged her to take another helping!

After casting four new actors in *Adam's Rib,* who contributed to its freshness, Cukor determined to use new faces whenever possible. The trouble with most Hollywood actors was that they looked and sounded like actors. Tom Ewell didn't look like an actor, but the combination of him and Holliday didn't sound "appetitlich." Ewell was such an odd-looking fish that audiences might think his unattractive looks were the reason for his marital breakup. William Holden was an "agreeable chap," but he lacked the reality for the part; besides, he was "too goyish." As for Danny Kaye, his audience was conditioned to expect songs and high jinks.

Of course, they all wanted Marlon Brando, feeling it was time for a little change of pace for him. Brando's "Rocky Graziano approach" would bring reality and vitality to the picture. Cukor knew he could do wonders with Brando, but he teased the Kanins that using Brando might change their script into the story of a girl who married an introspective moody fellow and thereby got herself into trouble. Cukor joked about Brando because he knew the chances of getting him were nil.

The timing seemed perfect for making a star out of an unknown. Indeed, the role was finally cast with Aldo Ray, formerly Aldo da Re, the constable of Crockett, a small town outside San Francisco. Endowed with an offbeat personality, Ray looked average and had an odd, husky voice. "I had a part in a football film," Ray recalled. "Harry Cohn wanted me to stay in Hollywood, but I said, 'No, I'm a big fish in a little pond. I'm going home.'" The next day Ray got a call from Columbia: "We'd like you to come down and make a test for Mr. Cukor; we think you have a future in the business."

Ray took another week off and returned to Hollywood. After a brief meeting at the studio Cukor took him home. "He started talking to me,"

Ray recalled, "just to get to know me. For one week, six full days, he tutored me." Cukor tested Ray on a thousand-to-one hunch; it certainly was a risk entrusting a lead part to someone with no experience, but Cukor found him real and fresh—if a little crude.

Ray went back to Crockett. "They called me," Ray recalled, "as soon as the Kanins saw the tests."

"Kid, resign your job," said Columbia's casting head.

"What for?" asked Ray.

"You can't wear two hats. You can either stay in politics or become a movie star."

Ray was perplexed, but when he was told that his costar was Judy Holliday, with Cukor directing, his response was: "OK. I'm in!" He added: "It was a big step for Columbia to gamble on me."

Back in Hollywood, Harry Cohn told Ray, "I've got one standing order for you. You are never to take an acting lesson." Ray always suspected the order came directly from Cukor. However, Cukor did recommend that Ray be sent to a ballet school because he walked too much like a football player.

Cukor flew on September 7 to New York, where four days later exterior shooting began. Working with an inexperienced lead, he asked for an extra five-day rehearsal. In the end they were able to complete the film in forty-five days.

The first day of shooting was rugged because Ray was scared. It was pretty trying for Holliday, too, but "she behaved like an angel." During their first screen kiss Ray asked Cukor, "What should one of these phony kisses look like?"

"A phony kiss looks like a phony kiss," Cukor retorted. "Now kiss her like you did the girls in Crockett."

Gradually Cukor helped Ray relax in front of the cameras.

Ray said Cukor "made a point to know his actors." In the two films he did with Cukor, *The Marrying Kind* and *Pat and Mike*, "he taught me everything I know about acting." Cukor created a natural atmosphere for Ray. "The key to acting is not to act," he told Ray, urging him to do "what comes naturally. Don't memorize words, memorize the idea, and for that you have to listen."

Cukor watched every little movement Ray made, giving him endless corrections: "Bring it up"; "Bring it down,"; "Don't be afraid to get emotional; A lot of actors are afraid to emote, but when you're heartbroken, you've got to show it." "Don't worry," Cukor said, "the camera catches everything. It's in there, it's in your eyes, whether you know it or not."

"We didn't do too many takes," said Ray. "The Kanins wrote good scripts. You didn't have to deviate much; everything was there."

In the movie the Keefers' marriage suffers from unrealistic expectations. In flashbacks each tells about their life together. One narrates a past incident, while the same episode is shown onscreen as it is remembered—quite differently—by the other. "It's all in what you remember and in your point of view," the judge tells the couple. The emphasis on subjective interpretation of reality was a recurrent motif in Cukor's work—most notably in *Les Girls,* a 1957 *Rashomon*-like picture.

One of the brilliant scenes was the flashback to the Fourth of July picnic. Their son, Joey, has gone off with other children to swim, but the camera doesn't follow him, zeroing in on Holliday as she plunks her ukulele and warbles a chorus or two of "Dolores." Then Cukor shows the legs of people running toward the lake in obvious haste. Holliday is oblivious until her little girl screams that Joey has drowned.

The scene ends with a powerful dissolve to the present, with Holliday relating the episode to the judge. Her crying and screaming by the lake dissolve into her crying and beating her fists on the table. Cukor's inspiration for this scene came from a production of Chekhov's *The Cherry Orchard.* He remembered the way Alla Nazimova, sobbing over the death of her child, threw herself on the young tutor. Nazimova sobbed as if the tutor were actually carrying her boy, as if he had just drowned. This scene had such emotional impact that Cukor stored it for future use.

"This is a key scene," Cukor told Ray. "You've got to think of something that would make you very emotional."

"At that time I didn't have a son," Ray recalled, "but I had a little brother, two years old, who was like a son to me." Ray thought about his baby brother during that scene. "I ran down there, grabbed the boy, and pulled him out of the water, screaming away. Everybody was in tears; they thought it was for real." Cukor saw violent rage in the frantic way Ray moved and had tears in his eyes. It was a rare occurrence for a director who took pride in being unsentimental.

Cukor's idea of putting a dream sequence into a realistic comedy was also interesting. Many of the Kanins' scripts for Cukor contain such a fantasy. In this one Chet has a nightmare in which he is sucked off his bed onto a conveyer belt that transports him to a mail chute. He surfaces in Times Square, where a firing squad composed of many images of Florence, dressed in a policeman's uniform, shoot at him. This sequence visualized Chet's anxiety and dehumanization caused by his monotonous job. "You just run across Broadway in your shorts," Cukor instructed Ray. "I did it without a blink," said Ray. "What the hell, I would do anything for George."

The Keefers' romantic illusions are shattered by the tragic death of their son. But the crisis, which initially drives them apart, also serves as the potential for their reconciliation, and confirming they are still the marrying kind, they stay together. The movie was made during a period when married couples in films had to sleep in twin beds. Cukor's solution in *Marrying Kind* was original: He set it up as if the furniture hadn't arrived yet, and they had to sleep on the floor. Garson wrote a charming line that Ray delivers wistfully, "Honey, couldn't we change the order to a double bed?"

When the rough cut was ready, Cukor invited Ray to watch the film. "He gave me a pad and pencil, and said, 'Mark down anything you see in there.' " As the film progressed, Ray made a couple of notes, and Cukor was impressed with their specificity. "When they get into the cutting room," Ray said, "they are often so close to the film, they don't see anymore."

Cukor sent Ray out on the road with the film, which was released during Senator McCarthy's hearings. "They were all pinkos, Judy, Garson, Ruth," Ray said, "and the American Legion and Veterans of Foreign Wars, who were really gung ho, were picketing all over the country." Ray toured more than twenty cities in ninety days. "I was the all-American boy," he recalled. "I would tell them, 'You guys are nuts. It takes six hundred people to make a film, and you're picketing because you think these three are pinkos? You're not even saying they're Reds.' " Ray claimed that he broke up every picket line and that almost invariably the demonstrators then apologized and asked for his autograph.

Like many other stars, Ray said that after two films with Cukor, "I became a pretty learned actor. I absorbed a lot in those fourteen weeks." At the end the only advice Cukor gave Ray was: "Just keep working. Don't worry about the size of your role. Whatever you play, hero or heavy, just put your heart and soul into it." Cukor knew from the outset that Ray was made for the movies. There was something special about the look in his eyes. He also cried well, something that was very difficult for most men to do. Ray could be funny and endearing at the same time, and he wasn't afraid to play unsympathetic men.

Before the opening of *The Marrying Kind*, Cukor said to the actor, "You're going to be around a long time." *The Marrying Kind* did make Ray an instant movie star. Interestingly Spencer Tracy used exactly the same words when they finished shooting his next movie, *Pat and Mike*. It was gratifying to Ray that a director of Cukor's stature and an actor of Tracy's concurred.

Cukor's next picture, *Pat and Mike,* was a welcome change of pace. The Kanins had written a script about a woman athlete who falls in love with a raffish sports promoter, a Runyonesque type. It was Kanin's idea to have a ladylike, high-minded athlete taken on by a gangsterish manager. *Pat and Mike* was a cross between *Woman of the Year* and *Guys and Dolls.*

The idea of working with Cukor again was appealing to both Hepburn and Tracy. After Hepburn's ordeal with John Huston on the set of *The African Queen,* it was a relief to work on a small film and in California. Her return also lifted the spirits of Tracy, who in her absence had started drinking again.

The script gave Hepburn a chance to display her athletic skills in golf and tennis. Always impressed by her physical prowess, Cukor told his friends how she swam in his unheated pool in the dead of winter. "The film was based on the fact that I could do all these athletic things," Hepburn allowed. "Gar and I were good friends; he wrote it for me."

Pat and Mike didn't have much of a plot, but the dialogue was witty, and the roles were tailor-made for its stars. In the film Hepburn demonstrates with physical strength what in *Adam's Rib* she proved with intellect: that women can be equal to men. A companion piece to *Adam's Rib, Pat and Mike* was also ahead of its time.

The picture was made under friendly, intimate conditions, and it shows: *Pat and Mike* is a more relaxed film than *Adam's Rib.* Cukor, the Kanins, Tracy and Hepburn were like an extended family working together, particularly now that Tracy was renting one of Cukor's houses. Early readings took place in Cukor's library. "Gar was interested in writing those stories," Hepburn said, "and I certainly enjoyed working on them. Spencer was interested, too," she said, "but unlike me, he didn't like the chores of sitting in on script conferences."

Shooting started in January 1952 at an L.A. country club, then switched to the MGM back lot. Like *The Marrying Kind,* the film boasts a quasi-documentary quality, using some authentic backgrounds. Cukor had Hepburn take on famous golf and tennis athletes Gussie Moran and Babe Didrikson Zaharias, who played themselves. And Frankie Parker, the glamour boy among tennis champions, taught Hepburn tournament form. "She was a little bit afraid about her form and thought she ought to use a double," Parker said, "but I told her there was no reason why she couldn't do all the shots herself." She did.

Hepburn played a gym teacher caught between her enthusiasm for sports and pressure to get married. The moment her fiancé, a bland macho figure, arrives on the scene, her confidence disappears and her game falls apart. As in *The Marrying Kind,* Cukor staged an interesting fantasy sequence: Pat's tennis game goes off because her fiancé is watching. The net suddenly becomes huge, her own tennis racket the size of a tablespoon, her opponent as big as a spade. Cukor got the idea from Bill Tilden, a great player who shared with him the impression one felt when not playing well.

Tracy's Mike, a Brooklynese sports promoter with dubious connections, tries to convince Pat to throw a golf match. But realizing she is incorruptible, he signs her up, along with a racehorse and a dumb prize-fighter (played by Aldo Ray). By gaining Mike's respect, Pat becomes his most commercial asset and is also free to be herself. Mike's support is based not on love but on admiration of a pro. The film, however, doesn't suggest that women can live without men. "Who wants to get along without men?" says Pat. There is no need for it if the relationship is, as Mike says, "Five-oh-, five-oh."

In an unguarded moment Cukor told the press he didn't know the first thing about golf. But he looked on his lack of familiarity as an advantage. Too many pictures dealing with golf had been approached from the expert's point of view, while he looked at it from the audience's. Cukor reasoned that if he could stage a golf match that interested him, it would also look good to the audience.

Though not as clever as *Adam's Rib*, *Pat and Mike* is one of the most engaging of Cukor's comedies. By 1952 Tracy and Hepburn had achieved such rapport that their sparring bouts were beautifully coordinated; their previous films seemed like a warm-up. *Pat and Mike* also doesn't work hard for laughs; Cukor let the chips fall where they might. Relaxed and low-pressured, the characters never use dirty words or cheap lines to get laughs.

One of the film's best bits was a product of Kanin's inspiration. Unhappy about a line in which Mike discusses Pat's physique, the script-writer came up on the spur of the moment with: "There ain't much meat on her, but what there is, is cherce [for choice]." This quip got a big laugh, even though Tracy delivered it while three-quarters away from the camera. The line was so strong that Cukor decided not to cut to a close-up of Tracy; he didn't even shoot a close-up.

An unassuming film, *Pat and Mike* deals in a light manner with the raffish side of sports as most of the characters are seedy. One of the gangsters was played by Charles Bronson before he became a movie star, when his name was still Charles Buchinski. The gangsters were written with a nod to Damon Runyon, whose tone suited Cukor.

Pat and Mike also tells a love story of two improbable people, whose romance doesn't compromise their professional relationships. Their interaction is less competitive than in *Adam's Rib*, where both are lawyers. In an unusually discreet romance they hardly touch each other and never kiss. Only once, when Mike massages Pat's leg, is there physical contact. Tracy has a naughty-boy look on his face when he tells Hepburn that athletes must abstain from sex.

Aldo Ray played a small but funny part, a dumb prizefighter, providing the comic relief equivalent of Holliday's frumpy housewife in *Adam's Rib*. Cukor introduced the actor to Tracy and Hepburn humorously, as the constable from Crockett. When Ray was assigned to *Pat and Mike*,

Harry Cohn demanded that MGM give him costar billing. But the two veterans were shocked. "What?" they said. "The constable from Crockett? Star billing with us?" But Cukor convinced them: "You watch, Aldo will be a big star when *Marrying Kind* comes out."

Once Ray's status was settled, however, the stars accepted him graciously, as an equal and pro. "They were beautiful," Ray said. "They watched over me. Great stars like Tracy and Hepburn are always easy to work with. If you're cocky and go in with an attitude, they would probably discipline you." But Ray was humble. "What the hell, I *was* the constable of Crockett."

Cukor's fondness for Ray did not lessen his expectations. One morning, when Ray showed up unprepared, he gave him one of his famous "little talks." "George lectured me about self-discipline: 'You've got to learn to discipline yourself; otherwise you're finished.' " On another occasion Ray was late because of a party the night before, and Cukor "admonished me, but gently; he was a very gentle man: 'When you come to work, you've got to know what you're expected to do and be prepared to do anything that's in the script.' "

Ray felt that Cukor was more relaxed with Tracy and Hepburn than with him. The director knew them better and respected them for their work. "George was like a big brother to Kate and Spence," Ray noted. "He was mother hen, nurturing them, holding them together."

In one funny scene, in which Ray explains how he won a fight, he had a solid page of dialogue to memorize. He and Cukor talked about how he was going to do this scene. In the script the character says: "I was looking at him. I was fighting him. I thought it was me, and I was beating up me." But every time Ray did the scene, Cukor broke up laughing, losing his own discipline. "He was laughing so hard I had to start all over again. But to break George up behind the camera pleased me. I knew I was doing a good job."

Ray also learned to avoid looking at his director. "If you looked at George," he said, "he could throw you." Some actors complained about Cukor's habit of mouthing their parts, but for Ray, Cukor's presence was important psychologically. "I was hoping we could have done at least one more picture," Ray said mournfully. "I had some great directors, but none was ever like George Cukor."

With Cukor's near-perfect direction, *Pat and Mike* receive good reviews and did moderately well. For some reason, the film is not as fondly remembered as *Adam's Rib,* though recently film critic David Denby singled it out as the best film of 1952.

Pat and Mike was Cukor's eighth and last feature with Hepburn. "We didn't work together in the 1960s," she said. "We couldn't find the right scripts." *Pat and Mike* was also Hepburn's last MGM role. Unhappy about Dore Schary's new regime, after Louis B. was ousted, she decided to go her own way. In contrast with her, who, in liberating herself from MGM, entered the most exciting era of her work since the 1930s, Cukor's career suffered tremendously when the studio system declined.

For Cukor, a good title for what was going on at Metro was "The Ten Days That Shook the World"—big decisions, big changes. He finally had a half hour audience with Nicholas Schenck, president of Loew's. In the nineteen years Cukor had worked there, all he had ever said was: "Good evening, Mr. Schenck, give my kindest regards to your wife."

In 1952, undeterred by previous experiences, Zanuck approached Cukor with a new project, My Cousin Rachel, based on Daphne du Maurier's novel about murder and intrigue. Zanuck had engaged Cukor twice before: for The Razor's Edge and for another film that never got made.

In a burst of misguided enthusiasm, Cukor gave up his vacation to research the film. Zanuck requested that Cukor stop in New York to talk to Garbo, whom he wanted to star in the picture. He believed that if anyone could talk Garbo out of retirement, it was Cukor.

On the telephone, however, Cukor was unable to convince Garbo that My Cousin Rachel was the right vehicle. She liked the story, but she was full of fears about her comeback. On April 4, 1952, hoping a face-to-face meeting would change her mind, Cukor met Garbo at the Plaza Hotel. His hope, however, was in vain. Cukor attributed Garbo's refusal to do the picture to "la maladie Swedoise—sheer stubbornness."

In New York Cukor also talked with Vivien Leigh, who was performing Shaw and Shakespeare with Larry Olivier. Leigh had already refused My Cousin Rachel, but when she learned that Cukor was signed, she was willing to reconsider. Cukor was delighted at Lady Olivier's announcement that his "entrance" put an entirely different "complexion" on the project.

After seeing a matinee of Anthony and Cleopatra on a Sunday, all three went to the Kanins' farm in Connecticut to discuss My Cousin Rachel. Leigh agreed to star, provided the entire film was shot in England; she wanted to avoid another painful separation from Olivier. However, Fox was against shooting in England, claiming it had lost money on previous attempts.

On April 8 Cukor left for London to meet with Daphne du Maurier. The next few weeks were frantically busy as Cukor moved around the Continent, trying to put My Cousin Rachel together. On April 9 he interviewed Richard Burton, after attending an impressive performance of Monserrat at the Lyric Theater. He arranged for Burton to have costume fittings and a photo session.

The next morning Cukor left for location scouting in Cornwall with

Du Maurier, then flew to Rome, where he engaged a woman to do further research into the 1830s. After a brief vacation in Milan he continued to examine different villas and gardens; architecture was important to the story.

Back in London for another series of talks with Vivien Leigh, Cukor told her that if she signed on, Zanuck would try to arrange for the production to be made in England. After two hours of discussion Leigh gave him her word. This was not a simple achievement, for she still had reservations, and there was opposition from Olivier. After lunch Cukor called Zanuck in Paris and informed him of Leigh's demands.

With all this business going on, Cukor made time to visit his English friends. He had lunch with Edith Sitwell to discuss *Fanfare for Elizabeth*, a project he still wanted to do. As fate would have it, Hepburn was also in London, appearing in Shaw's *The Millionairess*. As soon as he returned home, he called Laura Harding and Hepburn's father and reported of her great success.

On May 10 everything seemed to be coming together, and Cukor had dinner with the Oliviers to finalize the deal. But four days later Zanuck decided against filming in England. He now asked Cukor to go back to New York and see Olivia de Havilland, the new star for *My Cousin Rachel*. De Havilland immediately agreed. After the abortive attempt of *GWTW*, she would at long last work with Cukor, but he didn't think she had the necessary erotic appeal.

Frustrated that his trip had yielded no results with Garbo or Leigh, Cukor flew back to California on May 16. In the meantime, du Maurier finished a preliminary treatment. Much was still missing, but she indicated what additions were needed.

When the script arrived, both Cukor and du Maurier thought it departed from the book. "Quite desperate," du Maurier declared in a long critique. Cukor agreed with her points: The writing was flat and banal and missed the book's ambiance. The story needed to be elemental, more passionate, anything but a Victorian tale. Again siding with Du Maurier, Cukor disliked the phony humor, which was dragged in to lighten what was basically an atmospheric drama.

As usual, Cukor's protests went unheeded. Realizing he made no headway at all, he decided to withdraw from *My Cousin Rachel;* Fox's press release stated "artistic differences." Deeply disappointed, Cukor felt foolish, too. Not only had he wasted time in England, but he had also paid for his own fare! His "consolation" was to find some use for the extensive information he had gathered. Joking about the heaps of stuff about the South that were never used in *GWTW*, he now added the Cornwall materials to a growing pile.

While Cukor was in Italy, Ingrid Bergman had asked him to carry some presents to her daughter Pia Lindstrom. Bergman's friendship with Cukor proved important after she had left her husband and fallen in love with Italian director Roberto Rossellini. Cukor served as liaison between Pia and Bergman, who was viciously attacked by the press for her "immoral" behavior and blacklisted by the industry.

In May 1952 Pia visited Cukor to pick up her mother's presents, and he proudly showed her around the house. A charming child with lovely looks, Pia was endowed with the most agreeable manner. Cukor remembered that in his childhood the people he liked were those who gave him presents. He thus gave Pia some colored stones and foreign coins for her collection.

Bergman told Cukor he was the best package carrier she'd ever had and thanked him for providing details about Pia. The exiled actress longed to hear his reports because she hardly had any news about her daughter. Hoping things would go well for Bergman in the nasty court business over Pia's custody, Cukor contacted her lawyer and volunteered to testify about her deep concern for Pia.

Cukor kept in touch with the Rossellinis, congratulating them on the birth of first their son Roberto, and later their twin daughters, Isabella and Ingrid. It took Bergman some time to overcome the surprise of suddenly having a truly large Italian family. And she reported with joy how she adopted Cukor's advice to "carefully count 'em" before going to bed.

It was a quiet summer for Cukor; he even had time to engage in politics, which seldom interested him. The major event of the season was the spectacular emergence of Adlai Stevenson as a presidential candidate. A wavering Democrat by his own admission, Cukor had become an ardent supporter of Stevenson's under the influence of Irene Selznick. Cukor's faith in the Democratic party was suddenly revived. When he ran into Charles Brackett, a faithful Republican, the producer mentioned Stevenson's acceptance speech wistfully. Hedda Hopper, another staunch Republican, was reportedly suicidal after hearing it.

Because he was experiencing more and more difficulties putting together a new film, Cukor's dogs became the major joy of his life. Dealing with dogs was more emotionally satisfying than dealing with humans. His dogs were a great comfort to him. Cukor devoted an enormous time to his dogs, talking and writing about them as if they were his children; he reported their habits, favorite foods. In a 1952 letter to the Garson Kanins, he described in detail the habits of Sasha, a black poodle Ruth Gordon had given him. Cukor reproached the Kanins, while using Sasha's name: "Have they written—any news of 'em?" He then described how Sasha's tail dropped between its legs as the dog crawled into a corner.

Everyone admired Sasha, Cukor's favorite dog. One night actress Merle

Oberon, another dog enthusiast, vowed that Sasha was the most attractive poodle she had ever seen. Cukor felt that if there weren't so many classy people that evening, Oberon would have made a handsome cash offer for the dog.

Cukor's next picture, *The Actress,* based on Ruth Gordon's autobiographical play *Years Ago,* was a modest achievement. A period piece and nostalgic slice of Americana, it differed from his other films with the Kanins. Treating Gordon's personal story too reverently, Cukor ended up making an uncharacteristically sentimental picture.

Cukor conducted his usual extensive research, studying old snapshots of Gordon's family, incorporating every detail he could into the film. He went with her to Wollaston, Massachusetts, which she hadn't visited for forty years. He duly noted minute details, such as the number of doors in the kitchen; without such research, no set designer would have designed a kitchen with four doors. "There was a lot of talk about the preciseness of the research," recalled Teresa Wright, who was cast as Ruth's mother.

At first Cukor felt the major contender for the lead was Debbie Reynolds, who had become a star after the successful musical *Singin' in the Rain.* She seemed to have the right temperament and humor; she embodied the average girl. But Reynolds lacked finesse and was uneducated; she had never heard of Shakespeare: a big minus to Cukor. After seeing her in a stage appearance, singing "Aba Daba," Cukor was offended and appalled. All along he had doubts whether Reynolds was capable of portraying Gordon's fierce individuality. Kanin was also discouraged by Reynolds's test, which shattered his hopes and made him bitter toward Metro. The film ought to look as real as a family album; Reynolds's excessive emotionalism was inappropriate.

What worried Cukor was the damage Metro was causing to its actresses. The studio had wrecked such original talents as Judy Garland and June Allyson. Cukor held that no young actress could be exposed to Joseph Pasternak's musicals and a dose of Lillian Burns's tutelage without hurting her fresh talent.

Cukor eventually cast Jean Simmons, a lovely British actress brought to Hollywood after her Oscar-nominated Ophelia in Olivier's *Hamlet.* "I was amazed to get the part," Simmons said, "me, an English girl, to play Ruth Gordon?" Cukor got a charming performance out of her, though she was miscast. Simmons lacked the young Gordon's energy: her desperate urge to perform, her strong drive to succeed. Too attractive to capture Gordon's offbeat look, a girl like Simmons could never have been the indefatigable trouper who left her sea captain father and housewife mother at age fifteen.

Cukor realized all this, but left with no choice, he resorted to Hollywood's conventional casting. Nobody was ever really plain. Either plain girls were played by Olivia de Havilland, or pretty girls wore eye glasses, which someone took off to make them suddenly become ravishing beauties. Ruth Gordon, however, was immensely flattered. "Mad" about Simmons, she was confident the Britisher would be "absolutely great."

At first Cukor wasn't excited about Teresa Wright, who landed the mother's part. "The first time I met Cukor and Spencer, over lunch," Wright recalled, "they just kidded a lot. Cukor was very nice, very relaxed. It wasn't anything like, 'This is a difficult role; do you think you can handle it?' " Cukor's problem was that Wright was too young for the part; the age difference between her and Simmons was only eleven years. "It was my first character part," Wright said. "I was dying to play it, but I don't think I quite pulled it off."

Anthony Perkins, then an unpolished actor, made his debut in *The Actress*. Simmons recalled that Cukor was harsh on all the actors, but especially on Perkins because he was so inexperienced. Cukor had known his father, Osgood Perkins, from the stage. Perkins himself conceded that his first reading leaned heavily on the " 'Shucks, Ma' school." Cukor reproached the youngster for displaying so many "Ogunquit gestures." Offended at first, Perkins was in the final account grateful that Cukor took him "so firmly in tow. I don't think I shall ever stop being influenced by you," he told Cukor, hoping to work for him again.

Before leaving for Paris, the Kanins told Cukor the picture needed every possible cinematic device—camera angles and movement—to spruce up the story. At the risk of incurring their displeasure, Cukor complained ("me not like") about the proposal scene, which still needed some "subtle adjustment." Why not take another crack at it? After all, they had only done twenty versions. Within twenty-four hours the necessary changes were made. This kind of speed and efficiency marked the Kanins' collaboration with Cukor.

"For a filmmaker," Kanin said, "George had a rare respect for the text, striving always to provide entertainment for the ear as well as for the eye." He recalled how Cukor phoned him five times a day from the set in Hollywood to request minor changes. Once a single word was substituted; another time it was a two-line cut.

Cukor held that the primary function of a director was to establish an atmosphere for creative work. In this capacity he excelled more than other directors. In every correspondence the Kanins paid compliments to their director. Cukor was so good there was a new game in town, called "Cukor, Cukor, who's got Cukor?" The couple never ceased to be amazed by the thoroughness and energy with which Cukor approached their scenarios; that was why they wanted him to direct all of them.

The correspondence between Cukor and the Kanins had a relaxed

manner. Kanin teased Cukor, as the only truly cosmopolitan friend he
had in California. He had never encountered anyone who didn't know
Cukor, or hadn't dined with him, or whose dogs didn't know his dogs. As
for Gordon, she signed her letters with some funny name, like Darling
Flo, Lolita Robertson, Alvira Francis, Zelda Sears, Lulie May, Dainty
Marie, Bella Burnett. For his part, Cukor simply addressed them as Dear
Mama and Papa.

Despite the title, the central character in *The Actress* was the gruff
father. It was a richly textured part, both harsh and tender, which Tracy
played marvelously. "George and Spencer had a special rapport," said
Simmons. "There was great kidding between them. Once, when George
wanted to show Spencer what to do, the actor said, 'Now, George, stay
where you are, and let me do it my way.'" Wright also noticed that
"George knew exactly how Spencer worked, and he made him comfortable. Their kidding never became a match; it was just for the sake of
relaxation."

Tracy had a running gag about the misbehavior of the film's cat that
kept Cukor in stitches. "This banter with Spencer was so much part of
George's way of working, the kind of camaraderie that comes from
knowing and respecting each other. It was one of the happiest times of
my life," Simmons said. "George was so amusing, so stimulating there
was never a boring moment. He had a lovely New York theatrical humor.
His joy of life was infectious; one was always happy to be around him.
Some directors are calm and laid back, but not him."

Cukor always talked a lot, sometimes making outrageous statements,
but they didn't bother Simmons. "He would get up and show me what to
do, and I thought he was better than I could ever be." Cukor teased
Simmons about the way she walked, suggesting a new walk for her. He
said, "Jean, walk with excitement as if you were always dying to go to the
bathroom." It made perfect sense to her because "this girl was always in
a state of excitement.

"He was down to business," Simmons added. "When I did it right, he
was complimentary. George was a great conversationalist. He used bad
language, but he never used it in anger. He would say, 'Oh, you British,
you all behave piss-elegant, drinking your tea, but you screw like
minks.'"

"George used to tease me," said Wright, "that when I got nervous or
didn't feel comfortable, I would bury myself in whatever I was doing." In
one scene, noticing that Wright had her back to the camera, he said: "For
God's sake, Teresa, don't you know enough to turn around and get your
face on the screen? You're not getting this amount of money just to show
the back of your head."

Cukor didn't want Wright to wear any heavy makeup. "George was happy just to let me try to do it with acting. An older makeup at my age would have looked like high school. If you were very young or very old, you can do it without makeup. Otherwise it becomes not an acting job, but the makeup department job."

"None of us wore makeup," Simmons recalled. "There was one scene in the theater with Hazel Dawn and many extras. When George noticed that some of the extras came with makeup, he started to scream. He was so angry he sent them home and suspended shooting." Cukor was a perfectionist, checking everything down to the last detail of the extras. "He would be there with you on all the costume fittings," said Wright, "and I'm sure he had gone over these things ahead of time." But Cukor was "not neurotically perfectionist.

"In staging a scene, George had things worked out pretty much," Wright said. "If it wasn't comfortable for you, you could say, 'Would it be all right if I did such and such?' He would nod or ask why. I don't remember him as one of those adamant directors who say, 'This is it.' He had enough ego to be secure; he didn't feel challenged by these remarks."

Compared with William Wyler, with whom Wright made *The Little Foxes,* Cukor was more vocal with his praise. Wyler got his actors to reach their points of desperation. "With George, everything was much more relaxed; he seemed very easy with the crew. Wyler was crazy if he couldn't get the effects he wanted and the crew hated him, but George was liked by the crew."

"George had a great sense of film, as Hitchcock did," Wright said. Comparing him with Hitchcock, who directed her in *Shadow of a Doubt,* she noted: "Like most good directors, George liked to work with a good script and good actors. He was aware that film progressed by physical action and movement. That doesn't mean that the actors have to necessarily move, but the camera must move gracefully in a kind of choreography." Wright knew she was working with a man of great taste and a sense of refinement. "George was a great gentleman, yet he used sarcasm when somebody was not cooperative."

The Actress had a twenty-four-day shooting schedule, which Cukor missed by only a couple of days. In mid-January, with a week to go, the cast dreaded the end because every day had been "Happy Days in Dixie." Cukor had not worked in as euphoric an atmosphere since *Sylvia Scarlett!* Everyone admired the rushes, but a bit superstitious, Cukor knew this could augur a "perfectly stinking" picture.

The first preview of *The Actress,* or *Fame and Fortune,* as it was then called, was good, but Cukor faced two major problems. One was length—the audience was restless—and the other was sound. There was "throwaway dialogue," which caused some confusion, particularly in the first reel. "Viewers insist on understanding every word," producer Latorence Weingarten told Cukor as if he were telling him something new. As for length, Weingarten promised to make no cuts until he discussed them with Cukor. Weingarten thought that Cukor's direction was "truly creative," but despite his conciliatory tone, a battle with Cukor over the final cut was beginning, and it was anything but friendly.

Cukor concurred on the need to cut some scenes, but not those recommended by Weingarten. In an effort to put an end to the combative atmosphere, Cukor told Weingarten he was entitled to a very large share of the credit for his generous help and patience. Behind his back, however, Cukor described Weingarten as an ass, and not a very nice one.

Cukor firmly believed that it was this kind of giving in to an "ill-mannered and idiotic" audience of teenagers, as if the preview cards were gospel, that had brought the movie business to a low point. Although the preview audiences didn't like Jean Simmons much, he defended her, arguing that if an audience had similarly reacted to Hepburn's debut in *A Bill of Divorcement*, Hollywood would have missed a great star.

Running the new dubbed version, Cukor became even more furious. A deplorable job that distorted the film's high-quality acting had been done—despite his demand for accurate sound transference. Sound man Sidney Franklin imposed his ideas about Jean Simmons's voice that unfortunately resulted in the actress sounding older and without vitality.

Wright's homey voice was smoothed out as well, and lines Tracy threw away were hiked up so that the audience would hear them. A heavy, disagreeable hand had been laid on many good scenes, and the delicacy and individuality were dissipated. Cukor considered asking Tracy to step in and throw his weight—if his didn't count.

Another preview was held at the Fox Theater in Inglewood. Once again cards were distributed, and again, a majority of viewers said they would recommend the film. Cukor was furious, for whenever he talked to Weingarten, his answers were based on a "scholarly" analysis of the preview cards—Hollywood's new science.

In October 1953, after the Kanins had seen the film, they praised Cukor's imaginative work with difficult material. But they criticized Weingarten's foolish cutting, which made the story confusing. Aware of Cukor's battle with the front office, Kanin tried to console him: No matter how hard one worked, there came a time when the project was placed in the hands of "popcorn salesmen." "There was a very pernicious habit," Cukor later told Lambert, "that when you finished a picture, *everybody* had a panacea! People who hadn't contributed very much would say, 'Oh, you can cut this and that, and you'll fix everything.' "

What Cukor deemed as lack of "taste and discretion" in handling the picture was also reflected in the choice of title. Weingarten was in favor of *The Father and the Actress,* which was suggested by the New York office, but Cukor thought it "the all-season low." They might as well call it *Father's Little Actress,* following MGM's *Father's Little Dividend,* which also starred Tracy. Finally, Weingarten changed the title to *The Actress*—also a bad one.

None of the cuts was helpful. *The Actress* didn't do well at the box office. Though a critical success in England, the film was a "commercial frost" in the United States. "MGM just didn't know what they had in the film," said Wright. "They didn't publicize the film, and the word of mouth was not very good."

Vivien Leigh, who had come to Hollywood to do a picture, inquired whether she could rent one of Cukor's houses; he could charge her a huge rent because Paramount was paying. But rented on long leases, none of the houses was available, and Cukor invited Leigh to stay with him until she found the right place.

Cukor was then delighted to learn that she had spent hours talking about him with John Gielgud. He had not taken an instant liking to Gielgud, but his opinion about the Britisher changed; he was completely wrong about the insulting things he had said about him. He now found Gielgud to be amusing, and thanks to Leigh's mediation, a new friendship began.

Leigh attended an evening at Cukor's that had an interesting mix of celebrities. Moss Hart and his wife, Kitty Carlisle, were there, along with high-toned socialites such as Lord Astor, Lord Dunsany, and the Stewart Grangers ("neither lords nor socialites"). The conversation was on a very high literary plane; the guests never talked of anyone less highbrow than T. S. Eliot or Christopher Fry. Cukor, however, was right there punching, impersonating Joan Crawford and poking fun at the plot of her new film, *Torch Song,* in which her love interest was a blind pianist.

Ethel Barrymore was also there, despite the fact she had not been well. She was staying with Cukor until moving to a smaller house, which was less expensive to run. As with Billie Burke, Barrymore was working hard on her book. The publishers sent an editor to help out, but she was reluctant to reveal private things about her family. Cukor sympathized with Barrymore; many efforts to write a book about his life also failed because of his hesitancy to talk about *his* family.

In the meantime, Cukor's social reputation outside the film industry was steadily growing—as the result of his outgoing personality. In February 1953 Bosley Crowther, the influential *New York Times* movie critic, approached Cukor for help in collecting information for his new book on MGM. Cukor was selected as a "central" figure and director of MGM's top films. After their first meeting at the Plaza Hotel, Crowther was impatient to talk further, finding Cukor's observations "vastly stimulating" and "eminently sound."

Cukor suggested that Crowther talk with Margaret Booth, Thalberg's editor, and Weingarten. And he volunteered to arrange a meeting with Tracy, whom he described as a "diverting" fellow with the most original thoughts. With business slow in Hollywood, Cukor assured the critic that people would have a lot of time to talk about the good old days. Though it was time-consuming, Cukor enjoyed this task; he hoped that his stories about Garbo would help dispel some of the "hocus-pocus" about her.

Cukor liked to introduce his friends to one another. When Jack Cage planned a trip to Paris, Cukor sent a letter to his French friend Pierre Barillet, introducing Cage as one of his intimate friends ("do not hold that against him"). Cukor also wrote letters of introduction for a rich Italian businessman who was driving up to San Francisco to see if it was true what they said about the gay Mecca.

Cukor's friends performed the same service for him. Constance Collier brought Zsa Zsa Gabor, with whom she worked in *Moulin Rouge,* to his house. With his wonderful gift with women, said Collier teasingly, he could make Gabor even more interesting. A fellow Hungarian, Cukor found Gabor "full of beans" (yet another favorite Cukor compliment) and not as vulgar as her publicity.

Cukor was hard at work on his next film, *It Should Happen to You,* during postproduction on *The Actress.* The project had started at Fox with a Garson Kanin script, *Miss Nobody,* but Zanuck somehow "loused it up," as Cukor put it, with requests for rewrites. Still, when Zanuck was willing to sell the script for thirty-eight thousand dollars to Columbia, Kanin prepared a new screenplay, originally titled *A Name for Herself,* within a matter of weeks.

Cukor began shooting the Columbia picture in New York, on May 5, 1953. A raucous comedy, it is the story of Gladys Glover (Judy Holliday), an average woman who, afraid that life is passing her by, grasps at a chance to be somebody. A frustrated actress yearning for celebrity, Gladys spends all her savings to put her name on a Columbus Circle billboard. She also faces a romantic dilemma, having to choose between her affection for Pete (Jack Lemmon), an honest but poor documentary filmmaker, and Evan (Peter Lawford), a rich soap manufacturer.

Cukor saw *It Should Happen to You* as a frothy comedy about the hunger for publicity among people who lack any talent. He was also targeting his satire at excessive advertising and the increasing popularity of TV talk shows.

No script submitted to Cukor was ever accepted without demands for revision. In this case he thought that some of the dialogue was "too discursive and argumentative." He therefore asked for changes, specifically "a definite story progression" and a "fine emotional climax." Kanin originally wrote the script for Danny Kaye, but with Holliday aboard, it was changed to fit her qualities. The part had the kind of vitality and emotion that Holliday handled well.

Interestingly, Kanin had suggested for the lead Julie Harris, who scored a big success in *A Member of the Wedding* and now had "picture status." Over the last year the Kanins had "gone off" Holliday, who was becoming less interesting to them. Holliday at the time was suffering from a weight problem, which became known as the Fatso or FA (fat ass) operation. Cukor held a candid talk with Holliday's friends Adolph Green and Betty Comden, who told him that she had a habit of indulging herself and then absolutely starving herself to lose weight. Kanin resented talking about Holliday as if she were some magical creature like Garbo. Garbo was "irreplaceable," but Holliday, a good comedienne when she had a good part, was "highly replaceable."

When Holliday tipped the scales to 160 pounds, Cukor sent her a wire with a none-too-subtle message: "This is a delightfully light script—I hope you are too." The latest scoop on Operation FA was Holliday's confidence she could get herself down to the required weight of 145 pounds. Cukor told Harry Cohn not to pussyfoot around with her, perhaps even to threaten a cancellation. A good scare should help her; it was "unconscionable" of Holliday to let herself go in this way. Cukor was then glad to report that according to his April 7 bulletin, Holliday had lost 4 pounds. This started a countdown of the actress's weight on a daily basis. On April 16 the good news about the "Fatso Department" was that Holliday had lost another 7 pounds and was now down to 149 pounds.

Cukor felt uncomfortable about burdening the Kanins with silly complaints about his actresses' problems. But he remembered—not too fondly—a few "ticklish passages" during *The Marrying Kind* when he had to reassure the insecure Holliday of her greatness as an actress. This time the increasingly impatient Cukor was determined not to go into a similar "song and dance"; he was too old for that.

The trouble about Holliday's size filled Kanin with anger. The whole project was halted because of a "big slob who eats too much and has got too large a posterior." He believed that something dramatic must happen for the actress to wake up; she was just too apathetic, undisciplined. He didn't care if the picture was made with someone else; it might do her good to lose the part. Kanin now completely sympathized with George Kaufman's line "When actors get too trying, I tell them to try somewhere else."

On the first day Cukor shot around New York's Central Park. A heat wave, which brought all the mad people out to the park, only made matters more difficult. On the second hot day he invited the cast up to his suite at the Plaza Hotel for lunch. Suddenly Holliday breezed in. "I have to take a cold bath," she said, and she did so with her hat and makeup on.

Cukor was delighted that the Kanins were living it up in luxury in France. He wasn't bitter or angry that they had cooked up some ridiculous episodes in the script, like one causing him to spend three days—at a temperature of ninety-nine—shooting a white Jaguar going around and around Columbus Circle.

Holliday played her earlier scenes marvelously, perfecting her dumb blonde part with shrewd determination. The scene in which she drives around Columbus Circle, infatuated with her billboard, is both funny and chilling. After Gladys becomes famous, she's invited to appear on a TV show. Cukor cast the scene with his old friends Constance Bennett and Ilka Chase. He satirized the fatuous personality of celebrities who talk a lot but say nothing. TV guests pretend to be very original, but they're just interested in putting themselves across. Cukor hated TV shows in which everything was false, particularly the atmosphere of fake friendship.

Cukor's big discovery in *It Should Happen to You* was Jack Lemmon. Though he had some experience in television, this was Lemmon's first chance in movies. Because he was a novice, Lemmon was not easy to work with. After each reading Cukor would say, "Jack, give less, much less."

Exasperated, Lemmon finally screamed, "Don't you want me to act at all?"

"Dear boy," said Cukor, "you're beginning to understand the essence of film acting."

In an important scene, in which Lemmon and Holliday have a row, Cukor kept saying, "I don't believe one damn thing. Jack, what do you do when you get angry?"

"I get chills and cramps," Lemmon replied. "I get sick to my stomach, but you can't use that."

"Why not?" said Cukor. "Do that!" In the height of fury, Lemmon clutched his stomach. It made all the difference.

One of Cukor's trademarks was to make a scene seem spontaneous. The scene in which Gladys and Pete are talking between snatches of playing the piano seemed improvised, but it was actually well rehearsed. According to his work habits, Cukor watched what his actors were doing naturally, trying to catch them as they behaved instinctively; the most delightful moments from his actors were often the most unexpected.

Trying to seduce Gladys, Evan chases her around the room. He gets her on the couch and starts nuzzling her neck erotically, as if he were taking her clothes off. Evan takes one of her earrings off, but she picks it up and tries to escape. He chases her again, and she ends up on the couch, in the same position, with the earring back on. "May I help on this?" a property man said during shooting.

"Please do," Cukor said.

"Let her take the earring off herself," the propman suggested, "so he can nuzzle her ear again." It made the scene terribly funny—and erotic, too.

In the scene Gladys pours a glass of champagne down Evan's neck. Because Lawford had only four clean shirts, the crew could shoot only four takes. Holliday did it once, but it was a tricky shot, and the cameraman didn't get it. She then told Cukor that she couldn't help laughing. "If you do," said Cukor, "I'll kill you." Holliday didn't laugh, but she did giggle. Cukor had to admit it was great and kept the scene as is.

Although Cukor enjoyed working with Lemmon, he did not get along with Lawford. He had wanted a more accomplished actor, an American Rex Harrison. Lawford knew that Cukor didn't want him, and he also resented Cukor's continual talks. Producer Sam Marx later invited Cukor to visit the set of *The Thin Man,* a TV series starring Lawford. There were some problems with the characters of Nick and Nora, and he thought Cukor might help. Besides, Cukor was interested in observing the television medium, of which he knew little. It never occurred to Marx that anybody would mind. To his surprise, as soon as Cukor walked in, Lawford walked out, taking the TV director with him. Lawford simply refused to face Cukor; Marx never spoke to the actor again.

Despite the strain with Lawford, there were many funny moments on the set of *It Should Happen to You.* The script satirized every glamour bath that had ever been done in the movies. Shooting the bathing scene involved thirty-four men, with Holliday up to her dimpled chin in bubbles. One propman poured soap flakes into the tub, and another whipped up a mountainous froth of suds with an electric mixer. "It is quite a commotion just to get one girl bathed," Cukor said. "This is taking on the appearance of a mob scene from *Quo Vadis,* and we intend to prove the ancient Romans were pikers when it came to bathing." After several takes Holliday began to tire, but Cukor said, "We'll do it again, Judy, but this time try to give that bar of soap a more rhapsodic look. Gaze at it as though it is a necklace from Cartier's." Said Holliday: "All right, but I hope this take does it. I want to get out of here and take a nice clean shower!"

In the original script, the film ended when Pete and Gladys stop at a motel, and he points at a sign out the window, which reads MR. AND MRS. PETE SHEPPARD. But the studio came up with another ending, in which Gladys looks up and sees an empty sign. Kanin who knew nothing about the new ending until some mimeographed pages were delivered to him, allowed that his resolution wasn't perfect, but it was better than the studio's. At this point Cukor did not have the strength for another fight; he had simply come to the end of his energies. But the last scene struck him as dangerously tepid when he saw the preview.

Cohn didn't mind shooting a new ending, but he didn't think it would help; Kanin soon realized they had lost the battle. He read Cukor's letter with tears in his eyes, caused by frustration over the heartless and brainless injustice. That any executive could step in and take charge, "vetoing and overriding," was appalling to him.

In November the film's title was changed by the studio, behind Cukor's back; he got the information thirdhand from the cutter. Protesting to Jerry Wald that he was the last to find out, Cukor was beginning to get accustomed to being double-crossed and badly treated by Columbia. He vowed that he and Columbia would have to get along without each other in the future.

Kanin thought that overall *It Should Happen to You,* released on January 15, 1954, was their best collaboration. While their professional association ended here, the friendship continued for another twenty years, until their falling-out, caused by the publication of Kanin's *Tracy and Hepburn.*

CHAPTER EIGHT:

Cukor's Masterpiece, 1954–57

In the summer of 1953 Cukor enthusiastically accepted Sid Luft and Judy Garland's offer to direct their new musical version of *A Star Is Born*. *A Star Is Born* was to be Cukor's first musical and his first picture in color. The tale of a doomed Hollywood couple, she on the way up and he on the way down, was a remake of the 1937 film with Fredric March and Janet Gaynor, and it also resembled Cukor's *What Price Hollywood?* Cukor used his comedic skills to add some lightness to the story's more tragic elements.

In August Cukor spent a week in San Francisco, gathering strength for what he knew would be a pretty rugged picture. The production took about ten months: Shooting began in October 1953, and postproduction was not completed until July 1954. The deal between Luft's Transcona Enterprises and Warner's called for a film budgeted at $2.5 million, but it ended up costing $6 million, way above the average for the time. Cukor was blamed for the excessive budget, but he didn't care; making this film was so absorbing and so stimulating he could hardly wait to get to the studio each day.

Hoyningen-Huene, back from Spain to serve as the color consultant, was soon overextending himself and getting involved in all "matters of taste." He coordinated the color design, sets, props, and costumes. Hoyningen-Huene never understood why there was such a loose liaison among the various elements in color pictures. Cukor's model for this film was John Huston's *Moulin Rouge;* he attributed its success to the exciting use of color.

A Star Is Born was made for Garland; it was a comeback vehicle, for she hadn't made a film since MGM had dropped her from *Annie Get Your Gun* in 1950. Cukor's chief problem was casting the male lead, Norman Maine, the alcoholic actor, whose career is on the wane. Separately and jointly Cukor and Garland courted Gary Grant, who had serious doubts about the role.

One afternoon, sitting by the swimming pool, Cukor watched Grant read the part. He had tears in his eyes; it was the finest performance he had ever seen Grant give. "Please, think about it again," Cukor said. "It's a terrific part." This time he knew he was bound to lose. Grant was considering retirement, but Cukor knew there was another reason for his refusal. The plot was similar to Grant's career; his recent films were not successful, and the star feared the public might see the link.

At that time British actor Stewart Granger (nicknamed Jim) was informally approached by Cukor. "We started rehearsing in his garden, with his goddamn dogs licking at me," Granger recalled, "but the first line I ever said, George started correcting me. He said, 'No, no, no, not like that,' which completely threw me. He immediately corrected me, instead of letting me find my way."

There was no deal signed. "George would ring me up and say, 'Hey, Jim, let's rehearse tomorrow.' It was done very unethically. I should never have done it until I had a firm offer. And at the same time I was doing it, they were trying to get Cary Grant, so there was all that shit going on."

Granger rehearsed three mornings with Cukor, two with Garland. "If Judy was upset," Granger said, "she just popped a couple of pills. The whole thing was set for her," he explained. "Maine was subservient to Esther. In the original Fredric March was the important part, but Cukor's was obviously a film about the woman.

"In the end I couldn't take it," Granger said, "so I got a bit drunk one night, called George up, and said, 'I'm coming down to see you.' I drove to his house and said, 'George, sit down and shut up. Don't wag your finger at me, and I will tell you how to play this fucking scene.' I played the scene, and he said, 'Why didn't you do that before?' 'Because you wouldn't give me a chance. You can take the script and stick it up your ass.' And I walked out." Granger thought that James Mason was good, but he would have been much better. "I can play a shit, like Fredric March was. James is a wonderful actor, but he wasn't right; he wasn't a shit."

By the time Mason was cast, Cukor had been turned down by every major star, including Humphrey Bogart, Marlon Brando, and Montgomery Clift. Mason jumped at the opportunity. This was a prestigious project, for which he would receive his best pay to date, $250,000 for a twenty-two-week schedule. Cukor was pleased about Mason, whom he later described as hardworking, modest, and one of the most charming actors he'd ever worked with.

In public Cukor said Mason was a most agreeable actor, but in actuality he didn't approve of Mason's insistence on interpreting his role in his own way. After the first preview, however, Cukor reported to Mason that the audience was moved by his extraordinarily fine performance, but he added, "You see what comes of paying heed to your director." Mason was to receive the best reviews of his career and his first Oscar nomination.

Cukor had very specific ideas of how Norman Maine should be played, but Mason wanted to do something more personal. Mason's wife later said she had never known him to be so upset on a film; he was actually ill for two weeks. "George used to drive him mad," Granger said, "giving him intonations, telling him how to say his lines."

Eventually Cukor relented and let Mason do his own thing. In the scene in which Maine breaks down and decides to commit suicide, Mason asked Cukor just to keep the camera close on him for a long time, to register the many changes in his feelings. Cukor allowed this, and the scene became one of the film's most emotionally powerful.

From the beginning there were problems between Luft and Moss Hart, who was the scriptwriter. But Cukor stuck to his philosophy that it was courtesy to ask the author to do whatever rewriting or changes were necessary. Hart felt strongly that the scene when Danny talks Judy into going to the Shrine Auditorium should remain intact. In this well-written scene Danny says: "Took guts to do what he did, when he found he couldn't lick it—but he did it. And the one thing he was proudest of—the only thing he ever did in his life that paid off—you—you're tossing right back into the ocean after him. Who gives you that right? Because it hurts?"

The Catholic Legion of Decency gave A Star Is Born a Class B rating because it made a "mistake" and portrayed Maine's suicide sympathetically. It found in the dialogue a justification, even a glorification, of suicide. Still, despite pressures, Danny's lines remained as written.

Planning to start shooting on October 5, Cukor was happy that A Star Is Born would be done on a big screen and in glorious Technicolor. The results of the tests Cukor made on the still-experimental WarnerScope were "distinctly unpleasing." With Mason, the distortion was distracting; with Judy, disastrous. But Judy's tests in Technicolor were great; she looked radiant.

Though he was not the producer, Cukor strove for as much control as possible, taking care of every detail. He told the costume designers that Garland's dress for the Academy Award scene should be white, not black. And for the "Born in the Trunk" number, he proposed that Garland wear black tights under a voluminous coat, one that in the course of the number could be used to improvise another costume. Cukor suggested light colors for Garland because tests showed that some white near her face was very becoming. For the "Lose That Long Face" number, Cukor brought in pictures of slum children circa 1890 and suggested dressing Garland as a "Anna Magnani waif," with a little shawl over her head.

Shooting began on October 12, but on October 21 the production came to a halt so that expensive tests could be made with the new technology of CinemaScope. The news was at first shocking because the film was already in production, but once Cukor got used to Cinema-Scope, he found it challenging.

Cukor worked even more closely with Garland than with his other actresses. He allowed her to shoot at night, when she was at her best, even though he hated working after dark and it cost more money. During the day, whenever possible, he shot around Garland. She could look lovely one day and terrible the next. When she didn't show up, Cukor knew it was not self-indulgence; she wouldn't perform unless she was in terrific shape.

Garland's perfectionism was reflected in her insistence on endless re-takes. Like Cukor, she was endowed with a fiery temperament and frightening intensity. One day Ina Claire visited on the set. Watching Garland deliver "The Man That Got Away," Claire was horrified by the level of her energy. At lunch break Claire warned Cukor: "This girl should work for only two hours a day, then go home in an ambulance! She gives too much of herself."

Garland played the part with such raw emotions that it was often painful for Cukor to observe. In one scene she had to scream. "I've never screamed on the screen before," she told Cukor. "Do your best," he said. Garland then let out a scream as bloodcurdling as any he had ever heard.

Cukor got a great kick out of working with Garland. "Dazzled" by her talent, he found her amusing, too. She aroused his admiration as an actress and a woman, with her quick intelligence, captivating humor, brilliant creativity. An impeccable musician, Garland was, of course, a masterful singer, able to project her personality. It was exciting for Cukor to watch Garland discover things about herself, for despite her long career, she had never really tested her dramatic skills. And it was doubly rewarding that her first serious acting was in *his* film.

Cukor soon learned how to deal with Garland. One day everybody waited for hours for her to come out of her dressing room. Cukor, who never liked to fetch anyone, finally said, "I'll go and ask her to come out." When he walked into her dressing room, she was sitting at the table, her head down, resting on her arms. Since the four walls were mirrored, he also saw her face. "Is anything wrong?" he suddenly heard himself saying. But Cukor immediately realized how ridiculously silly his question was, and he burst into laughter.

Heaving with laughter, Garland said: "This is the story of my life. I'm about to shoot myself, and I'm asked if there's anything wrong." She then came onto the set and gave a wonderful performance.

In one scene Garland's character had to turn on a young actor. "Should I really let myself go?" she asked Cukor. "Yes," he said, "all the way." He then observed Garland's fury with amazement, never before having witnessed such an explosion of raw power. "Judy, that was glorious!" he exclaimed. "My blood froze. I had goose pimples."

Garland looked at him, with tears in her eyes, and said, "You are welcome to come to my house. I do that almost every day." That mordant wit, Cukor believed, was Garland's saving grace.

But there were terrible times when it was impossible for Cukor to get Garland to the studio, and shooting was halted for days. Depressed and unreachable, she stayed at home. Harold Arlen, who had written her famous song "Over the Rainbow," became Cukor's messenger because she had a special regard for him.

One of Cukor's "directorial secrets," an effective way of getting actors "on the beam," consisted of little talks, which have been mentioned earlier. In his "illuminating discourses," Cukor explained the psychology of the characters the actors played. But he could also make a fool of himself. Cukor talked about how to play a cheap waitress for half an hour to a woman testing for a waitress role in *A Double Life*. "But, Mr. Cukor," the actress said, "I worked as a waitress in a beanery for two years." This was an example of what he called "my cheap advice."

In *A Star Is Born* Cukor foolishly explained to Garland the psychology of an actress who has great difficulty sleeping or the reactions of a singer who gets standing ovations. Cukor could behave like a "congenial idiot" by his own admission. Once, explaining to Garland how a girl felt when she was desperately unhappy or going through marital troubles, she just looked at him and said, "Who will ever know better than I the tortures of melancholia?"

Cukor tried to ignore the rumors that Garland had fallen in love with the unwilling Mason. He knew she had problems with Sid Luft, and he noticed how she went out of her way to please the handsome Briton. Mason picked up on this but tried to be very patient with her. Though both stars were gifted, in most other ways Cukor saw them as opposites. Mason was the ultimate professional, always on time and ready with his lines. Garland was usually unreliable and unpredictable.

"I had the greatest possible faith in Cukor," Mason told the *Times* of London, "and an admiration, a sort of love, for Judy who was marvelous to work with." But he also conceded that he had difficulties with Garland, who sometimes "exasperated" Cukor, too. "Some mornings she couldn't start before eleven because of the pills, but once she was awake, she was great and joy to work with."

What Cukor enjoyed best was Garland's innate talent for telling stories; she was one of the wittiest raconteurs he had known. She confided her problems in a humorous way, with herself as the butt of the joke, always playing the stupid part in her stories. She could talk about the most devastating experiences of her life, including her traumatic childhood, and have her audience screaming with laughter.

During the lengthy shoot Cukor reported with "utmost humility" to Hart that they were getting exciting footage; could it be otherwise with a Hart script? Indeed, the initial response to the rushes was great. Jerry Wald thought that Cukor had the making of a superb picture, at once commercial and artistic. It was a thrill for Wald to see Cukor bringing Garland back to the screen as her old vibrant self, full of warmth and emotion.

Hart, too, could not contain his eagerness to see "Cukor's stuff," hearing from everybody this was his "magnum opus." Hart asked Cukor to save some energy for his new script, which he hoped Cukor would direct at Fox. This was not nearly as noble as it sounded; Hart was selfish. If by any good fortune Cukor directed both pictures, they could form a Hollywood branch of a mutual admiration society. Hart was planning to take a look at the picture in January to see if Cukor needed any rewrites.

But *A Star Is Born* was far from a smooth production. Cukor didn't relish starting the intricate job of editing without all the necessary material at hand. Before Jack Warner left for Europe, there were some unpleasant encounters, and Cukor congratulated himself for being firm. Warner didn't think it enough to be a rich showman; he also considered himself a great editor. Cukor respected his showman's instincts but not his taste. He pointed out to Warner that he knew the material better than anybody, that it was "unfair" not to take advantage of his experience.

Hart then protested vigorously the way that "The Fat's in the Fire" number was cut. It is the big scene, the one that kicks off Esther and Norman's relationship and establishes Norman's character. Whoever had cut it had taken all the character and juice out, making it a cliché. Cukor was also appalled by Warner's duplicity. Compared with the original scene, the new one was emasculated.

Hart felt he hardly deserved this kind of dismissal. He gave his hand whenever Cukor asked for rewrites, and he was willing to come out on his own to help. Shouldn't he expect the courtesy of being informed about the grotesque cutting of his script? In Cukor's view, Hart was absolutely right. Apparently Luft was responsible for the "shenanigans," but he remained elusive. Cukor didn't care much for Luft's ideas, but he was happy that Hart understood now how maddening it was to do business with such customers as Luft and Warner.

It was not the first time that Cukor, Warner, Luft, and Hart became embroiled over script changes. Luft tended to be slow sending Cukor new pages. After a few days Cukor demanded that Luft give the corrections right away to the production department. Cukor found himself one Monday morning, standing on the sidewalk at a telephone booth, outside a gas station in Laguna, waiting for Luft to call. Then and there he vowed never again to put up with such crap. Cukor later humorously said that he felt humiliated the way that Edda Mussolini must have felt, stranded on a snowy day near the Swiss border.

Cukor planned for the picture to wind up on February 13, so Garland could rest. Though exciting, this rugged operation seemed interminable; six months in production established a new record in Hollywood. By late March Cukor was engaged in assembling a rough cut, paying strict attention to Hart's notes. To his disappointment, the first cut was clouded. Cukor was distracted by one muddled scene after another; this was upsetting because he remembered the rushes as wonderful. In April Cukor and the cutters went over the whole picture again, polishing and tightening it.

A Star Is Born was the most demanding film of Cukor's career, perhaps because of his insistence to oversee every major and minor detail. Perceiving the film as an important event, there were good reasons for Cukor's insecurity. Boasting a large budget and scale, the film was his first musical, and he knew that younger directors, notably Vincente Minnelli, were competing for such projects.

In April Cukor held a long discussion of his options with his agent, Bert Allenberg. With his Metro contract up soon, Cukor would be free to do pictures at other studios. Sensing that his position as a director was declining, Cukor was determined to look at the New York theater and at the European scene as well. Once a free agent, he intended to take advantage of his "extensive" friendships with authors throughout Europe, as had been impossible before because MGM wasn't interested in outside material.

Katharine Hepburn was also a free agent, and soon Tracy would be. They all had talked about setting up a partnership with the Garson Kanins, their successful collaborators, for other movies. In fact, Hepburn had recently asked Cukor to direct the film version of G. B. Shaw's *The Millionairess*. Cukor was the first to predict she would score a success in this play in London. He took time to read Preston Sturges's script, which now included Hepburn's additions and thought it was proficient in keeping the play's good stuff.

Though interested in *The Millionairess*, Cukor didn't want to offend Harry Cohn because he was informally committed to direct *Pal Joey* at Columbia. However, when Allenberg went to Cohn to formalize the deal, the mogul started to hedge. Adamant at carrying Cukor at a large sum per week while looking for a cast, Cohn suggested transferring Cukor to another picture, *My Sister Eileen*. But Allenberg refused to let Cohn have his way this time.

For the first time in his long career Cukor had no commitments. His agent, Allenberg, talked to Metro's Eddie Mannix about getting two more weeks as paid vacation, but in view of the bad economic situation, he refused. Cukor decided not to hang around once he finished cutting *A Star Is Born*. Warner's wasn't prepared to pay him a salary for just sitting and waiting.

Cukor informed all his friends about his upcoming European trip. If on May 8, Cukor wrote to Oliver Messel, he happened to be looking out his window and saw "a fine figure of a man, tall, dark and handsome," that was Cukor.

On April 29 Cukor began a two-month vacation. He decided to take three weeks on his own, in addition to the six granted by Metro. He spent the first week in New York, the highlight of which was a cocktail party in his honor, given by *Vogue*'s editor and attended by Mel Ferrer and Audrey Hepburn, Garbo and George Schlee, Irene Selznick, and Moss Hart and his wife.

The only piece of business in this trip concerned *Pal Joey,* which Cukor regretted not having seen. Despite Harry Cohn's hesitations, Cukor promised to give his "all" to the movie, beginning with interviews with Marlon Brando and Mary Martin. Brando had shown an interest in playing Joey, but because he had never done a musical, he asked for an audition. He believed he could make a passable stab at both singing and dancing; Cukor thought it would be an original bit of casting.

Jerry Wald arranged for Brando to contact Cukor at the Plaza Hotel, but Brando failed to show twice. He wrote to Cukor a sweet letter of apology: "Such an oversight placed on top of another, leaves one with a distinct bad taste in the mouth." He hoped that Cukor didn't hate him and that he would be able to hold his head up next time they met.

The meeting between the two finally took place on May 4. Brando seemed interested in playing the part, and Cukor found him forthright and charming. Brando told Cukor he wanted to use a lighter touch than he had used in any previous role.

Cukor's friendly meeting with Brando stood in sharp contrast with his meeting with John O'Hara, the author of *Pal Joey*. O'Hara asked to be paid for his consultation, claiming that advice that costs nothing is worth just that. Irritated, Cukor refused to meet with him again. In his long career he had never met a writer who behaved so idiotically.

Wald and Cohn thought that it might tip the scale a little if Cukor had a personal talk with Mary Martin. Martin had some misgivings about doing a "fast" character, but Cukor reassured her that her wholesome personality was needed; otherwise the love affair would become sordid. Martin remained unconvinced.

Cukor was also unsuccessful with Moss Hart, who turned down the offer to do the script. Hart hoped his reaction wouldn't have a discouraging effect, but he found the story rambled. Except for two or three wonderful good songs, *Pal Joey* was overrated. Hart feared that whoever did the script would come off badly because he would be charged with spoiling the wonderful theatrical invention.

In the evening Cukor had dinner with his friend Mary Goldwater, and together they saw *Tea and Sympathy*. The next evening Cukor went to see *Ondine*, starring the ravishing Audrey Hepburn. He had a long talk with Audrey and her husband, Mel Ferrer, about filming *Bell, Book, and Candle*, in some sort of partnership. They had to proceed carefully, for Selznick had optioned the play. One thing was clear: It would be bad news to involve him.

Over the past couple of years Cukor had had on and off talks with Selznick about a possible collaboration. But now it was Cukor who was busy and had no time to reply to Selznick's queries. Cukor apologized, but there was a snotty tone to his letters. He noted that despite his attempts to be a "stickler for good manners," his reply was delayed because he was "summoned" by his Metro superiors to discuss future assignments. Cukor knew his response would offend Selznick, but he didn't care.

On May 7 Cukor flew to London with Tracy and Hepburn. Tracy seemed to have forgotten his apprehensions about flying, vowing never to travel again by boat. He was also now talking about treating his alcoholism in an Italian resort. One day, when Tracy was in one of his more open-minded moods, Cukor took the initiative and spoke up against Tracy's routine of coffee, Dexedrine, and sleeping pills. It was of no help.

This was the first time that the Garson Kanins, Cukor, and Tracy and Hepburn were in London at the same time. They went out to fancy dinners, saw many plays, had fun. Cukor teased the Kanins about staying at Hanover Square; he couldn't afford having "déclassé" friends who lived on the wrong side of the tracks.

It just happened that many of Cukor's friends were in London that week. He had lunches and afternoon strolls with Audrey and Mel Ferrer, then, in the evenings, late suppers with Gladys Cooper and the Oliviers, all of whom were performing onstage. On May 10 Cukor saw *The Sleeping Prince,* which had the elements of a popular film with Marilyn Monroe—if *he* directed it.

On May 11 Cukor went with high anticipation to see *Pal Joey* for the first time. He was disappointed; the supper that followed with the Oliviers was more enjoyable. In the next week he went to the theater every night, and afterward he had late suppers with his friends: Oliver Messel, Peter Glenville, John Gielgud, Allan Davis.

Cukor's friendship with the Oliviers blossomed in the 1950s. He was always closer to Vivien Leigh than to Larry. When the couple visited Hollywood, Cukor threw dinner parties for them. He generally invited members of the British colony—Gladys Cooper, David Niven, the Ronald Colmans, and the Stewart Grangers—and, of course, his regulars: Tracy and Hepburn, Ethel Barrymore.

Back in California in July 1954 Cukor plunged headlong into postproduction of *A Star Is Born*. Concerned with the studio's premature enthusiasm, from the top brass down to the salesmen, Cukor was willing to settle for just a small part of the extravagant predictions made. Modest or not, Cukor informed his friends that his picture would be unveiled to the "waiting world" in September.

In August Warner's held the first preview of what Cukor now called "that little quickie" he had been working on for a year. Though Cukor was always nervous on such occasions, the film went extremely well in spite of its length. Garland's performance generated hysteria and immense applause from the screaming viewers. Cukor thought the response excessive, but he was carried along with it, too.

It was at this preview that Cukor first saw Jack Warner's cuts, the result of using a "heavy, inept, insensitive" hand. Warner had succeeded in muddying things up, making scenes incomprehensible. For example, because he cut out the scene in the car driving from the club to Esther's motel, the audience knew nothing about her background, leaving the effect of Maine just being on the make.

Many of Garland's finest moments were also "brutally and stupidly" taken out. The slashing cuts reduced the running time from 181 to 154 minutes. Unfortunately Warner also tampered with the dubbing, emasculating some scenes by flattening the sound.

Although he despised Warner's cuts, Cukor himself wished the film were shorter because of his belief that "Neither the human mind nor the human ass can stand three hours of concentration." He claimed that he could easily sweat out twenty minutes and no one would be the wiser. He suggested, for example, cutting the proposal scene on the recording stage; it had charm but was anticlimatic after the passionate scene in the nightclub. Warner, however, wanted to have his way.

Working in Pakistan on a new picture, *Bhowani Junction*, Cukor couldn't attend the premiere of *A Star Is Born*, which Hoyningen-Huene described as "a double wow." Hollywood had never seen anything like it. Traffic was blocked off for several streets on either side of the Pantages Theater. The streets crawled with police officers, and the sidewalks with spectators. On the roof of the theater six enormous searchlights converged at a center, their beams forming an immense star that could be seen miles away. The front of the building was bathed by more lights than were used in the picture itself. With more stars in attendance than ever before, Cukor's absence was deeply felt.

After the show, in which scene after scene was greeted with sincere applause, there was a big party at the Cocoanut Grove, which lasted until five in the morning. Warner sent a telegram to Cukor in India: "Opening last night was fantastic acclaim for Judy. Everyone beyond anything anyone ever witnessed in a theater. Thanks again for the wonderful contribution you made." On October 3 Garland telegrammed: "Premiere smash. Opening tremendous success with thanks due to you. Will send clippings."

Cukor's friends Sonya Levien and Zoe Akins came away from the film bigger Cukor fans than ever before. His handling of the details of such an overwhelming production seemed the work of a genius. It showed off Cukor's multiple skills as politician, statesman, psychiatrist, magician, painter, writer, animal trainer, nurse, elocutionist, dancer, mathematician, musician, cameraman, dressmaker—everything but Garland's husband! They believed that *A Star Is Born* was Cukor's, not Garland's, picture.

Two telegrams relished by Cukor came from actors he had never worked with. "You're the goddamnest director that ever was, is, and will be. Don't you dare ever die, we need you," Frank Sinatra wrote. And Kirk Douglas was so impressed with Mason's work that he wrote: "May I please work for you, please? I'll learn to sing, dance, rollerskate or any damn thing you want."

Columnist Sheilah Graham surpassed other applauding critics with her prediction: "Here's a nomination for next year's Oscar—Judy Garland— she can't miss!" The film proved to the world the depth and range of Garland's talents as a dramatic actress. For Cukor the tragedy of her career was that she was never able to realize that potential fully. "It was all Judy," Cukor said, giving her full credit; "it was there when I got on the set."

At Oscar time *A Star Is Born* received six nominations, including Best Actor, Actress, Art Direction, but Cukor failed to receive a nomination for what many people consider his finest work. The film to sweep most of the awards that year was *On the Waterfront*, starring Marlon Brando. "It's one of the great sorrows of my career," Cukor later said, convinced that the picture's cuts cost Garland the Oscar that was undeservedly given to Grace Kelly for *The Country Girl*.

Occasionally Cukor heard about the existence of an uncut print and went chasing after it, only to be disappointed. It took twenty-nine years for the film to be restored by film curator Ron Haver and be shown as Cukor wished.

*   *   *

By the time the glorious reviews of *A Star Is Born* were out and its box-office records tabulated, Cukor was deeply involved in *Bhowani Junction,* an on-location romantic melodrama, set amid India's shifting politics. Before going to India, Cukor felt like crying, "Unclean! Unclean!" because he was "a walking repository of every known disease." He got shots for typhoid, cholera, and yellow fever, so that he wouldn't contaminate India's inhabitants—or maybe it was the other way around.

Ava Gardner, then MGM's most popular star, was cast as Victoria, the Anglo-Indian woman who has affairs with three men: Patrick, a young Anglo-Indian (Bill Travers); Ranjit, an Indian prince (Francis Matthews) who wants to marry her; and the British Colonel Savage (Stewart Granger). There was something genuinely tragic about the heroine, though in those days she seemed too promiscuous.

In January 1955 the rough draft for *Bhowani Junction* was submitted for the censors' approval. This time, they complained that there was too much emphasis on Victoria in a girdle, a bra, and panties. They asked for rewrites of her account of her attempted rape to stress the rapist's insanity rather than its sexual inference. Even a line like "I jabbed him hard with my elbow, he moaned and bent forward" was deemed suggestive. To Cukor this was all nonsense.

Cukor split his work between the script of *Bhowani Junction* and the play *The Chalk Garden.* Irene Selznick had given him Enid Bagnold's play, which he found "entrancing," and he immediately became interested in directing it. He was flattered when Irene told him no one else could direct the play as well. It touched his imagination more than other plays, and he how hoped a leave of absence from Metro could be arranged.

In late January 1955, before leaving for India, Cukor spent a couple of days in New York, settling into the Plaza Hotel. On February 1 he had lunch with Marilyn Monroe and Uncle Morris, who had asked to meet the star. Throughout lunch Cukor's uncle, unable to utter one coherent word, kept ogling Monroe. Cukor had never seen his uncle behave in such a bizarre way. Later that day Morris called to say the meeting with Monroe was one of the most interesting events of his life.

That night Cukor left for London, where he again stayed at the Savoy. The next day he met with Ava Gardner to discuss her hair, lipstick, and makeup. In the evening he had dinner with her, Hoyningen-Huene, Allan Davis, and Cecil Beaton, assigned to design the sets for *The Chalk Garden.*

When Cukor auditioned Indian actors, they all seemed like "Armenian opera singers." Cukor said, "You can't take somebody blond and have him play an Indian, but if the coloring and the shape of the face and the manner seem right, then makeup and acting can bring it off." Thus the Indian roles were played by Europeans.

"One of my favorite stories," said Allan Davis, who shot tests for the film, "is about Francis Matthews, who played Ranjit, the young prince. In the wedding scene Matthews was acting away, all dressed up with diamonds and wonderful clothes. George said to him, 'Listen, Francis. I want you to make it more down-to-earth, more real.' But Francis said, 'Well, I've been acting this way in the theater lately.' 'Now, listen, Francis,' Cukor said abruptly, 'that kind of acting would be pretty shitty any place!' "

John Mills was disappointed when Cukor informed him that the role of Patrick had been cast. Cukor was disappointed, too, for Mills would have been wonderful, but the part had already been cast with another Briton, Bill Travers. MGM was excited about Travers, hoping he would become an international star. Cukor did not share that enthusiasm, and as it turned out, he was right.

Because of time pressure, Sonya Levien and Ivan Moffat were forced to write the script out of continuity. They first worked on the outdoor sequences, then wrote the more intimate scenes. Cukor disliked their script; it conventionalized the characters and missed the book's humor. Not knowing what else to do, he sent the draft to John Masters, the author of the novel on which the film was based, "under the table," strictly on his own. There was no better way of capturing the book's quality other than to get his advice. For some mysterious reason, however, it was considered heresy in Hollywood to have anything to do with the original author.

On *Bhowani Junction* Cukor worked for the second time with cameraman Freddie Young, for whom he had the highest regard, recalling happy times on the set of *Edward, My Son*. Young was in complete control of the cinematography; Cukor assured him that Hoyningen-Huene, his color consultant, would not encroach on his work.

Bhowani Junction's shoot began on February 17, 1955, and ended eight weeks later. With the exception of *Edward, My Son,* which was shot in England but on a studio lot, Cukor had never made a movie outside the United States. He did not relish the rigors of India; it meant being away from home for five months. But he had gone on so much about "artistic integrity" that he had to be consistent.

It was a challenge for Cukor to work on location. Ever since *GWTW* he had been waiting for the opportunity to show Selznick, and his other critics, that he could direct a spectacle, an outdoor film with plenty of action and crowd scenes. Cukor boasted how he never had a scene with fewer than a thousand extras.

The Indian press and industry were opposed to the production, and the government refused to grant permission to shoot there because of a disparaging line in the script about Indian politicians. Afraid that this opposition could continue indefinitely, producer Pandro Berman switched the movie to Lahore, Pakistan.

Perceiving India as the leading character, Cukor devoted a lot of time to the visual look. The on-location shooting grounded the production in authenticity; using the dominant color of a brownish tone, Cukor helped to display the country in a new light. "There was so much there," he later said, "you just had to look." Cukor became aware of the contradictory sights: on the one hand, exposed electric wires and utter poverty and, on the other, the grandeur of a great palace like the Taj Mahal.

The picture took a great deal of effort to make. But *Bhowani Junction* contains impressive sequences that are unique in Cukor's work: the verisimilitude of the Indian atmosphere, the crowd scenes, people caught up in social upheaval. Cukor conveyed effectively a restless country of "thousands of people swarming around." Wherever he went, there were "people, people, people!" In the scene where the passive resisters lie down in front of the train, Cukor actually shot how the army pissed and poured shit over them, but fearing censorship, the studio later excised this scene.

The exteriors of the picture were shot in Pakistan, and the interiors at London's Elstree studio, but Cukor wasn't sure which of these settings was tougher. During the shoot the scenes seemed to have the right "feel," but with no facilities to see the rushes, he was "dancing in the dark."

Bhowani Junction was one of the few films in which Cukor was defeated by casting. In the past he had always been in control; he considered casting his specialty. But in this film Stewart Granger was signed before he was. Cukor thought that Granger was miscast and, worse, that he brought out the movie queen in Ava Gardner.

After making three bad films in a row, producer Berman asked Granger to choose a project. Granger had read John Masters's books and suggested all of them, but Berman opted for *Bhowani Junction* because it was more modern. "I'm in his office one day," Granger recalled, "talking about the part, and in walks George. Pandro says, 'We're lucky we've got George Cukor.' And I said, 'Oh, no, you fucking don't, I'm not working with him.' And George looked at me and said, 'Oh, come on, Jim, we'll get on all right, I promise you. And who am I to turn down George Cukor, who had done all those wonderful films? So I said, 'All right.'

"George didn't want me," said Granger. "He thought I was wrong. Well, he could have had Trevor Howard, and the film would have fallen on its ass, because Trevor is a wonderful actor, but he's not a romantic actor, and this needed romance." Granger resented Cukor's lack of respect for him: "George thought the only actor who ever existed was Barrymore or Tracy; he thought that my pictures were shit. I should have walked off the fucking film, and he'd have been taken off. I should have done what Clark Gable did, just walked off, but I'm not quite as arrogant as I seem. And I kept on saying to myself, 'You can't do that,' because George directed the beloved Spencer and Kate in many successful films. But this was a time when George had lost his talent."

Spencer Tracy had warned Granger, "Jim, he's a very good director, but don't let him tell you how to say your lines. He does it to me sometimes, and I say, 'All right, George, I'll direct the film, and you fucking act in it!' We get to India, and George starts from the beginning to tell me how to play it."

Granger was deeply disappointed: "George was a woman's director, so when he is telling an actress how to say her lines, she is not copying him because she's a woman. But here he is, a little homosexual Jew from Brooklyn, and I'm playing an English colonel, and my father was a colonel in the Indian Army, and I was in the English Army, and he's telling me how to say the lines."

Granger hated his performance: "I yell and scream too much. I'm a good actor, but an English colonel doesn't yell at women."

Cukor would say, "Do what you're told."

"We don't do that in England," Granger would say.

"I don't give a shit," Cukor said.

"One thing about George," said Granger, "he used worse language than I do, which endeared me to him. 'You are a cunt,' he would tell me.

"George took five months to make that fucking film," Granger noted. "To me, he was an insufferable director, going on and on, doing thirty-five takes. He drove me up the wall." The movie didn't make any money because it cost so much. For Granger, *Bhowani Junction* wasn't good, because "it wasn't the book. The book is a sexy romance between the colonel and Victoria. When he takes her out, his India is the most romantic thing. They screw up on a tree; they screw on safari.

"All that's out because George's boyfriend, Huene, did the costumes. Huene made the wedding the biggest fucking thing in the film; in the book it's a little side thing. George fucked up that film. It was too long; it went off in too many directions. The audience was interested in the relationship between Ava and me, and there wasn't enough of that.

"Ava was not an Anglo-Indian," said Granger. "If all Anglo-Indians looked like her, there would be nothing to worry about. Ava was wonderful with George," he recalled. "She thought he was a pain in the ass, too, but she joked about it." She told Granger, "George goes on, but I don't listen, I just do it my way." For her, it was amusing for a man to play a woman.

"George did the same with James Mason," said Granger. "James couldn't stand him. He said, like me, 'George is a brilliant man, but I wish he wouldn't tell me how to say my lines.' George never did it with Spencer Tracy—*never*—because he respected him. He knew Spencer would say, 'George, go fuck yourself.' He sure as hell wasn't a man's director because the ones I've talked to couldn't stand him, except for Spencer, but Spencer had an entirely different relationship with George. It was all right for Spencer to say, 'George, shut up,' but I was a new boy, and he made it obvious very early he didn't hold much esteem for me."

When I mentioned to Granger that Rex Harrison (who starred in Cukor's *My Fair Lady*) liked him, he said, "Don't forget, George wouldn't tell Rex anything. Rex was established; he knew how to do his part. And I'm sure that what Rex would admire about George, which is what I admire about George, was his attention to detail. He didn't care about the camera and the angles; he was worried about the acting. George was an actor's, or rather actress's, director.

"George's weakness," said Granger, "is that he would always have pages in his hand and stand behind the camera and act with you. I would say to him, 'I can't act with you behind the camera,' and he would say, 'Well, what am I supposed to do, go out because you can't fucking act? Go on, do it, do it.' And you had to do it his way."

But even Granger conceded that Cukor's greatest quality was his excitement. "He was enormously enthusiastic about everything. On the set, if the camera crew was setting up, he wouldn't sit and relax. He would say, 'Come on, let's talk about the scene, let's run it once more.' 'George,' I said, 'the script doesn't have shit and fuck.' 'You know what I mean, you know what I mean,' he would say. 'Let's do it again.' "

Granger said Cukor was not a technical director; he relied on Young for the camera setups. "George had a general idea of what he wanted, but he wasn't a technical genius like Willie Wyler, who was cutting in his head. He would just shoot a lot and then see it with his editor. George's talent was working with actors. He would get the best performances, though he didn't get my best."

Years later Cukor confronted Granger at a party. "I hear you didn't like me," the director said.

"You're an absolute prick," said Granger.

"Oh, well, fuck you," Cukor said.

The relationship ended just like that with "not much love lost between us," said Granger.

Despite his frustrations with Granger, Cukor's major reward was creating a climate in which Ava Gardner did her best work to date, giving a "full-bodied" performance. The more he saw Gardner's work, the more depth, dignity, and feeling he found in it; seeing a performance like hers was "the acid test." Because of censorship, Gardner was very discreetly dressed, but she was the kind of actress who could think "untrammeled things" and the audience would understand. There was a kind of electricity when Gardner came on the screen, and it wasn't just her dazzling beauty.

Shooting ended on April 7, 1955, on an extremely hot day—ninety-seven degrees and climbing. The next day Cukor left on a small chartered plan. He didn't go with the stars, who flew via the posh airlines, but with "the little people," the crew.

During postproduction John Masters kept reminding Cukor that he had not gone to Pakistan to make the film "large" but to make it "real and gritty." Masters advised him to emphasize the underlying sexual tension and the heat. The glare of the sun should hurt people's eyes when they talk, and people in India don't stand still; they shift uncomfortably.

At a meeting of Metro's international executives, only the exciting parts of the rough cut (the rape) were shown. Dore Schary and the others all were "high" on the film. "High-shmigh," Cukor joked. He had never been handed a script without being told that Schary was "high" on it.

Cukor's first cut was too long, two hours and forty minutes. That created a strain with Berman. "I would be the first to fight for a long picture," Berman recalled, "if I believed it was better in that length." But he thought some of the scenes were superfluous and distasteful. Cukor himself wasn't pleased with the "muddled" picture; it lacked clarity.

The first preview in San Francisco confirmed both their fears: The picture was too long and too confusing in depicting Victoria's going from one man to another. Granger recalled that the audience was baffled and that MGM decided to reshoot a happy ending, so that Gardner would end with Granger. "George didn't like that at all, but I loved it! I said, 'You see, I was right!' "

The drastic cutting took place in Projection Room Eight, a small, stuffy room, which reminded Cukor of the spot over the gutter where Gardner had to wait before making her entrance. Cukor was forced to excise some daring scenes, like the one on the train when Victoria shows her attraction for the colonel. In the original she dips his toothbrush in scotch and cleans her teeth while staring at him.

To Cukor's disappointment, the audience seemed unsympathetic to Victoria's story, forcing him to turn *Bhowani Junction* into the colonel's story. As a result, the saga was rearranged—i.e., set in flashback with the colonel's voice over. But the oversimplified narration contained unnecessary exposition, and it made the film more sentimental. "I had to do narration," Granger allowed, "because they realized it was a fucked-up script."

Because Cukor wished to do another picture with Gardner, his new favorite actress, his agents sent her books to read, including Herman Wouk's *Marjorie Morningstar*. With nothing interesting in the foreseeable future, Cukor offered his services to Gardner as "an old, not-too-efficient, houseboy."

People in Hollywood knew Cukor was close to Gardner and used him as a mediator. Writer-director Jean Negulesco (*Johnny Belinda*) asked Cukor to send a book that he wanted to adapt to the screen for the star. Negulesco realized Gardner was busy, but he knew that Cukor's Hungarian charm and the affection of people for him were invaluable assets. Negulesco was convinced that anything Cukor recommended would have a good chance with Gardner.

In decline at his own studio, Cukor was trying to come up with new ideas, such as reteaming with Gardner on *The Female*. John Lee Mahin was going to write a script, an adaptation of Paul I. Wellman's novel, which Metro had owned for years. The story was set in Constantinople in the sixth century; its heroine, Theodora, was the courtesan who became the consort of Justinian the Lawgiver.

Another possible project with Gardner was *Carmen,* to be shot on location in Spain. Critic Kenneth Tynan had sent Cukor an outline, which he liked. However, MGM's top brass thought the story had been done too many times to make it "palatable" at the box office again. Cukor's promise that it wouldn't be a hip-swinging Carmen and that the film would cast new light on the character met with deaf ears.

Toward the end of *Bhowani Junction*'s lengthy shoot, Cukor began to think about the play he had committed himself to direct, *The Chalk Garden*. Back in London for two months, he spent the earlier part of June on readings and discussions with producer Irene Selznick, playwright Enid Bagnold, and designer Cecil Beaton. His meetings with the flamboyant Beaton were surprisingly harmonious. There was no display of Beaton's notorious ego and outrageously queenish conduct that Cukor was to experience later on the set of *My Fair Lady*.

Above all, Cukor was looking forward to working with his friend British actress Gladys Cooper, who was cast in the lead. Cukor admired Cooper, who was businesslike and intelligent, as both an actress and a woman.

In July Cukor was still working on the retakes and final touches of *Bhowani Junction*. He managed to find time and go to Stratford to see "theatah," like *Macbeth* with Olivier. Cukor's companion was the endlessly chatty Clifton Webb, whom he befriended in California and who was one of the regulars at Cukor's all-male parties.

Cukor had planned to start rehearsals on *Chalk Garden* in New York in late July, but the recutting of *Bhowani Junction* took longer than scheduled. Irene Selznick gave him a hard time and "real drama," for the actors were already cast and theaters were booked in New York and on the road. At first he had misgivings about plunging right away into the play without his usual preparation, but under pressure he consented.

On September 17, the day after Cukor checked into New York's Hotel Stanhope, at Fifth Avenue and Eighty-first Street, Allenberg informed him that he had to report to MGM in two weeks for more work on *Bhowani Junction*. Cukor knew Irene Selznick would be furious. Late as it was, he was determined not to leave the results of almost a year's work to the mercy of studio cutting. After *A Star Is Born*, he firmly believed he was indispensable to a picture's final cut.

It felt very strange to direct an intimate play after the epic proportions of *Bhowani Junction*, where he had been giving orders like "Set the whole station on fire, make the five thousand extras riot, wreck the train." One day he received a card on a piddling tray that said, "Mr. Cukor, we paid $75 for this, and we can only afford $50."

During one particularly bad rehearsal the actors fell all over themselves. Suddenly it seemed that a director of his caliber was not necessary for a play of such "puny scope." Sitting in a dirty dressing room, Cukor asked himself, "What the hell am I doing here?"

Angry and disappointed, Irene Selznick decided to fire him. "I don't think George lost interest in the theater," Katharine Hepburn explained. "He just found motion pictures more interesting." In her view, "*Chalk Garden* came to an end because it just bored George. Irene didn't think George was very good at it," she said, "but he wasn't fired; it was terminated by mutual agreement. George didn't think much of it, one way or the other."

After one dismal week of rehearsals, a relieved Cukor flew out west. It was one of his most joyful flights ever. In the future, when people asked if he was going back to the theater, Cukor's answer was firm: "Not if I'm in my right mind. I shall stay right where I am and be what I am: a movie director!"

Despite their disagreement, Irene Selznick and Cukor remained close friends. The following year she suggested that they go to the Soviet Union together. At first it struck Cukor as an outlandish idea, lest Adolphe Menjou, Hedda Hopper, Ward Bond, and the other good Republicans hear about this. However, had it not been for the long idleness caused by the delays in the start of his next film, *Les Girls*, he might have been tempted to join her.

Upon returning from New York, Cukor heard from the other Selznick. David sent him a script of *Tess of the D'Urbervilles*, hoping to do it with the distinction and success of the 1939 classic *Wuthering Heights*. Selznick had developed *Tess* for Jennifer Jones after Metro had rejected it. However, if Metro knew Cukor was interested, it could be set up as an English production of high quality and significantly lower cost. Two weeks later Selznick changed his mind and was now inclined to make *Tender Is the Night*. Cukor decided to take his time to think about directing the movie.

Cukor was then involved in the effort to film a biopicture of *Laurette Taylor,* with Judy Garland, but he had gotten a most emphatic no from Metro to Garland as Laurette; as a matter of fact, it was no to Garland for anything at Metro.

Mary Martin was also considered for the Taylor part, but she had some reservations. Martin felt she was fine for the first part of Taylor's life but too young for the later years. In all candor, Cukor thought Martin was right for the older woman as well; after all, she was forty-five.

Desperate to have some kind of project in the works, Cukor called Harry Cohn. The mogul was not overwhelmed with joy at hearing his voice, but he was at least cordial. Cukor spoke enthusiastically about the Laurette Taylor project, but Cohn remained aloof.

With characteristic humor, Cukor suggested a provision that the portrayal of his persona in the biopicture would be in good taste and a "dignified" manner. Cukor's wishful thinking was to be one of the leads; it never hurt to have a "fascinating character," he bragged, recommending that his part be played by Marlon Brando or Burt Lancaster, but not someone like Yiddish actor Maurice Schwartz.

Knowing that they would have to deal with his private life, Cukor was a bit apprehensive. He had made nasty jokes about *Night and Day,* the phony 1946 biopicture about Cole Porter (played by Gary Grant) that never even hinted at the composer's sexual preference. Still, Cukor demanded that any departure regarding his character should be subject to his written approval.

On his way to Europe Cukor stopped in New York to see the smash hit musical *My Fair Lady* with the Garson Kanins on July 6, as a celebration of his birthday. He, of course, had no idea that in ten years he would direct the film version, for which he would win his only Oscar.

On July 8 Cukor flew to London to scout locations for the musical *Gigi.* There was some talk that Cukor might direct the movie, which he later lost to Vincente Minnelli. By the time shooting began on *Les Girls,* on January 3, 1957, Cukor had experienced the longest time—two years—without making any movie. It was the beginning of his decline.

The story "Les Girls" had been purchased by producer Sol Siegel for MGM as early as 1955. Like *A Star Is Born,* the film was an original and unconventional musical, created directly for the screen. With Cole Porter writing the music and Cukor signed to direct, Siegel was aiming for an all-star cast, which would feature Gene Kelly, Leslie Caron, Cyd Charisse, and Carol Haney. However, of these prospective performers, only Kelly was in the picture.

Les Girls had an amusing premise. It begins in a London courtroom where Lady Sybil Wren (Kay Kendall), a former show girl, is faced with a libel suit after publishing her memoirs about an act called Les Girls. All three women in the act—Sybil, Angele (Taina Elg), and Joy (Mitzi Gaynor)—are amorously involved with their manager and star, Barry Nichols (Gene Kelly).

Sybil, Angele, and Barry take the witness stand and in Rashomon-like style tell their version of the "truth." As the stories unfold, the film moves back and forth between the courtroom, the stage, and their personal lives. In Rashomon, a film Cukor greatly admired, Akira Kurosawa argues that all people are liars. Cukor suggested that people try to tell the truth but do it in a subjective manner. Les Girls was appropriate material for Cukor. "I love doing low comedy," he said. "To me, a kick in the pants is just as good as a bon mot, if it's done right."

The film featured Porter's last score, which was not vintage Porter, who was extremely ill during preproduction. Saul Chaplin had to finish the score. The sophisticated air and ingenious rhyming were intact, but the music was too reminiscent of Porter's previous endeavors. "Ça C'est l'Amour" echoed "C'est Magnifique" from Can-Can. But there was one standout number, "Why Am I So Gone About That Gal?," a parody of Marlon Brando's 1953 motorcycle film The Wild One. Performed by Kelly in black leather, with Mitzi Gaynor as his moll, it imitated Brando's arrogant hood. The number was played against a red barroom background with a chorus of Brando-like types.

As soon as rumors spread that three female parts were available in Cukor's movie, his old stars contacted him. Paulette Goddard scheduled a "polite" lunch with Porter, though she didn't dare ask him if there was a part for her. But she did ask Cukor; it would "mean so much" to her to return to Hollywood for him.

Cukor had his own ideas about casting, which he was determined to stick to after the mistakes of Bhowani Junction. He wanted to cast Kay Kendall, but married to Rex Harrison, the actress didn't want to leave New York, where Harrison was appearing in My Fair Lady. At the same time he had seen a young Finnish actress, Taina Elg, in Metro's commissary and asked if she could play an English girl. Elg was thrilled at the prospect of working with Cukor, and they carefully worked on some scenes before shooting her test.

In the meantime, Kendall decided to do the film if she could spend long weekends in New York. Knowing it would be disappointing to Elg, Cukor now asked her to rehearse for the French girl. Leslie Caron was supposed to do it, but she had differences with Cukor about her costumes and Elg inherited her role.

The casting of Mitzi Gaynor as the third girl was a major drawback, forcing Cukor to work with a colorless and inadequate actress—"one of

MGM's flat tires." He was offended because Metro had engaged Gaynor after he was assigned. Siegel admitted he was wrong, but the bottom line was that Gaynor remained as the lead.

The studio's inconsiderate conduct was an indication of how Cukor would be treated in the future. At first Cukor made up his mind to quit, but when the studio realized it wasn't easy to replace him, its attitude became more amendable. Cukor resented "being pushed" into something he didn't feel right about.

Hoyningen-Huene was also dismayed." Three "unimportant" girls, he told Cukor, don't sell a picture no matter what the music and costumes are. He urged Cukor not to let himself get bullied into another Lana Turner picture. If Cukor did all the studio wished him to do, he would be out on Pico Boulevard, unemployed. Hoyningen-Huene held that a mediocre picture at this point in Cukor's career could harm him; he was better off with another "little comedy" with Judy Holliday.

There was another problem to solve before shooting began. Cukor was initially asked to work with the costume designer he least liked, Helen Rose. Rose was an intrigant—which might be overlooked—but she was devoid of talent, and that, for Cukor, was "the most deadly sin." He was able to persuade MGM to use his friend the talented Orry-Kelly, but he found it illuminating how the executives "worked their wits." Rather than tell Rose directly she wasn't wanted, the studio told her no decision had been made yet.

The picture's nominal star was Gene Kelly, who had never worked with Cukor before. Kelly did not want to star in the film; it was his last musical at MGM. *Les Girls* wasn't a typical Kelly musical because the story focused on the women. And Cukor's label as a woman's director, combined with the film's title, made Kelly extremely nervous even before rehearsals began.

Kelly had never worked with choreographer Jack Cole either. This also created tension because Cole tried to stage scenes that wouldn't be "typically Kelly." The choreographer wanted to create a more sophisticated, less bravura style, but the dancer was unwilling to change.

Cukor respected Cole as a choreographer, though his method irritated him. Ironically Cole was like Cukor, a perfectionist who worked slowly. Cole's habit was to rehearse individual phrases, but he avoided putting a number together until it was ready to be shot. Cukor got impatient as he wanted to see the entire number. In mid-production, when Cole contracted hepatitis and had to leave, Kelly took over, but now Kelly seemed more interested in staging the numbers than dancing them.

Kelly's relationship with Cukor was no more than cordial. "George can spend a couple of hours going over a scene which needed no explanation at all," the actor later complained. "I'm conscientious, too, but there's a limit to how long you can go on discussing a line." Every once in a while Kelly interrupted to say: "For christ sake, George, let's just shoot the goddamn thing!" Kelly could see that "there's a canny method to his madness, because by the time he's through explaining what he wants out of a scene, you feel you know everything there is to know about it, and you go out and play it with confidence." But for Kelly, it was a luxurious way of working, too time-consuming.

The women, by contrast, admired Cukor's method. "We had numerous rehearsals and wardrobe sittings with Mr. Cukor," Elg said. Cukor personally supervised the makeup, demanding test after test until he got it right. For Elg, new to acting, the in-depth analysis that irritated Kelly was a revelation. "Mr. Cukor gave examples from life that would color whatever lines you had. You could call them master classes in film acting. Every little detail, every word in the script were discussed."

Kay Kendall also appreciated Cukor's guidance, though she had other misgivings. Kendall was reluctant to accept the role because she had to sing and dance. Although she came from a musical background, she didn't feel very confident about her ability to sing or dance. Cukor assured her that she wouldn't have to sing much, and Kelly worked with her on the dance numbers.

One afternoon the insecure Kendall went to Jack Cole in a panic. "Don't be a fool," Cole told her. "Just be yourself. Who the hell cares if you can sing and dance? You dominate the screen anyway." Indeed, Kendall's crackling comic sensibility distinguished her delightful performance—"a natural clown with a marvelous comedic instinct," Cukor said.

Cole was right. In Kendall's big number with the other women, "Ladies in Waiting," her presence is so strong she steals the scene. Tall, blithe, and beautiful with thoroughbred features, Kendall had star quality, that "something extra" that Gaynor and Elg lacked. In her number with Kelly she seemed to be outdancing him and having an easy time of it. Kendall was also an original. In a scene in which she gets out of a cab, her enormously chic black hat was caught by accident, but with a gesture and a look, she turned it into a marvelously funny bit. The problem was that Kendall's role was not big enough to sustain the whole film.

Again Cukor found himself giving unexpectedly funny directions. He once said to Kendall with absolute solemnity, "For God's sake, stop thinking!," by which he meant, "Don't worry too much." If anything Cukor usually made a point of telling his stars, "Unless an actor thinks, the scene won't make sense." He now had plans to do more pictures with Kendall, promising to build her into the American Anna Neagle; unfortunately Kendall died prematurely in 1959.

Elg remembered that Cukor loved to tell amusing stories on the set and laughed all the time. His sophisticated humor was a little bawdy, and on occasion he used salty language. After a rude comment to Kendall, Cukor had to apologize: "You sure taught me a lesson, no more flip off-color remarks!"

Cukor wasn't always well mannered on the set. "He lost his temper," Elg noted, "when somebody wasn't professional or didn't understand what he wanted, even though he had explained it clearly." Once, when he shouted at Elg, a colleague said, "How can you take it?" "Why?" said Elg. "I'm flattered that he shouted at me."

Elg said: "Mr. Cukor didn't take any nonsense from the crew, but because he demanded, everybody was willing to do their best. The electricians, cameramen, everybody was the tops. We all worked like a beautiful machine." The ambience on the set was professional but very friendly. "On the set Mr. Cukor would whisper. He would ask you to come to some corner, or he'd come to your room. Mr. Cukor helped you to relax; he gave you the feeling of confidence if he liked what you did." At the same time Cukor could be dictatorial. "I could tell from the expression on his face if he liked what I did," said Elg. "I was so keen on trying to please him that he could have shouted, no matter how much. I was very young, and he was this great director. I was afraid of him.

"Once," Elg recalled, "I got extremely nervous in a scene where I had to cry, but nothing would make me cry. Finally Mr. Cukor desperately said to me, 'Your child has died, your husband has died, your dog has been killed.' " His comments, however, only made Elg laugh—until she realized he was getting impatient. Frustrated and angry, she withdrew to her room, where the tears began to flow. At that moment Cukor called, "Come out, Taina, it's time to cry." But again she couldn't cry and instead laughed hysterically. Finally, after many unsuccessful takes, she had to use menthol spray in her eyes.

Initially Cukor planned to shoot some scenes on location: in Paris, Granada, and London. However, to save money, *Les Girls* was entirely shot in Hollywood. Cukor did go to Paris with his artistic collaborators, Gene Allen and George Hoyningen-Huene, to prepare the film. "We trudged up six flights of stairs into one cramped apartment after another," he later recalled, "and put all the details into the set." The costumes were witty and tacky, just like the Folies Bergère. Cukor's observation of how the show girls at the Folies scrambled around catwalks and just barely got onstage on time also made its way into the film.

Hoyningen-Huene came up with interesting ideas for the film's classy look. One day he blew a puff of cigarette smoke and said, "The whole thing should be this color, the background, the set."

"Won't that be drab?" asked Cukor a bit worried.

"No, no, no," said the photographer-designer in a voice that imitated the director; Cukor realized that it was color used with discipline.

Hoyningen-Huene also proposed that the makeup of the chorus girls would be sloppy and exaggerated, in contrast with the show girls, who were more carefully made up.

As standard procedure, Cukor had to submit Porter's songs for ratings before shooting began, and a number of changes were dictated. Porter's ribald song "Ladies in Waiting," with words like "nizzle-nozzle" and "foodle-doodle," was deemed "suggestive." The song was toned down, but remained funny because of Kendall's assured comic style. Cukor thought the censors' demands—when Sybil hangs out her laundry, panties and brassieres were to be omitted—were downright ridiculous. In October 1957, *Les Girls* was given Class B rating because of its provocative dialogue and costumes.

Les Girls lacked the energy and exultation that permeate Hollywood's best musicals. For one thing, it simply didn't have enough musical numbers (80 percent of the film was book). But released at a time when musicals were at a low ebb, it stood out. The Oscar nominations for art direction and costume design certified the picture as an art film. And there was the minor reward that *Les Girls* was selected for Britain's Royal Command Performance, an honor bestowed on only one picture a year, usually British.

CHAPTER NINE:

A Replacement Director, 1957–62

In 1957, DISSATISFIED WITH WILLIAM MORRIS, CUKOR DECIDED TO change agencies. He told his longtime agent, Bert Allenberg, that Morris had been "well compensated for whatever services had been rendered," especially since his ongoing MGM contract predated his relationship with the agency. At first Allenberg refused to release Cukor, but under continued threats from Cukor's lawyers a settlement was finally reached.

With a newfound sense of freedom and relief, Cukor began an association with Irving "Swifty" Lazar, a Hollywood celebrity in his own right. Known primarily as a literary agent, Lazar made his first effort for his new client the film version of Tennessee Williams's prizewinning play *Cat on a Hot Tin Roof*.

MGM had purchased the play for Liz Taylor, then its most popular star. Cukor, however, envisioned Vivien Leigh, who had won an Oscar for her excellent performance in Williams's *A Streetcar Named Desire*. He had been waiting for decades for the right project to do with Leigh. In October 1957 Cukor informed Leigh that MGM has assigned him to direct *Cat on a Hot Tin Roof,* but he hadn't accepted yet because of misgivings about the censors' demands, which threatened to injure the play's integrity and effectiveness.

Eventually Cukor pulled out because he couldn't live with the changes imposed by the censor. He wanted to do the film exactly the way the play had been done onstage, dealing up front with the issue of homosexuality, but in the 1950s the word "homosexual" couldn't even be mentioned onscreen. Indeed, when the film was made by Richard Brooks in 1958, the play's third act was completely rewritten.

Cukor's next project was *Wild Is the Wind* at Paramount, with Hal Wallis as producer. The film was originally slated for John Sturges, who became ill and was forced to withdraw. With a starting date of April 1, Wallis began a hasty search for a replacement. Anna Magnani, who had won an Oscar for her first American film, *The Rose Tattoo,* and was the star of *Wild Is the Wind,* had director approval. When Wallis mentioned that Cukor was available, she immediately consented. Having seen and liked Cukor's films, she was excited at the prospect of working with him.

Wild Is the Wind tells the story of Gino (Anthony Quinn), a widowed Italian sheep rancher who marries Giola (Anna Magnani), the Italian sister of his deceased wife, and brings her to Nevada. But expecting Giola to be a duplicate of his wife, he treats her insensitively. Conflict arises when Giola falls in love with Gino's adopted son (Tony Franciosa), though in the end she and Gino reconcile.

Throughout the film Cukor had to stand with a whip to keep his performers from acting all over the place. As soon as casting was announced, insiders in Hollywood made jokes about the film's "heavy-breathing, high charged" actors. Franciosa was trained in the moody depth-probing Method acting, and Magnani subscribed to it, too. Known for his aversion to Lee Strasberg's much-touted Method, Cukor couldn't tolerate overacting and excessive emotionalism.

Anthony Quinn recalled that Magnani was supposed to show up in Carson City, Nevada, where Cukor and the other actors were already staying in a motel. Every day they were told Magnani was coming the next day, but she didn't show up for a whole week. Finally a big car brought Magnani, who went straight into her cabin. "There was a lot of anticipation," Quinn recalled. "All the actors were looking through the windows of their cabins."

Half an hour later Magnani sent notes inviting Cukor and the cast for a spaghetti dinner at her cabin. "We were all excited," said Quinn. "It was a great honor to meet Miss Magnani." Magnani poured wine as they made small talk. "Suddenly Anna said, 'You know, on Monday we start this picture, and I've been working on the script with my dialogue coach, but I don't know Mr. Quinn, and I've just met Mr. Cukor. I would like to know more about all of you.' 'You're not going to ask us a lot of questions, I hope,' Cukor quipped drolly. 'No, no,' Anna said. 'In Italy, we have a game, it's called the truth game. We sit around and ask each person a question, and he has to answer truthfully, because if he doesn't, it will smell in the room and create bad feelings. I will start asking questions, and then we go around the table.' "

"Excuse me," Cukor immediately said. "I'm leaving."

"The hell with him," Magnani said, "we know all about him. Now,

Mr. Quinn, I'm gonna ask you the first question: Do you want to fuck me?"

"No," said Quinn.

Then she asked Dolores Hart, "Do you want to fuck Tony Quinn?" Hart turned pink and stammered. "Well—"

Anna interrupted, "You better tell the truth 'cause if you don't, you're gonna be terrible in this picture."

So Dolores said, "Yes!"

Then Magnani turned to her dialogue coach: "Have you ever been fucked in the ass?" and the poor girl had to say yes. Finally Anna turned to Franciosa and said, "Mr. Franciosa, do you want to fuck me?"

And he said, "Absolutely."

So Magnani said, "OK, everybody, the game is over!"

The next day, told the story, Cukor wished he had stayed.

Cukor elicited a powerful performance from Magnani in her second American film. "No actress possesses the magic and the fire of Anna," he said. "She didn't know English, but she has such a wonderful ear that it didn't make a difference." Magnani was extremely talented but also "perversely unpredictable." Cukor never knew what she would do. She could be temperamental and difficult, but Cukor was used to handling temperamental stars.

Cukor's reputation as Hollywood's best woman's director made Quinn fear he would concentrate on Magnani. On the first day of shooting they filmed a scene in which Magnani gets off the plane from Italy. "Anna started talking Italian and a whole ad lib," Quinn recalled, "and I ad-libbed right along with her. When we walked off the camera, Anna turned to me and said, 'I'm gonna have trouble with you.' Cukor, who overheard the conversation, said to her, 'You certainly are because he can ad-lib as well as you do.'" From that point on Cukor and Quinn had an excellent relationship.

"George was a wonderfully sensitive director," said Quinn. "He was not only great for women; he was great for men. It's also unfair to say he was just a great actor's director because he told a story magnificently with the camera." Quinn liked Cukor's ability to communicate with rich language. "It's interesting," he said, "that George didn't get along with Gable, but he did with Tracy; Gable probably didn't understand his poetic imagery."

Cukor had a very good sense of what a scene needed in order to be effective. One day Franciosa said, "I wanna make this moment very important." "What do you mean, Mr. Franciosa?" asked Cukor. "It is *my* moment," the actor said, to which Cukor responded, "Your moment? You just have to look over and walk away." "No," Franciosa insisted, "I want to stay here and react." Finally the impatient Cukor said, "You can stand there and react as long as you want because I'm gonna cut it later to two seconds!"

Quinn enjoyed an utmost respect from Cukor, who gave him the freedom to experiment. "Basically George liked a good script," the actor said, "but of necessity he would sometimes improvise. Even if you say the script's lines, you still have to improvise the movement and the attitude."

Cukor was also open to Quinn's suggestions. "There is a scene where I dance alone with the guitar. I couldn't put my arms around my wife, and the only thing I could do was hug my guitar. George thought that was very good, and he let me do it. But he also turned me down when I was not thinking of the script, when I was thinking only of *my* part."

In style *Wild Is the Wind* was a departure. For the first time Cukor attempted naturalism; there were scenes of training sheepdogs and of a lamb's birth (which created censorship problems in some cities). Also uncharacteristic of Cukor was the overly explicit symbolism. Giola develops a special affection for a wild stallion because, as she says, "This horse and I speak the same language." Like the stallion, Giola embodies an individualistic spirit, resisting efforts to tame her.

Wild Is the Wind builds with a brooding tone of a Eugene O'Neill tragedy but is marred by a sentimentally contrived happy ending, which Cukor reportedly detested. Yet, as critic Gene Phillips notes in his book, the film features a prevalent theme in Cukor's work: illusion versus reality. Gino refuses to accept that the past is buried, that the irrepressible Giola isn't a copy of his wife. But he must face the truth and give up his fantasy of reliving his first marriage.

The sweet smell of Oscars unmistakably hovered over the picture, released in December. Magnani and Quinn were nominated for acting awards. Quinn took his first Best Actor nomination with a sense of humor. "Win, lose, or draw," he told Cukor, "you're still my buddy." Magnani was equally grateful to Cukor's intelligent and sensitive help, noting that if the picture had any success, it would be thanks to him. For his part, Cukor told Magnani that working with her was one of the most deeply satisfying experiences of his life and that he really wished to work with her again.

The opportunity to work with Magnani again seemed to materialize almost immediately. In 1957 Lazar made a deal for Cukor to do two pictures at Paramount: *Two Women* and *Heller in Pink Tights*. Based on Alberto Moravia's novel, *Two Women* is the heart-wrenching story of an Italian mother and her shy daughter, both brutally raped by Moroccan soldiers during World War II. "It's my Italian period," Cukor joked. To get a sense of the film's look, Cukor requested photographs of Italy during the war. He planned to go to Rome for preliminary work, hoping to shoot *Two Women* the following spring with Anna Magnani and Sophia Loren.

Casting difficulties, however, prevented him for doing the film. Magnani thought that Loren was too strong-looking to make the mother-daughter relationship convincing. If Loren was definitely set for the daughter, Magnani would have to decline the mother role—despite her respect for both Cukor and Loren. Moreover, fearing the picture might be thrown to Loren, she demanded approval of script, stressing that her decision had nothing to do with the size of her part.

Cukor thought that Magnani made a valid point but that the problem could be resolved with Loren's performance and makeup. In his view, Loren's part was too one-dimensional; if anything, it was her role that needed additional facets for dramatic tension. Cukor held it would be "fatal" if Magnani were in the "driver's seat"; her demands were unacceptable.

Cukor believed Magnani was not acting in good faith because when she sent her agent to express her concerns, she knew Loren was set for the picture. He also resented Magnani's playing hard to get, trying to jockey them into a position where they'd be on their knees. He didn't know the history of her enterprises but suspected they all started with refusals, counteroffers, and shenanigans.

For Loren, the prospect of playing Magnani's daughter was a coup. Excited to work with Cukor and with "the doyenne" of Italian actresses, she tried to convince Magnani to do the film, but to no avail. Magnani's rejection was persistent; she refused to perform with a daughter who was taller than she was.

In January 1959, the University of Southern California made Cukor an honorary member of Delta Kappa Alpha, a national fraternity that named one industry leader each year in recognition of his or her achievements. Past winners included John Huston, Cecil B. De Mille, and George Stevens. Cukor was paid tribute at a fancy banquet, with speeches by Judy Garland, Charles Brackett, and several USC chancellors.

Humorous messages from many celebrities were read. "You were at Warner's so many years in the making of *A Star Is Born* that the place just doesn't seem the same without you," wrote Jack Warner. "Your influence on the studio was profound. Before you came to us, we were thought of as a business corporation, but our calm reaction when the picture ran a little over schedule and a trifle over budget, gave the impression that Warner's had become a non-profit foundation for patronizing the arts."

Recalling *GWTW*, Cukor termed himself living proof that one can survive one's failures. But listening to the tributes, he had the feeling he was at his own funeral. "What words of wisdom can I say," he said. "Strive for success, but don't be afraid of failure; if you have had it, it gives you freedom and the greatest boldness to proceed." Alluding to the fact that he had never won an Oscar, Cukor said he went to work each day with "anticipation and hope."

Cukor reciprocated with the establishment of a fellowship that provided a year's tuition for a graduate student at USC. He also gave Georges Braque's painting "Still Life," valued at eighty-five thousand dollars, to USC. "It is particularly rewarding," said Norman Topping, the university's president, "when such generosity as that of Mr. Cukor turns toward an institution of private higher education, which so often does not have the funds to acquire such art treasures."

Cukor got to work with Sophia Loren in his next Paramount film, *Heller in Pink Tights*, the only western he ever made. The label is misleading, for the film was actually a comedy about show business, with some satirical commentary on the western genre.

The film was based on a novel by Louis L'Amour, whose romantic stories of the American frontier were very popular. Loren was perfectly cast as Angela Rossini, the leading lady of a theatrical troupe touring the frontier. The flirtatious Rossini was inspired by the real-life actress Adah Menken. Cukor's focus in the story was consistently on Loren's character. Angela charms the theater's owner in believing that *La Belle Hélène* cannot possibly violate Cheyenne's moral standards. But she also makes trouble for the company with her deceptive flirtations.

The most remarkable dimension of the film, which was shot on location in Tucson, Arizona, was its visual style. Cukor devoted more time to ambiance than plot. For example, the color scheme of the casino sequence gives it the aura of a fairy tale: The casino is red, all the men wear black, and Angela's dress is white.

Cukor artfully conveys the peculiar magic of the theater as a way of life. The best sequences are the presentations of the operettas *Mazeppa* and *La Belle Hélène*. The latter is most amusing because of its mixture of styles: Loren wears a white wig and a togalike costume, and Quinn a military uniform of an unspecified era.

"*Heller in Pink Tights* was an unfortunate film," said Quinn, who played Tom, the theater's manager. "George was a man of great substance, but even a comedy had to have contents for him, and contents were missing from this movie." Quinn never understood why he was cast in the film: "I was basically playing a homosexual." He recalled: "Cukor worked more with Sophia than with me. Maybe it was the role, or maybe she was more demanding of his attention."

By this time Cukor had become the master of orchestrating great entrances for his female stars. The first glimpse of Loren begins with a detail shot of a woman's foot in an elegant shoe. The camera tilts up from the shoe to her face, as she steps out of a wagon. Tom introduces the troupe, saving Angela for last, when Cukor cuts to a close-up of her face. Angela titillates the crowd with a succession of colored scarves, revealing her beautiful face only in the split-second intervals between scarves. For Cukor, Angela was the embodiment of the spirit of play onstage and off.

As the movie begins, the troupe is forced to flee the last town it played because of some missing funds. Similarly, at the end the company has to leave town to avoid trouble after the theater's safe has been robbed. But far more entertaining are the witty exchanges between a hard-edged aging actress (Eileen Heckart) and the company's ingenue (Margaret O'Brien). In one hilarious shot the women prepare to leave town with as many of the company's costumes on them as possible. In the last sequence the company puts on another performance of *Mazeppa,* and the spectacular climax involves Loren's mounting a horse and riding off the stage.

Cukor had a lot of fun making *Heller in Pink Tights,* though he resented Paramount's pressure to speed up the action; it was never meant to be a plot-driven film. The final cut deviated from the film Cukor envisioned. He protested against the studio's stupid cuts and senseless snips, which clouded the story, but he lost the battle.

Heller in Pink Tights was still in postproduction when an unexpected turn of events led to Cukor's next assignment at Columbia, *Song Without End* (originally *The Magic Flame*). Director Charles Vidor died suddenly of a heart attack, with only about one tenth of the film shot. With its $3.5 million budget, each day of idleness was costing the studio some $30,000. As soon as the initial shock was over, producer William Goetz approached Cukor to take over—within twenty-four hours Cukor consented.

By that time Cukor had developed a reputation as a replacement director. In 1958 producer Hal Wallis asked him to reshoot the ending of *Hot Spell,* a Shirley Booth vehicle, directed by Daniel Mann. Cukor didn't know that the reshoot was done in secrecy behind Mann's back. "George's career was then in decline," said Mann, "and he did it as a favor to Wallis, but I didn't expect such behavior from a gentleman like him." To Mann, Cukor was a "letdown" and his behavior "most upsetting," though before that he had great respect for Cukor's professional and personal integrity.

Shortly after this incident Mann met Cukor at a party. Cukor wished to shake his hand, but Mann was so upset he refused. "George was shocked, he was really embarrassed," Mann said. "I wouldn't shake hands with you," Mann told him, "because you're not a man." Cukor was perplexed and hurt, thinking Mann was alluding to his being gay. Years later, when they met again, Cukor explained that had he known the full story, he would have never involved himself.

Paramount sent Cukor along with a rough cut of *Heller in Pink Tights* to Vienna, so that he could complete the film, while shooting *Song Without End* there. After a horrible flight the SAS plane landed at six-thirty in the evening. Exhausted and irritated, Cukor was the last passenger to deplane. Bill Goetz had arranged a fanfare greeting at the airport, complete with media coverage and a caravan of limousines. *"Bitte"*—a Viennese TV cameraman rushed up to Cukor—*"schauen Sie die Script, Herr Regisseur."*

A publicity man then whispered, "Make like you're reading the script."

"Oh, certainly," said Cukor with a wide grin, "that would seem to be an intelligent beginning." Everyone smiled in relief.

Cukor found a troubled set, with a badly demoralized cast. His first decision was to let cinematographer James Wong Howe go. Howe had fumed endlessly about the problems of lighting interiors of baroque Hapsburg palaces and black cathedrals. Charles Lang, an equally good photographer with a better disposition, replaced him.

Under Cukor's guidance, most of the "high falutin crap" was weeded out of the script by Alfred Hayes. Cukor had found the film's opening scenes unbearable, insisting they be rewritten. Tired of clichés in music biopictures—the musician sits at a piano, wearing an agonized expression, grabs a pencil, and suddenly writes ferociously—Cukor brought a fresher approach. He remembered seeing composer Jerome Kern sitting and writing at a desk in a producer's office. He made Dirk Bogarde, who played Franz Liszt, do the same.

Despite these improvements, Cukor was never really emotionally involved, so the picture didn't wear him out. *Song Without End* was not the kind of story he would have chosen to direct. Nor was the production he took over up to his standards. The sets were banal, and the costumes far from Jean Louis's best.

Cukor did enjoy directing his two stars, Dirk Bogarde and Capucine. Bogarde embraced the composer's role because he was tired of playing charming and boyish fellows. "I am sick and tired of being the Loretta Young of England," he told Cukor. Bogarde was impressed with Cukor's skill and taste as he worked to put the derailed production back on track. Working with one of Hollywood's masters was exhilarating. "You were entirely responsible for opening my eyes to the magic of cinema and screen acting," Bogarde told Cukor, "you and you alone."

Capucine, who was making her film debut, said Cukor was "terribly amusing. You never had a boring second with him. He was very bright and had one of the greatest sense of humors I've come across." She recalled a scene in which her character, after making love for the first time, goes to church to confess. Cukor wanted her to be remorseful, but not too much. "Listen, darling," he told Capucine with typical bluntness, "don't give me that Loretta Young bit. Remember, you have been fucking all night!"

"It was my first picture and in English, and I was in awe of him," said Capucine. "I couldn't have been in better hands. Dirk Bogarde was already a confirmed actor, but I was stagestruck." Though inexperienced, Capucine was the kind of actress Cukor loved. He immediately saw her indefinable magic, the kind that lights up the screen, her "love affair" with the camera.

"Every scene was meticulously rehearsed," recalled Capucine. "He even paid attention to the bit players who announced the czar's entrance. George realized that actors could be frightened. He didn't paralyze actors; he was terribly sensitive to their feelings. What he loved was innuendos," said Capucine. "He didn't like performers who were flat. He always told me 'to go the essence of my feelings.' "

Capucine remembered an incident with actress Genevieve Page, who had a small part and was making a nuisance of herself. One day Page confronted Capucine: "Aren't you lucky? You are the star." Capucine was intimidated, but Cukor, who had overheard the remark came to her rescue. "That's enough," he said. "Let's get on with it." This was Cukor's typical reaction to unnecessary pettiness.

The production stayed in Vienna for two months, then moved back to the States for another month of studio shooting at Columbia. When Cukor took over as director, he stipulated that he was not to get screen credit. The film's concept belonged largely to Charles Vidor, who had worked on the project for a long time and shot some of its key scenes.

Cukor turned to Frank Capra, then president of the Directors Guild of America (DGA), for permission to waive his credit. "I feel very strongly, that no matter how much of the picture I will have shot—and I don't want to minimize my efforts—the screen credit should go to the man whose conception I have followed." DGA's board granted Cukor's request and expressed its deep appreciation of his motives. It was an easy decision for Cukor, who didn't want his name attached to a film he didn't like. Columbia, however, expressed its gratitude; Cukor's name appeared in the credits in type of the same size as Vidor's.

Cukor's friends were more generous than the critics. Claudette Colbert, who found the film incredibly beautiful, told Cukor that Capucine would bless him forever. And Goetz informed that opening day at Radio City had broken all records. Those records are "mighty fragile," Cukor quipped. "They're *always* being broken."

As the decade drew to a close, Cukor was worried about Ethel Barrymore's livelihood. He had been instrumental in establishing in 1956 Barrymore Fund at USC, and to which he asked his close friends Tracy and

Hepburn and the Garson Kanins to donate fifteen hundred dollars each year.

When the Barrymore Fund needed "replenishing," Cukor didn't hesitate to nudge his rich friends, albeit with customary flattery. He addressed Whitney Warren as a San Francisco "art lover and distinguished agriculturist!" Or thanking Alex Tiers, Cukor stressed how the collection was fast becoming an important tool for scholars. It was gratifying that Tiers, who was also urged to donate artworks to USC, asked the school to identify him not by name but as an "admirer of George Cukor."

Cukor had proposed that Barrymore make recordings, but she couldn't cope with the exacting work. It was a struggle for her just to keep going day by day; Cukor witnessed a gradual diminution in her interest to live. When Barrymore died in 1959, she left him a precious present: a John Sargent drawing of her.

As usual Cukor started planning his Christmas cards in the fall. For the 1959 card George Hoyningen-Huene came up with the idea of Cukor and his dogs sitting in a baroque theater box right out of *Song Without End*. But Cukor thought the idea, though fanciful, was not right; he had sent a similar card before. Besides, *Song Without End* wasn't really his picture. When Cukor asked for another of Hoyningen-Huene's brilliant ideas, the latter proposed to blow up a photo from *Heller in Pink Tights* but showing, instead of the theatrical troupe, Cukor and his troupe of dogs. It turned out to be one of his best-remembered Christmas cards.

Cukor thanked Alex Tiers for the gorgeous belt, flattered that its size was 32. He might not look like the stars of *Maverick*, but he sure felt as tough as they seemed. It was also a useful incentive to reduce! Cukor was then on one of his periodical diets, determined to keep that 32 waist.

Fat or thin, Cukor never really liked the way he looked. He always cracked a joke if someone took a picture of him. "We're a motley crew," Cukor told Joshua Logan about a photo of directors who won a popularity poll of a film magazine. There was a touch of criminality about all of them: Zinnemann looked the smuggest, Sidney Lumet pretty unappetizing, Logan too sincere, and himself plain stupid. On another occasion, thanking Harry Cohn for some stills, Cukor complained they didn't "catch" him at all; he came out looking a "fattish, grayish, oldish gentleman of a certain religion."

Taina Elg's son, Raoul, was born shortly before rehearsals for *Les Girls* began. One afternoon Cukor asked to see the child, so she brought him to the studio. She recalled: "My baby took one look at Mr. Cukor and started to scream, but he thought it was funny because it was from a child." Cukor later said, "Taina's son took one look at me and screamed of fright."

"George had that extraordinary owlish face, with big circles under his eyes," said Efrem Zimbalist, Jr., who appeared in *The Chapman Report*. Cukor reminded Zimbalist of the woman who had headed the actor's drama club: "You could have put George in drag, and he would have fit the role, though there was nothing effeminate about him."

Despite Cukor's jokes, he was self-conscious about his appearance, particularly now that he was again losing his battle against weight. His black humor was a survival tactic for a gay man, who not only was surrounded by attractive people but himself attributed the utmost importance to physical beauty.

If the late 1950s were not a good time for Cukor professionally, there was an interesting development on the personal arena: He met a young man, George Towers, who changed his life. Cukor's friends believed that Towers, a stunningly WASPish-looking blond, was a hustler. "There was at that time a well-known hustler circuit for the upper Hollywood echelon," said one friend. "A famous guy managed the whole thing, usually by the telephone. I know that Towers was part of this person's stable."

"The only long-standing relationship George had," said another friend, "was with George Towers. Towers was his protégé, and George put him through law school at USC," he explained. "He was in love with Towers, but they never lived together. George would never live with anybody. It went on for years, until Towers got married. But even after his marriage they continued to be friendly. George became a godfather of one of Towers's children, who were always coming over to the house."

"The relationship lasted probably several years," noted Lambert, "but they never lived together. George never talked about this relationship, and people never asked about it." Lambert explained: "Since I knew him well, I would try discreetly to make him open up about Towers, but he just wouldn't. He didn't get angry; he would just change the subject. It was just clear it wasn't something he was going to talk about to anybody." Lambert added: "But George was very curious about my life. He would ask me very direct intimate questions, and I would answer. But he wasn't prepared to answer these questions if I asked him. I would invite him to open up, saying something like 'I know you were very close to Towers; that must have been wonderful,' but he just wouldn't pick up on it; he turned me down."

"George had a strong sense of values," Capucine allowed, "but we never touched the subject of his homosexuality. He was very discreet about what people did with their bodies; he respected their intimacy. There was a threshold of discretion he wouldn't cross."

"By the time I knew him, he was a man of a certain age," Elg said. "Everybody knew he was gay, but I never saw him around young boys or making any overtures. People didn't talk behind his back because they respected him; he commanded a certain authority. I'm sure that if somebody had done any damage to him or started rumors, he would have been very capable of just shutting them up."

Towers was the ideal man for Cukor—blond, virile, decidedly not gay in his behavior (Cukor was known for his attraction to the "rough trade"). Towers was also the type of man Cukor could display at his straight parties. And because Cukor was used to paying for sex, providing Towers with a "good education" seemed like a worthy cause.

The beginning of the relationship was somehow rocky because the person who brought Towers to Cukor's house noticed that the host instantly became smitten with him. There was some brouhaha as "eventually George pulled Towers away from this person, who took it very badly and didn't speak to George for years." But Cukor was so infatuated that he didn't care; he believed this was one occasion where his ungentlemanly conduct seemed justified.

None of Cukor's intimate friends liked Towers, who was often standoffish. "In the final account," claimed one friend, "Towers was well paid for his services: George left him his money and Alan Searle left him Somerset Maugham's estate." But another friend doubted whether Towers exploited Cukor. "If you're really in love with somebody," he said, "you're willing to do a lot. Whatever George did for Towers, he did it because he wanted to."

Towers was perfectly comfortable with Cukor's gay friends. "He would come to our Sunday evenings by himself," recalled one regular guest, "and sit and chat with us." Said another: "They behaved like a couple, though. George was not the demonstrative type." Cukor never talked about this relationship—to anyone—and he very seldom took Towers to his friends' houses.

Upon Towers's graduation from law school, Cukor was instrumental in finding him a job with his lawyers' office. And after he formed a production company, GDC, Towers worked as its executive secretary, handling the legal aspects of some properties. Later Cukor arranged for Towers to become a partner of the J. William Hayes law offices.

After working with Anna Magnani in *Wild Is the Wind* and Sophia Loren in *Heller in Pink Tights,* Cukor continued his cycle of films with Italian actresses when Gina Lollobrigida was cast as the lead in *Lady L.* Set in London and Paris at the turn of the century, this was a comedy about the kind of heroine he liked: strong and morally "disreputable."

However, Cukor didn't look forward to working with Lollobrigida, whom he found stupid, cagey, and untalented. Still, his tests for the star brought out finesse, a quality she had never shown before. Externally Lollobrigida always could pass as Lady L., but Cukor hoped that now her internal department, her intelligence, would match.

Since there were serious problems with the script, in August 1959 Cukor was informed that *Lady L* was being pushed back to the spring. Producer Julian Blaustein's periodic reports that the script was moving at a good pace proved less and less encouraging as the months rolled by and a scenario remained to be seen. Work on the script continued for another year.

In August 1960 Gene Allen was sent to Europe to scout locations. But a few days after Allen left, Cukor sent him an alarming letter. While he'd gotten used to work for no salary, Cukor didn't want to lose too much money on these uncertain projects. MGM had balked at paying Cukor's preproduction expenses, and unfortunately his agent, Swifty Lazar, accepted its decision too easily. All this meant that the scouting trip couldn't stretch for too long. Cukor saw in MGM's mistreatment yet another indication of his declining standing in the studio.

Lady L was going to be shot in Hollywood, with some on-location shots in Europe. After Allen laid the groundwork, Cukor was to go to London in August to approve the exteriors. From there he would go to Paris to scout locations, then end in Nice in September with a well-deserved vacation.

Cukor had always wanted to work with Ralph Richardson, and *Lady L* seemed to offer the opportunity. But the distinguished actor wouldn't accept the deal unless he was able to read his part. While in London, Cukor talked Richardson into going to California to discuss the (still-unfinished) script and his wardrobe. Richardson arrived with his agent, Constance Chapman, and with his charm Cukor made their visit enjoyable.

Because Lollobrigida and costar Tony Curtis were put on the payroll in January 1961, the studio was anxious to start shooting. By May, however, there was still no script, for changes were still being made by S. N. Behrman. When Behrman's version was finally submitted, the producers were dissatisfied, and Noel Langley (who had cowritten the play *Edward, My Son*) was brought in.

In the meantime, Lollobrigida was demanding to see the script, claiming she needed plenty of time to learn her lines in English. Cukor was annoyed with interviews she gave to the press, denouncing the current script as being so bad she ought to be in mourning. Always the professional, he couldn't understand an actress's sabotaging a project she was committed to and, in his mind, overpaid for.

Cukor was as upset as Lollobrigida about the script, however. On April 11 he sent Sol Siegel one of his strongest letters. In his whole career, Cukor wrote, he had never faced a situation like this, and despite his sincere efforts not to be affected, his morale was completely shaken. Aside from lack of wit and style, the story was unclear. Questioned by the actors about vital points of the plot, Cukor was unable to give answers. Worse yet, in his conferences with Curtis and Lollobrigida, he was put in the awkward position of having to sit by silently.

Cukor's request to comment on the script's changes before his stars saw them was denied. He waited in his office for the telephone to ring, but no one called for days. When Blaustein finally phoned, he told Cukor he wished to talk to Curtis and Lollobrigida in Cukor's absence. Outraged, Cukor failed to see how he was to handle his stars with firm authority when he was being bypassed in such a humiliating way.

Ultimately a good script for *Lady L* never materialized. MGM spent more than one million dollars on the sets and costumes. With so much money spent and nothing to show for it, the endless postponements were meant to save the studio's face with the stockholders. Cukor was expected to start shooting with an unacceptable script. Unable to reconcile this problem, he asked to be relieved. Cukor saw nothing but disaster ahead. With his best efforts, he would be unable to make even a passable picture. The film was eventually shelved.

During the prolonged deliberations over *Lady L,* Cukor busied himself with *Let's Make Love,* his first film with Marilyn Monroe. This was Cukor's third musical. His first, *A Star Is Born,* was such a distinguished picture it cast a shadow on his subsequent attempts. Like *Heller in Pink Tights, Let's Make Love* was a light film with serious overtones and strong visual style.

Initially known as *The Billionaire,* the musical had an entirely negligible plot. A French billionaire playboy, Jean-Marc Clement (Yves Montand), finds out that an off-Broadway company is planning a satirical revue based on his life. He intends to take legal action to stop the show, but upon meeting the leading lady, Amanda Dell (Marilyn Monroe), he is instantly infatuated. He passes himself off as a down-at-the-heels actor who bears a resemblance to Clement. The ensuing story describes the preparation of the show and Clement's romance with Amanda.

Though the material is slight, the film features one of Cukor's dominant themes: the magic of show business. He therefore gives stronger visual attention to the theatrical setting than to the characters, effectively conveying the chaos of rehearsal as well as the excitement of performing. At the end the spirit of the play conquers Clement and shakes his bureaucratic world, a moment captured by Cukor in a long shot of his formal office.

Let's Make Love showed once again Cukor's expertise in staging special entrances for his female stars. Monroe's introduction begins with her legs shinnying down a pole center stage; she is rehearsing her big number, the Cole Porter classic "My Heart Belongs to Daddy." Cukor alternated shots of Amanda and an all-male chorus, emphasizing the whiteness of

Monroe's skin and blond hair. Lighting is a key factor in this sequence, with spotlights illuminating Monroe's features. The scene also encourages voyeurism: Watching the show, Clement fantasizes about performing the sexually suggestive song with Amanda.

After *A Star Is Born*, Cukor's mise-en-scène, specifically the use of space and color, became more deliberately pronounced. Here he employed camera movement and color to intensify the impact of Monroe's song. Amanda's red dress, signaling her sexuality, is contrasted with her white face, her naïveté. The scene in which Monroe's chiffon dress, moved by a blast of air, billows out from her waist, paid homage to her famous moment in *The Seven-Year Itch*. Cukor consciously exploited Monroe's photogenic looks and the viewers' familiarity with her screen persona.

Having scored a huge success in *Some Like It Hot*, Monroe was at the height of her career. Cukor did not have to mold her image; he took it as a given. *Let's Make Love* was one of the few films in which Cukor had no influence over its star. In fact, he benefited from Monroe's popularity, onscreen and off. There were always press people on the set, and Cukor and the film got plenty of publicity.

Cukor found Monroe intelligent, if tough. To him, she was a reincarnation of Harlow, possessing the same mixture of simplicity and overpowering femininity. Like the 1930s star, Monroe had the ability to create an "exaggerated feeling of enchantment." Her natural gift for comedy also resembled Harlow's: She said her lines as if she didn't quite know what they meant. However, Monroe was more profoundly distressed than the even-tempered Harlow. "Marilyn was quite crazy," Cukor once said, "full of bad judgment."

At the same time, Cukor was amazed at Monroe's "reckless intensity" as a performer. In one scene, wearing her usual high heels, she ran as though her life depended on it. Cukor placed himself beside the camera to stop her from colliding with it and injuring herself.

"Marilyn's face moves," Cukor told Kenneth Tynan, "it catches the light—it's genuinely photogenic. And she thinks boldly, as a dog thinks. Her mind is wonderfully unclouded—she doesn't censor her thoughts. Like all great performers—whenever she enters, it's an occasion." But Cukor was also playful at her expense. Asked in a party game what food Monroe reminded him of, Cukor immediately replied, "A three-day-old Van de Kamp Bakery angel cake."

Jack Cole, who choreographed the numbers in *Let's Make Love*, recalled: "It was a terrible ordeal for everybody. Cukor was not crazy about Marilyn for a number of reasons. He was not good for her. Josh Logan [*Bus Stop*] was good for her. Logan would get everybody onto the set, lock the doors, get everybody crazy and then start photographing." But Cukor didn't work in such a way.

The first couple of weeks were "lovey-dovey," and Cukor hoped it would continue that way. Then Monroe came down with the flu—80 percent flu and 20 percent terror, Cukor told a friend, or maybe it was the other away around. Realizing how insecure Monroe was, Cukor forced himself to be extremely gentle.

Cukor's special treatment was appreciated, for during the shoot he received a letter from Arthur Miller, Monroe's husband at the time. The picture was important to her, wrote Miller, but immeasurably more important were the precious weeks of her life, which Cukor's patience and skill and understanding had made humanely meaningful for her. Miller had never known his wife to be so happy at work, so hopeful, so prepared to cast away her worst doubts. Confiding in Cukor why Monroe was so dear to him, Miller also complained about his long, forced bachelorhood.

As usual, Cukor and his stars also had fun on the set. On June 17 he sent a birthday telegram, signed by Monroe and Montand, to their mutual friend the French director René Clair, who had asked Cukor to tell Monroe how much he admired her. Cukor knew that Monroe and Montand were having an affair; it was almost expected of them. The mood changed dramatically, however, once Montand's actress/wife, Simone Signoret, arrived to look after her husband.

On May 27, 1960, shooting ended, except for the musical numbers. Cukor was busy doing postproduction work with the cutter, what Montand in his charmingly poor English called "dumbing" (dubbing). Once again Cukor encountered censorship problems. The Legion of Decency gave *Let's Make Love* a Class B rating, for its suggestive costumes, dancing, and lyrics. On June 10 Frank McCarthy, Fox's publicity director, asked Cukor to let some censors see a rehearsal of the number "Let's Make Love," because the lyrics were deemed unacceptable. In what seemed a miracle to Cukor, this sexually provocative number remained intact.

Let's Make Love enjoyed wonderful notices and a smash opening in Los Angeles, with long lines at the Grauman Chinese Theater.

While Cukor was shooting *Let's Make Love,* Vivien Leigh was enjoying her success in Jean Giraudoux's *Duel of Angels.* The play did so well in New York that the producers decided to bring it to L.A. Press agent Walter Alford was sent to the West Coast to set up the ad campaign and make arrangements for the company. Leigh also assigned Alford a sensitive job, one that eventually fell into Cukor's hands. She asked Alford to send a telegram to the Associated Press, to announce her consent to give Olivier a divorce so that he could marry Joan Plowright. Leigh knew that the "bombshell" would break in the American papers on Monday, and she wanted to be away from the inevitable media onslaught.

But Leigh was worried about mutual friends she and Olivier had in Hollywood, about who would remain her friend and who would shun her. She was particularly nervous about the opening night of *Duel of Angels,* which was sure to be a star-studded event since it marked her first appearance in L.A. in years. Cukor seemed the right person to handle the delicate situation. "Get in touch with George," Leigh told Alford. "We are very good friends."

"I called on George," Alford recalled, "and he couldn't have been more gracious. He took charge of the whole thing." Cukor got hold of the seating plan and put the two gossips, Louella Parsons and Hedda Hopper, on the same row at opposite ends of the aisle. When the theater got requests for seats, they simply turned them over to Cukor. Knowing everyone in Hollywood, Cukor used his social skills to avoid awkward pairing of celebrities. He also helped steer Leigh through the gala party, telling her whom to speak to first, whom to avoid. "Coming to the aid of his friend was a great pleasure for George," said Alford. "He thoroughly enjoyed arranging that evening."

When *Let's Make Love* premiered, the *Lady L* project was still up in the air, with no final script or starting date. In the meantime, Selznick had a more ambitious project for Cukor: Scott Fitzgerald's *Tender Is the Night.* But Lazar notified Selznick that Cukor was still committed to *Lady L* and to another picture at Fox, *Goodbye Charlie* with Monroe. Selznick was bitterly disappointed: It seemed a pity that a man of Cukor's talent would waste himself on "junk" like *Lady L,* placed in production solely on Lazar's salesmanship, while a masterpiece like *Tender Is the Night* was available.

Selznick almost accepted the fact that *Tender Is the Night* was a dead issue, but unexpected developments prompted him to reopen talks with Cukor. The chief obstacle in the past was the lack of an appropriate male star, but with Glenn Ford that problem could be solved. Selznick told Ford that Cukor was "easily the best choice" for the subject, but it was important for Ford to get some feedback directly from Cukor. Selznick suggested a meeting with Ford, who was now a key to the whole project.

Selznick also sent Cukor the first draft of Thackeray's *Vanity Fair.* There were many companies where he could set this project up, but because he wanted to do it with the least possible delay, Selznick asked Cukor to read the draft. Alas, as in the past, nothing came out of *this* round of talks. Cukor was simply uninterested in lending his services to Selznick.

Cukor was hoping to complete *Lady L* in time to do the Monroe picture *Goodbye Charlie,* but the delays made this impossible. When Cukor didn't report on time, Fox filed a breach of contract suit. In

February 1961 MGM and Fox began a legal battle over Cukor's services. In the first litigation in years to pit one studio against another, Fox sought an injunction to force Cukor to do its picture first. MGM's executives claimed that their contract with Cukor gave them the right of preemption. To settle the suit, Cukor accepted another assignment at Fox, *The Chapman Report*, with Richard Zanuck as producer.

The Chapman Report, however, was not destined to be made at Fox. "The film switched studios," Zanuck recalled, "as at that time my father, Darryl Zanuck, was no longer running Fox. There was a lot of turmoil at the studio; it was the beginning of the *Cleopatra* debacle. They were very disorganized and they decided it was too risky and had no foreign potential. We were pretty far advanced in the production, though we hadn't started shooting," Zanuck said. "It took one telephone call from my father to Jack Warner, who took it right away."

Cukor gave Zanuck some humorous but savvy advice. "When you come on a studio lot," Cukor said, "the first couple of days are critical. Ask for as many things as you need on the first day, and you'll get everything you want, because after a while they forget you, you become part of the background." Cukor was right. "I made a lot of demands, and since we were the new kids on the block, we got everything," said Zanuck.

Based on Irving Wallace's scandalous novel, *The Chapman Report* has an episodic structure, dealing with the sexuality of a cross section of American women. A team of sexologists, not unlike the Kinsey researchers, unearths some startling behavior about the "respectable" married set in Brentwood. By today's standards the material is mild, but back then there was a great outcry about how shocking and indecent the book was. Despite the hype it received—heralded as the "sexiest" movie ever made in America—the salaciousness was never there.

As expected, the Production Code office expressed its strong concern with "the quality of the sex episodes and the treatment of each incident." Any one of the four sex episodes—concerning a nymphomaniac, an adulterous wife, a frigid woman, a dissatisfied wife—would be sufficient for one controversial move, but piled into one and discussed in clinical language, they were unacceptable.

To upgrade the project, Zanuck decided to hire a top filmmaker. "Cukor was an important director," he recalled, "one of the finest. Getting him was a coup." Cukor immediately took to the "lively, kinky, and very much of today" material. He knew the picture was trashy, but he wasn't apologetic; he needed to work.

As lowbrow as the material was, Cukor treated it with care, elevating it with perceptive casting and tasteful direction. He used three first-rate actresses: Claire Bloom, Shelley Winters, and Glynis Johns. The fourth actress, Jane Fonda, showed potential but was not yet established.

But if the casting was nearly perfect, the script was not. "We had a poor script," Zanuck concurred. "George and I and Gene Allen worked very hard on it right up to shooting." As many as seven writers were involved, but in the end Wyatt Cooper and Don Mankiewicz were credited for the script, and Grant Stuart and Gene Allen for adaptation. In actuality Allen wrote the final script.

In the past Cukor had a terrible prejudice against the children of famous stars because as he put it, it wasn't difficult to believe they got where they did because of parental influence. But this was definitely not true of Fonda. Originally she auditioned for the nymphomaniac; she came dressed and made up as a streetwalker. Cukor found Fonda's screen test amusing, but he was more intrigued by casting her against type. He saw through to Fonda's WASPish upbringing, which convinced him to assign her to Kathleen Barclay, the frigid widow with a pathological fear of sex, exacerbated by hunger for love.

"I wanted to play the nymphomaniac, which I'd heard was the only good part in the film," Fonda told Hedda Hopper. "So I dressed in style, but Cukor looked at me and laughed. 'You are going to play the sophisticated widow,' he said. But if I'd gone in my frigid widow clothes, I don't think he'd have hired me." Claire Bloom, who ended up playing the nymphomaniac, recalled that Cukor told Fonda, "Go to the bathroom and take all that terrible stuff off right away."

Fonda wanted to do the film because of Cukor: "You might have to wait a lifetime to work with him." Indeed, something exciting was happening to her on the set. With Cukor's support, Fonda came into her own—this, after five years of serious doubts. *The Chapman Report* was a turning point in her career.

"I'm beginning to visualize it through a glass darkly," Cukor told Fonda. "I see your part as mostly large gorgeous close-ups of Kathleen laughing, crying, pouting, running the gamut!" Cukor worked closely with her, always providing invaluable advice: "Restrain your natural exuberance before the cameras." He said later: "I don't mean to flatter myself, but I brought out something very fine in Jane. It may have been already there, but she brought it out with *me*." Fonda always spoke favorably of Cukor: "You know he'll protect you. He has impeccable taste and a sense of subtlety. He forces himself to love and believe in you."

After the movie was done, Cukor invited Fonda to his house. "I've let you do certain things now," he said, "that if you did three years from now, I'd knock your teeth in." Fonda was an "American original," but her "problem" was how to hold her talent in. Cukor taught her discipline and, once again, showed his wonderful eye for detecting talent. Within a decade Fonda went on to win two Oscar's and become the best actress of her generation.

Because he worshiped English acting, Cukor used Claire Bloom and Glynis Johns. Johns had just undergone major surgery for cancer, but she came out of the hospital early. "I was supposed to stay in bed with a nurse to look after me," she recalled, "but I got a call from George, who heard from Jane Fonda I was interested in the movie." He said: "Obviously, you can't have me as a visitor, but I'd love to have a chat with you when you feel better." Without a moment's hesitation Johns said, "I can see you right now!" And she did.

Just a day after her release from the hospital, Cukor visited Johns. She recalled: "I told my nurse to go out and get something to make me look tanned. I put on a black dress cut down, with no bra and no stockings, and I wore high-heel sandals. I put on Frank Sinatra as background music, opened the door and said, 'Good afternoon, Mr. Cukor.' " Cukor was stunned. "Glynis," he said, "only a great actress can do what you did. You've got the part."

Johns had one difficult but funny seduction scene with a muscle beach boy, played by Ty Hardin. "It was quite a long scene and rather physical," she recalled. "We had to grasp each other, fall on the sofa and roll off it, and I had to get up, run out, and get into my car. Normally a director would shoot it in two or three shots and then cover it with over the shoulder and close-up shots. But Cukor said, 'This is going to be done in one shot.' We did only one take, and that's the one he printed."

Early in the shoot Cukor was staging a lecture scene with the four women taking notes in the front and many extras in the background. "George loathed crowd scenes," Johns said. "He had deep hatred for anyone who was extra because he knew they were all frustrated actors."

Johns had a couple of lines, but she couldn't make them work. "It was early in the process, and I was not in my character yet." She knew Cukor had absolute faith in her abilities, but a perpetual worrier, she needed to speak to him. Johns waited for a moment when Cukor wasn't surrounded with people, patted him on the shoulder, and said, "George, I am being rather bad in the scene." Cukor just glared at her for a second and said, "So, for Christ's sake, be good. You know how!"

Claire Bloom had never met Cukor, but he knew of her from Vivien Leigh. Cukor wanted an actress who looked like a lady but could also play a whore. He wanted to avoid the obvious choice of casting a sexy bombshell, fearing the character would be too vulgar. "When one reads that part, one doesn't think, 'Hmm, Claire Bloom will be good in it,' " Bloom said. "The result was interesting; the part points to someone who seems to be one thing but really is another. With every part you learn a certain aspect about yourself," she added. "From this one I got a kind of sexual freedom. I've often been asked to play that kind of part since, but never *before*."

If *The Chapman Report* is interesting today, it is mostly for its acting, especially Bloom's. Coming from the theater, Bloom had dazzling skills. Cukor's first impression of her was of a polite girl, somehow mysterious, who rarely talked above a whisper. During rehearsals the sound men complained they couldn't hear her. "Claire is not a nice Nellie," Cukor said, "she has no inhibition, and she is not as cold as some people say." Bloom even received the greatest compliment Cukor could pay an actor: "Claire is a creature born for the screen."

As usual, if Cukor had something to say, he came up and whispered it. "In my scenes," Bloom said, "he whispered that I should be feeling sexually alluring. He was very clear about precisely what he wanted, and then he would kind of act offscreen. On the other side of the camera, he would mime what he wanted you to do."

One day Cukor sensed something was wrong. "Take off your bra," he said. Bloom was stunned but obeyed. Cukor put her into an unfitted black dress so that her breasts could move freely; the effect was erotic; her dress was always falling off. Without a bra she moved in a way that told a lot about her character's hopelessness and looseness. "He wanted me to look distinguished but to be very much a whore," said Bloom. "He did ask me if I'd mind wearing a see-through, but I couldn't have cared less. I was in the hands of a great director; I would do anything for him. For most other directors, I'd say, 'No, I'd rather not,' but if George thought it right, you would say, 'Of course.'

"George was mentally interested in actors," said Bloom, "particularly actresses. A lot of directors aren't."

"Cukor was very precise, very detail-conscious," Zanuck said. "A lot of directors don't have that assurance. They wing it a lot, and hope to get lucky. George never improvised," he said. "He knew exactly what he wanted and was very stubborn about it."

On the set Cukor was also very discreet. One of the actors was "physically utterly filthy and had breath to knock fifty people over for a hundred miles," according to Bloom. "I just can't do it," she said to herself, so she took Cukor aside and said, "George, he smells like a raccoon, and his breath is just terrible. Couldn't you tell him at least to use a mouthwash?" Cukor told her, "No, this is not really what he's like; he's getting in the mood for the part he's playing." But the next day Bloom noticed that the actor had brushed his teeth. "That kind of thing was special of Cukor: 'Don't complain about other actors.' He was so political about this fellow. I didn't believe all that rubbish about being dirty because you're playing someone dirty, but George took it from the actor's point of view."

According to Bloom, "Cukor was very interested in issues of female sensitivity. He lived vicariously through certain of the tenacious feelings that I played. He experienced the material in a different way because he was homosexual. Like many highly tuned artists, he knew what it was to be a man *and* a woman."

Efrem Zimbalist, Jr., who played the psychiatrist, also emphasized Cukor's different way with women: "Physically women were the embellishment that moved around while the men remained motionless. Like a dancer, the man was there to lift the ballerina. Sometimes the man had his back to the audience; he was there to service the woman. One of George's secrets was to feature the women, to make tableaux of them. If only for this, he was Hollywood's greatest woman's director."

Cukor thought that women showed off better if they were in motion. "None of the men were very mobile in a Cukor film," said Zimbalist. "He would ask you to stand in one place, while the woman moves around you. George saw his job in showing the women off, but then he had some gorgeous women in his career."

"George was very conscious of the look of the picture," Zanuck said, "and that's where Allen and Hoyningen-Huene came in. He had great faith in them and would totally rely on them." The costumes were designed by a very good designer, Orry-Kelly. Each woman wore one dominant color all the way through. For example, Bloom's color was brown, and Winters's black. At first Cukor thought the viewers would become too aware of it, but then he realized it also would make each woman stand out.

Bloom had never known anyone who took such care over costumes as Orry-Kelly. "I remember him painting my shoes himself so that they should be exactly the same tone as my dress. That kind of care—and shoes don't even show—that kind of detail characterized the whole picture." Zanuck concurred: "George was very picky, but in the good sense. He would stay there and do it over and over again until he got what he wanted."

There were never any conflicts or harsh words between Cukor and the cast. Zimbalist recalled that for the most part Cukor was extraordinarily patient. "There were occasions when it seemed he was putting up with more than he had to. I remember saying to him, 'How do you manage to keep your patience and put up with these things.' 'Well,' he said, 'that's my job.' "

Zimbalist also singled out the quiet encouraged on a Cukor set. "Nobody talked unnecessarily," he said. "Everyone was a bit scared, a bit awed. There was just no monkeying around. You knew he meant business, and you respected him and his reputation. People restrained themselves, not because he demanded it; it was something you instinctively felt on his set. There was always a threat he could suddenly start screaming. This cowered people."

For example, in a scene with Glynis Johns, Ty Hardin couldn't remember his lines. "They went over a number of takes," Zimbalist recalled, "and George was reaching the boiling point after containing himself for some time." Hardin finally got his lines right, and George printed it. Then the actor asked for another take, at which point Cukor absolutely exploded. "It was like dynamite, TNT, atom bomb, and everything else put together," said Zimbalist. "For half an hour George just screamed not very complimentary things. Hardin just leaned against the wall and listened patiently. When George finally ran out of steam, Hardin said, 'OK, cowboy, let's get serious now.' The term 'cowboy' for George delighted everybody because he was such an urbane man. Cukor roared with laughter, and everybody joined him."

Bloom conceded that Cukor sometimes had a frightfully violent temper that lit up extremely quickly. "He had a volatile temper," Zimbalist remembered. "He would scream at the top of his lungs when something upset him." On one occasion Cukor asked Jack Warner to come down for the dubbing of a scene. Zimbalist was in the dubbing room, where the microphones were, and Cukor was in the soundproof booth. Cukor got so annoyed that Warner didn't come that he started screaming, jumping up and down. The actor could hear him through the soundproof glass, he was yelling that loud.

"George's language was a peculiar thing because it was so uncharacteristic of him," said Zimbalist. "That kind of language shocked you; it just did not compute. Cukor's direction was very casual; he would just go over a page of dialogue, with funny little comments, and interspersed would be these dreadful four-letter words. It wasn't that he was angry; he just used some crazy words that made no sense at all. Then he would say, 'Now, go in there and do it again.' "

Capucine recalled how Cukor said time and again, "I'm not going to take bullshit from anyone." She said: "George had a distaste for anything superfluous. He would dismiss a lot of what he heard as 'crap' and 'shit.' He'd take one look at you and know exactly how honest or dishonest you were. What annoyed him most was people making fuss over nothing."

Lambert noted that "George loved to use 'shit' and 'fuck' a lot—socially." As Cukor grew older, his language got worse, and he swore a great deal on the set; it was somehow more permissible in the open climate in the 1960s. Allan Davis's first impression of Cukor was of "a very bossy and irascible man." Irene Selznick once told Davis that "the reason George was so irascible was that he was meant to be a fat man, and he's made himself into a thin one."

"George was so damned brilliant," Johns said. "He didn't need to have psychological discussions. 'Say the lines and get off,' he would say; he didn't believe in Method acting." Bloom said: "He kept the camera on me for a long time. He admired actors." But the actors knew that no matter how good they were, Cukor would never print the first six takes. This didn't mean he would print take seven; Cukor could shoot as many as twenty takes. "He directs like Maureen Stapleton eats," Fonda once said. "She selects a huge table of food, then picks and chooses what she wants from it."

"The difference between George and other directors," said Bloom, "was that he was an extremely sophisticated European gentleman, with irony, wit, and delicacy. He had been in the theater all his life, and he'd kept his wit, his standards, his independence. You can't live in this place, as I found out, without being damn tough."

Bloom was immensely sad when shooting ended; it had been a wonderful experience. Enormously in awe of him, she wanted to ask Cukor about his work with Garbo, but she thought it was a corny question and never did. Bloom is one of the few actresses who did *not* keep in touch with Cukor. "I was very shy of him," she said. "I admired him more than I could say."

"George cared very much," said Johns. "He covered it up with all kinds of remarks, but underneath he was vulnerable and perceptive with a very loving nature. He either cared about you or struck you off the list; he used to give me lectures on how I should behave with men." Johns gained from Cukor confidence, the "confirmation" that a great director felt she had talent. "It was a wonderful boost from a director of his ilk that you are there not by chance."

"This movie was important," said Bloom. "It was what's called a stretch; my part was different from any I'd had."

Directing *The Chapman Report* was more time-consuming than Cukor thought. "Those modern classics demand all of you," he complained, "especially when they're done at Warner's." Displeased with the first cut, Cukor recut the film himself. Zanuck said Cukor changed the tempo and pacing, personalizing it with his style. "For George, editing wasn't a question of taking things out, but a question of order and aesthetics."

It was obvious to Zanuck that there were going to be censorship problems. The Legion of Decency questioned the value of "a pseudo-scientific survey of female sexuality whose only purpose seems to be sensationalism." Zanuck recalled: "The committee wanted to give us an X rating. To get the proper rating, George had to tone down scenes that were too graphic. That upset him. The movie was pretty tame, but it was considered controversial then."

Indeed, the PCA officials fulfilled their "promise" to "scrutinize the film with minute care." One of their agreements was that the word "sex" would be eliminated wherever possible, to avoid the impression that the story concentrated heavily on sex. But to their dismay, "sex" was used excessively—as much as five times on two pages—and the word "intercourse" was used in too outspoken a manner.

Cukor was volatile about censorship, particularly when Warner's decided to change the ending. For him, his film actually proved that the American woman was a "kinky" item. In the new version, however, Andrew Duggan and Zimbalist were going over IBM cards, and Duggan had the following line: "Well, I think by and large the American woman's pretty normal, wouldn't you say?" Zimbalist was supposed to say, "Yes, completely normal."

Warner's brought in another director to reshoot the ending, but Cukor came back from his vacation in Hawaii. "George would rather have control," said Zimbalist, "even though he hated the ending; he was turned off by those lines. When Duggan says, 'Well, I think American women are pretty normal?' George said in his crackling way of talking, 'Andy, don't be such a goddamn peach.' 'Beg your pardon, George?' Andy said. George repeated, explaining that this line, unbearable to begin with, was being made even more unbearable by Andy's pompous delivery. George didn't want him to sound quite so wonderful."

A lot of film ended up in the cutting room. What was really first-class in the film, Cukor told Lambert, were long sustained interviews with the women who confided their sexual problems. The scenes were extremely well played; Fonda had an emotional scene that was particularly good, but it was "cut, cut, cut!"

The company went for a preview to San Francisco, where Zanuck had been lucky with audiences on other pictures. "I liked to get out of town," he said, "because when you sneak a picture in L.A., you don't really get a true audience." The response was so positive that they all met upstairs in the manager's office. "After we got through talking about the picture," Zanuck recalled, "Jack Warner right then and there offered *My Fair Lady* to Cukor. George was very excited; it was something he had really desired."

Comparisons with other screen versions of books by Harold Robbins and Jacqueline Susann were in Cukor's favor because of his tact and taste. "*The Chapman Report* was never a great film," said Zanuck, "but George made it much better than it ever aspired to be as a book."

Despite Cukor's frustration over *The Chapman Report*'s cuts, it was a mild experience compared with the ordeal of his next film, *Something's Got to Give,* starring Marilyn Monroe.

Hoping to make the film without breakdowns or interruptions, for which Monroe was notorious, production head Peter G. Levathes met all her demands. First, she wanted producer David Brown to be dismissed. Then the script had to be rewritten; this cost the studio more money.

Levathes also accepted Monroe's choice of Dean Martin as the leading man, and when she became displeased with director Frank Tashlin, he brought in Cukor at a cost of $250,000.

Initially called *Goodbye Charlie*, the film was a remake of *My Favorite Wife*. In this version Monroe plays a lost aviator and the mother of two, who comes back to her husband (Dean Martin), now attached to another woman (Cyd Charisse). Cukor wanted to reveal a new facet of Monroe in her scenes with the children. Knowing that Monroe loved, but was unable to have, children, he worked extensively on her scenes with the kids, observing with delight Monroe's rolling on the floor and giggling with them.

A replica of Cukor's house, including his famous swimming pool, was built on the Fox lot. In the renowned pool episode Monroe was trying to woo her ex-husband by exposing her charms in a brief skinny-dipping sequence. Cukor first asked her to do it in a flesh-colored bikini, but the subterfuge was transparent. When he suggested doing it in the nude, she agreed without a murmur. Monroe looked exquisite; she had recently trimmed down, back to her great 37-22-35 measurements.

Tight security gripped Fox's Stage 14: Cukor cleared the set of hangers-on and asked the electricians to look away. Clutching the pool's rim, Monroe was more bashful about showing off her stroke than her figure. "All I can do is dog-paddle," she said. "That will be just fine, darling," Cukor said. Later Cukor vowed never again to have swimming scenes in his movies. Garbo did her much-publicized swim in *Two-Faced Woman*, which turned out to be her last picture. And then Monroe!

On January 21 the film was eight days behind schedule, and Fox had already invested $1.5 million. At first Monroe called in sick, but then the calls stopped coming, and she simply didn't show up. "We can't afford her and *Cleopatra*, too," Fox officials said; Liz Taylor's absences were boosting *Cleopatra*'s budget to $30 million. By April *Something's Got To Give* was thirty-two days behind schedule, costing Fox $2 million extra. Monroe's record showed just five performance days out of seven weeks of shooting. Of her five days, only two were good.

Cukor was irritated by Monroe's coach, Paula Strasberg, who hung around and gave him and the crew a hard time. Her line "My Lee [Strasberg] says, 'It's what's on the screen that counts'" was often ridiculed by Cukor at his parties. That was what she said when Monroe appeared for a few hours once in three weeks. In Cukor's dictionary, Madame Strasberg was a pretentious bore.

In April out of the thirty-two working days, there were only seven and a half usable minutes. When Monroe did show up, she was nervous about being late. At first Cukor was reassuring, telling the insecure actress not to worry, that it had been worth waiting for her.

When Monroe was out, Cukor did cover shots of Dean Martin and Cyd Charisse. But they soon ran out of material; Martin had reacted to the script girl and anybody else they could find. Cukor was especially furious when one Thursday Monroe scampered off the set to a helicopter and flew to Inglewood's airport to jet to New York. This was two days before President Kennedy's birthday party at Madison Square Garden. Her trip threw a crew of 104 people out of work for half a day on Thursday and all day on Friday. Monroe claimed Fox had been notified months in advance, but the studio denied ever giving her permission to go.

Cukor was even more annoyed when Monroe didn't show up on Monday, June 4, this after making an appearance at a Dodgers' game on Friday night. For Cukor, she had the nerve and ruthlessness to send a huge crew home. "Here are these men," Cukor told Hedda Hopper, "and I hate to sound patronizing, but they have children, and they have to sit and see this money thrown away."

Cukor thought Fox should have replaced Monroe weeks before, but the studio was run by incompetent people who had no experience. Levathes said to Cukor in the midst of the crisis, "If we can get her in for just one day." Cukor retorted, "What about the other days?" He resented Monroe's shenanigans, plotting and bullying everybody with her outrageous demands. "Fox was weak and stupid and deserved everything it got," Cukor said off the record.

On June 8 Monroe's attorney notified the studio that the star was "ready and eager to go back to work in two days." Widespread reports that Fox was preparing a replacement had apparently scared Monroe, supposedly recovering from her most recent "illness." In the meantime, Cukor heard that Monroe was busy furnishing a new beach house, making daily trips to the stores.

"Please forgive me, it was not my doing," Monroe wrote to Cukor in her June 8 telegram. "I had so looked forward to working with you." On June 11 Cukor and associate producer Gene Allen packed up their stuff. "The picture is in a state of contingency, there is no salary and we cannot accept other jobs," Cukor told a reporter. "We just sit and wait." He was actually relieved by the turn of affairs because even if he'd finished the film, it would not have been much good.

In an honest talk with Hedda Hopper, Cukor said that no company should take this from a star and that Monroe's willful behavior stemmed from being "over the hill." A reliable source told Cukor that Monroe was in the seventh floor of the hospital, where the windows were barred—for violent cases. Recalling that when Sinatra became engaged, Monroe went mad, knocking her head against the wall, Cukor realized there was no sanity to her conduct.

Cukor felt sorry for Monroe. Unstable, she fired her staff, then took them back. What was terrifying was her wish to do the picture but her complete loss of control. It was obvious to Cukor from her brief appearances that she couldn't function anymore. By afternoon under the influence of alcohol she couldn't remember her lines. Monroe was intelligent enough to know she was no good and Cukor predicted it was the end of her career.

Cukor perceived Dean Martin, one of the "Rat Pack," as a Sinatra disciple, with the same gangster mentality. Martin bellyached to Cukor about how impossible it was to work with Monroe. At the same time he made outrageous statements to the press, boasting to be the "highest-paid golfer in history."

From the beginning Cukor had a strong hunch that the enterprise with Monroe was doomed. He wasn't surprised when Monroe was found dead in August 1962. Hollywood couldn't be held responsible for her death, he said later, because Hollywood made her a star. Ruthlessly exploited by her associates, Monroe simply couldn't live up to the image that was created of her.

In the next few months, wherever Cukor went, people asked about Monroe. He realized he didn't please her fans with his standard explanation of her death: "She was a girl fraught with crises. There was a crisis every day of her life, and perhaps one night was more critical than the others."

On at least one level Cukor enjoyed the gossip about Monroe: It put him at the center of a big media scandal. Whenever he worked with stars like Garbo, Garland, or Monroe, he was guaranteed free, immense publicity.

Preparing a trip to London, he promised Judy Garland and Dirk Bogarde to go into "fascinating" details of his "trials and tribulations" with Monroe. It was nice of them to think of an old pal who had had the rug pulled out from under him. But just when he thought it was "curtains," from somewhere over the rainbow came his chance for a "comeback." Cukor left the good news to the very end: "Jack Warner has selected me to do that musical, based on, I believe, a stage play called *Pygmalion*."

It was absolutely the best news that Cukor could deliver at this juncture of his declining career.

CHAPTER TEN:

The Second Peak: My Fair Lady, 1963–65

ALAN JAY LERNER AND FREDERICK LOEWE'S MY FAIR LADY WAS A mega stage hit. Acclaimed for its witty book, adapted from Bernard Shaw's *Pygmalion,* and for the melodic sweep of its score, the musical received a sensational reception at its 1956 opening and enjoyed a record run of 2,717 performances in New York. Not surprisingly the struggle to acquire the film rights from the Shaw estate went on for years. It ended in February 1962 when Jack Warner paid an all-time record price of $5.5 million.

The most expensive musical ever made, *My Fair Lady* was initially budgeted at twelve million dollars, but by completion its cost had risen to seventeen million, a huge figure in the 1960s. Warner announced that he personally would supervise the production, using the finest talent available for the most ambitious project the studio had ever launched.

As soon as the rights were secured, casting began. Lerner proposed that Rex Harrison and Julie Andrews re-create their stage roles. The young Andrews had a beautiful voice and exquisite diction. In the theater her melodic singing against Harrison's "uttering" of his songs had proved a winning combination. Warner, however, didn't want Andrews, who wasn't known enough in the United States.

Audrey Hepburn, a well-respected actress, was Warner's choice for Eliza Doolittle from the beginning. There was nothing mysterious about his decision to cast her, Warner told the press. Julie Andrews was "just a Broadway name," but Audrey Hepburn was an international movie star. "In my business I have to know who brings people to the box office."

Hepburn was cast in May 1962, a few months before Cukor, who was not the first director to be offered the film. Both Lerner and Warner wanted Vincente Minnelli, who had directed many successful musicals, among them *Gigi*, which had swept the 1958 Oscars. But Warner thought he should have an alternate, just in case he couldn't make a deal with Minnelli. "I jumped in," Lazar recalled, "and suggested George, who was my client and had a reputation for doing good movies."

Negotiations began with Minnelli, but as Warner suspected, a deal was not easily cut. Badly advised by his agent, Minnelli demanded a lot of money and final cut. "He knew that Lerner wanted him," said Lazar, "but mistakenly thought nobody else could direct the film. Minnelli underestimated Warner's power; he thought he had him in a bind." Warner's decision was also influenced by the big failure of Minnelli's last film, *Four Horsemen of the Apocalypse*.

Warner called Lazar and said, "I'm having trouble making a deal with Minnelli. What about George Cukor? How much do you want for him?"

"Whatever you say, I'll take," Lazar said matter-of-factly.

Lazar knew that Cukor needed the picture desperately. It was a bad time for him: *Heller in Pink Tights* had been a failure, and *The Chapman Report* had barely recouped its expense. According to Lazar, "George wasn't easy to sell because his popularity had declined. Getting *My Fair Lady* was the most important thing that could have happened to him." Lazar knew that Warner's offer would be fair. When the mogul offered half a million, he immediately consented. "It was a very big coup of mine. George was ecstatic."

The first conversation about the film between Warner and Cukor took place on an airplane, on their way to a preview of *The Chapman Report* in San Francisco. "How would you like to do *My Fair Lady*?" the mogul said.

Without a moment's hesitation Cukor replied, "I'd love to—and let me tell you, Mr. Warner, you're making a most intelligent choice!" There were good reasons for hiring Cukor. Known as the best woman's director, Warner hoped he would "handle" Hepburn, bring the best out of her. And it helped that Cukor's last Warner's film, *A Star Is Born*, had been a musical and a huge success.

Because Cukor was having difficulty in finding suitable properties, he decided in 1962 to establish his own company, GDC (George Dewey Cukor) Enterprise, with the goal of acquiring stories and preparing scripts. It was also good for tax purposes. In July Cukor's law firm arranged for GDC to lend his services to Warner's to direct *My Fair Lady*, his forty-fourth film. The basic deal was fifty-two weeks for five hundred thousand dollars, Cukor's highest fee to date.

A day after he signed, Cukor cabled Audrey Hepburn: "At long last, I'm delighted at the prospect." The actress was ecstatic: "We waited the longest and got the best." Determined not to lose any time, Cukor sent her the play and suggested that she look carefully at the 1938 British film, which starred Leslie Howard and Wendy Hiller.

Casting the film generated a great deal of publicity. It was almost as big a kudo as that for *GWTW,* except that this time Cukor was more in control. All summer rumors continued to fly about who was going to play Higgins; at first Warner suggested Trevor Howard, who had been originally thought of for the play. And Cukor talked to Jimmy Cagney, who has just retired from the screen, about Alfred Doolittle. But both names received a "calm reaction" from Warner's.

Cary Grant was also approached for Henry Higgins, though Cukor expressed some reservations about his peculiar manner of speaking—"a little Cockney creeps in." Grant was offered the part but in his gentlemanly fashion turned it down, claiming, "It was Rex's and only Rex's part." Grant told Warner that he wouldn't even see the film if anybody but Harrison played the role.

In the meantime, Lerner had met Peter O'Toole, the new star of David Lean's forthcoming epic *Lawrence of Arabia.* After seeing a rough cut of *Lawrence,* Cukor became immediately convinced that O'Toole, with whom he got on like a "house on fire," should play Higgins. At Lerner's suggestion, Cukor met O'Toole and Jules Buck, the actor's manager, in London. Buck was guarded, but Cukor sensed O'Toole was "crazy" to do it. However, Buck made such excessive demands that Warner, a shrewd negotiator himself, refused them.

Audrey wasn't the only person already involved in the film when Cukor came on board. Also signed on was Cecil Beaton, the noted designer, whose involvement was secured at the onset by William Paley, who negotiated the deal with Warner's. Beaton had created only the costumes for the stage production (the set design was by Oliver Smith), but they so richly evoked the Edwardian era that he garnered a lot of publicity. Cukor realized that not only had Audrey and Beaton been engaged before he was, but their participation was perceived as more crucial than his— two hard facts his ego had to swallow.

Cukor told Beaton that he planned to shoot some exteriors in London, trying to correct the impression that he was opposed to working abroad. True, in the past, Cukor had found Metro's Elstree studio disorganized, but he had no preconceived notions. It's really what's on screen that counts, he said; "to hell with everything else."

It was also important to get as many scenic shots of London as possible. Realizing that Warner would not do any interior shots there, Cukor proposed to get extras in Hollywood who carry off the style of the period. This could be done if they got "tough" with the hairdressing and makeup department. Cukor also urged Beaton to use his longtime art director,

Gene Allen, who was practical and experienced. Having started as a blueprint boy years before, Allen knew the ins and outs of the industry. Allen understood that Beaton was the designer, but he was anxious to lend himself in any way. With such praise, and a bit of informal pressure, Beaton consented to use Allen.

In August 1962 Cukor decided to take George Towers to Europe as their relationship had become more intimate. He asked Alan Searle to make arrangements for Towers to stay at an hotel near Maugham's villa, but Searle insisted they both stay with them. Cukor described Towers modestly: a nice man who'd make a most agreeable guest, but he knew that Searle would take to Towers's stunning looks.

On the way to Europe, they stopped in New York, and Cukor showed his young companion the city and introduced him to his friends. They went to a matinee of *My Fair Lady* with his friends Bob Wheaton and famed Hollywood publicist Stanley Musgrove. This kind of traveling was eye-opening for Towers, who was unsophisticated at the time.

They continued to Madrid, where they socialized with Ava Gardner, all attending a flamenco performance. In Barcelona, accompanied by Allen and Hoyningen-Huene, they did some location scouting for *Olympia*, a comedy that was to star Gardner. After three days in Milan, they arrived in Munich and settled at a comfortable hotel.

For the next three days Cukor and Towers spent most of their time with Maugham and Searle. They dined in one expensive restaurant, then another, and as usual, Cukor picked up the bill. Cukor could tell that both Maugham and Searle were charmed by Towers.

After a short stop in Paris they went to England. On September 9 Cukor, Allen, and Beaton had a thorough look around London, curious to see if they could find streets that, in a long shot, might pass as London circa 1910.

That night the market was deserted, except for a few policemen hanging around in the empty arcades. The three wandered around Covent Garden, looking for "local color," before attending the evening performance of *My Fair Lady* at the Drury Lane. Beaton wanted to impress Cukor, to overcome his dislike of making pictures in England. Many scenes, Beaton felt, should be filmed with the authentic look and sound. "Yes, yes, we will certainly shoot some of the scenes here," Cukor said. But Beaton, knowing Cukor's old complaint that the English were always breaking for a cup of tea, sensed he needed extra conviction.

The lack of market life in the evening struck Beaton, trying his hardest to stage-manage the outing, as a personal affront. He even had trouble locating some favorite landmarks. "I think St. Paul's Church is at the end of the arcade," he said, "but just in case it isn't, I'll ask the policeman."

Trying to calm him down, Cukor said reassuringly, "You are a fine guide."

A snob, Beaton was unimpressed with Gene Allen, whom he described as "a former policeman, stocky and apple-faced, with a bullet head and a child's starry eyes of wonderment." But he liked Allen's idea to take an effective shot of the Opera House facade, with the green wrought-iron framework of the market buildings alongside. A semblance of the film was beginning to take place, and Beaton's fears that the real London might not be used were momentarily allayed. From London, Cukor and Allen went to the Ascot racetrack to see old pictures of the place.

In October Cukor spent a long weekend in San Francisco, on an artistic binge, staying with his friend Whitney Warren. On the first night they went to the opening of the Bolshoi Ballet. The next, they attended a Stravinsky opera, followed by a fancy supper on Telegraph Hill. The next day they saw a matinee of *Don Giovanni*. By the end of the weekend all this high culture and dressing up had driven Cukor up the wall. He was ready to go home and start working.

As late as October Cukor still had no idea who would play Higgins. When the negotiations with O'Toole foundered, Harrison's name was again at the top of the list. Harrison was a fascinating actor, but Cukor was concerned that he might be too old. Moreover, Warner didn't want him. "Jack Warner was very anxious not to have the stage people in the film," Harrison recalled. "Besides, I did it for three years onstage and thought it was enough." Still, Cukor kept in touch with Harrison, then vacationing in his Portofino villa.

"Cukor called me one day and asked for photographs," Harrison recalled. "My younger son took some shots. One showed me with a Chianti bottle covering my genitals, another reading the *New Statesman*." The actor sent these "happy snaps," taken in and around the villa, so the director could see the "decay" he was in. But Harrison was dismayed by the studio's request that he test; tests signaled trouble. Cukor concurred with Harrison, and with a little prodding, Warner saw his point. Cukor thought that even the photographs had been unnecessary, but he knew they would facilitate the decision.

Once a decision to cast Harrison was reached, Cukor informed the actor that the pinup picture with the bottle had done the trick. With his inimitable humor, Cukor said he had ultimately ruled out the *New Statesman* picture because it had too much dignity. "So all's well that ends well," Cukor concluded, stressing the film's magical cast and great old director.

Cukor was pleased with the casting, thinking that if he could capture what Harrison did onstage, he was home. He told Audrey that he didn't think Rex could be improved upon. "You sought the dauphin and you found the king," Audrey wrote back. Harrison was ecstatic at the prospect of working with Cukor; it had always been one of his great ambitions.

Harrison was concerned about the way Cukor was planning to shoot the musical sequences. He favored moving about, using his body and hands, and he thought close-ups of his singing would restrict the wit and impair the freedom of his performance. Cukor said humorously that he planned to have Harrison sing on his knees, but he promised to see to it that the actor was comfortable in every way.

Audrey had a different kind of request: She wanted to know if Beaton could send the designs for her shoes. Since her days in ballet she had had trouble with her feet unless they were properly shod. Over the last ten years she had her movie shoes made in Paris. More concerned with acting than shoes, Cukor suggested that she work on her cockney accent with a famous voice coach.

Cukor researched the film extensively, using volumes of notes and sketches for each scene. He spent hours with Beaton, looking at photographs for the Ascot, Covent Garden, and other scenes. Cukor was aware of the problem of translating a "big whopping success" onto the screen. The material was also well known: "You can't change the damn thing and you mustn't overwhelm it." It was a matter of delicate balance: "You have to keep confidence in the material, preserve what it has, and yet not flatten it out. You dare not break the unity, and yet you have to move it. You take everything good and, as best as you can, transcribe it with care."

Cukor was somehow upset by the definition of *My Fair Lady* as a play with music. For him it was a musical play, because the songs were integral to the progression of the story. What attracted Cukor to the material, beyond the writing, was the fact that *My Fair Lady* was one of the few romantic musicals in which the principals had no love song; like *Pat and Mike,* the romance was not overt.

As usual, Allan Davis tested nearly every character actor in England; because it was such a "prestigious operation," that was not hard. "I particularly was pleased," Davis recalled, "to find a character actress, Mona Washbourne, whom I knew George would love." Cukor, who had always wanted to work with Washbourne, thought that as the housekeeper, Mrs. Pierce, she was perfect: warmhearted, sympathetic, and motherly. "George trusted me absolutely about casting," said Davis, who also helped cast Jeremy Brett as Freddie.

Cukor finally got to work with his friend Gladys Cooper, who was signed to play Higgins's mother. The only strain over casting concerned Wilfred Hyde-White as Colonel Pickering. Jack Warner didn't want him, but Cukor made a strong case, using the actor's "real personality and period style." Even for the bit parts of Higgins's servants, Cukor himself interviewed twenty finalists.

The casting was completed by the end of the fall, and Cukor settled into the Christmas holiday season. When he was not shooting, he entertained a lot. "George's house was large and quite comfortable," said Rex Harrison. "He was a great host, but the food was average, and the wine was really bad, but then California wine is filthy."

Cukor showed a remarkable knack for successfully mixing different kinds of people at his gatherings. One evening found Stravinsky and Mary Pickford dining at the same table. Pickford told stories about Adolph Zukor and Hollywood of yesteryear and at one point became too emotional to continue. Insecure, the aging Pickford admired everything about Cukor. She hoped she lived up to his expectations, for her dress made her look fat. For Pickford, the most outstanding moment was when Cukor whispered in her ear that her acting of fifty years before was as modern as today's.

For a gala dinner in honor of Whitney Warren, Cukor invited the Poglisis (Merle Oberon and husband), the Pressmans (Claudette Colbert and husband), the Reeds (Carol and his wife), Clifton Webb, and Lillian Hellman. Hellman seldom went out, but when an invitation came from Cukor, she accepted it with pleasure.

Cukor had engaged in correspondence with Maureen O'Sullivan ever since she had starred in *David Copperfield*. In 1946 O'Sullivan and her director husband John Farrow asked Cukor to be the godfather of their daughter Mia. "George was our closest friend," she recalled. "He was a very responsible man, and we knew he would be caring, we knew he would be there." Cukor said he would be delighted but reminded them he was still Jewish. "We were Catholic, but it wasn't an issue," she said. "George was just happy to do it; he felt close to the family."

Mia was christened in a modest ceremony in L.A. "George was very funny," O'Sullivan said. "With his camera eye, he saw the knurled hand of the archbishop with a big ring holding up this tiny baby. 'Wouldn't that be some shot for a camera?' he said." She added: "George was very perceptive. When Mia was born, she was a strong-willed child. Holding the tiny baby, George quipped, 'I think I'm carrying Eddie Mannix [the tough MGM executive].' "

Cukor attended every important event in Mia's life. On June 9, 1962, he went to her commencement exercises at the Sacred Heart of Marymount School. He never forgot the Farrow family. "When my son was killed," O'Sullivan recalled, "George was wonderful; it was a Jewish tradition to bring food. And of course, he came to John Farrow's funeral in our car." After Farrow's death, O'Sullivan and her children moved back to New York, but the distance didn't lessen their bond.

Cukor invited O'Sullivan to dinner when she was in California, often just the two of them. "He had such exquisite taste. He always did things right, wonderful service, superb silver. I didn't like to talk about my work," she said. "It was just personal. George would always talk about the children. 'You have such perspective on your children,' he would say with a gleam in his eye, but then the whole issue made him laugh.

"My husband had left very little money," said O'Sullivan. "George knew that, and he created a very interesting job for Mia." Unaware that Mia was interested in show biz, Cukor asked her to cover stage plays for him in New York. But once he learned she was studying acting, he advised her to let nothing interfere with her ambition.

Always willing to help, Cukor offered Mia a stipend of four hundred dollars a month until she got established. Cukor couched the gift as if *she* were doing him a favor. As he wasn't in the "first flush of his youth," he said, at some future date he might ask his rich goddaughter to send a couple of bucks now and then. This was Cukor's way of saying that something would be expected in return for his support.

When Mia Farrow got her first job in a New York revival of Oscar Wilde's *The Importance of Being Earnest*, she rushed to tell Cukor. Every once in a while she would drop him a note, like: "Dear Uncle George, thanks for the check. The months, I don't know where they've gone. It's frightening, soon I shall be old." When she arrived in L.A. to do a pilot for a TV series based on *Peyton Place*, Cukor was the first person she called. Full of doubts, she got plenty of encouragement from him. In fact, the TV series became so popular that Cukor didn't have to support her any longer.

Among Cukor's friends were several foreign directors he had met in his trips to Europe. When they visited Hollywood, he was the first person they contacted. He was their point of reference and chief connection in the industry. Cukor contributed a statement for the seventy-fifth birthday of the Danish director Carl Dreyer, whose silent film *The Passion of Joan of Arc* he admired. Dreyer was a "towering figure" of the film world, wrote Cukor. His work was a reflection of his "great and generous human spirit." In the 1960s, wishing to work for an American studio, Dreyer turned to Cukor for help, but with all his connections, Cukor couldn't assist.

Another director who benefited from Cukor's generosity of spirit was Robert Bresson. Cukor first came to Bresson's aid in 1951, when the director was having difficulty finding a distributor for *Diary of a Country Priest*, which won the Venice Festival Award. American distributors saw the picture as an art film and were skeptical about its commercial appeal. At the risk of "abusing" Cukor's kindness, Bresson asked for advice.

Cukor was appalled by the distributors' wish to cut the film; this type of slick thinking had brought the American industry to its lamentable state. He immediately showed the film to other distributors. He also turned to Louella Parsons, who commanded the attention of millions of readers and thus had great power, and asked her to see the film, promising it would be a memorable experience.

Bresson admitted to Cukor that he had many catastrophes because of his refusal to engage movie stars. But in 1964 he asked Cukor to contact Burt Lancaster and Natalie Wood as possible stars of his new film, *Lancelot of the Lake*. "You know how much I admire and respect you as a director," Cukor noted. "It pleases me that you ask me to make inquiries for you." When the script arrived, Cukor sent it to Lancaster and Wood, noting that he didn't feel guilty about his interference because Bresson was a "distinguished" director.

In 1964 Cukor received out of the blue a strange request from Henry Miller, asking him to forward a letter to Ava Gardner. The writer conceded that at his age he felt "at liberty" to do foolish, sentimental, and romantic things. Cukor informed Miller about Gardner's comings and goings and gave him her address in Spain so that he could send her letters and presents directly.

Cukor admired writers, particularly those who didn't look down at the film industry. Since Miller was a confessed movie fan, Cukor provided him quite a thrill when he invited him home for a dinner attended by Vivien Leigh *and* Simone Signoret.

Cukor functioned as both a social and an informational center. When colleagues needed information, they turned to him. For example, Olivier asked him to name the best horticultural establishment in Hollywood. Olivier recalled that Ronald Colman had a "night scented jasmine" in his gardens that he wished to give to some friends in Italy. Cukor informed Olivier of the plant's Latin name and made arrangements for the plant's delivery; the bill was charged to his account.

Cukor spent a great deal of time writing letters, never forgetting opening nights. He sent beautiful azaleas to Charles Brackett at the Cedar Sinai Hospital, a birthday wire to composer Irving Berlin, a telegram to Noël Coward for opening night in New York, and another one to Jane Fonda ("Knock 'em dead")—all on the same day.

When not working, Cukor could spend four hours a day on his correspondence. "He was an avid letter writer," Irene Burns recalled. "He didn't like to do letters but nevertheless spent a great deal of time writing to his friends. The letters tell you almost everything about him."

Cukor wanted his letters to be models of "grace, polish, and wit." But he admitted that his style was similar to Hedda Hopper's: "Never use one word when ten will do." He applied Voltaire's description of a bore— "The secret of being a bore is to tell everything"—to himself. This was one reason he was impressed with Mel Ferrer, whose writing was clear and well organized. Cukor's letters, by his admission, were "meandering, elliptical, with a joke here and there," but they seldom came to grips with the subject at hand.

As Cukor grew older, he found it increasingly difficult to write letters: "I reread what I've dictated and it doesn't really say what I mean. They embarrass me so I do 'em again. Then I have several more go's at it, none of them seems satisfactory. And finally I telephone." The result was desk littered with unfinished letters, friends and business neglected, and a troubled conscience.

Cukor didn't neglect his duties as a neighbor either, always anxious to know the ins and outs of his street. He took the initiative to welcome John Gilligan (at 9232 Cordell Drive) into the exclusive Cordell Association. They had been called snobbish and uppity, Cukor told him, because their standards were so high, but Gilligan belonged right there among them.

The deaths of two very close friends in 1963 upset him. Cukor received a long, detailed letter from Maria, Aldous Huxley's wife, describing the last days of his life and his request to die under the influence of LSD. She described the injection of drugs and how he felt he was "going forward, toward the light, toward a greater love." Huxley accepted his death with real tranquillity. He died the way he wanted to, as described in *Island:* as a continuation of his work. Cukor had known Huxley since 1939, when he wrote the script for *Madame Curie,* which Cukor was going to do with Garbo.

Huxley was the first of Cukor's close friends to die. Over the next five years his most intimate friends and associates died: Cole Porter, David O. Selznick, Somerset Maugham, George Hoyningen-Huene, Spencer Tracy, Vivien Leigh, Tallulah Bankhead, Judy Garland, Bill Goetz.

Cole Porter's death was a more severe blow than Huxley's because he was a closer friend. The musician had an amputated leg and didn't want to see many people, but Cukor took Vivien Leigh to see him shortly before he died. When they arrived, Porter was in bed and couldn't move. Wearing a colorful dress, Leigh tried to be entertaining. Cukor had never seen her like that. From time to time they had to leave the room, so the nurses could give Porter shots for his pain. When they left, Leigh asked to sit up front in the car, next to the driver, and Cukor could tell she was sobbing. In Porter's memory, Cukor later established an annual scholarship at USC.

In May 1963 Audrey Hepburn arrived in Los Angeles for preproduction work on *My Fair Lady.* Because millions had seen the musical, she was faced with a tremendous challenge. Her portrayal of the lady was not problematic—after all, she had beauty and elegance—but Eliza's cockney accent, so crucial in the film's first half, proved to be an obstacle. In preparation for the role, Audrey had been taking diction lessons with a voice coach.

One Sunday afternoon Cukor, Lerner, and Beaton were invited to Audrey's house. The conversation was cordial, and the star was, as always, charming. After some chitchat she came straight to the point. "Are you going to use my voice for the songs?" she asked, indicating it was an issue of great concern to her. Having sung in several of her films (*Funny Face, Breakfast at Tiffany's*), she wanted to do her own singing in *My Fair Lady*.

What the actress didn't know was that Marni Nixon, who had previously sung for Deborah Kerr in *The King and I* and Natalie Wood in *West Side Story,* had been secretly approached for the job. Cukor explained that perhaps some of her singing would be interpolated with another voice, used for the higher notes she could not sing. He told her that Minnelli had effectively used this technique with Leslie Caron in *Gigi*. Audrey Hepburn said she would continue to work hard on her singing.

Later in the afternoon Audrey again ruffled her guest, though unintentionally. "This picture is one we must all remember," she said. "Wonderful talents, everyone right. It's the high spot for all our lives. Let's enjoy it!" Cukor was a bit annoyed but tried to conceal it. This was the kind of speech ordinarily delivered by the director, not the star, and it was prematurely made.

Alan Lerner was upset; he never liked the idea of Audrey Hepburn as Eliza. When the film went into production, Lerner kept his visits to the set to a minimum. His associates later claimed that he really hated the film.

On June 4, 1963, Cukor attended a press conference whose purpose was to announce the movie's auspicious beginning, but it turned out to be a nightmare. Beaton, fussy and particular, was appalled by the low-quality food and plastic flowers. With the two stars at hand, the press ignored Cukor, who sat there like an uninvited guest. At one point a photographer screamed at Cukor when he walked in front of Harrison. Uncomfortable to begin with, Cukor yelled back.

Audrey was asked embarrassing questions, like "Why didn't Julie Andrews play the part?" or "How much of it will actually be *your* voice?" The press didn't spare Harrison either. One journalist rudely asked: "Since you made such a success as Higgins, do you play every part exactly the same way?" Harrison's cool reply was: "Of course, that's exactly how I played Caesar and the pope." However, when asked whether his approach to the movie would differ from his stage interpretation, the actor exclaimed, "Indeed, it will! The movie audiences will be closer; they will see a more intimate portrait of the fellow. I, therefore, must go deeper into the characterization than I ever did on the stage. But then I've rehearsed the part for three years."

Cukor became so sensitive to his film that when Truman Capote wanted to do a piece on *My Fair Lady,* his initial reaction was to oppose it, fearing Capote might do something satirical. But Capote clarified that what he had in mind was a brief piece to accompany Beaton's photographs, nothing in the vein of his long articles for the *New Yorker.* Assuring Cukor that Audrey and Beaton were friends of long standing, Capote wouldn't consider hurting them in any way. Noting his solid respect for Cukor, Capote promised to show him the piece before publication.

The four-and-a-half-month shooting schedule began on a hot Friday, August 13. "This is one time when we can't afford to be superstitious," Jack Warner quipped. In the first week Cukor was annoyed by the lack of rapport between his stars. Harrison was formal and reserved; Cukor knew his reservations about Audrey. Rehearsals were also handicapped by Harrison's forgetting his lines and Audrey's struggling with her accent. Audrey broke the ice between them when she gave her costar a red bicycle with a special basket for his script. As time went by, the atmosphere on the set improved.

Spending months in Hollywood designing the sets and costumes and overseeing their execution, Beaton worked hard. He spent hours examining periodicals and visiting museums, but he accomplished wondrous results. At first, working closely with Cukor, Beaton showed respect for the director's professionalism, enjoying the "greatest creative experience" of his career. Horrified by the sets of other Warner's films—"the Himalayan mountains of bad taste and artificiality"—Beaton kept a very close eye on the work.

During the shoot Lerner and Beaton often lunched at Cukor's pool, and "sparks of brilliance" emerged from Lerner amid endless digressions. "We seem to trigger him off and he enjoys our help after working in solitary confinement," Beaton noted. Out of such meetings came the film's more inspired moments, like the idea to open it with a flower sequence.

Admiring Beaton's taste and expertise, Audrey knew it was he who made her look beautiful. Enchanted by his sketches, she immediately wanted to parade in her costumes. One day Beaton showed her a mannequin of herself wearing Eliza's shabby green coat. Completely taken by the costume's detail, she started to cry. Soon Beaton was behaving like a Svengali, giving orders about eyelashes, selecting a brooch or a trinket. Insisting on authenticity, Audrey legitimized Beaton's tendency to argue over every detail.

Under Beaton's rigorous scrutiny, every scene had to be tested and retested because the essence lay in Audrey's gradual transition to a lady. She sat for hours with the makeup people, then gave up lunch to work with her coach. Audrey was patient and polite, but Cukor could tell she was tense.

Beaton was disappointed when he learned there was not going to be location shooting in London. Increasingly homesick, he began to feel imprisoned in Hollywood. That Cukor gave too many instructions—in a stream of bad language—only made things worse. Cukor's habit of talking before entering a room and seldom completing a sentence also upset him. "I can't think how I will feel about George at the end of it all," Beaton confessed.

There were severe tensions between the two men. Beaton had decorated his office with photographs of himself with Jackie Kennedy and Garbo. A dandy, Beaton wore Edwardian suits and broad-brimmed panama hats, and his mannered flamboyance was a marked contrast with Cukor's ordinary gray slacks and open shirt. "Cecil was too fussy," Harrison said. "George was modest and down-to-earth." The main problem was that Beaton never saw himself working for or under Cukor. He considered his position independent of—if not superior to—Cukor. Opinionated and imperious, both men enjoyed temper tantrums; their spats often sparked derisive comments from the crew: "these two queens" or "these fags."

"George was very anxious about the look of the film," Harrison recalled, "but at the end he let Cecil have his way. Otherwise there would have been one constant clash of two very strong personalities." Once the visual conception was established, Cukor didn't have to speak to Beaton anymore. And he didn't.

Beaton was a master salesman of his work, and that became another source of strain. "At first Cukor failed to realize that Cecil was selling himself," Harrison said, "but soon he began to resent the publicity Cecil was getting just for himself." Cukor once asked Harrison, "Why don't we take a tip from our artistic friend, who is getting an awful lot of mileage from *My Fair Lady*?" Apart from selling photographs and articles to the *Ladies' Home Journal* and *Vogue,* Beaton designed textiles and wallpapers and made drawings for galleries—all while working on the picture.

Beaton's habit of coming onto the set to take publicity photos showed his lack of sensitivity and deference to Cukor. "The long photo sessions irritated George," Harrison said; "they were a waste of time." Gene Allen, who worked closely with Beaton, concurred. "There are all kinds of ways and times to do publicity shots, but you don't interrupt the director's day to do them. That's never taken place in the history of the business. It may be with some lesser directors, but you don't take Audrey Hepburn away from George Cukor. George was used to working with professionals," Allen said, "which is different from photographing celebrities, but Cecil saw no reason why he couldn't take Audrey off the set." In Allen's view, that was the "big blowup" between the two men.

"George got really furious. He never wanted to see Cecil again," Allan Davis said. "He wanted Audrey when she wasn't shooting to be resting. This is the most important part that applies to George: When he was working, nothing else mattered except the job in hand. This was his great strength, the work, and what it called for dominated his life."

Allen worked with Beaton the same way he always did: "I would design, show George, and then get Cecil's approval. It was certainly everything through George first." Allen doesn't know exactly when Cukor and Beaton stopped getting along, but it happened early. "I never had one ill word with Cecil," he said. "I just didn't have time to get involved in any personal problems. It was such a big picture; there was so much to do.

"George didn't tell me what an evil man Cecil was," Allen said, "and I don't know how the actors felt about it. Audrey was as sweet and lovely an actress as there ever was one, and so fond of George. But I'm sure she was just as fond of Cecil for his contributions. Some of those egos may have gotten between George and Cecil." They weren't speaking at the end; Beaton left Hollywood before the shooting was over.

Cukor resented the fact that Audrey was closer to and more dependent on Beaton than on him, and he could never get over the fact that Beaton had been hired before he was. The perception that Beaton was more vital to the film than he was made the rift between them greater. Cukor, after all, would have preferred to work with George Hoyningen-Huene, his frequent consultant and friend.

Beaton also violated Cukor's professional code: As soon as he departed, he began to trash Cukor and the crew. Cukor resented Beaton's tales of the "absolute truth" about the "strains" and "despairs" of working on *My Fair Lady,* how against all odds he had managed to put some taste into the picture. Beaton spoke patronizingly about Hollywood's "skilled technicians" (not artists) on the order of Gene Allen.

It was a ticklish subject from the beginning. When Cukor talked to Allen about *My Fair Lady,* he foresaw that for all his work, there would be little acknowledgment. Cukor didn't realize then how greedy Beaton was. Allen contributed a lot to the picture, way beyond art direction: He supervised the construction and painting of the sets, shot the main titles, did second-unit work, and helped with the cutting. Allen confirmed that he'd never been so busy shooting a picture of that size: "I worked with George on how the picture was going to be filmed, shot by shot, frame by frame."

In later years Cukor pigeonholed Beaton as CCC, "Classed as Cunt by

Cukor." He told his friends, "We were happy making it, with one minor but very irritating exception: The initials are C. B. and it's not De Mille." Alan Jay Lerner reproached Cukor for making snappish remarks about Beaton in public, but Cukor thought they were fair, considering what a "blackhearted" villain Beaton was.

Still, when Mel Ferrer mentioned the possibility of Beaton's designing Cukor's next picture with Audrey, Cukor assumed a professional approach: Whatever was good for the picture was OK by him. The reason why they didn't get along, Cukor reminded Ferrer, was Beaton's failure to realize that film was a collaborative effort.

Despite the strain with Beaton, it was a relief for Cukor to work on *My Fair Lady*. After the "madness" of Monroe and Fox, it seemed easy and smooth. He was impressed with Audrey's hard work and beautiful manners: She was never late and always knew her lines. Audrey had none of the usual selfishness, stupid demands, and tiresome suspicion of other stars; she had Cukor eating out of her hand. "All is going smoothly, 'unberufen,' Progress, Harmony, and Peace," Cukor reported shortly after shooting began.

Cukor told Audrey that if he ever opened an Academy of Dramatic Arts, there would be a very important chair for her to teach a course on actresses' behavior. There was a lot of talk about how directors handled actresses, but equally important was the issue of how actresses handled directors. Realizing he talked too much, Cukor suggested Audrey include in her course tips to directors on how *not* to make "bores" and "nuisances" of themselves.

A snob, Cukor admired Audrey's refusal to exploit her origins; her mother was a Dutch baroness. Part Dutch, part Hungarian, and part Irish, Audrey represented a good balance of the proper elements. He described her as a mixture of "horse-sense, imagination and nobility." A giggler, she could go in for high jinks. In one scene the assistant director had to keep her wet, but one day Audrey grabbed the hose and let him have it good!

The script was storyboarded, scene by scene, with specific instructions for camera movement and angles. Cukor decided to shoot the story more or less in continuity, an unusual practice, so that Audrey could develop from the cockney girl to the society lady. It was a costly procedure, but it was essential to her performance. Indeed, as shooting progressed, Jack Warner got increasingly nervous about the budget. In a confidential memo he urged Cukor to work more efficiently, reminding him that Audrey's twenty-four weeks ended on November 30; from then on it would be forty-two thousand dollars per week!

Audrey's attempt to sing some of the numbers resulted in smiles of embarrassment and uncomfortable feelings among the crew. No one wanted to tell her that her voice was not right—even in the lower register. Refusing to admit defeat, she continued to record for another month. Cukor knew all along it was a waste of time, but he didn't want to be the villain. In the end Audrey provided about 2 percent of the singing.

Somehow a rumor spread that she had actually sung half the songs, and a row followed. Marni Nixon's husband issued a statement calling the reports unfair and inaccurate. The whole thing was a "great bore" to Cukor; it was "mischievous to make a Federal case out of it." In the future, asked about Marni Nixon, Cukor would say, "She is where she belongs, appearing with Liberace."

Because the atmosphere on the set became tense, intruders were forbidden. On each of the six sound stages, a sign hung out: Positively no visitors. Audrey asked for a white picket fence to surround her dressing room and the crew had to keep out of her sight. Nobody was allowed to enter her eyeline range while she was acting. Cukor obliged, setting up screens around the set, but the crew resented it.

There was also strain between Audrey Hepburn and Mel Ferrer. Cukor heard quarrels from her dressing room. Her press agent, Henry Rogers, tried to keep the trouble from the press, but Cukor knew the couple was having marital problems; a frustrated actor, Ferrer was simply jealous of his wife's success.

Eliza was, in fact, the most difficult role Audrey had ever undertaken, transforming a cockney girl of the gutters into a lady at the embassy ball. Cukor had never seen an actress work with such dedication, sometimes rehearsing twelve hours a day. She took singing lessons, cockney lessons from a UCLA phoneticist, then worked with musical director André Previn. There were endless fittings and makeup tests. Cukor soon became disturbed about Audrey's health; in the last month of shooting, she lost eight pounds. Realizing this was their biggest picture to date, both Cukor and Audrey felt immense responsibility for the film's enormous budget.

Once a decision was made not to shoot exteriors in London, Cukor moved toward greater stylization. "It's not a realistic picture," he said. "People don't walk up and down Wimpole Street and sing." The race scene was deliberately stagy. Cukor had decided not to be adventurous and grabbed as much as he could from the stage, but taking elements from the stage and making them flow onscreen was not easy.

Cukor was typically sparing with close-ups so that the few used would be effective. When Higgins commands Eliza to say, "The rain in Spain," Cukor thought that if the camera cut to her face, it'd let the audience know that she was going to say it correctly. He instructed Audrey to say it away from the camera.

Cukor saw his primary job as creating a "conducive climate" for his actors. Harrison knew his part inside out; there was no point in telling him how to read his lines. The problem with Harrison, though, was that he tended to give his energy away in the rehearsal, and after five or six takes he'd had it. Cukor asked him just to go through the mechanics and "save" the real emotion for the camera. In the end Cukor thought Harrison rendered a more deft performance in the film version than on stage.

In contrast, Audrey improved steadily with each try and liked to do many takes. Cukor decided to shoot Harrison's close-ups first. By the time his were done, Audrey was surer of herself, and he shot hers. He thus violated an old custom: He generally gave the women the courtesy of doing their close-ups first so that they could appear fresh.

"I usually did my songs first," Harrison recalled. "I did my numbers live, which is unusual, and I did them without a cut, in long takes." He was careful about overacting. "The essence of screen acting is in thinking rather than projection," he said. "The moment I started to project big, George would tell me."

One morning, while shooting "I've Grown Accustomed to Her Face," Cukor didn't get what he wanted from Harrison. He could tell by the pitch of his voice that he was off the beam. By noon Harrison was in a state of terror. "What's wrong?" he asked. "You've lost it. You'll never be able to do it again," Cukor answered. "Don't tease me. This is serious," said Harrison. "Let's take a lunch break," Cukor said. After lunch Cukor explained to him, "This morning, when you did the line 'Damn damn, damn,' you simply weren't angry." Harrison grasped what Cukor meant, and the scene was done in two takes.

On November 22, while the song "Wouldn't It Be Loverly?" was being filmed, a crew member came on the set with awful news: President Kennedy had been shot in Dallas. Cukor was stunned, but always the optimist, he said without thinking, "No, he isn't dead. He's just wounded." Audrey insisted that something must be said to the crew, but Cukor simply couldn't trust himself. Gathering her strength, she borrowed a mike and announced: "The President of the U.S. is dead." Absolutely thrown, Cukor had tears in his eyes. They decided to continue business as usual, but an hour later Audrey broke down, and work was suspended for the rest of the day.

Cukor couldn't help thinking about the "incredible waste," as he had met Kennedy and was full of admiration for his magnetism. Cukor had received from Whitney Warren an expensive unframed chrome of Kennedy in a profile shot. One day Audrey said, "George, you should have a frame. It should be a wide silver one from Tiffany's. Let me get it for you." She wrote a simple inscription and handed it to him. Years earlier George Hoyningen-Huene had given Cukor a miniature American flag, with its mast topped by a golden eagle. The two ornaments proudly stood on Cukor's Americana shelf in his library.

Another piece of sad news was the death of Henry Daniell, who was playing the British ambassador in *My Fair Lady*. A good, stylish actor, he had appeared in many Cukor movies (notably *Camille*). One day Daniell did not feel good and went home early; that night he died. Cukor was very sad, but he had to replace him immediately. By ten o'clock the next day they were shooting with another man; and audience never noticed that two different men played the role. It should teach us a lesson, Cukor told the crew mournfully; they can do without us all.

Postproduction on *My Fair Lady* began after the holidays. Cukor spent most of January 1964 at a Todd AO laboratory, dubbing the film. He went through "I'm an Ordinary Man" twenty times and found Harrison great every single time. Cukor had never worked on this six-track process before and found it remarkable for its depth and detail. Some lines, like the dialogue in the opening rain sequence and a line in the bathroom sequence that was covered by steam noise, had to be postsynched.

In the spring Harrison submitted his critique of the rough cut. With the exception of the opening, which "dragged its ass a little bit," he found the first half stunning. The second half, however, was overlong. It had good numbers but no *real* plot, no advancement of the story. The curtain had to come down as the line of his number "Why Can't a Woman" was spoken; that was when no dry eye existed in the theater. It was the giving in of the man that was moving—not a close-up of a girl in a Beaton hat. Harrison asked that the curtain fall on Higgins laughing—but laughing longer—and after the interval show Higgins still laughing. Cukor took many of Harrison's suggestions, but he didn't change the intermission; supported by Warner, he thought it was in the right place.

While cutting the film, Cukor had to take care of unpleasant personal business: firing his agent, Irving Lazar. At his request Lazar was advised not to undertake or negotiate any commitment that involved Cukor's services. Lazar was urged to comply, to avoid misunderstanding and embarrassment.

Cukor didn't discuss the issue with Lazar. His lawyer sent a letter to Lazar, who was in Hong Kong. When Lazar got the bad news, he was shocked; in his mind there was no question of his loyalty and devotion. He asked for a chance to explain; after all, Cukor had been an important part of his life. Lazar simply wouldn't allow their friendship to end by a lawyer's letter; "it will take a papal decree to separate us."

To this day Lazar claims to have no idea why he was fired: "I never asked George, and he never told me why. I was very hurt. I thought that wasn't very stylish for a gentleman like George to do." Lazar didn't protest; he just thought Cukor's conduct was shabby. "If not for me," he said, "George could never have gotten *My Fair Lady,* and he should have known it." But Lazar conceded that Cukor was annoyed by his frequent travels.

Cukor went back to the William Morris agency, but after a short time he decided not to use it either. He bitterly criticized it as "preoccupied, lackadaisical, and bumbling." The agency was not sorry to lose him; aging and declining, Cukor had ceased to be a viable client. Cukor then asked Kurt Frings to handle negotiations for particular pictures.

In September, a month prior to the opening of *My Fair Lady,* Cukor went to see *Mary Poppins.* The talk of the town, because of Julie Andrews's debut, the movie performed marvels at the box office. He went to a matinee with Merle Oberon and her children. "I am not meanspirited or envious," he told Harrison, "but me no likee." Cukor found the picture charmless and only intermittently funny. It had no style, and even the flying was just a gimmick, for it wasn't integral to the story. Andrews sang prettily, but Cukor found her earthbound and prim. His criticism was the minority opinion among his friends: Katharine Hepburn said she wept at the end of the movie, and Gladys Cooper went to see it three times.

Cukor embarked on an extensive tour for *My Fair Lady,* with premieres in Chicago, New York, Los Angeles, and Washington, D.C. It was easier, however, to work on the film than promote it. Cukor hated those publicity-drumming shindigs, but commanded by Warner, he obeyed like a "good soldier."

Before the first show, Warner gave Cukor Higgins's custom-designed hat to express his appreciation of what he labeled "the greatest box-office attraction in motion picture history." Cukor thought he looked better ("a dandy") in the hat than Harrison did and promised to choose the spots when and where he'd wear it. This time it was "tougher" for Cukor to write because it came from his heart. After thanking Warner for choosing him to do the picture, he repeated "immodestly" that the mogul's choice was the "right" move. Above all, he was grateful for Warner's refusal to settle for anything but the best and for backing it with hard cash.

For the New York premiere, on October 21, Cukor invited Irene Selznick, describing it as "the Premiere to End All Premieres." It was in New York that he saw the picture on a large screen for the first time with a hip, sensitive audience. Cukor went with mixed feelings: excited but also nervous. A "beating of drums" had whipped up a great state of anticipation; he now hoped it wasn't going to be a letdown. But when word of mouth started, Cukor began to enjoy the experience. Knowing that a success like *My Fair Lady* happened rarely, he enjoyed it "to the hilt," doing his best not to get "the big head."

"It was a very emotional day," Irene Burns said about the press screening of *My Fair Lady* in L.A. "My husband and I were invited, and we went to see it. That was my favorite film Mr. Cukor directed while I was with him. Congratulating him, I was moved to tears."

The West Coast premiere at the Egyptian Theater, telecast live on Wednesday, October 28, was also a thrilling event, which was a benefit for the Motion Picture Relief Fund. Jack Warner was the honorary chairman, and Arthur Godfrey the emcee, as he had been in New York and Chicago. As cochairs, Frank Sinatra and Natalie Wood raised $130,000; every seat of the house was sold at $125. The long forecourt of the Egyptian Theater was bedecked with flowers. Cukor found himself making bombastic statements like "This is not a movie; it's a motion picture."

The L.A. premiere had "a miracle" of an audience, warm and sympathetic, that made the picture feel like a breeze. It was followed by a big plush party at the Beverly Hilton Hotel. Audrey stayed with Cukor during the L.A. festivities. They got home at three in the morning, and exhausted as they were, she said, "Let's put up our feet and just sit and enjoy it!"

Even those who admired Julie Andrews in the role of Eliza had to give Audrey some credit. The consensus, however, was that she was better as the lady than the guttersnipe. Pauline Kael thought that her total lack of conviction as the cockney girl worked against the story's credibility. Cukor never got over Kael's review, which hit in the areas in which he was most vulnerable: pace and length. Kael wrote: "The musical staggers along, it seems to go on for about 45 minutes after the story is finished."

"I would much prefer to do it with Julie Andrews," Harrison said. "Audrey had no voice and didn't sing, which was sad. Being Dutch, she didn't understand the cockney accent. George was very patient," the actor noted. "He tried to get her to play with that accent, but she simply couldn't, and he gave up."

The critique of the *New Republic* reviewer, Stanley Kauffmann, was as harsh as Kael's: "Cukor's direction is like a rich gravy poured over everything, not remotely as delicately right as in the Asquith-Howard 1937 *Pygmalion*." Kauffmann thought that the word "great" has been too generously applied and that only Harrison's work deserved the term: "[H]is first name never seemed more apt."

The strongest criticism was that Cukor failed to use the medium. "I wish I knew what they meant," Cukor said. "If, by way of analogy, a man were to stage *Pygmalion* as Shaw wrote it, without songs and dances, should we therefore condemn him for having failed to use the full resources of the theatrical medium?" Defensive, Cukor stressed there were many scenes in his film that brought out emotions through the distinctive use of the medium, camera angles, close-ups, cuts. He gave himself good marks for being clever enough to take full advantage of the wonderful things in the stage production. He was also prepared to take bows for "tidying up" the play here and there.

The mixture of styles (the semirealistic Covent Garden scene, the semi-abstract Ascot) was criticized, too. Cukor's visual sense flagged: When he took the cameras outdoors, the Beaton exteriors clashed with one another a little too cheekily. Except in the hate song "Just You Wait," where a squad of guardsmen troops into Eliza's mind to execute Higgins, Cukor didn't employ his cinematic imagination. "George was more of a theater director," Harrison said. "He was not a figure like Hitchcock or David Lean behind the camera."

Cukor's defenders claimed that he used the medium self-effacingly to re-create a theatrical experience in the cinema. It was not his fault. Most of the action was confined to one set, as was not true of most screen musicals. To Cukor's fans, a measure of his effective staging was that the audience didn't feel the smallest twinge of claustrophobia.

At the time Harrison had no overall view because "as an actor you don't think about the film as a whole." However, when he later caught it, he had strong reservations. In the final account Harrison said, "the original stage production was more important than the film, which was pleasant, but not exceptionally good."

More important than the critics' was the reaction of Cukor's colleagues. Frank Capra wrote: "It is a masterpiece of art and entertainment, long may it play." William Wyler noted: "*My Fair Lady* is the most wonderful job of film making. You make me proud of my profession."

Vivien Leigh had great fun seeing the film in London with Harrison. Thrilled about the glorious success, she found Harrison's performance impeccable. However, *My Fair Lady* received worse reviews in Britain than in the United States. Cukor was taken aback at the carping of the British critics. They must think it "pretty damned impertinent" of Americans to touch any English subject, he told Allan Davis; "to have it done with taste is unforgivable."

Surprisingly, it was the *Times* of London that spoke disparagingly and unfairly about Beaton's contribution. What a pity, its critic charged, that George Hoyningen-Huene didn't work on the picture. Cukor could not figure out why a marked clipping was sent to Hoyningen-Huene by—of all people—Beaton himself.

As was his pattern, if Cukor liked an actress, he immediately looked for other projects to do with her. This was definitely the case with Audrey Hepburn. Two projects were under consideration: a remake of *Peter Pan* and a remake of Cukor's 1938 *Romeo and Juliet*.

Cukor sent Audrey a new edition of *Romeo and Juliet*, asking her not to be intimidated by its weight. Elliott Morgan, head of the MGM library, presented it to him as souvenir for his long tenure there. The play was followed with a recording, with Albert Finney and Claire Bloom, which Cukor asked Audrey Hepburn to listen to "with prejudice." He was enthusiastic about Terence Stamp for Romeo, believing that after *The Collector* he would be a "name." Cukor sent Audrey Stamp's photo so that she could see what an arresting face he had. Cukor had no doubt that the chemistry between the two would be explosive. But Stamp's agent rejected Cukor's offer; at this stage of his career Stamp should not attempt a classical film. Cukor then considered Albert Finney, who could be a good Romeo, provided he had a strong director to restrain him. When Finney turned it down, Mel Ferrer decided not to go forward with *Romeo and Juliet.*

Cukor started all over again, searching for the right property for Audrey. Ferrer asked Cukor to reexamine the idea of a movie about the Egyptian queen Nefertiti, to be filmed on location. Since Cukor's knowledge of the subject was sketchy, he asked Hoyningen-Huene to supply books; after reading them, Cukor found the books too "high falutin" for his taste. On the basis of these scholarly works, Cukor feared they would be in hot water with the Production Code. "It wasn't easy for poor Nefertiti," Cukor quipped, "being the king's wife and mother," though to him she looked like Edna May Oliver.

As for the remake of *Peter Pan,* Ferrer suggested approaching Walt Disney, who owned the rights, in a friendly level; that meant that Kurt Frings was not the right man. At Cukor's request, Gene Allen made a rough estimate of a four- to five-million-dollar budget for the film, a figure, they hoped, would scare Disney off, who had never spent so much money on a picture. But Disney was notorious for protecting his properties, and that project soon died.

Cukor's early winter was an award-giving season, replete with cocktail parties, elegant dinners, and receptions. The Hollywood Foreign Press Association, New York Film Critics, the Directors Guild all were busy handing out their awards for the year's achievements. Cukor had never gone this route before, and some of the occasions were embarrassing, but a good trouper, he decided to do them all.

At the request of Warner, Cukor agreed to accept the New York Film Critics Award for Best Picture. On his way he stopped in Washington, D.C., for the swearing in of the President. It turned out to be an exciting event. The ceremonies were wonderful, if a bit absurd, with drum majorettes, brass bands, and floats. Usually not given to claustrophobia, he had a few apprehensive moments that day. Cukor went to some great parties, where he hobnobbed with Governor Nelson Rockefeller and other celebrities. He stayed at the Sheraton Hotel, which had the biggest hoop-de-do because that was where the President was to wind up at the inaugural ball.

Cukor's friends thought it was corny to go to Washington, but they were wrong; he found it an extraordinary experience. The overall impression was moving; Cukor was present at a festive, inspiring occasion, sharing it with many of his countrymen. When one of his friends said, "George, you're beginning to sound like a politician," he turned back and said quietly, "In that case, I'd better stop here." Nothing was more offensive to him than politics and politicians.

Cukor was never a political animal. "Occasionally he would talk about politics," Katharine Hepburn observed, "but not too much—unless it was the style or unless something came up, like McCarthyism. He was liberal in his attitudes," she allowed, "but he was not as outspoken as I was." Indeed, Cukor's career never suffered as a result of his politics.

Cukor thought the Democrats had done well in the 1964 elections. He later received a letter from Robert Kennedy, thanking him for "the consideration shown in memory of the late president." Cukor joked about how Irene Selznick "spoiled" him with name-dropping, measuring events by the caliber of their celebrities.

At the New York Film Critics ceremony, Harrison was singled out, but the best actress was Kim Stanley (*Séance on a Wet Afternoon*). Cukor was a "true sport," putting on a smiling face when Stanley Kubrick got the directorial award for *Dr. Strangelove*. The thirteen voting critics were friendly, but Cukor was particularly fond of The *New York Times'* Bosley Crowther, whose favorable notices of his films had furthered their friendship over the years.

All in all it was a dismal occasion. The snowstorm made a piker of D. W. Griffith's *Way Down East;* Lillian Gish hadn't had it as hard as Cukor had, trying to get a cab. He and Irene Selznick braved the elements to go to Sardi's, a restaurant Cukor hated for its combined smell of stale Italian cooking and toilet disinfectant. They arrived on the dot at ten-fifteen and hung about for a lackluster ceremony that began at midnight.

There was, however, a high-drama confrontation at the party when Irene Selznick snubbed Crowther for allegedly damaging the reputation of her "saintly" father, Louis B. Mayer, in his book *The Lion's Share*. Cukor had never read the book, though he had helped Crowther collect information. Cukor couldn't care less because, as he put it, "Louis B. was not my favorite, though I wasn't his."

In February 1965 the New Yorker Theater, on Broadway near Eighty-eighth Street, planned a Cukor Film Festival. Organizer Daniel Talbot asked Cukor to help get some of his earlier movies. "A *Cukor Festival*!" the director wrote to David Selznick. "I never thought I'd see the day!"

He then asked Selznick for the rights to screen *A Bill of Divorcement* and *Little Women,* two of their RKO movies. Some saw poetic justice in Cukor's riding high while Selznick was all but forgotten; Selznick's last feature, *A Farewell to Arms,* had been made in 1957.

At the Golden Globe awards, given by the Hollywood Foreign Press Association, Carolyn Jones, complete with her *Addams Family* fright wig, and Roddy McDowall, a close friend of Cukor's, handed Cukor the best director trophy. "Aren't you glad I suggested using an unknown Irish script," wrote Alan Jay Lerner, who still thought Cukor should have used Julie Andrews for the lead. Irene Selznick said that if she weren't superstitious, she'd put a whole shelf for the awards to come, alluding to Cukor's winning the most coveted one—the Oscar.

During this award season Cukor realized he possessed a "Dore Schary side" to him, one that sought publicity and awards. He now coveted everything—plaques, statues, citations—and it made no difference who was giving these honors. Indeed, a few weeks after the Golden Globes Cukor was singled out by the Directors Guild. It was an important award, if only because it served as a good predictor of the Oscar. At the ceremony Cukor tried to express what the DGA meant, but words failed him. "When I am safely behind a camera," he told the DGA president, George Sidney, "I can talk a blue streak; it's the microphone that intimidates me."

In February the Academy of Motion Picture Arts and Sciences (AMPAS) announced its Oscar nominations. *Mary Poppins* led the nominations with thirteen categories, followed by *My Fair Lady* and *Becket,* each with twelve nominations. Cukor got caught up with the Oscar fever. At first he thought he could resist the hype, but he soon confessed to have gotten the bug. "I go anywhere, any time I'm asked, TV, radio, ladies' luncheons. It's gotten so bad that, if I see four people congregating, I join 'em, just in case." One day he found himself on the steps of the Federal Building praying. He even attended the premiere of *My Fair Lady* in Las Vegas.

Cukor knew that AMPAS's failure to nominate Audrey was "hell" for her, but she behaved like a "queen." The actress made herself inaccessible during the nominations; she went to Lausanne to escape the hectoring press. But a major Hollywood row broke out over the academy's snub. "Outrageous!" exclaimed Jack Warner, taking it as a personal affront. Unfortunately, Audrey had fired her press agent, Henry Rogers, and had remained aloof during the most crucial phase of the Oscar contest. Some of her friends began a campaign to get her nomination as a write-in, but it failed.

It was Cukor's idea that Audrey replace Patricia Neal as the Best Actor presenter at the Oscar ceremonies when Neal was convalescing from a stroke. Despite her initial intention to avoid the awards presentation, Audrey finally agreed. Her professional standing and reputation had not been in the slightest harmed, but her decision to appear in the show, for Cukor an indication of her "rare grace," created a furor. It was the academy that cut a sorry figure; Cukor saw its stupid oversight as one of those "periodic flaps" and "blunders" that afflict Hollywood.

It almost made Cukor change his mind about the merit of the awards. In the past he had praised the Oscars as being absolutely on the level. It was glorious, for example, that Harrison and his wife, Rachel Roberts, were nominated for 1963 Oscars (he for *Cleopatra*, she for *This Sporting Life*). Both richly deserved it, but as he told Harrison, "I don't see either the French or—let's be frank about it—the English, being so impartial with their accolades.

"I've been around a long time," Cukor said, "and never in my experience has anyone offered me a bribe, or tried in any way to influence me in how I voted. You may think that you will vote for a pal, but when the chips are down and you are alone with your God and your ballot, you find yourself voting for what you really think." In the long run the AMPAS choices withstood the test of time. For Cukor the Oscar was the most valuable award because it was dearly won, reflecting a professional judgement that was at once the most merciless and the most generous.

Ina Claire once told Cukor that as a younger actress she was introduced as a "great American actress" to Sarah Bernhardt. "Oh, no," said Claire modestly, "I just happen to be a popular actress." Bernhardt reportedly replied: "Very well, very well, first come popular, then come great." In Cukor's view, Bernhardt was absolutely right: The public is never wrong. True popularity means something; it cannot be faked.

The thirty-seventh annual Oscar ceremonies took place on April 5, 1965, with Bob Hope as emcee. Judy Garland made a special appearance, singing a Cole Porter medley, in tribute to his recent death. The academy's president that year was Cukor's longtime colleague MGM producer Arthur Freed, and several of his leading ladies were on hand as presenters: Deborah Kerr for writing, Joan Crawford for directing, and Audrey for best actor.

"Nineteen sixty-five was a big year for the movies," Bob Hope said in his opening remarks. "This was the year lovely Julie Andrews made her motion-picture debut . . . in the big hit called *Mary Poppins* . . . or 'How I Learned to Stop Worrying and Love Jack Warner.' Before you can pick up your Oscar, you have to show your passport; twelve out of the twenty acting nominations went to foreigners. But we're not worried. We still lead the world in the production of popcorn."

Hope introduced Crawford as "one of the great all-time stars but also the best-looking business tycoon you'll ever see." Crawford immediately announced the five nominated directors: Peter Glenville for *Becket;* Stanley Kubrick for *Dr. Strangelove;* Robert Stevenson for *Mary Poppins;* George Cukor for *My Fair Lady;* Michael Cacoyannis for *Zorba the Greek.* With all the brouhaha about the large number of foreign nominees, it wasn't a particularly strong year for directorial achievements. Cukor was by far the best known; the others were all first-time nominees.

"I had no idea what I was going to say if I won the Oscar," Cukor said afterward, "except that I knew I would mention Audrey." After the Oscar he sent the same telegram to everyone: "It was mighty fine to catch up with that elusive Oscar—at long last. It made me very happy. But it was the affection, the joy with which my friends greeted this happy event that touched my heart!" When people commented how thin he looked on TV, Cukor quipped, "What is the name of your set? I must get one immediately."

Katharine Hepburn is not sure how important it was for Cukor to win an Oscar. "Maybe it was," she said. "I'm not a good judge of that sort of thing. When you win the Oscar, you really win it because the script is good, something is advocated in the script. *My Fair Lady* had a good script, and George's work was very good."

Truth to tell, it was extremely important for Cukor to win. He was honored with the award at his fifth nomination, and he was sixty-five years old. Many believed that his Oscar was compensatory, Hollywood's long-overdue tribute to a distinguished career. Cukor had been nominated four times before: *Little Women* in 1933, *The Philadelphia Story* in 1940, *A Double Life* in 1947, and *Born Yesterday* in 1950. "It is good for the soul, if not very pleasant," Cukor once noted, "to sit there with your nomination and be turned down in front of a hundred million people. But when you do get it, it is a glory. Mine seemed to be an inordinately long time coming, but when at last I got it, it meant more to me than any other award I have received."

Among the thousand telegrams, from all over the world, was one from Sam Goldwyn: "It was about time and I am delighted." Irene Selznick cabled: "You did it. You did it. I told you you could do it." Elia Kazan wrote: "I've always thought you should have had an Oscar for *Philadelphia Story,* which is a masterpiece and one of the best films of its kind ever made in this country." William Inge noted: "You got your just desserts." Said Joan Crawford: "What a brilliant production. You're still the greatest director of all."

When Arthur Freed congratulated him on a "masterful job," Cukor said: "I did have great material to work with, a glorious cast, and the understanding and help of a producer with a great big open purse." Cukor told producer Ross Hunter: "You see, I give the producer all the credit that is due him! Remember this the next time you are casting about for a director."

Among all this praise, Cukor didn't forget his tailor, Sid Sanders. What turned the trick, he told Sanders, what really put *My Fair Lady* over, was his chic appearances in his varied coats. In the afternoon it was the tweed coat; in the evening he knocked 'em dead in the black number with the velvet collar and the red lining; if it rained, he wore the elegant raincoat.

By Oscar time *My Fair Lady* had settled in for an indefinite run at the Egyptian Theater. In twenty-five weeks, with total grosses of $1.65 million, it set a new house record. The old record holder, *Ben Hur,* had reached its first million in fifty-three weeks. *My Fair Lady* ended its tenure in February 1965, after a sixty-eight-week run. In its first year the movie grossed more than $50 million worldwide.

"*My Fair Lady* was George's best-known, but not greatest, film," Gene Allen said, "but it certainly was a fitting one." Allen didn't think Cukor would necessarily consider it his best. "For George not to have won awards, when his actors won awards in his films, was always a puzzle." Allen thought Cukor actually had two full careers. "The span of years and the ups and downs were tremendous," he elaborated, "but no painter paints the same quality." It was one of two Cukor films Allen was most pleased with: "*A Star Is Born,* my first picture with George, was a tremendous learning process, but *My Fair Lady* was the one I enjoyed the most."

After the Oscar, reason slowly returned to the troubled world. There were other matters, "trivial ones," Cukor joked, to be settled, like riots in Santo Domingo, the trial of the Ku Klux Klan. After half a decade of being in the dark, Cukor's visibility suddenly increased.

The Oscar represented the peak in Cukor's career, but unfortunately after this height he experienced the worst years of his career.

Cukor *(left)* didn't know anything about sports before directing *Pat and Mike,* but he learned from his leading lady, Katharine Hepburn, and tennis champion Frankie Parker.

Rehearsing Spencer Tracy, Jean Simmons, and a dog on the set of *The Actress,* based on Ruth Gordon's autobiographical play. This is the only sentimental picture in Cukor's oeuvre.

Cukor gets to know Judy Garland on the
set of *A Star Is Born,* which is his masterpiece and features Garland's most
impressive dramatic performance.

On his knees in Pakistan, Cukor guides Ava Gardner and
Francis Matthews *(left)* in *Bhowani Junction,* Cukor's only
epic costume drama.

Even the naturally elegant Kay Kendall was instructed how to move by Cukor in the stylish musical *Les Girls*.

Anna Magnani goes over her lines with her acting coach *(left)* while Cukor, for a change, quietly observes on the set of *Wild Is the Wind*, an assignment he took over at the last moment.

Always the meticulous professional, Cukor examines Sophia Loren's mutilayered dress and stockings in *Heller in Pink Tights,* Cukor's tribute to the performers in the Old West.

Playwright Arthur Miller *(right)* visits his wife, Marilyn
Monroe, and chats with Cukor during *Let's Make Love*.
COURTESY OF THE ACADEMY OF MOTION PICTURE ARTS AND SCIENCES

Again on his knees, this time Cukor shows Glynis Johns and Ty
Hardin *(left)* how to convey sexual tension in the trashy soap
opera *The Chapman Report*.
COURTESY OF THE ACADEMY OF MOTION PICTURE ARTS AND SCIENCES

Cukor rehearses *(left to right)* Rex Harrison, Mona
Washbourne, and Audrey Hepburn in *My Fair Lady,*
Cukor's Oscar-winning, though decidedly not best, film.

COURTESY OF THE ACADEMY OF MOTION PICTURE ARTS AND SCIENCES

Maggie Smith's heavy makeup created some tensions on the
set of *Travels with My Aunt,* a film originally designed for
Katharine Hepburn.

COURTESY OF THE ACADEMY OF MOTION PICTURE ARTS AND SCIENCES

Cukor rehearses Elizabeth Taylor *(center)*, Cicely Tyson *(left)* and some children in the Russian-American coproduction of *The Blue Bird*, his weakest—and only embarrassing —film.

In London with Katharine Hepburn and Sir Laurence Olivier for his first made-for-TV movie, *Love Among the Ruins*. Getting Olivier to costar proved more challenging than actually making the picture.

In 1978, the Lincoln Center Film Society
honored Cukor with a career achievement
award, and it was Katharine Hepburn's turn to
lecture, shaking the finger that Cukor had used
so many times when he directed her.

COURTESY OF THE ACADEMY OF MOTION PICTURE ARTS
AND SCIENCES

Cukor poses with two beautiful leading ladies, Candice
Bergen *(left)*, whom he
admired, and Jacqueline
Bisset, whom he disliked,
during the shooting of
Rich and Famous, his swan
song. This also marked a
return to MGM, where he
began his career and made
most of his films.

COURTESY OF THE ACADEMY OF
MOTION PICTURE ARTS AND SCIENCES

the
Cukor
George and Whitney

Cukor with Whitney, his last and favorite dog.

CHAPTER ELEVEN

The Worst Years of His Career, 1965–69

WITH CUKOR'S HELP, GEORGE TOWERS BEGAN WORKING AT EXECU-tive Business Management under Earl Wright and Bill Hayes, Cukor's longtime lawyers. At first Towers handled a few productions and the Maugham properties, but the idea was to involve him more and more in Cukor's company, GDC. Once Lazar was fired, Kurt Frings was em-ployed as Cukor's agent, but Frings did not have exclusive rights to sell GDC's properties; he was to get paid only if he negotiated a deal.

After George Hoyningen-Huene's death, Cukor's sole artistic collabo-rator was Gene Allen, who also functioned as his associate producer. For a studio director, Cukor had created something unique: an artistic team that included Hoyningen-Huene and Allen. This intimate collaboration was responsible for Cukor's continued development as a filmmaker, spe-cifically in the visual domain. Cukor's peers were quick to notice a more lavish and sumptuous style in the 1950s and 1960s; the turning point was *A Star Is Born,* his first color film.

My Fair Lady, however, was Allen's last movie with Cukor. Allen's contract continued, but no film materialized. "We weren't doing any-thing," Allen recalled, "so we mutually agreed just to do it project by project." They stayed in touch, but they mostly saw each other at AMPAS functions. With Cukor's encouragement, Allen became actively involved in the industry. "He pushed me to become a governor and then president of the academy," Allen said. "In all of these positions I proudly used knowledge gained through years of working with George."

Cukor had used the studio system to his advantage. For years his motto was: "Just give me a fair budget and a decent script, and I'll shoot a good movie." According to Allen, "George was the kind of director who needed a Jack Warner or Harry Cohn to say, 'Let's do it.' " Cukor couldn't help harking back to the good old days of the powerful studios heads, though he never thought that of all people, *he* would be sentimental about Louis B. and Harry Cohn, but he was. He liked working where there was no "anarchy," he said, when the head of a studio has been a showman.

Cukor discussed the new Hollywood with Tracy and Hepburn, and they all agreed that times had changed and they'd better "roll with the punch" (another typical Cukor expression). The industry was now all deals, promotions, and packaging. Cukor compared it with Rome's Via Veneto: "a little tricky and maybe shady, too." But he didn't know how to adjust to the changing context, and it didn't help that he had had many failures over the past decade.

"The 1960s were changing times," said Allen. "George was not getting the properties he wanted, perhaps he wasn't aggressive enough. But he was not the only idle director; many marvelous directors were sitting at home during those times, from the Willie Wylers to the Billy Wilders."

Katharine Hepburn believed that Cukor never really understood the system: "George lacked capacity to butter up the right people, like Louis B. He was a very cultivated man, but he didn't have the gift to make friends with Mayer; he was friends with his daughters. I was a master at getting on with the moguls, but George wasn't. You have to play politics with the money; you have no choice. If they don't like you, you don't get hired. George didn't know how to play politics," she elaborated. "It's a talent you either have or not."

Hepburn contrasted Cukor with John Huston, who understood the system: "Huston had a nose for presenting himself as a brilliant figure, which indeed he was. He knew how to sing the song, how to promote himself. It's a very subtle thing, but George didn't understand how to sell himself." Hepburn held that "one can look at George's record and see when he began to lose it. He lost it when the scripts he got weren't interesting."

With no prospects for directing original scripts, Cukor turned again to adapting some of Maugham's stories. But this time he had to deal with Searle because Maugham was too frail. Years before Cukor had talked to Maugham about making a "bang-up" picture out of *Cakes and Ale,* but the author countered that the heroine was a nymphomaniac. Times had changed, and with the decline in censorship, Hollywood was displaying an "ever-increasing parade of dissolute heroines." Cukor liked the idea of Shirley MacLaine in *Cakes and Ale;* she could be raffish, funny, and moving. She was enormously talented, with unexplored depth and range, and as for her deficiencies, something could be done about her accent, and there were "falsies" for her flat chest.

Maugham's death, in 1965, put all these plans on hold. The writer's unstable behavior and sickness had upset Cukor for years. When Cukor spent some time with him in California, Maugham seemed vague and remote, but then suddenly he would talk lucidly about his friendships with Henry James or Rudyard Kipling. In the last couple of years life in the villa was terrible for him and his companion, Alan Searle. Maugham lived in a strange world of terror; his sickness had gone on for too long. Imprisoned in the villa for years, Searle too wished the end would come soon, for Maugham himself longed to die.

Cukor tried to reawaken Searle's interest in life, advising him to change his environment, perhaps even find work. He even offered him a consulting job on the Maugham project—if it materialized. Cukor was now hoping Vivien Leigh would show interest in Maugham's stories. Wouldn't it be wonderful if they could at last work together?

Cukor invited Searle to stay with him, promising a much-needed rest and some "pleasant relaxation." In his previous visits Searle spent a lot of time running around with Towers, to whom he was attracted. Cukor believed that Searle brought out the worst in Towers and was a bit jealous though he tried not to show it.

As he grew older, Cukor enjoyed Searle's company less and less. He could never forget a nasty quarrel between Maugham and Searle at his house. Upset over something, Searle charged: "I'm going to leave you and marry a rich wife." The writer gave him a cold look, then said bluntly: "Living with a rich wife is hard work, and you simply don't know how to do it."

Searle and Cukor could not have been more different. Searle would indulge himself in food, rich lunches at the Beverly Hills Hotel, then come home and sleep for hours. After dinner he went out again, sometimes until the early hours of the morning. He was too wild, selfish, and flamboyant for the disciplined Cukor. Worse yet, nothing irritated Cukor more than complaining, and Searle complained all the time.

In the same year that Maugham died, Cukor lost another important person, David Selznick. Characteristically Selznick left a memo with directions for his own funeral. Though not a devout Jew, Selznick asked for a rabbi, but one who didn't know him well so that he wouldn't talk too long and bore his friends.

The crowd attending the Selznick funeral was too large for the small temple in Forest Lawn Memorial Park, and the ceremony was moved to a larger place. Cukor acted as director, but he could not control the service; Samuel Goldwyn, who was an honorary pallbearer, aggressively elbowed himself to the front of the procession.

"David's friends and colleagues will not be surprised to learn," Cukor said in his eulogy, "that the occasion which gathers us here today was consistent to his attention to details, the subject of a memo. But I think his generosity would have permitted us to stretch a point—which instructed brevity—impossible brevity to honor an excitingly energetic, enchanting man. Enchanting was his world, his presence, and his life. We have lost an irreplaceable individualist, who was as tender as he was tenacious, as courageous as competitive, as inventive as ingenious, as sensitive as stalwart."

Cukor didn't mention *GWTW* or other movies, all "public facts and part of our cultural history." But he singled out Selznick's unique qualities: his down-to-earth acumen and virile ambition, daring showmanship, and, above all, bedrock principles of quality. Selznick's image as a filmmaker, Cukor concluded, "does us all honor."

Cukor corresponded with Selznick's son, Daniel, sending him books to read. For his part, Daniel referred to him as Uncle George, the "wittiest" observer of the family, who still possessed the same well-worn smile and engaging voice. He particularly appreciated Cukor's description of his father as "the most generous of friends." The Selznicks honored Cukor with a special present for his devotion to their father, a Gentleman's Gruen's dress pocket watch, which Selznick had received from his Republic managers back in 1920. Cukor was deeply touched.

With plenty of time in his hands, Cukor began to think for the first time about an autobiography, with the help of Jane Wilkie. In the past he had been hesitant because he hated being a "name-dropper," a species that bored him, as well as an "I-dropper," which was even worse. Cukor loathed interviews; he knew that nobody was interested in *him*. "I have spent a lifetime shoving actors through their paces," he said, and it was these actors who fascinated the inquisitors. Cukor complained that interviewers always put words in his mouth, such as "Garbo is mysterious," "Barrymore is a ham," missing the point that Garbo was shy, not mysterious, that Barrymore was a ham, but also gentle and charming.

But Cukor quickly lost interest in Wilkie's work; she asked too many questions about his private life. He then asked Hoyningen-Huene to do the layouts for an illustrated book that was to deal with the legendary personalities he had directed. Nothing came of this idea either.

Then another writer, Louise Tanner, showed interest in collaborating on Cukor's book. Cukor thought that a book of candid shots, showing him with his stars in "action," might be "telling" about his work and also funny. His often outrageous faces and peculiar gestures, all unconscious, made these shots different from the "carefully posed" pictures of the "director at work," which were usually listless and conventional.

To protect himself, Cukor asked his lawyers to inform Tanner that the writing of the book was "unilaterally" undertaken, with no commitment for compensation. And no materials based on his life were to be submitted to any publisher without his approval; what Cukor had in mind was a ghostwriter, not a biographer.

Tanner was shocked by Cukor's letter; she had had no intention of asking for money or publishing a book without his consent. If she had stewed over the book, she explained, it was because he wasn't easy to catch. Tanner believed she deserved a better treatment from a director who prided himself on decency and courtesy. Nonetheless, in 1966 Cukor's lawyers informed Tanner that her work was terminated. This ended the first, but by no means last, effort at a biography. There were to be many more attempts—all futile.

Frustrated by his passivity as a director, Cukor turned his attention to *Bloomer Girl*, a movie about Amelia Bloomer based on the Broadway musical. After being slaves of fashion, Bloomer and her friends wanted freedom from hoopskirts and heavy crinolines. They were impractical for leading an active life, and being laced tightly was bad for bearing children. The story was set in 1850, when these women invented bloomers to make their life easier. "It's a bang-up subject," Cukor said. "It says things that are relevant today with wit and fun."

In March 1966 preproduction on *Bloomer Girl* began. Cukor was to get paid $175,000 and a small percentage of the profits, a major reduction after *My Fair Lady*. But he was promised a long rehearsal period and no fewer than eighty-six shooting days. Cukor got permission to shoot in Cooperstown, New York, a city that approximated the story's locale, Cicero Falls. He hoped that Arthur Laurents, the gifted writer, would produce a good script, but when Laurents showed no excitement, he turned to John Patrick.

Almost every major star was considered, though Cukor wished to get Shirley MacLaine, then at the height of her career. MacLaine was a diverse actress who could also dance; besides, her mother was a descendant of women in the story. Fox was pushing for a big party to announce the casting of MacLaine and Harry Belafonte, but Cukor thought it was premature.

In the summer Cukor asked Bob Fosse to do the choreography, assuring him that his work would be well publicized and would be a step forward in his desire to become a filmmaker. But Fosse expressed his concern about earlier promises to Agnes de Mille, who had done good work on Broadway with *Bloomer Girl*. Fosse thought that she should do the film, noting that he would have been crushed if somebody else had made movies out of his musicals. Cukor dismissed Fosse's "curious" sense of loyalty and told him to regard the project on its own merits, without excessive emotionalism.

Since Cukor could be insensitive, even cruel, he cited the reviews for de Mille's choreography in *Carousel*, which were respectful, but the crackle of excitement was missing; her last show also hadn't fared well. Cukor feared that the combination of de Mille and him would be old hat; Fosse's young blood was needed as counterbalance.

Upon learning of the shenanigans behind her back, de Mille was stunned; she had already filled notebooks with ideas. If it were MacLaine's choice of Fosse, she told Cukor, she could accept this. That would be like Wimbledon. Fosse won—and fairly. But if it were anything else, she couldn't hear the disappointment. Notified by a cable about the termination of her work, de Mille was humiliated by Cukor's reversal of decision.

Over the next two weeks de Mille wrote to Cukor every day, dismissing all of John Patrick's allegations of disloyalty and denying she had broken trust or belittled the project. How could she have? Her trust in Cukor was absolute. She was willing to sign a contract, script unseen, only because Cukor was in charge. *Bloomer Girl*, however, was never made because of budget and cast complications.

Another frustrating project that never materialized was Lesley Blanch's *The Nine-Tiger Man*, with a script by the British playwright Terence Rattigan. Cukor reminded Rattigan's agent, Harold Freedman, that in 1934 he had dined at London's Garrick Club with the prince of Liechtenstein. A young playwright, a protégé of the prince, who knew nothing about theater, sought Cukor's advice about an agent. You're lucky, said Cukor, because Freedman, the finest literary agent, happens to be at the Savoy. He arranged for a meeting between them, and a contract was signed. The "finest" agent was Freedman, and the playwright Rattigan. Cukor didn't ask for any "kickback" or "special treatment," but he didn't want Rattigan to forget the story. Cukor couldn't afford to pay the outrageous amount Freedman demanded and instead offered ten thousand dollars as commission.

In his visits to California, Rattigan was crazy about the boys at Cukor's house; he obsessed about this and that blond he had met there. Knowing Rattigan's infatuations, Cukor delighted in teasing him, reporting about a mutual trick who had come in for a swim and dinner, an anecdote about a colleague, etc.

When Rattigan left for vacation in Italy in August, Cukor determined to visit him, "by hook and by crook," whether or not the writer invited him. Cukor joked that although he hadn't worked since *My Fair Lady*, he was willing to scrape together the necessary funds, put himself in debt, even pocket his pride and ask his enemy Cecil Beaton for a loan. Far more important was the question of the circles in which they would be moving: Would he be required to dress as a fisher lad or more like Burt Lancaster in *The Leopard*? Cukor preferred to stay in a small hotel, close to Rattigan's park, so that he could watch the comings and goings of his boys.

Rattigan promised to have his job cut out by September, but further delays pushed the project into winter. "George spent a great deal of time testing and talking about *The Nine-Tiger Man*," Allan Davis recalled. "I introduced him to writer John Mortimer, who worked on this project. A lot of money was spent developing the script, but it was never made."

When Rattigan proposed Liz Taylor for a role that would be a departure for her, Cukor was reserved. Offered every part and limitless money, Taylor was spoiled. Cukor preferred to direct Taylor in *Sappho*, a novel that had long haunted him; in the 1940s, he and Garbo had talked about a screen adaptation. What made the project unique was its fresh and poignant love story, and Taylor could be wonderful—the perfect meeting of actress and role. But the star found the book old-fashioned and refused to commit herself until she saw the final script.

There was no point in doing Sappho unless there was a uniquely suited actress. When the negotiations with Taylor failed, Cukor turned to Sophia Loren, who had recently become an international star. He sent the script to her producer husband, Carlo Ponti, hoping the couple would be enthusiastic. Six months later, impatient and disappointed that Ponti had not responded, Cukor demanded to know if Loren was still interested. Finally, Ponti gave his verdict: It wasn't advisable to invest any money in the development of *Sappho*.

Another idea was to adapt Arthur Schnitzler's novel *Casanova's Homecoming*, about the legendary lover, for Rex Harrison. In November 1967 Cukor embarked on a three-week business trip to Paris, where he met with producer Alexander Salkind and Harrison. The meeting went well, and Cukor signed an option for *Casanova's Homecoming* as a joint venture with GDC. But soon all of Cukor's British writer friends, including Peter Shaffer and John Osborne, declined the project. A suitable script was never produced.

Going from one unsuccessful project to another, Cukor believed he had struck bad luck. Next in line was *The Right Honorable Consul* (or *Dilke*), also with Rex Harrison. John Osborne had done one third of the script but then had a falling-out with producer Sam Spiegel, who was now making a fresh start with John Mortimer. Like the other projects, the film was never made.

Though supportive of the two major film schools in Los Angeles, USC and UCLA, Cukor was always more involved in USC's operations. In 1967 he was asked to talk to its students. "The students are full of beans," he later said, "but they are inclined to be arty and to resist conventional filmmaking. They are in a great danger of being influenced by avant-garde snobbery, the sort of thing they read in very intelligent, but very slanted, cinema magazines." Cukor told the students that many of the foreign directors they considered innovative were actually experimenting with techniques already used—and discarded—by Hollywood.

On April 18, 1967, UCLA decided to bestow an honorary degree, Doctor of Fine Arts, on Cukor. Doctor or president, he told Vivien Leigh, at heart, he was the same "gentlemanly kid" she'd met on the back lot of the Selznick studio the night Atlanta burned.

This modesty was false: He was very proud of the degree. "Look at this, look at this," Cukor said to Allan Davis in London later that year. "What do you think of this? See, I'm a doctor now?" To Davis's surprise, Cukor pulled out an eight-by-ten photograph of himself with other distinguished gentlemen wearing gowns. "Oh, George, how marvelous," said Davis. "I'm a doctor, you see. I'm a doctor now." Cukor said again. "What are you a doctor of?" asked Davis innocently. "Fine Arts, you cunt," said the irascible director.

In the 1960s Cukor began regular correspondence with Joan Crawford. With both their careers in decline, they reminisced about old times. Crawford never ceased to be amazed at how exciting it was to be in Cukor's presence and how magnificent his style of entertainment was—a "lost art." She was grateful for many things Cukor has given her, but mostly his talent. For his part, Cukor thanked Crawford for sending him a box of fancy-shaped scented soaps and promised to have a ball keeping clean. In the following year he received from the star a dessert called Bon Appetit—Joan Crawford Peaches.

Practically every female star who worked with Cukor remained in touch with him. Ava Gardner was no exception. She often consulted with Cukor about her career, as when Mike Nichols asked her to play Mrs. Robinson in *The Graduate*. But Cukor was unfamiliar with Charles Webb's novel.

One evening Cukor went to see Marlene Dietrich's act with the Kanins and Rosalind Russell. For Cukor, Dietrich was no great singer and had little humor. He thought Mrs. Fiske's quote "the firm, firm touch on the wrong, wrong note" aptly described the aging Dietrich. He could hardly keep a straight face during her opening speech: "I was a schoolgirl in Berlin when the American director saw me." But the show was sold out, and Cukor envied her. In the final account it was Dietrich who got the last laugh—and a hundred thousand dollars for two weeks.

Indeed, after the collapse of the studio system, Cukor was jealous of anyone who had business skills and knew how to survive. Told that Claudette Colbert was getting 20 percent of her play's grosses in New York, he snapped, "She is not French for nothing."

In his correspondence with Colbert he jokingly proposed to film a story titled *Frenchy* or *Mam'zell from Barbados*. "Ze leetle French immigrant girl that becomes ze beeg beeg movie star, and the kid from the Eastside ghetto who is first a movie director, then sees the light and becomes

Reverend George Cukor (they'll decide on the sect later)." Colbert would, of course, play the heroine at all ages, but who could do justice to Cukor? Charlton Heston was too goyish; Lee J. Cobb, too Jewish. Cukor signed his letters to Colbert "Your friend from Pilgrim Hill," alluding to their presumed childhood meeting in Central Park.

Of his gay friends, Cukor admired the company of Christopher Isherwood and Don Bachardy; Isherwood was the only friend who could make Cukor shut up. In the 1960s he was a regular guest at their Santa Monica house. Because he hated driving, Cukor was driven to their house by Hoyningen-Huene or Stanley Musgrove, who became his publicist. A bad driver by his own admission, Cukor had some minor accidents, so friends usually arranged to pick him up. Bachardy did several drawings of Cukor, which he later displayed in a gallery. He recalled that "George was amused to be scrutinized and passive, as he had been used to be so active all those years of standing behind the camera."

Snobbish about his connections to the literary world, Cukor took immense pride in his bonds with writers all over the world. In Paris he had befriended Pierre Barillet, the successful playwright of boulevard comedies (*Cactus Flower*), and Marcel Achard. Cukor's interaction with actors was easier to maintain, but literary friendships with the likes of Edith Sitwell, Noël Coward, Terence Rattigan, and Tom Stoppard were more challenging to cultivate.

Cukor considered it a privilege to read Thornton Wilder's *The Eighth Day* in galleys and told the author that the humanity and nobility of his book would surely place it among the world's great novels. He was truly flattered when Wilder said he had no better judge than Cukor for the screen potential of his book.

In 1967 and 1968 a good deal of Cukor's time was taken up by funerals and memorials. He went to so many that he believed he had become a friend of every dead person in the world. "I have my own kind of religion," he said; "it's going to funerals." With so many of his friends dying, he sympathized with Noël Coward's saying "If your friends just last through lunch."

For a whole year Cukor and Katharine Hepburn went to a funeral almost every weekend. A "conscientious funeral girl," Hepburn had a special costume for these events—black slacks. During the services Cukor listened to all the prayers and thought how wonderful it was that people really believed they were off to heaven.

Cukor was amused by the show biz "comic" aspect of funerals. He and David Selznick joked about those mortuary ads that stressed the earth quality: "Warm, dry soil, no seepage!" Catholic funerals were the most tricky: "There was a moment when you had to sink your knees in front of the altar, but the *fine* point is you must lower your head very respectfully *before* you sink to your knees. It took real timing, and you could easily miss your cue."

Spencer Tracy's death, in June 1967, was not a shock but still a very sad event. Cukor had known Tracy for three decades and directed him in six movies. He watched with admiration as Hepburn took care of the actor, forgetting all about her career. Cukor was touched when so many people wrote condolences for Tracy to *him*. Anthony Quinn had only a passing acquaintance with Tracy, but he held the actor in high regard. Quinn wrote to Cukor: "You gave Spencer the only things he really praised: love and friendship."

Lucille Ball wanted to do something special on her daughter's birthday, so she took her to see *The Actress*. Enchanted by its "nostalgic quality," Ball found the experience refreshing, after all the "trash and sex-ridden monstrosities." She told Cukor that one of her unfulfilled desires was never having had the pleasure and fortune to have been directed by him. Cukor made the most of Ball's letter, first reading it, word by word, to Hepburn, who was moved. He then showed it to Ruth Gordon, who was also delighted. Going to the trouble of writing such a letter proved again what a generous human being Ball was.

The good news for Cukor after Tracy's death was that Hepburn was in a mood to work—for the first time in years. In the past Hepburn didn't even want to read anything; she simply was unavailable. But in the next two years she enjoyed a great comeback. Indeed, in April 1968 Cukor accepted the Oscar for her for *Guess Who's Coming to Dinner?* After the show he called Hepburn in France, where she was shooting *The Lion in Winter* (for which she won another Oscar). It was 7:30 A.M., and the actress, characteristically, was having an early-morning swim. Hepburn saw the award as a tribute to Tracy in a film that was his swan song. She told Cukor, "This one is for the two of us."

The major event in spring 1968 was a tribute to Vivien Leigh on March 17. Cukor always believed that Leigh was underrated—"a consummate actress hampered by beauty." Furious when people said that Olivier "carried" her, he always reminded her detractors of her deservedly won not one but two Oscars.

Cukor found Leigh's company captivating, particularly the way she told outrageous jokes in a cool voice that made him weep. Leigh also had great talent for gardening and for creating beauty around her. She had true breeding: When she invited people for dinner, everything was perfect. Cukor held that Leigh's need for order compensated for an underlying disorder; there was something tragic even when she was at her happiest. In fact, he wasn't surprised when she died (Hepburn said, "Thank God!"). Leigh was so miserable after her divorce that she once confided in Cukor that she would rather live a short life with Olivier than a long one without him.

Cukor treasured Leigh's contribution to Louise Tanner's attempted biography. She had described him as "a director brimful of ideas, and with such facility of expressing them." Touched by her eloquent portrait, Cukor promised to try to become the "paragon of virtue" she believed he was.

An intimate friend, Leigh sometimes stayed with Cukor. When she came to L.A. to shoot *Ship of Fools*, Cukor rented a big Beverly Hills house for her, and before she arrived, he filled the house with personal things and artworks that he knew she liked. Cukor and Leigh were always planning to do films together. "Of course, I want to do a film," she wrote periodically. "I read and read, but you know how damned difficult it is to find the right thing. Why have you no part for a veteran actress who adores you?"

"George adored Vivien the most," recalled Allen Davis. "The last time I saw her was at a cocktail party in her flat. There was this exquisitely beautiful woman, smoking and drinking martinis, entertaining everybody around her bed. 'Have you heard from George?' she asked. 'Why doesn't the bastard ring me?' " Leigh insisted that Davis tell her over and over again Cukor's honorary degree cunt story. She then roared with her throaty laughter.

After her death Cukor planned a big Hollywood celebration that he aptly called "An Appreciation of Vivien Leigh." USC's Friends of the Libraries sponsored the event, the fourth in a series of tributes that have previously honored other friends of Cukor's: Aldous Huxley, Somerset Maugham, and Cole Porter.

The audience got a special thrill when Leigh's test for *GWTW* was shown. Cukor hadn't seen the test since 1939 and was curious about it himself. Upon re-viewing the test, he found it obvious why "this accomplished and beautiful creature got the part; it couldn't have been otherwise." There was an unexpected humorous note as well. Cukor was so busy giving instructions that his chair slipped out from under him and he found himself on the floor. He somehow had the feeling that Leigh herself joined in the laughter.

Cukor kept in touch with Leigh's mother in London, sending her clips from the tribute, which for him was the most emotional of the four he had supervised. "The best I can say," Cukor said after the event, "is that Vivien would have been pleased for the most part, amused at times, and irked very seldom."

George Hoyningen-Huene died a few months after Vivien Leigh. His contribution to the look of Cukor's films was invaluable, though many remembered him only as the designer of Cukor's Christmas cards. The year Hoyningen-Huene died was the only one Cukor did not send any cards. The noted photographer left his body to USC, but he didn't take care of the papers, and USC would not accept it. Cukor had to act quickly, so he sent the body to a funeral home; he later felt bad about burying his friend in a run-down cemetery.

On the way to the funeral, Cukor wrote some lines and asked Hepburn to read them, but she said she couldn't. However, when the coffin was put into the vault, Hepburn stepped forward and with streaming eyes said a few poignant words. She then took Cukor's lines and gave them an eloquent reading.

The year 1968 was particularly bad as far as funerals were concerned. In December Tallulah Bankhead died. "Tallulah was a truly magical creature," Cukor said. "I'm very grateful for the enormous amount of fun I had with her. She was sensitive, diverting, and touching." When Bankhead's estate was liquidated, Cukor was bequeathed a painting by Ambrose McEvoy and some art objects she knew he had admired.

By 1969 Cukor had not made a film in five years, the longest stretch in his career. Then, out of the blue, came an offer from Richard Zanuck to take over the direction of a problematic film, *Justine*.

Based on a modern classic, *The Alexandria Quartet*, a four-volume fiction by Lawrence Durrell, *Justine* was meant to present a rich tapestry of life in Alexandria, Egypt, in the 1930s. Fox had purchased the rights of the books for $50,000 and spent $750,000 on the screenplay. After eight years and numerous attempts by different writers, Lawrence Marcus was finally signed to do the script.

Marcus consolidated the four volumes. The final script was half *Justine*, the first novel; the other half was a combination of the second and third books. An attempt was made to heighten the poetic style by selecting dialogue from the books. The film, however, followed a straight-line approach rather than Durrell's more subjective style.

There were many jokes about shooting in Alexandria because the last time Fox had shot there had been for *Cleopatra*. Joseph Strick, who had adapted *Ulysses*, the literary masterpiece that was considered unfilmable, was hired to direct. Shooting began in September 1968, but in November, after six seeks on location, there was little usable footage, and Strick was fired. The production was temporarily halted, awaiting a replacement for Strick. "I wasn't pleased with the way the film looked," Zanuck recalled. "I had the unfortunate task of relieving Strick of his duty and shutting the picture down."

Zanuck's first call was to Cukor, who was, of course, available. Cukor said he would do it and in a week or so shooting started again. "George knew I was in trouble," Zanuck said, "but I don't think he would take a material that he really thought was awful. He wouldn't put his name if he didn't like it."

"There's no great stigma to being replaced as a director," Cukor told reporters. Close friends, however, knew that he took the picture on because he hadn't worked in years—many projects had fallen through—and he needed the money.

Zanuck immediately noticed a difference between Strick's work and Cukor's. As soon as Cukor came in, "the film started coming to life and the performances got better. Everything was like night and day: the way the picture looked, the way the camera moved." The thing that always amazed Zanuck about Cukor was his tremendous vitality and enthusiasm, even as he was growing older.

"It was difficult for George," Zanuck noted, "because when he came in, the picture had been cast. He was stuck with a lot of footage that had been shot before him, of which he kept about twenty-five percent." But he did change the costumes and some of the sets. Zanuck conceded that *Justine* was not a typical Cukor movie: "He came in late and didn't have the chance to really make it a Cukor movie."

In the final cut the location work is Strick's, and the studio sequences are Cukor's. Cukor disliked the location footage, because it was antiseptic; the streets of Alexandria looked cleaner than Beverly Hills. He wished he could have shot the film in Alexandria; it would have been much more Mediterranean.

Bound by these restrictions, Cukor opted for atmosphere rather than authenticity. Most of the picture was finished on Fox's back lot; Alexandria's streets were reconstructed in the studio from stills. Cukor cast the street people (Egyptians, Greeks) with the great resources Hollywood had. The interiors of Justine's town house were also wrong. The downstairs looked like an unsuccessful hotel, so they played most of the scenes upstairs, with a different kind of furniture.

Cukor's opening scene in *Justine* was excellent in establishing the decadent ambience. Anna Karina is belly-dancing with other women. Then suddenly she starts screaming and runs into the street; she has taken ill. Another excellent scene is the costume ball, which stood out for its accuracy. Cukor couldn't afford to reshoot everything, but it was still a compelling sequence.

Cukor wanted to create a child brothel but feared the picture would get an X rating. Indeed, the censors tried to cut the "balls" off the picture. Zanuck brought in the youngest-looking teenagers he could find, but Cukor was not pleased. Then somebody suggested using midgets. They used children on the outside, but inside, one only saw the midgets. Cukor held that it would have been much more shocking if they all had been children.

The film was kinky, but not kinky enough. Cukor thought that had he made the film in 1971, instead of 1969, the story would have been bolder and sexier, and the humor more hard-bitten, as American movies radically changed in those few years.

The major problem with *Justine* was that the script lacked a clear structure; it didn't make much sense. Cukor's efforts to create a coherent movie out of a confused script were unsuccessful.

Moreover, some of the actors were inadequate, and the leading lady, French actress Anouk Aimée, was a disaster. The hollow-cheeked actress became an international star after *A Man and a Woman*. "It is a role that comes up only once or twice in your life," said Aimée, but that was before shooting began—and before she fell in love with Albert Finney. "It was the only time I've ever had anything to do with somebody who didn't even try," Cukor complained. "Anouk was indomitably refined—wouldn't do the coarseness of it." She also had trouble with her costumes, which were designed by Irene Sharaff. Perceiving her as a "monster of selfishness," Cukor referred to Aimée as "the cunt."

"George could be quite catchy and testy," Lambert said. "He hated Anouk's unprofessional behavior. He became angry with her because he thought she didn't want to play the part; she just wanted to be beautiful. To talk in such a way about a star was quite exceptional for George, and some of it even got into print." Lambert recalled a party that he attended where he ran into Albert Finney. "We were talking, and George suddenly came up and said, 'So you divorced Anouk?' And Albert said, 'Yes, I did.' 'Quite right,' George said. 'You're well rid of her; she was a terrible cunt.' "

"George didn't get along with Anouk," Zanuck concurred. "She was having problems, and she wanted to leave the picture before the end. I had to inform her that we would sue if she did. She was just starting her romance with Albert Finney and was uncooperative—always late and unprepared."

By contrast, Cukor was happy to work again with Dirk Bogarde though, like the first time, in *Song Without End*, he wasn't responsible for his casting. "George is completely and utterly dedicated to the picture," the actor told the press; "he doesn't think, breathe, drink, or eat anything when he's working." Bogarde said Cukor taught him how to act for the camera. Cukor used the simplest words, like "If you lift your finger, open a door, stir a cup of tea, always make it interesting." But Bogarde, like James Mason before him, also thought Cukor was inflexible: "Every word has to be said, you can't change the script."

Cukor liked Bogarde's performance for its power, originality, and edge. Whether those glorious things Bogarde said about him were true or not, Cukor teased the actor. Cukor considered his interview a firm commitment to employ him as director on his next film—"When do I report, where and how much."

Justine's shoot was completed on February 3, 1969, and a few weeks later cutting began. Cukor ran the same gamut at every editing session: He was first pleased, then a bit excited, but at the end plunged into gloom. He now hoped the audience would like the picture better than he did.

The audience seemed to like *Justine*, previewed in May in San Diego. Fox's executives developed high expectations for the film's box-office appeal, but Cukor thought the movie still needed clarification and discreet cutting.

In late July Cukor flew to New York for the film's premiere. Staying at the St. Regis Hotel, he made only one request: not to be given the Cecil Beaton suite. That was not because of his feelings for Beaton, but because it was hideous, uncomfortable. Still, he reveled in Hepburn's stories about how Beaton drove her up the wall with her costumes in the musical *Coco*. Cukor had never heard Hepburn express such detestation of anybody; there was no doubt in his mind that Beaton deserved every bit of it.

Being in New York, Cukor missed Garson Kanin's evening, *Remembering Mr. Maugham,* a dramatization of his book, at the Mark Taper Forum. Wishing Kanin good luck, Cukor sent him Maugham's handkerchief with a note: "I did not steal it, Willie gave it to me." Kanin had earlier asked Cukor to join him in nominating Ruth Gordon for "The Woman of the Year," not because she needed it but because by honoring her, they would be honoring themselves. Cukor immediately wrote to the *Los Angeles Times,* nominating Gordon for "The Woman of Any Year," noting that at seventy-three, Gordon was "completely contemporary, wise, witty."

On August 4 *Justine* was shown to the New York press. Cukor answered the questions as politely as possible, but he was bored. Asked what his next movie was, Cukor had to come up with a quick answer. He said he was too superstitious to announce future projects, but the sad truth was he had none in sight.

In New York Cukor visited old friends. Over tea with Joan Fontaine in her Seventy-second Street apartment, Cukor was curious to know why the lovely-looking actress was not performing. "It's a pity," he told Fontaine. "You're too good an actress to be idle." When Fontaine said, "All I'm offered is grandmothers and bit roles," Cukor seemed to understand her dilemmas as an aging but proud actress.

Justine's world premiere took place on August 8, with the reaction of the press mixed. The *New York Times'* Vincent Canby was kind, under-standing what Cukor had faced when he took over a troubled produc-tion, particularly the problem of creating exoticism on the studio lot. "*Justine* didn't open well," said Zanuck. "It wasn't successful." Cukor's fears and misgivings about the reaction of British press to his "imperti-nence," meddling with an English classic, proved justified: The British reviews were worse than the American.

CHAPTER TWELVE:

A Comeback, 1970–72

IN 1970 CUKOR WAS ENGAGED IN A BIG PROJECT, *THE MOVIES*, PRO-
duced as a benefit for the Motion Picture and Television Relief Fund.
Cukor chaired a committee that included Philip Chamberlain as producer, Gary Essert as technical director, and Robert Epstein as historian.
"We met at George's house two or three times a week," Essert recalled,
"and after the project was over, we all became friends." The compilation
was a great success, but it was not easy; the clips were from hundreds of
features, which had to be projected separately. "It was insane to run,"
Essert said. "It took eight projectionists and many machines, but when
the audience watched it, it looked like one film.

"We all sort of did it together," Essert said. "Cukor suggested some
clips, but the majority of clips from his movies were suggested by Epstein." The only problem they had with Cukor was that "he always
wanted his clips to run too long; he didn't want to cut his." Originally
there were more clips of Cukor, but Essert had to persuade him to take
some of them out because "it wouldn't have looked right to have more
of his films since he was the only director on the committee."

Cukor had excellent segments in the show. For Part One they chose the
premiere of *A Star Is Born*, followed by Judy Garland's rendition of
"Swanee." For the "Comedy" section they showed the clip from *The
Women* in which Rosalind Russell bites Paulette Goddard and the gin
game between Broderick Crawford and Judy Holliday in *Born Yesterday*.
For the "Battle of the Sexes" segment Cukor was represented by two
scenes: Hepburn and Grant in *The Philadelphia Story* and Hepburn and
Tracy in *Adam's Rib*.

The three-hour program consisted of film clips from 1907 to 1970. Cukor hoped that the assemblage conveyed "the dazzling range, vigor, and glory of Hollywood." The program was so successful that it was run again at the Los Angeles Music Center and the Academy of Motion Picture Arts and Sciences (AMPAS). Shown with big electric signs over the theater, it was a "super-duper" show, with Princess Grace's patronage and stars like Frank Sinatra and Barbra Streisand. Though it was late, Cukor was surprised to see so many "intrepid souls" watching the show to its end.

While they were showing the film, ABC Television contacted the group with the idea of preparing it for a network special. The proceeds would also go to the Motion Picture and Television Relief Fund, for which the show had been originally designed. Thus began a long process of putting the original negatives on one film.

The Movies added a "panache, style and tradition" to the evening, not to mention the "Cukor verve," wrote Gregory Peck, as president of AMPAS. Through his activities at AMPAS, Cukor befriended the Pecks and was often invited to their parties. For him, the Pecks were a wonderful family: He was a successful actor and public-spirited man; Veronique was a devoted, intelligent wife. "Ah, harmony, harmony," Cukor said about them.

For years Cukor was on the Board of Governors and cochair of the Foreign Language Picture Committee of AMPAS. Apparently there had been "shenanigans, political and otherwise," in the choices of these films. Cukor joked about how he had been asked to add some fresh and young blood to the committee's more veteran members.

In 1970 Cukor gave a lunch for the foreign directors at the request of Gregory Peck. Wishing to include "hot directors," he invited Sam Peckinpah, whose films he did not like, but Peckinpah was in Mexico City. Fearing the occasion might be just Old Hollywood, Cukor also asked Paul Mazursky, another rising director.

It was an extraordinary occasion, with a "sense of closeness," as he put it, no generation gap or international misunderstanding, just movie directors, delighted to be in one another's company. For Mazursky, it was one of the most exciting afternoons of his life; he immediately made himself available for future luncheons. For Mark Rydell, who also attended for the first time, it was moving just to be present in such a distinguished gathering. There was a sense of camaraderie that seemed nourishing.

In 1971 Cukor again hosted the foreign directors' luncheon. That year the guest of honor was Spanish filmmaker Luis Buñuel, and the gathering was particularly impressive, including big shots like John Ford, George Stevens, and Alfred Hitchcock. Cukor recalled that when he and Buñuel were at Metro, the Spaniard was not given anything to do because of rumors he was on a B list of directors. Cukor went to Irving Thalberg and told him it was a shame a genius like Buñuel was treated this way. "Why, there isn't any B list," Thalberg reportedly said, "but I'll see to it that he is taken off!"

On April 8, 1971, Cukor attended the Oscar ceremonies with Liz Taylor. There was always a great to-do about security because of Taylor's emeralds, which Cukor nicknamed hemorrhoids. Cukor complained that his eyes were impaired by the endless barrage of flashbulbs to which Taylor was subjected. Ironically, the photographs with Taylor brought him more fame and attention than he had ever had.

Liz Taylor had become Cukor's frequent companion on social events. One evening they went to see a play in which a couple of nude people were onstage, rolling on the floor. Taylor remarked that the actors were unappealing and made love as if they were sexually frigid. Cukor couldn't agree more. "In the good old days, the girls who exposed themselves had good figures, but now that had no bearing at all; the most lamentable girl would undress."

One afternoon Taylor suggested they go to Disneyland. Their wonderful day brought back memories of his boyhood, when he was taken to Coney Island. Disneyland held the same magic for him. Never was he taken by anyone so dazzling, Cukor told the star, who in his view possessed that rare virtue "simple kindness." When he needed company, Cukor could forget what he had said about Taylor ("a limited actress who made some silly movies").

Out of The Movies came an important creation, Filmex, an international film festival. At first Cukor thought it would be a good idea to bring the entire New York Film Festival to L.A. He had talked to the people in New York, but they said it would be difficult because of logistics. When Cukor heard Essert and Chamberlain's idea to create an L.A. festival, he got excited. Together they conceived a larger event that wouldn't just pick the cream of the crop—the usual French and Italian films—but would go far afield and run a diversity of films.

The word "exposition" was chosen over "festival" since the event was noncompetitive and no awards were given. The nonprofit Filmex was funded by private and organizational grants, from AMPAS, the American Film Institute, the Los Angeles County Museum. Cukor agreed to serve as spokesman, and with his assistance, Essert and Chamberlain started to raise money. The festival ran for thirteen years, from 1971 through 1983, when some of the founders left to create the American Cinematheque.

The first Los Angeles International Film Exposition opened on November 4, 1971, with Peter Bogdanovich's The Last Picture Show. The entire cinematic spectrum—old and new, feature-length and short—was represented, creating an environment for people to see, talk about, and appreciate movies. The diverse program of forty films included John Ford and Chaplin classics but also Andy Warhol.

Because of his international reputation as a director and his involvement as the festival's founding trustee, Cukor was considered the father of Filmex. Initially Cukor was very involved in board meetings and fund raising. At the beginning of the festival he stood up onstage and welcomed the guests or introduced a film. Cukor's participation was vital in the first years. "He was aware of film preservation," Essert said, "that certain of his films had deteriorated and that there were no good prints." He was also aware of the bad projection of films in theaters.

"We occupied a lot of his time," said Essert. "He did a lot of the strategy meetings, devised a plan on how to create the organization, where to raise money." But once the plan was put together, Essert implemented it. Cukor seldom attended events besides opening night. Halfway through the festival there was usually a directors' lunch when most of the directors were in town. Cukor threw an informal lunch, sometimes at his house, sometimes at a restaurant.

On June 24, 1970, Cukor flew to Dallas, where he was honored with the Golden Plate Award at the ninth annual Salute to Excellence by the American Academy of Achievement. In tribute to his extraordinary career, Cukor had been chosen as one of fifty "national giants of accomplishment." The academy, honoring exceptional leaders in science and art and dedicated to inspiring America's youth, placed Cukor in the company of such past honorees as astronaut James Lovell.

The weekend included a tour of the aerospace facilities, a luncheon at the Dallas Women's Club, symposia about the "exchange of great ideas," and a barbecue ranch party. The highlight of the event was a black-tie banquet at the Fairmont Hotel, a salute to the "gathering of the greats." Cukor looked at the whole affair with characteristic humor, commenting later that it was all very "reassuringly Republican—none of those pinkos there."

The tone of the event went against the grain of Cukor's politics. "I am not a Nixon man," Cukor said in a rare political statement during the Vietnam War. He believed that the Watergate scandal and other filth happened because Nixon and his "sanctimonious, mealy-mouthed hypocrites" were running the country. On another occasion Cukor said that Jack Warner never forgave him for being one of those "despicable characters—a Democrat."

This was one of the greatest contradictions in Cukor's nature: He disliked Republican politics, but he enjoyed socializing with the rich and famous, who were in Hollywood, as in most places, Republican. Said George Eells: "George had many rich, conservative friends, like Whitney Warren, and he would joke about how the talk was always very conservative Republican right wing." But Cukor never let politics interfere with his professional or social life; cultivating friendships was his talent and specialty.

With the exception of a few attractive gay men, who could be uneducated and unsophisticated, Cukor's friends were either high achievers or wealthy.

Taken to dining at the houses of the rich, Cukor spent an evening at Alfred Bloomingdale's. He was placed one seat away from Ronald Reagan, then governor of California. Nancy Reagan and Cukor were on kissing-cousin terms, but Reagan gave him a cool and distant look, knowing the director was unsympathetic to his philosophy.

Cukor had not seen Nancy in years, but every time he encountered her, he couldn't help thinking of her MGM screen test. Spencer Tracy had asked him to test Nancy Davis, the daughter of the actor's physician. Cukor shot the test and told the studio Nancy had no talent, but she was hired anyway. In later years he made nasty remarks about the "no talent" Nancy: "If I only had a nickel for every Jew Nancy was under, I would be rich."

Cukor found Reagan a bore, and an insistent one at that. Reagan "talks at you," he told a friend, and he wasn't interested in what anyone else might have to say. At the Bloomingdale dinner party Reagan described a students' demonstration at Berkeley as he was walking to a Board of Regents meeting. There were protesters on both sides, and for all his toughness, he found this walk difficult. Cukor got the impression that Reagan really believed in what he was doing, apart from the wheeling and dealing for his own benefit.

Cukor's old friend Billie Burke died on May 14, 1970, at the age of eighty-five. The last years of her life were pretty dreary; she was too feeble to get out of bed. At the memorial service Cukor said a few "halting" words that evoked Burke's charm and distinction. He recounted how she met Flo Ziegfeld on her way to her furrier to repair her coats. There was a sable, a mink, and a chinchilla on the floor of the car. "You're the only person in the world more extravagant than I am," Ziegfeld reportedly said. "I think we should get married." Cukor recalled Burke's selfless devotion on the set of A Bill of Divorcement at a difficult time, when Ziegfeld was dying.

In the 1970s the only survivor of the old moguls was Jack Warner, who sent Cukor tickets for movie premieres, to which he took Frances Goldwyn. Upon seeing the remake of Lost Horizon, Cukor told his friends to avoid the commonplace and banal film like "the plague." In contrast, Cukor anticipated with pleasure the grand reopening of My Fair Lady. He reminded Warner of what he said when offered to direct the film: "Mr. Warner, you're making a most intelligent choice!"

Characteristically, Cukor was closer to Warner's wife, Anne, than to the studio head. Thanking her for her gift of porcelain works, he noted his weakness for anything that had a "touch of fantasie." Visualizing a love affair with her, Cukor compared her to Mrs. Tchaikovsky because they never met but only exchanged flowers. A flatterer when he needed to be, Cukor ascribed "miraculous" qualities to the ravishing white roses Anne Warner sent him from her garden.

Of all the movie stars he had worked with, Cukor kept up an active correspondence with Joan Crawford. Every Christmas there was a ritualistic exchange of presents and notes. Crawford's generosity took care of everything: For his intellectual life she gave him a splendid pen to write poems, and for his greedy nature, delicious pistachio nuts.

Cukor also didn't neglect Crawford's old MGM rival Norma Shearer. "To me you are like a king," Shearer once said after dining at his house, "living as you should be in your beautiful castle." Cukor sadly realized that Shearer had become a recluse, but in public he vehemently denied rumors she was ill, reassuring everybody she was still beautiful, still possessing her zest.

In the 1970s Cukor became closer than ever to his friend of fifty years, Frances Goldwyn; Irene Selznick once noted that she was willing to take second place only to Frances. "My mother was jealous," said her son, Sam Goldwyn Jr.; "she needed and demanded George's attention." When the younger Goldwyn called from overseas, his mother first told him the news of the immediate family, his father's business, but she then always said something about Cukor. "George was part of my growing up," Goldwyn Jr. said, "and he became close to my children. He was always there to help and advise—when needed.

"My mother was frail," Goldwyn, Jr., said. "If anybody left her for ten minutes, she couldn't take it. George forced my mother to go out." When Frances was sick, Cukor called from Russia or from wherever he was. "She kept beside her bed a picture of George as a little boy (one finger in the air) about five or six years old." Goldwyn, Jr., often saw his mother holding that picture close to her chest.

The night the senior Goldwyn died, in 1974, Cukor was the first to be informed. "At the service for my father, my mother said to me, 'You are probably amazed to find out that George has a plot with us.' There were four plots: three for my family and one for George."

After Frances's death in 1976, Cukor was distressed. "He tried not to show it," said Goldwyn, Jr., "but you could notice his depression." When Goldwyn, Jr., read Scott Berg's biography of his father, he told the writer, "You need to put in more of George." Berg put in more stuff, but Goldwyn, Jr., still believes "there isn't enough about him in the book."

Cukor went to the Hollywood Wax Museum for the unveiling of a new wax figure of his friend Mae West. It coincided with West's eagerly awaited comeback in the campy *Myra Breckinridge,* based on Gore Vidal's novel about a sex-change operation. At the preview Cukor witnessed long limousines and a mass of West's hysterical fans.

After a brilliant opening (of five minutes), *Myra Breckinridge* went steadily downhill. "I know that taste is an archaic word," Cukor told a friend, "but they sure don't have any of the good variety in this picture." About one third of the picture consisted of clips from West's earlier films, which made the new one seem uninteresting. For Cukor, Michael Sarne's movie was so stupid and vulgar that he was embarrassed to call West after the show.

Mae West was always fun to be around. Cukor orchestrated the famous meeting between Garbo and West in his house. Garbo had wanted to meet West, though she didn't anticipate West would shockingly kiss her on the mouth.

Cukor once went to a distinguished soiree at Roddy McDowall's where the guests included Beverly Sills, Mae West, and Liz Taylor. The dialogue between West and Sills was hilarious. In one of her films West sang "Mon coeur s'oeuvre à ta voix," an aria from *Samson and Delilah.* "Who did the actual singing for you?" asked the diva. "I did," answered West. "I have a trained voice." Then West asked Sills if she was acquainted with the opera. "Yes," said the singer, "but I hadn't sung it for quite a while." West replied: "It wasn't easy." Cukor almost fell on the floor.

Cukor had met Roddy McDowall when he was a child actor at Metro and always continued to describe him as the "most famous kiddie of them all." The two really became friends in 1963, when the actor went to a Fourth of July Party at Cukor's house. They saw each other frequently, after McDowall moved to California in 1971. McDowall rented a house that Cukor had inherited from Hoyningen-Huene and was in the process of buying it when it burned down.

"We struck up a friendship," McDowall recalled, "and remained close friends until he died, sharing mutual respect and enjoyment. We met everywhere, in New York, at my house, at his house. We also corresponded. George would send funny postcards from his travels. George had a very quick mind," said McDowall. "He had an amazing curiosity; everything interested him. He was one of the most practical filmmakers, he knew that in order to function, you have to be aware of the commercial base on which the profession rested. A realist, George approached work with a common sense that went hand in hand with deep artistry."

McDowall would have loved to work with Cukor, but it just never happened. "We talked about my performances," he said. "George always was very encouraging about one's work and one's future. He provided constant acting insights. He would talk about his work, but not in the sense of a career; it would just be in the sense of specific scenes or actors, and he always was funny about it.

McDowall related to Cukor on the basis of their friendship and the people they knew. "I never delved into George's past," he said, "other than what he chose to tell me. He was very discreet about his life and about your life. That's why he had so many friendships. He was probably my closest friend, but we never discussed his personal life. Our friendship was provocative and educational. George was a great lesson in life. In essence I learned how to stand up and be counted, how to be brave in a profession that is full of pitfalls; it's like walking on shifting sands. I learned how to run the course, which is one of the hardest things, not to think that everything depends on this or any movie. The overreaction in our profession, the overdamnation and praise, are phenomenal.

"George knew who he was; he knew his accomplishments. He wasn't shy, but he was modest. If you complimented George, he would make fun of it. He had enormous respect for people he considered talented. One reason George was held in such affection was his treatment of everybody—it didn't matter who they were—as if they were at the pinnacle of their achievements." Indeed, Cukor occasionally referred to *Los Angeles Times* critic Kevin Thomas as a "modern-day Hazlitt."

Cukor was loyal, generous, and candid in his advice. Allan Davis met Cukor in 1951, when he was lecturing at drama departments in the United States. An experienced stage director, Davis was invited after this trip to MGM as a film director. He did a minor picture and asked Cukor to see it. "You're a comedy director, kid," Cukor said. Recalled Davis: "This was very important because I was young and I still wanted to change the world. And nobody had specifically said that to me before." Davis went back to London, where he directed many successful comedies, but he was forever grateful to Cukor for his advice and for asking him to do screen tests for *Bhowani Junction*.

Cukor enjoyed helping his friends. When Kevin Thomas went to Europe, Cukor called Alec McCowen in London and gave the critic letters of introduction to his friends all over Europe. Days before he left, Thomas learned that a retrospective of Cukor's work was planned at the County Museum. "I've got to cancel my trip," said Thomas, but Cukor characteristically said, "No, no, no, Kevin, there is such a thing as too much publicity."

In the 1970s Cukor realized there was strong interest in the Old Hollywood. "Oh, the blessed enthusiasm of the young," he would say. A young interviewer, who knew more about Cukor's pictures than he did, made Cukor feel as if he were writing his obituary. People wondered how Cukor had lived under the tyranny of the Old Hollywood, but actually he lamented the passage of the big studios: The old system was comfortable; its facilities enormously helpful. "Cukor benefited from the system," agent Ben Benjamin said; "the studios respected him."

Cukor missed the good old days, when the studios were arranged with some kind of order, and now perceived the old moguls as "great showmen with curiously good taste who created something extraordinary." Louis B. was never nice to Cukor, but "he cared and was organized and he knew how to develop stars." Harry Cohn had terrible reputation offscreen for being tough and stingy, but "he was also intelligent and encouraged you if you had anything to give."

At present a hit movie went very quickly; after a week it was forgotten. That was the reason why the new movie stars lasted for such a short time. The sad thing for Cukor was the lack of training for the new stars to develop their talents. Garbo had had a chance to develop as an actress, but nowadays a star made a quick success, got public attention, and was immediately given too much power.

With all his criticism, however, Cukor remained hopeful, ever denying the film industry was dead. "Not by a long shot," he said. "It's different, but it still has enormous vitality." In one specific way, the movie industry was better than in the past: It was more respectfully treated by the critics and public.

One of the old institutions Cukor did *not* miss was the Production Code. He remembered all too vividly the nonsense he had to go through— timing a kiss with a stopwatch or checking Crawford's décolletage within a sixteenth of an inch. When a husband and a wife were in a nuptial bed, one of them had to have feet planted on the floor. As for a nonhusband and wife in a nonnuptial bed—heaven forbid!

Cukor confessed that he was taken aback by the new films. "I'd hate to take Mama to see *Last Tango in Paris,* even though it had wonderful things in it." As for nudity, Cukor held there was more eroticism generated by women like Crawford fully clothed. The new vulgarity, sacrificing everything for the fast buck, upset Cukor; the pernicious effect of this tastelessness was that it alienated the family audience.

Cukor read all the new fan journalism at his chiropodist. The lurid magazines there would have had to close up shop if they hadn't had Jackie Kennedy and Liz Taylor. Asked why there were no great film personalities, he replied, "Where are the great personalities in life? This is not the age of overwhelming personalities."

His taste was admittedly conservative. Cukor's movie queens were devastatingly pretty, but the new stars were not presented at their best; the world had toughened them up in an unattractive way. In "this revolution," Cukor claimed, the men looked a hell of a lot better than the women. He couldn't tell whether the new stars were pretty or not; from the way they were presented by their directors they seemed to lack charm and dignity. Cukor talked at length about the "lack of looks" and the "craze of nudity."

Cukor's point of reference was Mike Nichols, the new genius in Hollywood. He didn't like Nichols's first film, *Who's Afraid of Virginia Woolf?* because Richard Burton missed much of the humor, and Liz Taylor played Martha as a whore. He detested the way Anne Bancroft was presented in *The Graduate,* though he liked Dustin Hoffman. Nichols's *Carnal Knowledge* was shrewd but still a "hateful" picture about cheap cynicism—the kind of life he always thought was a bore. "Marilyn Monroe, walking across the screen, not trying to be sexy, had more eroticism than Candice Bergen in *Carnal Knowledge.* Her character was hard and stupid and she didn't act well."

To Cukor, this cult of ugliness, with unappetizing-looking women, was hideous, as if the audience were watching someone sitting on a toilet. To do a scene that required sex, actors had to be charming or erotic. "A love scene has to be a *scene,*" he explained, "but today it's all exhibitionistic and pointless." Hope, love—the human scale—were simply missing from the new American movies.

Surprisingly, Cukor found a lot of charm and humor in Paul Morrissey's *Trash* and *Flesh*. "George was a fan of my pictures," Morrissey allowed. "He gave interviews saying he'd liked *Flesh,* which was very nice. You feel you're really in the league when somebody like Cukor likes you. What George really liked," Morrissey explained, "was performances that were natural and seemed unactorish. It was the same qualities he looked for in his actors, that they surprise him, that they show spontaneity. The performers in my films seemed lifelike, and lifelike was what he admired."

By the summer of 1970 Cukor was hard at work on his next movie, based on Graham Greene's novel *Travels with My Aunt.* Cukor read the novel in 1969 and was instantly drawn to it. It was a rare combination of robust adventure and funny comedy, he said, "a good story in which, for once, Greene does not find God." The tale follows the adventures of Aunt Augusta, an eccentric Englishwoman in her seventies, as she travels about the globe with Henry, her straitlaced nephew in tow. The "disreputable" Augusta introduces her stuffy middle-aged nephew to a life of freedom and fun.

Cukor liked the novel's freshness and was particularly intrigued by the character of Augusta: "An old woman who's been through the mill, she's very wrong-headed and commits follies." Augusta was in many ways like Cukor himself: "She lived a sinful life, but she's not meanspirited. And despite her tribulations, she is not sour or bitter." Augusta, like Cukor, rejected age the way she would an unworthy suitor. Cukor had a strong aversion toward depressed people—in his life and in his films.

There was no question in Cukor's mind that Katharine Hepburn, then in her sixties, would make a perfect Augusta. If Augusta were played by a middle-aged actress, the film might too closely echo *Auntie Mame*, a pitfall Cukor wanted to avoid. The novelty of an elderly woman involved in marijuana, sexual freedom, and interracial romance, all topical ingredients, would be really funny. With Hepburn in the lead role, Cukor hoped to make a stylish, relevant movie. It wasn't difficult talking Hepburn into playing the zany septuagenarian. She immediately realized what a wonderful part it was; parts like this did not often come along for someone her age. It was a year, however, before Hepburn committed herself to the film.

As expected, Graham Greene sold the book outright and would have no role in the production of *Travels with My Aunt*. A joint venture was thus established between GDC and Robert Fryer Productions. With MGM behind the project, and a $3.5 million budget, the search for a writer began. Cukor wanted Peter Shaffer, the renowned English playwright, but they couldn't come to terms with him. Instead Hugh Wheeler, also British, was chosen.

Cukor knew that the novel's odyssey structure would translate to the screen, but the important thing, the force that propelled the characters, was still missing. Because the narrative rests on a number of "revelations"—that Augusta might not be Henry's aunt but possibly his mother—the picture should have the "do you believe this?" camp quality of movies like *Tom Jones*.

Wheeler submitted the first script draft in July 1970 and for the next months worked closely on its development with Cukor. Hepburn, or "Miss Coco," as Cukor called her because of the musical she was doing, read the draft and made suggestions, too. The actress soon became active in developing her part.

In August Cukor left to spend a week in New York, where the Museum of Modern Art honored him with a retrospective. He stayed at the Garson Kanins' apartment on Central Park South. In a week of nonstop activity, Cukor combined business and pleasure, visiting friends and having meetings related to new projects. The evening of his arrival, Cukor dined with a friend, Bob Linden at one of his favorite Manhattan restaurants, the Running Footman. The next evening he dined with several male friends at the Diners Club. As was his habit, he methodically recorded the expenses: That night the cost was $42.80, plus $2.55 tax and $7.50 in tips.

On August 24 Cukor had a meeting with MOMA's curators to discuss the retrospective. The following day was equally hectic, beginning with a meeting with a literary agent, to discuss his biography. In the afternoon he met with MOMA's Gary Carey and film critic Pauline Kael.

Amid his nonstop schedule, Cukor was able to meet with Wheeler and discuss the progress on the script and the changes that he and Hepburn had requested. Cukor spent the early part of the evening with Laura Harding, who had played a society girl in *A Bill of Divorcement*. He humorously told her that he still thought it a pity that she had given up a promising career.

The MOMA retrospective opened on August 26 with a screening of *Holiday*. It reflected Cukor's choice; MOMA originally wanted to begin the series with a "gutsier" statement, *Sylvia Scarlett,* but he opted for a more "respectable" attraction. There was a comic note in MOMA's choice, for when *Sylvia Scarlett* opened, it had been a disaster, as noted earlier. Cukor, who had never liked the film, couldn't understand how "by some curious alchemy" the film had acquired a cult status.

A reception at the museum followed the screening. Cukor had invited his friends quoting the immortal words of Mrs. Joe E. Brown: "Just because I'm Mrs. Joe E. Brown, I don't want you to think that *I* think I'm any better than you." He hoped he didn't put a strain on his old friends, but it was important for him that they attend. Paul Morrissey, Roddy McDowall, and old friends like Irene Selznick and Mary Goldwater all were there.

The airing of a documentary, *The Life and Times of George Cukor,* coincided with the MOMA retrospective. In a letter to Garbo Cukor joked about how he'd reached that advanced stage in life when people made documentaries, but he wouldn't consider a fair representation of his work without *Camille*. Offended that Garbo didn't respond, he complained that she was as "elusive" as ever. Not knowing how the documentary had turned out, Cukor asked his friends to see it at their own risk. He did like its last scene, which ended on a personal note, with Hepburn firmly nailing a flag at his house.

On August 30 Cukor flew back to L.A. and immediately threw himself into *Travels with My Aunt*. Despite Wheeler's efforts to retain much of the novel, Hepburn had strong reservations about the text. In Spain, recovering from a face-lift, she received a cable from Cukor: "Script en route. Changes being made. Please phone after reading." Everyone associated with the project wanted Hepburn to do the picture. MGM's Russell Thatcher thought they should go to the very end of the line with Hepburn, so that no one could ever say they hadn't done everything possible to accommodate her.

A visit to Hepburn in Spain was the first stop on a trip to Europe Cukor began in the fall. As soon as he arrived in Madrid, he lunched with

Hepburn at the hotel. They went over the most recent changes in the script; it seemed to be going well. In London Cukor stayed in the luxury executive suite at the Grosvenor Hotel, which was nice and its price right. It was good-bye to the Savoy Hotel, without regrets. The last time at the Savoy Cukor had been given a noisy suite and been overcharged, after years of staying there. He took a greater suite than the usual in order to interview people and asked MGM to share in the cost.

Irene Burns was instructed to keep after Metro so that it would not be delinquent in its payments. This issue made Cukor feel like a character in an early Arthur Wing Pinero play, a ne'er-do-well, always waiting for a check that sometimes came and sometimes didn't. That was Cukor's history with Metro, always humiliated for having to call up. But this time he resolved: No more nonsense.

In Paris Cukor was met by Simone Signoret and Costa-Gavras. He lunched with René Clair at Yves Montand's, went to the theater with Claudette Colbert, and had dinner with playwright Pierre Barillet. Cukor also met George Towers and his wife, Sharon, in Paris. After Towers got married, their relationship changed, but they continued to be friends.

Neither Cukor nor the producers were satisfied with Wheeler's third draft. The feeling was that in dialogue and character definition, he couldn't give what Cukor was asking for. However, Thatcher was hesitant to bring in a new writer, fearing that ego would force any writer of stature to make drastic changes. Thatcher therefore undertook to rewrite the dialogue and make the characters sharper, offering to work with Cukor, scene by scene, page by page, to get the script exactly as the director wanted it.

In April 1971 *Coco* opened in L.A., and Cukor went to see it again. He found the production brisk and lively; begrudgingly he even complimented Cecil Beaton's work as "creditable." Most of his praise, however, was reserved for Hepburn, whose achievement was in creating a believable and entrancing woman. Hepburn's vitality and joyous performance overcame the compromising material—and devastating reviews. *Coco* was to close in the summer, at which time Cukor expected Hepburn to turn her full attention to *Travels*.

Casting Henry was trickier because the part was not as well written as Augusta. Looking for an actor in his forties, Cukor thought that although Paul Scofield was first-class, he was too "dreary." Alec McCowen was ultimately chosen on Allan Davis's recommendation. "I was the one who suggested McCowen," Davis said. "George was worried at first because he wanted John Gielgud." McCowen read his part one afternoon at Hepburn's apartment. "It was like an audition," he recalled. "When I finished reading, I expected to get fired, but instead everybody applauded."

Casting seemed less problematic than the continuing ordeal with the script. By September 1971 Cukor reported to Thatcher that the script had been improved, if not shortened. In weak moments Cukor believed the Holy Spirit itself was needed to bless this endeavor. Screenwriter Chester Erskine was then brought on board to work on the script. In December 1971 Cukor reported that at the risk of sounding optimistic, the script was now sophisticated, funny, plot-clear, and shootable and carried out the author's intention, if he'd had any.

But after months of agonizing about the script, Cukor's temper was beginning to flare. After one heated telephone exchange with Erskine, he received a terse response to his queries. The character of Aunt Augusta in his script could be easily explained: She was Hepburn. As for costumes, they should be ultramodern, though this was Cukor's problem, not Erskine's. Erskine's job was to make order out of chaos. These arguments, however, were never too serious—"just an exercise in nerves." They lasted a few minutes, then were forgotten. Working ten or twelve hours a day, both men were tired and cranky.

Ironically, after months of working on the script, much of which was intended to accommodate Hepburn, she never appeared in the picture. She was fired before shooting began. The star was never happy with the revisions imposed by MGM's James Aubrey. MGM refused to comment on her departure, and Cukor also declined to talk about it. In public he said that Hepburn's leaving was based on an "honest disagreement" and that everyone was very "civilized." It was not true.

"It was public knowledge that he was going to leave *Travels with My Aunt* when Kate was fired," said Roddy McDowall. "That's an extremely moral behavior. For George, you don't start a project, if you have any mettle, with one person who's a close friend and have him scuttled. It's a person of lesser fabric who will say, 'You're fired, I'll go on with another person.' "

After the picture was completed, Cukor felt freer to talk about the scandal. It wasn't Hepburn's fault; she was badly dealt with by the studio. "She's a generous, scrupulous, noble creature—one of the few extant." Cukor thought Hepburn behaved with the greatest generosity. "You should wham them with a big damage suit," he told her. "They cheated you. You have a way of being above this sort of thing, but in this case don't be above 'getting the dough' for all the work you did."

"I worked a long time on the script," Hepburn confirmed. "Then I guess they thought I was too bossy. The studio believed I told George what to do; they didn't want an actor to be telling him, 'Do this, do that.' Before they fired me," Hepburn noted, "George said, 'If you don't do it, I'm not going to do it.' He wanted to withdraw, but I wouldn't let him."

Fortunately Cukor was able to replace Hepburn quickly. After a brief consideration of Angela Lansbury, they turned to British actress Maggie Smith, who was available. Cukor knew Smith's work on stage and in film, and she had recently won an Oscar for *The Prime of Miss Jean Brodie*. When Smith was criticized for taking Hepburn's role, Cukor defended her as an innocent bystander. "We were damned lucky to get her; everyone but the wretched MGM behaved impeccably."

Scouting locations in Portugal began in November. Looking at some possible sites for the film's Panama sequences, Cukor drove to Setúbal, about forty minutes from Lisbon, to see the area near the waterfront, but he did not feel it was tropical enough. The Portuguese locations were never used.

A major chunk of the budget was trimmed by constructing a production unit in Madrid and allowing just one major move to England. Most of *Travels with My Aunt* was shot at an abandoned railroad station. "It's the station that changed costume every day," McCowen noted. Of the thirteen-week schedule, there were six weeks in the studio and seven on location, including a few days in London. With sixty-eight shooting days and a script of 102 pages, Cukor was expected to produce 1.5 page per day. It was manageable.

Cukor received a living allowance of a thousand dollars per week above his director's fee. Knowing he would be on location for months, he packed well. He took with him his double-breasted blue and brown suits, silk lounging pajamas, a gray terry-cloth robe, black and brown shoes, six books, sleeveless sweaters, a red dressing gown, eighteen shirts, six silk handkerchiefs, and long johns.

The cast settled into a nice shooting routine, though not before a flare-up about Maggie Smith's makeup. "To get the effect of being a seventy-year-old woman," McCowen said, "she had to wear pounds of rubber makeup. It was terribly uncomfortable, and if it stayed on too long, it burned her skin."

For various reasons, Cukor had to shoot at night. This was absolutely hell for him because his vitality was always low at night. Cukor enjoyed working with the two pros, Smith and McCowen, who knew each other well from the theater. It also helped that both had a thorough grasp on their characters' eccentricities.

But directing novice Cindy Williams was another story. Williams read for Cukor when he couldn't find an actress to play the ingenue. "He offered me the part two days later," she said. "They were hard pressed as they were leaving for Spain."

In his instructions to her Cukor was direct and succinct. "Mr. Cukor liked to talk about each line," said Williams. "It was his way of bringing the vision out of his mind and into the material. We did the first scene inside the train, when I was crying about being pregnant, thirteen times."

McCowen was getting tired after the seventh take, but Cukor screamed, 'Do it again, again!' " Before rolling the cameras, Cukor asked her, "Do you have the words? Now forget everything I said, and do it your way." Williams recalled: "I went into a state of panic. I was young. I could not draw from anything in my past to do the scene."

Cukor could be harsh and cruel. "I don't think I grasped the enormity of the project," Williams noted. "I didn't put it in my head that I was so inexperienced. Mr. Cukor was bigger than life; his was a very savvy direction to be given at the age of twenty-three. Oddly enough," she said, "I went from Roger Corman to George Cukor. It was an entirely different experience and extremely frightening."

According to the actress, Cukor wanted to get results quickly. "He resented the fact that he had to wait for me to be ready for a scene." Not knowing the script was sacred for Cukor, Williams made a mistake and argued over a line, saying her character wouldn't say "fuzz" but "cop." Cukor jumped on her: " 'What does the script say?' He wanted it true to form, like art history, you don't change anything. At the end I just nodded to everything he said; he was pleased with that."

Williams was terrified of her big scene at the train station. Cukor told her over and over, "You can do it, damn it."

"It just overwhelmed me," Williams recalled. "All I wanted was to please him, but I couldn't. Alec came to my caravan to console me and invited me to his hotel for a drink. Later Mr. Cukor sent someone to get me, he wanted to talk about the scene, but I wanted to avoid him at all costs. I left the caravan and hid behind it for some time."

McCowen acknowledged that Cukor was "extremely impatient with Cindy because he didn't trust her. And he did it in front of the whole crew, which was embarrassing. George lost his temper and took a personal antipathy to her."

"I didn't understand that Mr. Cukor was trying to train me," said Williams. "I guess he had to be cruel to be kind. He was like a tough football coach, trying to prepare me for my career. It was a major test. I was thrown into fire."

McCowen was an experienced stage, but not film, actor. What he mostly remembered about Cukor is "the way he could relax me. Before each take, George would whisper in my ear a useful advice, like 'Drop your shoulders' or 'Don't pop up your eyes.' It was mostly physical things, but he did it very discreetly."

Knowing everyone's job, Cukor interfered in the jobs of the sets and prop people. "If something wasn't right," said McCowen, "he demanded changes. He would tell the propman, 'Aunt Augusta would not use book matches; she would use box matches,' and then would proceed to name specific match companies."

At the same time Cukor hated to be helped. "If the cameraman would make a suggestion, George would jump and scream, 'Don't teach me how to do my job.' Strangely, George was slow in staging the simple scenes, like moving the action from one room to another. It seemed he had forgotten how to get people around. Somehow things became easily confused, and he got upset. He lost his temper at least half a dozen times."

In Madrid Cukor was staying at the luxurious Palace Hotel. "We often ate in a bachelor group in George's suite," recalled Walter Alford, who was in charge of publicity. "He would keep food up there, and we would bring good wine." They met at the hotel almost every night because there was nothing else to do. "George never liked to be alone," Alford said. "He liked to have people around to eat and talk with." In these informal sessions the guests would listen enraptured to Cukor's anecdotes about his work. Alford was close to Cukor but "only as a worshiping acolyte."

Beginning a relationship that in tone was like that "between uncle and nephew," McCowen also got close to Cukor. "George showed interest in my career; he came to see all my plays." One evening he brought Gregory Peck and Kirk Douglas to see *Equus*. "George used to make fun of me because I was born in the small town mentioned in *The Importance of Being Earnest* and because I had lots of aunts."

One of McCowen's fondest memories is the "look on George's face when he saw chocolate because he was always on a diet." The actor also noticed the director's well-known frugality: "Even though he was staying in a luxurious suite that was paid for, at the end of the evening he would put the old tonic back in the refrigerator." Friends who went out with Cukor were often embarrassed when he asked the waiter to pack his dessert if he couldn't eat it.

Shooting six days a week, Cukor came in only one day over schedule. In April Metro's bosses were reportedly enthusiastic about the rushes. Cukor warned, however, "Beware when the crew breaks up with laughter on the set." He couldn't help remembering the enthusiasm during *Sylvia Scarlett*—and what a disaster that turned out to be.

During the shoot Cukor kept in close contact with his secretary. As was his practice, he asked Burns to send some food supplies, like Romanoff's MBT instant mix for prime broth. She kept him abreast of the affairs at 9611 Cordell Drive. The house was included in a grand tour sponsored by a museum, and the housekeepers had spent a whole week beautifying it. It was a huge success. There were no damages or mishaps, and the two thousand people who showed up were filled with admiration for Cukor's taste.

Knowing Cukor's attachment to his dogs, Burns wrote about them in great detail. Her reports, especially the stories about Cappy, his favorite dog, made him homesick. She described how Cappy lay on the terrace waiting for Lee, the gardener, to walk him out. Cappy greeted him with a magnolia leaf in his mouth, then rushed to the closet for his leash. After his mother died, Cukor found that she'd kept every single letter he had written to her. It was almost the same dull letter over and over again, but she didn't mind them. He now hoped that Burns would be just as indulgent as his mother had been.

The ending of *Travels with My Aunt* was problematic and unsatisfactory. Cukor did consider another ending: what went on inside Augusta's head as the coin was flipped. He wanted the audience to wonder, What is going to happen? Who will influence whom? But it was a comedy, and when he came to a certain point in the story, that was the point to stop.

A select group of "typical" moviegoers—no show business types— gathered at the studio on September 25 for a preview. The picture played well, and the audience was completely engrossed, Cukor told McCowen: no wavering of interest and no bad laughs. There were plenty of good ones in the right places.

For the next two weeks Cukor was on the road, hustling *Travels with My Aunt*. He went to Toronto, Detroit, Philadelphia, and other cities, hoping to come back in "one piece." Cukor did it of his free will; MGM's "white slavers" didn't force him. In his publicity tours Cukor told the press that he consciously chose a romanticized version of the hard-bitten book. Cukor also singled out Smith's brilliance as an actress; he'd had to temper what he said to her because she could do anything. Cukor placed Smith in the pantheon of that rare breed of performers who were great stage and screen stars.

Though Cukor liked Smith, he was still angry at the way Hepburn had been mistreated by Metro. "Your scenes played wonderfully," Cukor told Hepburn; "they were funny, moving, and adroit. I'm not being disloyal to Maggie—she is really splendid, skillful—but the glory that you'd have given it is not there."

Anxious to get Hepburn's response to the film, Cukor was disappointed when she was no more than polite. "I didn't think it was brilliant," Hepburn said, "you can only be as good as the script, but if the script is mediocre, anything you do is mediocre."

The film's notices were mixed, though Pauline Kael's review was really condemning. "The film seems to run down before it gets started," she wrote. "Maybe the material couldn't have made it anyway, but for it to have a fighting chance the director should have a ravishing style and the actress who plays Aunt Augusta needs a charismatic presence; both are impossible to fake, and in this movie George Cukor and Maggie Smith don't have them—though they try exhaustingly hard." Cukor struggled for a light touch, but the camera seemed to go off on its own. His movie was too diffuse, failing to keep the viewers involved in the story.

Kael disliked Smith's performance, which was "full of busywork, and many body tilts and high-piping vocal effects." Smith badly overacted; everything in her character was italicized; she seemed to mimic the great English actress Edith Evans. The London critics also attacked Smith for being too mannered and falling back on technical tricks. Ironically they savaged Smith's performance on the very day she received an Oscar nomination for the role.

To Cukor's credit, *Travels with My Aunt* wasn't as stale as Rosalind Russell's vehicle *Auntie Mame,* but the movie went overboard. Uneven in quality, it appeared as if Cukor weren't in control. And of course, everyone seemed to agree that an older woman should have played the part. "When you begin to speculate about who should have played a role," Kael noted, "it means that the person on the screen doesn't touch your imagination."

A Christmas release, to qualify for the Oscars, *Travels with My Aunt* was nominated, aside from Best Actress, for Art Direction, Costume Design, Cinematography, and Song. The movie won one Oscar, for Anthony Powell's costumes, which Cukor accepted for him. Standing next to Greer Garson at the grand finale, Cukor joined everybody's singing of "You Ought to Be in Pictures."

The year 1972 was for Cukor a year of getting recognition as a filmmaker. In September the Los Angeles County Museum presented a retrospective of twenty-one of his films. An article by Charles Champlin in the *Los Angeles Times* did a lot to promote the tribute and elevate Cukor's status: "Cukor is one of the most literate storytellers, remarkable not least because he continues to work and work well after all his contemporaries have retired or found it impossible to cope with a changed Hollywood."

Ron Haver, the curator who organized the tribute, recalled how he introduced Cukor as "the man who was fired from *Gone with the Wind*." Said Haver: "George gave me a strange look; he didn't like it. I could tell I committed a major breach, but I was trying to be funny." After this incident Cukor labeled Haver "wise-ass." Haver said: "You didn't mess with George. You had to be careful. He demanded good manners and appreciated good breeding."

On November 17 Cukor flew for a retrospective of his work at Washington's Kennedy Center for the Arts. Flattered that it was the first time films were shown there, he found the place impressive. The critics were completely wrong to criticize the auditorium's size; the packed audiences for his old movies proved his point.

These retrospectives coincided with the publication of the first book about him, *On Cukor,* by Gavin Lambert. "It was initiated by the AFI [American Film Institute]," Lambert recalled. "They felt it was important, particularly when the directors were getting on in years, to interview them and to get a general rundown, from the horse's mouth, of their careers." Lambert agreed to do the interview on the condition that he could also publish it as a book.

Lambert had met Cukor after *My Fair Lady* through a social contact, and they "personally clicked on." Cukor had always wanted to film a novel by Lesley Blanch, *The Nine-Tiger Man*. He wanted Lambert to do the script, but he couldn't get it off the ground. What struck Lambert about Cukor was that "unlike other directors of his generation, whose careers were beginning to wind down, George was so unbitter. He was interested in the new generation, terribly eager to recognize talent when he saw it. Talent of any kind just turned him on. He loved to see talent, to respond and encourage it. His record shows how many unknown people he launched in his movies."

The working procedure for the book was that the day after a screening, they would talk about the particular movie screened. Lambert suggested that when he didn't think the movies were particularly good, and Cukor agreed, they wouldn't be included. He didn't want his book to be a total rundown of Cukor's career, thinking it would be more interesting, since it was done in the dialogue format, to talk about the movies they both liked.

Sometimes Lambert liked a movie better than Cukor did. In the case of *Sylvia Scarlett,* the critic had to persuade Cukor it was interesting enough to be included. "Like other directors," said Lambert, "when there was a notorious commercial flop, George preferred not to think or talk about it. It was the only sign of insecurity in George I ever saw. He got nervous about discussing a failure." Lambert also noticed that when Cukor wasn't pleased with a film as a whole, he looked for something incidental he liked, like the character actors.

The two got along very well. "I could only do this with someone I felt rapport with," Cukor told Lambert. "Somebody else tried to do a book about me, and it didn't work because I couldn't open up." Cukor felt he could open up to Lambert, though the latter played it safe by deciding to write a book about his movies, not his life.

Later Cukor asked Lambert if he would do a biography of him. "I decided not to," Lambert recalled, "because I knew he would never talk about his personal life. He had worked in an era when you had to be very secretive about homosexuality. It wasn't a secret about George, but it was never publicized. There was a kind of agreement between the studios and the gossip people," Lambert noted. "If somebody was really important, they wouldn't touch him."

Indeed, another writer, Hector Arce, began a biography of Cukor. Arce had published a piece about Katharine Hepburn in *Women's Wear Daily,* which Cukor thought was witty and funny. When he read the piece aloud to his friends, it played remarkably well. Cukor anticipated "gnashing of teeth" all the way from London, for Hepburn had not even mentioned Beaton (who designed her costumes in *Coco*). This by-product of the story still tickled Cukor.

Arce submitted an outline of the proposed book, titled *Getting On,* to Atheneum in 1971, but the results Arce produced, after six months of work were not satisfactory. While in Madrid, Cukor gave Walter Alford a draft of Arce's book. "George asked me to read one chapter and tell him what I thought of it," Alford said. "I took a day off and read the entire manuscript." Alford told Cukor that Arce had flattened out every anecdote he had told so vividly: "George was a great raconteur; he would keep us in stitches."

In August 1972 Cukor worked on the introduction of the book, which was going to begin with some telling observations: "I have discovered that everything—including affection and respect—has to be earned in life." Cukor conceded that his friendships usually started with business relationships, but the lines often blurred. His friendships flourished for the most part in his own house. "I only ask people I really like to come here, to be unguarded and at their best. My house is an enormous responsibility, one I relish in, a living organism, like a string of pearls that has to be constantly worn to retain its beauty."

The table of contents was revealing, too. The introduction, "Flashbacks from a Women's Director," was followed by chapters like "Insights" (Tallulah, Hepburn, the Judys, Bergman, and Magnani), "Elegances" (Ethel Barrymore, Norma Shearer, Audrey Hepburn, and Gladys Cooper), "The Symbols" (Harlow, Gardner, and Monroe), "The Leading Men" (Barrymore, Grant, Tracy, Colman, Harrison, and Bogarde). There were also going to be chapters on "Studio Heads" (Mayer, Thalberg, Cohn, Warner, Selznick), and "The Literati" (Maugham, the Sitwells, Walpole, and Barrie). The last section of the book was appropriately titled "House and Garden."

But as in the past, there was not much there to base a contract on. The editor understood the difficulties of getting down on paper the style of a man as complex as Cukor but, on the basis of what was written, it did not seem like an interesting book.

Cukor was very pleased that *On Cukor* came off well. But the book was not highly publicized because Putnam's, its publisher, was going through some changes. It sold moderately, but not as well as Cukor had hoped. He sent reviews of the book to his friends, adopting this habit of clipping articles from the Garson Kanins. Whizzes on publicity, they had an elaborate system of sending out flattering notices; that was how their friendship with Cukor had begun after *The Philadelphia Story*. Cukor now joked about being "infected" with the Kanins' shameless mania for publicity.

Cukor was offended by Charles Higham's review in *The New York Times,* which questioned his status as an artist. Higham's observation "Lambert does not quite settle that crucial question which the director himself would embarrassedly avoid: Is Cukor an artist?" was hard for Cukor to swallow. Fortunately his friend George Eells came to his defense and in a letter to the *Times* cited Katharine Hepburn in a BBC interview: "You were and are totally an artist."

But the question of what kind of artist Cukor was still remained. "David Lean was a master of moviemaking," Hepburn said. "I don't think Cukor had that mastery, the pictorial imagination that Lean had. Lean's pictures have incredible vision; they are thrilling." According to her, Cukor never starred himself. "John Huston took himself very seriously; so did Hitchcock, who had respect for his own work. But I didn't feel Cukor thought he was brilliant; he probably thought he was very good at what he did."

Auteurist critic Andrew Sarris writes in his influential book *The American Cinema:* "When a director has consistently dished up tasteful entertainment of a high order for half a century, it's clear he's more than a mere entertainer; he is a genuine artist." Sarris doesn't include Cukor in his highest category of "Pantheon Directors," a place reserved for John Ford, Alfred Hitchcock, Orson Welles, and their like. But Cukor appears in Sarris's second category, "The Far Side of Paradise," along with Frank Capra and Preston Sturges, "directors who fall short of the Pantheon either because of a fragmentation of their personal vision or because of disruptive career problems."

French director François Truffaut, who admired Cukor's work, held that along with Elia Kazan, Cukor was the best actor's director in Hollywood. But even Truffaut noted that "Cukor isn't the kind of director you write about; he's someone to talk about with friends on the street or sitting in a café." The French filmmaker did not mean this in a derogatory way, but he put his finger on a recurrent problem in film criticism: What to do about Cukor and how to evaluate his work? Cukor's oeuvre is so commercial, seamless, and effortless that it erroneously appears to be without distinctions.

Movie magazine, in a recent "talent histogram," ranked Cukor below Howard Hawks and Alfred Hitchcock but had virtually nothing to say about him. "Cukor has presented a problem," Edward Buscombe observed. "He is a great director, but there is, literally, nothing to say about him." Only those who admire self-effacement, a light touch, and invisibility as a style single out Cukor's greatness.

Cukor was neither the author of his narratives (like Billy Wilder or Joseph Mankiewicz) nor the producer of his films (like Otto Preminger or George Stevens). His career and status resemble William Wyler's, another underrated director. Like Wyler (*Dodsworth, The Little Foxes, The Letter*), Cukor believed in faithfully transposing to the screen the works of other writers. And like Wyler's "style without style," Cukor's self-effacement deprived him of the reputation he undoubtedly deserved.

No matter how one looks at Cukor's work, he was an auteur—thematically and stylistically. The preoccupation with the theater world as a thematic locale enabled him to comment on the tension between reality and illusion, the collision between fact and fantasy. As Sarris notes, Cukor's work is "committed to the dreamer, if not to the content of the dream." Cukor's dreamers exist within multiple layers of deception and confusion, striving to achieve a more realistic sense of self. Reflecting the complexity and hardness of everyday life, Cukor's movies stress the necessity of making choices and the ironic conviction that even seemingly secure identities and relationships always shift and change.

Larger than life, Cukor's characters are imbued with extraordinary humanity that makes them eccentric yet accessible. Stylistically, too, Cukor is interesting: His elegant approach, taut narratives, lively and fluent dialogues, and flawless acting all are qualities of his best films. Cukor's camera moved smoothly, serving the text rather than him or his actors—all the more amazing because many of his players were big stars. In their style Cukor's films refrained from exhibitionism; his camera did not intrude with sharp cuts or tricky angles.

Cukor himself provided the best explanation of his approach: "In my case, style must be largely the absence of style." There may have been a director "whose reputation is based on a certain hallmark which he imprints on all his work to subject every new story and scene to his own style and personality." But such directors—Hitchcock, Ford, Welles— were rare. In contrast, Cukor perceived himself as an interpretive director "whose end is to extract the best that all his fellow-workers have to give, and who is best pleased when the finished picture shows to the layman in the audience no visible sign of direction." He told Lambert: "The text dictates the whole style, which may not be to the director's advantage because it means his touch is not immediately recognizable."

At their best Cukor's movies are intelligent, witty, unmanipulative, and respectful of their audiences. His sophistication served him well in balancing the comic and dramatic aspects of his narratives. He was great at satirizing human foibles and self-delusions. He also excelled at sustaining the right emotional pace (he called it momentum) of his varied pictures. In his evaluation Champlin describes Cukor as "one of the most literate storytellers the movies have yet produced. Few directors are more adept at dealing with articulate characters, or at placing them in the well-observed and accurately reproduced milieus which both shape and help to explain the characters."

Despite singular achievements, Cukor always defined himself as a product of the studio system, a "typical Hollywood director" whose aim was no more—but no less—than entertainment. He subscribed to the notion of film as a collaborative art and of the director as coordinator or supervisor of the writer, actors, and crew. But Cukor's art goes beyond passive collaboration. "He was smart enough to get good material and good writing," said James Lee Herlihy. "He knew how to get stars to bring their charm and talent to his movies." Cukor's greatest talent was "knowing the importance of other people's work and getting the best available people."

But being a generous collaborator worked against Cukor. Gary Carey's book was unfairly titled *Cukor and Co.* as if Cukor's collaborators were more responsible than he was for his films' quality. It may be valid to claim that Cukor's personality in film is subservient to that of his writers and actors and that his sensibility can best be grasped from the type of collaborator with whom he worked most felicitously. But it's unfair to deny Cukor his genuine talent—and taste—in bringing out the best of every artist he worked with.

Unfortunately, even critics who detect a distinctive Cukor style have deprived him of the credit he deserved. In the final account it was Cukor who shaped his films, and his work does bear his own signature. Working with different editors and cinematographers suggests that the "special look and charm" of Cukor's films cannot be attributed to one or a few artists. The consistent display of coherent style shows that an idiosyncratic vision defined Cukor's films.

Holding that good directors are versatile, Cukor directed a wide range of movies, making forays into psychological thrillers (*Gaslight*), film noir (*Keeper of the Flame, A Double Life*), literary classics (*Little Women, David Copperfield, Romeo and Juliet*), plays (*Edward, My Son*), and musicals (*A Star is Born, Les Girls*). However, Cukor was at his best with sophisticated comedies (*Holiday, The Philadelphia Story*), which became his defining genre and his most important contribution to the American cinema.

Cukor admitted he was "green with envy" reading about the star-studded parties publishers gave to other biographies, but the "inept, cheap, and listless" Putnam's did little to promote *On Cukor*. He complained about Putnam's minimal advertising and its neglect to stack the book in the stores. It was MGM, not Putnam's, that sent copies to reviewers, hoping the book would help promote *Travels with My Aunt*. Cukor almost threw in the towel, but his better nature told him to hustle the book. John Dodds of Putnam's explained that he'd had the "devil's time" in lining up TV shows. Dodds thought that unless they got major shows, there was no point in doing the small radio and TV daytime interviews. Cukor was disappointed.

The British edition of *On Cukor* came out at the end of 1972 and its publisher did a "more enterprising" job than the wretched Putnam's. The book's promotional line, "Cukor Tells All," amused him, for readers might be led to believe he was going to reveal as tantalizing episodes as Cecil Beaton's "Love Story with Garbo." With the book's failure to generate interest, Cukor now hoped for a greater success with a full-fledged biography. He was frustrated; many movie stars were writing their memoirs, and the market for scandalous biographies was expanding.

The evidence was provided by the popularity of Garson Kanin's book *Tracy and Hepburn*, which detailed the lives of the two stars. Cukor was terribly upset with Kanin for writing the book. In his view, the writer had turned on his friends by revealing information that should have remained private. Told that Kanin has been suffering from migraine headaches, Cukor quipped it was all conscience; he didn't remember Kanin being troubled by them before *Tracy and Hepburn*. Thinking of all the fun they had together, Cukor was inclined to be sentimental, but then reason took over and his heart got hardened.

There was an additional reason for Cukor's fury. He resented the fact that when Kanin was introduced at a retrospective for Tracy and Hepburn, he spoke at length about the scripts but hardly intimated that a director had worked on those films.

Kanin took Cukor's complaints seriously and, before permitting their long friendship to die, proposed an honest exchange of views. It was painful for him to hear stories of Cukor's vilification of him; he heard that Cukor was upset because he wasn't sufficiently noted in the book. This even more irritated Cukor, who went out of his way to deny these rumors, but he continued to hold a grudge. After this incident Cukor and the Kanins occasionally met, but their friendship was never the same.

CHAPTER THIRTEEN:

A TV Director, 1973–79

AFTER FINISHING *TRAVELS WITH MY AUNT*, CUKOR HIRED A NEW AGENT, the noted Ben Benjamin of ICM. Benjamin became Cukor's agent by default. Cukor had come into Ashley-Steiner Famous Artists, where Benjamin was an agent, to sign contract papers with Iris Steiner. However, Steiner had just left the agency, and suddenly he had no agent. "George was bewildered and bothered by it," Benjamin recalled. "He came into my office and said, 'Well, you know, Ben, why don't you represent me— that is, if you'd like to?' "

Benjamin represented Cukor for the next ten years, until his death. These were by no means Cukor's best years. "I came into his life late," the agent said. "It was the decline of his career. George suffered under this terrible business of being labeled a woman's director." "They were making all these action pictures, and there were no pictures for him to direct."

Over the years Benjamin and Cukor became friends in the way business associates often do, but the agent never considered himself a member of Cukor's inner circle. "I would go in and try to sell him a script," he said. "I was there on the business side, but often, when you're with a man of that stature, pretty soon the business end of it is transcended into friendship."

Aware that he himself wasn't a good businessman, Cukor relied heavily on Benjamin, his business manager, Bill Hayes, and George Towers to guide him in his business and financial affairs. "Cukor would say, 'Ben, just do the best you can. Whatever amount of money you get is fine with me.' George just accepted what I said the price was going to be."

But money was increasingly a big issue in Cukor's life. "If you had ever seen his house, you would understand what a great taste the man had," Benjamin said. "George always needed money because he was such an admirer of beauty. He wanted to buy art, and he was always spending beyond his means. It took an awful lot to keep up his magnificent home, with all the servants, cooks, gardener."

In the 1970s Cukor wasn't making a lot of money. His track record and reputation had no clout in the New Hollywood. "I guarantee that if you contact half a dozen studio executives today," Benjamin noted, "and you say, 'Do you remember George Cukor?' they wouldn't know who the hell he was. The kind of movies that he used to make are out today.

"There were not many scripts he refused because we didn't get enough of those offers. I would send him scripts to read just to give him something to do, let him know he was still in the business." It wasn't easy for Benjamin, who at first thought he just had to point out Cukor's qualities. How many people in Hollywood had credits as great as George's? "It wasn't just a matter of finding the right material," said Benjamin. "It was also competing with the younger directors coming up; George was identified as old hat."

Benjamin had the greatest admiration for Cukor, always keeping a picture of him with his dog in his office. "Cukor was really beloved by the people who knew him well," Benjamin said. "But he was difficult to work with; he could be tough and inflexible. He could be mean, too; he could throw out a pretty mean line at you."

In 1973 Cukor got caught in the middle of an argument between Gavin Lambert and the Selznicks over Lambert's book *The Making of Gone with the Wind*. When Lambert began the book, he asked Daniel Selznick if he could look at the Selznick files for his research. Selznick first agreed but later changed his mind. He was apparently furious when Lambert decided to proceed without his help and interview everyone connected with the picture who was still alive. For some reason, the Selznicks believed that no book on *GWTW* could be written without their supervision. Later, when they obtained a copy of Lambert's book, they were very upset.

Daniel Selznick decided to involve Cukor. He told him his mother wasn't happy about the book and asked him to send a message to Lambert. Without thinking, Cukor cabled Lambert in Morocco and asked him to do what he could to satisfy the Selznicks. Startled by the telegram, Lambert explained that he had rejected the family's cooperation after Irene Selznick demanded he go through the book, page by page, with her. With too many implicit conditions attached, Lambert stood firm on his principle: that he wouldn't be told what to write by anyone.

Cukor didn't know at the time that Irene Selznick had complained that

Lambert's book was too pro-Cukor. "Can one be too pro-Cukor?" the writer replied. The publishers were against giving in to the Selznicks' demands because their objections seemed to be more on interpretation and point of view than facts.

A few days later Cukor had pangs of conscience, and in a second telegram he asked Lambert to forgive him for sticking in his nose. Cukor not only sympathized with Lambert's irritation but actually delighted in his toughness, praising the writer for giving the Selznicks the "brush off" they deserved. Cukor deplored Irene Selznick's perception of herself as the "ultimate repository of TRUTH." Irritation moved to anger when she intimated that Cukor was feeding information to Lambert. Cukor, who had always been generous about his involvement with *GWTW*, informed Daniel Selznick that he felt imposed upon and wished not to involve himself with the matter any further.

Irene Selznick's suggestion that Cukor and Lambert were in cahoots was unfounded. Cukor had spent hours with Lambert talking about his work, but he adamantly denied making disparaging remarks about David Selznick. Lambert's more objectionable quotes, from the Selznicks' point of view, came from Vivien Leigh's letters to her husband at the time. Making matters worse, however, Cukor told everyone that the book not only was accurate but did justice to the subject.

This reminded Cukor of another unpleasant episode with Irene Selznick: her reaction to Crowther's MGM book. She was intelligent enough to know that her father, Louis B. Mayer, was no angel, but Cukor understood that it must have been painful for her to see it in cold print. Despite her qualities, Cukore now saw her as a woman with plenty of time on her hands to think of suspected injuries done to the family.

It was not the first time that Cukor was angry with Irene. A year earlier he was both furious and offended when the Selznicks neglected to invite him to Daniel Selznick's wedding, as he had been present at his birth. This time, however, he had the guts to confront Irene. Lambert's book did rekindle some difficult memories. Cukor liked the book immensely, finding it eminently readable, beautifully written, even entertaining, but *GWTW* was not a subject he liked to dwell on. He thought he was at last out of *GWTW*, but periodically the issue raised its ugly head; it became an irritation and a bore.

After many years of gentlemanly behavior about *GWTW*, Cukor was disappointed by Irene's pettiness. He realized this might mean the end of their friendship, but he was fed up. He told Lambert that if *he* asked her to go to some trouble for him, she would very tactfully but firmly decline. It was probably the Louis B. blood in her, wanting to have her own way at all costs. It was too bad, Cukor held, that certain people didn't improve with the years—like Hepburn, Mrs. Roosevelt, and himself. As the years passed and the incident dimmed, Cukor rekindled his friendship with Irene, though it was never back to normal and it didn't last long. In 1978, when Cukor was in New York for a few days, he didn't call her. Irene was so upset she made an international scandal out of it. "George could hold grudges," said Morrissey. " 'This stupid woman,' he said. 'Why is she mad at me?' I don't think they ever spoke again. Irene built this incident up as some sort of treachery," Morrissey said. "Tough on such matters, George hated when his friends acted silly; you could never catch George being stupid or unintelligent."

Roddy McDowall concurred: "George knew how to be a friend, when to be supportive, when to be severe. George would lose his temper, but mostly at the stupidities his friends did. He couldn't tolerate stupid behavior, being less than what you were capable of. If you behaved in a manner less than your potential, George would pick you up on it; he would reproach you not to be silly."

When I tried to interview Irene Selznick for this book in 1989, she wouldn't talk to me. "George Cukor was no close friend of mine," she said in anger. "When did he have time to see me in the last thirty years?" Bitter and frustrated, she held grudges against Cukor even after his death. "George changed; he became very strange; he wasn't the man I used to know," she said.

Cukor did not work from 1972 to 1975, when he made the TV movie *Love Among the Ruins*. In those years correspondence with his friends took a major portion of his time, as well as trips to London, which had always been Cukor's favorite European city.

In April 1973 he went to London again. Cukor attended the theater every night, for some of his friends were always performing. This was the trip he saw *Equus*—a fascinating experience with a great performance by McCowen. But Cukor was unkind to Olivier's production of the Italian play *Filumena*, starring Joan Plowright. Its actors spoke with "push 'em up" Italian accents, reaffirming his belief that English actors were not good at accents.

The primary focus of the trip, however, was business. For some time Cukor had been corresponding with Peter Dunlop, director of the Fraser & Dunlop agency, about doing a film about Virginia Woolf, with Maggie Smith in the lead. Wishing to have creative control over the project, Cukor and Smith secured the rights to Quentin Bell's biography of Woolf, determined to produce the movie despite the difficulties of getting studio support. Dunlop had summoned Cukor to London to discuss the project, in another journey undertaken as a "gamble," with Cukor paying his own expenses.

Cukor's major concern, as always, was to find a suitable screenwriter, who had to be young and unorthodox in his method. (He added with typical acerbic humor that the only one permitted to be old was the director.) That proved to be difficult. Cukor's choice was Tom Stoppard, but the brilliant playwright was forced to pull out because of a time conflict over a play he was doing for the Royal Shakespeare Company. Maggie Smith then suggested Alan Bennett, who was less expensive than Stoppard, but Cukor feared he would be too "jokey." Instead, he chose Peter Shaffer, then in vogue because of *Equus*'s great success, but nothing came of it.

Dunlop also offered Cukor Anthony Shaffer's *Black Comedy,* a witty farce that could be done quickly in England. Cukor put himself to work right away, hoping the public would be delighted to see something jolly after all the "torments and degradations" of eroticism, police brutality, and other unappetizing subjects then on display in theater and film.

But the holiday season came and went, and little progress was made on *Virginia Woolf* or *Black Comedy*. In March 1974 Dunlop thought that taking a second option on Bell's biography was unwise since the British film industry was still depressed. It was hard to generate enthusiasm—or financing—for any film. After more than a year's work the two projects were shelved.

Cukor's next project, a TV movie called *Love Among the Ruins,* was born in a talk show and was full of unanticipated turns. During Katharine Hepburn's 1972 celebrated interview with Dick Cavett, he asked her if she regretted never having played opposite Laurence Olivier. In her straightforward and acerbic manner Hepburn quipped, "Well! Neither Larry nor I are dead yet!" The comment proved to be prophetic; within months Hepburn's costar was Olivier, though the pairing did not come to life easily.

James Costigan's script for *Love Among the Ruins* had been written for Alfred Lunt and Lynn Fontanne, but when the famed couple retired, the project was shelved. It was Hepburn's idea to involve Olivier. "You know," she told Cukor, "it must be played by somebody in the public's eye, somebody important." Cukor, too, held it would be more touching if the actors were "gorgeous ruins" with whom the public could identify. Aware that casting was crucial for TV movies, Cukor hoped that with these stars they would make a "bang-up" show.

Persuading Olivier to accept the role was not easy, however. The actor felt bad about disliking the script; his view was an "absolute polarization" from Cukor and Hepburn's. "Try as I may," he noted, "I just can't change my opinion or make my love and deep admiration for you both alter it to come into line with yours." Cukor told his agent: "As you can see, his lordship says, nay, but he is making a big mistake." Said Benjamin: "Larry definitely didn't want to do it, but George really talked him into it."

Cukor told Benjamin: "Larry turns us down ever so regretfully, ever so affectionately, ever so respectfully. I'm sure he'd have liked to work with us all and is disappointed. There's a chance that he might change his mind. I have no basis for saying this, but I have a hunch he might." Cukor was right.

Cukor and Hepburn proceeded to write a long letter to Olivier that consisted of a series of questions: "Do you find the relationship—thus cast—not interesting? Do you find it not funny? Do you find it too trivial? Would there be any particular thing which could make you do it? Say it's just hopeless, and we will both blow our brains out." Cukor decided to be cute and mention their biggest failures. "What a combo! The star of *Romeo and Juliet;* the girl was so successful in *The Lake;* and the director, fresh from his success of *GWTW.* Irresistible!"

Olivier changed his mind after receiving their "enchanting" letter. Concerned that it would be a feature film and demand formidable strength, the ailing actor was relieved to learn it would be a TV movie. In the winter of 1973 Cukor proudly announced that he had got England's best actors to work for him. Ralph Richardson showed strong interest in *Black Comedy,* and Olivier had committed himself to do *Love Among the Ruins.*

Allan Davis recalled how he was asked to produce *Love Among the Ruins.* Cukor said, "I'm going to do this movie for TV in London, and we want an English producer. I'd like you to do it." Davis replied: "I'm doing a play. I don't know if I can." Just out of curiosity Davis asked: "Who's going to be in it?" Calmly Cukor said: "Laurence Olivier and Katharine Hepburn." Caught off guard, Davis said, "Yes, of course, I'm free. When do we start shooting?"

Set in the Edwardian period, *Love Among the Ruins* told an unorthodox love story of an English barrister (Olivier) and a world-famous actress (Hepburn). Olivier played Sir Arthur Granville-Jones, the elderly barrister who reencounters the love of his youth. Cukor thought the title was "tricky" because they all were of a "certain age."

Shooting at London's Pinewood studios went on for six weeks. "It was a lovely experience for all of us," Davis recalled. "The audience saw parts of old London with all these wonderful horses and carts." The problem was they could shoot in those areas only on Sundays, and that meant they had to work on weekends. Initially Ben Benjamin, who was also Olivier's agent, said, "Larry never works on Sunday." But Davis went directly to the actor and bought him a drink. "Does this mean we'll finish the film sooner?" Olivier asked. "It certainly does," Davis said. "Then I will do it," Olivier said.

The script was filmed pretty much in sequence except for the exterior shots. Cukor asked the TV people, "How does one shoot for television?"

They said, "Shoot it just the way you would shoot a picture." Cukor didn't have to modify his style in any way; the film was intimate, with most of the story set in a courtroom.

"The first person to arrive at the studio was George," Davis recalled. "He would be prowling around the studio at six in the morning, looking at the set, pacing back and forth, but never looking through the camera." Davis never saw Cukor look through the camera. He was much more concerned about the acting and pacing of the dialogue. "I've got experts to do the camera," he said. "I don't need to ask them if they have got the corner of the chair in." Davis noted: "George simply didn't want to be bothered with that."

Davis recalled fondly a scene in the lawyer's office. Hepburn, who never kept her mouth shut, said, "George, you've got the camera in the wrong place. If you had the camera over there, you'd see me and Larry, and then you'd see my sister in the background. It would make a lovely shot. What do you think, Larry?" Cukor responded firmly: "Kate, this is not a subject for vote." He later conceded that he didn't do it because *she* suggested it. "Hepburn and Cukor were funny when they argued," Davis added. "Everybody would laugh ruefully about their bickering. Their relationship was love and argument."

The worst argument occurred when Olivier arrived one Monday morning and said to Davis, "I've been rewriting the scene that we're to do. I've had it typed out, and I want you to give it to George." When Davis read it, he said to himself, "It's just as bad as what we've got." But he gave it to Cukor, who looked at it and said, "No, no, no, it is no good." Davis went back to Olivier to report: "I've shown it to George, and he thinks that what we've got is better." The actor wasn't pleased, but he did the scene the way Cukor wanted it—and he did it well.

In one scene, which called for a fire burning, Hepburn said, "No fire ever burns like that. It's ridiculous, George. Have that altered." Cukor said: "Miss Hepburn, I know you're a great actress and expert on many things, but I didn't know you were an expert on fake fires." Everybody laughed, and that was the end of it.

Hepburn did her big scene near the end too tearfully. "You're going to cry eventually," Cukor said, "but don't cry now, don't break here." Hepburn was resistant. "I'll be so flat if I don't cry," she said. "No, no, no," Cukor insisted, "just do it as I say." She said: "I'll do it, but with grave doubts." But as in the past, Hepburn came in matter-of-factly and cried exactly on cue.

Cukor liked to shoot an immense footage, refusing to say what to print. "Print them all," he would say. "How can I tell now?" He ended up with "mountains of rushes," but this was television and he had to do it on time and on budget. "We were only one day over the allotted time," said

Davis. "The shoot was only three weeks, but we shot seven days a week. George was completely demanding," he added. "There was never anything else on his mind. All the people in the film were also supposed to be totally committed to it."

Love Among the Ruins became a unique experience for its wonderful casting; all the people, down to those who played the small parts, were charming. "The movie is really a puffball," said Davis, "just wonderful performances." Cukor and his stars, who had always wanted to work together, all had marvelous time.

The presence of the two charismatic stars almost redeemed the slight plot. "When the movie came out," said Benjamin, "you could tell that all the people involved had enormous respect for each other." The production was a testament to Cukor's unfailing good taste. "Seeing the movie," said Benjamin, "you realized that George must have picked out the best costume designer, the best set decorator. Everything was the best; he was a perfectionist."

However, telecast on March 6, 1975, *Love Among the Ruins* received mixed reviews. One critic remarked, none too kindly, that Cukor should have switched the professions of the two protagonists to make them more convincing. It was one of those entertainments in which the actors seemed to have more fun than the audience. "Did anyone dare send you *The New York Times?*" Davis asked Cukor. "If they didn't, and you can face them, let me know, but no need to depress yourself unduly."

There was no doubt, however, that the public loved it, and of course, the response of Cukor's friends was more gratifying than any printed review. Anita Loos reported from New York that "last night, half the town stayed in to see *Love Among the Ruins;* it was sheer delight to escape from the everyday ugliness and violence. Bravo!"

Olivier and Hepburn received Emmy awards for their acting, and Cukor for direction. Now he was a certified show biz director, having won both an Oscar and an Emmy. Filming in Jamaica, Olivier was unable to attend the Emmy ceremonies, and Cukor accepted the award for him. Longing for his enthusiasm and energy, Olivier wished Cukor were directing his new movie.

After winning the Emmy, Cukor wrote jokingly to Olivier that the voters were dazzled by the realization that he had taken "two unknown and inexperienced kids" who'd been at it a long time with little success. Cukor boasted about whipping his stars into giving respectable performances for the first time in their "lackluster" careers. Olivier was a wonderfully accomplished actor, Cukor later said, but he'd never seen him play with such simplicity and vulnerability—entirely the result of *his* artistry as a director.

*   *   *

The first feature project Benjamin got Cukor as his client was actually initiated by producer Edward Lewis. Based on Maeterlinck's 1908 fantasy play, *The Blue Bird* was a film about two children's search for the true bird of happiness. It had been done twice before: first as a silent in 1918, then as a Shirley Temple vehicle in 1940. Now it was planned as an American-Soviet project.

It took five years to set up the coproduction through the persistent efforts of Clara Reece, a Cleveland businesswoman with extensive investments in the USSR. Lewis, who owned the rights, developed the deal with Reece. *The Blue Bird* was chosen because of its apolitical nature. When Reece first broached the idea to the Soviets in 1969, she met with a cool response, but the situation changed after relations between the two countries began to thaw. "She was a tower of strength," Cukor said of Reece, "and so was I."

With a budget of $8 million, Fox put up the above-the-line costs; the Soviets contributed the rest. Because no money was exchanged—it was hard to put a value on the dollar and ruble—the deal was easier. The movie was planned as an Easter 1976 release. Benjamin negotiated the far-from-lucrative deal, with Cukor receiving $150,000, or one third of what he was paid for *My Fair Lady*.

Hugh Whitemore revised the script, first adapted by Alfred Hayes, which was then translated into Russian by Alexi Kapler. Allan Davis had introduced Cukor to Whitemore, and the two became close friends. "That was a great friendship, of which I am very proud," said Davis. "One of Hugh's children is called George, and George is his godfather."

Cukor was apprehensive about the project, hoping not to fall flat on his face. He may have aspired too high, but he saw it as a major enterprise, politically, if not artistically. Cukor decided to cast the film with an all-star cast. Thus, for the role of the dog, he considered every English actor, from Alec Guinness to Paul Scofield, Peter Sellers, and Trevor Howard. For the role of the cat, his choices included Maggie Smith, Shirley MacLaine, and Jeanne Moreau. None of these performers, however, was cast. In the end, Liz Taylor, Ava Gardner, Cicely Tyson, and Jane Fonda all appeared in the film.

Cast as the Night, Fonda had only a cameo role, appearing onscreen for less than ten minutes. But she felt she owed Cukor a favor; he had been the first director to recognize her talent in *The Chapman Report*. Besides, as Benjamin said, "Jane was crazy about George; she would do anything for him."

Cukor took with him to the USSR: three boxes of Finn Crisp, two pairs of gloves, two pairs of rubber boots, a three-quarter-length jacket. Later, Irene Burns provided additional supplies: toiletries, twelve jars of herbs and spices. Douglas Strock, of the U.S.-USSR Trade and Economic Council, arranged for food to be flown to Russia. Cukor told Strock that because of his diplomatic skill, several American movie queens—and he—would be saved from malnutrition.

On his way to the Soviet Union Cukor stopped in London, where he rented a fur-lined overcoat and hat for six months. He also subscribed to the *International Herald Tribune* and arranged for the *Times* of London to be airmailed. In the evenings he watched the screen tests that Davis did for *The Blue Bird*.

Shooting began on September 22, 1975. Unfortunately there were myriad difficulties from day one: language barriers, inferior equipment, a slow shooting schedule, cast illnesses, personnel changes. Producer Lewis was kicked upstairs to an executive position in mid-shoot and replaced by Paul Maslansky. Despite an awkward beginning, however, Cukor hoped the film would soon get its tempo and momentum. It never did.

The shoot was long and painful, and Cukor realized the movie should have been more carefully prepared. On a personal level Cukor liked the Soviets—they were kind and cooperative—but they had different ways of working: They were less organized and slower than Americans. "Time means nothing to them," he noted; "we're used to working at a certain clip." Also, the Soviets' limited equipment and technique in no way compared with those of the Americans.

The squabbles on the set were trumpeted by Rex Reed in the *Ladies' Home Journal,* but Cukor thought that to rebut Reed would be beneath his dignity. "If the picture is good," he said, "that would be the only rebuttal." Cukor dismissed the negative accounts with one word: "Bullshit." He added: "We were pioneering, it's bound to be easier for the next people who go over." The "myths" did the film a disservice; everything was exaggerated.

Jay Preston Allen, who visited on location, reported that Cukor was not wilting despite the reputedly nightmarish ordeal of directing the movie and that he was proud of his contribution to détente. "George was on top of the world," Allen reported. "I never saw him look better." Cukor somehow managed to conceal the problems by serving her a feast from Fortnum and Mason.

Cukor's own stories about the USSR were not derogatory, except that staying there was hard. "He was not a fan of the Soviets, by any means," said Benjamin. "It was long before *glasnost*. The film was a disaster for everybody, especially for George's psyche. George never should have done it at his age. That kind of weather and that script, the whole thing just didn't work. It was damaging and too hard on a man of his age." When the disparaging reports continued, Cukor went out of his way to prove he was in high spirits and undaunted.

While in the USSR, Cukor kept up his correspondence with his close friends. Thanking him for the glorious postcard from Russia, Joan Crawford noted that *The Blue Bird* was the type of film there should be more of those days. Sick of horror movies, she was hoping Cukor would help change the trend. "How you are missed," Katharine Hepburn noted. "We all resent your going away for so long—it interferes with so many lives." She had received a card from Whitney Warren, furious that his visit to L.A. was not to be.

Cukor's gay friends kept him informed about trivial matters. One friend described a birthday party in which Cukor's comrades took to drag like a duck to water. Hollywood was chock-full of rumors about the movie. Is it true, he asked, that there was a ballet with Liz Taylor on point? Cukor's friends wanted to send him Colt's calendars, but they feared an international incident. . . .

Allan Davis got a funny picture of Cukor "threatened" by all those sissy Bolshoi boys. Davis didn't go to Russia, but Mona Washbourne, who was in the movie, told him that Cukor was "appallingly rude," that he swore really badly on the set. "It was terribly hard on him," said Davis, "a rotten script, bad scenery, everything possible went wrong. The most George would ever say about it," Davis recalled, was: " 'They were very pleased in Washington that I made the first American-Russian co-production.' " Fortunately most people didn't see it.

Returning from the Soviet Union, Cukor advertised himself as "a six-day wonder," not the "tottering old creature" everyone expected to see. It had been rugged, he said, but not nearly as tough as the newspapers would have had it. "I'm still in one piece," he said, "not quite the dashing young man, but I'm O.K." But Cukor did look bad. "I was rather shocked," Richard Zanuck observed. "George looked frail and had lost a lot of weight. He told me what an awful location it was, but he always had a gleam in his eye, and he'd say it jokingly."

After a long absence Cukor enjoyed being back at home. He saw friends, went to the movies, and read his favorite genre of books, historical novels. He found Stanley Kubrick's *Barry Lyndon* ravishingly beautiful but thought that it was too grand, with too carefully composed shots; he longed for some "carelessness, disorder, evidence of humanity." Kubrick was talented, but the picture defeated itself because it had so little story.

The month of March was the season of movie parties. Every year, before Oscar night, Cukor hosted a lunch for the foreign directors. Cukor regretted having missed the 1975 occasion at Perino's, at which Frank Capra was asked to preside. Billy Wilder later told Cukor that he had missed a riot, as the Hungarian director spoke in German, the Polish in French, etc. Wilder provided a running translation from French and German into English and then translated the comments of the Hollywood directors into these languages.

For Cukor the main event of the season was the Washington premiere of *The Blue Bird*. But the next couple of days proved not only exhausting but embarrassing. On May 4 he had an interview at the Washington *Star*, then at lunch met a delegation of American and Soviet politicians. In the afternoon there was an international premiere at the Kennedy Center, followed by a formal dinner. The next day he was summoned to meet the Soviet ambassador. On May 6 Cukor flew to New York, where he had interviews with *The New York Times* and CBS TV. MGM's Alan Ladd thanked Cukor for his contribution to the Washington premiere; once again he had shown he was a stalwart, with unfailing charm.

For the first time in his career Cukor had no idea how bad a film of his was. At the very least, he hoped *The Blue Bird* was "genuinely touching." But it soon became clear that the film's greatest failure was the lack of unified style. Critics wondered why Cukor had taken the project in the first place. Nothing in his distinguished career showed he liked fantasy films, and it was known he didn't like to work with children.

"It got quite a publicity as the first Russian-American film," said Benjamin, "but it got nasty comments that offended George very much." Benjamin quoted one snide remark: "It works so hard in making history that it forgets to make sense." Or worse: "If you have naughty children you want to punish, take them to see *Blue Bird* and make them sit all the way through it."

It was a miscalculation, Cukor later admitted, though initially he thought there was something touching about the play. "We probably didn't do it right. We miscast it, it just didn't work, the audience remained cold to it." Cukor still believed the film was unfairly treated by the press and badly marketed; it should have been sold as a Disney movie. Angry at the press, Cukor complained it was out to get him, saying all sorts of stupid things, "all nonsense."

The Radio City Music Hall opening was part of a special benefit for the Lincoln Center Library for the Performing Arts. On Sunday evening Cukor was honored with an award from the New York Public Library. Liz Taylor presided, as Cukor presented a script of *The Blue Bird* to the library. The evening began with Aaron Copland's overture *Fanfare for the Common Man*, conducted by Sarah Caldwell, and continued with a speech from the library's president.

On this trip east Cukor went to Rochester, anxious to see how he would react, for he had not been there for years. In Rochester he was presented with the George Eastman Award, which made him sentimental; memories of half a century earlier flashed through his mind. Rochester was the place where he had begun his stage career.

Cukor flew back home on May 15. He kept the usual detailed journal, which included almost hour-by-hour expenses (even telephone calls he made). He complained to the accounting office of the Pierre Hotel regarding a restaurant bill of $41.02, charged to him by error. Cukor was able to document that he had neither lunch nor dinner that day!

In early June Cukor flew to the USSR again for the Moscow premiere of *The Blue Bird.* It was a short and strenuous visit. The Soviets, he reported, were great in entertainment, consuming enormous amounts of vodka. And while he was not enthusiastic about their way of life, he once again found them to be endearing.

Cukor then took a quick trip to Hungary, the land of his forefathers. He found Budapest as beautiful as ever and its people spirited, but there was a pall, as though they were in bondage to a strange political system. As usual Cukor paid most attention to the women's looks and conduct. He found the women working at the airport too aggressive and bullying to his taste, not a very positive image for the modern Hungarian woman.

In Paris, his next stop, Cukor hustled *The Blue Bird* on TV. After Eastern Europe, Paris was the beautiful world that he had been accustomed to. Still, when he got home, he felt like sinking to his knees and singing "God Bless America." No matter where Cukor went, he always enjoyed coming home. He never lost the feeling of patriotism he had acquired as a child from his grandparents.

Most of Cukor's efforts in 1976 and 1977 were centered on a new film project, *Vicki,* or *Victoria Woodhull,* about the first woman to run for President in 1872. James Toback was working on a screenplay for a film to star Faye Dunaway. An adventurous woman, who preached and practiced free love, Woodhull precipitated a big sex scandal by accusing a well-known preacher of immoral carryings-on. Cukor found it interesting that from obscure beginnings, she ended up a rich stockbroker. The film showed, he said with amusement, that adventurous, wicked ladies, after having had a high old time, do not always come to bad ends.

Cukor's first impression of Dunaway was negative—an "all-time cunt," "a routine actress." Whenever he met Dunaway, she was high, "crazy with cocoa," he said, quoting Tallulah Bankhead's famous line. Worse yet, she could be pretentious. But after seeing Dunaway in *Chinatown* and *Network,* he changed his mind about her abilities.

Cukor continued to host AMPAS's foreign directors luncheon. On March 28, 1977, the event included Frank Capra, Milos Forman, Rouben Mamoulian, Vincente Minnelli, King Vidor, and others. Stories about the old Hollywood were, as expected, in abundance. But the novelty that year was Lina Wertmuller, the first woman director, American or foreign, ever to be nominated for an Oscar (for *Seven Beauties*). "This is going to be the year when we break this all-male chauvinist club," Cukor quipped, noting disappointedly that the Italian director was in San Francisco.

Following Cukor's introduction of the foreign directors, Capra said, "Here is a guild of directors who love each other." "Except when they're young and talented," Cukor interrupted. "There are hundreds of cinema schools," Capra continued, "and everybody is learning to be a director. There'll be eight million directors, and where will we be?" Cukor said that the United States was the "best goddamned country in the world because in no other place would they give another nation the Oscar with such complete generosity."

"The Oscar is just a simple little idea," Capra said, "but it proves the power of an idea, not the power of money." "Because it's honest," Cukor said; "it's absolutely on the level." Capra then recalled how in 1944 *Wilson* was supposed to be the biggest winner but was not. "*Wilson* was a bore," Cukor said, failing to realize that its director, Henry King, was present. "I owe you an apology, and I'm going to shut up from now on," Cukor said, but he continued to dominate the event just as usual.

Cukor showed his respect for film personalities by organizing memorials and tributes to their careers. In April 1977 Cukor took on himself the impossible task of asking Garbo to send a wire to Clarence Brown, honored by the Directors Guild. Garbo never responded, which upset Cukor, as Brown had directed her in many films.

Veteran actress Lillian Gish involved Cukor in getting Henri Langlois, founder of the Cinémathèque Française a special Oscar, for a life dedicated to film preservation. Cukor immediately spoke to the Board of Governors and got it to act. He later helped in honoring the Museum of Modern Art with a second similar Oscar, in 1980.

Cukor and Gish suggested an award for director King Vidor, who had been nominated five times but never won. Having some clout at the academy, Cukor managed to get Vidor an honorary Oscar. In February 1979 Cukor organized a tribute for Lewis Milestone at the Directors Guild, sharing memories of his work as a dialogue director on *All Quiet*, half a century before.

Cukor kept in contact with Joan Crawford up to the last months of her life. For her part, she adored his "articulate and visual" letters. Unaware of Crawford's illness and of her becoming a recluse, Cukor once called her. The voice that answered the telephone, pretending to be her secretary, sounded familiar. Not to embarrass her, Cukor pretended he didn't recognize the voice and hung up, sadly realizing the pathetic state of the once-proud actress.

A month after Crawford died, Cukor arranged a tribute for her. A great protector of stars' reputations, he wished to offset the unkind things written about her. In fact, Cukor had never approved of Crawford's horror movies, reasoning that it was a pity and shame to destroy the audience's illusions and memories of her as a major star.

The celebration of Crawford in film, fact, and fond memories took place at the academy's Samuel Goldwyn Theater, on June 24, 1977. It was the first time that the whole industry, guilds and unions included, came together to honor a movie personality. Myrna Loy presided, along with John Wayne, Robert Young, and Steven Spielberg, who had made his debut on a TV show that starred Crawford. "We strove for a kind of coffee klatch atmosphere," Myrna Loy recalled. "Cukor was in charge. Anybody who dared begin with 'It gives me a great pleasure'—out!" The tribute comprised an extraordinary range of people and engendered an overwhelming outpouring of affection.

"I know it sounds odd," Cukor said, "but somehow I did not believe Joan Crawford could ever die. She was the perfect image of the movie star, and as such largely the creation of her own indomitable will. She had very remarkable material to work with. A quick native intelligence, tremendous animal vitality, a lovely figure, and above all, her face, that extraordinarily sculptural construction of lines and planes, finely chiseled, like the mask of some classical divinity from fifth-century Greece. It caught the light superbly, you could photograph her from any angle, and the face moved beautifully."

Cukor had had a strong influence on the career of Crawford, who, in his view was a glorious movie queen as well as an accomplished actress. "These people had a good deal of character," Cukor said; "they had to live with the seven fat years and the seven lean years. The camera saw a side of Joan that no flesh-and-blood lover ever saw. The nearer the camera, the more tender and yielding she became: Her eyes glistened; her lips parted in ecstatic acceptance."

Cukor quoted Katharine Hepburn's dictum that "every big real star has the talent to irritate." Crawford had that, too. Whether one liked or didn't like her, one could not ignore Crawford's existence or deny her quality. "As long as celluloid holds together and the word 'Hollywood' means anything," Cukor concluded, "she will live!"

The publication of Christina Crawford's poisonous *Mommie Dearest* irritated Cukor. He refused to read it because he believed it treated Crawford very shabbily. As far as he was concerned, Joan Crawford was an "admirable creature," nice to work with and a good friend. It was a shame that such a nasty book was written—and by her own daughter.

Occasionally Cukor was asked to write an obituary or a book review of a celebrity. He reviewed, for example, *Hello I Must Be Going: Groucho and Friends,* by Charlotte Chandler, for the *Hollywood Reporter.* "I was a fan of Marx," Cukor's review began, "but my only personal contact with him was when he set fire to my own dining room." Cukor had invited Olivia de Havilland, who was visiting from Paris, and she asked if she could bring a guest; the mystery escort turned out to be Groucho

Marx. Very animated during dinner, Marx paid too much attention to the pretty girl next to him. The two lingered at the table after the guests had left the area. Suddenly the butler, pale and shaken, announced there had been a fire in the dining room. Getting up from the table, Groucho apparently had tossed his napkin lightly on top of a lit candle. Typically Cukor never let Marx know about the damages.

In 1977 Cukor reviewed Rosalind Russell's book *Life Is a Banquet* in the *Hollywood Reporter*. The book was just like Russell: "warm, funny, romantic and down-to-earth." She took illness and pain in stride with "indomitable courage." Her supreme common sense helped her to cope with everything. Work was the real tip-off. "You get to know those you work with very thoroughly," Cukor wrote, "not always for the best." With Russell, however, their work together only intensified his liking and admiration. Cukor had been instrumental in getting Russell a 1972 special Oscar, the Jean Hersholt Humanitarian Award, for her charity work.

Cukor kept in touch with all the aging movie queens of his past. Myrna Loy thanked him for a lovely evening, noting that he certainly knew how to "handle a woman." In 1981, when Loy returned to MGM, thirty-four years after her last film there, Cukor hosted a lunch for her at the commissary.

From New York Anita Loos complained that her social life was stymied by traffic and muggers. For his part, Cukor thanked her for sending him the 1978 Calendar of American Writers, promising to fill each day with "tantalizing" items. The week of January 9 was his favorite because that was where the picture of Loos appeared. When Cukor got the volume *Native Voices,* he resented the fact that the voice of an eloquent writer— Loos herself—was not there.

On October 5, 1977, the American Film Institute (AFI) organized a seminar with Cukor, following screenings of *Camille* and *The Philadelphia Story.* "Be very easy on me," Cukor told the students; "don't ask any difficult questions." Everybody had to sit down because Cukor couldn't stand people walking around, and his attention span was short. In the midst of the questions, Cukor screamed, "Lock the door, I wish people would not come in. You're going to see a difficult Hollywood director," he told the students. "I've done it before, and it's all rather vague, unless you ask me definite and specific questions."

Cukor repeated what he had said before: that a scene had to be believable. He urged the students always to ask themselves, when they finished a scene, "Do I believe it?"

"You've had such an illustrious career through the years," one student started to say. "See," Cukor interrupted with pleasure, "he's very intelligent, that's a good question." But when another student inquired about his working relationship with movie stars, the director noted, "That's a whole goddamned story, I'd be here ten weeks. I'll tell you in one word: I'm always right, and they're always wrong."

But Cukor really disliked the next question: "Do you think the fundamental strength of theater is different from that of film? And if that's true, aren't you shortchanging film when you do an adaptation?" Cukor replied: "That's not a very good question," Cukor relied. "This talk, fundamental truth and fundamental this, is pretentious."

As for the state of the American cinema, Cukor said he deplored its new vulgarity and monotony; four-letter words were simply not very witty. He found the new films limited, failing to show the range of human experience; Hollywood was trying to play it too safe. Films should deal with "human disappointment, human laughter. You see all the gangsters, but you're never caught up in the affairs of the heart." Talking about eroticism onscreen, Cukor suddenly said, "I'm giving you all sorts of secrets—how to teach an actor to become sexy. Do you appreciate it?"

Asked whether it was experience that gave him his film instincts, he said, "I don't think I've mastered it. I'm still insecure." All training was good, Cukor stressed; "everything you see in life, everything you've experienced is all grist for your mill. Don't narrow yourself down. We do narrow ourselves down eventually; life does that to us. But the more you see, and the more you free yourself, the bigger you will become."

When the AFI's James Powers mentioned that French director Jacques Demy (*The Umbrellas of Cherbourg*) was present, Cukor said modestly, "I don't put myself in a class with him; his films are charmingly made." Cukor hoped Demy wouldn't dazzle the students and make him look a dud. Demy said that Cukor was absolutely loved in France, where there was a cult of his films. Demy had seen *Camille* when he was nine years old. "And it changed your life?" Cukor quipped.

"Is there a style that I have?" Cukor asked.

"Certainly," said Demy, "it's true what they say about elegance and character and also being women's director."

"I am not aware of that. I just go into a day's work. I'm not thinking, 'Oh, this one's going to knock 'em dead,' though I hope it will. It's all filtered through one's sensibilities, what you think is funny, what you think is touching."

Cukor's recommendation was: "Just work, work hard, don't be too highbrow. If you can get jobs and get experience, just stick to it, and don't be too discouraged. There are an awful lot of kicks in the ass as you go up the hill, but just have courage. It's a happy life, but it's not an easy life."

Cukor was such an entertaining speaker that the AFI organized another seminar with him, in February 1978, this time with actress Ann

Rutherford of *GWTW*. "We were all in absolute awe watching the way you worked," the actress recalled, "because many of us had worked with martinets, with tyrants who came on cracking their little quirts. They just demanded you to do things, but they never explained why. George would let us rehearse; then he would quietly call one person after another aside to discuss the scene."

Around that time Cukor acquired an assistant, Daniel Woodruff, an intelligent actor who was only twenty-one when they met. Despite the enormous age difference, they shared some habits. "We were both high-strung," said Woodruff. "We were both impatient." Cukor told him with a big smile on his face, "You're the only person I know who eats faster than I do." He also pointed out that Uncle Morris's wife had been named Cora Woodruff. Soon Cukor asked Woodruff to move in and, as was his habit, began corresponding with his parents, assuring them that he was gearing their son toward a promising career as a director.

Cukor took special liking to Woodruff—and so did Katharine Hepburn, who was still living in one of the houses. Cukor watched the two with admiration as they hiked their daily four miles. The three spent many evenings together; one night they had fun watching *The African Queen* on TV. What Cukor liked about Woodruff was that he was a smark-alecky kid, always candid in his opinions.

They went to the movies in the afternoon, then frequented the bookstores. "I wasn't worldly," Woodruff allowed. "Cukor gave me education, a taste for art and music." Cukor was stimulating company. Woodruff recalled how he would crack jokes about Christopher Reeve, who foolishly dreamed of being the next Cary Grant. Watching TV, Cukor would imitate the newspeople with their phony smiles and mannerisms and make astute observations.

Cukor took Woodruff to New York twice. On September 22, 1979, Hepburn and Cukor gave him a special tour of the city. That afternoon they saw *Sweeney Todd* and went backstage to meet Angela Lansbury; in the evening they had dinner with Maggie Smith at Hepburn's house. The next day Hepburn drove them to Boston for lectures at Harvard and Boston University. It was exciting for Woodruff: Christmas party at Neil Hartley's (producer of Cukor's *The Corn Is Green*) with David Hockney; lunch at John Schlesinger's with Isherwood, Bachardy, and Michael York in attendance; dinner at Roddy McDowall's with Vincent Price. On the second trip to New York, Cukor and Woodruff went with Hepburn and Laura Harding to see *Romantic Comedy*. Afterward they went backstage to meet the comedy's stars, Mia Farrow and Tony Perkins. The next night they saw Stoppard's *Night and Day* and met Maggie Smith after the show.

Cukor often asked Woodruff to drive his Rolls-Royce, bought with money me made for *My Fair Lady*. The young man wasn't paid for his services; Cukor got him some jobs, for which the studio usually paid. Woodruff asked to read for a part in *The Corn Is Green*, but Cukor ruled he wasn't right. When Cukor came back from Ireland, where *The Corn Is Green* was shot, Woodruff was employed in postproduction. "It was kind of an exchange," he said. "I was never on the payroll, but George taught me a lot about dubbing and mixing while we worked together."

Hepburn had told Woodruff that when Cukor was young, everybody loved him and he'd had a wonderful personality. But Woodruff noticed that as Cukor got older, he became "cranky and cantankerous. He was on pain-killers for his back and sleeping pills and would go to the dentist three times a week, but he didn't like to complain." Cukor told Woodruff one of his mottoes: "Nobody cares about how you feel except for your mother, and when she's dead, you're on your own." When Woodruff got upset, Cukor typically said, "But why? Life is just a bowl of cherries."

Woodruff lived on the premises for three years, but he tried to leave Cukor a couple of times. "I wasn't getting anywhere," he said. "I couldn't spend with him all the time that he needed, and he was becoming more and more demanding, more and more dependent on me." Finally Hepburn interfered and without Cukor's knowledge told Woodruff, "You've got to get out of here."

"I felt terrible about leaving. It took me a whole year to decide. George was persistent and persuasive; he knew my weaknesses. He would say, 'Ava Gardner is coming tonight for dinner. Why don't you join us?' But I needed to live my life. George wasn't taking my career seriously enough."

On June 28, 1980, Woodruff left while Cukor was at his barber's. Cukor's gardener took him to the barber every Saturday; Cukor boasted about how he was treated by Reagan's barber. Woodruff expressed his gratitude for all Cukor had done but explained that he had to make a career for himself. Cukor was reportedly humiliated and devastated. "George resented that I left him," Woodruff recalled. "He thought I was unappreciative."

After he left, Richard Stanley took over, but Cukor missed Woodruff. Stanley was nice and responsible, but not nearly as intelligent and provocative company as Woodruff. In his will Cukor left some money to Woodruff but none to Stanley.

A year after Woodruff's departure Cukor called him at AMPAS, where he was now working, because the director needed clips for a documentary. He made one last attempt to get Woodruff back. "Let's go on now," Cukor begged. "I never thought I would need you for my career." The two met occasionally for lunch, but their interaction was mostly on the telephone. "I made it clear," said Woodruff, "that I didn't have the time, but he would say, 'Stick with me for just another picture.' He didn't want to let me go."

Cukor's second TV movie, *The Corn Is Green,* also came to fruition under strange circumstances. The idea originated in 1977, when actor-playwright Emlyn Williams visited Cukor in California. Seeing Cukor's beautiful home by daylight for the first time, Emlyn noticed it was filled with a tranquil comfort. They talked about old plays in a casual manner, and *The Corn Is Green* came up. Later that year Cukor told Williams he was interested in doing his play with Katharine Hepburn. The playwright was, of course, ecstatic.

For once it was not hard to get studio backing for the project. "Warner's respected George enormously," Benjamin said, "and they wanted to establish prestigious TV movies. *The Corn Is Green* was a famous play and a famous movie, too." Cukor was praised by his colleagues for saying out loud, "What's wrong with doing a good TV movie?" Dreading the pressure of a feature, Cukor went for TV, but he was not defensive about moving to television. It was easier and faster to get financing for a TV movie.

Cukor asked Hepburn if she would work with him on another TV movie. She reread the play and found it hopeful, powerful, and also politically correct, propagating education of the masses and generosity of spirit—values that she stood up for in her movies and in her life.

Hepburn played the spinster schoolteacher, Mrs. Moffat, who comes to teach in an illiterate Welsh mining village and discovers that one of her young miner students has unusual talent. Hepburn knew it was a great role: Ethel Barrymore played it in New York, and Sybil Thorndike in London. Ironically, in the 1946 movie Bette Davis was too young (thirty-six) for the middle-aged Moffat, and in 1979, Hepburn too old (seventy).

Irving Rapper shot the 1946 Warner film on the studio lot, but Hepburn suggested doing it in its proper locale, in Wales. She went with Cukor to London and Wales to search for the right cast and proper location. Cukor didn't mind traveling; after his harrowing experience in the Soviet Union, everyplace else seemed easy.

British actress Toyah Wilcox, who played a secondary part in the movie, complained that Cukor intimidated her and the other young performers. But she praised Hepburn for coming to her rescue. "She saw I was frightened and that Cukor was coming on strong," Wilcox recalled. "She told him not to bully me." Though it was their tenth collaboration, Cukor and Hepburn continued to argue, but their arguments were good-natured. "Our relationship is give-and-take," Cukor said. "I give and she takes."

Though Allan Davis had worked out extremely well on Cukor's *Love*

Among the Ruins, he did not produce *The Corn Is Green;* the producer was Neil Hartley. "It would have been better if I had been," Davis said. "I was disappointed with it. They kept coming to me with questions about casting, but I didn't get involved."

The work on *The Corn Is Green* was overshadowed by a major social event in April 1978. "I'm to receive the great honor from the Film Society at Lincoln Center," Cukor told a friend. "It's a very prestigious business; they've only had four before me, nobodies like Chaplin and Hitchcock." Cukor called Ina Claire in San Francisco and invited her to escort him. At eighty-six, Claire was lucid and beautiful, a living proof of Cukor's long-held theory that actresses were indestructible. Two weeks before going to New York, Cukor began working on his speech. "I'm awfully good at telling other people exactly what to do," he told Davis, "but when I do it myself, I get really scared."

The big lunch was on Saturday, April 29, at Le Côte Basque, to which Cukor invited "only ladies!" He knew only a "courageous or foolhardy" man would undertake this but still hoped it would be fun. The guests included Cukor's all-time favorite women: Katharine Hepburn, Ina Claire, Anita Loos, Maureen O'Sullivan, Joan Fontaine, Gloria Swanson, Myrna Loy.

The highlight of the lunch was Hepburn's arrival. When the food was served, she said, "No, thanks, I've just had lunch," but then she proceeded to eat from soup to nuts! Cukor wondered how she still hung on to that lovely girlish figure of hers. Gloria Swanson brought her own lunch in a bag, which reminded Cukor of all those years he carried his own diet food to Hollywood's parties. Cukor had a wonderful time with the women. "George listened with rapt attention," O'Sullivan recalled, "as each one of us talked about what we were doing in our lives. We, of course, reminisced about our first meeting with George."

Cukor was genuinely touched by the speeches at the gala, on Saturday evening, April 30. "I made my first picture with George," Hepburn said, "and we've lived through a lot together, up at the top, trembling, and down a bit. I want you to know he's a truly modest man. And the reason his pictures are wonderful, both for the audience and for the writers and actors who make them, is that his joy to make them shines."

"I learned more about acting from one sentence of George Cukor," Fontaine remarked, "than from all my years of acting lessons." Cukor had advised her: "Think and feel and the rest will take care of itself." Amused by Jack Lemmon's appearance, Cukor reminded him that he was the one to eliminate the "shtick" out of his work: "It was sweet of you to go on about me, showering me with praises (deserved)."

On January 29, 1979, when *The Corn Is Green* premiered on TV, the reviews were far from praising. Cukor's direction was not as strong or tight as in his first TV movie. Even Hepburn's work was not lauded; strangely, she brought no new insights to the part. Cukor didn't think the British critics were appreciative of his efforts, but then they seldom were. "They're inclined to be bitchy," he told Allan Davis. "I see some crapola British TV, but Americans are generous about it. I suppose we're too ignorant to know the difference."

A videocassette of the movie was sent by Cukor to Emlyn Williams, with a note: "It was a thrill to work on such wonderful material. It played." Seeing the TV production was a lovely experience for the writer; he wished the real Miss Moffat could have seen Cukor's version. Telling Cukor it represented his "finest work," Lillian Gish was even more admiring: "Every inch is perfect, flavor, acting, beauty, music—everything. It's your and Katie's moment."

Following the premiere of *The Corn Is Green,* Cukor's life settled into a quiet routine. In 1978 his longtime Czech servants departed from the house. They were good cleaners, but they lacked the foggiest notion about working in a big house. Cukor needed somebody desperately, for in recent years he had been running a boardinghouse. There was such fast turnover that the guests' beds weren't even permitted to grow cold. Fortunately a Hungarian cook, Margaret, appeared. When Cukor heard that she had worked for eight years for Jascha Heifetz, he was encouraged. Heifetz had a reputation for being difficult and for entertaining a great deal.

In spring 1979 Cukor embarked on a special trip to Israel. He had been wanting to go to the Holy Land for years. The opportunity came when his friend Sara Mankiewicz expressed interest in joining him. Cukor decided not to stay at the Carlton Towers, because it was too expensive; $112 struck him as outrageous for Israel. He joked about spending the money he saved on hotels for buying mezuzoth for his Jewish folks in Beverly Hills.

Before his trip to Israel, Cukor was planning to lose weight. It simply became a daily struggle to get into his old wardrobe. He was now hoping that the kosher food in Israel would do the trick. Sara Mankiewicz was much more excited about the trip than Cukor, reflecting the way many goyim felt about the Holy Land; for her it was a pilgrimage. Always ambivalent about religion and unsure about his own feelings, Cukor was apprehensive about the trip. With no plans after Israel, he jokingly said he might settle in a kibbutz and start a new life.

On his way to Israel he stopped in London for a couple of days, but this time he asked Allan Davis to arrange only quiet dinners for him. The Israeli jaunt turned out to be disappointing. Cukor was afraid he would be struck by lightning for not being moved by the Holy Land. But he wasn't: He disliked the hotel, the food.

Hepburn and her longtime housekeeper, Phyllis Wilbourn, had been living in one of the houses on Cukor's estate since 1975, when she arrived to star in *Rooster Cogburn*. After their return from Wales, Cukor confided in the actress that he had to sell the house; he needed the money. Cukor begged Hepburn to buy it, but she knew she wouldn't make many more films, and without work in California, there was no point in keeping a house. "I don't know if she paid any rent," said Benjamin, "but I do know that she got mad at George for selling the house." Cukor then sold the place, and the new owners asked Hepburn to move out her belongings. It was the end of an era for both Cukor and Hepburn.

CHAPTER FOURTEEN

The Swan Song, 1980–83

THE DAWN OF A NEW DECADE FOUND CUKOR IN GOOD HEALTH, STILL energetic, and in full possession of his sharp, often caustic humor. He found great solace in the fact that some of his contemporaries were still around and kicking. When he heard that his friend British actress Cathleen Nesbitt was rehearsing *My Fair Lady* for a Broadway revival, he congratulated her for not sitting back or putting her feet up. As "a mere boy of eighty," Cukor gave himself long afternoon naps but didn't approve of them.

Asked by a reporter, "What do you fill your time with?" Cukor said jokingly, "Oh, I pay the rent, I've got things to do. It doesn't matter how old you are, you make it stimulating by seeing what's going on in the world, and hope that something good will turn your way." Cukor missed the old days because a lot of people he liked were gone, but he wasn't nostalgic: "You can't dwell on the glorious days."

For Cukor, the principal thing remained work, but getting assignments was increasingly difficult. With his long period of inactivity, rumors started to circulate that he was on the verge of retirement. "I have never considered to stop making pictures," Cukor said, vehemently denying the rumors. "I simply worked on a number of projects that never turned out." Cukor continued to lead a busy life with an active schedule to his death.

Cukor never lost his passion for film, maintaining his sharp curiosity, willing to see anything that promised to be interesting. But he wished the new pictures weren't so hopeless, that they would be more emotionally involving: "You see pictures where you don't really care if anybody lives or dies." Cukor's companions marveled at his ability to single out some achievement in every film he saw, even in bad ones.

Cukor knew that his prospects as a director were limited, for the industry was becoming younger and younger; most of his peers were dead or retired. Asked to comment on changes in American cinema, he was quick to reply: "Film may be more advanced technically, but a good, witty script is still the basis for a great performance." Though he highly praised advancements in special effects, his preference still was for good stories. *Star Wars* was a "bang-up picture," but he was just too old for such thrills. Never having liked sci-fi, he dismissed Lucas and Spielberg with "I don't believe any of that stuff of spaceships and flying."

Cukor continued to go to the movies but disliked most of what he saw. He often said, "Who are these persons in the movie? They can't act, and they look awful; it's like having a nightmare of monsters." Cukor regretted the loss of movie stars who had class and charisma, qualities that for him were absolutely necessary for making good pictures. When people accused him of placing too strong an emphasis on looks, he reminded them that Marie Dressler and Spencer Tracy were not beautiful but had "something" special.

Cukor believed that real movie stars had an innate superiority. Acting talent, for that matter, was mostly inborn; one couldn't learn how to be an actor in school. He found many young actors pretentious because they claimed to study their parts seriously. Did one ever hear of John Barrymore and Garbo studying their parts? he once remarked. The new actors showed a lot of effort, but little charm or class.

For Cukor, humor was the key to great screen personalities. Reading a piece about *The French Lieutenant's Woman,* he thought he was reading about the Second Coming of Christ; it was described with such "cathedral hush." And while he thought Meryl Streep was very charming, he joked about how much she had suffered making the film.

After five decades of a busy career it was hard for Cukor not to work. "Cukor was old, but he was very strong in his mind," said Morrissey. "He always made an effort to be with it. He was never a person to look depressed, be depressed, or go in the corner and sulk. He was rigid about his schedule, following the same routine: He woke up every day at the same time, had lunch and dinner at the same time. You could see that he was running his life as a pattern; this is how he got through."

Cukor never seemed lonely, but he was. "Do you miss me in any way?" he once asked Hepburn. "There isn't a morning when I open my eyes that I don't think, 'what is dear Kate doing today?'" But he wasn't a complainer. When people bitched and moaned, he criticized them in public: "Oh, you're crying about this, you're crying about that."

Fortunately Cukor's life was stable and comfortable. The people working for him formed a supportive community, a sort of substitute family. There was Irene Burns, his secretary from 1945 until he died, and he had strong relationships with his cook, Margaret, and her husband, Joseph, the gardener. A considerate employer, Cukor felt it impolite to exploit his staff. He wanted his nightly dinners to be over on time, not only because he was rigid but also to free Margaret from the kitchen. Once in a while Cukor lost his temper—usually at his younger servants—because they didn't perform as expected. He also hollered at guests who came late for dinner. He had always had a strong temper, and as he grew older, he became less and less tolerant.

"He really was a nice man," said Morrissey. "It was hard for journalists to make up stories about him." This was a problem Morrissey confronted when he attempted a biography. "Everybody has something they are ashamed of," he said, "but whatever George might have done when he was young, he himself paid no attention to it. George had a healthy attitude about everything; he had no blind spots."

Cukor was renowned for never being sick. There was a famous story about this. Twenty years before he died, he went for a checkup, and the doctor told him he had cancer and didn't have long to live. Cukor reportedly screamed at the doctor, "You son of a bitch, how could you say this to me?" For years he just mentally blocked the idea of being sick or of ever dying.

As Cukor grew older, he increasingly liked to be surrounded with younger people. In January 1980, when Laszlo Benedict invited him to give a series of lectures at the New York University Film School, Cukor readily accepted. His enthusiasm was contagious as he guided students through re-creations of scenes from his favorite films—*The Women, Gaslight*—to demonstrate acting and directing techniques. The students were thrilled to have such a legendary figure in the class.

During a break a student said with awe: "It was an honor to have the same man who yelled at Tracy, Barrymore, and Gable yelling at us." Cukor worked with the students in the same way he had worked with his actors, alternately cajoling and scolding them as they went through their parts. Although the director encouraged the students to ask questions, he was a little frustrated after the first session. "They're babes in arms," he said. "I find them touching; they're just shy." Cukor told them there was no such thing as a dumb question, but when a student asked what actors in his career he had found the easiest to direct, Cukor replied in his inimitable way, "Now that's a dumb question."

The winter of 1980 was awards season again, and Cukor found himself onstage quite often, as either a recipient or a presenter. In the last decade the film world had come to realize the great cinematic talent he was. In 1978 the Film Society of Lincoln Center had honored him with its Life

Achievement Award. And in February 1980 Cukor, Capra, King Vidor, and William Wyler were honored by the American Society of Cinematographers at its annual gala. Stanley Cortez, the society's vice-president, said he deemed it a great honor to pay tribute to these "Beethovens of the film world."

In the following month Cukor received the D. W. Griffith Award, bestowed by the DGA, "for lifetime contributions to film." He became the thirteenth recipient—in three decades—of this prestigious award, conferred on such legendary directors as Ford, Capra, George Stevens.

In March 1981 Cukor was asked to copresent with King Vidor the directorial award at the fifty-third Oscar ceremonies. Emcee Johnny Carson introduced them as "two directors who are still active and whose monumental careers add up to a hundred and eighteen years of movie making." With the music playing "Hooray for Hollywood," the two veterans walked onstage. "Isn't that a nice reputation, George?" said Vidor. "Very gratifying," Cukor replied. "Do you suppose it's for our work or for our age?" "Well, we're not getting any younger," Vidor noted. "Did you remember the envelope?" "Certainly," Cukor said, "and let's get on with it." "Action," Vidor exclaimed before announcing the nominees and then the winner: Robert Redford (for *Ordinary People*).

Redford approached the podium and took the Oscar without even acknowledging their presence. Said Morrissey: "It was insensitive and impolite not to make any reference to being given an award from Cukor and Vidor, two giants." Cukor never liked Redford as an actor ("too stiff"), and this incident made it worse. He and Vidor looked foolish; nobody paid attention to them. "George didn't say anything," Morrissey recalled. "If he was insulted, he wouldn't say. That was his personality."

Finding himself with ample time, few projects in the works, and no offers on the horizon, Cukor once again turned his attention to an autobiography. The idea of writing his memoirs was still appealing even though numerous attempts had failed. In 1979 he had again attempted a biography, this time with *Time*'s critic Richard Schickel, whom he respected after watching his TV series *The Men Who Made the Movies*, which contained "illuminating" (Cukor's word) insights into his career.

Schickel arrived in L.A., at Cukor's expense, for two weeks. The idea was for him to work closely with Cukor but do all the writing himself. Alas, this attempt also failed, and for the same reasons that the previous ones had proved futile: Cukor was reticent about his personal life. Schickel held that Cukor had spent a lifetime protecting his homosexuality, and he was so guarded in their meetings that even "safe" stories about his work or friendship with Somerset Maugham lost their punch.

At one time Schickel was tempted to "break the strange and unnecessary silence" and tell his gracious host, "I know you are homosexual and it doesn't matter." But he didn't, probably out of respect.

The 1980s brought a renewed interest in a book about his life. Cukor was undoubtedly influenced by the proliferation of biographies and autobiographies of prominent Hollywood personalities. The high-profile memoirs of Lauren Bacall and Shelley Winters catapulted them to the best-seller lists.

Cukor had deep respect for the art of writing and had spent much of his career working with Hollywood's best writers. However, attempts at writing about his life had never progressed beyond discouraging starts. "It's not laziness on my part," he conceded, "but I've never written anything or even attempted a book."

The idea now was to work on a biography with Morrissey. "I like him, and he likes me," he told a friend, "so we're hoping that this time we'll be able to get on with it." Morrissey recalled: "I went through George's letters, and even though I knew him well, there really was no story there. You can always tell the story of somebody who's had a terrible life, fought with this and overcame that. But Cukor's life was not wrought with crisis. What gifts he had, he understood and handled well. He never had terrible problems, which left any real drama out."

The real story, Morrissey thought, was not so much in Cukor's life as in the gallery of his friends, which included Hollywood's most legendary personalities. Because Cukor had saved every letter he had received, Morrissey suggested compiling a book based on his personal correspondence, amplified with new anecdotes. He hoped Cukor's distinct wit would be reflected in a book about the way he presented and dealt with these celebrities. It was going to be a companion to *On Cukor,* in which he talked about his films.

They spent days tape-recording his recollections, but soon Morrissey ran into the problems of earlier biographers. There was little personal information in the letters, and Cukor was unwilling to talk about his personal life. He would not share intimate details, even though Morrissey was a trusted friend. Insights into his emotional and sexual life were not forthcoming. Cukor rigorously avoided anything about his homosexuality or how being a gay director had affected his life. He regarded his sexuality as his business. "Whatever it was, it was something that was strictly his."

Morrissey compiled what personal anecdotes Cukor gave him, added some letters, and set out to find a publisher. The book was submitted by agent Robert Lanz to Jacqueline Onassis, who had recently joined Viking in a much-publicized return to the work force. Lanz, however, wasn't optimistic. He told Morrissey matter-of-factly, "I love George, and I love this book, but no publisher will take just a book of letters. Besides, no book of letters has ever made a penny for anybody." Lanz's fears proved true. Unable to find a publisher, the book died.

In the 1980s Cukor increased his involvement with AMPAS. He always had a special relationship with the academy, as a member of its board and cochairman of the Foreign Film Committee. In April 1980 Cukor again hosted his annual luncheon for the foreign directors nominated for an Oscar. Over the past decade these luncheons had become one of AMPAS's most felicitous traditions. This one took place on a sunny Saturday afternoon at Sunset Boulevard's fashionable Le Dome restaurant. It was the first to include women directors: Margarethe von Trotta and Nancy Walker.

The foreign artists exchanged quips and ideas with veterans like Allan Dwan, Billy Wilder, Rouben Mamoulian, William Wyler. Mamoulian was applauded when he spoke about a brotherhood of artists that transcended national ideologies. "With the world the shape it's in now," he said, "the one hope for understanding is through the arts." They all raised their glasses in a special toast to Allan Dwan, who had just turned ninety-five. At the end Wyler told the contenders: "I've been nominated among the five directors in America, but you've been nominated as the best five in the world. So how can any one of you be a loser?"

On July 11, 1980, a select group of industry people was invited to a gala reception in Cukor's honor. The occasion was the presentation of his personal papers to the academy's library. With prospects of a biography dimmed, Fay Kanin, a close friend and then AMPAS president, was finally able to convince Cukor to donate his vast archive, which included forty leather-bound shooting scripts, forty-two unbound screenplays, seven thousand location photographs, personal letters, research materials, and other memorabilia. More than two hundred people attended the reception, including Jack Valenti, president of the Motion Picture Association of America, directors King Vidor and Robert Wise, and actors Jack Lemmon, Roddy McDowall, Gregory Peck, Cathleen Nesbitt, and Gale Sondergaard. Cukor also invited Gene Allen, his secretary, Irene Burns, his lawyer, George Towers, and other close friends.

The reception began at five-thirty on a Friday afternoon, with a welcome from William Schallert, president of the Screen Actors Guild. Fay Kanin commented that it was "proper" that the collection reside at the academy, in the community where Cukor lived, worked, and developed as an artist. "The quality and diversity of his work is [sic] staggering. It's just awesome," said Kanin. "This is a very exciting occasion for us; it's a small way of thanking George for this wonderful gift.

"I love the way they are bound," she continued. "Expensive," noted Cukor. "We have a chance to see how your salary grew." "Not enough," quipped Cukor. Relating how shamelessly the academy had courted

Cukor for his collection, Kanin concluded with a lovely surprise: Samuel Goldwyn, Jr., had donated ten thousand dollars, earmarked for the loving care of the George Cukor collection.

"My speech will be very brief," Cukor told his friends. "It's a great privilege and a thrill that I'm permitted to give one of these valueless things, no more than my right eye, to the academy. I hope to God young people will use them and really benefit by them. I give it with my great pleasure. I see all my loving friends here, who are far too young. I've known them when they were children."

The reception also served as a birthday party: Cukor had turned eighty-one a few days earlier. He cut the huge cake, which was decorated with fifty candles, celebrating his fiftieth anniversary as a filmmaker. While Cukor blew out the candles, some frosting came off onto his coat. "We will either have it cleaned or buy you a new coat," Kanin said. But Cukor thought it somehow looked more real—and better.

The most significant event in Cukor's eighty-first year, which marked his golden anniversary as a director, was an offer to direct *Rich and Famous.* The film had been in the works since 1976, when producer William Allyn optioned the rights for a remake of *Old Acquaintance,* a 1943 Bette Davis vehicle based on John Van Druten's Broadway play. In the original Davis played a long-suffering writer of serious fiction, and Miriam Hopkins her shrill friend, who ended up writing potboilers and becoming more famous than her rival.

When Universal decided not to do the film, Allyn sent the script to Jacqueline Bisset, hoping that with her name attached to the project, he could attract financing more easily. Bisset loved the script and agreed to defer her salary if Allyn could raise the money. In exchange, she would not only be the star but also be involved behind the cameras. In May 1980 a production company was formed with Bisset as coproducer. When American businessmen insisted on approving every aspect of the production, which would have delayed the process, Allyn decided to seek out major studio backing. Fortunately MGM agreed to budget it without deferring salaries. The picture was set for a fifty-five-day-shooting schedule and a budget of eleven million dollars; it ended up costing less.

Robert Mulligan was signed to direct, with Bisset and Candice Bergen in the lead roles. "The movie is not a remake," Allyn said. "It has been inspired by the play, but Gerald Ayres updated the story." In the new film Bisset had the dowdy Bette Davis role, while Bergen donned the jewels and furs of the bitchy Hopkins part. The film starts in 1959, when the two women are roommates at Smith College, and works its way up to the present. Bisset is a serious writer, but she can't get her private life together and suffers from long fallow periods of depression and writer's block.

Bergen, on the other hand, writes trashy novels in the afternoon, while her kid is asleep and her husband is away. In the Judith Krantz tradition, her works are best-sellers, and she's a hit on *Merv Griffin*. Despite all these changes, the two women remain friends through the years.

Bisset had never worked with Bergen before. "I liked what I saw of her," said Bisset, "but I was a bit wary before meeting her. My generation was reared to have a slight distrust of other women." Indeed, Hollywood wags predicted fireworks on a set that featured two female stars, but the fireworks never occurred. Bergen was quick to praise Bisset's generosity and lack of competitiveness. "We were in instant sympathy with each other," she recalled, "long typecast for our looks and ready to break out of our restrictive roles. We worked closely with each other throughout the film, a tight two-women team. I think our friendship was reflected in our performances."

From the beginning, however, Mulligan had difficulties with Bisset. "She doesn't trust me," he complained to Allyn. "I am unable to communicate with her." Her involvement behind the cameras contributed to the tension, as what exactly Bisset's "coproducer" status entailed was not clearly established. She took the role seriously, and David Begelman, MGM's top executive, may have encouraged her too much. Allyn, however, didn't really consider her a coproducer. "Because of that credit," he recalled, "she had the illusion she could interfere as much as she wanted. But it was more of a courtesy to her; it was my money, my development."

Labor disputes resulting in a Screen Actors Guild (SAG) strike forced the production to shut down after only one week of shooting. The strike was not resolved for ten weeks, and Mulligan, who was unhappy over the situation with Bisset and had other commitments, used it as an excuse to withdraw from the picture.

At the end of August Cukor was contacted. Visiting his home to talk about the project, Allyn spent the whole afternoon looking at Cukor's remarkable collection of photographs. As irascible as ever, when the conversation came around to Cecil Beaton, Cukor remarked, "And you surely have heard about that cunt." Fifteen years after *My Fair Lady*, he still couldn't resist the opportunity to trash Beaton.

An announcement was made on October 10 that Cukor would replace Mulligan. The official statement was that Mulligan would no longer be associated as the result of circumstances arising from the SAG strike, but insiders knew that Mulligan had left because he disliked Bisset. Cukor had no qualms about taking over. "I've replaced other directors and other directors have replaced me," he said. "If I wasn't sure that I was still able and ready to direct a picture, I wouldn't have agreed to do it." Asked if he was nervous about tackling his first feature film since *Travels with My Aunt,* nine years earlier, he noted: "Not one damn bit. It's an awfully attractive project. If it's no good, it's nobody's fault but my own."

Cukor told his friends about the offer to do *Rich and Famous* in a typically self-derisive humor: "Allyn called me and said, 'George, you know, we have this film, and the director left. How would you like to direct it?' I said to him, 'You must be really scraping the bottom of the barrel; you must be desperate.' " There was a measure of irony in Cukor's quip because few people knew that he needed to work for financial reasons. Maintaining a house with a large staff and continuing his luxurious life-style were expensive propositions.

Cukor's business manager, Bill Hayes, often called Benjamin to ask, "Ben, is there anything in the offing for George? He needs money." But as a client Cukor didn't make demands. "The only time he got upset," Benjamin recalled, "was when I said, 'George, there's this picture to be done in England. I'm embarrassed to even bring this to you, but it's a deal, and it's a hundred thousand dollars.' "

Furious, Cukor exploded, "How dare you offer me anything for so little money?" Two hours later Cukor's secretary called and said, "That wasn't George who was talking to you. He's so full of pain-killers, and he's just so sick. I know he loves you, and he would never talk to you in that manner." The next day things were back to normal, and "there was no longevity to the bitterness," according to Benjamin.

"All he wanted was good scripts," said the agent, "though he wouldn't do youth-oriented movies." Benjamin claimed that Cukor had trouble making TV movies, which were easier to find, because he was used to twenty-week-productions, and in television a movie had to be made in several weeks.

Cukor was thrilled to do *Rich and Famous;* a stylish comedy about women's life choices, it was the kind of material he was drawn to. But he denied that he wanted to do the film because it had two strong parts for women. "I hope people don't get hung up on the idea that it is a woman's movie, it's our version of *Butch Cassidy and the Sundance Kid.*" Cukor wanted to direct it, he said, because "it was one of the wittiest scripts I've read in a long time. I still find a witty, intelligent script irresistible.

"Of course," he said wistfully, "the offers don't come fast and furious," but then added mischievously, "I think they made a very intelligent choice." Bisset concurred: "Candy and I are thrilled that George has agreed. His aesthetic sense will enhance the picture, as it's been doing for pictures for the past fifty years." And Bergen felt "it was wonderful to have worked with a director of that caliber. He was one of the great mandarins, and it was an honor to have done a film with him, much less his last film."

One afternoon Ayres went to Cukor's house to discuss his script. "Go ahead," the director said, "let's hear what you have in mind." Ayres had come to hear Cukor's ideas, not to voice his own, but Cukor asked him to read the entire script out loud. "He ended up correcting my performance," Ayres recalled, "emphasizing the rhythm." Cukor loved the script so dearly that not one line was changed. "I stuck right to the text," he noted. "I don't come each day with new lines of my own scribbled on the back of an envelope."

By the time Cukor came aboard, all the casting had been done. Initially Cukor was pleased with his leading ladies. "Jackie and Candy will bring beauty and simplicity back to the screen," he said. Bergen and Cukor were not strangers. He had known her father, Edgar Bergen, the famed ventriloquist; she was like a little sister to Charlie McCarthy, the wise-cracking dummy. Bergen recalled: "I was someone he had a frame of reference for, having grown up in Hollywood, with parents who were in show business and with a father whose sense of humor and talent he respected. We had a kind of common language, knowing a lot of the same people."

As for Bisset, Cukor had met her fifteen years earlier, when she was at Fox's talent school for young actors. He had been assigned to find a scene for her, and they had even worked together at his office for several days. But then Bisset's agent had sent her to do a test with another studio. "I'm afraid there was a big brouhaha," Bessit said; "everyone got offended. George took heavy umbrage, and he was furious with me." Back then Bisset didn't really know who Cukor was or the extent of his fame in Hollywood: "I was young, and not very schooled in the American cinema." When they met socially, Cukor was polite but slightly "standoffish." Bisset always believed he was offended that she hadn't paid him the homage he expected.

Rich and Famous, Cukor's twentieth film for MGM, went back into production on November 10. Cukor had last worked on the MGM lot as a director in 1957, on *Les Girls.* In the intervening years a great deal had changed; a new generation of filmmakers was working at the studio. As a joke, Cukor carried a list of his credits with him—lest they forget who he was.

After fifty years of filmmaking, one might expect Cukor's energy and enthusiasm to wane, but this was not the case. He thoroughly embraced the whole process. "He enjoyed the attention he was getting at this age," Bisset said. "It gave him a reason to be out there. He enjoyed having young people around him."

The first day Cukor arrived at the MGM commissary, the waitresses were all over him, kissing his hands. One day he ran into Cary Grant, whom he had not seen in years. The encounter brought back rich memories of their work in the 1930s. After some chitchat, Grant said,

"George, how would you like to do a remake of *Sylvia Scarlett*?" referring to their disastrous film. "Cary," Cukor retorted, "it was a lousy picture then; it's a lousy picture now."

On the set Cukor enjoyed the kind of respect he always had: The minute everything was ready, all eyes turned to him. "That's the way it should be," he said. Cukor reshot the entire film, which took about two months, including two weeks on location in Malibu, downtown L.A., and the airport. Only Mulligan's opening sequence at Smith College, where the story begins, was kept.

Cukor had the distinction of being the oldest filmmaker ever to direct a major studio release, supplanting a record held by Chaplin, who was seventy-seven when he filmed *A Countess from Hong Kong*. He derived tremendous pride from being Hollywood's most senior member. "I planted the rest of the bastards!" Cukor boasted to Sam Goldwyn, Jr. At eighty-one, however, Cukor lacked the stamina of his youth, which affected the way he worked. "I am magical in the morning," he said, "but I go home after a ten- and twelve-hour day with my ass dragging."

Every day Cukor snatched a quick nap during his lunch break; it was an old habit. On the first day of shooting Cukor was sitting on a chair resting, but people thought he was asleep. Allyn tiptoed quietly toward him. "I'm not dead yet," Cukor snapped back. He knew that people were gossiping about his age and health.

Aljean Harmetz of *The New York Times* contributed to the buzz. She visited the set on a day when Cukor happened to get confused about the script. "What year are we?" Cukor asked, referring to the narrative. Harmetz thought he was talking about the present and reported Cukor wasn't in control. There were also stories that Bisset stepped in to exercise control when Cukor proved infirm. According to Bisset, "George did fall asleep a few times, but he didn't behave like an old man. He was extremely sharp and on the ball most of the time."

Ayres vehemently denied that Cukor wasn't in control. "Even if he sticks his finger from an oxygen tank, he'd still be better than other directors." Bergen also denied the reports: "The whole crew worked overtime to accommodate whatever efficiencies George had in terms of energy and concentration. Everyone bent over backwards; the crew worked as fast and as hard as they could. He would sound off at them very often, but really they're the ones who did the most to accommodate him.

"He was really a hawk," Bergen said; "he didn't miss anything. When he heard us laughing, he had to know immediately what we were laughing about; he hated being left out. He was tremendously impatient with getting on with it," she continued. "He just didn't have time to wait around for the endless setups that you have in a film." She always remembered his saying, "Can we get on? Can we go now?" He was anxious to keep the shoot moving, drive it forward.

One day, shooting at the UCLA campus, Cukor raised his fists high up in the air and shouted, "Can we go now?" Suddenly his pants fell down to his ankles. Without a blink or embarrassment, he just stooped down, pulled up his pants, and, unfazed by the experience, continued to scream.

But Bergen and Bisset did not enjoy the kind of relationship Cukor had had with his former leading ladies. "We got on very well," Bergen said, "but he was not in great shape. Cukor began losing energy each week. It was exhausting, though he did phenomenally well considering the physical limitations."

When they were shooting in New York, Cukor sometimes dosed off behind the camera, but by then the actresses were used to working on their own. The two blocked out the scenes early in the morning with the assistant director. They rehearsed it and showed Cukor their work, and he either corrected them or shot it. "George didn't come in first thing in the morning," said Bisset. "When he came in, the scenes were often mapped out, and he would then add the camera moves."

From the very beginning Cukor complained that Bisset worried too much and that it was not good for her acting. "Cukor thought Jackie's seriousness was a bit pretentious," Ayres said. "Candice was shrewder, and she possessed such astonishing personality that anyone would get along with her." Cukor respected Bergen's intelligence and sensitivity. Whenever Allyn suggested a close-up of Bergen, Cukor would say, "Whatever you want, my dear boy." Cukor gave Bergen simple but effective advice for her close-ups: "Just look into yourself very carefully."

"George mostly worked on the pace of the performances," Bergen said. Cukor considered sluggish pace the major fault of many films. "Americans pick up things fast," he would say, "even things they don't know anything about!" Cukor was obsessive about speed, always driving things faster. Bisset remembered: "His most frequent comment to us was, 'At a good clip, now, ladies, at a good clip.' He was there with a whip," she elaborated. "He would crack his whip and say, 'Come on, girls, faster, faster, pick up the pace.' "

Cukor hated acting that was imbued with self-indulgent intervals; he often spoke about "actors and their greedy pauses." He didn't want anything to slip through the dialogue. When Cukor thought his actresses were slowing down, he would say, "Oh, I could send a train through there," or, "You've lost the back of the audience; they've all left." Ayres recalled: "In the midst of the most dramatic scene, Cukor would interrupt Jackie and scream, 'Faster, louder.' This kind of thing would have infuriated any actress, let alone Jackie, who wasn't very secure." Bisset didn't take these interruptions well.

Morrissey, who spent some time on the set, was intrigued by Cukor's method. "He did something wonderful, which is the reason why actors, when working with him, were much better than when they were in other films. It was a kind of child psychology, a way of getting what you want without going in directly for it."

At a big party scene at the beach, Morrissey recalled, Bisset had to walk all the way across a room to the bar, stopping along the way to wave to somebody. Cukor didn't like the way the scene was working and called for reshoot. "He just sat and rested," Morrissey said, "but when the setup was ready, he got up and, with all the energy he had, hollered at them, 'OK, girls, let's do it again! But remember: Personality! Personality! Personality!' " Bisset did the scene again, but this time, when the take was over, Cukor told her, "Jackie, the camera's still running. Go right back to your place and let's shoot it again."

"That's the most disconcerting thing you can say to an actor," said Morrissey, "because the camera's running. They have to turn around and get back in their mood. He wanted her to do it again without thinking, so she wouldn't be so tight. So here is Jackie not only acting but wasting stock as a coproducer, and that's a lot of film to waste." Cukor wanted Jackie to relax, it was a simple tactic to get her to stop "acting." For Cukor, the biggest trick was not to get caught acting.

Bergen loved every day of shooting; she couldn't wait to get to the set. "I respected my director," she recalled. "Never had I felt such security, such confidence, such joy in my previous work in films. It was maybe the performance I was the happiest with because I had a wonderful time with that character."

Cukor brought out Bergen's comedic flair. On the second day of shooting he declared that comedy was her strong suit. In the past, he claimed, directors had capitalized on Bergen's stunning looks and cool patrician image, but they missed her hilarious side. But the quality Cukor admired most about Bergen was her class. Bergen reminded him of Vivien Leigh: She could do and say the most ridiculous things yet remain elegant.

It was the first time Bergen had ever done a character part; Merry Noel wasn't a leading lady. Cukor approved of her choice of a broad accent and broad body language. For her part it was a relief to work in a film in which she wasn't glamorized. She was also pleased that for a change the nude scenes belonged to the men. "Fantastic and about time," she guffawed. "They can have my falsies, panties, and body stockings any time."

Bisset, in contrast, insisted on maintaining her glamorous look. Because her role ranged in age from twenty-two to forty-two, Cukor suggested that in the later scenes she would play "sans makeup," but Bisset didn't take to it well. According to Allyn, Bisset saw the film as a publicity stint for herself; there were at least four press agents on the set every day.

She even suggested having only female journalists because it was a film about women. But her idea backfired when the film was marketed as a woman's picture.

Bisset resented Cukor's preferential attitude toward Bergen. "He was lighter with Candy," she said, "because he knew her father. Also, Candy was not in my position, and she was perpetually in a good mood. She was having a wonderful time, she loved the part, and she enjoyed George, but she, too, knew he could be grumpy."

There was a lot of press about Cukor's legend. "God damn it," Bisset was quoted as saying, "if the picture is any good, he'll get all the credit." A friend said: "George didn't get along with Jackie. He was furious when he came back from lunch one day and found that she had told the cinematographer to take some close-ups of her." Cukor described Bisset in his dinner parties in no uncertain terms: "that cunt."

Bisset was full of demands, wanting the camera higher, lower, on the side. She thought she wasn't getting enough close-ups. "Why is she so mean to the cameraman?" Cukor wondered. "He's made her a vision of beauty." Bisset recalled: "George was very authoritative and didn't like any discussions with the actors. He would appear to discuss some things, but in fact, he wasn't." Bisset asked Cukor once if she could change a line, but he didn't want her to interfere. She accepted his verdict and managed to make it work.

Worse though, Bisset alleged, was Cukor's refusal to hear her name except as an actress: "He couldn't bear the idea that I was a coproducer. If I said anything about anything, he hated it. He interacted with me strictly as an actress. I tried to correct certain things that I thought were not right. Some of the sets were too lavish. Merry's place in Malibu looked to me like they were billionaires; it was a very Hollywood set, compared to the reality of what those houses cost at the time. I just said this looks like they've made it, and they haven't. There was a hell of a hullabaloo over it, and George got fed up. He really loathed it if I was in any way involved; he just wanted me to shut up."

Bisset wasn't sure that Cukor's behavior was a result of his old age. "George was not particularly different when I first met him in the 1960s," she noted. "He was always autocratic. I've heard that consistently. That was his style. He was grand, and he was the head. He was just a product of another school, used to an era when actors didn't have much to say. We had a combative relationship," Bisset conceded. "It wasn't easy."

Enraged at Bisset's "increasing interference," three weeks into shooting, Cukor threatened to quit, informing Allyn: "I will not have a third-rate actress tell me what to do." On a number of occasions Allyn had to take Bisset away and tell her "to let up." Allyn said: "Jackie never understood that George was an old man and we had to protect him, that the crew had to rally around him." Allyn was concerned that the film would fall apart because of the tension with Bisset.

Even Allyn finally lost patience with Bisset. "Jackie could be gauche," he said. "She was self-indulgent, demanding numerous takes, even when there was no need for it." Allyn was shooting an exterior at a railroad station at four one morning. Cukor didn't show because it was too cold. "I'm too old for that," he told Allyn. During the shoot Bisset came to Allyn and demanded a close-up. "You are not nineteen!" Allyn said. Bisset got really angry.

But Allyn also admitted that Cukor could be intimidating to the extras. If he caught someone chewing gum, he would scream, "No chewing gum on my set!" Bergen said: "He certainly could be very vicious, though he never lost his temper with me." Bisset concurred: "George could be a tremendous bully with the extras. He had a very low patience level."

"Being old certainly didn't help him," Bergen noted. "He was not especially sensitive in the way he treated people. I don't think he was really open to much from anybody, and I would never have presumed to suggest anything. I just came with what I'd prepared, and he seemed to like it." But when Bergen's new sense of professionalism asserted itself in a request for a retake, Cukor didn't find it so funny. He glowered at her fiercely and sputtered, "You Swedish fanatic."

The sets had been designed according to Mulligan's specifications, but Cukor didn't like them, so everything was made grander and slicker. Cukor redecorated Merry's suite at the Waldorf, putting the piano in the middle of the huge room. He also painted Liz's apartment white, to lighten its previously dreary look. "George glamorized the sets considerably," said Bergen. "He got a bigger house and furnished it much more lavishly."

Mulligan wanted to do a film that was darker and more realistic, but Cukor saw it as a fast-paced comedy with a cutting dialogue and a glamorous feel. Bergen thought that if Mulligan had directed, the film would have been a more serious treatment of a love-hate friendship. "Jackie saw it more as a portrait, but I was more comfortable with the tone that George wanted."

Both actresses wanted to wear wigs at the beginning of the film, but Cukor always hated wigs. When Bisset refused to change her hairstyle and insisted on wearing a wig, Cukor screamed again, "No one wears wigs in my film!" This was an old obsession of Cukor; one of his contributions to *The Wizard of Oz* had been to get rid of the horrible blond wig that had been designed for Judy Garland.

After the L.A. sequences were completed, the shooting moved to New York. A special-effects team had to blow forty tons of crushed ice all over the sidewalks to look like snow. Cukor thought he was prepared for the cold weather of New York, making jokes about having enough warm clothes from his stint in the USSR, but he was wrong. It was so cold that his lips turned blue; the cameraman had to lift him off the curb to the warmth of the waiting truck.

The sexuality in *Rich and Famous* was much more explicit than it was in the 1943 film or, for that matter, in any previous Cukor film. There were two embarrassing scenes in the picture. In one, Bisset picks up a man (Michael Brandon) on an airplane, they have sex in the rest room, and become members of the infamous "Mile High Club." Cukor wanted it out because it was a lapse of taste.

The second scene showed Bisset picking up a hustler (Matt Lattanzi) on Fifth Avenue. Allyn wasn't allowed on the set because of the sexual explicitness. Bisset had a nudity clause in her contract and insisted on wearing a bra. "Jackie pretended as if she has never had intercourse," Allyn recalled. "She rehearsed it out loud, walking around and saying, 'First, I have three moans; then I come.' " Mortified by what he saw, Cukor tried to stay calm.

"Cukor was reasonably shy in that area," Bisset allowed. "He kept saying, 'Aren't we being modern?' putting his hand up by his mouth and going 'hee-hee' kind of thing, like, aren't we being naughty boys?" Bisset thought that Cukor was scared of the film's sex scenes, because "he staged them from a distance." Still, it was Cukor's idea that the hustler should take his clothes off. Technically the scene is very good, displaying Cukor's masterly mise-en-scène and expertise in conveying erotic tension.

There was some discussion on whether the hustler scene should be cut. Allyn didn't like the scene because "rhythmically" it was wrong. And Katharine Hepburn, who saw a rough cut, thought the scene slowed the story. But asked for advice, she said, "I wouldn't presume to tell you what to do." The editors kept it in.

Allyn tried to make the whole experience as pleasant as possible. As a tribute to the veteran director, he involved many of Cukor's friends. And Roger Vadim, Barbet Schroeder, Christopher Isherwood, Paul Morrissey, and Don Bachardy played themselves in the Malibu party scene. And the literary party scene included another set of honorary figures: writer Ray Bradbury, Bergen's mother, and Randal Kleiser (director of *Grease*). It was part of the publicity campaign but also an attempt to please Cukor, to pay homage to him.

Cukor loved people coming on the set. One day Liz Taylor arrived. "Ladies, be careful," Cukor said spontaneously, "there is an actress on the set who wants your parts." Then, turning to Taylor, he said, "Look at all these diamonds." Taylor smiled, but the crew could tell she was embarrassed.

As company, Bergen found Cukor witty, perceptive, cultivated but also caustic. He came every day with his Labrador dog, Whitney, and Bergen brought hers, a mongrel. "Most of our personal conversations," she said, "were about our dogs. I gave his dog a Christmas present from my dog, a big basket full of doggie toys." It also helped that Cukor adored Bergen's husband, French director Louis Malle, who was often on the set. "My husband had a better time with George than anyone else," said Bergen.

According to Bergen, Cukor was not especially "generous of heart or affectionate, he may have been a fierce and loyal friend, but I didn't get to know him personally. I don't know that he was someone I would have been too compatible with, although certainly we could have bantered at dinner parties together."

Both leading ladies expressed concerns over Cukor's longtime reputation as a woman's director. "I don't know that he liked women especially," said Bergen. "I'm not sure who he liked exactly because he enjoyed directing the men better." Bisset also thought the men got more attention possibly because their parts were smaller. "We had the more solid parts," she explained, "and Candy and I had rehearsed so much together that we were pretty much off on our own gig."

What was beyond doubt was Cukor's respect for talent and wit. Bergen claimed that Cukor was attracted to the women's strong characters, that the film was "really Cukor material." The women he liked in his life were like the women in *Rich and Famous*. "These two girls are humdingers!" he said. "George wanted them to have grace, wit, and guts," Bisset said. "He didn't want them to be sappy or weak."

Both actresses readily acknowledged their gains from working with Cukor. Bergen learned a "lesson in behavior" rather than technique: "George never hesitated to speak out his mind, but he was also abusive to people. He would tell people exactly what he thought, and they would come back for more. George said exactly what he felt about everything and not only got away with it but also was respected for it."

Rich and Famous gave Bergen a new perspective on her career, a new confidence in playing comedy. When she first read the script, she found Merry "unsympathetic and unnecessarily strident and shrewish," but after working harder than she ever had on any character, she had a great time with it: "I loved finding the character. I could have played her forever."

Bisset singled out Cukor's "strong sense of what was visually right. George understood beauty and style; he wasn't just assuming that it would be there because there was a camera in front of you." The experience, however, left her baffled and hurt. "I was hurt by his closing down the hatches so abruptly. Occasionally George was rude, and I replied. I didn't want to take it, so once or twice I talked back. He hated it." Bisset's performance was stiff; there was no edge to it. He accepted her interpretation because he knew her limitations as an actress.

In directing *Rich and Famous*, Cukor felt challenged to stay away from its melodramatics. Asked whether it was comedy or drama, he typically answered, "It's a comedy, of course." And he directed it this way, changing the narrative's tone. Ayres was later criticized for writing a glossy melodrama, but he claimed that "they didn't shoot what I wrote. I didn't write it as a Hollywood movie." It was hard for the writer to talk about it because of his respect for Cukor: "Here was this master of cinema, and I was so flattered that he directed my story." Ayres wrote his script more in the spirit of the British film *Darling*. The title was meant to be ironic, but Cukor changed it into "something else."

The cutting and editing of *Rich and Famous* took longer than the usual. "George had me sit and watch a rough cut of the film," Ayres recalled, "and he liked my suggestions so much that he told me, 'You work with the editor and show me the results.' " In this manner about twelve minutes of the movie were deleted.

One day Cukor announced that Hepburn was coming to see the film. Now that her house was sold, she stayed with him. Cukor was in a curious state of anticipation of her remarks. At the end of the screening, after a moment of silence, Hepburn said, "George, you have made a very, very sexy film. But let me tell you how I would play the last scene." She then proceeded, grabbing Ayres's shoulders. "I would kiss her on the mouth and laugh." Once business was over, the two veteran friends reminisced down memory lane. Cukor re-created his first meeting with Hepburn, when she arrived in Hollywood as a big society girl wearing white gloves.

On October 4, the day *Rich and Famous* opened, Cukor gave an interview in the Los Angeles *Herald Examiner* that turned out to be explosive. The interviewer began by talking about the new technology in movies and the minimization of character, quoting Pauline Kael. This irritated Cukor immensely. "Oh, f—k Pauline Kael," he exploded, "f—k her—and I don't use that language all the time. I don't care what the hell she has to say. She's a b——h. She's spiteful and she's wrong." It was not a shrewd comment to make, particularly as the film had not opened yet.

The premieres of *Rich and Famous* in Los Angeles, New York, and San Francisco launched a week of prerelease activities on behalf of the film. The festivities began in L.A., on Sunday, October 4, with a world premiere and black-tie dinner, hosted by MGM's CEO David Begelman. Following the showing at MGM's Main Theater, four hundred of Hollywood's own rich and famous (including Cary Grant and Liz Taylor) mingled at a party on Stage 28, the historical stage that had once housed the sets for Cukor's *Pat and Mike* and *Les Girls*.

On Tuesday, October 6, the New York premiere took place at the Ziegfeld Theater, under the auspices of the Museum of Modern Art. After the screening the party moved to Studio 54. It was Cukor's first visit to Studio 54 or, for that matter, to any disco, but he seemed oblivious of the blare of the loud music and dark space.

On October 8 Cukor flew to San Francisco—its international film festival was celebrating its twenty-fifth anniversary with a special premiere of the film, honoring Cukor's fiftieth anniversary as a director. The gala began with a cocktail party at Francis Ford Coppola's home, followed by a screening at the Castro Theater and a party at Maxwell's Plum.

The screening in the Castro area, the heart of gay life in San Francisco, was absolutely wild. "When George, Candy, and I went up onstage," Bisset recalled, "we got such a great reception it was unbelievable." The producers knew that *Rich and Famous* would get a special reception from gay audiences because of its subject matter and because it was directed by Cukor, who always had a loyal gay following.

Cukor protected himself by not reading reviews. Only once, in a moment of weakness, he asked Ayres: "Do you think the picture was OK?" "Of course, it was," the writer replied.

Pauline Kael condemned the film and Cukor's lack of understanding of women. To this day Bergen said she had not even touched Kael's review because the critic was "so brutal to all of us."

Sarris, the influential critic for the *Village Voice*, thought that Kael made a viciously homophobic attack on Cukor for his not "understanding" women presumably because of his "disabling deviation." It was a strange charge, after a lifetime of Cukor's being labeled as a "woman's director." What worried Sarris was that "with the trend in contemporary gossip toward pinpointing everyone's sexual predilections, the critic may find it hard to decide where the descriptive ends and the derisive begins."

Distributed by United Artists, the movie went into wide release on October 9. Despite high hopes, however, *Rich and Famous*, received mixed reviews and didn't perform well at the box office. Cukor was deeply disappointed.

In January 1982 Cukor was decorated as a commander of the Order of Arts and Letters by France's minister of culture, during a special ceremony at the Cinémathèque Française. It was the highest order the French government could bestow upon an artist. A special prerelease screening of *Rich and Famous* opened an impressive retrospective, from *Grumpy* in 1930 all the way to the TV movie *The Corn Is Green* in 1979. "When George was knighted," Allyn recalled, "they gave him a green ribbon, and in the evening he danced and played with it like a child."

Bisset was in Paris for the event. "There was quite a tension between us at that point," she said. "It was not easy." Indeed, in London before a screening at the British Film Institute, Cukor was furious. "I will not go on the same stage with her," he told Allyn. "She is a liar." By now Bisset's name had been added to the actresses he held in contempt: Gina Lollobrigida and Anouk Aimée.

Cukor traveled in Europe with his new companion, Richard Stanley, and Sam Goldwyn's old hat, which Francis Goldwyn had given him after the mogul's death. Many journalists wanted to interview him, but all they wanted to hear was gossip about movie stars of yesteryear. Cukor knew they were not interested in him. Once, when a noted French director wanted to know how he met Garbo, Cukor said, "You know, it is an old fucking boring story," and simply walked away.

With *Rich and Famous*, Cukor proved he could still make movies, despite his advanced age. Wishing to direct at all costs, he managed to set up a new project in February 1982, *Where's Percifal,* a two-million-dollar comedy-drama for producer Alexander Salkind, written by his wife. The movie fell through, but Cukor didn't give up. On the day of his death he was considering another project—a TV remake of *Anna Karenina* with Sophia Loren and her son.

Cukor died of a heart attack on January 23, 1983. "For years he had a heart condition that nobody knew about," said his friend and doctor Hans Kohler. "He had a heart attack in the 1950s, but he never talked about his physical problems." Kohler found out about Cukor's problem accidentally. Shortly before he died, Cukor went for some tests at St. John's Hospital in Santa Monica. A friend of Kohler's at the hospital asked Cukor, "What is a nice Jewish guy like you doing in a Catholic hospital?" Cukor immediately responded, "It's a secret. I've converted." Said Kohler, "George's mind was lucid and quick up to his last day."

The underlying cause of the heart attack could never have been anticipated. Cukor was having major dental work and allowed the dentist to pull two or three teeth at the same time. At his age, eighty-three, this weakened him substantially. Secretary Irene Burns held that if Cukor had not had this dental work, he could have lived longer.

According to Burns, Cukor slowed down only in the last few weeks before his death. He led a quiet life, spending a lot of time in his room, reading or watching television. But he was still active socially. "People would come in to see him. He would still have simple dinner parties with his close friends, who were a great comfort." During *Rich and Famous* Cukor forged close relationships with Bill Allyn and Gerald Ayres, who joined his circle.

Cukor tried to be jovial; that was one of his most admirable qualities. Though he had disappointments in his life and long periods when he didn't work, he didn't show bitterness. "He was full of humor about the disasters in his life," neighbor and friend Roddy McDowall recalled. "Any man who'd been fired from *Gone with the Wind* and managed not only to survive it but to retain all those friendships is pretty remarkable." Cukor was a realist; this was a key to his survival. "He knew who he was," said Morrissey. "He never felt insecure around people. He always radiated a kind of common sense."

Lon McCallister happened to visit Cukor on the last day of his life. The two men were old friends, and though McCallister lived in Northern California, they usually spoke on the phone every Sunday. McCallister arrived at the house unannounced, and Burns told him Cukor was sleeping. "Don't disturb him," said McCallister, "just tell him I came by, and that I will call him later in the week." But Burns insisted on checking and found Cukor awake. Cukor asked his friend to come into the room. In all their years of friendship it was the first time McCallister had seen Cukor unshaven. He looked tired, but his spirits were almost as vibrant as ever.

McCallister sat on the edge of Cukor's bed and told him about his wonderful life in the country. "I wish you lived nearer, Lenzo," Cukor said.

"I know," McCallister replied, "I miss our time together, George."

It was obvious Cukor was ill, but they made plans for him to visit Little River, where McCallister lived. When Cukor began to tire, McCallister decided to leave. Cukor never really liked any show of affection between men, but McCallister leaned over and kissed him on his forehead. This time Cukor seemed to enjoy it.

Around six o'clock Burns went to Cukor's room to say good night. Cukor smiled cordially at her and seemed at ease. She went home, but a few hours later, about nine o'clock, the housekeeper called to inform her that Cukor had been taken to the hospital.

Cukor had dined that evening with his close friends Harris Woods and Tucker Fleming. Both were neighbors who spent a good deal of time with him, especially in the evenings; they were like family. The night Cukor died was much like any other. As he often did, Cukor excused himself after dinner and retired to his room to rest. Usually after fifteen minutes he would rejoin the party and continue conversing. When he failed to reappear, Woods went back to his room, expecting to find him sound asleep. Instead he found him unconscious. Cukor was rushed to the emergency room of the Cedar Sinai Hospital Medical Center and died of heart failure at ten fifty-eight.

Private funeral services were held on Friday at Forest Lawn Memorial, with more than sixty Hollywood celebrities gathered at the Little Church of the Flowers in Glendale to offer their respects. Among the mourners were Ina Claire, who had starred in Cukor's *The Royal Family of Broadway*, fifty-three years back, and Lew Ayres and William Bakewell, stars of

All Quiet on the Western Front, the first film he had worked on as a dialogue director.

Cukor's friends attended a public memorial held at the Directors Guild the following Wednesday. "We had a small memorial," said Ben Benjamin. "It was a very intimate group of people close to George. We were just reminiscing about him, anecdotal material mainly." Other friends found more private ways to express their sadness. Shortly after Cukor's death Burns received a call from Allan Davis that brought tears to her eyes. "I am going to miss him for the rest of my life," Davis said, "but it isn't the jobs, it's the jokes that I'll miss."

Burns continued to work at the house; there was a lot to be done. George Towers, whom Cukor stipulated as trustee of his estate, began the business of executing the terms of Cukor's will. Burns was left a trust fund of $125,000 and $1,000 a month. Monetary gifts to some of Cukor's friends were stipulated in the will, including $10,000 each to actresses Madge Kennedy and Signe Hasso.

In November Cukor was honored posthumously at the twentieth annual tribute dinner of the Friends of the USC Libraries, an association of which Cukor was a founding member. Jack Lemmon, Garson Kanin and Ruth Gordon, Irving Lazar, and many others joined in the homage to Cukor. The program was interspersed with clips from his motion pictures.

Katharine Hepburn, who was recovering from an automobile accident, delivered a characteristically no-nonsense message in a videotaped interview from Manhattan. In her strong, distinctive voice, she said that the widely held perception of Cukor as a woman's director was "just a bunch of bunk." She said: "Look at the men he's directed," citing Jimmy Stewart, Ronald Colman, Spencer Tracy, James Mason. "George's greatest gift was knowing how to present a star." That knack had had the greatest single impact on Hepburn's career.

Indeed, Cukor's films contain some of the best performances in the American cinema. And if he was not as well known as the stars he featured, that, according to Hepburn, was how he wanted it. "The only really important thing I have to say about George Cukor—because I worked with quite a few of the so-called famous directors—is that all of those directors 'starred' themselves. But George 'starred' the actor. From the beginning that's the way he saw it. He wanted the actor and the story to be fascinating. In life you either star yourself or somebody else. John Huston starred himself, David Lean starred the camera, but George Cukor was brilliant on the performance. He didn't want people to say, 'This great director'; he wanted them to say, 'This great actor.' "

Perhaps the greatest honor paid to Cukor was the presentation of the restored version of *A Star Is Born* at the Radio City Music Hall, on July 7, 1983. Cukor's masterwork became the most stirring event of that season. While there were disputes about the 27-minute footage that Warner's had trimmed from the original 181 minutes, there was no doubt about the film's high quality and emotional impact.

David Denby, film critic for *New York* magazine, represented many others when he lamented: "Childishly, I thought that if the studio heads could only see this—6,000 adults concentrating on a 30-year-old film that meant something to them emotionally—they might feel some distaste for the movies they have released this summer. This kind of directorial bravura and self-confidence," Denby elaborated, "this kind of emotionally saturated narrative, with its darkly neurotic compulsions, its cynicism and sentiment, its svelte, easy, inside-show-business knowingness, music of this quality composed freshly for a movie—such glories have all but vanished from the American cinema."

At long last George Cukor had the last word, as befits his stature as a filmmaker and his personality as a man.

Filmography*

1930

GRUMPY

Paramount. Codir: Cyril Gardner. Sc: Doris Anderson, based on Horace Hodges and Thomas Wigney Percyval's play. Ph (B&W): David Abel. Ed: Cyril Gardner. Pr: August 1930. *74 min. Cast:* Cyril Maude ("Grumpy" Bullivant), Phillips Holmes (Ernest Heron), Paul Cavanagh (Jarvis), Frances Dade (Virginia).

THE VIRTUOUS SIN

Paramount. Codir: Louis Gasnier. Sc: Martin Brown, based on Lajos Zilahy's play *The General.* Ph (B&W): David Abel. Pr: October 1930. *80 min. Cast:* Walter Huston (Gen. Platoff), Kay Francis (Marya), Kenneth MacKenna (Lt. Sablin), Jobyna Howland (Alexandra). With Paul Cavanagh, Eric Kalhurst, Oscar Apfel, Gordon McLeon, Victor Potel, Youcca Troubetzkoy.

THE ROYAL FAMILY OF BROADWAY

Paramount. Codir: Cyril Gardner. Sc: Herman J. Mankiewicz and Gertrude Purcell, based on George S. Kaufman and Edna Ferber's play. Ph (B&W): George Folsey. Ed: Edward Dmytryk. Pr: December 1930. *82 min. Cast:* Ina Claire (Julie Cavendish), Fredric March (Tony Caven-

---

* Pr: producer; Ass Pr: associate producer; Dir: director; Codir: codirector; Sc: screenplay; Ph: photography (B&W: black and white); Ed: editor; Pr: premiere. Names of main characters are in parentheses. Video availability is indicated by *.

dish), Mary Brian (Gwen Cavendish), Henrietta Crosman (Fanny Cavendish), Arnold Korff (Oscar Wolfe). With Frank Conroy, Charles Starrett, Royal G. Stout, Elsie Edmonds, Murray Alper, Wesley Stark.

1931

TARNISHED LADY

Paramount. Pr: Walter Wanger. Sc: Donald Ogden Stewart. Ph (B&W): Larry Williams. Ed: Barney Rogan. Pr: April 1931. *80 min. Cast:* Tallulah Bankhead (Nancy Courtney), Clive Brook (Norman Cravath), Phoebe Foster (Germaine Prentiss), Alexander Kirkland (DeWitt Taylor), Osgood Perkins (Ben Sterner), Elizabeth Patterson (Mrs. Courtney.)

GIRLS ABOUT TOWN

Paramount. Pr: Walter Wanger. Sc: Raymond Griffith and Brian Marlow, based on Zoe Akins's story. Ph (B&W): Ernest Haller. Pr: October 1931. *82 min. Cast:* Kay Francis (Wanda Howard), Joel McCrea (Jim Baker), Lilyan Tashman (Marie Bailey), Eugene Pallette (Benjamin Thomas). With Allan Dinehart, Lucile Gleason, Anderson Lawler, Lucille Browne, George Barbier, Robert McWade, Louise Beavers.

1932

WHAT PRICE HOLLYWOOD?*

RKO. Pr: David O. Selznick. Sc: Jane Murfin and Ben Markson, adaptation by Gene Fowler and Roland Brown, based on Adela Rogers St. Johns's story. Ph (B&W): Charles Rosher. Ed: Jack Kitchin. Pr: June 1932. *88 min. Cast:* Constance Bennett (Mary Evans), Lowell Sherman (Max Carey), Neil Hamilton (Lonny Borden), Gregory Ratoff (Julius Saxe), Brooks Benedict (Muto), Louise Beavers (The Maid).

A BILL OF DIVORCEMENT*

RKO. Pr: David O. Selznick. Sc: Howard Estabrook and Harry Wagstaff Gribble, based on Clemence Dane's play. Ph (B&W): Sid Hickox. Ed: Arthur Roberts. Pr: September 1932. *80 min. Cast:* John Barrymore (Hillary Fairfield), Billie Burke (Margaret Fairfield), Katharine Hepburn (Sydney Fairfield), David Manners (Kit Humphrey). With Bramwell Fletcher, Henry Stephenson, Elizabeth Patterson, Paul Cavanagh, Gayle Evers.

ROCKABYE

RKO. Pr: David O. Selznick. Sc: Jane Murfin and Kubec Glasmon, based on Lucia Bronder's play. Ph (B&W): Charles Rosher. Ed: George Hively. Pr: November 1932. *71 min.* **Cast:** Constance Bennett (Judy Carroll), Joel McCrea (Jake Pell), Paul Lukas (De Sola), Jobyna Howland (Snooks), Walter Pidgeon (Comm. Howard). With Virginia Hammond, Walter Catlett, June Filmer, J. M. Kerrigan, Clara Blandick.

1933

OUR BETTERS

RKO. Pr: David O. Selznick. Sc: Jane Murfin and Harry Wagstaff Gribble, based on Somerset Maugham's play. Ph (B&W): Charles Rosher. Ed: Jack Kitchin. Pr: March 1933. *83 min.* **Cast:** Constance Bennett (Lady Grayston), Gilbert Roland (Pepi d'Costa), Charles Starrett (Fleming Harvey), Anita Louise (Bessie), Grant Mitchell (Thornton Clay), Hugh Sinclair (Lord Bleane), Alan Mowbray (Lord Grayston), Minor Watson (Arthur Fenwick), Violet Kemble-Cooper (The Duchess), Tyrell Davis (Ernst). With Virginia Howell, Walter Walker, Harold Entwhistle.

DINNER AT EIGHT*

MGM. Pr: David O. Selznick. Sc: Herman J. Mankiewicz and Frances Marion (additional dialogue by Donald Ogden Stewart), based on Edna Ferber and George S. Kaufman's play. Ph (B&W): William Daniels. Ed: Ben Lewis. Pr: August 1933. *110 min.* **Cast:** Marie Dressler (Carlotta), John Barrymore (Larry Renault), Wallace Beery (Dan Packard), Jean Harlow (Kitty Packard), Lionel Barrymore (Oliver Jordan), Billie Burke (Millicent Jordan), Madge Evans (Paula Jordan). With Lee Tracy, Edmund Lowe, Jean Hersholt, Karen Morley, May Robson, Phoebe Foster, Grant Mitchell, Elizabeth Patterson, Phillips Holmes, Harry Beresford, Hilda Vaughn.

LITTLE WOMEN*

RKO. Pr: David O. Selznick. Sc: Sarah Y. Mason and Victor Heerman, based on Louisa May Alcott's novel. Ph (B&W): Henry Gerrard. Ed: Jack Kitchin. Pr: November 1933. *115 min.* **Cast:** Katharine Hepburn (Jo), Joan Bennett (Amy), Paul Lukas (Prof. Bhaer), Edna May Oliver (Aunt March), Frances Dee (Meg), Jean Parker (Beth), Henry Stephenson (Mr. Laurence), Douglass Montgomery (Laurie), Spring Byington (Marmee). With John Davis Lodge, Harry Beresford, Nydia Westman, Marion Ballou, Mabel Colcord, Samuel Hinds.

1935

DAVID COPPERFIELD*

MGM. Pr: David O. Selznick. Sc: Howard Estabrook (adaptation by Hugh Walpole), based on Charles Dickens's novel. Ph (B&W): Oliver T. Marsh. Ed: Robert Kern. Pr: January 1935. *133 min. Cast:* Freddie Bartholomew (David Copperfield—boy), Frank Lawton (Copperfield—man), W. C. Fields (Micawber), Edna May Oliver (Aunt Betsey), Lionel Barrymore (Dan Peggotty), Maureen O'Sullivan (Dora), Madge Evans (Agnes), Lewis Stone (Mr. Wickfield), Elizabeth Allan (Mrs. Copperfield), Roland Young (Uriah Heep), Basil Rathbone (Mr. Murdstone), Elsa Lanchester (Clickett). With Violet Kemble-Cooper, Lennox Pawle, Jean Cadell, Jessie Ralph, Una O'Connor, Hugh Williams, Herbert Mundin, Hugh Walpole, Harry Beresford, John Buckler, Renee Gad.

1936

SYLVIA SCARLETT*

RKO: Pr: Pandro S. Berman. Sc: John Collier, Gladys Unger, and Mortimer Offner, based on Compton Mackenzie's novel. Ph (B&W): Joseph August. Ed: Jane Loring. Pr: January 1936. *90 min. Cast:* Katharine Hepburn (Sylvia Scarlett), Cary Grant (Jimmy Monkley), Brian Aherne (Michael Fane), Edmund Gwenn (Henry Scarlett), Natalie Paley (Lily), Dennie Moore (Maudie Tilt).

ROMEO AND JULIET*

MGM. Pr: Irving G. Thalberg. Sc: Talbot Jennings, based on Shakespeare's play. Ph (B&W): William Daniels. Ed: Margaret Booth. Pr: August 1936. *140 min. Cast:* Norma Shearer (Juliet), Leslie Howard (Romeo), John Barrymore (Mercutio), Basil Rathbone (Tybalt). With Edna May Oliver, C. Aubrey Smith, Andy Devine, Reginald Denny, Ralph Forbes, Conway Tearle, Violet Kemble-Cooper, Henry Kolker, Robert Warwick, Maurice Murphy, Virginia Hammond.

CAMILLE*

MGM. Pr: Irving G. Thalberg (ass pr: David Lewis). Sc: Zoe Akins, Frances Marion, and James Hilton, based on Alexandre Dumas's play. Ph (B&W): William Daniels and Karl Freund. Ed: Margaret Booth. Pr: January 1937. *108 min. Cast:* Greta Garbo (Marguerite Gauthier), Robert Taylor (Armand Duval), Lionel Barrymore (Monsieur Duval); Henry Daniell (Baron de Varville), Elizabeth Allan (Nichette), Laura Hope Crews (Prudence), Lenore Ulric (Olympe), Rex O'Malley (Gaston). With

Jessie Ralph, Russell Hardie, E. E. Clive, Douglas Walton, Joan Brodel, Marion Ballou, Elsie Esmonds, Fritz Leiber, Jr., June Wilkins.

1938

HOLIDAY*

Columbia. Pr: Everett Riskin. Sc: Donald Ogden Stewart and Sidney Buchman, based on Philip Barry's play. Ph (B&W): Franz Planer. Ed: Otto Meyer and Al Clark. Pr: June 1938. *93 min. Cast:* Katharine Hepburn (Linda Seton), Cary Grant (Johnny Case), Doris Nolan (Julia Seton). With Lew Ayres, Edward Everett Horton, Jean Dixon, Henry Kolker, Binnie Barnes, Henry Daniell.

1939

ZAZA

Paramount. Pr: Albert Lewin. Sc: Zoe Akins, based on Pierre Breton and Charles Simon's play. Ph (B&W): Charles Lang, Jr. Ed: Edward Dmytryk. Pr: January 1939. *83 min. Cast:* Claudette Colbert (Zaza), Herbert Marshall (Dufresne), Bert Lahr (Cascart), Helen Westley (Anais), Constance Collier (Nathalie). With Genevieve Tobin, Walter Catlett, Rex O'Malley, Rex Evans, Robert Fischer, Ernest Cossart, Dorothy Tree.

THE WOMEN*

MGM. Pr: Hunt Stromberg. Sc: Anita Loos and Jane Murfin, based on Clare Boothe's play. Ph (B&W, color): Oliver T. Marsh and Joseph Ruttenberg. Ed: Robert J. Kern. Pr: September 1939. *134 min. Cast:* Norma Shearer (Mary Haines), Joan Crawford (Crystal Allen), Rosalind Russell (Sylvia Fowler), Mary Boland (Countess DeLave), Paulette Goddard (Miriam Aarons), Joan Fontaine (Peggy Day), Lucile Watson (Mrs. Moorehead). With Phyllis Povah, Ruth Hussey, Virginia Weidler, Florence Nash, Margaret Dumont, Dennie Moore, Marjorie Main, Hedda Hopper.

1940

SUSAN AND GOD

MGM. Pr: Hunt Stromberg. Sc: Anita Loos, based on Rachel Crothers's play. Ph (B&W): Robert Planck. Ed: William Terhune. Pr: June 1940. *115 min. Cast:* Joan Crawford (Susan Trexel), Fredric March (Barry

Trexel), Rita Hayworth (Leonora Stubbs), John Carroll (Clyde Roches-ter), Ruth Hussey (Charlotte), Nigel Bruce (Hutchins Stubbins). With Bruce Cabot, Rose Hobart, Constance Collier, Marjorie Main, Dan Dailey.

THE PHILADELPHIA STORY*

MGM. Pr: Joseph L. Mankiewicz. Sc: Donald Ogden Stewart, based on Philip Barry's play. Ph (B&W): Joseph Ruttenberg. Ed: Frank Sullivan. Pr: December 1940. *112 min. Cast:* Katharine Hepburn (Tracy Lord), Cary Grant (C. K. Dexter Haven), James Stewart (Mike Conner), Ruth Hussey (Liz Imbrie), John Howard (George Kittredge), Roland Young (Uncle Willie), Virginia Weidler (Dinah Lord), Mary Nash (Mrs. Lord). With Henry Daniell, John Halliday, Rex Evans, Lionel Pape.

1941

A WOMAN'S FACE*

MGM. Pr: Victor Saville. Sc: Donald Ogden Stewart and Elliott Paul, based on Francis de Croisset's play. Ph (B&W): Robert Planck. Ed: Frank Sullivan. Pr: May 1941. *105 min. Cast:* Joan Crawford (Anna Holm), Melvyn Douglas (Dr. Gustav Segert), Conrad Veidt (Torsten Barring), Osa Massen (Vera Segert), Reginald Owen (Bernard Dalvik), Albert Basserman (Consul Magnus Barring). With Donald Meek, Connie Gil-christ, Richard Nichols, Marjorie Main, Henry Daniell, Charles Quigley, Clifford Brooke.

TWO-FACED WOMAN*

MGM. Pr: Gottfried Reinhardt. Sc: S. N. Behrman, Salka Viertel, and George Oppenheimer, based on Ludwig Fulda's play. Ph (B&W): Joseph Ruttenberg. Ed: George Boemler. Pr: November 1941. *95 min. Cast:* Greta Garbo (Karin Blake), Melvyn Douglas (Larry Blake), Constance Bennett (Griselda), Roland Young (O. O. Miller), Ruth Gordon (Miss Ellis). With Robert Sterling, Frances Carson, Connie Gilchrist.

1942

HER CARDBOARD LOVER

MGM. Pr: J. Walter Ruben. Sc: John Collier, Jacques Deval, Anthony Veiller, and William H. Wright, based on Deval's play. Ph (B&W): Harry Stradling and Robert Planck. Ed: Robert J. Kern. Pr: July 1942. *93 min. Cast:* Norma Shearer (Consuelo Croyden), Robert Taylor (Terry Trindale), George Sanders (Tony Barling), Frank McHugh (Chappie Champagne), Elizabeth Patterson (Eva), Chill Wills (Judge).

KEEPER OF THE FLAME*

MGM. Pr: Victor Saville. Sc: Donald Ogden Stewart, based on I. A. R. Wylie's novel. Ph (B&W): William Daniels. Ed: James E. Newcombe. Pr: January 1943. *100 min. Cast:* Katharine Hepburn (Christine Forrest), Spencer Tracy (Steven O'Malley), Margaret Wycherly (Mrs. Forrest), Richard Whorf (Clive Kerndon), Forrest Tucker (Geoffrey Midford), Frank Craven (Dr. Fielding). With Steven McNally, Audrey Christie, Percy Kilbride, Darryl Hickman, Howard Da Silva, William Newell, Donald Meek.

1944

GASLIGHT*

MGM. Pr: Arthur Hornblow, Jr. Sc: John Van Druten, John L. Balderston and Walter Riesch, based on Patrick Hamilton's play. Ph (B&W): Joseph Ruttenberg. Ed: Ralph E. Winters. Pr: May 1944. *114 min. Cast:* Ingrid Bergman (Paula Alquist), Charles Boyer (Gregory Anton), Angela Lansbury (Nancy), Joseph Cotten (Brian Cameron), Dame May Whitty (Miss Thwaites). With Barbara Everest, Emil Rameau, Eustace Wyatt, Edmund Breon, Halliwell Hobbes, Heather Thatcher, Tom Stevenson, Lawrence Grossmith, Jakob Gimpel.

WINGED VICTORY

Twentieth Century-Fox. Pr: Darryl F. Zanuck. Sc: Moss Hart, based on his play. Ph (B&W): Glen MacWilliams. Ed: Barbara McLean. Pr: December 1944. *130 min. Cast:* Lon McCallister (Frankie Davis), Jeanne Crain (Helen), Edmond O'Brien (Irving Miller), Don Taylor (Danny "Pinky" Scariano), Judy Holliday (Ruth Miller), Jane Ball (Jane Preston), Mark Daniels (Alan Ross), Lee J. Cobb (Doctor). With Red Buttons, Barry Nelson, Karl Malden, Gary Merrill, Martin Ritt.

1947

A DOUBLE LIFE*

Universal. Pr: Michael Kanin. Sc: Ruth Gordon and Garson Kanin. Ph (B&W): Milton Krasner. Ed: Robert Parrish. Pr: December 1947. *104 min. Cast:* Ronald Colman (Anthony John), Signe Hasso (Brita), Edmond O'Brien (Bill Friend), Shelley Winters (Pat Kroll), Ray Collins

(Victor Donlan), Millard Mitchell (Al Cooley), Philip Loeb (Max Lasker), Whit Bissell (Dr. Stauffer), Charles La Torre (Stellini), Joe Sawyer (Pete Bonner).

1949

EDWARD, MY SON

MGM. Pr: Edwin H. Knopf. Sc: Donald Ogden Stewart, based on Noel Langley and Robert Morley's play. Ph (B&W): Freddie Young. Ed: Raymond Poulton. Pr: March 1949. *112 min. Cast:* Spencer Tracy (Arnold Boult), Deborah Kerr (Evelyn Boult), Ian Hunter (Dr. Larry Woodhope), Leueen MacGrath (Eileen Perrin), James Donald (Bronton), Mervyn Johns (Harry Simpkin). With Felix Aylmer, Walter Fitzgerald, Harriette Johns, Clement McCallin, Tilsa Page, Ernest Jay.

ADAM'S RIB*

MGM. Pr: Lawrence Weingarten. Sc: Ruth Gordon and Garson Kanin. Ph (B&W): George J. Folsey. Ed: George Boemler. Pr: November 1949. *102 min. Cast:* Spencer Tracy (Adam Bonner), Katharine Hepburn (Amanda Bonner), Judy Holliday (Doris Attinger), Tom Ewell (Warren Attinger), David Wayne (Kip Lurie), Jean Hagen (Beryl Caighn), Hope Emerson (Olympia La Pere). With Clarence Kolb, Elizabeth Flournoy, Polly Moran, Will Wright, Emerson Treacy.

1950

A LIFE OF HER OWN

MGM. Pr: Voldemar Vetluguin. Sc: Isobel Lennart. Ph (B&W): George J. Folsey. Ed: George White. Pr: August 1950. *108 min. Cast:* Lana Turner (Lily Brannel James), Ray Milland (Steve Harleigh), Ann Dvorak (Mary Ashlon), Louis Calhern (Jim Leversoe), Tom Ewell (Tom Caraway), Barry Sullivan (Lee Gorrance). With Margaret Phillips, Jean Hagen, Phyllis Kirk, Sara Haden, Hermes Pan.

BORN YESTERDAY*

Columbia. Pr: S. Sylvan Simon. Sc: Albert Mannheimer (and Garson Kanin—uncredited), based on Kanin's play. Ph (B&W): Joseph Walker. Ed: Charles Nelson. Pr: November 1950. *102 min. Cast:* Judy Holliday (Billie Dawn), Broderick Crawford (Harry Brock), William Holden (Paul Verrall). With Howard St. John, Frank Otto, Larry Oliver, Barbara Brown, Grandon Rhodes, Claire Carleton.

1951

THE MODEL AND THE MARRIAGE BROKER

Twentieth Century-Fox. Pr: Charles Brackett. Sc: Charles Brackett, Walter Reisch, and Richard Breen. Ph (B&W): Milton Krasner. Ed: Robert Simpson. Pr: November 1951. *103 min. Cast:* Jeanne Crain (Kitty Bennett), Scott Brady (Matt Hornbeck), Thelma Ritter (Mae Swazey), Zero Mostel (Wixted), Michael O'Shea (Doberman). With Helen Ford, Dennie Moore, Frank Fontaine, John Alexander, Jay C. Flippen, Maude Prickett, Ken Christy, Jacqueline French.

1952

THE MARRYING KIND

Columbia. Pr: Bert Granet. Sc: Ruth Gordon and Garson Kanin. Ph (B&W): William Daniels. Ed: Charles Nelson. Pr: March 1952. *108 min. Cast:* Judy Holliday (Florence Keefer), Aldo Ray (Chet Keefer), Madge Kennedy (Judge Kroll). With Sheila Bond, John Alexander, Phyllis Povah, Rex Williams, Mickey Shaughnessy, Peggy Cass, Griff Barnett, Susan Hallaran, Wallace Acton, Elsie Holmes.

PAT AND MIKE*

MGM. Pr: Lawrence Weingarten. Sc: Ruth Gordon and Garson Kanin. Ph (B&W): William Daniels. Pr: June 1952. *95 min. Cast:* Spencer Tracy (Mike Conovan), Katharine Hepburn (Pam Pemberton), Aldo Ray (Davie Hucko), William Ching (Collier Weld), Sammy White (Barney Grau), George Matthews (Spec Cauley), Loring Smith (Mr. Beminger), Phyllis Povah (Mrs. Beminger). With Jim Backus, Chuck Conners, Frank Richards, Charles Buchinski (later Charles Bronson), Owen McGiveney, Joseph E. Bernard, Lou Lubin, Carl Switzer, Gussie Moran, Don Budge, Frank Parker, William Self, Beverly Hanson, Helen Dettweiler, Betty Hicks, Beverly Hanson, Babe Didrikson Zaharias, Alice Marble.

1953

THE ACTRESS

MGM. Pr: Lawrence Weingarten. Sc: Ruth Gordon, based on her play. Ph (B&W): Harold Rosson. Ed: George Boemler. Pr: June 1953. *90 min. Cast:* Jean Simmons (Ruth Gordon Jones), Spencer Tracy (Clinton Jones), Teresa Wright (Annie Jones), Anthony Perkins (Fred Whitmarsh). With Ian Wolfe, Kay Williams, Mary Wickes, Norma Jean Nilsson, Dawn Bender.

1954

IT SHOULD HAPPEN TO YOU*

Columbia. Pr: Fred Kohlmar. Sc: Garson Kanin. Ph (B&W): Charles Lang. Ed: Charles Nelson. Pr: March 1954. *87 min.* Cast: Judy Holliday (Gladys Glover), Jack Lemmon (Pete Sheppard), Peter Lawford (Evan Adams III), Michael O'Shea (Brod Bennett). With Vaughn Taylor, Connie Gilchrist, Whit Bissell, Walter Klavun, Arthur Gilmore, Rex Evans, Heywood Hale Broun, Constance Bennett, Ilka Chase, Wendy Barrie, Melville Cooper.

A STAR IS BORN*

Warner. Pr: Sidney Luft. Sc: Moss Hart, based on Dorothy Parker, Alan Campbell, and Robert Carson's 1937 screenplay from William A. Wellman and Robert Carson's story. Ph (color, CinemaScope): Sam Leavitt. Ed: Folmar Blangsted. Pr: October 1954. *Originally 181 min., but released at 157 and 140 min., restored in 1983 to 181.* Cast: Judy Garland (Esther Blodgett/Vicki Lester), James Mason (Norman Maine), Jack Carson (Mat Libby), Charles Bickford (Oliver Niles), Tommy Noonan (Danny McGuire). With Irving Bacon, Lucy Marlow, Amanda Blake, Lotus Robb, James Brown, Hazel Shermet.

1956

BHOWANI JUNCTION

MGM. Pr: Pando S. Berman. Sc: Sonya Levien and Ivan Moffat, based on John Masters's novel. Ph (color, CinemaScope): Frederick Young. Ed: Frank Clarke and George Boemler. Pr: May 1956. *110 min.* Cast: Ava Gardner (Victoria Jones), Stewart Granger (Col. Rodney Savage), Bill Travers (Patrick Taylor), Abraham Sofaer (Surabhai), Francis Matthews (Ranjit Kasel). With Marne Maitland, Peter Illing, Edward Chapman, Freda Jackson, Lionel Jeffries, Alan Tilvern.

1957

LES GIRLS*

MGM. Pr: Sol C. Siegel. Sc: John Patrick, based on Vera Caspary's story. Ph (color, CinemaScope): Robert Surtees. Ed: Ferris Webster. Pr: October 1957. *114 min.* Cast: Gene Kelly (Barry Nichols), Mitzi Gaynor (Joy), Kay Kendall (Lady Sybil Wren), Taina Elg (Angele). With Jacques Bergerac, Leslie Phillips, Henry Daniell.

WILD IS THE WIND

Paramount. Pr: Hal B. Wallis. Sc: Arnold Shulman, based on Vittorio Nino Novarese's novel. Ph (B&W): Charles Lang. Ed: Warren Low. Pr: December 1957. *114 min. Cast:* Anna Magnani (Gioia), Anthony Quinn (Gino), Anthony Franciosa (Bene), Dolores Hart (Angie), Joseph Calleia (Alberto), Lily Valenty (Teresa).

1960

HELLER IN PINK TIGHTS*

Paramount. Pr: Carlo Ponti and Marcello Girosi. Sc: Dudley Nichols and Walter Bernstein, based on Louis L'Amour's novel. Ph (color): Harold Lipstein. Ed: Howard Smith. Pr: March 1960. *100 min. Cast:* Sophia Loren (Angela Rossini), Anthony Quinn (Tom Healy), Steve Forrest (Cline Mabry), Eileen Heckart (Lorna Hathaway), Edmund Lowe (Doc Montague). With Margaret O'Brien, Ramon Novarro, George Matthews.

LET'S MAKE LOVE*

Twentieth Century-Fox. Pr: Jerry Wald. Sc: Norman Krasna, with additional material by Hal Kanter. Ph (color, CinemaScope): Daniel L. Fapp. Ed: David Bretherton. Pr: September 1960. *119 min. Cast:* Marilyn Monroe (Amanda Dell), Yves Montand (Jean-Marc Clement), Frankie Vaughan (Tony Danton), Tony Randall (Alex Coffman), Wilfrid Hyde-White (John Wales). With David Burns, Madge Kennedy, Milton Berle, Gene Kelly, Bing Crosby.

1962

THE CHAPMAN REPORT

Warner. Pr: Richard D. Zanuck. Sc: Wyatt Cooper and Don M. Mankiewicz, adaptation by Grant Stuart and Gene Allen, based on Irving Wallace's novel. Ph (color): Harold Lipstein. Pr: October 1962. *125 min. Cast:* Efrem Zimbalist, Jr. (Paul), Jane Fonda (Kathleen Barclay), Claire Bloom (Naomi), Shelley Winters (Sara Garnell), Glynis Johns (Teresa), Ray Danton (Fred Linden), Ty Hardin (Ed Kraski), Andrew Duggan (Dr. Chapman). With John Dehner, Harold J. Stone, Corey Allen, Henry Daniell, Cloris Leachman.

1964

MY FAIR LADY*

Warner. Pr: Jack L. Warner. Sc: Alan Jay Lerner, based on Alan Jay Lerner and Frederick Loewe's musical from Bernard Shaw's play *Pygmalion*. Ph (color, Super Panavision): Harry Stradling. Ed: William Ziegler. Pr: October 1964. *170 min. Cast:* Audrey Hepburn (Eliza Doolittle), Rex Harrison (Henry Higgins), Wilfrid Hyde-White (Colonel Pickering), Gladys Cooper (Mrs. Higgins), Stanley Holloway (Alfred P. Doolittle), Jeremy Brett (Freddie Eynsford-Hill). With Theodore Bikel, Mona Washbourne, Isobel Elsom, Henry Daniell.

1969

JUSTINE*

Twentieth Century-Fox. Pr: Pandro S. Berman. Sc: Lawrence B. Marcus, based on Lawrence Durrell's *The Alexandria Quartet*. Ph (color, Panavision): Leon Shamroy. Ed: Rita Roland. Pr: August 1969. *116 min. Cast:* Anouk Aimée (Justine), Dirk Bogarde (Pursewarden), Anna Karina (Melissa), Robert Forster (Narouz), Michael York (Darley), Philippe Noiret (Pomball). With John Vernon, Jack Albertson, Cliff Gorman, George Baker, Elaine Church, Marcel Dalio, Michael Dunn.

1972

TRAVELS WITH MY AUNT

MGM. Pr: Robert Fryer and James Cresson. Sc: Jay Presson Allen and Hugh Wheeler, based on Graham Greene's novel. Ph (color, Panavision): Douglas Slocombe. Pr: December 1972. *109 min. Cast:* Maggie Smith (Aunt Augusta), Alec McCowen (Henry Pulling), Lou Gossett (Worsworth), Robert Stephens (Visconti), Cindy Williams (Tooley). With José Louis López Vásquez, Corinne Marchand, Valerie White, Raymond Gerome, Robert Flemyng.

1975

LOVE AMONG THE RUINS (TV MOVIE)*

ABC. Pr: Allan Davis. Sc: James Costigan. Ph (color): Douglas Slocombe. Pr: March 6, 1975. *102 min. Cast:* Katharine Hepburn (Jessica Medlicott), Laurence Olivier (Sir Arthur Granville-Jones), Colin Blakely (J. F. Devine). With Richard Pearson, Joan Sims, Leigh Lawson, Gwen Nelson, Robert Harris, John Blythe, Peter Reeves.

1976

THE BLUE BIRD

Twentieth Century-Fox/Lenfilm. Pr: Paul Maslansky and Alexander Archansky. Sc: Alexi Kapler, Alfred Hayes, and Hugh Whitemore, based on Maurice Maeterlinck's play. Ph (color): Ionas Gritzus and Freddie Young. Pr: May 1976. *99 min. Cast:* Elizabeth Taylor (Mother Witch), Jane Fonda (Night), Ava Gardner (Luxury), Cicely Tyson (Cat), Todd Lookinland (Tyltyl), Patsy Kensit (Mytyl), Will Geer (Grandfather), Mona Washbourne (Grandmother). With Harry Andrews, George Cole, Robert Morley, Richard Pearson.

1979

THE CORN IS GREEN (TV MOVIE)*

Warner/CBS. Pr: Neil Hartley. Sc: Ivan Davis, based on Emlyn Williams's play. Ph (color): Ted Scaife. TV pr: January 29, 1979. *99 min. Cast:* Katharine Hepburn (Lily C. Moffat), Ian Saynor (Morgan Evans), Anna Massey (Miss Ronberry). With Bill Fraser, Toyah Willcox, Patricia Hayes, Artro Morris, Bryn Fon.

1981

RICH AND FAMOUS*

MGM. Pr: William Allyn. Sc: Gerald Ayres, based on John Van Druten's play. Ph (color): Don Peterman. Ed: John F. Burnett. Pr: October 1981. *117 min. Cast:* Jacqueline Bissett (Liz Hamilton), Candice Bergen (Merry Noel Blake), David Selby (Doug Blake), Hart Bochner (Chris Adams). With Steven Hill, Meg Ryan, Matt Lattanzi.

Movies Cukor Worked On as Dialogue Director

River of Romance. Paramount, 1930
All Quiet on the Western Front. Universal, 1930.

Movies Cukor Worked On but Didn't Get Credit for

One Hour with You. Paramount, 1932
No More Ladies. MGM, 1935.
I Met My Love Again. UA, 1938.
Gone with the Wind. MGM, 1939.
I'll Be Seeing You. Selznick International, 1945.
Hot Spell. Paramount, 1958.
Song Without End. Paramount, 1960.

Unfinished Movies

Something's Got to Give. Twentieth Century-Fox, 1962.

Cukor Movies Nominated for the Best Picture Oscar Awards

Little Women   1933
David Copperfield   1935
The Philadelphia Story   1940
Gaslight   1944
Born Yesterday   1950
My Fair Lady   1964   (won)

Cukor's Nominations for the Best Director Oscar Award

Little Women   1933
The Philadelphia Story   1940
A Double Life   1947
Born Yesterday   1950
My Fair Lady   1964   (won)

Notes

George Cukor, Master of Elegance is based on a wide variety of sources and materials:

1. The Cukor Special Collection (CSC, see note below)
2. Descriptions of Cukor's fifty features and made-for television movies, based on repeated viewing of these films
3. Detailed reconstruction of the production process of Cukor's filmmaking, particularly of his important and popular films
4. Examination of articles in various newspapers (*The New York Times*, Los Angeles *Times*, etc.) and magazines for the sections dealing with the critical reaction to Cukor's films when they were made
5. Interviews with Cukor's colleagues and collaborators: directors, actors, writers, art designers, editors, and cinematographers (see page 436)
6. Shooting screenplays of Cukor's movies and other archival documents about his work and personal life
7. Trade publications (*Variety, Hollywood Reporter*) to establish the commercial (box-office) appeal of Cukor's films
8. Biographies and autobiographies of actors and directors

These materials were collected over the last five years at the libraries of the Academy of Motion Picture Arts and Sciences (AMPAS), the American Film Institute (AFI), Lincoln Center Library of the Performing Arts, the Film Division of the Museum of Modern Art (MOMA), and the Archives of the Directors Guild of America (DGA). The book's photographs (of Cukor's films and life) are taken from the George Cukor Special Collection and the Stills Collection of AMPAS.

The George Cukor Special Collection (CSC)

The George Cukor Special Collection is an invaluable treasure trove, which Cukor donated to the library of the Academy of Motion Picture Arts and Sciences in 1980. The CSC consists of four types of files:

1. Correspondence (hundreds of files with numerous letters)
2. Stills (a large number of photographs of Cukor's family, friends, Broadway plays, Hollywood movies)
3. Shooting scripts (which differ from the final version of scripts)
4. Production notes or notes Cukor made about casting; working methods with different actors and actresses; suggestions for art, set, and costume design, ideas for editing, reviews of his films, interviews he gave while directing particular films, etc.

Personal Interviews

More than a hundred interviews were conducted over four years (1988–92) for this book. These lengthy interviews provide rare information about and invaluable insights into Cukor as an artist and a man. The most revealing and challenging interview was with Katharine Hepburn in February 1989; the noted actress is known for her reluctance to give interviews. The following is a list of the major interviewees:

Walter Alford, publicist and Cukor's friend
Gene Allen, Cukor's art director on many films
William Allyn, producer, *Rich and Famous*
Gerald Ayres, screenwriter, *Rich and Famous*
Lew Ayres, actor, *All Quiet on the Western Front, Holiday*
Don Bachardy, artist, companion of Christopher Isherwood, Cukor's friend
William Bakewell, actor, *All Quiet on the Western Front*
Ben Benjamin, Cukor's agent in the 1970s
Joan Bennett, actress, *Little Women*
Candice Bergen, actress, *Rich and Famous*
Pandro S. Berman, producer of Cukor's *Sylvia Scarlett*
Jacqueline Bisset, actress, *Rich and Famous*
Claire Bloom, actress, *The Chapman Report*
Dirk Bogarde, actor, *Song Without End, Justine*
Mary Brian, actress, *River of Romance*

Irene Burns, Cukor's secretary from 1947 to his death in 1983
Capucine, actress, *Song Without End*
Claudette Colbert, actress, *Zaza*
Robert Cushman, AMPAS archivist
Allan Davis, producer of Cukor's TV film *Love Among the Ruins*
Olivia de Havilland, actress, *Gone with the Wind*
Agnes de Mille, choreographer
Edward Dmytryk, editor, *Royal Family, Zaza*
George Eells, entertainment editor for *Life* magazine, Cukor's friend
Taina Elg, actress, *Les Girls*
Gary Essert, film curator, Filmex and American Cinematheque
Mia Farrow, actress, daughter of Maureen O'Sullivan
Tucker Fleming, Cukor's neighbor and friend
Joan Fontaine, actress, *The Women*
Ava Gardner, actress, *Bhowani Junction*
Stewart Granger, actor, *Bhowani Junction*
Rex Harrison, actor, *My Fair Lady*
Signe Hasso, actress, *A Double Life,* Cukor's friend
Ron Haver, film curator for the Los Angeles County Museum
Eileen Heckart, actress, *Heller in Pink Tights*
Audrey Hepburn, actress, *My Fair Lady*
Katharine Hepburn, star of ten Cukor movies, his best friend
James Leo Herlihy, author of *Midnight Cowboy,* Cukor's friend
Samuel Goldwyn, Jr., son of Sam and Frances Goldwyn, Cukor's friend
    from the late 1920s to her death
Harry Horner, Cukor's art designer
Ruth Hussey, actress, *The Philadelphia Story*
Glynis Johns, actress, *The Chapman Report*
Deborah Kerr, actress, *Edward, My Son*
Hans Kohler, Cukor's friend and physician
Gavin Lambert, Cukor's friend, author of *On Cukor*
Irving ("Swifty") Lazar, Cukor's agent in the 1960s
Arthur Lubin, director, Cukor's friend
Lon McCallister, child star of *Romeo and Juliet,* later Cukor's friend
Alec McCowen, actor, *Travels with My Aunt*
Roddy McDowall, actor, Cukor's close friend
Joseph Mankiewicz, director of *All About Eve,* producer of *The Phil-
    adelphia Story*
Daniel Mann, director (Cukor took over *The Hot Spell* from him)
Elliott Morgan, MGM's librarian, Cukor's friend
Paul Morrissey, director, Cukor's friend
Maureen O'Sullivan, actress, *David Copperfield,* Cukor's friend
Gene D. Phillips, author of book about Cukor, friend

Anthony Quinn, actor, *Wild Is the Wind, Heller in Pink Tights*
Deborah Raffin, actress, Cukor's friend
Aldo Ray, actor, *The Marrying Kind, Pat and Mike*
Richard Schickel, film critic for *Time* magazine, contracted by Cukor to write a biography in the late 1970s
Irene Selznick, David O. Selznick's first wife, Cukor's close friend from the early 1930s
Jean Simmons, actress, *The Actress*
Kevin Thomas, film critic for Los Angeles *Times*, Cukor's friend
Cindy Williams, actress, *Travels with My Aunt*
Chuck Williamson, Cukor's friend and neighbor, at his house the night he died
Shelley Winters, actress, *A Double Life, The Chapman Report*
Danny Woodruff, Cukor's personal assistant in the 1970s
Jerry Wunderlick, decorator, friend
Teresa Wright, actress, *The Actress*
Richard Zanuck, producer, *The Chapman Report*
Efrem Zimbalist, Jr., actor, *The Chapman Report*

Chapter One: A Life in the Theater

Interviews as they appear in the chapter:

Claire Bloom
Stewart Granger
Katharine Hepburn
Signe Hasso
Claudette Colbert
Samuel Goldwyn, Jr.
Candice Bergen
Paul Morrissey
Glynis Johns
Aldo Ray
Capucine
Taina Elg

Cukor's observations about New York and Los Angeles are taken from *Current Biography,* 1949.

Cukor genealogy and childhood is based on an unnamed document, produced by his grandfather, Joseph Cukor, available in the Cukor Special Collection (CSC) at the library of the Academy of Motion Picture Arts and Sciences (AMPAS), Los Angeles.

Most sources list Cukor's birth date as July 7, 1899, and this is the date etched on his gravestone. In a few sources, however, the date is July 14; Cukor joked about his birthday being close to, but not quite, France's greatest day.

Cukor's adolescence and initiation into the theater world draw on extensive interviews and personal correspondence between Cukor and his friends, also CSC.

Cukor's relationship to his family also draws on my interview with Katharine Hepburn.

Cukor's friendship with Frances Howard is based on my interview with her son, Samuel Goldwyn, Jr.

"Rochester was a very American city . . ." is from Bernard Drew, "Cukor Remembers Rochester," Rochester *Democrat and Chronicle* (August 17, 1969).

Discussion of Cukor's early years in Rochester draws on Clune, *The Rochester I Know.*

Cukor's advice to Frances Goldwyn, "Run, don't walk . . ." is from Brown, *Let Me Entertain You,* p. 56.

The first meeting between Cukor and Somerset Maugham is reconstructed from Maugham's file in CSC, as well as Calder, *Willie,* Morgan, *Maugham,* and Curtis, *Somerset Maugham.*

Quote on Maugham's attempt to control is from Calder, *Willie.*

Cukor's conversation with Louis Calhern is taken from his letters in the CSC.

Cukor's theatrical career on Broadway and the chronicle of his 1927 season in Rochester are based on theater archives at the Lincoln Center Library for the Performing Arts in New York. "I study my new parts until three in the morning. . . ." is from Mildred Harris, *New York Sunday Telegraph,* July 27, 1927.

Bette Davis's association with Cukor in Rochester and her dismissal from the Lyceum Players are based on several books about the actress, including Higham, *Bette;* Quirk, *Fasten Your Seat Belts;* and Stine (with Davis), *Mother Goddamn.*

"She had her own ideas . . ." is from Quirk, *Fasten Your Seat Belts,* pp. 22–24.

"Davis seemed to know the way . . ." and Cukor's giving in to pressure to let Davis go are from Higham, *Bette,* pp. 26, 30–31.

Cukor's work with Ethel Barrymore in *The Constant Wife* is drawn from theater archives at the Lincoln Center Library, as well as her autobiography, *Memories.*

"Willie, I ruined your play . . ." is from Calder, *Willie,* p. 195.

Discussion of Cukor's humor and friendships draws on my interviews with director Paul Morrissey. Section on Cukor's laughter is taken from my interviews with Aldo Ray, Capucine, and Taina Elg.

Laurette Taylor's work in *Her Cardboard Lover* and her friendship with Cukor are reconstructed from correspondence and her daughter Marguerite Courtney's book *Laurette*, as well as material in the Lincoln Center Library.

The discussion of *Coquette* comes from Barrow, *Helen Hayes* and Abbott, *Mister Abbott*.

Chapter Two: The Making of a Movie Director

Interviews as they appear in the chapter:

Mary Brian
William Bakewell
Lew Ayres
Gavin Lambert
Joseph Mankiewicz
Kevin Thomas
Edward Dmytryk
Katharine Hepburn

Louis B. Mayer's conversation with Cukor about his homosexuality is taken from Brown, *Let Me Entertain You*, p. 56.

Discussion of *The Royal Family of Broadway* draws on Lambert, *On Cukor* and Quirk, *The Films of Fredric March*.

Cukor's observation on Ina Claire is from Lambert, *On Cukor*, pp. 35–63.

Dmytryk on editors is taken from my interview with him; "Cutters had a tendency to act tough . . ." is from his autobiography *It's a Hell of a Life*, p. 16.

Cukor's view of Tallulah Bankhead is based on various sources, including Lambert, and Israel, *Miss Tallulah Bankhead*. "Watching Tallulah on stage . . ." is from Lambert, *On Cukor*, p. 38.

Bankhead's remarks about Cukor as director are from Zeitlin, *Photoplay* (February 1933).

"I could have fallen flat on my face . . ." is from Cukor's observation at his golden anniversary, from 1981 tape at AMPAS.

"What if the audience wonders . . ." is from Lambert, *On Cukor*, p. 40.

Cukor on Tashman is from Lambert, *On Cukor*, p. 40.

Conflict with Ernst Lubitsch on the set of *One Hour with You* is based on court documents in the CSC.

"A young man in a hurry . . ." is from Irene Selznick, *A Private View*, p. 171.

Discussion of *What Price Hollywood?* draws on Lambert and the film's files at AMPAS.

"He's a rare thing . . ." is from Constance Bennett's interview with Zeitlin, 1933.

"It's all right, Mrs. Selznick . . ." is from Behlmer, *Memo from David O. Selznick*, p. 17.

Irene Selznick's description of Cukor as a young man is from her memoirs *A Private View*.

Hepburn's casting in *A Bill of Divorcement* is from Behlmer, p. 43, and memo from Kay Brown, May 26, 1932.

There are many versions of Cukor's first meeting with Hepburn. I draw on my interview with her, Cukor's recollections at a 1973 retrospective at the University of Connecticut, and various books about Hepburn, among them Carey, *Katharine Hepburn*.

"Miss Hepburn, I've seen the test . . ." is from Kobler, *Damned in Paradise*, p. 264.

"Jack, the man is happy . . ." is from Lambert, *On Cukor*, p. 60.

Cukor and Selznick's observations about Lukas and McCrea in *Our Betters* are taken from memos October 3, 1932, and December 6, 1932.

"If you go into the moving picture business . . ." is from Behlmer.

The discussion of *Our Betters'* style draws on Carey, *Cukor and Co.*

King Vidor's comments on *Our Betters* is from an RKO memo, February 4, 1933.

Chapter Three: The First Peak

Interviews as they appear in the chapter:

Joseph Mankiewicz
Maureen O'Sullivan
Ruth Hussey
Katharine Hepburn
Joan Bennett
Pandro S. Berman
Lon McCallister

Cukor's remarks on Jean Harlow in *Dinner at Eight* are from Lambert, *On Cukor*, p. 63.

"She was a real actress . . ." is from *Mademoiselle* (March 1973).

John Barrymore's descriptions of his character in *Dinner at Eight* are taken from various books, especially Kobler, *Damned in Paradise*, p. 374.

"Well, it ought to be . . ." is from 1973 TV series *The Man Who Made the Movies,* also published as a book by Richard Schickel.

Herman Mankiewicz's comments about *Dinner at Eight* were conveyed to me from his brother Joseph in an interview.

Charles Brackett's observation on Cukor's contribution to screen acting is from Tynan, "The Genius and the Girls," *Holiday* (February 1961).

The section on screen acting is based on my interviews with Maureen O'Sullivan and Ruth Hussey.

The discussion of *Little Women* draws on Lambert and my interview with Hepburn.

"It was always considered a little girl's story . . ." is from Ehrlich, "Interview with George Cukor," at AFI.

Cukor's observation on Beth's dying scene is also from Ehrlich.

The interaction between Cukor and Hepburn on the set of *Little Women,* including his slapping her, comes from transcribed Cukor and Hepburn interviews at AMPAS, and Lambert, *On Cukor,* p. 99.

Joan Bennett's casting in *Little Women* comes from my interview with her.

"In New England there is always a poinsettia . . ." is from Ehrlich.

The making of *David Copperfield* draws on Behlmer, *Memo from David O. Selznick,* pp. 72–75, and my interview with Maureen O'Sullivan.

The casting of Charles Laughton in *David Copperfield,* and his work with Cukor is drawn from his wife's autobiography, *Elsa Lanchester Herself,* p. 125.

"This was the only movie part . . ." and ensuing Fields quotes are from Monti, *W. C. Fields,* pp. 43–45.

Cukor's work with W. C. Fields draws from Lambert, *On Cukor,* p. 86.

Cukor's observations on Jackie Cooper and Freddie Bartholomew are taken from Crowther, *The Lion's Share,* p. 214.

Discussion of *David Copperfield*'s style draws on Lambert, *On Cukor,* p. 87.

Cukor's remark about the British version of *David Copperfield* is from Ehrlich.

Discussion of *David Copperfield* preproduction and Cukor's trip to London is reconstructed from articles in the *Hollywood Reporter* (May 8, 1934), the *News-Chronicle* (May 16–17, 1934), the New York *Journal* (June 12, 1934), and *The New York Times* (June 18, 1934).

The section on Cukor's house here, and in later chapters, is based on "In Seven Living Rooms and One Bedroom," *Country Life* (June 1937); *Current Biography* (1949); *Flair* (1950); English, "Cukor Enlarges House to House Art Treasures," Los Angeles *Times* (May 27, 1951); and Tynan, *Holiday* (February 1961).

Cukor's correspondence with Laurette Taylor is taken from her daughter, Marguerite Courtney, *Laurette*.

Discussion of *Sylvia Scarlett* is based on my interviews with Hepburn and Pandro S. Berman.

"I can quit the business . . ." and the re-creation of the disastrous *Sylvia Scarlett* preview are from Freedland, *Katharine Hepburn*, pp. 48–49, and the Hepburn interview.

Casting of Norma Shearer and Leslie Howard is taken from Lambert, *On Cukor*, p. 104.

Shearer's work in *Romeo and Juliet* draws primarily from Quirk, *Norma*.

Cukor's interaction with Barrymore in *Romeo and Juliet* is taken from Kobler, pp. 304–05.

Discussion of *Romeo and Juliet*'s art design is from Quirk, *Norma*, p. 170 (lack of Italian flavor), and Lambert, *On Cukor*, p. 104.

Shooting of the potion and parting scenes in *Romeo and Juliet* is based on Quirk, *Norma*.

Discussion of Cukor's projects with Garbo is based on Behlmer, pp. 75–77.

Information about censorship problems of *Camille* is based on correspondence between Joseph Breen, director of Production Code Administration (PCA), and MGM, May 18, 1936, June 5, 1936, October 26, 1936, and November 7, 1936, available at PCA Special Collection at AMPAS.

Cukor's analysis of Armand in *Camille* and discussion of Robert Taylor's casting are taken from a 1977 AFI seminar.

"George, she's awfully good . . ." is from Ehrlich.

Cukor's work with Garbo draws from Ehrlich and Lambert.

Background information on the making of *Camille* is drawn from Lambert and Morden, *The Hollywood Studios*.

Cukor's observations on Garbo are from Ehrlich and an interview with Dr. Bernard Cantor (USC) at AFI, as well as innumerable interviews Cukor gave about the actress over the years.

Shearer's reaction to *Camille* is from Quirk, *Norma*.

Garbo's refusal to look at rushes is from Lambert, *On Cukor*, p. 113.

On the revaluation of *Camille*, see Morden, *The Hollywood Studios*, pp. 99–100.

Chapter Four: The Greatest Disappointment of His Life

Interviews as they appear in the chapter:

Katharine Hepburn
Claudette Colbert

Edward Dmytryk
Joan Bennett
Joan Fontaine
Olivia de Havilland
Gavin Lambert
Paul Morrissey
Gerald Ayres

Discussion of the preproduction of GWTW draws on Behlmer, *Memo from David O. Selznick*. Most of Selznick's quotes in this chapter are from this book.

Research for GWTW is also based on Lambert's *The Making of Gone with the Wind;* Harwell, ed., *Margaret Mitchell's Gone with the Wind Letters;* and Crowther, *The Lion's Share,* as well as biographies of actors involved in the film.

Mitchell's complaints about the "burden" of GWTW is from her letter, October 16, 1936, in Harwell.

Mitchell's letters to Cukor are also from Harwell.

"You charmed all the regions . . ." is from Mitchell's letter, April 1937.

"Under no circumstances . . ." is from Selznick memo, August 16, 1937.

Cukor as "Boy Test Director" is from Selznick memo, October 25, 1933.

Susan Hayward's screen test for GWTW is from Linet, *Susan Hayward,* pp. 34–45, and LaGuardia and Arceri, *Red,* pp. 21–30.

"Life, at present, is not as exciting . . ." is from Hayward's letter, while she was still named Edyth Marrener, in Linet, p. 45.

The section on *Holiday* uses information from Lambert, *On Cukor.*

Hepburn as "box-office poison" is from Freedland, *Katharine Hepburn.*

"I believe in the detached approach . . ." is from Lambert, *On Cukor,* p. 152.

"On the stage you can play for laughs . . ." is from ibid, p. 122.

Description of the making of *Zaza* is taken from my interviews with Claudette Colbert and Edward Dmytryk and from Lambert.

"Cukor was a whiz with dialogue . . ." is from Dmytryk, *It's a Hell of a Life,* p. 43.

Fanny Brice's work with Colbert is from Lambert, *On Cukor,* p. 134.

"Act simple, Bert . . ." is from Lahr, *Notes on a Cowardly Lion,* p. 186. "Use that funny laugh . . ." is on p. 187.

Dmytryk's observations on the censorship problems and the cutting of *Zaza* are from his interview and Dmytryk, p. 40.

"I think the biggest black mark . . ." is from Selznick memo, September 21, 1938.

"He is as much concerned . . ." and Selznick on Gable are from Selznick memo, October 19, 1938.

The section on Gable's casting and relationship with Cukor uses Tornabene, *Long Live the King: Clark Gable,* as well as Cukor's interviews about the actor.

"Any money we waste is going to be unavailable . . ." is from Selznick memo, October 21, 1938.

Shearer testing is from Quirk, *Norma,* as well as Selznick memos, March 23, 1937, and September 20, 1938.

Hepburn's comments about *GWTW* are from my interview with her.

"Take it easy, Tallulah, relax . . ." is from Brian, *Tallulah, Darling,* pp. 78–80.

"Tallulah just was not fresh enough . . ." is from Israel, *Miss Tallulah Bankhead,* p. 181.

Louella Parson's "George Cukor, her friend, is going to direct . . ." is from ibid., p. 169.

Joan Fontaine's screen test for *GWTW* is based on my interview with her.

Cukor's casting and direction of Olivia de Havilland in *GWTW* were described to me by the actress in a interview.

"If we finally wind up with any of the stars . . ." is from Selznick memo, October 21, 1938.

"We simply cannot fool around another day . . ." is from a Selznick memo.

"Projection-room surprises" and Selznick's demands to see rehearsals are from Selznick memo, February 8, 1939.

"I was the director, after all . . ." is from Lambert, *On Cukor,* p. 89.

"The only solution . . ." is from Selznick memo, February 14, 1939.

"I was put off because David . . ." is from Lambert, *On Cukor,* p. 88.

"George's work was simply . . ." is from Irene Selznick, *A Private View,* p. 216.

"I am informed by MGM that Gable refuses . . ." is from Selznick memo, December 8, 1938.

"I'm not sure that Gable thought I was any good . . ." is from Lambert, *On Cukor,* pp. 88–89.

Discussion of Cukor's dismissal from *GWTW* draws on my interviews with Katharine Hepburn, Olivia de Havilland, Paul Morrissey, and Gavin Lambert, and Lloyd Shearer, *New York Times Magazine* (March 30, 1947).

"It is nonsense to say that I was giving too much attention . . ." is from Robyns, *Light of a Star,* quoted in *D.O.S.,* p. 192.

"I was an awful bitch on the set . . ." is from Lambert, *On Cukor,* p. 149.

Vivien Leigh's interaction with Cukor during *GWTW* draws from Lambert, *On Cukor,* pp. 89–90, 149.

"I've long ago reconciled . . ." is from Lambert, *On Cukor.*

Frances Goldwyn's comment on Cukor is from Tynan.

"The most innocent jokes . . ." is from Loos, *A Cast of Thousands,* p. 167.

"Cukor could detect hidden qualities . . ." is from Loos, p. 168. Other observations are from Carey, *Anita Loos,* pp. 183–86.

The casting of Crawford and Cukor's work with her in *The Women* are taken from Thomas, *Joan Crawford.*

The Crawford-Shearer knitting story is from Quirk, *Norma,* p. 205; the Russell-Shearer gum-chewing story and Lubitsch story are also from this book.

Rosalind Russell's work with Cukor in *The Women* draws heavily on her autobiography, *Life Is a Banquet.*

"Look, kid, just forget those female tricks . . ." is from Loos, p. 168.

Joan Fontaine's experience in *The Women* is based on my interview with her.

Hedda Hopper's comment on *The Women* is from her book, *From Under My Hat.*

Cukor on stars is from Lambert, *On Cukor,* p. 181.

Margaret Mitchell comments to Cukor on the opening night of *GWTW* is from January 9, 1942, letter, in Harwell.

Chapter Five: The End of an Era

Interviews as they appear in the chapter:

Joseph Mankiewicz
Gavin Lambert
Teresa Wright
Joan Fontaine
Claudette Colbert
Lon McCallister
Joseph Mankiewicz
Katharine Hepburn
Ruth Hussey
Joan Fontaine
Elliott Morgan
George Eells
Hans Kohler
Gary Essert
James Leo Herlihy

Kevin Thomas
Allan Davis
Arthur Lubin
Don Bachardy
Signe Hasso

Cukor's self-definition as a director and his choice of material are taken from various interviews, but primarily Ehrlich, including "It's disconcerting to people . . ."

"There's nothing more awful than being preached at . . . ," including comments on Richard Lester and John Ford, is from interview in *New York Post* (August 8, 1969).

Observations on Cukor as a woman's director by Joseph Mankiewicz, Teresa Wright, Joan Fontaine, and Claudette Colbert are taken from my interviews with them.

"I'm staging a one-man rebellion . . ." is from an interview in New York *Daily News* (September 16, 1949).

The discussion of *Susan and God* draws on Lambert, *On Cukor*, as well as Quirk, *The Films of Fredric March*.

Hepburn's role in the play and film version of *The Philadelphia Story*, is drawn from Freedland, *Katharine Hepburn*, pp. 80–81.

Cukor's work with Jimmy Stewart, including quote "If I appear in a bathing suit . . ." is from a taped interview between Cukor and Katharine Hepburn, at AMPAS.

Cukor's approach to *The Philadelphia Story* derives from Lambert, *On Cukor*, pp. 123–26.

Cukor's work with the actors in *The Philadelphia Story* is based on my interviews with Katharine Hepburn and Ruth Hussey.

"The best times of my life . . ." and Cukor's descriptions of his Sunday luncheons are from an interview in *Architectural Digest* (April 1978).

"The only difference . . ." is taken from Chase, *Past Imperfect*, pp. 70–71.

"Katie and I used to go nearly every Sunday . . ." is from Kobal, *People Will Talk*.

Anita Loos's first Sunday brunch is taken from her autobiography.

"We both felt bad and had to apologize . . ." is from Simone Signoret's autobiography, pp. 317–18.

Cukor's talk about his house is from *Flair* magazine (January 6, 1950).

Cukor's meeting with Shirley Temple on the set of *The Blue Bird* is from her autobiography, *Child Star*, p. 298.

Crawford's casting in *A Woman's Face* is from Thomas, *Joan Crawford*. Cukor's work with Crawford is from Lambert, *On Cukor*, pp. 161–63, the quote, "No, no, no it's still got emotion . . ." is on p. 163.

"Open the windows . . ." is from *The New York Times* review of *Two-Faced Woman* (January 1, 1942).

The censorship problems of *Two-Faced Woman* are reconstructed from the PCA Special Collection, at AMPAS.

Cukor's early friendship with Ruth Gordon is based on her autobiography, *My Side,* as well as correspondence between them in CSC.

Louis B. Mayer's comment and Cukor's interaction with Shearer on the set of *Her Cardboard Lover* is from Quirk, *Norma,* pp. 225–26.

For background information on *Keeper of the Flame,* I draw on Anne Edwards, *A Remarkable Woman.*

"The screen is a powerful factor . . ." is from an undated Cukor interview in *The New York Times* (1942) available in the *Keeper of the Flame* file at AMPAS library.

"Kate had to float in . . ." is from Lambert, *On Cukor,* p. 172.

Information on Cukor's military service as well as Selznick and Tracy's letters of reference is from CSC.

The correspondence between Cukor and Hedda Hopper is from the Hopper files at AMPAS.

Chapter Six: Up and Down and Up

Interviews as they appear in the chapter:

Gavin Lambert
Gene Phillips
Lon McCallister
Irene Burns
George Eells
Signe Hasso
Shelley Winters
Deborah Kerr
Irene Burns
Katharine Hepburn

"You just had to take a firm stand . . ." is from Lambert, *On Cukor,* p. 182.

"But of course Greta wouldn't have sent the telegram . . ." is from Bergman and Burges, *Ingrid Bergman,* p. 122.

Cukor's work with Bergman in *Gaslight* is drawn from interviews with Ehrlich, Kobal, *People Will Talk,* p. 469, and *Mademoiselle* (March 1973).

"Slaves bound in golden chains . . ." is from Cotten, *Vanity Will Get You Somewhere,* p. 57.

The discovery of Angela Lansbury and Cukor's interaction with her, including quoted material is from Bonano, *Angela Lansbury*, pp. 10–13.

Lansbury's "I was really very young . . ." is from the 1978 tribute to Cukor at the Lincoln Center Film Society.

The story of Cukor's reshoots on the set of *I'll Be Seeing You* is taken from Black, *Child Star*, pp. 364–66.

"Willie has written this thing . . . ," "It's antipragmatic writing . . . ," and "The actors should pick up one another's cues . . ." are from Lambert, *On Cukor*, pp. 228–35.

The other quoted materials on the Cukor-Maugham interaction come from Calder, *Willie*, Chicago *Tribune Magazine* (May 1, 1966), and the Beverly Hills Citizen (July 17, 1969).

The observations on Cukor as an employer, particularly on his letters, is taken from my interview with Irene Burns.

"Now I know who will come to my funeral . . ." is from Cukor interview, *Pasadena Star News* (June 8, 1972).

"Much to my disappointment . . ." is from Tomkies, *Robert Mitchum*.

Cukor's dismissal and LeRoy's work in *Desire Me* is from LeRoy, *Take One*, p. 196.

"Don't worry about whatever curious effects . . ." is from Lambert, *On Cukor*, p. 197.

Cukor's view of Colman as an actor is from Juliet Benita Colman, *Ronald Colman*, pp. 225–26.

Cukor's work with the actors in *A Double Life* is based on my interviews with Signe Hasso and Shelley Winters.

Cukor's interaction with Tennessee Williams is from letters in CSC and Williams, *Memoirs*. The meeting with Garbo is taken from Williams, p.138.

The casting of Gloria Swanson in *Sunset Boulevard* is taken from her autobiography, *Swanson on Swanson*.

"Billy, I have the ideal Norma Desmond . . ." is from Zolotow, *Billy Wilder in Hollywood*, p. 160.

Ethel Barrymore's note to Winston Churchill is in her file at AMPAS.

Cukor's research for *Adam's Rib* draws on Lambert, *On Cukor*, pp. 200-01.

"You've got to be funny, but to elevate the comedy . . ." is from Lambert, *On Cukor*, p. 201.

The making of *Adam's Rib* is based on my interviews with Katharine Hepburn and Lambert.

Cukor's description of his research for *Adam's Rib* is from the Ehrlich interview.

Analysis of Cukor's cinematic techniques uses Bernardoni, *George Cukor*, pp. 47–66.

Analysis of gender in *Adam's Rib* draws on Haskell, *From Reverence to Rape.*

Cukor's comment on Cole Porter is from Eells, *The Life That Late He Led,* pp. 172–73.

Chapter Seven: Collaborating with the Kanins

Interviews as they appear in the chapter:

Gavin Lambert
Harry Horner
Arthur Lubin
Jerry Wunderluck
Aldo Ray
Katharine Hepburn
Teresa Wright
Jean Simmons

Cukor's observation on Lana Turner is from my interview with Gavin Lambert.

Discussion of *Born Yesterday* draws on correspondence between Cukor and Garson Kanin in the CSC, Lambert, and Kantor interview. Cukor's comments about role of Billie Dawn are from Lambert, *On Cukor.*

Discussion of the art design for *Born Yesterday* is taken from my interview with Harry Horner.

Cukor's observations on the Oscar Award are taken from various interviews on the subject.

Cukor on the adaptation of *Born Yesterday* is from a transcript of a 1978 seminar at AFI.

Discussion of the censorship issues in *Born Yesterday* is based on materials in the PCA Special Collection, AMPAS.

Cukor's work on Edith Sitwell's *Fanfare for Elizabeth* is based on correspondence with the writer as well as Sitwell, *Taking Care of.*

Charles Brackett's "phony, phony, phony" is from Tynan, *Holiday* (February 1961).

Discussion of *Gigi* draws on Loos, *Memoirs.*

The correspondence between Cukor and Darryl Zanuck draws from Harris, *The Zanucks of Hollywood.*

Most of the information on *The Marrying Kind* is drawn from my interview with Aldo Ray.

Cukor's observations on the post office scenes and his use of Nazimova as an inspiration are from Lambert, *On Cukor,* p. 202.

The section on *Pat and Mike* is based for the most part on my interviews with Katharine Hepburn and Aldo Ray.

"She was a little bit afraid about her form . . ." is from *Citizen News* (January 15, 1952).

Cukor's observations on sports films is from *The New York Times* (January 10, 1952).

The comparison of *Pat and Mike* and *Adam's Rib* draws on Haskell, *From Reverence to Rape.*

The section on *The Actress* draws from Lambert, *On Cukor,* and Ruth Gordon, *My Side,* and *An Open Book.*

Casting for *The Actress* draws on Lambert, *On Cukor,* p. 212.

"For a filmmaker, Cukor had a rare respect . . ." is from *The New York Times* (February 6, 1983).

Detailed discussion of Cukor's work with the actors is based on my interviews with Teresa Wright and Jean Simmons.

"There was a pernicious habit . . ." is from Lambert, *On Cukor,* p. 213.

Background material on *It Should Happen to You* comes from Cukor's and Kanin's correspondence in the CSC.

"Jack, give less, much less . . ." and other quotes about Lemmon are taken from Widener, *Lemmon,* pp. 111–13.

Cukor's interaction with Peter Lawford is taken from Patricia Lawford, *The Peter Lawford Story,* pp. 108–109.

Chapter Eight: Cukor's Masterpiece

Interviews as they appear in the chapter:

Stewart Granger
Pandro S. Berman
Allan Davis
Gene Allen
Katharine Hepburn
Taina Elg

Discussion of *A Star Is Born* uses Ron Haver's *A Star Is Born,* as well as Lambert's and Cukor's interviews during the making of the film.

Cary Grant's reading for *A Star Is Born* is taken from Wansell, *Grant,* p. 225.

Stewart Granger's audition for *A Star Is Born* is based on my interview with him.

Cukor's work with Judy Garland on *A Star Is Born* draws from many published sources, primarily Frank, *Judy,* and Cukor's comments about her in various interviews.

Ina Claire's observation on Garland is from Frank, p. 377.

"I've never screamed on screen before . . ." and Cukor's observations on Garland's personality are from Ehrlich interview.

"Do I really scream . . ." and "This is the story of my life . . . ," including Cukor's dressing-room talk with Garland, are from Frank, pp. 378–80.

James Mason's work with Cukor on *A Star Is Born* draws from Morley, *James Mason,* pp. 104–106; *Times* (London) quote is on p. 105, Mason's observation on Garland is on p. 106.

The correspondence between Cukor and Moss Hart is taken from their letters in the CSC.

The cutting of *A Star Is Born* draws from Lambert, *On Cukor,* and Haver's book on the 1983 restoration of the film.

The discussion of *Bhowani Junction* is based on Lambert, *On Cukor,* and my interviews with Pandro S. Berman and Stewart Granger.

"You can't take somebody blond . . ." is from Lambert, *On Cukor,* p. 227.

"Thousands of people swarming . . ." is from ibid., p. 221.

The casting of *Bhowani Junction,* including the story about Francis Matthews, is taken from my interview with Allan Davis.

Discussion of the censorship problems on *Bhowani Junction* are based on the PCA Special Collection, AMPAS.

Cukor's work with Ava Gardner, including description of scene that was cut, comes from Kass, *Ava Gardner.*

Cukor's work on *The Chalk Garden* draws from his correspondence with Irene Selznick, as well as from her book *A Private View.*

"George can spend a couple of hours . . ." is from Hirschhorn, *Gene Kelly,* p. 220.

"Don't be a fool. Just be yourself . . ." is from ibid., p. 220.

"For God's sake stop thinking . . ." is from the Kantor interview.

Discussion of *Les Girls* draws on my interview with Taina Elg, as well as books about MGM musicals and Gene Kelly.

Hoyningen-Huene's observations on the cast of *Les Girls* is based on material in the CSC.

Gene Kelly's strained relationship with Cukor is taken from Hirschhorn, *Gene Kelly.*

Chapter Nine: A Replacement Director

Interviews as they appear in the chapter:

Anthony Quinn
Daniel Mann
Capucine

Dirk Bogarde
Taina Elg
Gavin Lambert
Don Bachardy
Gene Allen
Walter Alford
Richard Zanuck
Claire Bloom
Shelley Winters
Efrem Zimbalist, Jr.
Glynis Johns

"No actress possesses . . ." is from Philips, *George Cukor,* p. 123.

The symbolic motif in *Wild Is the Wind* are from ibid., p. 122.

Casting problems with Anna Magnani and Sophia Loren in *Two Women* is drawn from correspondence in CSC and Levy, *Sophia Loren.*

A chronicle of the USC honorary aware bestowed on Cukor, including his address, is taken from USC files, AMPAS.

Discussion of *Heller in Pink Tights* is based on my interview with Anthony Quinn.

Analysis of *Heller in Pink Tight*'s visual style is based on Bernardoni, *George Cukor,* pp. 113–29.

Cukor's work on *Hot Spell* is reconstructed from my interview with director Daniel Mann.

Cukor's relationship on and off the set with Capucine during *Song Without End* is based on my interview with the actress.

Dirk Bogarde on Cukor as director comes from my interview with him and Beverly Hills *Citizen,* June 7, 1960.

The *Lady L* experience is reconstructed from interviews with Gene Allen and the film's file in CSC.

Cukor's work with Marilyn Monroe in *Let's Make Love* draws from several sources, including the Ehrlich interview and Kobal, *People Will Talk.*

"Marilyn's face moves . . ." Cukor's observation on Marilyn Monroe is taken from Tynan, *Holiday* (February 1961).

"It was a terrible ordeal . . ." is in Kobal, p. 606.

Discussion of the color scheme in *Let's Make Love* draws on Bernardoni, pp. 105–109.

Story of Vivien Leigh and *Duel of Angels* was related to me by Walter Alford.

Making of *The Chapman Report* is based on my interviews with Richard Zanuck, Efrem Zimbalist, Jr., Claire Bloom, Glynis Johns, and Shelley Winters.

"You might have to wait a lifetime . . .," "I am beginning to visualize . . .," and "He's a mystical character . . ." are from Spada, *Jane
Fonda*, p. 35.

"I don't mean to flatter myself . . ." is from Guiles, *Jane Fonda*, p. 80.

"I've let you do certain things . . ." is from Hadad, *Jane Fonda*,
p. 85.

"Claire is not a nice Nellie . . ." is from Cukor's comments in *Daily
Mail*, April 29, 1972.

Cukor's notes about Marilyn Monroe in *Something's Got to Give* are
based on Walter Bernstein, *Esquire* (July 1983), Ehrlich, and a conversation between Cukor and Hedda Hopper in June 1962.

The swimming pool scene is reconstruction from *Life* (June 22, 1962).

Chapter Ten: The Second Peak

Interviews as they appear in the chapter:

Rex Harrison
Audrey Hepburn
Irving "Swifty" Lazar
Gene Allen
Allan Davis
Maureen O'Sullivan
Mia Farrow
Irene Burns
Katharine Hepburn

Discussion of *My Fair Lady* draws on my interviews with Rex Harrison
and Audrey Hepburn, specifically their casting and work with Cukor.
Additional material was drawn from an interview he gave at the AFI.

Cukor's work with Hepburn also draws on Woodward, *Audrey Hepburn*.

The assignment of *My Fair Lady* to Cukor is reconstructed from my
interview with Irving Lazar.

Beaton and Cukor's meeting in London during preproduction of *My
Fair Lady* is reconstructed from Buckle, *Cecil Beaton Letters*, and Vicker,
Cecil Beaton; quotes are from Buckle, p. 355.

The interaction between Cukor and Cecil Beaton in *My Fair Lady* is
drawn from my interviews with Gene Allen and Rex Harrison, as well as
Beaton, *Self-Portrait with Friends* and Vicker, *Cecil Beaton*.

Casting of Mona Washbourne is based on my interview with Allan
Davis.

Section on Cukor's relationship with Maureen O'Sullivan and Mia Farrow is based on my interviews with these actresses.

Discussion of Cukor as a letter writer draws on my interview with Irene Burns, Cukor's longtime secretary.

Discussion of the preproduction of *My Fair Lady,* the issue of Hepburn's singing, and the famous press conference draws on Higham, *Audrey,* pp. 163–70.

The strain between Cukor and Beaton is drawn from my interviews with Gene Allen, Rex Harrison, and Allan Davis and from Vicker, *Cecil Beaton.*

Cukor's view of the differences between the stage production and film version of *My Fair Lady* is from his interviews with Ehrlich and Kantor.

The congratulatory correspondence to Cukor after the premiere of *My Fair Lady* are taken from the film's files at AMPAS.

Cukor's comments on the Directors Guild award and the Oscar are from the Academy Awards file of *My Fair Lady* at AMPAS.

Discussion of the 1965 Oscar ceremonies is taken from *Variety* and the *Hollywood Reporter* and Levy, *And the Winner Is.*

Cukor's view on the Oscar are taken from interviews, specifically *Los Angeles Times* (October 28, 1966).

The telegrams congratulating Cukor on winning the Oscar are taken from the Academy Awards file of *My Fair Lady* at AMPAS.

Chapter Eleven: The Worst Years of His Life

Interviews as they appear in the chapter:

Gene Allen
Katharine Hepburn
Hans Kohler
Allan Davis
Rex Harrison
Claudette Colbert
Richard Zanuck
Dirk Bogarde
Gavin Lambert
Joan Fontaine

The section on Cukor's career in the 1960s draws on my interviews with Gene Allen and Katharine Hepburn.

Cukor's correspondence with Alan Searle is drawn from letters in the CSC.

The discussion of the Selznick memorial is based on interviews given by Cukor as well as Cotten, *Vanity Will Get You Somewhere.*

Discussion of proposed Cukor biographies of Cukor is drawn from letters in the CSC.

The discussion of *Bloomer Girl* is drawn from the film's production file in the CSC.

Cukor's interaction with Bob Fosse and Agnes de Mille concerning *Bloomer Girl* draws on the film's file in the CSC.

Cukor's talk with the students at USC is drawn from materials available at the library of the University of Southern California.

"I have my own kind of religion . . ." and Cukor's ensuing comments on funerals are from Lambert, *On Cukor,* pp. 129–30.

The discussion of Cukor's friendship with Vivien Leigh is based on my interview with her close friend Allan Davis.

The discussion of Cukor's arrangement of the tribute to Vivien Leigh draws on her file at the USC Library.

". . . a consummate actress hampered by her beauty . . ." is from Lambert, *On Cukor,* p. 145.

The section on Hoyningen-Huene's funeral is taken from Lambert, *On Cukor.*

"There's no great stigma to being replaced . . ." comes from an interview with syndicated columnist Bob Thomas, June 5, 1972.

Cukor's observation is from Brian, *Tallulah Darling,* pp. 66–67.

Reconstruction of the making of *Justine* is taken from my interviews with Richard Zanuck and Dirk Bogarde.

Creation of decadent ambience and use of midgets in the making of *Justine* draws on Lambert, *On Cukor,* pp. 251–52.

Cukor's comments about Anouk Aimée are taken from my interviews with Richard Zanuck and Gavin Lambert.

Bogarde's comments on Cukor as a director are taken from my interview with him and from his memoirs.

The conversation between Cukor and Joan Fontaine in 1969 is taken from my interview with her.

Chapter Twelve: A Comeback

Interviews as they appear in the chapter:

Gary Essert
Katharine Hepburn
George Eells
Samuel Goldwyn, Jr.
Roddy McDowall

Kevin Thomas
Allan Davis
Ben Benjamin
Hans Kohler
Paul Morrissey
Irene Burns
Alec McCowen
Cindy Williams
Walter Alford
Ron Haver
Gavin Lambert

Discussion of Cukor's participation in *The Movies* and later in Filmex draws on my interview with Gary Essert, cofounder of Filmex.

The discussion of Cukor's role in the Foreign Picture Oscar and his luncheons for the nominated foreign-directors is taken from files available at AMPAS.

The discussion of Cukor's politics is based on various interviews given by the director as well as my interview with Katharine Hepburn.

Cukor's friendship with Francis Goldwyn draws on my interview with her son, Samuel Goldwyn, Jr.

Cukor's friendship with Mae West is from letters in the CSC, as well as my interviews with Roddy McDowall and Kevin Thomas.

The section on Cukor as a friend draws on interviews with Roddy McDowall, Allan Davis, Hans Kohler, and Kevin Thomas.

Cukor's comments on the studio era are from various interviews given by the director as well as his dialogue with Joan Crawford published in annual volume of *Daily Variety*, 1969.

Cukor's view of the New Hollywood draws on my interview with Paul Morrissey.

"A love scene has to be a *scene* . . ." is from Ehrlich, "Interview with George Cukor."

The section on *Travels with My Aunt* is based on my interviews with Alec McCowen and Katharine Hepburn and the film's production files at AMPAS.

"An old woman who's been through the mill . . ." and Cukor's observations on Graham Greene's book are from Ehrlich.

Cukor's comments on the Graham Greene book *Travels with My Aunt* and the meaning of the project to him is taken from an interview in the *Los Angeles Times* (July 23, 1972).

The casting of *Travels with My Aunt* is taken from my interview with Allan Davis.

Katharine Hepburn's dismissal from *Travels with My Aunt* is reconstructed from my interviews with the actress and Roddy McDowall. "Honest disagreement" is from Cukor's interview with Bob Thomas, June 5, 1972.

Cukor's interaction with Cindy Williams on the set of *Travels with My Aunt* is based on my interview with the actress.

The observations on Cukor's life off the set during the filming of *Travels with My Aunt* draws on my interview with Walter Alford.

Cukor's comments on his treatment of the book on film is from an interview in the *New York Post* (December 23, 1972).

Cukor's assessment and treatment of Maggie Smith are from an interview in *Mademoiselle* (March 1973).

Pauline Kael's panning review of *Travels with My Aunt* was published in the *New Yorker* (January 13, 1973).

The discussion on the preparation and publication of *On Cukor* is mostly taken from my interview with the book's author, Gavin Lambert.

"Cukor is one of the most literate storytellers . . ." is from Charles Champlin, *Los Angeles Times*, September 10, 1972.

The section on Hector Arce's attempted biography of Cukor draws on my interview with Walter Alford and an unpublished document regarding the work in the CSC.

The discussion of Cukor as an artist draws primarily from my interview with Katharine Hepburn.

"When a director has consistently dished up . . ." is from Sarris, *The American Cinema*, p. 89.

"Cukor isn't the kind of director you write about . . ." is from Truffaut, *The Films in My Life*, p. 105.

"In my case, style must be largely . . ." is from Ehrlich.

Chapter Thirteen: A TV Director

Interviews as they appear in the chapter:

Ben Benjamin
Gene Allen
Gavin Lambert
Paul Morrissey
Roddy McDowall
Irene Selznick
Allan Davis
Dirk Bogarde
Alec McCowen
Katharine Hepburn
Irene Burns

Richard Zanuck
Kevin Thomas
Mia Farrow
Danny Woodruff
Maureen O'Sullivan
Joan Fontaine

The discussion of Cukor's status as a director in the 1970s is based on interviews with Cukor's agent at the time, Ben Benjamin, and his long-time collaborator Gene Allen.

Cukor's involvement in Lambert's book *The Making of GWTW* draws on interviews with the author and Paul Morrissey.

The correspondence among Cukor, Hepburn, and Olivier with regard to *Love Among the Ruins* is based on files that Ben Benjamin, who was also Olivier's agent, shared with me.

The making of the TV movie *Love Among the Ruins* draws from my interviews with Katharine Hepburn and Allan Davis, as well as the film's production file at AMPAS.

The discussion of *The Blue Bird* is based on the film's production files at AMPAS.

Cukor's observations about the Russians are from an interview with Karin Winner, *W* (November 28, 1975) and Joseph McBride, *Action* (November–December 1975).

Reports of the ambience on the set of *The Blue Bird* are drawn from Rex Reed, "Elizabeth Taylor Sees Red in *The Blue Bird*," *Ladies' Home Journal* (October 1975).

The political significance and publicity surrounding premieres of *The Blue Bird* are from a Fox press release, "A Fantasy Becomes a Reality for George Cukor," 1976.

Comments by Capra and other participants in the foreign directors' luncheon are from AMPAS files on the foreign language pictures nominated for an Oscar.

Reconstruction of the Joan Crawford memorial and Cukor's speech is from press coverage of the event in *Variety* and the *Hollywood Reporter* as well as my interview with Kevin Thomas.

"We strove for a kind of coffee klatch atmosphere . . ." is from Loy, *Myrna Loy*, p. 328.

Cukor's discussion with film students at the American Film Institute is from seminars at AFI in October 1977 and February 1978.

The discussion of *The Corn Is Green* is based on my interview with Katharine Hepburn and Cecil Smith, "Interview with George Cukor," *Los Angeles Times* "Calendar," January 28, 1979, as well as the film's production files at AMPAS.

"Our relationship is give-and-take . . ." is from Edwards, *Katharine Hepburn*, p. 395.

The section on Cukor's receipt of an award from the Film Society of Lincoln Center is based on files at the Lincoln Center Library for the Performing Arts as well as my interview with Maureen O'Sullivan.

Chapter Fourteen: The Swan Song

Interviews as they appear in the chapter:

Paul Morrissey
Ben Benjamin
Allan Davis
Hans Kohler
Richard Schickel
William Allyn
Gerald Ayres
Candice Bergen
Jacqueline Bisset
Samuel Goldwyn, Jr.
Irene Burns
Roddy McDowall
Lon McCallister
Katharine Hepburn

The discussion of Cukor's life in the 1980s and his lack of work draws on my interviews with Paul Morrissey, Ben Benjamin, and Allan Davis.

"Who are these persons in the movie? . . ." is from my interview with Paul Morrissey.

Cukor's attitude about illness, including his comments on being told he had cancer, is from my interview with his doctor, Hans Kohler.

The discussion of the attempts to write a biography of Cukor are based on my interviews with Paul Morrissey and Richard Schickel, *Time*'s movie critic.

The ceremony, on July 11, 1980, in which Cukor donated his archives to the AMPAS Library is reconstructed from a tape of the proceedings, available at AMPAS.

The discussion on the making of *Rich and Famous* draws on interviews with producer William Allyn and screenwriter Gerald Ayres, as well as the film's production files at AMPAS.

Cukor's comments on *Rich and Famous* come from Kevin Thomas's interview with him in the *Los Angeles Times* (December 24, 1980).

"I stuck right to the text . . ." is from Gene Philips, *George Cukor*.

"Jackie and Candy will bring beauty and simplicity back to the screen . . ." is from an MGM publicity release for *Rich and Famous,* 1981.

Cukor's work with the actresses on the set of *Rich and Famous* is based on my interviews with Candice Bergen and Jacqueline Bisset as well as Bergen, *Knock Wood.*

Candice Bergen's remarks on her typecasting appeared in a Rex Reed, "Bosom Buddies," *Marquee* (September 10, 1981).

Discussion of the premieres and parties for *Rich and Famous* use information from the *Los Angeles Herald Examiner* (October 6, 1981), and the *Hollywood Reporter* (October 8, 1981).

Cukor's comments on Pauline Kael are from an interview in the *Los Angeles Examiner* (October 4, 1981).

David Denby's review of the reconstructed version of *A Star Is Born* appeared in *New York* (July 25, 1983).

Katharine Hepburn's remarks on Cukor's qualities as a director are taken from my interview with her.

Bibliography

Abbott, George. *Mister Abbott*. New York: Random House, 1976.

Anderson, Christopher. *Citizen Jane: The Turbulent Life of Jane Fonda*. New York: Henry Holt & Co., 1990.

Arce, Hector. "Interview with Katharine Hepburn." *Women's Wear Daily,* 1969.

"Architectural Digest Visits George Cukor." *Architectural Digest,* January 1978.

Bainbridge, John. *Garbo*. New York: Doubleday, 1955.

Bakewell, William. *Hollywood Be Thy Name: Random Recollections of a Movie Veteran from Silents to Talkies to TV*. Metuchen, N.J.: Scarecrow Press, 1981.

Bankhead, Tallulah. *Tallulah: My Autobiography*. New York: Harper, 1952.

Barrow, Kenneth. *Helen Hayes: First Lady of the American Theater*. Garden City, N.Y.: Doubleday, 1985.

Barrymore, Ethel. *Memories: An Autobiography*. London: Hulton Press, 1956.

Bart, Peter. *Fade Out: The Calamitous Final Days of MGM*. New York: William Morrow, 1990.

Beaton, Cecil Walter Hardy. *Cecil Beaton's My Fair Lady*. New York: Holt, Rinehart & Winston, 1964.

———. *Self Portrait with Friends: The Selected Diaries of Cecil Beaton, 1926–1974*. New York: Times Books, 1979.

Behlmer, Rudy, ed. *Memo from David O. Selznick*. Hollywood: Samuel French, 1989.

Berg, Scott A. *Goldwyn*. New York: Knopf, 1989.

Bergen, Candice. *Knock Wood*. New York: Linden Press, 1984.

Bergman, Ingrid, and Alan Burgess. *Ingrid Bergman: My Story*. New York: Delacorte Press, 1980.

Bernardoni, James. *George Cukor: A Critical Study and Filmography*. Jefferson, N.C.: McFarland, 1985.

Bernstein, Walter. "Marilyn Monroe's Last Picture Show." *Esquire* (July 1973).

Billquist, Fritiof. *Garbo: A Biography,* tr. Maurice Michael. New York: Putnam's, 1960.

Black, Shirley Temple. *Child Star.* New York: McGraw-Hill, 1988.

Bogarde, Dirk. *A Postilion Struck by Lightning.* New York: Holt, Rinehart & Winston, 1977.

———. *Snakes and Ladders.* New York: Holt, Rinehart & Winston, 1979.

———. *Voices in the Garden.* New York: Knopf, 1981.

———. *An Orderly Man.* London: Chattus and Windus, 1983.

———. *West of Sunset.* London: A. Lane, 1984.

———. *Backcloth.* New York: Viking, 1986.

———. *A Particular Friendship.* London: Viking, 1989.

Bogdanovich, Peter. *Piece of Time: Peter Bogdanovich on the Movies,* New York: Arbor House, 1973.

Boller, Paul F., and Ronald L. Davis. *Hollywood Anecdotes.* New York: William Morrow, 1987.

Bordwell, David, Janet Staiger, and Kristin Thompson. *The Classical Hollywood Cinema: Film Style and Mode of Production to 1960.* New York: Columbia University Press, 1985.

Braun, Eric. *Deborah Kerr.* New York: St. Martin's Press, 1978.

Bragg, Melvyn. *Rich: The Life of Richard Burton.* London: Hodder and Stoughton, 1988.

Brian, Denis. *Tallulah Darling: A Biography of Tallulah Bankhead.* New York: Macmillan, 1980.

Brown, Curtis F. *Ingrid Bergman.* New York: Galahad Books, 1973.

Brown, David. *Let Me Entertain You.* New York: William Morrow, 1990.

Buckle, Richard, ed. *Self-Portrait with Friends:* The Selected Diaries of Cecil Beaton, 1922–1974. New York: Times Books, 1979.

Burke, Billie, with Cameron Shipp. *With a Feather on My Nose.* New York: Appleton-Century-Crofts, 1949.

———, with Cameron Shipp. *With Powder on My Nose.* New York: Coward-McCann, 1959.

Buscombe, Edward. "Review of *On Cukor.*" *Screen* (Autumn 1973).

Calder, Robert. *Willie: The Life of W. Somerset Maugham.* London: Heinemann, 1989.

Carey, Gary. *Cukor and Co.* New York: Museum of Modern Art, 1971.

———. *All the Stars in Heaven: Louis B. Mayer's MGM.* New York: Dutton, 1981.

———. *Katharine Hepburn: A Hollywood Yankee.* New York: St. Martin's Press, 1983.

———. *Anita Loos: A Biography.* New York: Knopf, 1988.

Chase, Ilka. *Past Imperfect.* New York: Doubleday, 1942.

Cimons, Marlene. "Feminists Dissect *The Women.*" *Los Angeles Times* (October 18, 1971).

Clark, Virginia. *Aldous Huxley and Film.* Metuchen, N.J.: Scarecrow Press, 1987.

Clarke, Gerald. *Capote: A Biography.* New York: Simon & Schuster, 1988.

Clune, Henry W. *The Rochester I Know*. New York: Doubleday, 1972.

Colman, Juliet Benita. *Ronald Colman, A Very Private Person*. New York: William Morrow, 1975.

Conway, Michael, Dion McGregor, and Mark Ricci. The *Films of Greta Garbo*. Secaucus, N.J.: Citadel Press, 1974.

Cotten, Joseph. *Vanity Will Get You Somewhere: An Autobiography*. San Francisco: Mercury House, 1987.

Coward, Noël. *The Noël Coward Diaries*. London: Weidenfeld & Nicolson, 1982.

Courtney, Marguerite. *Laurette*. New York: Atheneum, 1968.

Crawford, Joan, with Jane Kesner Ardmore. A`*Portrait of Joan: The Autobiography of Joan Crawford*. Garden City, N.Y.: Doubleday, 1962.

Crotta, Carol. "Conversation with George Cukor." Los Angeles *Herald Examiner* (October 4, 1981).

Crowther, Bosley. *The Lion's Share*. New York: Dutton, 1957.

Cukor, George. "Close-up on Katharine Hepburn." *Photoplay* (March 3, 1947).

―――. Interview in *Flair* magazine (July 1950).

―――. Interview in *The New York Times* (January 20, 1952).

―――. AFI Seminar, October 5, 1977.

―――. AFI Seminar, February 16, 1978.

Cukor and Joan Crawford Dialogue. *Daily Variety*, Thirty-seventh Anniversary Issue (1970).

"Cukor's House." *House & Garden* (January 1990).

Curtis, Anthony. *Somerset Maugham*. New York: Macmillan, 1977.

Davidson, Bill. *Spencer Tracy: Tragic Idol*. London: Sigwick & Jackson, 1987.

Deachner, Donald. *The Films of W. C. Fields*. New York: Cadillac, 1966.

De Havilland, Olivia. "Dialogue on Film." *American Film* (December 1974).

Dent, Alan. *Vivien Leigh: A Bouquet*. London: Hamish Hamilton, 1969.

Deschner, Donald. *The Films of W. C. Fields*. New York: Cadillac, 1966.

―――. *The Films of Cary Grant*. New Jersey: Citadel Press, 1973.

Dmytryk, Edward. *It's a Hell of a Life*. New York: Times Books, 1978.

Douglas, Melvyn, and Tom Arthur. *See You at the Movies: The Autobiography of Melvyn Douglas*. New York: University Press of America, 1986.

Downing, David. *Charles Bronson*. New York: St. Martin's Press, 1983.

Drew, Bernard. "Cukor Remembers Rochester." Rochester *Democrat and Chronicle* (August 17, 1969).

Dunaway, David King. *Huxley in Hollywood*. New York: Harper & Row, 1989.

Eames, John Douglas. *The MGM Story: The Complete History of Fifty-four Roaring Years*. New York: Crown, 1979.

Easton, Carol. *The Search for Samuel Goldwyn: A Biography*. New York: William Morrow, 1975.

―――. *Judy Garland: A Biography*. New York: Simon & Schuster, 1975.

Edwards, Anne. *A Remarkable Woman: A Biography of Katharine Hepburn*. New York: William Morrow, 1985.

―――. *Vivien Leigh*. New York: Simon & Schuster, 1977.

Eells, George. *The Life That Late He Led*. New York: G. P. Putnam & Sons, 1967.

———. *Robert Mitchum: A Biography*. New York: Franklin Watts, 1984.

Ehrlich, Henry. "Interview with George Cukor." *AFI Files* (no date).

Eyles, Allen. *James Stewart*. New York: Stein & Day, 1984.

Falk, Quentin. *Travels in Greenland: The Cinema of Grahame Green*. London: Quartet Books. 1984.

Flamini, Roland. *Scarlett, Rhett and a Cast of Thousands*. New York: Macmillan, 1975.

Flint, Peter B. "George Cukor, 83, Film Director Dies." *The New York Times* (January 26, 1983).

"Focus on Cukor." *Mademoiselle* (March 1973).

Fontaine, Joan. *No Bed of Roses*. New York: William Morrow, 1978.

Frank, Gerold. *Judy*. New York: Harper & Row, 1977.

Freedland, Michael. *Katharine Hepburn*. London: W. H. Allen, 1984.

———. *Jack Lemmon*. New York: St. Martin's Press, 1985.

———. *Jane Fonda*. London: Weidenfeld & Nicholson, 1988.

Frewyn, Leslie. *The Late Mrs. Dorothy Parker*. New York: Macmillan, 1986.

Friedrich, Otto. *City of Nets*. New York: Harper & Row, 1986.

Fryer, Jonathan. *Isherwood: A Biography*. New York: Doubleday, 1977.

Gabler, Neal. *An Empire of Their Own*. New York: Crown, 1988.

Gallagher, Tag. *John Ford: The Man and His Films*. Berkeley: University of California Press, 1986.

Gardner, Ava. *Ava: My Story*. New York: Bantam, 1990.

"George Cukor." *Current Biography* (April 1943; March 1983).

Gielgud, John, Sir. *Gielgud: An Actor and His Time [A Memoir]*. New York: C. N. Potter; distributed by Crown, 1980.

———, ed. Ronald Harwood. *The Ages of Gielgud: An Actor at Eighty*. London: Hodder & Stoughton, 1984.

Gillett, John, and David Robinson. "Interview with George Cukor." *Sight & Sound* (Autumn 1964).

Ginsburg, Mark. "Interview with George Cukor." *Interview* (April 1983).

Glendinnings, Victoria. *Edith Sitwell: A Unicorn Among Lions*. New York: Knopf, 1981.

Godfrey, Lionel. *Cary Grant: The Light Touch*. New York: St. Martin's Press, 1981.

Goldstein, Malcolm. *George S. Kaufman: His Life, His Theater*. New York: Oxford University Press, 1979.

Gordon, Ruth. *Myself Among Others*. New York: Atheneum, 1971.

———. *An Open Book*. New York: Doubleday, 1980.

———. *My Side: The Autobiography of Ruth Gordon*, introduction by Garson Kanin. New York: Primus/Donald Fine, 1986.

Greist, Kenneth. *Pictures Will Talk: The Life and Times of Joseph L. Mankiewicz*. New York: Scribner's, 1978.

Gronowicz, Antoni. *Garbo*. New York: Simon & Schuster, 1990.

Hadleigh, Boze. *Conversations with My Elders*. New York: St. Martin's Press, 1986.

Harmetz, Aljean. *The Making of the Wizard of Oz*. New York: Knopf, 1977.

Harris, Marlys. *The Zanucks of Hollywood*. New York: Crown, 1989.

Harrison, Rex. *Rex*. New York: William Morrow, 1975.

Harwell, Richard, ed. *Margaret Mitchell's GWTW Letters, 1936–1949*. New York: Macmillan, 1976.

Haskell, Molly. *From Reverence to Rape*. New York: Holt, Rinehart & Winston, 1974.

Haver, Ron. *A Star Is Born: The Making of the 1954 Movie and Its 1983 Restoration*. New York: Knopf, 1988.

Hayes, Helen. *Gift of Joy*. New York: M. Evans, distributed by Lippincott, 1965.

———. *On Reflection: An Autobiography*. New York: M. Evans, 1968.

———. *Twice Over Lightly: New York Then and Now*. New York: Harcourt Brace Jovanovich, 1972.

———. *Loving Life*. New York: Doubleday, 1987.

———. *My Life in Three Acts*. New York: Harcourt Brace Jovanovich, 1990.

Highman, Charles. *Ava: A Life Story*. New York: Delacorte, 1974.

———. *Kate*. New York: Norton, 1975.

———. *Warner Brothers*. New York: Scribner's, 1975.

———. *Audrey. A Biography of Audrey Hepburn*. New York: Macmillan, 1984.

———. *Bette: The Life of Bette Davis*. New York: Macmillan, 1984.

———. *Cary Grant: The Lonely Heart*. San Diego: Harcourt Brace Jovanovich, 1989.

Hirschorn, Clive. *Gene Kelly*. Chicago: Regnery, 1975.

———. *The Warner Bros. Story*. New York: Crown, 1979.

———. *The Universal Story*. New York: Crown, 1983.

Holden, Anthony. *Olivier*. London: Weidenfeld & Nicolson, 1988.

Holtzman, Will. *Judy Holliday*. New York: Putnam's, 1982.

Hollywood Reporter: reviews of Cukor's films and articles about his career.

Hopper, Hedda. *From Under My Hat*. New York: Doubleday, 1952.

Howard, Leslie Ruth. *A Quite Remarkable Father*. New York: Harcourt Brace, 1959.

Israel, Lee. *Miss Tallulah Bankhead*. New York: Putnam's, 1972.

Jackson, Carlton. *Hattie: The Life of Hattie McDaniel*. New York: Madison Books, 1989.

Kael, Pauline. *I Lost It at the Movies*. Boston: Little, Brown, 1965.

———. *Kiss Kiss Bang Bang*. Boston: Little, Brown, 1968.

———. *Going Steady*. Boston: Little, Brown, 1970.

———. *Deeper into Movies*. Boston: Little, Brown, 1973.

———. *Reeling*. Boston: Little, Brown, 1976.

———. *When the Lights Go Down*. New York: Holt, Rinehart & Winston, 1980.

———. "Rich and Famous." *New Yorker* (October 26, 1981).

Kanin, Garson. *Remembering Mr. Maugham*. New York: Atheneum, 1966.

———. *Tracy and Hepburn: An Intimate Memoir*. New York: Viking, 1971.

444   Bibliography

———. "George Cukor's Loving Marriage to the Movies." *The New York Times* (February 6, 1983).

Kantor, Bernard. Interview with George Cukor. AMPAS (no date).

Kauffman, Stanley. "My Fair Lady." *New Republic* (November 4, 1964).

Kelley, Kitty. *Elizabeth Taylor.* New York: Simon & Schuster, 1981.

Kilday, Gregg. "Risque Bisset." *Vanity Fair* (July 1989).

Knight, Arthur. Obituary of Cukor. *Hollywood Reporter* (January 28, 1983).

Kobal, John. *People Will Talk.* New York: Knopf, 1986.

Kobler, John. *Damned in Paradise: The Life of John Barrymore.* New York: Atheneum, 1977.

Kotsilibas-Davis, James. *The Barrymores.* New York: Crown, 1981.

LaGuardia, Robert, and Gene Arceri. *Red: The Tempestuous Life of Susan Hayward.* New York: Macmillan, 1985.

Lahr, John. *Notes on a Cowardly Lion: The Biography of Bert Lahr.* New York: Knopf, 1969.

Lambert, Gavin. *On Cukor.* New York: Capricorn, 1973.

———. *The Making of Gone with the Wind.* Boston: Little, Brown, 1973.

Lanchester, Elsa. *Elsa Lanchester Herself.* New York: St. Martin's Press, 1983.

Lasky, Betty. *RKO: The Biggest Little Major of Them All.* New York: Prentice-Hall, 1984.

Latham, Aaroin. *Crazy Sundays: F. Scott Fitzgerald in Hollywood.* New York: Viking, 1970.

Lawford, Patricia Seaton, with Ted Schwarz. *The Peter Lawford Story.* New York: Carroll and Graf, 1981.

Leamer, Laurence. *As Time Goes By: The Life of Ingrid Bergman.* New York: Harper & Row, 1986.

Leaming, Barbara. *If This Was Happiness: A Biography of Rita Hayworth.* New York: Viking, 1989.

Lehmann, John. *Christopher Isherwood: A Personal Memoir.* London: Weidenfeld & Nicholson, 1987.

Leroy, Mervyn, as told to Dick Kleiner. *Mervyn LeRoy: Take One.* New York: Hawthorn Books, 1974.

Lesley, Cole. *The Life of Noël Coward.* London: Penguin Books, 1979.

Levy, Emanuel. *And the Winner Is: The History and Politics of the Oscar Award.* New York: Crossroad, 1987; paperback, 1991.

———. *John Wayne: Prophet of the American Way of Life.* Metucken, N.J.: Scarecrow, 1978.

———. *Small-Town America in Film.* New York: Continuum, 1991.

Linet, Beverly. *Susan Hayward: Portrait of a Survivor.* New York: Atheneum, 1980.

Logan, Joshua. *Josh: My Up and Down, In and Out Life.* New York: W. H. Allen, 1977.

———. *Movie Stars, Real People, and Me.* New York: Delacorte Press, 1978.

Loos, Anita. *Cast of Thousands.* New York: Grosset & Dunlap, 1977.

Loy, Myrna, and James Kotsilibas-Davis. *Myrna Loy: Being and Becoming.* New York: Knopf, 1987.

McBride, Joseph. "George Cukor—The Blue Bird." *Action* (November–December 1975).

McCowen, Alec. *Double Bill*. New York: Atheneum, 1979.

——. *Young Gemini*. New York: Atheneum, 1980.

Madsen, Axel. *William Wyler: The Authorized Biography*. New York: Crowell, 1973.

Marion, Frances. *Off with Their Heads: A Serio-Comic Tale of Hollywood*. New York: Macmillan, 1972.

Meyer, William R. *Warner Brothers Directors: The Hard-Boiled, the Comic, and the Weepers*. New York: Arlington House, 1978.

Milland, Ray. *Wide-Eyed in Babylon: An Autobiography*. New York: William Morrow, 1974.

Mitchell, George J. "Making All Quiet on the Western Front." *American Cinematographer* (September 1985).

Monti, Carlotta, with Cy Rice. *W. C. Fields and Me*. Englewood Cliffs, N.J.: Prentice-Hall, 1971.

Mordden, Ethan. *The Hollywood Studios: House Style in the Golden Age of the Movies*. New York: Knopf, 1988.

Morgan, Ted. *Maugham*. New York: Simon & Schuster, 1980.

Morley, Sheridan. *James Mason: Odd Man Out*. New York: Harper & Row, 1989.

Morrow, Susan Stark. "Architectural Digest Visits George Cukor." *Architectural Digest* (January–February 1978).

Myrick, Susan. *White Columns in Hollywood: Reports from the GWTW Sets*. Macon, Ga.: Mercer University Press, 1982.

New York Times: film reviews of Cukor's features and TV movies.

Nichols, Beverly. *A Case of Human Bondage*. New York: Award Books, 1966.

Olivier, Lawrence. *Confessions of an Actor*. New York: Simon & Schuster, 1982.

Overstreet, Richard. "Interview with George Cukor." *Film Culture* (Fall 1964).

Parish, James Robert, and Ronald L. Bowers. *The MGM Stock Company: The Golden Era*. New York: Arlington House, 1973.

Payne, Robert. *The Great Garbo*. New York: Praeger, 1976.

Phillips, Gene D. "George Cukor." *Film and Filming* (January 1982).

——. *George Cukor*. Boston: Twayne, 1982.

Power-Waters, Alma. *John Barrymore: The Legend and the Man*. New York: Julian Messner, 1941.

Quirk, Lawrence. *The Films of Fredric March*. Secaucus, N.J.: Citadel Press, 1971.

——. *The Great Romantic Films*. Secaucus, N.J.: Citadel Press, 1974.

——. *Norma*. New York: St. Martin's, 1988.

——. *Fasten Your Seat Belts: The Passionate Life of Bette Davis*. New York: William Morrow, 1990.

Robinson, David. "The Hepburn Years." *The Times Saturday Review* (November 24, 1973).

Robinson, Edward G., with Leonard Spigelglass. *All My Yesterdays: An Autobiography*. New York: Hawthorn Books, 1973.

Robyns, Gwen. *Light of a Star*. London: Leslie Frewin, 1968.

Rollyson, Carl E., Jr. *Marilyn Monroe: A Life of the Actress*. Ann Arbor, Mich.: UMI Research Press, 1986.

Roppolo, Joseph Patrick. *Philip Barry*. Boston: Twayne, 1965.

Rubin, Sam, and Richard Taylor. *Mia Farrow: Flower Child, Madonna, Muse*. New York: St. Martin's Press, 1989.

Russell, Rosalind. *Life Is a Banquet*. New York: Random House, 1977.

Samuelson, David W. "Freddie Young, BSC, Talks About Photographing *The Blue Bird*." *American Cinematographer* (December 1975).

Sarris, Andrew. *Hollywood Voices: Interviews with Film Directors*. New York: Bobbs-Merrill, 1967.

———. *The American Cinema: Directors and Directions*, 2d ed. Chicago: University of Chicago Press, 1989.

Schary, Dore. *Heydey*. Boston: Little, Brown, 1979.

Schatz, Thomas. *The Genius of the System*. New York: Pantheon, 1988.

Schickel, Richard. *The Men Who Made the Movies*. New York: Atheneum, 1975.

Schwartz, Charles. *Cole Porter: A Biography*. New York: Da Capo, 1977.

Selznick, Irene Mayer. *A Private View*. New York: Knopf, 1983.

Sennett, Ted. *Lunatics and Lovers*. New York: Arlington House, 1973.

Shapiro, Doris. *We Danced All Night*. New York: William Morrow, 1990.

Shepard, David H. "Review of *On Cukor*." *AFI Report* (November 1973).

Sitwell, Edith. *Taking Care: The Autobiography of Edith Sitwell*. New York: Atheneum, 1965.

Stine, Whitney, with Bette Davis. *Mother Goddamn: The Story of the Career of Bette Davis*. New York: Berkley Books, 1975.

Swanson, Gloria. *Swanson on Swanson*. New York: Random House, 1980.

Swindell, Larry. *Charles Boyer: The Reluctant Lover*. New York: Doubleday, 1983.

———. *Spencer Tracy: A Biography*. Cleveland: World Publishing Company, 1969.

Taubman, Howard. *The Making of the American Theatre*. New York: Coward-McCann, 1967.

Thomas, Bob. "Pat and Mike." *Citizen News*, Beverly Hills, Calif (January 15, 1952).

———. *King Cohn: The Life and Times of Harry Cohn*. New York: Putnam's, 1967.

———. *Selznick*. New York: Doubleday, 1970.

———. *Joan Crawford: A Biography*. New York: Simon & Schuster, 1978.

———. *Golden Boy: The Untold Story of William Holden*. New York: St. Martin's, 1983.

———. *Clown Prince of Hollywood: The Antic Life and Times of Jack L. Warner*. New York: McGraw-Hill, 1990.

Thomas, Kevin. "George Cukor: At 81, Still Young at Heart." Los Angeles *Times* (December 24, 1980).

Thompson, Howard. *James Stewart*. New York: Pyramid, 1974.

Thorne, Robin. "His Fair Ladies." *California* (July 1983).

Tomkies, Mike. *Robert Mitchum Story*. Chicago: Regnery, 1972.

Tornabene, Lyn. *Long Live the King: A Biography of Clark Gable*. New York: Putnam's, 1976.

Tozzi, Romano V. "George Cukor." *Films in Review* (February 1958).

Truffaut, François. *The Films in My Life*. New York: Simon & Schuster, 1978.

Tynan, Kenneth. "George Cukor." *Holiday* (February 1961).

Variety: reviews of Cukor's films and articles about his career.

Vickers, Hugo. *Cecil Beaton: A Biography*. Boston: Little, Brown, 1985.

Vidor, King. *A Tree Is a Tree*. New York: Garland, 1977.

Viertel, Salka. *The Kindness of Strangers*. New York: Holt, Rinehart & Winston, 1969.

Walker, Alexander. *Garbo: A Portrait*. New York: Macmillan, 1980.

———. *Joan Crawford: The Ultimate Star*. London: Weidenfeld & Nicolson, 1983.

Wansell, Geoffrey. *Cary Grant: Haunted Idol*. London: Collins, 1983.

Watson, Thomas J., and Bill Chapman. *Judy: Portrait of an American Legend*. New York: McGraw-Hill, 1986.

Widener, Don. *Lemmon: A Biography*. New York: Macmillan, 1975.

Wilk, Max. "Donald Stewart in Exile." *American Film*. (July–August 1982).

Williams, Paul. *Ernst Lubitsch's American Comedy*. New York: Columbia University Press, 1983.

Williams, Tennessee. *Memoirs*. New York: Doubleday, 1975.

———. *Five O'Clock Angel*. New York: Knopf, 1990.

Winters, Shelley. *Shelley: Also Known as Shirley*. New York: William Morrow, 1980.

———. *Shelley II: The Middle of My Century*. New York: Simon & Schuster, 1989.

Woodward, Ian. *Audrey Hepburn*. New York: St. Martin's Press, 1984.

Zec, Donald. *Sophia*. New York: David McKay, 1975.

Zeitlin, Ida. "A Director Looks at the Stars." *Screenland* (February 24, 1933).

Zierold, Norman. *Garbo*. New York: Stein & Day, 1969.

Zolotow, Maurice. *Billy Wilder in Hollywood*. New York: Putnam's, 1977.

Index